Tribal Library
Saginaw Chippewa Indian Tribe
7070 E. Broadway
Mt. Pleasant MI 48858

The Art of Tradition

The Art of Tradition

SACRED MUSIC, DANCE & MYTH OF MICHIGAN'S ANISHINAABE, 1946–1955

Gertrude Kurath
Jane Ettawageshik
Fred Ettawageshik

EDITED BY
Michael D. McNally

Michigan State University Press · East Lansing

Copyright © 2009 by Gertrude Kurath, Jane Ettawageshik, and Fred Ettawageshik

⊗ The paper used in this publication meets the minimum requirements of ANSI/NISO Z39.48-1992 (R 1997) (Permanence of Paper).

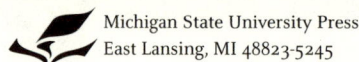 Michigan State University Press
East Lansing, MI 48823-5245

Printed and bound in the United States of America.

18 17 16 15 14 13 12 11 10 09   1 2 3 4 5 6 7 8 9 10

LIBRARY OF CONGRESS CATALOGING-IN-PUBLICATION DATA
Kurath, Gertrude Prokosch.
The art of tradition : sacred music, dance, and myth of Michigan's Anishinaabe, 1946–1955 / Gertrude Kurath, Jane Ettawageshik, Fred Ettawageshik ; edited by Michael D. McNally ; foreword by Frank Ettawageshik.
p. cm.
Includes bibliographical references and index.
ISBN 978-0-87013-814-0 (cloth : alk. paper)
1. Ojibwa Indians—Michigan—Religion. 2. Ottawa Indians—Michigan—Religion. 3. Indian dance—Michigan. 4. Ojibwa Indians—Michigan—Songs and music. 5. Ottawa Indians—Michigan—Songs and music. 6. Ojibwa Indians—Michigan—Folklore. 7. Ottawa Indians—Michigan—Folklore. 8. Michigan—Social life and customs. 9. Michigan—Folklore. I. Ettawageshik, Jane, 1915–1996. II. Ettawageshik, Fred, 1896–1969. III. McNally, Michael David. IV. Title.
E99.C6K87 2007
299.7'83330774—dc22
2007023823

Book and cover design by Charlie Sharp, Sharp Des!gns, Lansing, Michigan
Cover art is used courtesy of the Archives of Michigan (negative 11162).

g green press initiative Michigan State University Press is a member of the Green Press Initiative and is committed to developing and encouraging ecologically responsible publishing practices. For more information about the Green Press Initiative and the use of recycled paper in book publishing, please visit *www.greenpressinitiative.org*.

Visit Michigan State University Press on the World Wide Web at *www.msupress.msu.edu*

CONTENTS

- *vii*   Foreword *by Frank Ettawageshik*
- *xi*   Editor's Introduction
- *xli*   Editorial Principles and Orthography
- *xlv*   Authors' Acknowledgments

The Setting
- *3*   CHAPTER 1. Peninsular People
- *31*   CHAPTER 2. Public Festivals

Dance and Music Heritage
- *57*   CHAPTER 3. Contemporary Dance Patterns
- *91*   CHAPTER 4. Native Songs by Modern Singers

The Christian Legacy
- *141*   CHAPTER 5. Odawa Feasts
- *185*   CHAPTER 6. Ojibwe Methodist Camp Meeting and Hymn Singing
- *213*   CHAPTER 7. Hymn Tunes and Texts

Beliefs
- *239*   CHAPTER 8. Indigenous Lore
- *269*   CHAPTER 9. Odawa Myths

Interpretation
- *389*   CHAPTER 10. Interpretation

- *431*   Notes
- *443*   Works Cited and Suggested Reading
- *453*   Index

FOREWORD

My thoughts about the importance of this book can be quickly illustrated by a story. Just last evening, April 29, 2006, we held the Return Dinner in Harbor Springs, Michigan. Until recently this feast was held at the Holy Childhood Parish Hall, but now it is held in the commons area of the new Tribal Administration Building. The Return Dinner is held each spring, and it is hosted by the three kings chosen at the Three Kings Dinner held each January. These three people are the ones who received a dime, a nickel, or a penny in a small piece of frybread at the January dinner. Fifty-three years ago, at the age of four, I received the dime. In January 2006 I received the dime for a second time. That this tradition survived virtually unchanged throughout this half-century period is a testimony to cultural continuity.

These two feasts are part of a year-round feast cycle that has the appearances of being Christian—more specifically, Catholic. While these feasts coincide with events on the Catholic calendar, they also happen to follow closely the seasonal feasts held by Odawa traditionalists. A broad cross-section of the tribal members attend these feasts irrespective of their various beliefs—for the most common and strongest belief is respecting one's family, and we have strong kinship ties throughout the tribal community.

A culture that is completely quantifiable and static is one that is not alive. The Waganakising Odawak community (also known as the Little Traverse Bay Bands of Odawa Indians) remains multifaceted and diverse while it is also clearly evolving and growing. New practices and traditions are built upon older ones each year, but they are always a unique reflection of our history and culture.

At a young age I participated in one of the festivals about which my parents wrote. I was little Hiawatha in the pageant held at Ottawa Stadium in July 1953. Although this memory is from my childhood, the Odawa community of the Waganakising Odawak is far from fading into memory.

Today we have organizations such as the private nonprofit Odawa Institute, which annually hosts a festival where attendees participate in the culture and do not just observe. The Crooked Tree Arts Center in Petoskey, Michigan, has an Anishinaabe Festival in the fall of each year that mounts a different month-long art exhibit followed by a well-attended feast at which all members of the Odawa and non-Odawa communities are welcome. A whole department within the tribal government is tasked with cultural preservation and with archives and records preservation.

I was well into my adult years before I realized that I had been quietly taught a world view that differed a great deal from that of non-Odawa individuals. Stories, songs, the physical presence of items of my family's and the tribe's antiquity in my life and home—all were a part of my understanding of creation and daily life. In addition, I grew up listening to many interesting discussions at our dinner table and in our living room. Our family's book shelves included works by Vernon Kinietz, Frank Speck, Francis Densmore, and Paul Radin. We were visited by government officials and university professors.

Today, songs are sung and the drums sound, but this is not only the music of long ago. New songs are being composed and dreamed, and new singers are eagerly participating in a revival of both men's and women's roles in honoring the sacred. Outside scholars have written much about our community, but all along we have shown a strong ability to record our own stories as well. Andrew Blackbird, Joseph Shomin, my father Fred Ettawageshik, and more recently, Wesley Andrews are all tribal members who have written articles and books telling our stories.

I'm proud of the work of my parents. I'm glad that my mother's wishes are being realized with the publication of this volume. I first met Michael McNally years ago when he came to visit and told me of finding this manuscript and how he wished to work on getting it published. After a long talk in my home I told him of my mother's wishes to see it published. I also came to believe that McNally possessed an insight into the cultural understanding held by my parents and by other elders within this community.

In 1994 President Clinton signed into law Public Law 103-324, an act that reaffirmed that the Waganakising Odawak, the Little Traverse Bay Bands of Odawa Indians, had always had a government-to-government relationship with the United States. This ended a 120-year legal battle that had been waged by generations of our leaders.

I often speak about accidents of history as I outline the history of our tribal treaties and how we got to where we are today. But in our traditional beliefs there are no accidents. Everything has a purpose for us to understand. It was no accident that the Carlisle Indian School was created. Many lives were affected and my father's was one. Having traveled to the east, his subsequent friendship with Frank Speck led him to marry my mother. Her presence in our community at Little Traverse led to the research and writing that was so helpful in winning our battle with the U.S. government in 1994 and the subsequent growth in our tribal opportunities. Michael McNally's discovery of the long unpublished manuscript and recognition of the appropriateness of its message for today's scholars and community members is but another event in this chain. All of these were seemingly accidents of history, but like reeds woven together, they help make a part of the community tapestry upon which we build for tomorrow. It is important to know and understand our past to create the possibilities for building the tribe's future.

Today, I serve as the elected tribal chairman. I've served in one way or another in tribal leadership since 1989. When reading this book, the reader can get a glimpse of the richness of our Odawa community but cannot experience or capture its entirety. Like a rock skipping over the surface of the water at the shore, this volume only begins to reflect what we live and hear today at our feasts and powwows, at councils and lodges, at conferences, and in our homes.

Yet the stories like this one about our Odawa community are not isolated. Similar stories are found in nearly every Indian community across North America. This volume may well give insight to members of those communities and to those who live with and study them. I believe this book demonstrates that our Odawa culture has not been lost as it has evolved, but rather that we continue to embrace change within our own unique world view. Our culture is alive. Its contributions to the collective future of all people are as yet unknown but will be exciting and filled with promise.

FRANK ETTAWAGESHIK

EDITOR'S INTRODUCTION

I first encountered this work in the solitude of an archival reading room, but over the past years, as I have worked on this project, the authors have posthumously introduced me to a number of people whom I have been privileged to know: Frank Ettawageshik, Philip Mason of Wayne State University, the staff of Michigan State University Press—especially Martha Bates, Kristine Blakeslee, Julie Loehr, and Fred Bohm—and James McClurken, who offered generous advice and located lost materials, and who continues to model sound scholarship in the service of Native communities. I am also grateful to the authors' heirs, especially Ellen Kurath and Frank Ettawageshik, who not only allowed but worked hard to encourage this project to happen. In preparing the text, I am grateful for the advice of John Nichols and for the tireless and thoughtful work of a number of Carleton College students: Alison Traffanstadt, Adam Koren, Jacob McKnite, and especially Matt Hooley. Above all, I am grateful to Devon Anderson, for believing in me and in the possibilities for relevant, connected scholarship, and to our children, Svea and Coleman. At various stages of the project, Svea and Coleman, then babies, served as my muses as they sat on my lap while I worked at the keyboard. Who could wish for a better family? Along with Frank Ettawageshik, Ellen Kurath, and the folks of Michigan State University Press, I hope and trust that this book will be of considerable service to Odawa and Ojibwe communities today in their artful stewardship of tradition. To all, *miigwech*.

The Artfulness of Tradition

It is surely one of the principal ironies of American history that Native Americans have survived as distinctive peoples. In spite of the sustained, concerted effort by missionaries and governments to eradicate the ceremonies, languages, songs, dance traditions, and communal identities of diverse Native nations, not to mention the overt policies of genocide and land dispossession, Native communities throughout the United States have entered the twenty-first century in the midst of a tremendous renewal of interest in the languages, ceremonies, and traditions of more than five hundred tribal identities.

This book offers a window into the cultural dexterity with which certain twentieth-century Native American elders worked to ensure the survival of Michigan's Native communities and their cultures. It documents the traditions of music, dance, myth, and ceremony of Native communities in Michigan in the 1940s and 1950s. This was a crucial, if largely unsung, period for Native Americans when the renewed pride in Native ethnicities and cultures characteristic of the later twentieth century drew on a crucial generation of elders who had grown up speaking Ojibwe and Odawa at the feet of grandparents who had lived most of their lives in the nineteenth century, but who had come of age in boarding schools and attained their own eldership amid strong pressures of assimilation—partly as a result of overt U.S. policies of assimilation and partly as a result of more subtle and insidious processes of economic and cultural integration.

In this book, the reader will find a valuable compilation of Anishinaabe rituals, songs, dances, myths, legends, stories, and medicinal knowledge, documented with a modicum of interpretive overlay on the part of its authors, Gertrude Kurath, Jane Ettawageshik, and Fred Ettawageshik. Yet the materials they collected are anything but timeless traditions frozen in amber as museum pieces on the eve of their disappearance. Nor are they documents of what anthropologists of the time identified as the stuff of "acculturation," evidence of a tradition's erosion by the forces of assimilation.

Instead, the songs, dance steps, and stories collected here are fluid evidence of the dynamics of *rekindling* culture, the artful work of maintaining and breathing new life into traditions by indigenous artists and elders, often in venues and contexts that were anything but traditional and perhaps were even hostile to tradition. One entire chapter, for example, explores the way that Ojibwe and Odawa language hymns in Protestant and Catholic worship count as Native music. For many Anishinaabeg, these hymns had become part of a repertory of *traditional* Anishinaabe music. Other chapters consider older songs and dances of more direct indigenous origin in the context of their being brought to life by performance in such unorthodox settings as "Naming Ceremonies" and *Song of Hiawatha* pageants staged largely for non-Native audiences.

As scholars have begun to take seriously such performances of "Indian-ness" for the consumptive pleasure of non-Native audiences, we are coming to appreciate the agency of Native American actors in such pageants and shows, and to view the performances as complicated affairs involving both accommodation to Euro-American desires for and expectations of Indian-ness and some measure of resistance in this era of assimilation.[1] In rich profiles of the Native women and men who shared their materials with the authors, and in careful attention to the unorthodox contexts of performances of the songs, dances, and ceremonies documented herein, one glimpses the improvisation and the resourcefulness that lay at the heart of cultural continuity for many Native peoples.

The Hiawatha pageants can perhaps best illustrate the workings of Anishinaabe cultural dexterity in the confines of dispossession and colonization. The pageants came to Harbor Springs on Little Traverse Bay in 1905 from Ontario's Garden River Reserve of Ojibwe near Sault Ste. Marie, under the sponsorship of the Grand Rapids and Indiana Railroad, which was promoting tourism and, more importantly, land sales in the region. The pageant was really an operatic series of tableaux based on Henry Wadsworth Longfellow's 1855 poem *The Song of Hiawatha,* itself a romanticization of Anishinaabe oral traditions collected at Sault Ste. Marie in the 1820s, 1830s, and 1840s by Henry Rowe Schoolcraft, the region's U.S. Indian Agent. Perhaps more than any other work of literature, Longfellow's poem epitomized and popularized the romantic image of the vanishing Indian, the noble savage who must depart the scene upon the arrival of Euro-Americans. Not surprisingly, the most celebrated scene in the pageants was Hiawatha's departure by magic canoe into the setting sun, immediately following the arrival of the French Jesuit missionaries to whom Hiawatha entrusts his people. Ironically, while Native people were portraying on stage the "real Indians" of the romantic American imagination, they were also in effect performing their own *absence* as real Native people with existing claims to a region being parceled and sold by railroads, speaking their own language, and celebrating their own ceremonies.

But Kurath and the Ettawageshiks show that it was more complicated than this, that the Anishinaabe were active agents, not passive recipients, in this history. The Odawa men and women—like Joseph Chingwa, who proudly sang the role of Jibiabos—were publicly speaking their own language, singing their own songs, and subverting the colonizing grip of the performances with the audacious presence of the drum (the public performance of which was discouraged if not prohibited in that era), the pipe, and Indian humor. For example, while well-heeled tourists admired the romantic wedding of Hiawatha with the chaste maiden Minnehaha, the performers were smuggling in under the cover of their language the following song:

> *I wouldn't sleep if there was something I could drink*
> *I wouldn't sleep if there was something I could drink*
> *I wouldn't sleep if there was something I could drink*
> *I wouldn't sleep if I had someone to sleep with.*[2]

Although one ought not miss the process of folklorization implied in the construction of such performance contexts as Hiawatha pageants—for these stood in sharp contrast to the life of music and dance in aboriginal ways of life—the performers undertook this work as part of a conscious effort to celebrate and bequeath to their progeny these songs and these dances, even as they relied on these traditions to make a living in new ways.[3]

Michigan's Anishinaabeg: A Historical Sketch

Michigan is home to the Ojibwe (alternatively Ojibwa, Chippewa), Odawa (alternatively Ottawa), and Potawatomi, three distinct nations who viewed one another as relatives and allies under a confederacy of the Three Fires. The three nations refer to themselves collectively as the *Anishinaabe* (plural: *Anishinaabeg,* "the people"), as they share a common linguistic, cultural, and ceremonial heritage.

For the Anishinaabeg, living in Michigan and the regions surrounding the western Great Lakes is a profound religious calling. Among their more central narratives is that of their great migration from the eastern seaboard, a migration in response to a prophetic vision calling them westward, guided by a sacred *migis* shell apparition in the sky.

Anishinaabe communities initially encountered European Americans in the seventeenth century, when they first heard the message of French Jesuit missionaries and engaged with French fur traders. Although the traders and priests were reliant on Anishinaabeg and were relatively uninterested in changing an indigenous way of life based on a seasonal round of economic activities that included hunting, gathering, and trapping, this was still no benign encounter. Disease accompanied the Europeans to devastating effect and the ensuing century brought considerable social fragmentation to the equation of religious, cultural, marital, and economic exchange with the French, centered on the trading and mission villages at Detroit, Mackinac Island, Sault Ste. Marie, and other villages along the Great Lakes. In the 1760s many Ojibwe and Odawa joined French and other Native allies in the Odawa leader Pontiac's rebellion against British encroachment. They were called to anticolonial resistance under Pontiac's spiritual mentor, the Delaware prophet Neolin. In the 1810s a similar intertribal sacred resistance, which was inspired by Tenskwatawa, a Shawnee prophet, and led by his brother Tecumseh, mobilized many Michigan Anishinaabeg to join a broad intertribal alliance with the British against the aggressive advances of the Americans.[4]

But northern Michigan's Native communities met with increased American encroachment as the nineteenth century wore on. The lands inhabited by most of the communities in this book were ceded by the Odawa and Ojibwe at the Treaty of Washington in 1836, leaving small reservations, some of which were vacated by Anishinaabe communities later in the century. Even reservation lands fell prey to the axes of a timber industry bustling to feed the construction of railroads and cities, which made a subsistence based on the traditional seasonal round increasingly difficult for Native people. To survive, many Anishinaabeg turned to wage labor in lumber camps, on Great Lakes freighters, and on work details building the railroads and roads that would knit northern Michigan into the political economy of the United States. Still, Anishinaabe people proudly continued to practice seasonal fishing, hunting, berrying, and ricing, and they maintained a distinctive identity through those practices.

The Anishinaabe encountered Christianity first in French Jesuits in the seventeenth century, and again more intensely through stepped-up missions activity by Catholics and Protestants beginning in the 1830s. The Catholic inroads made in the seventeenth century, especially among those Anishinaabeg of mixed French and Indian heritage, were extended by the Slovenian priest Friedrich Baraga and his protégés in the region at Little Traverse and Keweenaw beginning in the 1830s and 1840s.[5] At Mackinac Island, Baptist, Congregationalist, and Presbyterian missionaries of the interdenominational American Board of Commissioners for Foreign Missions established and maintained a station and school in the same period.[6] Shortly thereafter, Methodists established a presence in the region by means of training and promoting circuit preachers of Anishinaabe heritage.

Although most Anishinaabe were baptized by the end of the nineteenth century, Odawa and Ojibwe people did not simply become what missionaries wanted them to be. Instead, they improvised and adapted Christianity in varying degrees to their own ends. For example, as Kurath and Ettawageshik discuss below, Catholic, Methodist, and American Board missionaries promoted translated Christian hymns in Ojibwe and Odawa as part of a campaign to supplant indigenous music, which they deemed savage, with what the missionaries took to be the "sounds of civilization." But once indigenized, especially in the prayer meetings and funerary wakes that took place beyond the control of non-Native missionaries, hymn singing took root in ways that helped negotiate distinctive Anishinaabe values, beliefs, and practices with the demands of Christianity and American culture.[7] At any rate, for an Anishinaabe to become Christian involved a much wider range of possibilities than imagined by missionaries who were convinced that to become Christian meant to cease being Indian.

Other Anishinaabeg in Michigan held fast to a markedly non-Christian religious identity, continuing to practice the *Midéwiwin* ceremonial complex and other traditional religious practices well into the twentieth century. But as the cultural assimilation to agrarian, Christian, patriarchal American society that Protestant missionaries had long preached evolved into overt U.S. Indian policy in the 1880s, it became increasingly difficult to publicly exercise those traditional Native religious practices. In that decade, the federal Office of Indian Affairs gave policy directives suppressing public dancing, drumming, and ceremonializing, with local enforcement at the hands of Indian agents who could restrict the entitlements due as treaty annuities to needy Anishinaabe families according to who remained within the agents' good graces on such matters.[8] Communally held lands on reservations were summarily allotted to plots held in trust for male-headed Indian households. And shortly thereafter, when non-Native speculators had won loopholes from Congress providing easier access to allotted Indian lands, many Native families suffering malnutrition and tuberculosis could ill afford not to sell their lands.

By the 1880s, the United States had also expanded its network of Indian boarding schools, in the confidence that removing Native children from the intricate ties of kin and seasonality would make them more receptive to assimilation. When the United States formalized its insistence on English-only education in 1887, children were shamed and sometimes beaten for speaking Odawa or Ojibwe. The elders whom we meet in the pages that follow were nearly all products of boarding schools, many of them spending years at the school in Mount Pleasant. That any of their knowledge of language and culture survived these totalizing institutions bears eloquent witness to their resolve, even as children, to hold on to cultural traditions deep within themselves.[9]

By the late 1920s a government-commissioned study confirmed what had become obvious: the colossal failure of assimilation and allotment policies. With the Indian Reorganization Act of 1934 and related legislation,

Congress formally reversed its assimilation policy, clarified the illegality of suppressing Native religious and cultural practice, and affirmed the value of distinctive Native languages and cultures. But in many respects the damage was already done, and deeply so. A generation of Native people who came of age after the Indian Reorganization Act had already been powerfully shaped by boarding school childhoods. Many boarding school veterans lost their language to the experience and the shame that went along with it, some still speaking English with an Odawa or Ojibwe accent. By the time Kurath and the Ettawageshiks were conducting their research, the Ojibwe and Odawa languages were indeed still spoken, but they were spoken less in public, less as languages of daily life, and by fewer people.

While the policy reversals of the 1930s abided, a second wave of assimilationist federal policy took hold in new forms. Believing that Native peoples' interests were best served by dissolving tribal status and identity and incorporating Indians more fully as citizens of the U.S. political economy, Congress terminated the legal status of a number of Indian tribes, including that of Wisconsin's Menominee (though it was reinstated decades later). Further reaching still was the federal government's relocation policy, which established a bundle of economic incentives for Native Americans to leave reservation homes and fill jobs in the nation's industrial cities. Although this process was just beginning at the time of this book's original writing, three decades later half of the American Indians in the United States were living off of reservations.

It was in this political environment that the Anishinaabe figures in this book tried to make a living and proudly maintain their distinctive cultural identity. Importantly, not all of the Indians in this book were members of Indian "tribes" that were federally recognized under the Indian Reorganization Act. While the Ojibwe of Baraga and Keweenaw Bay and of the Saginaw Band's reserve at Isabella did come under federally recognized status in the 1930s, the Odawas of Grand River and Little Traverse Bay originally did not. Instead of accepting the terms of recognition under the 1934 legislation—namely, to approve by election a tribal constitution whose text was generated by the Office of Indian Affairs and to organize community leadership in terms of an elected "tribal council" —the Little Traverse Odawas chose to remain Indian in their own way. For example, they articulated their personhood in community meetings, in the feasts and cultural celebrations described in this book, and through the creation of independent organizations like the Michigan Indian Defense Association, which sought to bring Michigan's various Odawa communities under a joint structure for purposes of dealing with state and federal governments.[10] Fred Ettawageshik, Joe Chingwa, and others whose stories, songs, and dance performances animate the pages of this book were deeply involved in the leadership of this association.

Although other Odawa communities in Michigan still seek the federally recognized status that hindsight showed was the preferred way to secure a land base and sovereignty, the Odawa children of those elders at Little Traverse continued their long struggle for acknowledgment as a people by petitioning for and eventually securing formal federal recognition in the 1990s. Kurath and Ettawageshik's manuscript played a role in the legal process of documenting the historical continuity of this Odawa community.

Traditional Anishinaabe Religion, Art, and Culture

This book was well-positioned to help document that continuity because it explores Anishinaabe art and religion amid the changed circumstances of mid-twentieth-century life in Michigan. Even in times of rapid culture change, the authors found, the Anishinaabe took the distinctive traditional posture that sought to fully integrate religion and art with the economic, political, social, medical, and ecological dimensions of what anthropologists would speak of as "culture" and what the Anishinaabe would refer to as the Anishinaabe *way*. Indeed, travelers among Michigan's Native communities today would doubtless encounter, as I have, a spirited insistence that the Anishinaabe do not have a *religion* in the conventional sense of the word, but rather a *way of life*. And yet, if not self-consciously religious, this unified way is and has been fundamentally ceremonious—spiritual, one might say.[11] The Anishinaabe, like other Native American communities, traditionally made no dichotomous distinction between the natural and the supernatural, the material and the spiritual, the profane and the sacred.

While honoring elders, making political decisions, and hunting deer could count as religion, since they involve ceremonious behavior and interior cultivation, the Anishinaabe did maintain a number of ceremonial complexes more overtly oriented toward sacred realities. The Midéwiwin, or Grand Medicine, society was and remains today an intricate complex of initiation and healing ritual that involves ritual death and rebirth, reenactment of the sacred migration stories, and herbal healing lore. The men and women who were initiates of the society held themselves to high ethical standards and were recognized for the extensive repertoire of hundreds of songs they memorized and herbal remedies they knew.[12] The Wabeno was another ceremonial complex demanding its own repertory of songs, dance, and ritual knowledge. The shaking tent ceremonial complex involved shamanic summoning and communication with tutelary spirits, leading to divination and healing. The doctoring ceremonial tradition involved ritualized identification and removal of illness-causing substances and spirits.[13]

But to classify Anishinaabe "religion" as the beliefs and practices isolated to these ceremonial complexes is to miss the point about how the religious undertone of an entire Anishinaabe way of life defies the dichotomy between sacred and profane upon which so many conventional definitions of religion rest. This is perhaps most clearly seen in the case of Anishinaabe music and dance, which have been so enmeshed traditionally with religious concerns and motivations as to be justifiably understood as forms of prayer. There have been, to be sure, more sacred and less sacred songs and dances, but because these arts serve as privileged mediums of exchange with the spiritual sources of existence, there has been no such thing as completely profane songs or dances in Anishinaabe tradition. Indeed, the melodies and texts of most Anishinaabe songs have no identifiable human composer and most dances no choreographer; instead they are regarded as "gifts" from the spirits through dream and visionary experience. Among the Anishinaabeg, not only have dreams and visions been considered "real" experiences; they have been "really real" experiences—revelations from the spirits that bestow the insights, ritual and healing knowledge, and power necessary for leading the good life. The melodies, texts, dance steps, and ceremonial directions imparted by means of dreams and visions, interpreted variously by elders and other religious adepts, and passed on in the oral tradition have been understood as containing a discrete kind of power, a power that could be generated in performance for the benefit of the people.

The aesthetics of Anishinaabe music and dance cannot be divorced from these considerations of power and the traditional associations with the spiritual sources of existence. While even the outsider might well treasure performances as hauntingly beautiful, a fuller, more contextual, appreciation of these Anishinaabe arts requires an understanding of the transformative power of ritual language, song, and gesture. Texts to traditional songs or dance choreography may seem at times flat, repetitive, and even simple, but they are hardly simplistic. Performances of the texts and steps are embedded in a sophisticated worldview that asserts that language, melody, and gesture, when properly performed, not only describe the world or express the inner states of the artist but can tap into sacred power to transform the world, to safeguard a journey, to heal the sick, to secure a successful hunt or harvest, or to renew the cosmos.

A number of examples found in this book help to show how the aesthetics of Anishinaabe artistic traditions are caught up in concerns about the sacred. First, the steady beat of the drum sets the rhythm and mood of nearly every musical and dance performance in Anishinaabe tradition, but the drum represents far more than musical accompaniment. As is viscerally felt in performances, the drum brings a *presence* to the music and dance—a power of the Drum in general and of certain drums in particular to effectively carry prayers to the spirits. When properly treated and invited to sing, the drum not only provides aesthetic texture to performance; it creates, according to Anishinaabe tradition, social and cosmic conditions conducive to sociality, healing, and well-being. In Anishinaabe languages, drums are not things but "persons," powerful subjects that require ceremonial feeding, clothing, and initiation at the behest of drum keepers and singers.[14]

Second, that the melodies of songs typically involve repetition of short phrases in sets of four or more reflects not only an aesthetic of repetition, or a culturally patterned sacred numerology, but an association with the transformative power of music and language in performance. Simply put, repetition can multiply the power generated by a musical phrase or a text, if such patterned repetition is not already a necessary structure of performance according to a song's origin dream or vision.

Third, the strings of discursively meaningless syllables often encountered in Anishinaabe songs—those "hey-ya-yas" that have so often been misconstrued as primitive utterances in popular caricatures of Native music—are "vocables" memorized verbatim as crucial, if not discursively meaningful, texts of songs. Associated as they are with spiritual sources, these vocables would be memorized and performed with the attentive care befitting the medieval monk's calligraphic reproduction of Christian scriptures.

A final example from the case of dance helps us appreciate a distinctive Anishinaabe aesthetic. Dance steps are repetitive, uniformly following a circular, and generally sun-wise, orientation. Although there may be other explanations tendered by other Anishinaabe sources, the sun-wise circular dance pattern in part reiterates the directions given to the primordial spirits by the Trickster following the flood. With the power of the Trickster's bidding, this dance recreated the habitable world by expanding the mouthful of dirt brought up from the depths of the flood by Muskrat.[15]

Anishinaabe convictions about the capacity for performative language, song, and gesture to transform the world cannot be reduced to magical manipulations of nature by incantation. At times, the authors themselves apply language associated with the study of magic. But while the authors' choice of the word "sorcery," for example, may be justified in certain contexts, it is better understood in the context of the fundamental ambivalence of sacred power in Anishinaabe thought. As is attested in numerous traditions the world over, the power to heal is of a piece with the power to harm, and traditional healers are regarded with a kind of distance and ambivalence befitting the power they bring to bear. Unlike "magic," the transforming power of performative language, song, and gesture in Anishinaabe tradition is embedded in a network of appropriate ethical relations with the spirits. The power granted people by the spirits in dream and vision is clearly regarded as a "gift," and as such involves a code of conduct that stands in stark contrast to a more mechanistic, magical control of nature. If people can generate power through song, dance, and ritual, the power still issues from spiritual others who can be perturbed by unauthorized use of gifted power.

This sacred power is also embedded in the network of proper relations between persons. Codes of conduct apply as well to those performing powerful songs and dances. Those who sing at a drum proceed according to a detailed code of respect toward the drum and befitting the sacred charge of keeping a drum and playing it, and good performances are those that issue from proper social relations and the proper intentions of those making the music.

Nevertheless, sacred song, dance, and ceremony for the Anishinaabeg have never been exclusively sacred, exclusively supernatural, or exclusively spiritual; they have always been simultaneously rooted in the material and natural concerns of life. Anishinaabe religion, if we are to refer to the Anishinaabe way in those terms at all, has been a markedly this-worldly enterprise. Although the Anishinaabe have had convictions of an afterlife, of an ultimate order of things that involved sophisticated moral and aesthetic sensibilities, the religious dimension of life has remained unapologetically concerned with the material conditions necessary to a healthy, well lived, long life. As Christopher Vecsey puts it, "survival in this life, this 'existence,'" was their "ultimate concern."[16]

By virtue of their origins and associations, songs and dances could be tied to specific uses, such as healing, mourning, divination, military prowess, or safety in canoe travel. Or they could be associated with ceremonial complexes ensuring cosmic renewal through the cyclical restoration of appropriate relationships and cosmic balance. In the case of other songs and dances, the power gifted to an individual or community could be brought to bear through performance for any occasion that could benefit from a blessing of supernatural power—hunting, fishing, or harvesting.

The logic of spiritual power generated through performance for material ends is, in part, the logic of "prayer" as conventionally understood from a monotheistic perspective, especially those prayers that recite sacred texts, like the Christian Lord's Prayer or the Jewish *Shema*. In this respect, songs sung and dances performed are "offered up" to communicate or to reaffirm relatedness with spiritual others. But underlying this logic also is an Anishinaabe worldview that departs dramatically from the modern West's clear distinction between the natural and the supernatural.

Anishinaabe languages assert a grammatical distinction between animate and inanimate phenomena. A being that is grammatically animate is spoken of as a *person* rather than a thing, a subject rather than an object, with a moral stature and a capacity for agency, sentience, and transformation.[17] Spirits, human beings, animals, plants, and stones are all grammatically animate, as are weather phenomena (wind, thunder, and so on), paraphernalia associated with music, dance, and ceremony (pipe, drum, and tobacco), and certain myths told only in wintertime, including those included in this volume from the cycle of trickster stories.

This grammatical distinction between animate and inanimate is more than a mere structure of language. According to contemporary Anishinaabe people, it fosters a kind of consciousness that the natural world is alive with sentience, far more than the system of objects that modern Western thought has imagined nature to be. On traditional Anishinaabe terms, to do well in the hunt, or in the harvest, or indeed in any life pursuit, is more than a matter of woodsmanship or skill; it requires the proper spiritual relations with the sentient, subjective persons that stand behind and within the natural order. And these relations are affirmed and maintained through ceremonious practices involving music, gesture, and sometimes dance. Put another way, proper songs, dances, and ceremonies of thanksgiving or blessing—conventionally understood as *supernatural* appeals—are tantamount to success in material terms, as were the ethical considerations of wasting nothing in order not to take more life than was needed to promote life. The power that courses through the created order to give life is a spiritual power, one that flows for those entrusted by the spirits with knowledge of sacred music, language, and gesture and who exercise proper relations and intentions.

Thus in Anishinaabe tradition the natural and the supernatural, the material and the spiritual exist on a continuum rather than in clearly delineated categories. From the perspective of such a worldview, the integration of Anishinaabe economy, politics, kinship, horticulture, music, dance, storytelling, and ritual into an ideal, ceremonious whole makes good sense toward *bimaadiziwin,* the concept of "the good life" that fuses the material, biological, and social attributes of the good, long life with the moral, aesthetic, and spiritual considerations of a life made sacred.

As the authors of this volume repeatedly make clear, this traditional posture toward integrating all facets of life had become increasingly difficult as Michigan's Anishinaabeg became more fully integrated into the wider American culture and political economy. Indeed, it was the authors' concern for the imminent loss of that integration that urged them on in their work to document the lives and repertoires of these elders. But before we hasten to draw a clear demarcation between aboriginal Anishinaabe tradition and that of the twentieth century, we should remember the three centuries of post–European contact history in which the Odawa and Ojibwe cultures proved their resilience and adaptability. We should also bear in mind the basic fluidity to Anishinaabe tradition, suspended as it was (and is) in the dynamic flow of oral tradition and resistant to the calcifying abstractions that literate, modern Western habits of thinking predispose us to seek.

Religion, Art, and Culture Change

While the concluding chapter refers to the religious beliefs and practices of aboriginal times, it is religion *and culture change* that we find at the heart of this project. Writing fifteen years before the resurgence of tradition that swept Indian country in the early 1970s, the authors considered Michigan's Anishinaabe people to be "highly acculturated" and situated them in "the last stages of adjustment to the dominant culture's way of life."[18] But surely the authors would be pleased to know how wrong their prognosis would prove to be, for all along it was the *perseverance* of tradition that interested them and to which they committed their scholarship. And it was to religion, along with its associated music, dance, and narrative forms, that they turned for evidence of cultural persistence. The "material aspects of culture" had become completely assimilated in their view, but they wanted to show how it was in "the spiritual aspects" that "Native customs and ideas have persevered in variously obvious or subtle manifestations."[19] Their claim that indigenous religion helped promote cultural continuity may seem all too obvious, if not for the remarkable way that Kurath and the Ettawageshiks considered indigenous religion to be necessarily aboriginal—that is, believed "unsullied" by contact with Euro-Americans. Indeed, the crux of their work lay in the way they amplify and render significant those "subtle manifestations" of the spiritual aspects of culture. Whereas the reigning functionalist approach of anthropology in their day understood religion chiefly in terms of its ability to maintain the social or cultural status quo against all change by collapsing history through myth and ritual, Kurath and Ettawageshik documented how indigenous religion in its subtler manifestations was at the heart of the process of negotiating culture change.

Although much of the text of the book speaks of the transition from aboriginal religion to Christianity or the transition from a traditional form and function of music and dance to the contemporary performances of those traditions in staged shows and pageants, Kurath and the Ettawageshiks did much to collapse the binary distinctions that governed discussions of Native American traditions in their own day: tradition and change, aboriginal and post-contact, pagan and Christian.

In the mid-1950s, it was accepted practice to discuss Native American cultural change in terms of *acculturation*. The language of acculturation captured the imagination of anthropologists who had been schooled to think of Native American tribes as organic cultural and linguistic wholes, but who encountered in their fieldwork anything but continuous cultural wholes.[20] Instead, they encountered communities that were beleaguered by the dispossession and violence of U.S. Indian policy, boarding school education, and the subtler workings of incorporation into the American cash economy.

The process of acculturation offered a useful framework for making sense of both the displacements that these historical changes brought and the tangible cultural continuities that these ethnologists found. Acculturation was that gradual, virtually inevitable eroding of timeless tribal cultural wholes as they collided with a unified Euro-American or "white" culture. What remained in the wake of this process—Native Christianity, fragmentary survivals of traditional culture, and the various syncretisms aggregating old and new—were seen as not only discontinuous but inferior to the traditions that had their fullest integrity before European contact.

An anthropologist working with Ojibwe communities in Manitoba, A. I. Hallowell, did much to develop the concept of acculturation in the authors' day. For Hallowell and his students, acculturation was a concept so plain, so real, that one could identify relative levels of acculturation among Native communities in differing proximity to Euro-American settlements by means of Rorschach inkblot tests. To their credit, studies of acculturation by Hallowell and others updated cultural anthropology with a sense of change over time, carried ethnographic writing some distance away from the old "ethnographic present" that made no reference to history or time, and to varying degrees recognized anthropological "informants" as historically situated actors in their own right rather than as nameless embodiments of "culture."[21]

The authors of this study were contemporaries of Hallowell and his students, and not surprisingly, they occasionally use the term *acculturation*. But Kurath and the Ettawageshiks show a fundamental discomfort with the category, especially the implied value judgment that assigns less integrity to the acculturated traditions of the contemporary day than to the traditional ways of aboriginal days. Perhaps because of the Ettawageshiks' personal connections to the Odawa community and because of Kurath's appreciation for the aesthetic of hybrid expressions of Anishinaabe song and dance, the authors seem conspicuously uneasy with the available anthropological language for culture change. While the authors do appeal to the language of acculturation to frame their work, they use it sparingly and only in muted passages at the outset and conclusion of book. I would submit that their discomfort with that language is a primary reason for the theoretical reticence of this book, which itself is arguably a reason for its not having been published when it was originally submitted in 1955. At any rate, the reader may agree that the interpretive portions that frame the book at beginning and end are the more wooden passages, unable to do justice to the complex, dynamic realities to which the rest of the book bears witness.

It is not simply a matter of the book's content that work against a narrative of acculturation; it is the authors' basic agenda. It is striking, for example, that Kurath has enough regard for Ojibwe and Odawa hymn singing *as Native music* to take it seriously. In this, she was alone among ethnomusicologists of her day and for several decades to come.[22] The dean of scholarship on Anishinaabe music, Frances Densmore, writing some forty years earlier, made no reference to Ojibwe hymnody in her two-volume work, *Chippewa Music,* despite the fact that her initial contact at the White Earth reservation was a Native Episcopalian priest who had compiled the *Ojibwa Hymnal.* Because she categorized them as Christian music, Densmore concluded that hymns in whatever language were the music of acculturation and thus not worthy of study. By contrast, in this study Kurath paid more respectful attention to the full musical repertories of Native peoples as encountered, regardless of the origin of the musical traditions, and in so doing reconceived the notion of what constitutes "Native" music.

This book is similarly remarkable for the way it takes seriously the contemporary dance of mid-twentieth-century Native people, even as that dance signaled dramatic changes from aboriginal days. During fifty years of beleaguering assimilation policies, many dances lost by attrition their conscious associations with ritual efficacy. By the 1940s many important dances in the repertory were performed in folkloric fashion, often staged for white audiences. Similarly, the Anishinaabe dance repertory had incorporated many dances from other tribes after cultural exchanges in these same kinds of nontraditional dance venues. But the authors of this book do not dismiss the full range of the dance repertory at mid-century, nor do they suggest that dance had lost all its aboriginal significance. Instead, they trace how nimble a medium dance proves to be, how it can embody the contradictions of culture change, and how it fluidly evades the wooden interpretive language of acculturation. This book thus helps complicate the emerging literature on Native American dance, especially the literature about the historical emergence of powwow culture in the Great Lakes region.[23]

From the perspective of late twentieth and early twenty-first century scholarship, we can, appreciate and amplify the ways these authors honored the integrity of the practices and beliefs of their Anishinaabe collaborators, however changed they were from aboriginal days. In part, the authors did so by simply letting the practices and narratives of the people we meet speak for themselves in all their integrity. Indeed, one encounters their integrity through the very improvisation and hybridity with which these cultural actors nimbly extend their tradition.

Again, Kurath and the Ettawageshiks recognized the counter-intuitive notion that Native religion could be at the center of negotiating tradition and change, of sanctifying those changes and conferring worth on them. And it is this attention to religion—chiefly here through its associated practices of storytelling, dancing, and singing—that constitutes one of the more significant interpretive moves of the authors. "What is the adjustive value," the authors ask, "of the religious customs, residual, blended, or modern?"[24]

As we have already seen, religion is a broadly integrative category in Anishinaabe life—at once pervasive and subtle—and the authors understood that. The authors also understood what conventional wisdom has denied: that Native American religions are *at home* in history. Too often, Native American religions have been seen as resistant to historical change, perhaps even antithetical to change. When change happens to them, they have been seen as no longer having an integrity as traditional religion and have been understood instead as acculturated, devalued survivals of traditions or, at best, syncretistic religions, unstable aggregates of fragments of aboriginal religion, Christianity, and new movements, but lacking a logic of their own.

Because the authors of this study had a keen, human sense of the integrity of their Anishinaabe consultants, friends, and relatives, this study considers modern Anishinaabe religion to be whatever modern Anishinaabe people in fact practiced. As the chapter headings demonstrate, their study alights on the "scattered lore, beliefs, tales, and linguistic tenacity limited to elders," especially in the narratives of the myth cycle of the trickster and perhaps more subtly still on the music and dance performed in the public celebrations of Ojibwe and Odawa culture in the late 1940s and early 1950s. There were three types of "gatherings with past or present religious connotations."[25] First, Native songs and dance were included in what the Anishinaabeg of the day were calling "powwows," "pageants," and "ceremonials," and what the authors chose to call "festivals." Second, "semi-Native, semi-Catholic feasts" along Little Traverse Bay set a range of indigenous ritual practices, including naming ceremonies, to the Christian liturgical year and made All Saints' Day, Epiphany, and Lent occasions for the performance of Odawa language, song, and dance. Third, the gatherings included Methodist-sponsored revivalist camp meetings in southern Michigan.

These gatherings were hybrid forms that defied a clean boundary between tradition and change and between indigenous religion and Christianity. The same is also true, if more subtly so, in the case of certain stories in chapter 8, in which the timeless trickster Nanabozho (Nanabojo in the authors' orthography) and European Americans mingle in myth time, where the sacred past and the profane present merge in concrete moments of storytelling.

All of this is not to say that the authors remain unmoved by the colonizing forces that conspired to fragment Anishinaabe communities, lands, languages, and religious traditions. Kurath and the Ettawageshiks mince few words concerning that dramatic loss of an aboriginal integration of religion, art, and economy. Native language hymn singing had incorporated the missionaries' disdain for drumming, dancing, and shrill indigenous musical styles. The songs and dance steps of the festivals and ceremonials had been stripped of their ceremonial function. Performers in the festivals ostensibly had become at the very least folklorists, reconfiguring the functions of their traditions in performance even as they tried to maintain their life. At their worst, these performers became showmen, holding considerable economic interest in the performance of songs and dances that previously had been considered communication with the spirit world. Such observations on the part of the authors hardly need further elaboration here.

What does need elaboration, or perhaps amplification, is the authors' insistence that Anishinaabe religion, as Anishinaabeg were practicing it at mid-century, was at the heart of Odawa and Ojibwe efforts to negotiate culture change on their own terms as much as possible. Even as they were undergoing a "transition from Native to modern religion," Anishinaabe people drew on both indigenous religion and Christianity in efforts to make that transition one of spiritual worth and communal continuity.[26] Kurath and the Ettawageshiks recognized that even the folklorists who consciously performed traditions in pageants and "naming ceremonials" were consciously saving "from limbo" certain cultural fragments that they had learned from their elders.

Ritual functions thus gave way to "nativistic functions," and in some cases indigenous ceremonies gave way to revivalist camp meetings, but the songs and dances and beliefs and practices remained as resources for the Odawa and Ojibwe communities to make as seamless as possible the continuity of culture and tradition amid fragmenting forces of dispossession. Kurath and Ettawageshik seem to recognize the fundamentally religious nature of such a project. But the authors did not come forward to say as much. They lacked the insights of subsequent scholarship and, more importantly, the benefit of twenty-first century hindsight, to recognize clearly that what they were witnessing was anything but the final stage of acculturation. At least they had the open-mindedness to conceive of their project as documenting a kinetic process of culture change rather than survivals of a pre-contact Anishinaabe culture on the brink of extinction.

To more fully appreciate their grasp of the complexity—perhaps even equivocation—involved in culture change, we must look not to the authors' theoretical language in their short interpretive discussions at the beginning and conclusion of the book but rather to their diligent attention to the complexity of the repertories, motives, and lives of Joe Chingwa, Susan Shagonaby, David Kenosha, Thomas Shalifoe, Jr., and the other Anishinaabe elders and traditionalists whose remarkable stories occupy and enrich the following pages.

Elders Making Tradition

We find these elders' stories first in the biographical sketches of "Peninsular People" in chapter 1. Joe Chingwa's nineteenth-century grandfather "had the power to call the bears from their dens." When he was a young boy, the railroad bought his family's land, probably for a song, and he spent three years stripped of family and community at the boarding school in Mount Pleasant. That same railroad sponsored the *Song of Hiawatha* pageants and paid him modestly for singing the role of Jibiabos. He pieced together his living from short-term wage labor, fishing in Lake Michigan, and living off the land. We learn later that he charmed his fishing hooks with herbs.

Comfortable in Native and non-Native worlds alike, he was elected head of the Michigan Indian Defense Association.

It was from the *Song of Hiawatha* pageants that Whitney Albert came as a youngster to learn some of his own repertory of Native songs, which was reportedly "the largest and most varied" in the state. While the authors called him "pagan at heart," he was an able singer of both Protestant and Catholic hymns. Albert, like the other elder men, pieced together a living in the woods, building interstates, selling handiwork, and appearing in "festivals," although it is clear that his enthusiasm was not solely a matter of pay. In his "show business" ventures with friend Eli Thomas, Albert went by the name of Chief Blue Cloud, but he told the authors he was "neither a chief nor Blue Cloud."

The picture of each of these and nearly twenty other remarkable figures is deepened in subsequent chapters, where we are introduced to their various repertories of songs, dance steps, and stories. They each occupy multiple cultural worlds with enormous dexterity and sense of humor. They impress the authors with their sincerity and conscious sense of themselves as custodians of sacred tradition, even while they perform for non-Native audiences. Perhaps in keeping with "the trickster logic" of Anishinaabe religion, centered as it is on the antics and boundary crossings of Nanabozho, they defy easy classification as traditional or progressive, or as Protestant, Catholic, or pagan, and they refuse to take themselves too seriously.[27]

Although the authors do not take an assertive interpretive posture to help make summary sense of such lives, and perhaps rightly so, these elders' life stories and the complex cultural repertories they perform are open to a fuller consideration of the logic of religion and culture change. On this point, two considerations are worth our attention.

First, we are at a moment in the scholarship where elders are regarded as authoritative arbiters of religion, culture, and tradition. Although I elaborate on this idea in the context of Anishinaabe religion and culture change elsewhere, I would contend that what is recognized by Native communities as tradition is precisely *what elders declare tradition to be* in concrete historical moments, if those elders are vested broadly by their community with this authority.[28] In the case of the twentieth century, the stakes for what constitutes tradition clearly run high and remain highly controversial. Nevertheless, there is considerable precedent in Anishinaabe history and worldview that religious and cultural continuity and change meet in the authority of elders.

Regarding the profiles in this volume, the stature of the figures in the estimation of their communities is what casts their performances in the light of tradition rather than simple invention or folklore. In short, the integrity of traditions improvised and performed in these contexts has much to do with the integrity and authority recognized in the performers by the broader tribal community.

Second, it is clearer today than it was in the 1950s that continuity and change are most nimbly negotiated through the nondiscursive performances of culture, especially music and dance. That is, it would be difficult if not impossible to elaborate in so many words how the performances of Native musical and dance repertory in a *Song of Hiawatha* pageant could be sincere or genuine expressions of culture. But the palpable "heartbeat" of the drum, the rustling of the jingle dress or the deer hoof rattles, the sun-wise, two-step movement, the high pitched singing of descending minor key melodies *make sense* in practice in ways that defy complete discursive comprehension.

No doubt this is why Native American peoples and other colonized communities find in traditional music and dance the possibilities for asserting the integrity of their tradition in performance contexts that are hostile to that integrity. Identity and tradition can be asserted in performance where they might be unthinkable, and might pass beneath the radar of colonizing powers that would not find such sovereign expression of identity and tradition to be legitimate.

The Artfulness of the Scholarship

It took unconventional scholarship to appreciate the subtlety and deftness with which Michigan's Anishinaabe elders in these decades did the hard work of maintaining the vitality and viability of tradition. Gertrude Kurath, Jane Willets Ettawageshik, and Fred Ettawageshik rose to that challenge. In the end, the unconventional nature of their work served to block the manuscript's publication in the late 1950s, but it renders their book more relevant still to a twenty-first century readership. Cultural anthropologists have made much of participant observation, of distinctions between approaches that attempt to tell of a culture by assuming the worldview of its participants and those that try to analyze the culture from a perspective that is decidedly external to the culture.

The nature of the collaboration of these three scholars, however, eludes such tidy classification. The outsiders are also insiders; the insiders also outsiders. The informants are interpreters; the interpreters are self-aware participants in the community they record. And the thread tying all the pieces together is an appreciation of art, of beauty.

Gertrude Prokosch Kurath

Gertrude Prokosch Kurath was born in 1903, graduated from Bryn Mawr College in 1928, and studied music and dance at Yale's School of Drama and in Providence, Rhode Island. Modern dance was her passion, but she became very interested in folk dance as well, in a manner consistent with other modern primitivist artists of her day. She thought of herself primarily as a dancer for the twenty years between 1923 and 1946, when she taught, performed, produced, and choreographed modern dance. Having moved with her husband, a linguist, to Ann Arbor, Michigan, she remained well connected to the world of dance and included Martha Graham in her circle of compatriots. Kurath drew heavily on European folk dance and Native American dance traditions in her compositions.[29]

In the mid-1940s, Kurath's artistic passions and tastes carried her into a more sustained career of studying the dance and associated musical traditions of the Anishinaabeg and other Native peoples. Although she had no formal academic appointment, a brief glance at the acknowledgments in her publications suggests how connected she eventually became in cultural anthropology and ethnomusicology circles. For a time she even served as dance editor for *Ethnomusicology*.

With one foot solidly planted in the world of dance performance, she regarded the Native people she met as artists in their own right; she considered the dance steps and ceremonial traditions she recorded to be aesthetic performances. Kurath appreciated the creativity of her Native teachers and she appreciated their traditions as artful acts of creation, not simply the reiteration of received traditions.

Kurath described this work retrospectively in terms of "dance ethnology," a genre that splits the difference between art criticism and ethnography. On the one hand, Kurath reflected, "two decades as a performing dancer have left me with the conviction that a scholar should consider dance in its own terms, as an art form." On the other, she possessed an ethnologist's interest in how "dance and its music express other cultural aspects," in placing dance in the context of culture.[30]

Perhaps because of her education in the traditions of the Michigan Native people she came to meet, Kurath was particularly interested in the juncture between art, religion, and economy. In an essay entitled, "Dance, Music and the Daily Bread," Kurath observed the following:

> Dance and music can be more than specialized arts; the "job" can be more than a grim task. The meeting of these two disparate aspects of modern life could give dance and music fuller significance and invest the struggle

for subsistence with an aura. In many parts of the world that is so. The arts have grown out of the economy. In such cultures they show myriad variations, yet pervading tendencies as to functions, aspect, cultural connections and dynamics. A few examples will pass in review, as ornaments on the stark universal theme of making a living.[31]

Thus, ethnology for Kurath was not simply a strategy for interpreting the cultural meaning of dance and music performances. It was a means for better appreciating the aesthetic textures of daily life in Native communities. An artist's passion for the traditions of others took Kurath to a striking range of communities. She wrote on a variety of indigenous traditions—the Yaqui, the Pueblos, the Haudenosaunee Iroquois, the Cherokee–on the Conchero and Matachines dance traditions that brought Indian and Christian traditions together, on European folk dances, and on the African American Holiness tradition (see bibliography for citations).

In her fieldwork, Kurath the artist could not abide the then conventional distinction asserted between the social scientist and the informant. She was an artist in conversation with other artists. She kept in view the larger cultural life of dance and music, but "culture" never became a faceless determinative force in music and dance. Cultures were performed, creatively, by people whom she knew to be too complicated to be simply instances or manifestations of a "culture." These people she came to admire, befriend, and even to host as guests in her own home. So much for "fieldwork" in the conventional sense of the word.

In the context of this study, Kurath noted that "five field trips came to *me* in Ann Arbor, as a result of my ways and means of bringing the Indians to this town." She wrote, "Many profitable sessions, though not true field trips, resulted from friendly visits by Indians to my home. Many observations on dances came about through stop offs en route to something else, or on family vacations."[32]

Kurath never felt as though she had perfected her own art of "dance ethnology." "Despite all the fieldwork and experimentation," she wrote in 1966, "the goal always seems out of reach. I really haven't figured out a clear device for integrating the artistic and cultural factors. It is a perpetual challenge, frustrating and exciting."[33] Perhaps it was her artists' reluctance to explain away the music, dance, and religion of the Anishinaabe that allows Kurath's scholarship on the subject to breathe even after fifty years.

Jane Willets Ettawageshik

Jane Willets Ettawageshik (1915–1996) was at work on the materials in this book for some years before meeting up with Gertrude Kurath. Born in 1915 in Millageville, Georgia, where her father and mother were stationed as physician and nurse under the U.S. Public Health Service (they had met in that capacity in the Philippines), Jane Willets grew up in Flowertown, Pennsylvania, outside Philadelphia. She graduated from Barnard College with a degree in composition and stayed in New York City to work in the publishing field, although the war effort during World War II found her testing airplane engines. After the war, Jane Willets followed a long interest in anthropology and archeology and enrolled in the distinguished anthropology graduate program at the University of Pennsylvania under Frank Speck.[34] Speck recommended three locations for fieldwork toward her master's thesis, from which she chose Harbor Springs, Michigan, where she was to call on Speck's friend, Fred Ettawageshik. As it happened, when she arrived in June of 1946, Fred's father had recently died, and in his grief Fred had gone off to be alone for several weeks. Jane resolved to begin her fieldwork nonetheless and met Fred when he returned. That summer they fell in love, and she returned again for more fieldwork in January of the following year. She completed her degree in 1948 and returned to Harbor Springs that year. As is evident from her account of the ceremony at which she formally received her Odawa name, Wabanokwe, Jane not only lived among Odawa people but she lived enthusiastically as a member of the community. She raised two boys, one of whom was christened with the name of her mentor at Penn, Frank.[35]

At the time this book was being compiled in the 1950s, Fred's failing health and hard times with the family business required that Jane get work to make ends meet. She commuted several hours south to Central Michigan University to receive her teaching certification. In 1959 the family moved an hour south to Marion, Michigan, where Jane became the primary breadwinner of the family.

Fieldwork and housework, the extraordinary and the ordinary, the professional and familial were necessarily, generatively, combined for Jane. "No part of this work can be considered finished," Jane wrote in her acknowledgments, "for I am constantly learning something new, or at times understanding some trait of culture that seemed inexplicable last week. Perhaps when one is dealing with people and culture the last and final word can never be said." This is particularly noteworthy as the study of Odawa culture was for Jane not simply an academic pursuit but one tied up closely with the well- being of her own family, her neighbors, and future generations of her community. If this study reflects uncommon rapport between scholars and subjects, it seems largely a result of Jane Ettawageshik's manner. Note, for example, how she credits her consultants in the acknowledgments. They were neighbors, friends, and relations—not objects of study or even "informants" in the conventional sense. Perhaps it is her sense of responsibility to them, to get it all exactly right, that kept much of the material of her study and her life out of the hands of publishers, despite the fact that, according to her son Frank, she wanted the work to make it into print for posterity.

Fred Ettawageshik

Fred Ettawageshik (1896–1969) stood at the center of the Odawa community on Little Traverse Bay. Born in Harbor Springs, he was highly regarded among his community, a fluent Odawa speaker and by descent related to the illustrious nineteenth-century leader Andrew J. Blackbird, or Mack-e-te-be-nessy. At the same time that he was bound deeply to his Odawa community and its language and traditions, he was hardly its prisoner. Able to deftly straddle multiple worlds, Ettawageshik had been schooled at the Catholic Holy Child School in Harbor Springs, the government Indian boarding school at Mount Pleasant, and at the flagship boarding school, Pennsylvania's Carlisle Institute. He worked for one year at the government's Indian boarding school in Pipestone, Minnesota, and served in the army during the First World War. After the war, he trained and worked as an executive with the Boy Scouts of America in New York City. In the 1920s, apparently while lecturing on fur-bearing animals at an exposition in Philadelphia, Fred caught the attention of Frank Speck, who invited him to lecture to his class at the University of Pennsylvania in 1926.

In the 1930s Fred suffered an eye disease that blinded him temporarily and permanently impaired his vision such that he could no longer drive. Along with his mother's death, this condition brought him back to Harbor Springs, where he lived with his father and took over the family business, a store that made and sold curios and handicrafts to the burgeoning tourist population that stopped by steamship in Harbor Springs or summered in the region. He also supplemented his work in the store in a range of ways that suggested his own dexterity: he sold Fuller brushes door-to-door, worked for a time in an automobile assembly plant in Flint, and gathered herbal medicines to sell to pharmacists. His education, experience, and familial prominence made him a community leader, and he was active in the Michigan Indian Defense Association, even chairing the community meetings that debated whether to accept the terms of federal recognition as a tribe through the Indian Reorganization Act. When the steamship traffic at Harbor Springs declined in the 1950s, so too did the retail business of the store. Cheaper "Indian artifacts" made in Asian factories undercut the family business. While he continued to operate the store on a seasonal basis until 1963, Fred turned his attention to the making of handicrafts for wholesale out of the family basement. Along the way, harmful fumes from newer paints may have exacerbated the respiratory problems that dogged Fred from then until his death at in 1969 at the age of 73.[36]

A conventional anthropologist of the 1950s might have regarded Fred as an "informant," a supplier of the data of tradition. But it is clear that Fred was a savvy, multilingual, at times poetic interpreter of his tradition. The fruit of his work is not objective "data," then, but the performance of tradition and, precisely because of that agency on his part, data more in keeping with indigenous modes of cultural transmission.

The Collaboration and the History of this Book

The manuscript that Gertrude and Jane submitted for publication to the American Philosophical Society in June of 1955 was a compilation of many years' work, including interviews in the field, in Detroit, and at Kurath's home in Ann Arbor.[37] As the web of connections between these scholars and the Native communities in question suggests, the collaboration was a documentary project that was overtly activist in its engagement with the cultural traditions it sought to document. They were at work when the "Naming Ceremonial" at Harbor Springs, hitherto sponsored by an all-Indian organization, came under the support and direction of the Michigan Indian Foundation, a group of non-Native doctors, lawyers, and men of affairs from Detroit who summered in the region and took a hobbyist interest in Indian culture and artifacts. In 1953, under the foundation's direction, much of the program was undertaken by white performers, the dancing even "taken over by a group of Detroit white boy scouts, the *Heyoka Wacipi.*"[38]

In May 1954, Gertrude said that she and Jane "spread propaganda" to encourage the Odawa to consider "the large number of genuine Ottawa songs and dances still in their repertoire" and to "undertake a revival entirely their own." Gertrude even drew on her own artistic sensibilities and proposed a "coherent and entirely indigenous program," which she and Jane presented to a group of Odawas who "passed it unanimously." Jane ran the business end of the venture and four performances resulted that summer. When the Michigan Indian Foundation protested the use of the stadium that they had built expressly for the pageants and ceremonials celebrating Indian culture, the City Council stepped in with its support. Kurath reported that what she and Jane "instigated" remained a "completely Indian" enterprise, one that grew into a stable movement dedicated to the "revival of their arts and lore."

More than an "intervention" in the lives of their informants, the episode and the refreshing candor with which Kurath and Ettawageshik write of their role suggest the rapport that developed between the studier and the studied in the collaboration and the sensitivity that the authors brought to these festivals and performances as something more than mere showmanship. This was hardly disinterested scholarship, but its candid interestedness gives it credibility and connects it with the community studied.

These two women were professionals who were also working at home. In her acknowledgments, Jane tellingly credits her sister-in-law, Julia Black, "who took care of my family while I made necessary trip to Ann Arbor in connection with this manuscript." By this time, she had become the main breadwinner of the family and could not afford the time she desired to work on the project and future revisions. Kurath lived in Ann Arbor and was married to a linguist on the faculty of the University of Michigan. Their daughter, Ellen, joined Gertrude on much of her fieldwork in northern Michigan and elsewhere in Indian country, and supported her mother's fieldwork with photography, film, and recording technical expertise. Gertrude was thoroughly part of the intellectual life of the university town in which she lived, although she held no formal academic appointment herself, a fact that is striking given how prolific and broad reaching were her publications.

The writing project itself was a joint one, although the final product reveals distinct voices pertaining to different chapters. Kurath wrote that, although copies of successive drafts were sent to one another and accrued considerable overlap, her "share" of the writing "covers dance, song, and associated ritual," while "Jane's embraces ethnology and folklore."

Although no document definitively explains why the manuscript was rejected by the American Philosophical Society, which had commissioned the research in the first place, Kurath indicated in a 1959 letter that "so far, the publisher's verdict has been too much cost for reproducing music and too meager sales for a book on Michigan Indians."[39] Yet given that publishers often use such language to couch subjective judgments about manuscripts in more objective terms, one cannot help but wonder whether the study involved too much attention to what then would have been called acculturated Indian culture, as opposed to the ostensibly "purer" forms of aboriginal traditions.

With their allegiance to documenting Michigan Native practices at mid-century in whatever performance contexts they found them, Kurath and the Ettawageshiks went far to emphasize the integrity of those supposedly acculturated practices. For aside from several pages at the outset and conclusion, this book lets the artists/elders and their songs, dances, and stories speak for themselves, and in so doing makes room for readers' appreciation of their defiance of dualistic categories like continuity and acculturation, tradition and history, art and handicraft, informant and interpreter.

Although the manuscript as a whole was not published, research from this body of work saw modest piecemeal publication in an occasional volume for the University of Michigan's Sesquicentennial, *Michigan Indian Festivals* (Ann Arbor, Mich.: Ann Arbor Publishers, 1966). Kurath also has several article-length publications on focused topics deriving from this research.[40]

The Uses of the Scholarship

Ironically, what may have hindered publication in the 1950s makes this study all the more interesting and valuable today. Precisely because the research documented and appreciated the deep continuity of Odawa and Ojibwe culture within these unconventional forums, without distilling the rich complexity of Native lives into formulas of "acculturation" or binary distinctions between "tradition" and "change," it served well in the hard-fought bid for federal recognition, won by act of Congress in 1994 for the Little Traverse Bands of Odawa Indians.[41] Like many other Native communities, the Little Traverse Odawas had to articulate the case of the historical continuity of peoplehood and culture in the face of counter-arguments that there are no more "real Indians" and hence no real claims to recognition when the language, religion, and culture do not appear, from a romanticized American perspective anyway, to be continuous. The manuscript that has become this book substantially documented the case made by anthropologist James McClurken in a more formal ethnohistory.[42]

It is certainly expected by this editor, the publisher, and the heirs of the authors that the release of this book will enrich efforts by today's Odawa and Ojibwe communities to further their knowledge of their traditions and language. Members of those communities and other serious researchers are encouraged to hear directly from the source the Native language songs and narratives that are archived at the American Philosophical Society Library in Philadelphia. There are more than twenty-two hours of these recordings, albeit of varying sound quality. The society has digitally reproduced all the recordings for easier use in research.

The effort that resulted in this volume is useful for a number of broader fields of scholarship as well. Students of twentieth-century Native American history will find, for example, a rich resource for telling at least one story in the development of the powwow tradition prior to its subsequent place in the further development of a pan-tribal Native American identity.

Students of ethnomusicology and cross-cultural dance will also find much to harvest in this book, both in terms of "data" and, perhaps more importantly, in terms of the intuitive feel that Kurath and Ettawageshik had for the vitality of dance, music, and story in the lives of twentieth-century Native peoples. Of value also is the authors' sensitivity to the hybridity of artistic repertories, specifically the way that the musical, narrative, and dance repertories of Native individuals traverse the conventional boundaries between cultures. As Judith Vander has demonstrated in the field of ethnomusicology, each person has a distinctive "songprint" that involves an array of cultural worlds in a single repertory.[43]

Students of anthropology will perhaps note the significance of this collaboration being somewhat before its time. If Kurath and the Ettawageshiks did not have at hand the nimbler vocabulary and analytical tools concerning performance theory and hybridity that cultural studies would make available thirty years hence, they did remain quietly reluctant to employ a meta-narrative of acculturation. What is more, the musical and choreographic data to which this collaboration attended, collected as it was in such unorthodox and apparently nontraditional settings as pageants and powwows, and the flavor of reportage, which took such performances seriously as evidence of real Indian traditions, commend both the acuity and the subtlety of the authors' insight. Perhaps this acuity and subtlety was missed by the editors at the American Philosophical Society Press, and perhaps the non-publication of this book itself instructs about the history of anthropology at mid-century and the fruit of the collaborative work between these women.

Conclusion: A Sacred Trust

Even as the Anishinaabeg came to conduct much of their life within the realm of writing and print, they have maintained sacred musical, dance, and narrative repertories in the oral tradition with a peculiar tenacity. No doubt this owes to the way that an oral tradition secures sovereignty over the transmission of sacred knowledge, but it also bespeaks a distinctive Anishinaabe belief in the renewable and renewing presence of tradition. That the Anishinaabe elders featured in this book entrusted their repertories to the recording instruments of Gertrude Kurath and Jane Ettawageshik–and through the technology of print to you the reader—indicates the rapport the authors earned and prefigures a kind of sacred trust in our responsibility as readers to read with respect. The reader is enjoined to recognize the integrity of fluid cultural traditions maintained in some of the least likely places, to suspend inclinations to privilege some cultural performances as pure and others as denigrated by acculturation. This is not to deny the very real and sometimes denaturing processes of change in which the historical Anishinaabe actors herein were caught. A successful encounter with a book like this, written as it was more than fifty years ago, will require open-mindedness, dexterity—even creativity—on the part of the reader. This approach is modeled, but ultimately not fully delivered, by the authors themselves, confined as they were to an analytical language now obsolete and deprived as they were of the hindsight that would demonstrate how the performances of these elders would provide a basis for the revitalization of traditional indigenous music, dance, and ceremony.

When the storied cultural anthropologist Paul Radin forayed into upper Michigan to collect data on aboriginal cultures, he determined that Michigan's Ojibwe and Odawa communities had become so acculturated that there was nothing there worth studying anymore. Meeting the likes of Fred Ettawageshik, Susan Shagonaby, David Kenosha, and Joe Chingwa, Gertrude Kurath and Jane Willets Ettawageshik got it, and concluded just the opposite. As the reader will perhaps agree, it is to their credit—and our benefit—that they did.

EDITORIAL PRINCIPLES AND ORTHOGRAPHY

Editorial Principles

As an editor, I present this book to the reader as a "primary" text and therefore have not acted on the impulse to "correct" what I might view as faulty statements or misguided interpretations in the content of the work. I have gone ahead and changed occasional expressions that are considered offensive today, such as "half-breed," but misguided predictions about the future of Native religion and culture and misnomers such as "sorcery" I have simply flagged in footnotes as signs of their times.

Similarly, I have engaged in modest copyediting to make the authors' ideas appear as cleanly and clearly as possible, but I have chosen not to alter basic content, even when an alteration might make for a more accurate interpretation of Anishinaabe religious and cultural history.

For the sake of clarity, I have made only brief remarks in the body of the book, restricting them to introductory notes at the outset of each chapter, to help frame the content and voice from a more contemporary perspective, to occasional interjections bounded by brackets ([ ]), and to the occasional footnote.

As for musical notation, it has seemed best to simply reproduce the manuscript notations made by Gertrude Kurath, even if there may be a number of inadvertent errors in the original manuscript. The alternative, which would surely be more pleasing to the eye, would have been to typeset them, but to do so would have raised the risk of making some ill-informed judgment calls in order to regularize Kurath's idiosyncratic notations. This editorial choice seems most in the interest of accurate and respectful documentation of Anishinaabe music.

A Note on Orthography

After considerable deliberation and consultation, I have chosen to let stand the orthographic transcriptions of the Odawa and Ojibwe language as they appeared in the original manuscript, despite the inconsistencies in this manuscript and the obsolescence of much of the orthography. Contemporary students of Michigan Odawa and Ojibwe languages will find rich resources in the interlinear translations of chapter 9, but likely will be frustrated that the representations of long and short vowels do not resemble most written resources used in learning the languages today (the original manuscript includes many accent marks atop stressed syllables, and these have been rendered as accents above the operative vowel. This is tantamount but not equivalent to transcribing long vowels). Since these transcriptions involve nuance and historical insights into the phonology of Michigan Anishinaabe dialects that are beyond my expertise, I hesitate to apply a hasty re-transcription. In my editor's introduction and in supplementary material authored by myself, I have used the common orthography found in Nichols's and Nyholm's (1995) work on Ojibwe. A more thorough re-transcription of Michigan Odawa and Ojibwe should begin afresh with a return to the audiotapes in the American Philosophical Society.[1] It remains for a scholar and/or community member to take on such a project.[2]

The reader will quickly notice just how variant are the transcriptions of the authors' various collaborators. Again, were I to forge ahead and hastily make the orthography uniform, it would not do justice to the authors. Instead, let me cite here what Jane Ettawageshik had to say concerning the various orthographies found in chapter 9 and elsewhere:

> The Odawa script which Fred uses is based on our English alphabet and his own interpretation of the way in which it should be used to write Odawa. He does not know just when he began to write Odawa. I am of the opinion that he was influenced by his father, Joe, who also wrote Odawa. I have seen Odawa written by my father-in-law and it is very similar if not identical to Fred's rendition.
>
> A number of Odawas write their language and there is considerable variation among them. The original desire to write Odawa was probably inspired by the Catholic priests. Andrew Blackbird speaks of his father in the early days of the mission schools, helping Odawas learn to write by devising an alphabet which he called "Paw-pa-pe-po" (Blackbird 1897, 31). Old Victoria Cooper still remembers a little about "paw-pa-pe-po" and at one time had a little book explaining it.

It is probable that modern writers of Odawa owe a debt to Fr. Friedrich Baraga, who translated hymnals and prayer books into Odawa in the mid-nineteenth century, yet I have not seen any recently written Odawa which is exactly similar to his. I have tried to pin Fred down a number of times about the origin of his Odawa script, but he usually ends by saying, "I write the words the way they sound to me."

If frustrations emerge from these difficult editorial decisions, the reader is invited to bear in mind that many Anishinaabe people, while embracing the possibilities of orthographic rendering in print, consider their languages to be fundamentally a matter of oral tradition. Perhaps the inconsistency of the orthography in the pages that follow will, in its own way, emphasize that point.

AUTHORS' ACKNOWLEDGMENTS

Distant tribes have preoccupied Michigan ethnologists, and Michigan tribes have been left in peace. A resident of Michigan, I also covered considerable mileage elsewhere. In 1948 I saw Cross Village for a day. After 1961 I began to wonder about the possibilities of Native patterns in this huge state. In 1965, plans for inquiry became a reality, thanks to a series of grants from the Michigan Academy of Science, Arts and Letters. In 1954 the American Philosophical Society lent further impetus by commissioning a joint manuscript by Jane Ettawageshik and me. From 1955 to 1966, observations and recordings grew out of a baker's dozen of field trips and Indian return visits. At first they confined themselves to the Lower Peninsula. In 1964 they reached to Baraga on Lake Superior, and in 1966, they extended to Nahma, Hannahville, and northern Wisconsin. Photography started in black-and-white, proceeded to color slides, and graduated to motion pictures. The more difficult photography is the work of my daughter Ellen. [These photographs were not part of the original ms.] At special sessions with David Kenosha on the Cross Village shore and with an Odawa group in the Ettawageshik garden, we followed a plan. Tape recordings and photography have been indispensable in analysis and interpretation. The recordings also were played back by the hour in translating sessions with singers, narrators, and special helpers: Fred Ettawageshik, and Evelyn and Kenneth Pike.

Linguistic analyses were beyond my training and my information on the dialects; but two approaches were within range. The terminology threw light on changing ideology. Some parallel spoken and sung renderings justified a comparative study of rhythm and melody. For the organization of our joint product, Jane Ettawageshik and I conferred on the occasion of every visit, and we mailed carbon copies of successive drafts to one another. My share covers dance, song, and associated ritual; Jane's embraces ethnology and folklore. Our treatments overlap in many customs and in the reference to history and ecology. On the whole, our shares called for separate chapters, but parallel conclusions have been combined. Pertinent materials have been exchanged. My transcriptions of her recordings are incorporated in the most appropriate places, either among songs or in the midst of Odawa feasts. The recordings have been edited and labeled for deposit in the Library of the American Philosophical Society. The tape duplicates of Jane's wire recordings are filed by themselves. Rearranged duplicates of my field recordings bear the labels of Native or Christian songs, texts of hymns, and narrations. One reel reproduces an evangelist meeting.

The first expression of gratitude goes to Dr. William E. Lingelbach and Mrs. Gertrude Hess of the American Philosophical Society, for without their efforts the manuscript would not have come into being. Equally essential was the financial support of the Michigan Academy of Science, Arts and Letters, through Dr. Frederick Sparrow, chairman of the Committee on Research, Frank X. Braun, and Dr. Pierre Dansereau, one-time secretary of the academy.

During the fieldwork, Jane and Fred Ettawageshik lent their invaluable assistance. To them, my thanks, as also to the Odawa and Ojibwe singers and dancers who cooperated so willingly. Dr. Allen P. Britton provided blank tape reels from the supply of the Archives of Regional Music at the University of Michigan, where one copy is deposited. Fred Anderegg provided cut rate photographic materials. Ellen Kurath photographed dance sequences in color. Thomas Bradley made discs for the Indians. Edwin Burrows and I exchanged recordings. In the preparation of the manuscript the following scholars and musicians helped ponder the problem of hymnody: Veronica Britton, Lester McCoy, Dr. Hans David, Fr. Paul Prud'homme, Dr. Martin Gusinde, and the officers of the Bishop Baraga Association. Evelyn and Kenneth Pike lent valuable linguistic assistance. The manuscript has passed through the hands of a number of readers, most of whom have made constructive comments: Dr. James Griffin, Volney Jones, James Howard, Nancy Solien, Estelle Titiev, Prod Wieck. To all of them I am obligated for the time spent on the perusal.

GERTRUDE KURATH

Many persons have aided in the preparation of this manuscript. Some of the information presented was obtained on my first field trip in 1946; some observations were added only yesterday as the result of a talk with Susy Shagonaby. No part of this work can be considered finished, for I am constantly learning something new, or at times understanding some trait of culture that seemed inexplicable last week. Perhaps when one is dealing with people and culture, the last and final word can never be said. My first meeting with Fred Ettawageshik was in the summer of 1944, when I was a graduate student in anthropology at the University of Pennsylvania. The late Frank Speck had known Fred for many years but had never visited Harbor Springs. It was his suggestion that I make a field trip to Harbor Springs in search of material for my master's thesis, and so I wrote Fred and came to Harbor Springs in June. A second trip sponsored by the University of Pennsylvania was made in January, 1947, and in the spring of that year Fred spent a week in Philadelphia under the joint sponsorship of the American Philosophical Society and the Linguistics Department of the University of Pennsylvania.

During this latter visit a number of the legends and myths in this book were recorded in Odawa for the Record Library of the American Philosophical Society. After completing my thesis, "Correlated Changes in Odawa Kinship and Social Organization," and receiving my Master of Arts degree in 1948, I returned to Harbor Springs in the spring of that year, sponsored again by the American Philosophical Society. I recorded more legends and myths, many of which have been translated and are included here. In 1954 I received a grant from the American Philosophical Society, which enabled me to prepare this account of Odawa religious beliefs and customs in collaboration with Gertrude Kurath.

My principal Odawa informant is, of course, my husband Fred, with whom I constantly check off every phase of Odawa culture. In addition, Susy Shagonaby sees the importance of recording information about Odawa culture before it is too late and is an enthusiastic informant. Joe Chingwa, now dead, was a mine of information. There are many other Odawas who should be mentioned and thanked for their help: old Victoria Cooper and her son Jim, the late Marian Kiogima (Susy Shagonaby's mother), Elizabeth and Joe Kishigo, Christine Otto (who died this year), Dorothy Sagataw, Betty and Vincent Cooper, and many others. In particular, I want to thank my sister-in-law, Julia Black, who not only was generous with information but also took care of my family while I made a necessary trip to Ann Arbor in connection with this manuscript.

I should also like to express my appreciation to my sponsors, the University of Pennsylvania and the American Philosophical Society, and to those whose advice and help were freely offered: Frank Speck, who taught me to appreciate the American Indian and introduced me to field work, and who directed my early attempts to cope with Odawa culture, and who gave me his Odawa field notes, which were based on conversations with

Fred in Philadelphia in 1926. A. I. Hallowell, Volney Jones, Emerson Greenman, Albert Spaulding, James Griffin, and others read my manuscript or were helpful in other ways. I am also indebted to the Bureau of American Ethnology for permission to use the unpublished Odawa notes of Truman Michelson and Albert S. Gatschet, and to Carl Wright of Harbor Springs and the Botany Departments of the University of Pennsylvania and Haverford College for help in identifying herbs.

My special thanks to Gertrude Kurath, who has been a good and generous friend through our association in preparing this manuscript. Her wide knowledge and experience in anthropology were an invaluable help to me, and she has also lent me books from her own library and from the University of Michigan, without which I would have been greatly hampered in my research. The photographs of Odawas presented are from a variety of sources [the original ms. did not include such photographs]. Some I took myself; others were given to me by informants or friends. Several photographs were taken by Voight Troup of Harbor Springs, a friend and professional photographer.

JANE ETTAWAGESHIK

The Setting

CHAPTER 1

Peninsular People

In this chapter, Jane Ettawageshik and Gertrude Kurath sketch the cultural geography and biographies that provide the setting for the music, dance, and narrative traditions described in the rest of the book. While fuller pictures of the authors' consultants emerge in subsequent chapters, the brief sketches that follow suggest the complicated ways in which each character is situated between inherited tradition and twentieth-century realities. The authors conclude the chapter with brief statements about their methodology and framework for interpreting culture change.

Since the dawn of history, the Michigan Anishinaabeg have roamed over the vast expanses of two peculiar land bodies, two peninsulas separated by a narrow strip of water, two peninsulas with different climates and different adjacent territories. The descendants, though now engulfed in a white population, betray in their cultural vestiges the effects of this topography. All but surrounded by four of the Great Lakes, the Natives benefited from the tampering changes in the maritime winds, from the fickle and often stormy climate that produced crops of maize, beans, and squash as far north as Mackinaw Island, in forests filled with game. They took advantage of the innumerable streams and lakes for fishing and for travel. The significance of the setting has been summarized by various experts:

> The Great Lakes and thirty-four primary river systems have shaped the economic destiny of Michigan.... The Michigan coast line is 3,117 miles long, of which 120 are harbor and inlet coast lines and 833 are island shore lines. The shores of the Upper Peninsula are generally rocky, picturesque, and even dramatic in appearance, varying as they do from dune and beach

to crag and precipice. The dunes of both Upper and Lower Peninsula are
... whimsically shifting, barren, sad, somber. (Works Progress Administration 1941, 18) ...

Start at the Monroe marshes and the flat, naturally wet plains in their hinterlands westward are the fertile reaches of Michigan's southern counties.... Northward lies a vast region of generally lean sands where, two short generations ago, stood the vast forests of pine.... Farther, the light soil types, where once northern hardwoods cloaked the hills.... Moving northward, across mighty rivers and past inland lakes by the thousands, the traveler reaches the Straits of Mackinac, dividing Michigan.... Hardwood pines were there, and sweeping areas of dark swamp growth sprawled over the eastern end of the Upper Peninsula, while on the ridges the rock commenced to emerge from the soil. To follow the rock toward Wisconsin and to see the increasing evidence of iron and copper riches is to realize the long distance and the many different areas that lie between this country and the marshes of the Ohio line. And on all sides, setting the State apart is a frame as blue as the Mediterranean—the great Lake Superior, hurling its mighty breakers upon the rocky ramparts of the Upper Peninsula; Michigan, snarling at the dunes; Huron, laving the golden beaches with its surf; and Erie, insistently nudging the rushes of the Monroe marshes. (Works Progress Administration 1941, 3–4)

On small parcels of these rich domains, there still live members of three important Algonkian tribes, often termed the "Three Brothers": the powerful nomad-hunters, the Chippewa or Ojibwe; the less numerous but enterprising hunters and cultivators, the Odawa; and the gentle, maize-growing Potawatomi. They occupy, respectively, rural Isabella Reservation near Mount Pleasant, coastal Little Traverse Bay, and a farming tract near Athens. They are scattered through many other areas, described in the narrative and shown on the map, and they have in small numbers migrated into industrial centers.[1] On the whole, they are content with their lot, for they remain on native soil and can follow Native pursuits, supplemented by the white man's work. They have embraced the white man's religion whole-heartedly. The Odawa have largely become Catholic; the Ojibwe of Isabella and the Potawatomi of Athens either Methodist or Presbyterian. Many of them combine a pride in their Indian heritage with education on European prototypes. The more fortunate Indians derive an adequate livelihood from their Native pursuits of fishing, hunting, cultivation of corn, beans, squash, tomatoes, and potatoes, plus work on railroads, road construction, and oil wells, and in factories, lumber camps, and tourism. Others located in more isolated, northerly areas, live in poverty. Even in humbler circumstances, electricity, radio, and television are indispensable. In camp gatherings, the army tents and electricity, and in shows, the ubiquitous public address system illustrates the Indian fondness for white man's gadgets.

They gather together for various reasons, for family and tribal feasts, evangelistic camp meetings, and powwows. The feasts, now limited to the Little Traverse Odawa, mingle cultural traditions. The religious camp meetings address Jesus instead of the spirits of nature. The powwows, despite a ritual origin, now include shows for the white man.

Migrations

The Michigan Anishinaabeg have always wandered over vast territories, and they still like trips. The wandering took the form of seasonal changes of habitat as well as of tribal shifts. The Odawa earned the name "traders." The Ojibwe (puckered moccasins) and Potawatomi (fire keepers) kept pace. Many other tribes temporarily resided in this area or rushed through in flight or conquest.

Traditions and history point to a southwesterly drift and increasing relationships with southern and westerly tribes. Legend tells of early migration from the northeast, with the *megis*, a seashell, as their guide (Warren 1885, 78ff).[2]

Many practices indicate prehistoric boreal connections: death rites (Wike 1952), dreams, shamanism, dog sacrifice, emphasis on hunting and animal cults, and bear ceremonialism. Before 1650, the Odawa occupied the eastern shore of Lake Huron and Georgian Bay. The many bands of Ojibwe had spread along the western shore of Lake Huron, all across the northern Lower Peninsula and the Upper Peninsula. The Potawatomi wrapped themselves around the southern shore of Lake Michigan.

About 1660, in a chain reaction resulting from white intrusion, the Iroquois drove these Anishinaabeg and the docile Iroquoian Huron tribe to the vicinity of Green Bay. Here the Three Brothers joined the Menominee, Sauk and Fox, Kickapoo, and the Siouan Winnebago (Kellogg 1925, 70, 99; Kinietz 1940, 308–10). Then some bands moved north to several locations on Lake Superior, including Keweenaw Bay and the Huron Mountains. Others returned east to the tribal melting pot and trading center, St. Ignace. Subsequent conflicts with the Dakota and Iroquois occasioned large scale retreats and advances, some Ojibwe spreading into Minnesota and others, called the Mississauga, occupying the tongue of Ontario just east of Michigan.

Connections between Michigan and Ontario Indians have extended all the way from Garden River Reserve, Manitoulin Island, and Parry Island to Walpole Island and inland reserves. They continue. The Huron, original inhabitants of that area, still were at home in Amherstburg in 1870 but have moved elsewhere in far smaller numbers (Barbeau 1915, 14). The easterly Five Nations Iroquois marauded Ontario and southern Michigan centuries ago and now have their most flourishing reservation in Ontario (Hinsdale 1925, 9, 14). The Ontario and even the New York State Iroquois keep in touch with Anishinaabeg through the camp meeting pattern.

A number of Central Anishinaabeg just to the south have now moved far from Michigan proximity. But in early historic times Shawnee settled in northern Ohio, along with some Seneca (Fenton 1940, 241). The Miami, in northern Ohio from 1650 to 1750, moved into Illinois, close to the Potawatomi and not far from the Great Plains (Fenton 1953, fig. 30; Kinietz 1940, 310). The Odawa migrated into Ohio and are still represented in Piedmont, Ohio, by five families (Br. Brown, personal communication). During the Green Bay Odawa period and throughout Ojibwe history, these Anishinaabeg adjoined the Illinois, notably on peaceable terms by way of the calumet.

With the Menominee next door on the Michigan-Wisconsin border, they have always been on peaceful terms. These close relations are most evident in the seventeenth century neighborliness at Green Bay. But Menominee traditions tell of remote, prehistoric connections. They trace the Menominee Wolf-Wave and Bear-Bald Eagle gentes to Michigan. Close religious and musical resemblances will be pointed out later on.

Contacts with the Sioux have been stormy. Odawa traditions have retained stories of Odawa attacks on the Winnebagos as far back as A.D. 1200 (Blackbird 1897, 85–89). In 1671 they were in turn driven east from La Pointe by the Plains Sioux (Wright 1917, 166–169). At the time of first white contacts the westerly Ojibwe and the Sioux were in constant guerilla warfare; then for a time they were on friendly terms and intermarried, first around 1680 and then again around 1695 through the intervention of French traders (Thomas 1903, 291; Warren 1885, 168ff.). In the eighteenth century they again molested one another, the Ojibwe driving to the Mississippi River, until they had to face a common enemy from across the ocean.

These westerly members of the Three Brothers, the Wisconsin Ojibwe and Potawatomi, have adopted many Plains traits and religious cults that never reached Michigan (Kinietz 1947; Ritzenthaler 1953b). They know the buffalo which never entered Michigan. They have received old war and recent powwow complexes from the Plains and from Oklahoma. Their dances and songs differ from those of Michigan's tribes, despite visits to Wisconsin powwows at Wisconsin Dells and other meetings.

Nomadism, historically compulsive, also characterized annual seasonal rounds of life and occupation. The Odawa and particularly the Potawatomi did accept some of the maize culture of their southern and eastern neighbors, but the Three Brothers shared an essentially hunting way of life. In the summer they moved to lakes and streams for fishing and wild plants: in the winter they disbanded for protected game areas. In the early spring they assembled in large numbers for the tapping of maples and for renewed sociability. This was very different from their sedentary life and their occupations of today. The economy and the associated religious customs were just as different from those of today.

White Contacts

Three centuries ago white intrusions arrived from the northeast, via the St. Lawrence River, along the Odawa River, across Lake Huron. The first Jesuit missionaries arrived at the Falls of St. Mary's in 1641 (Copway 1851, 197). The first associations with the French promoted good will, "for the Frenchmen . . . easily assimilated themselves . . . and respected their religious rites and ceremonies" (Warren 1885, 132–34). The later British and Colonial influences were almost entirely destructive.

By 1866 the Indians had ceded most of their lands and were concentrated in small settlements, Isabella Reserve being established in that year. Fur traders had depleted the game. Whiskey and disease had taken their toll. Many of the Indians tried to maintain their old ways and rites. Others turned to the established Catholic faith or to the new Methodism. Since that time, changes have been accelerating, each generation losing old beliefs and accepting new ways. In the new economy hunting and war rituals became obsolete; their vestiges became curiosities. Intermarriages with whites and migrations to cities completed the transformation.

Personalities and Their Homes

L'Arbre Croche

The history of the Odawa in old L'Arbre Croche has been tempestuous and varied. They have been alternately pagan and Christian, and have been strongly influenced by French, English, and white Americans as well as by surrounding Indian tribes. Today they are a highly acculturated group, but still rather strangely cling to some of the old Indian culture.

The Odawa language is spoken fluently by many and is understood at least partially by almost all of the group. Old ceremonies are for the most part obsolete, but some have been incorporated into and blended with Christian rituals—few still persist almost unaltered. Myths, legends, songs, and dances are known to some individuals, as are herbal remedies, sorcery, and superstitions based on ancient practices. Even the old manidos [spirits] are known at least by name, and in some cases vestiges of former attitudes toward them and beliefs concerning them are encountered.

It is not known exactly how long Odawas have lived in L'Arbre Croche. The name first appears in French accounts toward the close of the seventeenth century, but it does not seem to have been an Odawa settlement of any size until after 1742 when a considerable body of Odawas moved to the region from Mackinac Island (Kinietz 1940, 230). The name L'Arbre Croche was a French translation of the Odawa *Woganákasi* (Land of the Crooked Tree), said to have been given to the area because of a tall, bent pine that at one time formed a landmark on the sand dune above Middle Village. The original L'Arbre Croche was a string of villages stretching from Seven Mile Point on Lake Michigan to Cross Village; later it was extended to include Harbor Springs and Petoskey on Little Traverse Bay.

Foundations of a Jesuit mission, said to date from 1695, may still be found near Middle Village, but all records of the mission appear to have vanished with the priests who made them. It is quite probable that there were some Odawas living in the area at that time, and there must have been other Indian groups nearby. Just which Indian tribe or tribes it was that prompted the Jesuits to build a mission at Middle Village in this period is not known. In the literature concerning the proposed move of a group of Odawas from Mackinac Island in 1742, the region is spoken of as a wilderness.

The Odawa claim to have driven a tribe called the Maškódens from the area in a great battle that must have occurred, if at all, while the main body of the Odawa were living on Manitoulin Island and along the shores of Georgian Bay, where they were found by Champlain. In my section on Odawa legends (chapter 9), I discuss the problem of the Maškódens and conclude that they did exist, that they were a branch of the Prairie Potawatomi, and that the Odawas took the entire northwestern section of the Lower Peninsula from them by conquest. Whether or not there were still Maškódens in the area until the early 1700s is not known.

Jonas Shawanessi, an Odawa from Harbor Springs who is currently delving into Odawa tradition and history in connection with the Odawas' suit against the U.S. government for land claims, says that he believes the branch of the Odawa known as Sinágo (Grey Squirrel) may have been the Odawas who fought with the Maškódens and that they were the first Odawa group to settle in the region. Their town, he believes, was situated at the site of present Harbor Springs, and their nature was such that other Odawas who settled later in L'Arbre Croche proper, north of Harbor Springs, came to fear them.

Jonas said that his grandfather used to tell about his ancestors and the care they took to stay away from the harbor at Harbor Springs. Even though the L'Arbre Croche Odawa might have been traveling to a spot that would have made a trip through Harbor Springs or across the harbor the shortest route, they would make a wide circuit around Harbor Point, which forms the southwest side of the harbor. A mysterious drum was said to beat whenever Indians approached the Harbor Springs area; it was also said that a strange silence existed near the harbor that caused voices to carry a great distance. There is much truth to the latter belief: one can hear sounds from Petoskey five miles across the bay quite distinctly, but in Petoskey one does not hear noises from Harbor Springs.

Whether or not the Sinágo Odawa were responsible, the Harbor Springs area seems to have been regarded with a superstitious dread for many years. The L'Arbre Croche Odawa did not establish a town there until 1829 when it was decided to move the newly formed Catholic mission from Seven Mile Point to the Harbor Springs spot because of the fine harbor and safer mooring for boats. Other superstitious beliefs about Harbor Springs were the fear of a great whirlpool, which is said to have existed on Harbor Point, and the terror inspired by the Great Serpent, who was thought to have formed the harbor in the first place and was reported seen in the harbor from time to time.

Jonas, who is descended from a long and illustrious line of Odawa chiefs bearing the name Nısawákwatʻ ("three-pronged" or "forked"), tells me that the original Nısawákwatʻ came from the vicinity of Winnipeg, Canada, with a band of relatives and followers to settle at L'Arbre Croche. This probably took place about 1700 or shortly thereafter. Nısawákwatʻ's sister married a French trader named Langlade and in 1729 at L'Arbre Croche gave birth to Charles Langlade, the famous "mixed blood" who fought valiantly for both the French and the Odawa. From this and other evidence, Jonas deduces that L'Arbre Croche was already an important Odawa settlement before the addition of the Odawa band from Mackinac Island in 1742.

It is possible that Nısawákwatʻ's band of Odawa, who later settled at L'Arbre Croche, were among those who fled west in the seventeenth century before the warlike New York Iroquois. Odawas are known to have had settlements as far west as the headwaters of the Mississippi in this period. Jesuits also ministered to Odawas at Point St. Esprit and at other places in the western Upper Peninsula and in Wisconsin. By 1670 the Odawa began to trickle back eastward to St. Ignace and Manitoulin Island; shortly afterwards they were found at Mackinac Island, Saginaw, and Detroit and were apparently settling in the L'Arbre Croche area (Kinietz 1940, 230–31).

It is my belief that Odawa territory at the time of first contact included Manitoulin Island and the shores of Georgian Bay. During this same period (1615 or possibly a little later), the Odawa had settlements in the Saginaw Bay–Thunder Bay area in the northeastern Lower Peninsula. Odawa tradition says that they came from the east to these locations. Odawas today give the Montreal area as their original home.

At some time during the seventeenth century, Odawas took the northwestern section of the Lower Peninsula from the Maškódens by conquest (traditionally), but because of warfare with the Iroquois, they did not settle in the region in any great numbers until after the close of the century. Yet there were Indians in the L'Arbre Croche region in the seventeenth century—were they a branch of the Odawas, remnants of the Maškódens (or both), or some other tribe, possibly descendants of earlier inhabitants whose archaeological remains are yet to be found?

At the time the Odawas began to settle L'Arbre Croche it was apparently a paradise of virgin timber and fish-filled streams and lakes. Small game was plentiful, but for deer, bear, and moose Odawas left their villages in the winter to hunt in the Upper Peninsula and in the region of Grand River and St. Joseph. This semi-sedentary economy was maintained until about the mid-nineteenth century when pressure from both the missionaries and the U.S. government caused a gradual change to year-long residence in the villages. Following the treaty of 1855 in which the Odawas gave up their political status rather than move to the west, the old hunting economy began to break down completely. Large farms were allotted to heads of families under the terms of this treaty.

The location of L'Arbre Croche in the extreme northwestern section of the Lower Peninsula led to close ties between the Indians and the white fur traders and missionaries. Beginning with the French in the seventeenth and eighteenth centuries, contact with the traders was continuous through the short-lived British domination of the area and the establishment of the Astor fur empire. Odawas not only traded furs to Euro-Americans, but under the guidance of Fr. du Jaunay their gardens in the mid-eighteenth century supplied the Mackinac boats with corn for their fur trading ventures (Willets 1948, 114).

French Jesuits were known to the Odawa previous to Fr. du Jaunay—Frs. Menard, Allouez, Andre, and Marquette among others preached the gospel to them at Manitoulin, St. Ignace and at other village sites. But it was du Jaunay who seems to have had the greatest influence on the L'Arbre Croche Odawa. He it was who implanted Catholicism so firmly among them that even after more than fifty years without a priest, the memory of his teaching was so vivid that the Odawas requested the U.S. government to send them a "Black Robe" like du Jaunay (Shurtleff 1940, 23–24). Their desire was satisfied, and the mission and school were established in 1827 at Seven Mile Point, but soon moved to Harbor Springs (called Little Traverse then). The school is still in existence and is now the only remaining Indian boarding school in the Lower Peninsula. Other missions followed at Middle Village, Cross Village, and Petoskey, and in the mid-nineteenth century the Protestants finally got a foothold in the area through their establishment in Petoskey (Bidas'ge, "he is coming with a light").

White settlers, few in number throughout most of nineteenth century, poured into the area after the Homestead Act of 1875. They soon almost abandoned their farms in favor of lumbering, a booming industry until about 1910, when the grand old trees were all gone. Commercial fishing was also a big industry at one time, but was exploited to the extent of depleting the waters of their lake trout and whitefish.

Now L'Arbre Croche is almost exclusively a summer resort with many fine twenty-room cottages in such restricted communities as Harbor Point, Roaring Brook, and Wequetonsing. Lumber docks at Harbor Springs and along Little Traverse Bay have been torn down in favor of slips for cabin cruisers and sailboats; hotels and cabins have sprung up where lumber yards and saw mills formerly stood. For two months of the year, old L'Arbre Croche is a busy place in which all of the permanent residents labor for unbelievably long hours to satisfy the wants of the welcome summer visitors and to earn enough money to carry them through the winter.

Indians work during the summer as domestic help, handy men, clerks, and mechanics, mostly. Fred Ettawageshik operates a souvenir store in which his sister is employed and for which he buys many locally made Indian articles. There is also considerable sale of Indian handicraft at this time of year to other stores and to individual tourists. Such articles as porcupine quill boxes and black ash splint baskets are made during the winter for the summer trade. The Odawa Indian Pageant in the 7000-seat outdoor stadium in Harbor Springs draws large crowds in mid-July, and last summer an Indian group staged four additional shows, two at Cross Village and two at Harbor Springs.

When the summer season is over, however, the area is bereft of almost its only means of livelihood. Farming on the whole is not a profitable venture, and there is only one really sizable year-round industry—the Petoskey Portland Cement Company. Cross Village has no industry; Harbor Springs has a small lumber company and two minor industries. There are several additional industries in Petoskey but they are unable to offer employment to all who need it.

Many persons must tighten their belts a bit in the winter—live on unemployment insurance, credit, and whatever fish and game they can obtain. Young people, both white and Indian, are dissatisfied with such an economy and drift "down below" to the cities for steady and higher paid employment. There is talk, a great deal of talk, among all groups about the situation and its solution. Some fear industry because of possible alienation of summer resorters; others insist that more industry is the only answer. Currently Petoskey residents are planning to build or remodel a building for use as a community hall, in which large conventions could be accommodated. They point to Grand Rapids and Traverse City, which are deriving considerable income from the convention business. Indians have organized a club, an outgrowth of the shows presented last summer (1954), which plans to train dancers and singers for summer shows and to encourage and exhibit Indian handicraft.

But the old L'Arbre Croche region, like most of northern Michigan, is still a summer resort, with a very short season and no adequate means of livelihood in the winter. Historically the Indians left the area in the winter for better hunting grounds: Is this the answer for most whites and Indians today also? It certainly must be, unless new sources of revenue are made obtainable in the very near future.

Fred Ettawageshik

Fred was born in Harbor Springs in 1896, the third child in a family of five children. He attended the Holy Childhood school in Harbor Springs for a few years and was then transferred to the Indian boarding school which was then in existence at Mount Pleasant. Later he attended Carlisle Institute from which he graduated. Fred was subsequently connected with the Indian Service as a teacher and boys' counselor in such places as Pipestone and Tower, Minnesota, and Greenwood, South Dakota. In 1917 he joined the army in World War I, serving until 1919. He has held a variety of jobs, including that of tailor, painter and striper of autos, and salesman, and has lived in such widely separated parts of the country as Bloomsburg, Pennsylvania, and Bartlesville, Oklahoma.

For a number of years, Fred was active in Boy Scout work and was at one time a Boy Scout executive. In the early 1920s his father opened a souvenir store in Harbor Springs with which Fred was connected off and on until he finally assumed complete ownership and management of the store some years before his father's death in 1946.

Locally, Fred has been active in Indian affairs and was responsible for the organization of the Michigan Indian Defense Association (MIDA), an organization of local Indians who presented an annual pageant in the summer and were active in welfare work. The MIDA sponsored an annual Indian show in Harbor Springs, which later blossomed into the Odawa Indian Pageant held every July. Fred is one of the principal performers in the Indian pageant, acting as chief of the Odawa group.

No other Indian in the area has been so photographed nor so sought after as an after-dinner speaker on Indian affairs. He is generally considered to be the best informed Odawa about his people's culture and is frequently consulted by persons desiring information about Indians in general or the Odawa in particular. Fred has made radio and television broadcasts also and is probably the best known Indian in Michigan.

Joe Chingwa

Joseph Chingwa was born at Two-Mile Creek, not far from Petoskey, in a small log house on a seven-acre farm. While Joe was still a boy the Pennsylvania Railroad bought this land. Joe's father was an Odawa from Petoskey; his paternal grandfather was Mkkwániwi (Louis of the Bear Clan), who also gained a name because of his skill as a bear hunter. It was said that Mkkwániwi had the power to call the bears from their dens at Midwinter. According to Fred, Mkkwániwi's wife (Joe's paternal grandmother) was a Potawatomi Indian. Joe's mother was an Ojibwe from Manistique. She had a father whom Joe recalls, but he never saw his maternal grandmother.

Joe had little schooling apparently. He mentioned that he was in school in Mount Pleasant with his older brother from his eighth to eleventh year. During this time he says that he forgot "what his mother looked like." He worked for years for the city of Petoskey as a laborer. He was locally famous as a great fisherman and storyteller. He always knew where the biggest and best fish were to be found and was often called on by other fishermen for advice. His storytelling ability was known mostly to his Odawa friends and to anthropologists.

As a young man he was Jibiabos, the sweet singer, in the Hiawatha pageant given at Round Lake from 1906 on. He was with the company of players that toured the Midwest, appearing, among other places, also in Chicago. In 1930 he was elected chief of the MIDA.

Since the 1948 recordings by Jane, Chingwa has died. But his time as a dancer and singer remains. "You ought to have seen how he could raise his knees way up," said Susan Shagonaby. Joe was Fred's first cousin, a likable, friendly man with a great appreciation of the old Odawa culture and the ability to explain it to others. Joe is survived by his wife, Jennie, and four grown children, all but one of whom live in Petoskey.

Susan Shagonaby

Susy Shagonaby, a Harbor Springs Odawa, has been a constant source of information since we met in 1946. Married to Charlie, a Potawatomi from Hastings, Michigan, Susy has four living children, the oldest of whom is sixteen. Four other children were tragically burned to death in a fire some years ago. Susy is a graduate of the Harbor Springs high school. The family lives in outward poverty, yet there is always food on their table for themselves and for anyone else who may call. Both Susy and Charlie are gifted craftsmen, Susy being the more ambitious of the two. The Shagonabys are the principal manufacturers of porcupine quill boxes in Harbor Springs at the present time, and Susy has given demonstrations of the art at hobby shows and club meetings. Susy and Charlie live more in harmony with old Indian ways than any other Indians in Harbor Springs, outside of the old people.

Cross Village

Anemiawatigoning or Cross Village stands on ancient Odawa ground. David Kenosha and other Odawa claim their prehistoric residence on this site, but their claims are not supported by scientific evidence. The first white men found them around Georgian Bay and on the southwest shore of Lake Huron; from Manitoulin Island they raided the distant Winnebagos and ousted the Maškódens Around 1650 they retreated to Washington Island at the mouth of Green Bay and to Lake Superior at Chequamegon and Keweenaw Bay; in 1688 they returned to the Straits, always with members of the Huron tribe.

A small mission had been established at Middle Village in 1695 and again abandoned before a large migration of Odawa to L'Arbre Croche in 1742 and the establishment of their flourishing agricultural colony. The first mission was at Middle Village, or Goodhart, named after Chief Kaminoteyo (Good Heart). In 1765, Fr. du Jaunay moved it to Cross Village, and he left a year later. The mission was established in 1829 at Harbor Springs. A series of illustrious prelates served the Odawa: Fr. Frederic Baraga, Fr. Weikamp, and after 1884 a succession of Franciscans. In 1848 another church and convent were built in Cross Village and a new cross replaced the original one supposedly erected by Marquette (West 1934, 24; Wright 1917, 156–60).

The convent grain farm and grist mill, the lumber mill at Sturgeon Bay, and the fishing industry provided work for the Indians. But in 1883 Polish families began to move in and the Indians moved out to Harbor Springs, Petoskey, and points farther south. In 1917 there were still 325 Indians in Cross Village when a fire swept the village and lightning struck the convent. The lumber and sawmill were abandoned; lampreys impaired the fishing. Now nineteen Indians remain among the summer resorters.

David Kenosha

Born in Cross Village in 1892, David Kenosha is a true native of that area and has always returned to it after an absence. His Indian name is Shawenimiki (Yellow Thunder), whereas Kenosha (Pike) is his family name. He attended the convent school started by Fr. Weikamp in Cross Village, in the still extant building erected by Fr. Optatus. He learned Odawa, Ojibwe, and German from his parents and Latin at the high school in Petoskey. As a young man he worked at the lumber camp and sawmill at Sturgeon Bay and at the fisheries along the coast. During the First World War he served as quartermaster on Great Lakes vessels. In the 1940s he worked on the Detroit Express Highway, then for several years in the lumber camps near Mount Pleasant. For three summers he performed at the Wisconsin Dells Winnebago "Ceremonials." Since 1960 he has been back in Cross Village for the summer and winter, as "Chief" at the tavern, as a guide for tourists and hunters, and as a dancer.

He claims to have started the Cross Village Indian show twenty years ago together with another Odawa, Margaret Gilbert. Fr. Bartram took charge during Kenosha's summers at the Dells. Since 1960, Shawenimiki has been director, dancer, and singer. Now he is chief choreographer of the Odawa Sun Ceremony. In addition, he has danced in many camps and cities, including Chicago, St. Paul, Minneapolis, Lodi, Milwaukee, Detroit, and St. Louis.

He is one of the few Michigan Indians with a knowledge of Native dances and songs. He claims to have learned most of these from his grandfather and also some dances at the Dells. He knows Odawa hymns, can read music, and sings in the Holy Cross choir. He used to fiddle for square dances and, just for fun, has danced Indian style to jazz.

He stands between the two cultures, the Native and the white, the pagan and the Christian. He knows every inch of the ground on the beach and in the woods between Sturgeon Bay and Harbor Springs. He knows where to find arbutus, wild strawberries, blueberries, choke cherries, sand cherries. He can hear the slightest rustle of a deer in the leaves and sees a herd approaching the lake far across the bay. He knows the Native skills, can improvise a box from birchbark and a "tomahawk" from sticks and stones on the beach. He made a birch bark tipi, which now stands on the new dance grounds, and is highly skilled in bead work. Yet he has a hard time making ends meet during the long winter months and finds work on neighboring farms or wherever he can. He is an individualist and for that reason never married, for he likes to wander. He lives in the bygone days and subconsciously seems to hold the ancient beliefs and attitudes. Yet he must fit his activities into the present day and adjust his faith to that of the church, of which he is a good member. This conflict is both his charm and his tragedy.

Edward (Fred) and Louise Kenoshmeg

The Kenoshmegs (Long Pike) are the nuclear couple in Cross Village Indian activities. The Ghost Feasts always take place at their immaculate home. They are acclaimed as traditionalists and indeed they embody the most aristocratic of Indian principles. However, Fred knows only one dance, the Eagle Dance, which he performs when his asthma permits it. Louise (an Ojibwe from beyond St. Ignace) has never divulged any Native lore nor even biographical facts. Fred is shy and quiet, Louise lively and always near for laughter. In the summer they do well enough at work in summer resorts and on road construction; but during the winter, like most of their neighbors, they skimp along on savings. They are Kenosha's age mates and friends.

Odawa Catholics from the Area of Hart

Between Ludington and Muskegon there used to be a number of flourishing Odawa communities, which are now all but abandoned. Some outstanding folklorists come from that area but have moved elsewhere.

The Ottos

The Ottos lived in Scottsville, then Harrison, and now in Weidman near Mount Pleasant. They are the only family that has shared in activities of both the northern and southern groups of Odawas. S. Foster Otto, an amateur archaeologist and craftsman, is also a good dancer and has performed his Pipe Dance in Harbor Springs, Hastings, Mount Pleasant, and Ann Arbor. His young son, Donulus, is an excellent performer of the Eagle and War Dance, and shows good taste in his homemade costumes. Since 1953 he has been in the army, but is due to return to the powwows. The late Mrs. Otto was an expert at crafts and danced in the war dance groups.

The Chingmans

Anthony Chingman, one of the masters of ceremonies, grew up near Hart, and remembers the Midéwiwin and other Native practices. His wife Alvina is a native of Goodhart. They and some of their descendants, the Kings, live at DeWitt, north of Lansing, because there are job facilities in Lansing. Together with the Careys, their family constitutes a performing group that appears independently or together with the southern Indians. The Chingmans are well educated and have more knowledge of lore—tales and arts—than performing ability. With the aid of Whitney Albert, they give pleasant shows.

Cecilia Shagonaby Knox

Mrs. Knox is a native of Twin Bridges near Hart and a relative of the Potawatomi Shagonabys. She now lives in Ann Arbor and has given interesting accounts of the old Odawa ways, which resemble the family feasts of Harbor Springs. Neighboring Elbridge and Cobmoosa shared these customs. She is now a Methodist, satisfied with the white man's religion and comforts, and devoid of nostalgia for the passing of aboriginal customs.

Whitney Albert

Whitney Albert's Indian name is Žagežin (Crab), but he has taken the name of Chief Blue Cloud for show business. He says he is neither a chief nor Blue Cloud. He was born as a Catholic in Hart near Lake Michigan in 1890, but he now lives in a Methodist Odawa settlement at Mikado, not far from Oscoda on Lake Huron. In his younger days he worked as a lumberjack in (at that time) heavily wooded central Michigan, and he became an expert at "log rolling." In fact, he was a champion at balancing on a log in a stream and at forcing a competitor off of the log into the water. Annually he staged such a contest at Hastings with Eli Thomas. In the 1940s he worked, just as David Kenosha did, on the Detroit Express Highway, and at present he is employed in construction work, for he is very able-bodied. He is married and has two married daughters living in other communities.

He learned most of his songs and dances from his grandfather, and also a small number, including the Pipe Song and the Drinking Song, by watching the *Song of Hiawatha* pageant. For seventeen years he has been associated with Eli Thomas, first in educational programs in schools and now at the large powwows at Mount Pleasant, Hastings, and other summer places. Though not a showman and not an eminent story teller, he has the largest and most varied repertoire of Indian songs in the state. He constructed a birch bark tipi that is used at the shows. He is also an expert at beadwork and made himself a fine pair of moccasins, but he does not put this skill to commercial use. For the concessions he carves indifferently skillful hatchets.

In a way he ties together the northern and southern groups, but he has identified himself with the latter. He knows both Catholic and Protestant hymns, yet he is a pagan at heart. He is, however, little worried about his individual position and is poised, content, and affable.

Isabella Reservation

At the time of this writing, Isabella Reserve [was] the only true Indian reservation in the Lower Peninsula. It was established by agreements in 1855 and 1864, and it had a good Indian boarding school from 1891 to 1934. In 1927, when the Bureau of Indian Affairs withdrew its representatives from the state, it was placed under the jurisdiction of the Tomah agency in Wisconsin. Densmore gives the population as 435 (Densmore 1949, 33–34), but Eli Thomas sets it higher. Here is the story in Thomas's own words:

> [There are about] six to seven hundred people on the reservation, I'd say. What happened was ninety-nine years ago the government collect people from all over, the government says, "We'll give you land." I don't know why the government wants to give us land, after the Indians owned it all, the whole of Michigan. The Indian was so ignorant. They gave them forty acres apiece. They went over there; they put their names on there.

"What's your name?"

"O, Wabogishik. Put Wabogishik in. What's yours?"

All the names you put in there, the whole six townships, pretty near half the county. Now after the government given the land, they owned it. Then the lumberjacks come in, lumber companies. They want to buy not the land, just the timber.

"What's your name?"

"Wabogishik."

"Sign your name."

Cost nothing to sign it, get a little for signing it back. They were ignorant, they know nothing. The woods now are all second growth. Now, in that county they went on. Maybe they found out how many owned 40 acres, maybe 75 people owned 40 acres. Half a mile on other Indian land, plenty own that.

Now it's even worse. If you shoot a deer, they lock you up. You're not allowed to hunt there, you have to have a permit, costs $2.50. [They used to have an Indian school there too,] a government school. It was for Indians to learn English.

However, the tale of exploitation is not unmitigated. On August 28, 1937, the Tribal Council, represented by Elijah (Billy) Elk and Elmer B. Simonds, signed an agreement with Peru Fervor, agent of the Tomah agency, a "Corporate Charter of the Saginaw Chippewa Indian Tribe of the Isabella Reservation of Michigan" (also called the Black River Reserve). This is designed to protect the Indians from unscrupulous land speculators. Of late there have been investigations of the Indian claims, often with results advantageous to the Natives. So that at present their lands are increasing rather than shrinking.

As stated by Thomas, the original woodlands and hunting grounds were settled by a miscellaneous group of Indians, by a majority of Ojibwe from Lake Huron, especially Bay City and Saginaw districts. Its large area to the southeast of Mount Pleasant has been mostly denuded of its forests and has been converted into acceptable farmland. Despite their industry the Indians' own homes are conspicuously more humble than those of the surrounding white farmers. They have their own public school, sending the high school children to Mount Pleasant. In its southern part is a Methodist church; further north is a Nazarene church constructed by the Indians' own hands. In the center on a wooded knoll stands the community center, with the open-air tabernacle to the south and the powwow grounds to the north. The main floor of the Community House was turned into a chapel in 1955. Other rooms serve for Friday evening prayer meetings with refreshments and for Tuesday evening basket-weaving bees. Here also the women patch gifts of clothing and turn rags into quilts. The tabernacle is the site for the large annual Methodist camp meeting. The powwow grounds include a raised earth platform and an amphitheatre for the annual public pageant. The grounds are equipped for camping and picnicking.

The tidy aspect of these buildings and grounds, as in general the neatness of many homes, are symptoms of civic pride and cohesion, especially among the older, Ojibwe-speaking people. The new buildings and various improvements indicate rising economic status. Partly because of the cooperative spirit and partly because of its central location, Isabella Reservation attracts inhabitants. In this respect it contrasts with the Hart area, which has turned into a center of diffusion. The social visits and ceremonial gatherings are of short duration, from a few hours to a week. They entail communications with settlements many hundreds of miles away, and frequent contact with Grand Rapids, Oscoda, and Sarnia inhabitants. Permanent migrations from the Potawatomi centers at Athens and Bradley are frequent. The nomadic pattern also involves going out, but in round trips.

In view of this large sphere of contacts it is astonishing how little the Isabella and the L'Arbre Croche Indians see one another. Resentments do not seem to feature in this negative relationship. Evidently L'Arbre Croche feels self-sufficient in its religious and social events, which differ from those at Isabella.

Methodists

Eli Thomas

Eli Thomas of the Wild Goose gens bears the Indian name of Wašeškom (spelled by him, Washsuhkum), meaning approximately "Lightning Everywhere" (he made a scattering gesture during his explanation). Born in 1894 near Bay City on Lake Huron, he moved first to Oscoda and twenty-five years ago to Isabella Reserve. He has had little formal education. Both he and his aristocratic wife speak Ojibwe better than English and are expert singers of old Indian Methodist hymns. Both are skilled basket makers. Both hold on to certain Native practices, such as tobacco offerings, though they live in a frame house with electricity and follow modern ways.

Thomas may be considered the folklorist of his tribe. Fortunately his scant education has prevented the acquisition of exotic lore and has confined his knowledge to stories handed down from his ancestors and songs learned from Whitney Albert. For seventeen years he has been associated in show business with Albert. For five years he has been manager of the pageant at Hastings, which was formerly directed by Potawatomi from Bradley. He practically makes his living by giving shows at summer resorts, camps, and schools with a variable cast of his neighbors.

He is a superb storyteller in both Ojibwe and English, with most expressive inflections, especially in his native tongue. He is only a fair dancer and singer of Native songs but has a good voice for hymns. These he has learned by ear, for he cannot read music. He proved to be a skillful translator, though he never attempted this before November 1953. He is not only willing to permit tape recordings, but even eager to do so. He is indefatigable. His black bristling hair and dynamic manner belie his sixty years. Though content with modern ways, radios, and cars—he has seven used cars in his back yard—he is Indian in his way of thinking.

Isaac Pelcher

Isaac Pelcher (Pidendum, or Loud Noise) was born at Isabella Reserve but traces his ancestry to Saginaw and Sarnia on Lake Huron. His father was French but encouraged the preservation of Indian traditions. His Ojibwe grandfather taught him the few dances he knows. He remembers meetings of the Midéwiwin during his boyhood, but never was a member, for both he and his wife Lucy are faithful Methodists. His work with the highway department limits his participation in shows to weekends and holidays. He speaks Ojibwe perfectly.

His wife, Lucy, is of part Irish and part Indian ancestry. She runs the forty-acre farm, growing potatoes for sale (366 pounds last year), also wheat, corn, and hay, and tending a herd of cows. Two of her daughters live on the reservation; a third one and two sons live in Detroit, Battle Creek, and Ann Arbor. She was educated in music at Carlisle and is the chief pianist for Ojibwe hymn singing. Her own knowledge of Indian traditions and of the language is very limited.

Benedict Quignon

Originally a Potawatomi from Bradley, Quignon has identified himself with his present neighbors on Isabella Reserve. He is an ardent Methodist and is unfamiliar with his native tongues; yet he has studied the lore in a sophisticated and creative manner, by combining traditions with reading and original composition. He is program chairman of the annual Methodist camp meetings and also one of the most expert dancers. Still a young man less then forty years of age, he can do much to preserve Indian ways in his generation.

The Pamps and the Potawatomi Center at Athens

Near Athens is a fair-sized Potawatomi settlement, not a reservation. All of the Indians are ardent evangelists and the most ardent is Jack Pamp, who is in charge of the Indian mission, camp ground, and children's home on Highway 66. His white wife is even more fervent than he is. Nonetheless, he is well informed on Indian traditions. His brother, Charles Pamptope, was a renowned preacher until his death a few years ago. Charles' widow, Betty, and her children live at Mount Pleasant and spend the summers visiting camp meetings and the winters speaking at Indian and white churches. Betty knows the Ojibwe language, but very little of Indian lore. A highly educated and intelligent woman, she is trying to learn authentic facts and include them in the lectures. She even asked me for advice, literature, and information on dances and songs. She considers Thomas's shows undignified and distorting. However, like Jack Pamp and Quignon, she studies this as folklore, without residue of faith in the efficaciousness of Indian rituals, but rather with a mental reservation about "pagan practices."

James Shaffer

Though Shaffer is a mixed-blood Cherokee, he deserves mention here because he has identified himself thoroughly with the southerly Michigan Anishinaabeg. His family lives in Albion. James tries to reconstruct some Cherokee lore from his ailing grandfather. He works hard on costumes and paraphernalia, both Cherokee and Algonkian, and tries for authenticity. He received help from the ethnologist James Howard. At the Hastings and other shows, he and Don Otto were inseparable companions, being age mates.

Susan Ahgosa and Greensky Hill

South of Petoskey, all along Traverse Bay to the two jutting peninsulas, stretches an Odawa territory that now ties up more closely with the southern Methodist than with the Catholic tribesmen to the immediate north. In fact, several members of these Methodist communities, such as Mr. and Mrs. Enos Willis of Bayshore, shared our lunch at the Mount Pleasant camp meeting. It has not been possible to attend any of the camp meetings in that area, but the present minister of the Greensky Hill mission, Rev. Lloyd Schloop of Charlevoix, a young white man, recommended Susan Ahgosa as a representative of the old-time Protestant Indian.

Susan, neé Ona, was born in 1872 in Kiwedin and married the last chief of the illustrious Ahgosa family from Old Mission. Now a widow, blind, with her girlhood friends all gone, she keeps her house near Charlevoix in perfect order and depends for help on her kind Polish neighbors. She spends much of her time thinking of the past and is eager to hand on her precise information on the history of her area. She stands for an interesting transitional period in Indian religion. She says that the Indians are related to thunders, and used to make offerings of tobacco to thunders, though they do this no longer. She still can sing the old Ojibwe and Odawa Methodist hymns with a nostalgic memory of a period that is now giving way to complete anglicizing. She hums them to herself every day. They are the same as the hymns used at Mount Pleasant.

What follows is the tale she tells about Greensky Hill Mission. In 1836 the Old Mission Reservation was established all the way to Traverse City, by an agreement signed by five chiefs who went to Washington. In 1838 a Presbyterian missionary, Peter Dougherty, arrived. The chiefs wouldn't accept him right away. But Ahgosa's father, an old medicine man, said, "Accept this man. Soon white people come and my medicine be no good. I'm old, am going when thunder comes from south (summertime)." When the missionary came, they built a bark schoolhouse. The government opened the Point to white settlers in 1843. The missionary was ordered to go across to Omens Point and open a school. The old church, built in 1843, is still there on the way to Northport. Then came an Indian from the Sault, Peter Greensky. He got tired of the Presbyterian orderliness, gathered a group, and settled a Methodist mission across the bay. He picked a secluded piece of woods a few miles offshore, north of Lake Charlevoix, on a small pond, Susan Lake. First his adherents met in private homes at Big Village. Ten years later twenty-five families built the old log church that still stands in the woods. They hauled the logs by hand and built without nails, using beveled corners; they made their own shingles and a cedar bark ceiling that now needs renovating. According to Susan, the circle of trees in a nearby field remains from twenty-five of the twenty six families; it does not stand for thirty chiefs of thirty tribes as usually reported (Works Progress Administration 1940, 631). That took from 1862 until 1867.

The mission in its heyday was attended by Indians from Petoskey to Kiwedin. It has had Native and white ministers. Best liked was Rev. Walker, a white preacher of a generation ago, the father of Louise Walker (L. Walker 1950, 96–97). He was a powerful speaker. During his time Indians from far and near pitched their tents by the church and open air tabernacle for the summer camp meeting. Rev. Alexander, now at Elk Rapids, was there before Schloop. Now there are only fifteen members. The camp meeting held August 8–15, 1954, was poorly attended, partly because the Oscoda meeting ran through that same week. Also, the young people are forgetting the old ways and are not learning the Indian words. Instead they visit the Charlevoix beer gardens on pay day. The old members are getting to feud among themselves. But at Kiwedin there are big doings and big camp meetings.

Upper Peninsula

Margaret Lambert and St. Ignace

Margaret Lambert, a school teacher in St. Ignace, symbolizes this meeting point of Upper and Lower Peninsulas, of Lake Huron and Lake Michigan cultures. Her great grandfather, Chief Asignok, classed as a Huron, who came to St. Ignace from Manitoulin Island, was given the Great Partridge Medal in 1809 (she is very proud of this). Here Menominee and Ojibwe blood mixed with the Huron strain and with Scotch blood on her father's part—Lambert being a corruption of Lambeth. Her mother was an Odawa from Northport, a Methodist family still represented by the Smiths, Taylors, and Harringtons of Northport and Bayshore. Margaret adheres to her paternal Catholic faith.

Thomas Shalifoe and Baraga Bay

Far to the northwest of St. Ignace, the small town of Baraga lies on Baraga Bay at the southern end of the Keweenaw Peninsula. Three miles northeast on a forest dirt road a group of four Indian homes constitutes Beartown. In the third one Thomas Shalifoe lives alone, keeping his home and himself tidy and cheerful. He wears his eighty-seven years lightly, strides tall and erect, sings with a lusty voice, and fiddles with youthful zest. He is of three-fourths French extraction, but he speaks Ojibwe better than English and can read only in Ojibwe. In 1902 he married a second wife, Mary Jane, to whom he was intensely devoted, and whose death six years ago has left a lasting mark. He is proud of his nine children and 42 grandchildren, some of whom live next door. One son lives in Ionia, another, Thomas Jr., lives near Ann Arbor with his family. He and his sons have worked in the lumber camps in the Huron mountains. Also he used to be kept busy as fiddler for square dances. He knows both Native and Catholic songs and remembers from his youth many customs that have now died out. Both he and his son Thomas have given some interesting information on events and facts not to be found in books.

The Assinins Mission near Baraga was founded by Fr. Frederic Baraga in 1843 after this eminent prelate had left L'Arbre Croche. This was the same year as the construction of the Omena church. In 1868 he built a mission and started a model farm. A well-run orphanage, managed by sisters of the order of St. Agnes, and sponsored by the Diocese of Marquette, continues his work, rears abandoned children from as far as the Lower Peninsula and Wisconsin reservations, and sometimes sends them on to Haskell Institute. The Indian families in the neighborhood live in poverty, and for the most part in ignorance of their traditions. Only a few old-timers remember Indian wake songs. The same holds good for the entire surroundings of Baraga. In Shalifoe's boyhood, families would gather for New Year Feasts, *nimikwadadin*; now children wander about for "trick or treat" as at Halloween. Only the people of sixty or over know the language and hymns and remember the Squaw Dance.

Across the Bay and beyond L'Anse, the county and agency seat, a Methodist Indian settlement stretches along the rocky shore. It is focused on a brown wooden church in Zeba. There are two camp meeting grounds, one for the Methodists and the other for the Church of God. Among the Methodists many people sing Ojibwe hymns; some of the old-timers speak no English. But Indian lore has disappeared. The last singer of Native songs, Dan Curtis, died several years ago. The Church of God follows white patterns, graciously and gaily, as I had the opportunity to witness during a Wednesday night prayer meeting.

Economic conditions are difficult in that northerly region. No corn can be raised, only potatoes. During the winter, summer, and fall, many men, both Indians and Finns, find work lumbering; but between March and June the soft ground blocks the access. As in the old days, the Indians gather maple sugar in March, now in small family groups; in the summer they gather cranberries at Lighthouse Point and wild rice. They no longer sing Native songs during the wild rice pounding. In the fall they gather birch bark for containers.

As St. Ignace ties up with Ontario and the Hurons, Baraga connects with the western Ojibwe and Menominee and Sioux. Thomas Shalifoe Jr. went to school on the Bad River Reservation, Ashland, Wisconsin, and saw the dances there. He has visited many Wisconsin reservations. He tells stories of events before the coming of the white man, of feuds with the Sioux and of an Apache raid long, long ago. He tells of the working of copper by the Indians. Both he and his father tell about the French voyageurs who used to stop at the bay and who provided their ancestry and their name—a corruption from Charlevoix. They tell also about the succession of priests—Baraga, Terhaus, who translated hymns, and Fr. Prud'homme, who knew their language and has now moved to Isaac Jogues Mission at the Sault.

Nahma

Nahma (Sturgeon) spreads along the beautiful Bay de Noc of the northern Lake Michigan shore, at the tip of a peninsula. West of a neat resort village the shanties of some ninety Indians form a small, separate community. They appear indigent despite work in the woods and mill of the Bay de Noquette Company and in a small factory for playground equipment. The Catholic church is in disrepair and has services only every fortnight. Basketry making continues for tourist trade. Other Indian traditions are fast becoming a memory. Many of the young girls attend the convent schools at Harbor Springs and Assinins. Mary Weeden and Rose Bourasaw know Ojibwe Catholic hymns. Mrs. Weeden remembers customs resembling those of L'Arbre Croche, but she no longer has occasion to sing her hymns even at wakes.

Hannahville

A half-day's drive to the west, inland south of Harris, in Menominee County, 140 Potawatomi form a Methodist community, established in 1913. They have inadequate incomes: their 3,359 acres do not make good farms and the lakeside is far away, so most earn wages at saw mills or as day labor. Poverty is everywhere in evidence. The church was struck by lightning and never repaired. The adjoining tabernacle has not been used for two years, since the resident preacher, Betty Malone, moved south. Yet the inhabitants are intelligent and dignified people–the Petonquets, the Philemons. Eliot Petonquet joins the evangelistic caravans and was at Greensky Hill during my visit. Alex Philemon and his family constitute a powwow group, perform at the Indian Village in Escanaba, and make trinkets for sale. He is the disciple of Eli Thomas, and made the very honest comment that he does not believe in the old songs and dances but gives a show whenever he needs some quick money.

Frank Smart of Odanah, Wisconsin

Frank Smart, a member of the Bad River Reservation near Odanah, Wisconsin, has exerted such a perceptible influence on the Michigan powwow leaders as to deserve mention. He grew up in the neo-pagan pattern of northern Wisconsin but acquired an advanced education and considerable theatrical experience. We met at Lac du Flambeau, Wisconsin, where he spent the summer as powwow master of ceremonies. He had held an important position at the Dells "Ceremonials" and had in that capacity known David Kenosha and Eli Thomas. He taught Kenosha a considerable non-Odawa repertoire. He made a more superficial impression on Eli Thomas and, through him, on Alex Philemon. Another Odanah leader, Neganagijig, associates with Philemon, when he brings his dance group to the Escanaba Indian village. But he does not seem to have transferred any of his lore. Except for this small-scale infiltration, the boundary between the two states is real. Wisconsin Indian ritualism has not affected Michigan, and Michigan Indian hymns have not diffused to Wisconsin.

Pattern of Nomadism

Throughout their history and in their present network of travels, the Michigan Anishinaabeg show their mobility. Formerly the forced or voluntary migrations extended from Ontario to Minnesota. At the time of this writing, few individuals travel beyond the state. Within this network some communities have become centrifugal, others centripetal. Combating the tendency toward an exodus into southern cities, family ties and local solidarity keep many at home or prompt visits. Cultural fragmentation is prevented by large and small gatherings with a calendric recurrence. The three major types of meetings are the local Odawa feasts, the intertribal Methodist camp meetings, and powwows—they form the nucleus of this report.

The Problem: Adjustive Processes

The Michigan Anishinaabeg are highly acculturated groups, in the last stages of adjustment to the dominant culture's way of life.[3] In the material aspects, which do not concern the authors, the transition is complete, though not up to the highest standards. In the spiritual aspects, which form the thesis of this book, Native customs and ideas have persevered in variously obvious or subtle manifestations. These manifestations will be described and evaluated. They raise the question, What is the adjustive value of the religious customs—residual, blended, or modern?

They appear most strikingly in three types of gatherings with past or present religious connotations—namely, programs of Native dances and songs; semi-Native, semi-Catholic feasts; and evangelistic camp meetings. In addition, they include scattered lore, beliefs, tales, and linguistic tenacity limited to the elders.

Methodological Concerns

This study involves several stages of investigation. First, it involves gathering of facts from observation and interviews with cooperative individuals. Some of the facts appear as genuinely Native survivals, some as quasi-Native but actually manufactured items, and others as apparently acculturated patterns with Native undercurrents. The latter two types involve discrimination and weighing.

Secondly, it involves discrimination aided by research into origins, historical developments, and relationships with others tribes, and by a hypothetical reconstruction of aboriginal ritual and belief.

Thirdly, the reconstruction plus the observed modern phenomena suggest the processes of transition from Native to modern religion and factors in both religions that aided the transition. Many factors, ecological and political, enter into the kinetic process. Throughout this comparison we must bear in mind the aquatic location of the Michigan peninsulas, the heavy woodlands, the tempered shore climate permitting agriculture as far north as the Mackinac Straits, the combination of isolationism and traffic, the associations with tribes to the east, south, and west, and the migrations of the Odawa in particular. Also, we must remember the types of white associations in various sections, the types of religion introduced at various periods. With all of this as background we will try to find rhyme and reason in the ritual, musical, and choreographic changes in function and form.

Finally, the modern adjustments that are the end results of these processes must be evaluated with regard to the Indian and the white man. The key facets to be considered, by inference from behavior, or by direct questioning, are as follows:

1. Economic, that is, as beneficial or adverse to the financial status
2. Artistic, as productive of well-wrought art forms
3. Educational, as instructive in Indian ways to both younger Indians and white observers
4. Personal, as bolstering to the ego
5. Social, as favorable to tribal pride and cohesion and neighborliness
6. Nativistic, as a link with the tribal past
7. Adjustive, as oriented to new ways
8. Religious, as fulfillment of the need for communication with the supernatural

The present hypothesis favors a preponderance of beneficial nativistic effects as the result of a "conscious organized attempt . . . to revive or perpetuate selected aspects of its culture" (Linton 1943, 230). By Linton's criteria it would be a rational nativism, not a magical one, in part revivalistic, in part perpetuative. That is, the surviving fragments have in part been saved from limbo by conscious efforts of Native folklorists; and in part they have remained as tribal heritage though changed in form.

While the Indian merits first attention, the white student must not be overlooked. The study should have some significance to the science of human customs. The authors believe that detailed, sympathetic presentation of Michigan Indian religious patterns will make a definite contribution to problems of cultural clash and adjustment.

CHAPTER 2

Public Festivals

→ *This chapter, written by Gertrude Kurath, explores the events that served, along with the religious "camp meetings," as the performance contexts for the songs and dance steps detailed in subsequent chapters. Kurath chooses the term "festival" to describe what her consultants spoke of as "pageants," "powwows," and "ceremonials." To be sure, the different festivals staged indigenous music and dance within the frame of folklorization, attempting to perform indigenous traditions for largely non-Native audiences. Yet Kurath also makes clear that Native performers regarded these festivals with considerable relish, and not simply as opportunities for earning cash. That this is so is ultimately not surprising, for the events provided occasions for the gathering of Michigan Indians and significant public expressions of Anishinaabe culture. Although formal U.S. policies of cultural assimilation, along with the prohibitions against most ritual expressions of Native American music and dance, had been undone under policy changes of the so-called Indian New Deal, most of the performers were of a generation that knew few opportunities for the public articulation of tradition. It was, after all, in these gatherings that Michigan's Anishinaabeg came to constitute their "culture" and their "tradition," albeit in a folklorized frame. For example, a show performed on the campus of the University of Michigan unmistakably for non-Native audiences nonetheless was hallowed with a Catholic Native language hymn and one of the more significant indigenous rites of passage, the giving of an Indian name to someone's grandchild—perhaps someone whose parents worked at the Ford Plant in Ypsilanti and who could ill afford a drive north. In such performances, Michigan's Anishinaabeg in the 1950s showed remarkable resourcefulness.*

If the Anishinaabeg showed their dexterity in these performances, they also showed their resolve to control the articulation of Anishinaabe tradition. In their discussion of the Harbor Springs "Naming Ceremonials," the authors speak plainly about attempts by wealthy non-Native financiers to eclipse Anishinaabe performers with Boy Scout troops and other hobbyists playing Indians on stage, and consequent attempts by their Anishinaabe consultants to regain control of performances of culture—indeed to maintain control of the definitions of culture. As we see in this chapter, the authors themselves joined in the cultural politics.

Through three centuries of change, numerous dances and songs have persisted, some of them in modified form, virtually all of them in altered function. The extent of persistence and change can best be estimated by presenting descriptions of the festivals and dances, analyses of the songs, and the meager historical materials on these manifestations. In this presentation, the dances and songs have been rearranged from their order in the programs and reels to conform to the ideology evident in legends and in accounts of former rituals, an ideology which formerly motivated the dances and songs.

All of the extant Native dances and songs have been transferred to public festivals, programs for white spectators, called "powwows," "pageants," or "ceremonials" by the Indians. For working purposes they are called "festivals." In Michigan's Lower Peninsula the fine summer weather and tourist mobility encourage outdoor events. These occur annually at three nuclear locations and appear occasionally in other places. The annual festivals have been established at Cross Village and Harbor Springs on Little Traverse Bay, at Mount Pleasant's Isabella Reserve, and at Charlton Park near Hastings. The first of these is confined to the Odawa of that area and a few Potawatomi and Ojibwe residents. The second is a product of that reservation, with the assistance of Blue Cloud. The third brings together Indians from the entire Lower Peninsula, exclusive of Little Traverse. Analogous events have been reported for Escanaba and other places in the Upper Peninsula; they await future observation and description.

Cross Village

The "Annual Holy Cross Picnic and Carnival" featured Indian dances for many years. According to David Kenosha, he started it twenty years ago, together with Margaret Gilbert under the sponsorship of Fr. Paul. Of the series of resident priests, Fr. Bartram was the most interested, and he took over the management in competent fashion during Kenosha's absence in the 1940s. In 1953, Fr. Wolf was at the helm, but he withdrew church sponsorship for 1964 and finally withdrew to Harbor Springs. Fr. Bertram returned to an overjoyed flock late in the summer of 1954. He may reinstate ecclesiastical favor and could very likely give more explicit dates about this enterprise and its antecedents.

Though focused around two afternoon Indian programs, the festival has tended more and more toward a money-making fair for the church. In 1953 various booths run by Polish residents sold aprons and trinkets for the benefit of the church. One booth of Indian souvenirs, arranged by the Kenoshmegs, profited the Indians. Similarly, the church netted the proceeds from bingo and other games, from beef and chicken dinners served at noon in the community hall and donated by parishioners, and from sales at a beer truck parked on the grounds from 3 to 5 P.M. But the intake from a collection at the programs covered the Indians' expenses for a special bus and netted a few dollars.

The traditional date for this event has been the second Sunday in August, though in 1948 it was delayed to August 17. Formerly there could be as many as ten or twelve summer programs in Cross Village. Of late there has usually been only one. Two decades ago there were enough Indians in the community to carry the performances. In 1953 all of the participants except Kenosha and Kenoshmeg arrived at noon, unrehearsed, from Harbor Springs and Petoskey. Some of the young girls did the dances for the first time in their lives.

Kenosha had written down the dances for the two programs on a slip of paper; but there seemed to be a discrepancy between his list and that of an announcer who blared over a public address system. The two programs were to commence at 3 and 5 P.M., but they swung into action half an hour late. Perhaps Kenosha was to sing a number of accompaniments, but he sang only for the Eagle Dance and left the rest of the music to the drummer. He was director, dancer, and singer all in one. In between times he also obliged photographers.

The stage was a grassy plot south of the church. The background combined the white spire and white tipis set up for the occasion. The audience was held in check by a semicircle of rope. They stood, knelt, and sat around informally. Occasionally a photographer or child strayed beyond the magic circle. At times a member of the audience was drawn into participation for a Scalp Dance and an adoption. In general, informality prevailed and made up for lack of professional finish. The gaiety and the charm of the setting overrode the semi-commercial aspects.

In the program the soloists are especially mentioned. Group dances

Festival Sites

Cross Village
Harbor Springs
Petoskey
Greensky Hill
Charlevoix
Kewadin
Northport
Hart
Newaygo
Alto
Charlton Park
Bradley
Athens
Dewitt
Ann Arbor
Walpole Island, Ont.
Saginaw
Bay City
Mount Pleasant
Oscoda
Mikado
Houghton Lake
Burt Lake
St. Ignace
Sault Ste. Marie
Bay Mills
Garden River Reserve, Ont.
Manitoulin Island, Ont.
Zeba
Baraga
Hannahville
Washington Island

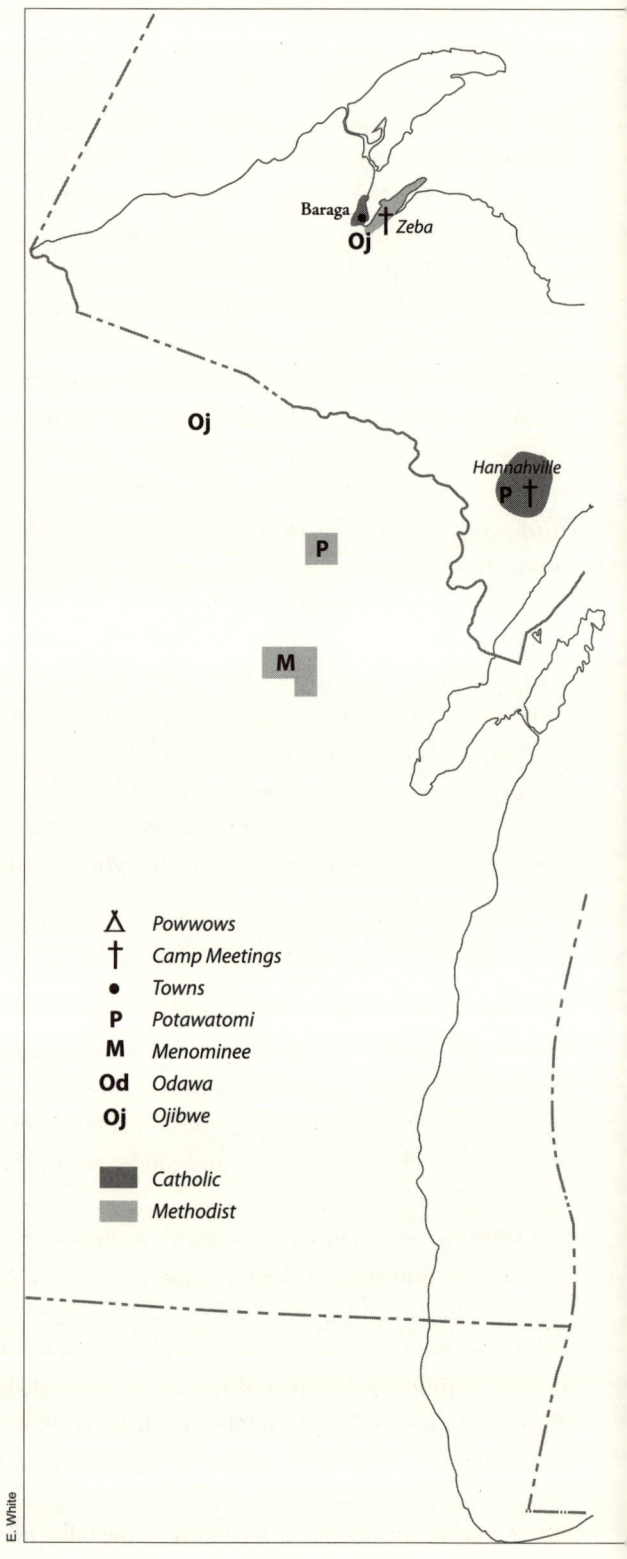

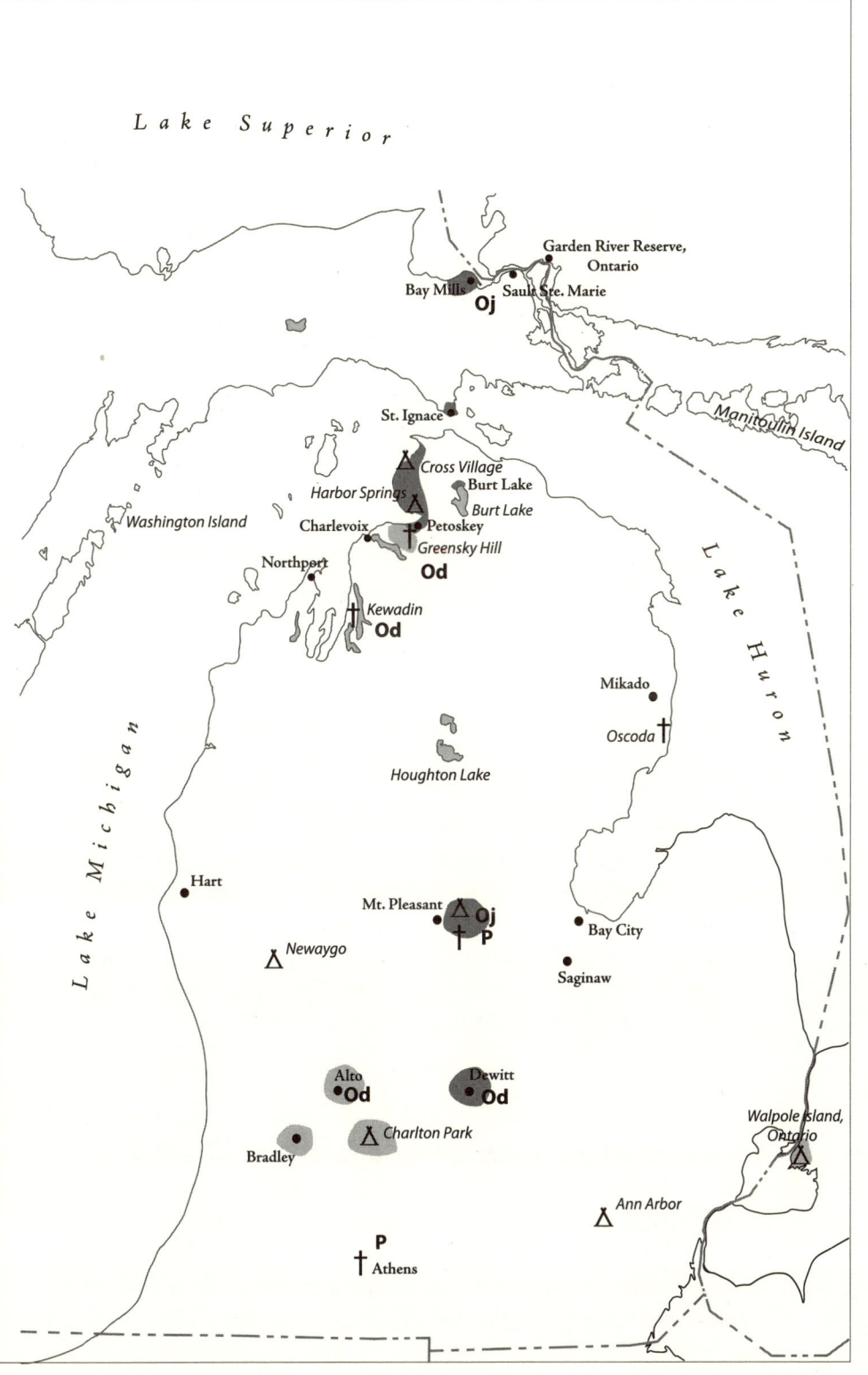

included the entire Shagonaby and Wemigwase families, Joe and Eliza Kishigo, Frankie Gasco, and a few others. The separate dances are choreographed in chapter 3.

Odawa Festival (August 9, 1953)

3 P.M.
1. Pipe of Peace Dance, *Richard Wemigwase and Dave Kenosha*
2. Kettle Dance, *Dave Kenosha*
3. Snake Dance, *Dave Kenosha and group*
4. Scalp Dance, *Richard Wemigwase and man in the audience*
5. Shield Dance, *four boys*
6. Sun Dance, *Dave Kenosha*
7. Eagle Dance, *Dave Kenosha*

6 P.M.
1. Naming of three white men and of Fr. Wolf, *group*
2. Pipe of Peace Dance, *Wemigwase, then Kenosha*
3. Snake Dance, *group*
4. Eagle Dance, *Kenoshmeg*
5. Scalp Dance, *Wemigwase, boys, and other man in audience*
6. Kettle Dance, *Kenosha and boys*

A Swan Dance and Bow and Arrow Dance had been planned, but were omitted because of miscuing. A Deer Dance and Buffalo Dance had been featured in some past performances but had to be canceled because of insufficient performer training. These and other previous dances had to be gleaned at a subsequent meeting with Kenosha—namely, at a picnic on Monday for him and the Kenoshmegs. The songs that did not appear on the programs were likewise produced at this gathering around a camp fire and during subsequent similar meetings.

Naming Ceremony at Harbor Springs (August 10, 1946)

A much publicized annual Naming Ceremony in Harbor Springs has mushroomed from modest beginnings some twenty years ago. The only reliable report concerns the August 10, 1946, occasion, which was witnessed and hereafter described by Jane Willets Ettawageshik. Every summer in July or August the Odawas of Harbor Springs have for a number of years staged a naming and adoption ceremonial. A prominent white person of Harbor

Springs or some other city in Michigan is given an Indian name and adopted into the tribe. There are dances and other ceremonies. This summer the ceremony was held again after a lapse of five years, the duration of the war, during which there were too many of the young people gone to present it. The ceremony is sponsored by the Michigan Indian Defense Association and is held on August 10.

There are a number of ceremonials and powwows held at this time in various parts of Michigan. The powwow in Cross Village was staged on the Sunday following the ceremonial in Harbor Springs. A *Song of Hiawatha* play was formerly given in Petoskey at this time every summer, but it was not presented this year because there were not enough actors available to take part in it. There was, however, a bazaar and auto raffle for the benefit of the Catholic church in Petoskey a week or so after the other ceremonials. The ceremonial at Harbor Springs was formerly held in conjunction with a Catholic church picnic, which has been given separately for some time. The picnic at the church was held this year on August 22.

There was really only one rehearsal, though plans were discussed previously. This took place on the Monday before the event in the Legion Hall, and the dances and order of events were worked out at this time. Most of the boys had never been in a ceremonial before so there was considerable worry over the result, but everyone in town seemed to agree that it was a big success. There were photographers and reporters present. There was a large audience even before the Western States, a cruise ship, arrived.

The ceremony was held by the tennis courts and the dock, where there is a cleared space, at 9:30 P.M. It followed a day of celebration in Harbor Springs, a water carnival, a beauty contest, sail boat races, and in the evening a boat parade around the harbor beyond the point and back. There was a row of small evergreen trees set up along the shore, with two tipis in front of them. Some distance in front of the tipis and about between them a council fire was laid and kept burning constantly. There were benches in a wide semi-circle for the participants near the entrance on Bay Street just in front of the tipis. A grandstand was set up near the entrance on Bay Street.

In addition to the soloists named, participants were Mrs. Christine Otto, John and Richard Gasco, Virginia Chingwa, and others. The dances in the following order of events are detailed in chapter 3.

1. Lighting of council fire and passing of peace pipe, *Fred Ettawageshik*
2. Announcements and greetings, *Fred Ettawageshik*
3. Welcome Dance, *group*
4. Scalp Dance, *Louis Wemigwase, Raymond Kiogima, and Gus Kiogima*
5. Eagle Dance, *Frankie Gasco (age ten)*

6. Snake Dance, *J. Foster Otto*
7. Adoptions; christening, *of Joe Chingwa's grandsons*; naming, *of several prominent men from Detroit and Ypsilanti*

At that time the ceremony was still in the hands of an Indian organization, the Michigan Indian Defense Association, but it soon fell into the hands of the Michigan Indian Foundation, a nonprofit corporation of white businessmen, with R. A. C. Wollenberg, M.D., serving as secretary. Their prospectus of the Annual Indian Pageant and Naming Ceremony sports photographs of prosperous executives in Sioux war bonnets, shaking hands with Odawa chiefs, bigger and better dinner dances, the Ottawa Indian Stadium (capacity 10,000), the unrecognizably remodeled Chief Blackbird home, a Hopi Snake Dance exhibited to the nuns of the Holy Childhood School. The aims, proclaimed in 1947, include the promotion of Indian welfare, "by good will, donation, bequest, endowment and contribution." These take the form of educational and other loans, which have to be repaid. The encouragement of "the study of ancient Indian history, customs, laws, manners, medicine, arts, crafts, music, poetry," etc. is manifest in the ceremonies that now take place at the stadium, remodeled in 1950. For instance, on July 24 and 25, 1953, the dancing was taken over by a group of Detroit white Boy Scouts, the Heyoka Wacipi. On July 22, 23, and 24th, white professionals enacted some excerpts from Chief Blackbird's History (Blackbird 1897) and sang parts of a song entitled "Rosemarie." A group of Hopi Indians gave some of their dances. It seems that the Odawa also performed a Scalp Dance and another item or two.

The transition was gradual. For several years the Odawa with professional aid presented a pageant in the stadium, an enactment of Longfellow's *Song of Hiawatha*.[1] This developed out of a Hiawatha pageant at Round Lake near Petoskey. Around 1905 this had been transferred from Garden River Reserve, Ontario (near Sault Ste. Marie), songs and all. At that time, local Odawa took prominent parts, for instance, Joe Chingwa played the role of Jibiabos.

In 1954 the Odawa were face to face with a choice, since the Holy Cross Church had withdrawn sponsorship and outsiders had taken over the Naming Ceremonial. The Indians could discontinue their Native song and dance portrayals or else undertake a revival entirely their own. During my field trip in May, Jane Ettawageshik and I spread propaganda for the latter course. I pointed out the large number of genuine Odawa songs and dances still in their repertoire and offered help in combining them into a coherent and entirely indigenous program. The scenario followed Baron Lahontan's description of the early eighteenth century sacrifices. It was presented to a large gathering of Indians assembled by Jane on June 27. The proposal was passed unanimously. Dave Kenosha was elected dance and song director and Joe Kishigo Jr. was elected manager. Much of the business, however, fell to the lot of Jane. An enthusiastic group of thirty-seven men, women, and children met once or twice a week around a camp fire at Mosquito Park in the Indian village. Despite various tribulations, four performances materialized. The worst obstacle was the objection of the Michigan Indian Foundation to the use of the stadium; the second worst was the expense of its ultimate use. The general public and the city council, however, lent their support, and the project proved a success. Little was cleared beyond costs, but each presentation was better than the one before. The effort at cohesion drew the Indians together and may grow into a permanent organization truly for the revival of their arts and lore. Beyond the initial instigation and a few subsequent suggestions on my part (some of them relayed by Jane), the enterprise has remained completely Indian.

There were variants on this general plan. When observed on August 22, the Swan Dance preceded the intermission, and the Buffalo Dance preceded the invocation. A Hoop Dance by Dick Wemigwase and another by Mary Wemigwase, both of them small children, were inserted. The Corn Dance did not materialize until the last performance. During the intermission, Fred Ettawageshik told legends, unhappily with the aid of a public address system due to the size of the space. A group of women sang an Odawa hymn, "Epitoweng nagamoda."

Four August performances were given on Sundays at 3 P.M. at alternating locations: Cross Village, on a grassy plot near the bluff, then in the Ottawa Stadium in Harbor Springs. One Sunday was omitted in the schedule because many of the Indians participated in a pageant of Pere Marquette's landing at St. Ignace.

Despite the more taut organization and the semi-professionalism of an admission charge, the same informality and leisureliness prevailed as in the 1953 Cross Village shows. This, in fact, constituted part of the charm and the sense of authenticity. In Cross Village the audience was drawn into the performances by the adoption of several individuals and by the impromptu clowning of Richard Wemigwase.

At times these performers have left their Native haunts and have appeared in other locations—thus a group of young men trained by Fred Ettawageshik in the 1940s and thus Dave Kenosha, who has appeared at the Wisconsin Dells and numerous cities. However, they cannot be regarded as professionals. They netted small profits and danced chiefly for the joy of it, in spare time from their regular occupations.

Isabella Reservation, Mount Pleasant

At Isabella Reservation Native songs and dances did not remain a constant tradition as among the Catholic Odawa. Rather, under Methodist teachings, they had died out and were revived only recently by Eli Thomas. For the past five years he has produced an annual "pageant" around the weekend of July 4. He learned much of this lore from Whitney Albert of Oscoda, and he has drawn this excellent performer into the local shows. Ike Pelcher has scoured his memory for recollections from his boyhood. A young Potawatomi, Benedict Quignon, has tried to reconstruct and compose dances from books and a fertile imagination, and he has aroused the interest of several boys and girls. Betty Pamp and her daughters are engaged in research concerning their Native traditions.

Eli Thomas is the unanimously acknowledged and very able manager of the pageant. Out of heterogeneous talents he builds a program that resembles a variety show more than a pageant. It contains no central idea and no script or specific cast of characters. With limited publicity he has usually assembled a fair audience in an attractive amphitheater near the community house and camp meeting tabernacle. He has erected totem poles and tipis, and Whitney Albert has brought along a birch bark tipi of his own construction. Thomas and Albert also function as drummers for the dances and as singers either with or without dance activity. At booths the inhabitants sell souvenirs, Native basketry, wild rice, frybread, coffee, tea, hamburgers, and other commodities. Everyone in possession of a costume wears it, whether he takes part in the program or not. In 1954 the Indians were on the grounds from Friday afternoon till Monday evening, excluding Sunday because of religious scruples. Some of them slept there. Thus Thomas and Albert spent the night in the birch bark tipi, largely in order to guard the artifacts. The Jackson and Chamberlain children ate under picnic tables. My daughter and I were among the campers and settled down in a grove of trees; but we moved onto the stage of the tabernacle in a downpour of rain. Mr. Chamberlain was kept awake at his hamburger stand practically all night by miscellaneous well-inebriated and noisy customers. In this setting the following programs took place Friday and Saturday nights and Saturday and Monday afternoons.

Ojibwe Pageant (July 2, 1954)

1. Welcoming Address and Procession, *Eli Thomas and group*
2. Hoot Owl Song, *Eli Thomas*
3. Medicine Man, *Billy Elk*

4. Hunter's Dance, *Benedict Quignon; Betty Pamp, narrator*
5. Methodist Ojibwe hymn, "Jesus Ishpeming," *unidentified woman*
6. Blanket Act, *Ike Pelcher*
7. Corn Grinding, *Mrs. Thomas*
8. Love Call from "Rosemarie," *Glenna Rickard*
9. Eagle Dance, *Benedict Quignon and narrator, with Johnny Quignon*
10. Adoption of radio announcer from Mount Pleasant, *Thomas and others*
11. War Dances, *all men*

The course of events on July 3rd and 5th was similar, with several improvements. Ike Pelcher gave the Pipe Dance instead of the Blanket Act. Albert, who had been delayed on July 2 by a car breakdown, sang and danced on the other occasions. On July 4, an Odawa Indian, Raymond P. Carey, performed a fairly expert Hoop Dance.

Charlton Park, Hastings

Five miles east of Hastings, a seemingly aimless dirt road leads to a secluded park on the Thornapple River. A wealthy farmer and Indian man by the name of Charlton donated the land to the public and erected small but good museum of Indian relics. A ballpark, a small sandy beach, picnic tables, and electric connections add to the attractions. Nearby there is an overnight campsite.

This idyllic spot is fairly centrally located in the state and between three large cities: Grand Rapids, Lansing, and Battle Creek. It has always been a center and at one time was the site of intertribal gatherings. On historic Potawatomi grounds, it is nearest to a modern Potawatomi settlement at Bradley. When intertribal councils lost their meaning, it became the setting for a "powwow" for white visitors, but it retains some of the aboriginal camp gathering pattern.

For a weekend in the middle of August, Indians from the entire Lower Peninsula congregate and pitch their tents by the woods on the river bank. They prepare their meals at the fireplaces provided in the park. They display baskets, bead work, tomahawks, birch bark dolls, and other objects of Native manufacture, but for tourist trade. During the daytime and through the early evenings they are kept busy by a succession of events, as on this given Sunday:

- 11:00 A.M.   More or less Methodist service by Jim Peters of Mount Pleasant; preachers' hymns with steel guitar by Jack Neomi and John Chevis; a capella by Eli Thomas, Benedict Quignon, and William Birch
- 1:30 P.M.   Log rolling contest in the river by Thomas and Albert
- 2:00 P.M.   Band concert
- 2:30 P.M.   Brief Indian show
- 3:30 P.M.   Baseball game
- 8:30 P.M.   Long Indian show initiated by "old time music" of square dance type

After the evening programs and, to an extent, early on Sunday morning, the Indians have time to visit, to gather around a campfire and tell stories, sometimes until a midnight chill sends them to their tents. That is the time when they feel in the mood for singing and are willing to record their songs.

The shows are under the experienced direction of Eli Thomas, who has to assemble on the spur of the moment a motley array of participants from various parts of the state. In addition, all kinds of mechanical chores keep him racing about, jobs like the installation of the public address system, the replacement of extinct light bulbs, etc. His cast features Whitney Albert and the most active dancers from Isabella Reserve, a group of Odawa from DeWitt just north of Lansing—Mr. and Mrs. Anthony Chingman, Mr. and Mrs. Philip King, and a young Cherokee, James Shaffer, whose father moved to Albion from Georgia. The Little Traverse Odawa are conspicuously absent, except for the J. Foster Ottos and their eighteen-year old son, Donald, but they have lived in Scottville and now in Weidman and have cast their lot with the more southerly Indians.

The audience gathers in a semi-circle around a campfire on a small field between the tents and the river. It is small enough to allow some intimacy. The fire would be bright enough for illumination. But a public address system and glaring electric lights are indispensable, it seems. The audience is served a fare exemplified by two witnessed programs. During an intermission they toss small coins into a hat that is circulated.

Intertribal Powwow (August 16, 1953)

1. Welcome Dance, *entire group*
2. Hoot Owl Song, *Eli Thomas*
3. Green Grass Dance, *entire group*; Song, *improvisation by Blue Cloud*
4. Folk Song with guitar, *Jack Neomi*

5. Snake Dance, *Dan Otto*
6. Turkey Dance, *James Shaffer*
7. Story of Corn, corn grinding and baking of squaw bread by women, *Eli Thomas, Mrs. William Birch, and Lucy Pelcher*; Song, *chanting by women and by Whitney Albert*
8. Eagle Dance, *Dan Otto*
9. Tobacco Invocation and Pipe Dance, *Billy Elk*
10. Story of Father on Hunting Trip, *Whitney Albert*
11. Blanket Act, *Ike Pelcher*
12. War Dance, *entire group, led by Whitney Albert;* Song, *improvisation by Eli Thomas*
13. Adoption ceremony and dance for two white men, *Eli Thomas and other men*
14. Social Dance, *entire group;* Drumming, *by Eli Thomas on a small Chinese tom-tom and by Whitney Albert on a Native-type log drum*

This program was recorded notwithstanding the distortions of an intermittently defunct loudspeaker.

Intertribal Powwow (August 14, 1954)

1. Story of the Origin of Porcupine, *Whitney Albert*
2. Procession, *entire cast*
3. Papoose Dance, *Johnny Quignon (age six)*
4. Green Grass Dame, *everyone;* Song, *improvisation by Eli Thomas*
5. Eagle Dance, *Benedict and Johnny Quignon*
6. Breadmaking, *Mrs. Birch*
7. Blanket Act, *Ike Pelcher*
8. Pipe Dance, *J. Foster Otto*
9. Medicine Man, *Billy Elk*
10. Hunter's Dance, *Benedict Quignon*
11. Adoption of chemical factory worker from Saginaw, *Eli Thomas and men*
12. Dog Dance, *Whitney Albert*
13. Hoot Owl Song, *Eli Thomas*
14. Contest Dance, *everyone*
15. Corn Grinding Dance, *unidentified woman and two young girls*
16. Acrobatic Dance, *a girl from Mount Pleasant*
17. Papoose War Dance, *Johnny Quignon*
18. Snake Dance, *Whitney Albert and children from the audience*

In the course of the summer, variable combinations of this cast, around the nucleus of Eli Thomas and Whitney Albert, appear at summer resorts in Houghton Lake and Oscoda, at centennials, and at camps. On Labor Day, 1953, the Chingmans assembled a group for an afternoon and evening show in Newaygo, following a centennial procession. They were encircled by a relatively small audience in front of the municipal auditorium, yet could not dispense with the public address system.

Newaygo Centennial (September 7, 1953)

1:00 A.M.—PARADE

2:30 P.M.—INDIAN PROGRAM
1. Welcoming Dance, *Don Otto, James Shaffer, and Philip King*
2. Eagle Dance, *Donald Otto, Mr. and Mrs. Philip King*
3. Story about Robin (opeche), *Anthony Chingman*
4. Green Grass Dance, *men and women;* Song, *Hoot Owl Song by Chingman*
5. Love Song, *Malvina Chingman*
6. Eagle Dance, *Don Otto*
7. The Dying Warrior, *James Shaffer*
8. Snake Dance, *Don Otto*
9. War Dance, *Don Otto, James Shaffer, Philip King, and Raymond Carey; Chingman drummed and sang variants of the Hoot Owl Song for all dances.*

9:00 P.M.
Indian program similar to the above, minus Don Otto and James Shaffer, plus a Fire Dance by Raymond Carey. Not witnessed.

Other Shows by Eli Thomas and Anthony Chingman

In the early fall, Eli Thomas makes the rounds of schools from Bay City to Lansing for the purposes of "booking." Then during the winter he follows up with educational programs for school children. He chooses from his collection the jalopy with the fewest rattles and piles in three or four helpers and a huge load of genuine Indian artifacts, basketry and porcupine quill work, and miscellaneous souvenirs. Generally he makes the round trip, including two or three shows, all in one day. He issues printed circulars and has devised a routine that varies somewhat with the four or five members of his company.

The program contains conversations in Ojibwe by Eli Thomas and Billy Elk, the Hoot Owl Song and the Grandfather Song, a Medicine Man scene by Billy Elk, a Pipe Dance (preferably by Ike Pelcher or Foster Otto), the Story of Hiawatha and of the Cradle in the Other World, a Corn Grinding Scene and Women's Dance (sometimes with Ike Pelcher burlesquing a woman), a Blanket Act by Ike Pelcher, a demonstration of basket weaving by Mrs. Thomas and any helper, a comic scene of the Coming of the Missionary, a War Dance by Eddie Jackson or another available assistant, and an Adoption Dance and farce with some child or adult in the audience.

Variants of this setup were witnessed in Ann Arbor on November 3, 1953, and March 11, 1954, through my machinations. Parts of this routine are combined with other numbers in the larger intertribal powwows.

Despite his good intentions, Eli Thomas has no sense for authenticity or coherence. He does not hesitate to include an Acrobatic Dance or a singing of "Pale Moon" by some youngster. But he is amenable to suggestions. When he was invited to perform at Michigan State University for the meetings of the Michigan Folklore Society on March 26, 1955, and again at the University of Michigan on July 5, 1955, he left out the nonsense. On both occasions he brought some ten performers and shared the program with Anthony Chingman and family. On the former occasion the program was called a Maple Sugar Festival; on the latter it was given the Indian title of "Apteneben" (Midsummer Festival). A study of the repertoires showed a hidden residue of aboriginal arts and lore. A topical arrangement and omission of the most obvious fakes gave a good picture of Native ceremonialism, though still in the frame of a show.

In the "Apteneben" the Mount Pleasant group, with Eli Thomas as master of ceremonies, presented plant ceremonies, a tobacco invocation and Pipe Dance, the story of birchbark, "thanks to the sugar maple," a medicine song, the story of herbs, and a Corn Dance in three parts. The DeWitt group, with Anthony Chingman as master of ceremonies, performed the Eagle Dance with a thunderbird legend, hunting and animal songs and tales, the Partridge Dance, Fire Dances, and the Snake Dance. Blue Cloud shone in both parts as singer of suitable songs. The Odawa group also performed a Catholic hymn and the naming rite of a grandchild. Appropriately, this event played in front of the Clements Library and was connected with an exhibit of Indian books.

Many miles to the north, on Hannahville Reservation, Alex Philemon gives the same program as Eli Thomas. He frankly admits that he learned the routine on a visit. The chief actors are his immediate family, including his grandchildren. For several years he was engaged at the Indian Village built west of Escanaba by Mark Sabuco, but in 1956 he refused to participate because of insufficient pay. He left the field to a group of Indians from Odanah, Wisconsin. But he has enough sporadic events to find show business worthwhile.

Changes and Trends

The changes in dance and music since aboriginal days have been revolutionary and pitiful. The segregation of these arts from religion and their commercialization is so complete as to obscure the aboriginal patterns. They can be reconstructed only with reference to historic accounts and to tribes with better-preserved patterns. The general trend has been toward disintegration, in keeping with the compartmentalization of the newly adopted culture. It took two centuries to segregate the arts from religion and economy. It took one to separate dance and music, audience and performer. This tendency was accelerated with the passing of each singer, but it was impelled by other factors, such as indifference and lack of rehearsals between singers and dancers.

Since 1953 this trend seems to have been arrested and even reversed. David Kenosha accompanies more dances with the songs in his repertoire, and Blue Cloud sings more solos and fits more of his songs to the related mime. Partly this is due to the two writers' interference in the natural course of development, but partly it can be credited to an awakening on the part of the Indians. This revival and new pride in Native lore has begun to improve the execution and even the costuming. Coherence departs when the Indian leaders are left to themselves; but it may return in time. Whether this folkloric trend will continue depends on two main factors.

One is economic. In 1955 and 1956 show business became more profitable. In the summer of 1956 two groups of Odawa and two of Ojibwe-Potawatomi were engaged at a flat rate of ten dollars a person by camps and resorts. Winter engagements are also on the upswing. This is a matter of no mean importance even to the most idealistic Indian. To some it is the only reason for performing and for rehearsing diligently in advance.

The other factor is psychological, partly conditioned by the economic. The leaders of the Indian groups have become more conscious of the value inherent in their non-Christian heritage. In this they have been encouraged by the realization of increased white interest and appreciation. With better pay they have given more time to research and to improvements. Thus any permanent rejuvenation is a project for the white audiences as

well as their Indian protégés. The trends are evident in several visual aspects that deserve attention in this chapter.

Costumes

The modern dance outfits function exclusively as costumes. As such they present a miscellaneous picture with an overbalance of Plains-derived items. Determining the provenance of each component is a task for a specialist. For the present purposes the probable origins can be used to classify the costumes into four main types. The first are of Anishinaabe derivation. These are in the minority and in part are recent developments.[2] The Wemigwases attempt reduction to aboriginal essentials, a breechclout with accessories. Richard Wemigwase and Dick Jr. wear a head ornament inspired by the roach. Dick adds leggings and a small cape. Louis Wemigwase adds a very cumbersome full-length war bonnet. Since 1955, Blue Cloud has been investing in a roach headdress. The most authentic apparel is Joan Pamp's of 1955, with the skirt-above-the-bust and shoulder strap style (Wissler 1915, 73–78; Cartwright and Douglas 1950).

The vast majority of the costumes are of Plains derivation. The men prefer huge war bonnets in gaudy colors—emblems of the typical Indian, but impractical for dancing. A bonnet is always presented to a new adoptee. For women a beaded headband and feather play the same role. A favorite male jacket is modeled on the Plains sleeved jacket with fringes, sometimes in one piece and of cloth (as in the case of Don Otto) and sometimes involving a button front and buckskin (as in the case of Blue Cloud). All are of the nineteenth and twentieth century tailored cut (Wissler 1915, 58). All women and girls wear Plains-type tunics, usually with leggings. Eliza Kishigo and Veronica Kishigo own fine, decorated hide costumes with horizontal fringed capes, of the Arapaho-Kiowa cut. The majority have to copy the tailored type with closed sleeves in cloth (Wissler 1915, 69–70, 87). They simulate hide in a preference for white or shades of tan, but some prefer red or robin's egg blue. Lengths and fringe patterns have many variants. Moccasins are of the Plains type, some heavily beaded.

A third type of costume is of southwestern inspiration. The influence of New Mexico has reached Michigan in diluted form only in the Eagle Dance costume. Don Otto's is the most faithful, with elaborate wings and beaked half-mask, and simple, with breechclout. Most performers have designed wings only, with fanciful and artistic painted decoration. Two winged Odawa girls wear long tunics.

Finally, other costumes can be considered hybrids. The hybrids compound nondescript tribal heritage with more or less white adjuncts. Next to the tunic, a vest or bolero is the most popular male garment, a derivative from white pattern with Indian beading and almost always in cloth. It is an Anishinaabe favorite, but extends from the New York Iroquois to sporadic appearances in Oklahoma. In Michigan it is, as a rule, worn over an ordinary white or brightly colored shirt, never in combination with a special smock for a "straight dance costume." Another garment with almost equal Indian distribution is the cloth legging-and-clout combination. Chingman has four flaps on his clout. In combination with multicolored war bonnets, these male costumes tend to be polychrome. Two costume types that have considerable vogue in Wisconsin and Iowa but have not reached Michigan Indians are the male pan-Indian bustle and the female appliquéd Anishinaabe tunic. Oklahoma-reared Indians in Detroit favor these styles but have not communicated them to the rural Indians.

The decorations are so individualized as to end up nondescript. The designs on necklaces, headbands, and other jewelry tend toward the geometric, but they can be anything. Ankle bells, spangles, and glass beads show white derivation. One distinctive article is Blue Cloud's antler-tip necklace. Face and body paint are out of fashion, but in 1946 Jane observed Louis Wemigwase's wild white, black, blue, and red body designs, with white all over the upper face. He used grease paint and lipstick, not Native materials.

Most of the costumes are the performers' handiwork. Some specimens were obtained on a visit to Dakota reservations. A few are heirlooms. Some of the Odawa women's costumes belong to the Harbor Springs Holy Childhood convent and have to be rented. The miscellaneous aspects and general types of costumes seem to have changed little among the Odawa since Jane's notes of 1946, though the southerly groups have introduced improvements within three years. Since 1912 the women's costumes have undergone change in a nativistic direction. Photographs in the program of the Hiawatha pageant show the older women in full cotton skirt and long-sleeved blouses but the men and younger women in Plains-style outfits, much as today. These pictures were taken at Round Lake near Petoskey by the Grand Rapids and Indiana Railway. Other photographs (Blackbird 1897; Lanzelère 1936) show men's headdresses with feathers stuck upright as a coronet. These few recent changes suggest the need for further research concerning interesting costume developments.

Accessories

An indispensable accessory is a peace pipe, usually a skillful copy of ancient models. Fred Ettawageshik produces perhaps the best specimens.[3] One of these, used in the 1946 ceremony, was described as follows by Jane Ettawageshik:

> Peace or Ceremonial Pipe in the ceremonial was made of wood by Fred. Twenty-three inches length of pipe. Eight inches length entire bowl, including "platform." Three inches length or height of bowl proper. Stem was

white ash (because it has a soft interior) with center hole made with hot wire, with tip shaped for lips. Brown stain was daubed on the stem so that it had a spotted appearance. The bowl was painted a dark red and shellacked so that it looked exactly like dark Catlinite and was shaped much like Catlinite bowls I've seen in the University of Michigan Museum. Just above the bowl proper, on the platform, the thunderbird was painted in yellow and blue. Just below the bowl proper were the three feathers in yellow acid blue, the chief's sign. The pipe bowl was drilled with a brace and bit. It was red cherry because it is hardwood and takes a nice finish, and tobacco can be smoked in it for a long time without setting the wood on fire. On each side of the bowl the crossed arrow and circle design for love and friendship was painted. Above the bowl a tuft of feathers (pheasant, pigeon) was bound on with strips of buckskin ornamented with blue and white Indian seed beads. A fan ornament, a partridge tail sewn to a top of buckskin, was bound to the pipe stem just above the feather tuft. The binding of the rawhide strips was attached to the buckskin top of the fan by Fred with a bobby pin. Several pendant strips of rawhide were also sewn on—four fringes to a side and one large blue or red wooden bead on each. A large piece of strip in the center of the top of the fan had two large beads, one red and one blue. There were four notches in the stem on each side of the feathers painted red, green, red, green, purely for decoration.

This pipe, modeled on the elaborate traditional calumets, has been superseded by simpler copies in present dances. The construction and proportions are analogous, but the pipe manipulated by Kenosha in the photographs (made by Fred) has no fan, only three fringes with strings of colored wooden beads. Its mouthpiece is painted white. Whitney Albert's fine old pipe is completely unadorned except for a narrow beaded band.

For corn grinding scenes, old wooden mortar and pestles of common Woodland type are used in all locations (Lyford 1945, 61). For the Kettle Dance, Dave Kenosha suspends an old iron kettle from a pyramid of three birch branches. Richard Wemigwase's scalping tomahawk and James Shaffer's wing fan constitute minor hand-wielded accessories. Noisemakers belong in the category of music.

Instruments

The instruments have deviated from the old-time types. A hundred years ago three types of drums were a *tewegun* or *dewigun* (struck-sound instrument), which was single-headed, for Wabeno ceremonies; a *mitgwakik* (wood kettle), double-headed from a two-foot hollow basswood log, for social dances; and a *buaukik* or *nibwəkik* (water kettle), a sixteen-inch-high log drum, tapering at the top with the top covered by a hide by means of a hoop, specifically for Midéwiwin rites (Schoolcraft 1848, 221–22; Copway 1851, 128; Jones 134, 154). These persisted into the twentieth century (Densmore 1913, 142; Jenness 1935, 63, 70). They have been described for Wisconsin tribes as the Menominee and Ojibwe (Hoffman 1896, figs. 3, 10; Kinietz 1947, plates 41, 62). Another important instrument identified from earliest times is the gourd rattle, called *shishigwan* or *chichicoué*, which is filled with pebbles or corn kernels and used for dances. Hoof rattles, *washkeinze* (Copway 1851, 87), rods with bells attached (Kinietz 1947, 282), flutes, and *pipigwan* have all been mentioned. These last and other forms of rattles have not been found in use in Michigan.

The variants of the above percussion instruments are now in use as follows. The Wabeno drum has not been observed at all. A water drum is in Eli Thomas's possession but is never used. Instead, Thomas beats a small Chinese drum.[4] Sometimes, however, Blue Cloud beats on such a drum in his own possession. Usually the Indians play on a double-headed tom-tom modeled on the *mitigwakik*, but called *puwahkik*. The usual type is sixteen to eighteen inches tall and about twelve inches in diameter, of wood or tin, covered at both ends with canvas or rubber inner tubing more often than with hide, and laced in zigzag like a southwestern log drum (Mason 1938, fig. 63). For recording, Blue Cloud used such a drum; David Kenosha used a smaller variety, only six inches high. These rubber-covered tom-toms have a surprisingly good tone and are excellent for recording because they are more subdued than hide drums. Charlie Shagonaby made two handsome drums that were beaten at the Sun Ceremony, one of them covered with birch bark. They were laced like the others, but were wider, about sixteen inches high and eighteen inches wide, more like the western powwow drums seen among the Meskwaki. The drum sticks are straight with hide-covered knobs, not curved or carved like the old ones.

The shaman's type of gourd rattle is apparently out of date, but small gourd rattles are sometimes shaken by dancers. Blue Cloud has a Dakota hide rattle (Mason 1938, fig. 105) and a small tortoise rattle with a handle.

None of the Iroquoian instruments have been accepted, neither the tiny, four-to-six-inch water drum nor the horn or bark rattles. Neither has the western Dream Dance drum penetrated Michigan, because the ceremony is unknown. Generally speaking, traditions are disregarded, and drums and rattles are made of handy materials in any convenient proportions. They may have developed from the Anishinaabe dance drum but changed in accordance with Plains and Pueblo designs. Except for a few valuable old specimens they lack ritual connotations or any sort of exclusiveness and are in fact reproduced for tourist trade. Yet they provide the bulk of the dance accompaniment.

Probable Provenance and Distribution of Dances

1. *Odawa (and Ojibwe?):* Sun Dance
2. *General Central Algonkian:* Animal Dances, former Mide, Wabano; sun-wise circuit, two-step, fourfold repeat, in N. Michigan.
3. *Eastern Woodland:* Women's step, counterclockwise circuit, SE Michigan.
4. *Northern Mississippi:* Pipe Dance, cardinal directions, clockwise
5. *Wisconsin:* Swan, Kettle
6. *Great Plains:* War type, Buffalo, Hoop; step-hop, toe-heel; mime without ground plan
7. *Southwest:* Eagle, Shield, effigy Snake, via Wisconsin; Corn (?)
8. *Southeast:* Snake, via Wisconsin
9. *White Men:* Square dances, tap

Evaluation

The statements on patterns and performers of the public festivals call for evaluation, largely because of certain questionable aspects. Ethnologists and lay spectators have at times expressed disapproval of the entire complex as well as of scattered items. They have given various reasons, such as commercialization, loss of ritual meaning, lack of significance in contemporary life, inclusion of fake numbers, careless performance technique, or deficiency in musical accompaniment. All such objections are justified. As rituals these programs are a failure. As professional exhibits they leave much to be desired. Yet the weaknesses can in part be condoned on the basis of changing purposes. And many deeper values escape the casual observer.

First of all, these festivals must be frankly regarded as shows, with admission fees in some form, payment of performers, and a series of events arrayed for exhibition. The fees are necessary for expenses, for compensation of time expended, and for addition to the all-too-small coffers. Fees are handled with tact, and often as collections, just as in church.

Since these Indians have joined the churches of their neighbors, they would be hypocrites to pretend religious motivation. Since they have been exposed to cultural loss over such a long period, they could not be expected to retain more than fragments. Of course, their shows are shows, but they are not professional performances. Only one Indian, Eli Thomas, makes a living from them. The rest must rehearse in odd moments. As they have no professional coach in their ranks, they perform as amateurs, with the virtues of spontaneity and the evils of carelessness.

The motivations of the various participants include the obvious ones and also some deeper ones. The reasons are shared in greatly varying proportions, as indicated by behavior and by explicit statements.

1. *For financial gain:* In all cases, but very little with David Kenosha and James Shaffer and very much with the Wemigwases and Alex Philemon
2. *For production of a work of art:* Secondary in all cases, nonexistent in some, important with Johnny Quignon
3. *To show off:* Secondary in few cases, important in most, evident with David Kenosha and Eli Thomas
4. *To educate the audience:* Probably less important than professed
5. *To meet other Indians:* An important factor in all cases, especially among the older individuals
6. *To fulfill a deeper meaning, as a link with the tribal past:* Very important with David Kenosha, a factor with all older Indians, less important with children
7. *For purposes of worship:* Much diluted, if at all; questionable even in the case of David Kenosha

These assertions would require systematic tests for reliable statistics. But they already indicate real values—economic, social, and to an extent artistic, but not religious. They affect the tribal members unevenly—most strongly the conservatives who are active participants, less strongly those who attend in a background capacity, and not at all the majority that stay away. Another form of evaluation involves the researcher and certain Indians in the capacity of informants. This is the identification of Native elements, specifically of local elements, the recognition of imported contents from other tribes or from Europe. A first glance and close scrutiny both reveal intense hybridization. One's first thought is to reject the many imports; the second thought is to welcome them as living examples of diffusion and assimilation—some ancient, some recent. The problem of cultural acceptance will course through the next chapters.

Dance and
Music Heritage

CHAPTER 3

Contemporary Dance Patterns

⎯ Gertrude Kurath begins her analysis of dances at Native festivals by observing that they "defy systematic analysis" because of the bewildering level of improvisation in their performances, on the one hand, and because the performers were often far from clear themselves—or better, far from articulate—about what was going on in the dances. The previous chapters equip us to appreciate how varied was the breadth and depth of cultural knowledge among Kurath's Anishinaabe collaborators, and how improvisation and cultural dexterity were necessary to the preservation of traditions in the first half of the twentieth century. Indeed, the dance repertory documented here turns out to be quite a mix of elements. A number of the dance performances would have turned off other serious students of Native American dances, due to their showmanship, even farcicality. Others are not so obviously of Anishinaabe origin, drawing instead on repertorial exchanges with people from other tribes in shows and festivals. At the same time, other dances still performed show clear provenance and significance from the deep past of Anishinaabe visionary and ceremonial tradition.

Yet precisely because Kurath documents whatever she encounters among mid-twentieth-century Anishinaabe consultants as "Anishinaabe dance," she directs our attention to an art form that remains deeply significant to the life of her Native collaborators. Perhaps this is precisely because the embodied, nondiscursive practice of dance is able to suspend—even embrace—the contradictions of twentieth-century Native existence, and to powerfully embody the wholeness of Anishinaabe peoplehood in spite of those contradictions. One could, through dance, outwardly perform what non-Native audiences would consume as "Indian-ness" while enacting steps and gestures laden with deep body knowledge of Anishinaabe significance.

Such indigenous significance was doubly charged. On the one hand, Anishinaabe people had long construed dance to be a privileged form *of spiritual expression, a form of "prayer" capable of generating sacred power by virtue of its fidelity to visionary origins, even while it promoted right relations among people. On the other hand, dance was a particularly charged art form given the cultural politics of federal assimilation policy. In 1921 the Commissioner of Indian Affairs formally authorized reservation authorities to exert educational and even punitive measures to curb dances that were "religious in significance," but he made room for—even attended himself—"folklorized" Native dance performances in powwows, Wild West shows, and the like (Browner 2002, 29–30). Two short decades later, the dance performances by Kurath's collaborators were doubtless still charged with these cultural politics, and they were accomplishing an immense amount of unstated cultural work. What a spectator might have seen as a folklorized, denatured version of a once religious ceremony a performer may have felt in her bones to be a genuine and forceful assertion of Anishinaabe identity. Kurath does not supply many interpretive comments to help clarify these subtleties of dance, but she makes readily available to her readers the varied repertory in all its complexity and the remarkable people who perform this repertory in all of their complexity.*

Choreographic field notes based on the festivals seem at first to defy systematic analysis because of the arbitrary arrangements of many of the programs and because of the hazy functional concepts in the minds of most performers. From the purely formal point of view the ground plans and steps resolve themselves into certain recurrent patterns. These unite various locations and characterize performers, but they do not offer a sufficient basis for arrangement. From the functional point of view the dances fall into categories, if one recognizes their remote past in barely legible documents and obscure memories of Indian leaders.

The former functions suggest arrangement into dances addressed to celestial phenomena and to animal spirits, dances concerned with human occupations and the cycle of life. Needless to say, the categories overlap. The dances impersonating the eagle and the swan aboriginally connected with the thunder and the heavens. The calumet ritual played an important role in almost all ceremonial and practical activities, and was closely associated with the war complex. Though these functions are now defunct, but for the Adoption Dance, the arrangement serves for working purposes.

Several significant dances will be missed, notably those belonging to medicine societies. They have been abandoned for so many decades as to have escaped the observation of even the elders of today. Thus they have no legitimate place in a series of descriptions dealing first of all with observed performances and secondarily with dances recently operative and described by informants.

Less common and more complex ground plans will be drawn next to the dance in question; likewise, all unusual steps. The sun-wise direction follows tradition. According to David Kenosha, all dances must follow the sun's course. Infraction brings bad luck. In his area this rule is followed so consistently that a counterclockwise circuit can be ascribed to error. On the other hand, at Isabella Reserve, the counterclockwise circuit is so common as to suggest a more fundamental reason—namely, a northwesterly type in northern Michigan and a southeastern Woodland type developed around Saginaw Bay (Kurath 1953a). This will be illuminated later on in connection with intertribal associations.

Many of the dances have no definite ground plan, but proceed in arbitrary fashion, a soloist according to his whim or a group in a helter-skelter intermingling. A drawing of the design would prove fruitless.

As to the distribution of steps, the step-hop predominates in all locations and the toe-heel prevails to a somewhat lesser extent. Other steps are specialties of certain performers, whose names are given next to this step. Some of these appear traditional; others, such as Benedict Quignon's, are invented.

The posture is generally fairly erect with a slight forward tilt, except in animal or war dances. Even David Kenosha, who usually dances erect, stoops considerably forward in the Eagle, Bear, and Buffalo Dances. Knees are also flexed very moderately except in the more violent Buffalo Dance and comic Scalp Dance. The arms hang relaxed except for special reasons, such as pointing at the sun, raising a pipe, or imitating a bird's wings. In general the dance style shows ease and restraint.

Dances to Celestial Phenomena

Dances of Offering

- *Occasion:* Odawa Sun Ceremony, 1954
- *Central idea:* Burnt offering to the supreme deity, manifest in the sun

DANCE OF OFFERING
- *Performers:* Entire assembly of men, women, and children
- *Accompaniment:* Double drum beat, speed 108
- *Choreography:* Ground plan 4 with step 1. Kenosha lights the fire,

then leads the circling group for 250 beats. As each person passes near the front of the fire, he or she mimes the tossing of an offering into the flames.

DANCE OF WOMEN
- *Performers:* Women and girls
- *Accompaniment:* Double drum beat, speed 100; song "Walking on the Green, Green Grass," with form of ABABAB ABBAB ABBABB AB, about 260 beats
- *Choreography:* Ground plan 3a and step 3b at first two programs
  Ground plan 3b and step 5 at last two programs

DANCE OF CHILDREN
- *Performers:* Boys and girls under twelve years old
- *Accompaniment:* Usual double drum beat, speed 84; both Hoot Owl songs, alternating thus: song 2 three times, song 1 thrice, song 2 once
- *Choreography:* Ground plan 4 with step 1

DANCE TO THE GREAT SPIRIT
- *Performers:* Entire assembly
- *Accompaniment:* Double beat by two drums, speed 120
- *Choreography:* Ground plan 4 with step 1. As each passes the fire, raise arms skyward in gesture of supplication.

These dances are based on aboriginal thought and procedures and follow traditional choreography; yet they are revivals rather than Native observances handed down from generation to generation. The dignified manner of the dancers evokes the sense of ritual activity.

Sun Dance

- *Occasions:* (1) Ottawa festival, Cross Village, August 9, 1953, 1955; (2) Ottawa Sun Ceremony, Cross Village and Harbor Springs, 1954
- *Performer:* Dave Kenosha
- *Accompaniment:* Double drum beat, speed 108
- *Central idea:* Salute the sun, follow its course from sunrise to sunset
- *Choreography:* Ground plan 1, proceeding from north to east, south, west, and back to north. (In first show the 1953 direction reversed, probably through error in confusion of the occasion.) Then circuit fire. Step 3b. At east, south, and west, shade eyes and point to sun. At east, start glancing straight ahead and raise eyes and hand; at west, reverse. At south, raise arms straight up.

According to David Kenosha, this is an ancient Odawa dance connected with the worship of the sun. The dancer varies the details on each occasion. Joe Chingwa described a variant of this dance for a group to Jane Ettawageshik as follows: "Start dancing to four winds, never back to audience. At start sun not up, come to center from south, half circle fire, go north, turn right and east to west, dance around fire. Sun comes up, catch sun in dancing; at sunset are all in, fall to ground. A lot can dance. Men carry whistle in mouth, blow like an eagle, women raise hands to sky. Originally four small fires in four directions."

Pipe Dance

- *Occasions:* (1) Ottawa Festival, Cross Village, 1953, 1955; (2) Sun Ceremony, 1954; (3) Hastings and Ann Arbor, 1953; Ann Arbor 1955; (4) Ann Arbor, March 1954; Mount Pleasant, July 3 and 5, 1954; (5) Hastings, August 1954
- *Performers:* (1) Dave Kenosha and Richard Wemigwase; (2) Dave Kenosha; (3) Billy Elk; (4) Ike Pelcher; (5) J. Foster Otto
- *Accompaniments:* Double drum beat, speed 108 or 112 as a rule
- *Paraphernalia:* a calumet, as described previously
- *Central ideas:* Tobacco offering to the sun and the Great Spirit for good fellowship and success in the venture
- *Choreography:* Ground plan 1a in all cases, except Ike's pattern 1b and a variant by Richard Wemigwase
  1. Kenosha and Wemigwase
     A. Kenosha, standing at north, raise pipe and smoke to 4 directions sun-wise
     B. Wemigwase repeat same procedure
     C. Wemigwase with step 1, proceed to south, west, across to east, blowing smoke at each point; return to north
     D. Kenosha with step 3b, dance to east, south, west, raising pipe at each point, then swing it low toward ground and proceed to neat point; dance to center, offer to sky and earth, then return north
  2. Kenosha
     With step 3b, dance to east, south, west, center as above; circuit sun-wise once around fire; exit north
  3. Elk—Drum tempo 96
     A. On knees, raise arms in prayer to Great Spirit
     B. Standing, lights pipe
     C. With step 1, circuit sun-wise for 14 hops, stand and puff; circuit

to north for 8 hops, stand and puff; circuit to east for 5 hops, stand and puff; circuit to south for 7 hops, stand and puff; circuit to west for 8 hops, stand and puff; circuit to Great Spirit for 6 hops, stand and puff; circuit to Earth for 3 hops, stand and puff

4. Pelcher

Start at north, proceed against the sun

A. Step 1 to west, holding pipe forward horizontally in both hands, 8 hops
B. Facing west, execute jump-hop in place, ending with quarter turn to face south, 8 double beats
A. Step 1 to south, raising pipe
B. Jump-hop in place, quarter turn to face east
A. Step-hop to east
B. Jump-hop, quarter turn to north
A. Step-hop to north
C. Raise pipe to sky and earth

5. Foster

A. At south end of dance ground it's announced that the pipe will be presented to west, north, east, south (an adjustment to the lay of the land)
B. With step 1, proceed to west and present pipe
C. Rush to microphone and utter some words in Odawa
B. Sun-wise circuit around fire, proceed to north
C. Repeat microphone act
B. Circuit ditto to east
B. Circuit ditto to south
D. In front of fire, present pipe to sky and to earth, holding it horizontally in both hands; exit, walking.

According to Kenosha, the Odawa originally only smoked and presented the pipe, without actually dancing. The dance came from the west. The traditional procedure of smoking and passing the pipe was enacted in 1946 by Fred Ettawageshik. As Jane Ettawageshik described it, "He lit the council fire with a birch bark torch; he welcomed the spectators and lighted the calumet from a brand of the fire. Pointing the pipe first to Mother Earth he took a puff on it, then pointed it to the sky and the four directions, taking a puff each time before pointing in another direction. The pipe was then passed to each of the participants (all men except one woman, 'a visitor from a distant tribe') on the benches, in a direction from east to west. Each person took the pipe from Fred, who said 'bi:ndá'konin' ('have a smoke') as he presented the pipe. Each time, after a single puff, the pipe was returned to Fred, who finally set it down at the place where he stood when talking." Such pipe passing is not enacted in the dance. Neither is the pipe actually lit; it is only make-believe.[1]

At the Petoskey Hiawatha play, a song was evidently used as accompaniment to a dance. It is not clear whether Joe Chingwa's song was used. According to Jane Ettawageshik, this is a really old Odawa song, perhaps not known to the Ojibwe. Joe Chingwa said his mother, who came from Manistique, taught it to him. During the *Song of Hiawatha* plays, in which Joe played Jibiabos for many years, he questioned many Ojibwe from the Upper Peninsula and could not find any who knew the song. Such a song could be sung at Midéwiwin ceremonials when the pipe is being smoked, perhaps by a welcoming delegation, at court trials, when asking for rain, at social meetings, etc. In the dance accompanying it, the chief dancer presents the pipe to the sky, the earth, and the cardinal points. Then he dances around the circle of the council, ending by giving it ceremonially to various members of the delegation. The dance step used is step, hop, step, hop. The song must be sung four times in a solemn manner. The singer strikes a rattle on his knee.

The solemnity pervades most of the performances. But Eli Thomas injects a special touch. I will quote from the tape recording made in Ann Arbor, November 3, 1953:

> While they're dancing and preparing for the great wars, Hiawatha he'll tell his people that wasn't right to do. He began to think about his people hurting each other all the time. So then he got on a high mountain. When he got up there he began to call (dramatic voice): "By the signal of the peace pipe I shall call my tribes from the south, the west, and the north, and then the east (inadvertent change)!" There he called his tribe together, and then by doing that he made peace. And then the medicine man will dance for you this afternoon one of the peace pipe prayer dances.
> Billy Elk: Wají.
> Eli Thomas: Ha há.

They converse in Ojibwe about lighting the pipe. They fuss with a stick and get frustrated. Thomas produces a cigarette lighter, audience laughs. He successfully lights pipe. During the dance he announces, "Now he's pointing to the north, then to the east, then to the south, then to the Great Spirit above, then to the Mother Earth." Meanwhile he drums on his tomtom. Finally young Eddie Jackson takes a puff and hands it to one of the men in the audience.

Owing to the jingle bells on Billy Elk's ankles, his moments of standing and his number of step-hops in each direction are clearly recorded, hence are accurately stated in the choreography. They vary in each direction and are obviously ad lib.

The ad-libbing carries through all of the versions. Not two renderings, even by the same man, are exactly the same. Not only does the count of steps vary, but even the sequence of sky and earth in relation to the cardinal points. Sometimes the cardinal points are mixed up, but the theory remains clear. According to Eli Thomas the order enacted by Billy Elk is correct. This was independently confirmed by David Kenosha. The gestures of pointing or swinging or doing fire circuits depend on the dancer's mood.

At present there is no accompanying song to mold the dance pattern. Even at Mount Pleasant and Hastings, where Whitney Albert is on hand with his knowledge of song, the two arts are not joined.

[Missing here in the authors' typescript is a complete page that begins a discussion of the Snake Dance. The discussion picks up as follows:]

3. *Accompaniment:* Double drum beat, speed 100 accelerate to 108
   Paraphernalia: Small jointed snake
   Choreography: Meandering course without spiral, due to absence of single file group
   A. Entrance and meander, for about 80 beats
   B. Pick up effigy snake, point at audience, 60 beats
   C. Exit meandering, wriggling snake in hands 70 beats
   Step 1.
4. *Accompaniment:* Same
   Choreography: Single file swerve C [clockwise], then CC [counterclockwise], then spiral CC; no unwinding, leader announced that now the serpent is coiled; step 4 used (run)

David Kenosha says the dance came from Wisconsin. He saw the Winnebagos and other Indians do the meandering dance at Wisconsin Dells. There have been Hopi Indians at the Dells and also at Harbor Springs with an imitation of their snake-handling dance. Kenosha was not explicit on the source of this item. He might also have gotten the idea from J. Foster Otto. According to Jane Ettawageshik, Otto handled a long wooden, jointed snake in 1946. He taught this to his son Don. At the Sun Ceremony in 1954, Richard Wemigwase had several grass snakes in a basket. At Cross Village, he released them as a sort of epilogue to create consternation, but he collected them again immediately before they escaped. No symbolism was attached to this transaction, despite the Indians' remembrance of serpent mythology.

Eagle Dance

- *Occasions:* (1) Cross Village, 1953, first show; (2) Cross Village, 1955, second show; (3) Photographic session, June 26, 1954; (4) Sun Ceremony, 1954; (5) Hastings and Newaygo, 1953; Lansing and Ann Arbor, 1955; (6) Mount Pleasant and Hastings, 1954
- *Performers:* (1) Dave Kenosha; (2) Ed Kenoshmeg; (3) Dave Kenosha; (4) Frankie Gasco (age eighteen); (5) Donald Otto, Raymond Carey, and Philip King; (6) Benedict and Johnny Quignon

  1. *Accompaniment:* Double drum beat, speed 108
     Central idea: Same as 2
     Choreography: Same as 2, except that Kenosha used step 3b (two-step)
  2. *Accompaniment:* Double drum beat and Eagle Song three times, speed 108
     Central idea: Imitation of soaring eagle, diving for prey
     Choreography: Ground plan as shown in drawing
     A. (First verse) Circling C, meander and sway from side to side, arms extended to side horizontally; at last measure, dive as for prey
     B. In center near audience, spiral upward C with 4 pivots, body and arms tilted toward right
     C. Flap arms and glide horizontally, swerving to exit; step 3a (glide)
  3. Same as 1, but abbreviated to entrance, dive, and two spirals; the dance carries out the illusion of approaching from a distance
  4. *Accompaniment:* Drum and theoretically Eagle Song, drum only, August 22
     Central ideas: Same as above, plus mime of being shot and killed
     Choreography: A, B, C in general, same as in 1 and 2
     D. Near plane of exit, dancer collapses, flutters "wings," and sinks to ground; this necessitates the singing of a fourth verse
     Step 3b (two-step)

On August 22, 1954, Frankie Gasco had a substitute, Jack Ramage. As this young man was not sure of the dance, Kenosha performed it with him, and hence Kenosha could not sing too. At the end they sank to the ground in rather awkward fashion, supported on their hands, with feet toward the audience. The complete form of Gasco's version was originally devised and executed by Fred Ettawageshik, then taught to Gasco. Jane Ettawageshik described the 1946 performance, when Frankie was 10 years old as follows:

The third dance was the Eagle Dance. It is Fred's variation of the widespread Eagle Dance, in which an eagle, circling around in the sky, alights and is trapped. He circles, but cannot free himself from the trap, and in this dance finally falls in exhaustion, only to arise once more and vainly circle trying to escape. Frankie is an excellent dancer so the dance was quite realistic, even though his costume was incomplete in that he had no wings.

This would involve a fifth dance section. In none of these enactments did the dancer use wings, but for the photography, Kenosha held a gourd rattle in his right hand and a cluster of gull feathers in his left, somewhat after the fashion of the Iroquois Eagle Dancers (Fenton and Kurath 1953).

This is evidently not an Odawa dance. Kenosha says it comes from the west. His version resembles that of the New Mexico Pueblos (Fenton and Kurath 1953, 270–71), but the Ettawageshik-Gasco version introduces another theme in the trapping. Fred attributes it to Antoine Bruneau, a Sault Ste. Marie Ojibwe.

> 5. *Accompaniment:* Double drum beat, speed 108; dancer's ankle bells, 132
> *Paraphernalia:* Pair of wings, made of a strip of canvas about a foot wide, reaching from finger tip to finger tip across shoulders, and decorated with multicolor painted designs; a row of fifteen-inch-long red-banded white feathers securely sewed on; on his head a skull cap of fluffy white chicken feathers with a protruding yellow beak at his forehead—an excellent imitation of the Pueblo half-mask
> *Central idea:* Imitation of eagle flight
> *Choreography:* Meandering course, as in 2A, body and wings tilting in direction of sway, sometimes with an up-and-down flapping of the wings; no dramatic portrayal, even when done by two or three dancers
> Step 2 a (toe-heel) done very lightly and too rapidly for the drummer

Though derived from Harbor Springs performances, the costume and toe-heel step are more reminiscent of the Pueblo type than any of the other versions. Don Otto's explanation of the origin was, "I picked it up in Harbor Springs."

> 6. *Accompaniment:* Duple tom-tom beat and reading of script prepared by Benedict Quignon; ankle bells in time with drum, speed 108

Paraphernalia: Both Quignon and his nephew wear elaborate wings of the same construction as Otto's, but they substitute huge war bonnets for the half mask—all in a red and yellow color scheme; their torsos are bare, but they add trousers to a breechclout

Central idea: Soaring, diving, and collapse of Ettawageshik version, plus feeding of eaglet and circuit by eaglet after death of parent, symbolizing the continuation of life by the new generation

Choreography: Ground plan CC circuit, with intermittent swaying and meandering, arid with a combination of straight-away and pivot

A. Circuit with meander and sway, then with straight-away and pivot
B. Dip for food and carry it to eaglet who is seated in front of fire; feed it with "beak," eaglet nibbles and flutters wings
A. Circuit as before
C. Father eagle mime hit by arrow, flutters, falls, trembles, lies still
A. Eaglet arises, circles with same straight-away and pivot as father

Though Quignon derived his idea from Bernard Mason's "Falling Eagle" (1940, 101–3) and combined it with some of Otto's costume and choreography, he has developed an original art product. In particular, the peculiar recurrent pattern drawn below is graceful and expressive. At first the reading is disturbing, particularly as the text includes some of Mason's "corny" words, such as "he struck the ground with a sickening thud." On second viewing this is less annoying. Nonetheless, it is an unnecessary and unsuitable adjunct. But for that, this dance would be thoroughly appealing and well designed.

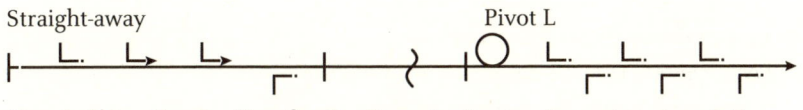

Step for'd L   Hop L   Step for. R   Repeat 4 times   6 running steps, L R . . .

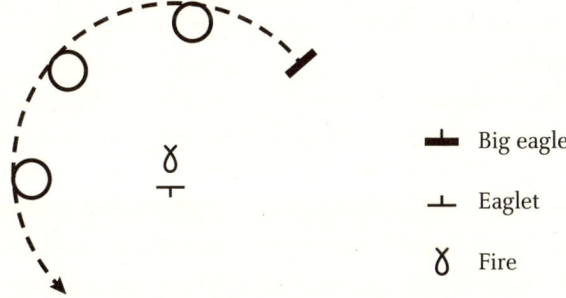

Swan Dance

- *Occasion:* Sun Ceremony, 1954
- *Performers:* Group of young Odawa girls, led by Evelyn Shagonaby
- *Accompaniment:* Drum by David Kenosha in various rhythms, speed 92
- *Central idea:* Imitation of flight and of descent with folding wings
- *Choreography:* Ground plan 3a, step 2a
    A. Flapping arms like wings, circuit once single file; drum with 40 toe-heel steps
    B. At starting point upstage, bend forward, kneel on one knee, fold arms forward in front of head; 10 beats
    A. Circuit as before, but with regular duple beat
    B. At starting point, fold wings again

Dave Kenosha had previously directed a Swan Dance at Cross Village, with a V-formation such as he had seen among the Winnebago at Wisconsin Dells. Though he taught this dance, he used a single file instead. Actually, either pattern conforms to swan habits, the V-form being used for long flights and a curving single file for short flights (Kortwright 1942, 70–74). The folding of the wings is also appropriate for settling down. This was Evelyn Shagonaby's contribution. Susan Shagonaby was the one who proposed this addition to the Sun Ceremony, for the simple reason that it is a pretty dance, suitable for girls. It was a good suggestion, for it contributed a well-executed and gracious number and provided variety in the monotony of the duple drum beat.

Bear Dance

- *Occasions:* (1) Photographic session, June 26, 1954; Cross Village, 1956; (2) Sun Ceremony, 1954
- *Performers:* (1) Dave Kenosha; (2) Five boys
- *Accompaniment:* Usual drum beat and Bear Song by Kenosha, speed 120
- *Central idea:* Imitation of posture and waddle of bear roaming in woods
- *Choreography:* (1) Enter from woods, upright, hands held up to chest like paws, fingers dangling loose; sun-wise circuit with waddling stomp (step 4); sniff about as approach foreground, bending low; at end of circuit, retire to woods (2) Ground plan 2, step 1
    A. Circuit for duration of song, holding hands like bunnies
    B. Break formation, wander and look about during repeat of song

This carries out the words of the song:

makkǫs ogiwéna ogášawan midéš ogiwéniyán
little cub   lost   his mother   so   he got lost

Kenosha connects the song and dance with the wooden bear traps made by his forefathers, though he has no perception of potential malevolence on the part of a bear spirit. The dance is not propitiatory but on the contrary emphasizes the humorous aspects of the beast—its quasi-human, erect posture, its functional forepaws, its relaxed gait. The song in particular stresses the helplessness of the cubs in tender fashion. Much of this can be based on his own observation, for he has seen bears in the neighboring woods, the Woodland black bears. But he also spoke of a traditional counterclockwise (!) dance for men followed by women, the men clomping, the women jumping onto their toes and then their heels.

Buffalo Dance

- *Occasions:* (1) Special session, June 26, 1954; (2) Sun Ceremony, 1954
- *Performers:* (1) Dave Kenosha; (2) Charlie Shagonaby, buffalo; Richard and Louis Wemigwase, hunters
- *Accompaniment:* Double drum beat, speed 120 at end of dancing changing to quadruple beat (𝄽𝄽𝄽𝄽) conclude with strong (𝄽𝄽)
- *Paraphernalia:* Real buffalo head with horns; Richard's tomahawk
- *Central idea:* Imitation of buffalo, his hunt and kill
- *Choreography:* (1) Without specific ground plan, lumber along, shake head and lower it as though butting; paw ground; exit (2) Improvisatory mime without ground plan
  A. Buffalo lumber in, jump off both feet, paw ground with one foot
  B. Stand in front of fire, raising arms (reason unknown)
  C. Step-hop (step 1) about, raising free knee high up, trying to elude hunter who pursues him
  D. Second hunter enters, buffalo gallops; farcical mime of pursuit
  E. Hunters close in; Richard Wemigwase mimes tomahawking, Louis Wemigwase shooting; buffalo falls

Kenosha claims that the Odawa had no Buffalo Dance, but that he learned it at Wisconsin Dells. This conforms to the statement of Frank Smart, the former Ojibwe master of ceremonies at the Dells. Furthermore, an authority on the distribution of the buffalo states that there are no evidences of its presence in Michigan, except temporarily in the extreme south (Roe 1951, 228, 254). From the mime, one would not infer that any of these dancers ever saw a buffalo in action. Shagonaby's mime is very lusty and comical, completely imaginative, shorn of any ritual connotations.

Raccoon Dance

- *Occasion:* Sun Ceremony, 1954
- *Performers:* Dave Kenosha and five other men
- *Accompaniment:* Duple drum beat, speed 120; end with sharp beats (𝄽 𝄽 𝄽 𝄽)
- *Central idea:* Tracking down of a raccoon by a group of hunters
- *Choreography:* Ground plan 2, step 1
  A. Circle for 80 beats
  B. Touch ground with right hand, smell it as though testing track while breaking formation; continue this for 120 beats

Kenosha mentioned this as a traditional Odawa dance. He has had direct experience with raccoons and is in a position to mime their pursuit.

Deer Dance

This dance has not been performed lately because of its difficulty, but according to David Kenosha, it used to be included in the Cross Village shows. Men and women galloped about and raised their knees high. To this day, deer have been plentiful in that neighborhood and could easily be imitated by the dancers. Dave remembers no ritual connections.

Dog Dance

This has no connection with the former ceremonial Begging or Dog Dance but is a farce enacted by Whitney Albert at Hastings. He step-hops around, barking. Then he stands in front of a young man and raises one leg in imitation of a conspicuous canine habit.

Wolf Dance

According to Chingwa, the Wolf Dance was western. The dancers wore "a wolf headdress, howled, criss-crossed as though trailing, stooped, touched toe to ground three to four times, then stepped. Have a strip down the beak for bank and tail."

Occupational Dances

The two chief categories of occupational dances belong to the two sexes: the hunt to men, corn raising to women.

Hunter's Dance

- *Occasions:* (1) Until recently at Cross Village[2]; (2) Mount Pleasant and Hastings, 1954
- *Performers:* (1) Frankie Francis; (2) Benedict Quignon
- *Accompaniment:* Duple drum beat, for Quignon also reading; speed 88
- *Paraphernalia:* For Francis a set of bow and arrow
- *Central idea:* Ambush and successful hunt

- *Choreography:* (1) Hunter looks around north, east, south, and west, releases arrow, gets quarry; (2) Ground plan ad lib; step 2a

This is how Eli Thomas tells the story: "A young hunter, the very first time he went out hunting, he's telling the big chief how he got it and he dance the action.

A. There he's out walking. Drum beat (⃗𝄻 ⃗𝄻)
B. There he's running and lookin' around. (⃗𝄻ˣ ⃗𝄻ˣ)
C. Then he goes across the creek. He didn't quite jump over the creek. He fell in the water and he had to drink water. Then he gets up.
D. So he looks down. On the bottom of the creek he sees that there's fresh track. Deer's just been goin' through there. Then he look where that track gone. He sees the deer afar off. He wants that deer.
E. He takes a bunch of leaves and throws them up. If they go east, wind is from the west. He goes way around and comes from the other side.
F. Then when he got his deer, he danced more because he's happy." Here dancer does step 2b, pivots and bends up and down

The Bow and Arrow Dance by Frankie Francis (nephew of John Chippewa) is supposed to be a traditional Odawa dance, but the Hunter's Dance is an invention of Benedict Quignon's. He does not seem to have dream inspiration from Bernard Mason this time, but to have drawn on his own experience. The modern Indians are still active and skilled hunters, especially around Isabella Reserve, though they have shifted to guns instead of bows and arrows. As in the case of the Eagle Dance, the text reading is an impediment to thorough enjoyment of this well-performed mime. Quignon and Whitney Albert have not gotten together on a coordination of movement and song.

Corn Dance

- *Occasions:* (1) Cross Village in former years; (2) Hastings, 1953; Ann Arbor, 1954; Lansing and Ann Arbor, 1955; (3) Hastings, 1954; (4) Sun Ceremony, 1954
- *Performers:* (1) Group of men and women, preferably four of each; (2) Mrs. Birch, Mrs. Jackson, and Mrs. Pelcher; (3) Betty Pamp, her daughters, and Glenna Rickard or an alternate; (4) Dave Kenosha, Louis Wemigwase, and fourteen men and boys; Kathleen Shagonaby
1. *Paraphernalia:* An ear of corn in right hand of each woman

Choreography: Straight line of men and women, in alternation
  A. Step-pat forward, shoulder to shoulder
  B. Step-pat back to original places
  This is supposed to be a traditional Odawa dance
2. *Accompaniment:* Pounding of pestles, drum beat by Whitney Albert; chant by all
  Paraphernalia: Old-type wooden mortar and pestle; iron frying pan
  Choreography: Rhythmic movement rather than strictly dance
  A. Two women pound alternately with two pestles, singing as they work, pretending to grind corn into meal; reverse pestles, when "hot"
  B. Same action continued while Albert joins in with drum and song
  C. Mrs. Jackson takes some dough (previously prepared) and cooks it in pan on fire; when done, distributes small pieces to audience; all this explained by Eli Thomas
3. *Accompaniment:* Duple drum beat and reading
  Paraphernalia: Mortar and one pestle
  Central idea: Women's activity of preparing maize and offering it as a sacrifice
  Choreography:
  A. Woman grinds meal, offers it to four cardinal points and to *Kiže Manido* (Great Spirit)
  B. She offers meal (mimetically) to first girl who rises from kneeling position (seated on her feet); girl takes it in cupped hands, bows, hands extended in front, thus offering it to Mother Earth; second girl, same action
  C. Girls dance CC with a grapevine step

Though mortar and pestle are no longer in use, the work of raising corn and preparing it for food is still actively engaged in by the Ojibwe women, especially at Isabella Reserve. The old Indian corn recipes are still used. Version 3 is Quignon choreography.

4. *Accompaniment:* Double drum beat
  Paraphernalia: Ear of corn held by each dancer
  Central idea: Celebration of successful harvest
  Choreography: Ground plan type 6 with additional complexities; step 1
  A. Circuit of men, paired in double file

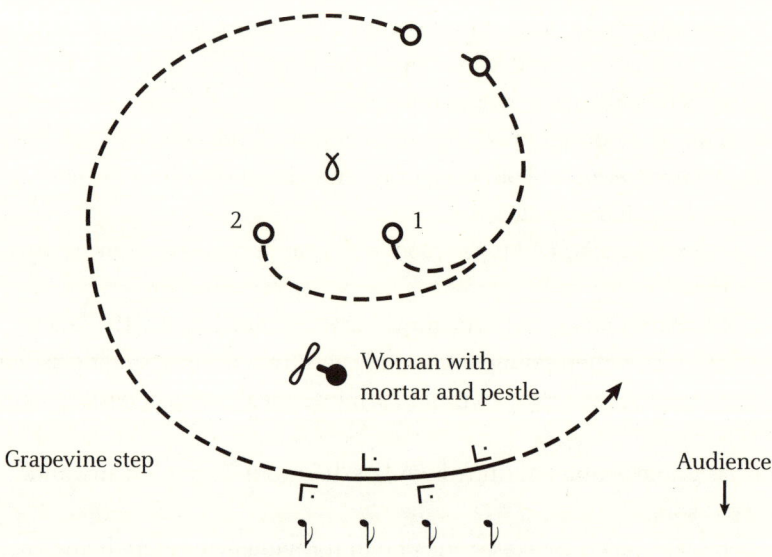

Grapevine step — Woman with mortar and pestle — Audience

B. Two files circle once in opposite directions, finish "upstage"
C. Men stand in two parallel lines, back to back; girl winds in and out of front line, then returns between two lines; as she passes each man, he faces about; she retires offstage
B. Men circuit double file as before and exit

This dance, which did not appear until September 6, was witnessed by Jane Ettawageshik during rehearsal and described by her. It is a Potawatomi dance from the neighborhood of Hastings and was transferred to the Odawa by Charlie Shagonaby. The Odawa version, according to Kenosha's outline, is different, though it shares the straight line. This pattern of parallel straight lines and the weaving course of the girl recall some of the New Mexico Pueblo dances and the concept of female fertility magic.

Kettle Dance

- *Occasions:* All Odawa programs
- *Performers:* Dave Kenosha and five men
- *Paraphernalia:* Iron kettle suspended on birch branch tripod
- *Accompaniment:* Double drum beat, speed 116
- *Central idea:* Tasting of food for feast
- *Choreography:* Ground plan 2, atop 1; men circle kettles, then in turn point index finger toward kettle, withdraw and taste, break formation

Kenosha brought this from the Wisconsin Dells.

War Dances

Strike the Post

- *Occasions:* Formerly at Harbor Springs and other programs directed by Fred Ettawageshik
- *Performers:* The Wemigwases and Kiogimas, all men
- *Accompaniment:* Even drum beat and song by Chingwa, speed 104
- *Paraphernalia:* Central pole; weapons (tomahawk, bow, etc.)
- *Central idea:* Boasting of martial exploits
- *Choreography:* According to Jane Ettawageshik's notes on Chingwa's Challenge Song, "The drummer sings the chant while dancers take on various warlike attitudes as though in battle. An old Odawa dance, the Strike the Post Dance, might be done to this. A large pole is placed in the center of the dance ground, representing a pole in a dance house. Each dancer strikes the pole with his weapon and dances around as though telling his exploits. Each man dances alone, one after another."

This mime was reconstructed by Fred Ettawageshik from accounts of seventeenth-century Strike the Post dances, with Jane's suggestions. It was not revived in 1953 or 1954.

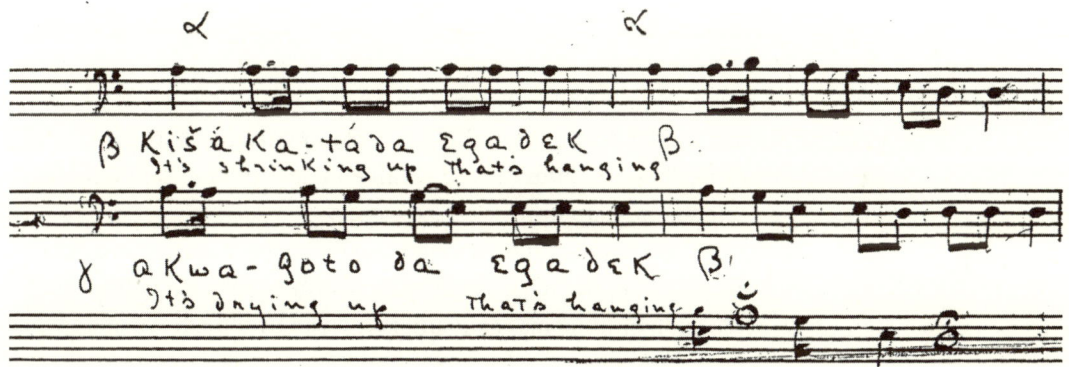

Shield Dance

- *Occasions:* (1) Cross Village, 1953, 1955; (2) Sun Ceremony, 1954
- *Performers:* (1) Four boys; (2) Richard and Louis Wemigwase
- *Accompaniment:* Even drum beats, speed 120
- *Paraphernalia:* Small round shields and feather-ornamented lances
- *Central idea:* Combat and victory for one contestant
- *Choreography:*
    1. Step 1

A. Circuit ground plan 2
B. Pair off for attack, advance and retreat as in attack
C. One victor in each pair dances around fallen opponent
2. Steps 1 and 2a and 2b, also running
Without ground plan and with improvised steps, two opponents mime their contest all over the dance ground until one collapses at any convenient spot. The victor raises his lance. On one occasion, Kenosha entered the arena for an unknown reason, perhaps in the role of a referee.

This mime was transferred from the Kiowa of Oklahoma via the Wisconsin Dells. It is a recent and now widespread Midwest and Plains dance. It is a specialty of the young men trained under Ettawageshik.

Scalp Dance

- *Occasions:* (1) Cross Village, 1953; (2) Sun Ceremony, 1954; also Naming Ceremony, 1946
- *Performers:* (1) Richard Wemigwase, scalper; white man from audience, victim; (2) Richard Wemigwase, scalper; Louis Wemigwase, victim; Gus Kiogima, medicine man
- *Accompaniment:* (1) Even drum beat; (2) Even drum beat, Scalp Song by David Kenosha, speed 92
- *Paraphernalia:* Scalper's tomahawk
- *Choreography:* Ad lib ground plan, step 1, menacing gestures
  1. Scalper hops in, grabs any accessible male, stretches him out and pretends to scalp him
  2. According to Jane Ettawageshik's notes on the 1946 performance, a brave out in the woods is attacked by an enemy. He falls in horrible agony minus his scalp and is revived by a medicine man who leads him away.
  A. Attacker sneaks up on victim—26 beats
  B. Attacks and fells him—23 beats
  A. (song repetition) Pretends to scalp him, dance of victory
  B. Dance of medicine man, who bends over victim and revives him

This is an imaginative reconstruction of a warlike expedition, a sort of victory dance. It is not like the traditional Scalp Dances, which circled around a pole with an enemy scalp or scalps. The idea is Louis Wemigwase's. Dick Wemigwase's 1953 play was pure farce.

War or Green Grass Dance

- *Occasions:* All performances except Cross Village and Harbor Springs
- *Performers:* All available dancers, sometimes women as well; in Ann Arbor, also several small boys following Eddie Jackson
- *Accompaniment:* Fast even drum beat and improvised chanting by Eli Thomas or Whitney Albert, speed 126; yelps and whoops, by dancers
- *Central idea:* Worship dance before setting out on a war expedition
- *Choreography:* Helter-skelter ground plan
  Steps: Most dancers step 1, occasionally with pivots
    - Blue Cloud (Albert) step 2 and b, with opposition of foot and arm (right foot forward, left hand forward)
    - Eddie Jackson and Eli Thomas step right, pat left side and forward; reverse

Eli Thomas says, "It was done the night before they met their enemies, the great prayer dance, a farewell. They didn't know whether they were going to come back." His confusion on the subject of the Green Grass Dance of the Plains—a War Dance—is evident in his explanation: "In the spring of the year, once more the grass is growing for our buffalo, deer, and ponies." The War and Green Grass Dances are identical in execution and are accompanied by the same type of song improvisation.

The Life Cycle

Naming Dance

- *Occasions:* Virtually all festivals, with variant choreographies
  1. Odawa Feasts (not always)
  2. Cross Village, 1953 and 1954
  3. All shows directed by Eli Thomas
- *Performers:* Master of ceremonies, adoptee, and group of celebrants
- *Accompaniment:* (1) Horn rattle in recorded instance, duple beat; (2) and (3) Drum, duple beat
- *Paraphernalia:* A war bonnet for male adoptee; beaded headband for female
- *Central idea:* (1) Naming of child, acceptance of white friend into tribe; (2) and (3) Honoring of a prominent white person, commonly for a fee
- *Choreography:* After a ceremony of initiation
  1. Jane Ettawageshik described her own adoption as follows: "As the

chief who has given the naming finishes his speech he may take up his rattle or drum, start to sing a chant and to dance slowly forward in a typically Indian dance such as a heel and toe step. Some of those witnessing the ceremony will probably join in the dance, following after the chief, with the person who has been named somewhere in the line of dancers. The group of dancers usually dances from one end of the room to the other and bank to the starting point."

2. Ground plan 5, step 4
3. Ground plan 2, but CC, step 1; thereupon War Dance with whoops

The Odawa invest this ceremony with dignity, but Eli Thomas turns it into a farce. He and Billy Elk feel the adoptee all over and ask embarrassing questions. They approve of him, "so then we'll honor you for one of our tribe." Elk howls like a wolf, adoptee imitates, then all dance.

Occupational and War Dances could be included under the life cycle but have been described separately.

Social Dances

Women's Dance

- *Occasions:* (1) Ann Arbor, 1954; (2) Sun Ceremony, 1954
- *Performers:* (1) Mr. and Mrs. Pelcher, the former disguised as a woman; (2) Group of women and young girls, led by Susan Shagonaby
- *Accompaniment:* (1) Usual duple drum beat by Eli Thomas; (2) Drum and song by David Kenosha
- *Choreography:* (1) Ground plan 3b, but in CC direction; step 6; (2) See Dances of Offering

Ike Pelcher claims this is an ancient Ojibwe women's step. He clowned and jumbled his feet. In the middle of the dance he faced about. Then, back to audience, he wiggled his hips with each foot twist.

Squaw Dance

- *Occasions:* New Year and other celebrations around Baraga (now extinct)
- *Performers:* Men and women
- *Accompaniment:* Partner Dance by Thomas Shalifoe, speed 116
- *Choreography (as described by Thomas Shalifoe Jr.):* Ground plan two

concentric circles, around central singer, women on outside moving CC, men on inside moving C, facing center, shoulder to shoulder; step for women type 5, for men side jumps and improvised steps

The songs for this and the following dances are included under the music by the respective singers, as they were not observed. The Squaw Dance may belong to the pan-Indian repertoire, which is now prominent in Wisconsin.

Courtship Dance

This song and choreography, adapted from a social dance to the scenario of the Hiawatha play, was described by Joe Chingwa to Jane as follows: "This was sung by Hiawatha and Minnehaha, he on one side of the fire, she on the other, very brief and fast (speed 104). Danced in Keweenaw County. Maiden dances, makes one circle, chooses partner. Then both dance. Another maiden steps in, does same, then another. Girl dances inside circle, man outside. They both turn and look at each other, they meet inside circle afterwards. They both circle as dance, give yell at same time: 'Don't flirt with your friend.'"[3]

Wedding Dance

For the Hiawatha play, a Drinking Song was combined with a social dance. This combination took place at Garden River Reserve, Ontario. Chingwa said, "This was danced at Hiawatha play in Petoskey when Hiawatha brought Minnehaha to his home, a Welcome Dance. All stand in circle facing inward (cf. ground plan 3b); men and women dance in place, women with the kind of step learned from Fred (toes out in opposite directions, toes in toward each other, round and round in circle) (cf. step 6). Men can do more. Dance usually given at night."

Chippewa Welcome Dance

At some of the Isabella and Hastings events the entire group opens the program with a replica of the War Dance, usually to a drum only.

Farewell Dance

Chippewa Farewell like Welcome Dance; Odawa Farewell like Naming Dance, with ground plan 5 and step 4.

Medicine Dance

The former esoteric dances for cure have dwindled to two farcical bits by the Odawa and Ojibwe. The former vestige is the resuscitation epilogue to the Scalp Dance. The latter is a travesty by Billy Elk with verbal obligato by Eli Thomas. Says he, "Now these herbs are not all good, some of them is poison . . . And now at this time we'll give you an idea of how the medicine man will gather herbs. (Ankle bells.) He's looking for the medicine. The medicine he's looking for is ginseng. Now he finds it. (Whoop.) When he finds it he carefully digs. He raise up again and goes another half hour looking for the medicine. (Rhythmic tinkle of bells, to drum beat.) There I see something! I see some more. There he goes again, walking and walking. (Ankle bells.) Sometimes he has to walk many hours before he can find it. Now he thanks the Great Spirit for that medicine he found. (Elk raises arms and chants.) Then he looks over the crowd, he said, 'Healthy men, boys, girls.'"

Ghost Dance

The song recorded by Joe Chingwa could belong to the Ghost Feast or to a Scalp Dance. According to Jane Ettawageshik, "This was sung and danced by a group in the Hiawatha play, but it may be a solo. The dancers pretend to be ghosts and wear white sheets and skeleton heads. Dance formation is flexible just so long as the dancers are in time tap the music." For the Scalp Dance version, "the [male] dancers are exposed from the waist up. The chief wears a headdress, the others not necessarily. The leader carries a scalp on a long pole, others carry knives, clubs. Can turn handsprings, etc." Kenosha describes Ghost Dance with ground plan 2, step 1, until tired.

Miscellaneous and Modern Dances

Hoop Dance

At the Odawa Sun Ceremony, little Dick Wemigwase did a Hoop Dance before the intermission and Mary Wemigwase repeated this after the intermission. Though well done, this will not be described, as it is a clear show of importation originating at the Standing Rock Reservation in the Dakotas and it spread to most tribes west of the Great Lakes. Raymond F.

Carey also performed this at Mount Pleasant, Newaygo, and Ann Arbor, with the hoop set on fire.

Modern Dances

Square dances are a favorite pastime of the Odawa and are held in the evening after the annual powwow, after weddings, and after feasts if space allows. In 1953, for instance, Indians danced in the Town Hall to the fiddling of an old Indian from Burt Lake. After the August 8 shows, the evening was given over to square dancing in the community hall to the music of a white band from the neighborhood. David Kenosha used to fiddle for square dances but has now no fiddle. These dances, which have regional specialties, would form a separate body. At Baraga, square dances also remain popular in homes, town halls, and open air platforms. Tom Shalifoe was a much sought-after fiddler and is still an expert with a fine rhythm.[4]

Round dances, such as fox trots and polkas, are interpolated between squares. *Jitterbugging* is less popular among the Indians, but was observed at the Cross Village tavern the evening before the powwow. One young man arose and did a tap dance. Kenosha says he sometimes does Indian steps to juke box music. This curious mixture was not observed.

The strict Methodist Indians permit neither square nor round dances.

Choreographic Variants

The juxtaposition of the dances shows recurrences, variants, and contrasts. These are both local and individual, especially the latter.

Local Variations

Perhaps the most obvious contrast between the Catholic northern and Methodist southern dance picture is the occasional inclusion of dances in Odawa feasts and also the enjoyment of social dances old and modern, the former as part of the Mosquito Park rehearsals. The restriction of dancing to shows among the Methodists goes a notch further among extremists like Quignon, who will not dance on Sundays.

Some items of repertoire are conspicuously recurrent, especially the Pipe, Snake, and Eagle Dances, and also the less common Corn Dance—that is, dances that David Kenosha claims are of western origin. War-type dances resemble each other in objective but not in form—thus the Odawa Scalp mime in contrast to the Green Grass Dance. Some are entirely local, such as the Odawa Sun Dance and Kettle Dance, and the Bear Dance and Buffalo Dance.

Though in theory, and usually in practice, all Pipe Dances progress sun-wise, the remainder of the repertoire reverses directions among the two tribal groups. The Odawa invariably progress sun-wise. The southern Ojibwe and Potawatomi progress counterclockwise, possibly by tradition or perhaps by virtue of new invention. Certain steps are ubiquitous, especially the step-hop (step 1) and to a lesser extent the toe-heel (step 2a). The same women's side twist (step 6) is known everywhere, though it is not practiced by all women. On the other hand, certain steps are unique in each location or, more exactly, appertain to one special individual. Types of posture and gesture are less variable.

Individuals

Individual dancers and choreographers differ in repertoire, steps, manner, attitude, and background. In what follows, I will characterize the main performers.

David Kenosha. David Kenosha's very special and exclusively Odawa dance is the Sun Dance; second is his variant of the ubiquitous Pipe Dance. The Bear Dance, less frequently performed, is known to him only, as are others now extinct (Ghost Dance, Deer Dance). All of these have highly ritualistic connotations and are enacted so ritualistically as to suggest subconscious faith in their efficacy. All of Kenosha's repertoire is traditional—either Odawa or Wisconsin Ojibwe. He is quite honest about the origin. Though he improvises on each occasion, he never invents a dance.

His choreography, likewise traditional, both gains and suffers from uniformity. All of his dances progress sun-wise with a step-hop or two-step, varying chiefly in accordance with personnel, and with mime such as raccoon tracking. The jiggling two-step is his trademark and recurs in his mimetic Eagle Dance and in his teaching of the Women's Dance. Likewise, the choreography gains and suffers from a certain vagueness, a casual drifting into the dance and out again without precise finish. This contributes informality and also an atmosphere of timelessness, but eliminates any chances of concise structure.

This indefiniteness and even dreaminess pervades Kenosha's entire style and approach. As a teacher he pays no attention to the others. As a soloist he usually remains self-centered. However, he enacts all mime with grace and with a sense of its meaning and at times injects a surprising bit of comedy. Though not an exciting performer, Kenosha may be Michigan's most important Indian dancer, for he reaches back into ancient tradition.

Fred Ettawageshik. This eminent folklorist, though no longer an active dancer, remains a force in Odawa dance revival. He frankly states that his choreographies are not traditional, but are compositions in good Indian style. He has trained a number of young men, notably the talented Wemigwases, and merits commendation for that achievement alone. His special creations are the dramatic Eagle Dance and the Strike the Post Dance.

Richard and Louis Wemigwase. These vigorous young men contrast completely with David Kenosha and have no regard whatsoever for this traditionalist. They infuse their performances with energy, comedy, and variety. Their rhythm is good, though at times too fast for an elderly drummer's ideas, and for that reason, they are occasionally at variance with the accompaniment. A little more coordination with the musicians and attention to spacing would result in better works of art. A little attention to Odawa traditions and to ritual meaning might enrich their repertoire and their style—limited at present to scalp and hunting mime. As is, they provide a much-needed element of burlesque and virility. It is hoped that these young men will continue to carry on their enthusiasm for dance and will encourage it in their equally gifted children.

The Shagonaby Family. The Shagonabys are indispensable in Odawa performances, not only because of their enthusiasm and because of Susan's efficiency, but also because of their intelligent and spirited performances. Susan and her daughter Evelyn lead the Women's and Swan Dances with precision. Evelyn in particular contributes some improvements, such as the folding of wings. Kathleen and Robert show signs of future leadership. So far, the Shagonabys have functioned largely under the direction of others. Yet Charlie has contributed the Potawatomi Corn Dance and has devised a boisterous Buffalo Dance.

Whitney Albert and Eli Thomas. Both of these men restrict themselves to a few War Dance steps, plus Albert's Snake Dance. They shine in other capacities, though: Albert as singer and Thomas as manager. They combine a practical attitude with genuine absorption in their Native arts.

Isaac Pelcher. This member of the Mount Pleasant contingent knows some traditional steps and executes a precise and light-footed Pipe Dance. Yet he stoops to such nonsense as the Blanket Act.

The Pamps. Betty and her daughters try to compensate for lack of tradition with ingenuity and hard work. Their Corn Dance is clean-cut in design, though only fair in rhythmic precision. They are the most independent southerly female dancers.

Some Younger Men. The fair number of promising young male dancers presents a heartening prospect. Don Otto, James Shaffer, Jack Neomi, Raymond Carey, and Victor King all combine good taste in costuming with neat, though limited, footwork. They prefer the western dance types—Eagle, War, and Hoop Dances. Shaffer is, however, seriously attempting a recreation of his ancestral Cherokee dances and costumes. Benedict Quignon, the most gifted and diligent of all, spent much care in planning and even typing out his excellent dance creations, but he has now retired from the field because of sudden religious compunctions. His steps and mime were always expressive and dignified. The several talented Wemigwase, Pamp, and other small children know only the exhibition dances taught them, but they practice diligently for neat execution. They deserve encouragement in their individual styles.

Perspective

Woodland Dance Affiliations

The posture is generally typically "Indian," erect with a slight forward tilt, more erect than west of Lake Michigan, about the same as the Iroquois. As everywhere, the women stand habitually erect, while the men may flex and crouch. This flexing and knee raising is most extreme in the Buffalo and Scalp Dances, which point to the Plains. But the flexion is less extreme and the style less frenzied than in the Plains or even than at Lac Court Oreilles. The dignity, with clowning at appropriate times, is reminiscent of the Iroquois and Cherokee, and the Meskwaki to the west.

While the placid women's style seems to conform to historical traditions, the men's dancing would seem to have calmed down. Modern shows present nothing as violent or fierce as the shamanistic or the warrior's enactments described by the old writers. Perhaps this is just as well. With the inner motivation gone, such frenzied gyrations would be objectionable to performers and audiences alike.⁵

With one exception, the Michigan ground plans are circular. The exception is the double line of the Potawatomi Corn Dance. In terms of direction, they are divided between the clockwise progressions of L'Arbre Croche and the counterclockwise compositions of the Isabella Reserve. The former has a firm foundation in religious symbolism of the sun and cardinal points. With Manitoulin Island as the most easterly boundary, this direction predominates in the entire northwest (Kurath 1953a, 60–63), whereas from the Iroquois southeast, the Woodland tribes dance widdershins (counterclockwise). In L'Arbre Croche this tendency is so consistent as to affect even the southeasterly Snake Dance, which everywhere else commences against the sun (even in Wisconsin), but among the Odawa starts sun-wise.

The Central Plains exception to the clockwise rule may help explain the eccentricities of the Isabella Reserve. The Fox of Tama, Iowa, go against the sun in their own traditional dances and in those derived from the southeast, but with the sun in Oklahoma dances. Before their hasty retreat before the Iroquois in 1650, the Sauk and Fox occupied the vicinity of Saginaw Bay, whence most of the Isabella Indians also migrated. It thus seems possible that the choreographic dividing line ran northeast to southwest through Michigan, grouping the Sauk, Fox, and Saginaw Ojibwe and Odawa with the Iroquois and other easterners, and the northern Odawa with the west. It should be possible to check on this theory by further field work.

The double file part of the Corn Dance suggests the Pueblos, but also the Shawnee, who sometimes perform in parallel lines (Erminie Voegelin, personal communication). This influence has already been suggested.

Ground plan-less dances concern original animal dances and war-type groupings of such obvious Siouan derivation as to take the name of Grass Dance. The same phenomenon holds good for the Iroquois and the Wisconsin and Iowa Algonkians previously observed. The arrangement of the sexes in file includes men alone, women alone, men, then women single file and double file. These same groupings prevail among the Iroquois, notably in their more esoteric dances (Kurath 1951b, 60–63). In Michigan the alternate arrangement of the sexes is missing—an arrangement common throughout Woodland social dances. Also, women never precede men as they do among the Sauk and Fox and in some other southeastern dances. These geometric characteristics and distinctions find confirmation in historical accounts wherever ground plans are mentioned.

Among steps, the common step-hop definitely ties up with the Plains and western Algonkians. Among the Iroquois it is limited to War Dances. The toe-heel and double toe-heel not only point west but can be identified as the official War Dance step of the Midwest powwow, including the Iowa Meskwaki. The Iroquois use it only in the Feather Dance and Wasase—both with westerly traditions. The two-step in David Kenosha's particular execution is unusual; if combined with an extra heel-bump, it resembles the Iroquois men's Drum or Thanksgiving Dance (Kurath 1951b, 5–6). The songs of this dance also share Michigan Anishinaabe characteristics. The stomp, which is rare in Michigan, recurs again end again in eastern Woodland rounds among the Iroquois, the Cherokee, and the Sauk and Fox. In the east it commences with the right foot. A corresponding step at Lac du Flambeau in, for instance, the Fish Dance starts with the left foot and goes sun-wise. In Michigan, this is arbitrary. The women's foot twisting, known throughout the state, is apparently an eastern step, the Iroquois women's step. It is also known to the Shawnee and Caddo now residing in Oklahoma but has not been observed among the Sauk or Fox (John Gillespie, personal communication).

Among nonexistent Michigan steps are the Iroquois fish type (Kurath 1951b, 65); a common heel-flat step of more southerly Algonkians—the Shawnee, Delaware, and their neighbors, the Tutelo—heel forward, then step on flat foot (Kurath 1953b, 154); and the virtuoso powwow steps of the entire Mississippi area.

Thus, the most common Michigan steps tie in with the west, while several less common ones tie in with the east. In addition, there are gaps, perhaps from disuse, and original steps that are individualistic products.

Plan of Odawa Ceremony to the Sun

(with quotations from Lahontan's "Voyages" of 1703 [Kinietz 1940, 290–91])

"The air must be clear and serene, the weather fair and calm, then every one brings his offering and lays it upon the woodpile."
1. Lighting of Fire, *Dave Kenosha*
   Dance of Offering, *entire cast*
2. Sun Dance, *Dave Kenosha*

"The women likewise make their addresses to him, and commonly, when the sun rises, . . . they present and hold up their children to that luminary.

Changing Dance Repertoire

DANCE	CA. 1950	1920	1850	1700	PREHISTORY
Sun	×	×	×	×	×
Pipe (5)	×	×	×	NW	
Offering	×		×	×	
Thunderbird	×	×	Pr	Pr	Pr
Snake (4)	×	SE		?	?
Eagle (6)	×	SW			?
Bear	×	×	×	Pr	Pr
Deer		×	?	Pr	Pr
Raccoon	×		?	Pr	Pr
Buffalo (2)	×	×			
Dog	×	×	×	×	×
Wolf		W			
Swan	×	W			
Hunter	×		×	×	×
Bow and Arrow		×	?	?	?
Corn (3)	×	×			
Kettle	×	W			
Rally		×	×	×	×
War	×	×	×	×	×
Strike-the-Post	×	×	×	W	
Scalp (2)	×	×	×		
Grass	W				
Shield	SW				
Hoop	W				
Naming	×	×	×	×	×
Dream Chant			×	×	×
Women's	×	×	×	×	×
Courtship		×			
Wedding		×			
Social	×	×	×	×	×
Begging		×	×	×	×
Cure			×	×	×
Ghost		×	×	×	×
Memorial		×	×	×	×
Mide			×	×	×
Wabano			×	×	×

Numerals = Number of versions. × = Performed at this time. NW, W, SW, SE = Northwest, West, Southwest, Southeast origin. Pr = Probably. ? = uncertain.
NOTE: Extinction of rituals and societies; rarity of persistent native dances; prevalence of introduced dances; persistence of size of repertoire (21–25 dances) but change.

3. Dance of Women, *group of women and girls, led by Susan Shagonaby*
   Song: "Walking in the Green Grass"

"When the sun mounts higher, the children make a ring around the woodpile."

4. Dance of Children, *five boys, led by Robert Shagonaby*
   Song: "Hoot Owl"

"And the warriors dance and sing around them till the whole is consumed."

5. Shield Dance, *Louis Wemigwase and Gus Kiogima*
6. Scalp Dance, *Richard Wemigwase, Louis Wemigwase, and Gus Kiogima*
   Song: "Scalp Dance"

"While the old men make their harangues addressed to the Kitchi Manitu, and present him from time to time with pipes of tobacco lighted at the sun."

7. Peace Pipe Dance, *Dave Kenosha (Interlude)*
8. Invocation, *Joe Kishigo Jr.:* "Great Spirit, Master of our lives, Great Spirit, Master of all things visible and invisible, whether good or evil; command the good spirits to favor thy children the Outouas [Odawas]."

"Preserve our harvests and our beasts."

9. Swan Dance, *group of girls led by Evelyn Shagonaby*
10. Buffalo Dance, *Charlie Shagonaby and Richard Wemigwase*
11. Snake Dame, *entire cast*
12. Eagle Dance, *Frankie Gasco*
    Song: "Eagle Dance"
13. Raccoon Dance, *group of men led by Dave Kenosha*
14. Bear Dance, *group of boys*
    Song: "Bear Song"
15. Corn Dance, *group of men and boys, led by Dave Kenosha and Louis Wemigwase with Kathleen Shagonaby*

"During the invocation all the guests eat." (Allouez, Journal)

16. Kettle Dance, *group of men, led by Dave Kenosha*

"When the sun is almost done, the warriors march out of the village, to dance the dance of the Great Spirit."

17. Dance to the Great Spirit, *entire cast, led by Dave Kenosha*

- *Singer:* Dave Kenosha
- *Drummers:* Louis Chingwa and Mitchell Masto
- *Reader:* Joe Chingwa Jr. (script prepared by Jane Ettawageshik)
- *Costume Mistress:* Susan Shagonaby
- *Others in Group:* Joe Kishigo, Sr., Eliza Kishigo, Hattie Sagataw, Veronica Kishigo, Victoria Francis, Betty Lou Seaman, Dick and Mary Wemigwase, and others

CHAPTER 4

Native Songs by Modern Singers

— In this chapter Gertrude Kurath undertakes a close analysis of the texts and musical structure of Anishinaabe songs, complementing the previous two chapters' study of the social context of the performance of the songs. Such analysis speaks for itself. But even close analysis of texts and music informs our sense of Anishinaabe musical culture, for Kurath organizes the chapter both by function and in terms of the respective repertories of her primary consultants. In doing so, she begins to identify what ethnomusicologist Judith Vander has characterized as the distinctive "songprint" of each singer, a document of each individual's repertory, and of the range of each singer's social and cultural experience (Vander 1988). The songprints in this chapter bespeak much of the loss sustained by Anishinaabe tradition in the era of assimilation. They also bespeak how individual agents of twentieth-century Anishinaabe musical culture embraced both tradition and change. Eli Thomas, a devout Methodist known for his renditions of Native hymns, sings a ribald version of the Drinking Song. Whitney Albert's songprint shows the importance of the Song of Hiawatha pageants to his knowledge of traditional songs.

A perusal of the choreographies shows an amazingly small number of dances with integrated song accompaniment. Of these, the Ottawa Eagle, Bear, and Scalp Dances could be said to have some traditional association. The women's and children's dances of the Sun Ceremony were combined with Walking in the Green Grass and the Hoot Owl Song simply because of the appropriateness. On the other hand, the Corn and War Songs of the southern groups are formless improvisations.

This is not because of a lack of Native songs, for more songs than dances have been found to survive. It is because the two arts have been separated and never rejoined, or more accurately, because the practitioners of the two arts have not troubled to sufficiently combine forces. Whitney Albert knows Pipe and Hunting Songs, but he has not placed them at Felcher's or Guignon's disposal.

Not only are the songs dissociated from the dances but on the whole they are conspicuously absent in the shows, even as vocal solos. The Hoot Owl Song is the only inevitable musical offering. Though the titles of the songs suggest an originally vital function, at present they seem to preserve no specific purpose. David Kenosha may sing his Maple Sugar Song at a sugar camp gathering or one of the animal songs for a naming. But Whitney Albert's large repertoire seems destined to amuse only himself as he drives along in his car.

This lapse in function no doubt accounts for lapses of memory and inaccuracies of rendering from verse to verse. The variations are often so great as to require special notation for each verse. On the other hand, Albert's animal songs usually recur with unusual accuracy, from some miraculous feat of memory. The texts as a rule are remembered even after the tunes have been forgotten.

Several points must be made before presenting the songs and the analyses. One is the great individual divergence in repertoire and style, so great as to preclude the parallel method employed with the choreographies. Only three songs recur in several repertoires: a Pipe Song, a Hoot Owl Song, and a Drinking Song. These are juxtaposed at the beginning. After this, the different singers display some analogous subjects and occasionally analogous patterns, but no truly comparable songs. Hence all the songs of each man are presented in succession, starting with Joe Chingwa, the earliest recorded musician in the nuclear Odawa areas; then David Kenosha, Blue Cloud, Whitney Albert, and a few songs by Eli Thomas. Then we add a few songs by Thomas Shalifoe, far to the north.

The texts, which are given with the songs and immediately translated, are important and often complicated. They are always meaningful and often expressive. On rare occasions they alternate or are followed by phrases of burden syllables [vocables], "heya" or "hi-i," depending on the whims of that particular singer. Whereas dance and song live independent lives, text and song remain thoroughly integrated.

After the presentation of all of the songs, they will be assembled and examined for their formal properties, for the salient factors of tonality, rhythm, structure, and contour. These forms and the styles of rendering characterize the various singers and possibly the area.

These qualities can be heard on Ethnic Folkways LP 1003 and in tapes [later digitized] held at the American Philosophical Society Library—Jane Ettawageshik's recording of Joe Chingwa's songs and my Reel 1 of Native songs.

Analogous Songs

Pipe Dance Songs

Joe Chingwa's version of the Pipe Song comes from his mother and hence from Manistique in the western Upper Peninsula. Whitney Albert learned it from Joe by listening. Yet the two versions are by no means identical. The greater length of Albert's rendering is due in the first place to insecure rendering and hence complete notation of the whole of the two verses. In the second place it is due to a longer text. Joe Chingwa has a text of one part, Albert has three parts. These reflect on the melodies. Chingwa transposes his fundamental theme with the fundamental words downward three times. Albert transposes only once, then varies his tune for the variant texts and starts all over again.

The end result of the two devices is a huge compass of twelve tones with intervals of a fourth and fifth for Joe Chingwa, as against a compass of a sixth with an initial fourth but thereafter seconds and monotone for Whitney Albert. The rhythmic motif is, however, conspicuously identical. And the structure is of the same type, descending phrases blocked into fours: four phrases, four verses.

The texts and translations show respectively the Odawa and the Ojibwe equivalents. (Though Whitney Albert is Odawa, he sings in Ojibwe).

Chingwa: sáko sako gíntuopwóganina*
   Let's you light our pipes

Albert: |:sak' ko:| gǽndopuə́ganina gí:sakowat gǽndopuə́ganina
   kazagǽskowamin (Odawa) kabi:ndákowmin
   Let's light our pipes after you lit up your pipes we'll have a smoke

**F. Ettawageshik corrects:* gindopwəganiwa [your pipes]

Hoot Owl Song

If a Michigan Indian, adult or child, knows any Native song, it is the Hoot Owl Song. Whitney Albert says, "This is the song they used to use when teaching our youngsters how to dance." Thomas says, "Long time ago when I was a small boy I was taught after the sun went down, I must be quiet, I must make no noise. They say to me, 'Don't do that. Owl going to come and get you.' That's the teaching I had when I was a small boy."

Thomas learned the song from Whitney Albert and sings virtually the exact tune with the text, though he adds a different nonsense coda. Their version is very like David Kenosha's, but not exactly. They all descend sequentially one octave, but Kenosha takes four phrases and the other men take three phrases, compressing Kenosha's second and third into a single phrase. The interval of a fourth is conspicuous, in the first phrase directly, in the others indirectly, by a cadence of 54 21 or 4 21. The rhythm, which recalls that of the Pipe Song, recurs throughout, except for a hold in

Kenosha's first phrase.

Thomas's text is shortest, David Kenosha adds a second idea, and Whitney Albert a third.

Thomas: kukukú'u   ningǫsa
           hoot owl   I fear
Kenosha: "   "   wábikukukú'u   ningǫsa
               white owl   I fear
Albert: I, II   "   "   III   "   "   IV   mičikǽkæ   ningǫsa
                                     great hawk   I fear

The codas (Z) are: for Thomas "heyo," with sustained notes; for Albert "hi-i" in a syncopated staccato pattern.

Second Hoot Owl Song

Another Hoot Owl song rendered by David Kenosha is included by way of contrast. It used to be a popular children's song in his boyhood and that of Fred Ettawageshik. But it is unfamiliar to most modern children. Like the other version, it encompasses an octave and descends sequentially. But the second phrase is only one tone lower than the first and includes a

semitone. Then the second theme B scans the entire octave in one swoop. A and B terminate with the same cadence of a downward fourth. In addition to these differences, the second version has a livelier rhythm with a dactylic figure, and in particular it has a unique text.

|: kukukú n'gúči gádenáŋ :| túda ningáguonaŋ n'gúči gádenáŋ
hoot owl I've got it by the leg   to be sure I I've got it by the leg

|: nekwaká n'diži dá:banaŋ :| túda ningaguonaŋ n'gúči gádenáŋ
to the woods I'm dragging him to be sure I I've got it by the leg

This is one of the few Michigan Indian songs reported in another location—namely, on Manitoulin Island. In 1936 and 1937, Rev. John F. Davidson found it there in the repertoire of Joseph Peltier, Sr. He says, "It is the spontaneous climax of a ten days' fast by an adolescent youth, when he finally meets his long awaited guardian spirit" (Davidson 1946, 303–4). The guardian spirit is a bluebird, not a hoot owl. Also there is no reference to the woods. Nevertheless, with several minor differences, the tune and text are the same as David Kenosha's. The connections between L'Arbre Croche and Manitoulin have been so close, despite the distance, that Ettawageshik claims kinship with the Peltiers. The point of origin and transmission of this song have been forgotten. Though Kenosha points out that the prehistoric Odawa were on L'Arbre Croche first, the European qualities of the second phrase in particular suggest an antiquity of no more than two hundred years.

Drinking Song

This is the song that Joe Chingwa recorded for the Wedding Dance of the Hiawatha pageant. It is an almost exact replica of a song dubbed "Carousal" by Frederick Burton in his study of Garden River Reserve songs (Burton 1909, 226). In that publication it is not specifically connected with the pageant, of which Barton was orchestra conductor. Before his recording, Blue Cloud announced it as a Peace Pipe Song, but afterwards, when pressed for the translation, he announced, "Someone misinterpret that. It isn't a Peace Pipe Song, it's a Drunkard's Song." The respective texts are as follows:

Chingwa: |: kanindanibási   nin :| kidagogóbanei   geinoǰinibásiwa
              I would not sleep   I   If there was anything   for which I could not sleep

Jane Ettawageshik comments that, "Some boys added to it, 'I wouldn't sleep if I had something to drink.'" Boys would add that just to clown.

Albert: |: kanindɑnibáiči :| kitagogóbænei waminikwǽyą
  I wouldn't sleep   If there was something I could drink

(Verse 4) " gáwiya nibáne owisǽną
       If I had   someone to sleep with

Though Whitney Albert picked up the tune at Round Lake, his treatment differs. Rhythmic figures and sequentially descending structures are the same. But, as in the Peace Pipe Song, Joe Chingwa's descent is more extensive and bolder. In five installments he again covers twelve tones, with the last phrase echoing the second phrase on a lower octave. Albert descends by only two installments and concludes with a rising and following phrase. This concluding phrase is shorter in the second, third, and fourth renderings than in the first, which was probably a sort of "priming." A Drinking Song by David Kenosha is so different from the above two versions, both in text and melodic texture, that it is best included in Kenosha's separate repertoire.

98   The Art of Tradition

All of these convivial songs are by their subject matter relegated to post-contact times and to a thoroughly secular objective. They are certainly at least fifty years old, since the "Carousal" song was already popular at the turn of the century. They could go back several centuries, for firewater lost no time in spreading among the Natives and even became indispensable for cures and offerings as long as two hundred sixty years ago (Kinietz 1940, 277, 307).

Thomas recorded a song different again from any of the above, so unique as to call for treatment with his special repertoire.

Repertoires of Individual Singers

The songs of five singers will pass in revue, along with texts and functional comments. They will be analyzed in comparative tabulations.

Joseph Chingwa: War Songs

Challenge Song. This is the song that could accompany the Odawa Strike the Post Dance. It has the same text but a different tune from another war chant of Joe Chingwa's.

|: kagowiya   ningásasi :|
no one   I'm not afraid of

War Chant. Jane Ettawageshik describes this as a "traditional Odawa war chant before a battle. Joe Chingwa singing and playing on tom-tom." The first rendering of the tune uses burden syllables [vocables]. On the other hand, a monotone, staccato second part, in the nature of a coda, uses the same words as the tune proper. The second tune is more conservative than the first in the compass—an octave as against eleven tones, and a consequent shrinkage of intervals. The Challenge Song descends in two installments, usually by fourths; the War Song shrinks from a fourth to thirds and from a second to a monotone. It is less conservative in its melodic treatment, with the variability of the sections A.

Coward's Song. No texts or explanations are available for this song. The melody is bolder and probably more recent than that of the two War Songs. The previously noted steep descent by installments to a twelfth below here shows a variation. After the second phrase, a rising and falling part B is inserted. The last phrase is a replica of the second an octave lower. The final phrase is strangely curtailed, ending on the fourth and leaving a sense of tonal uncertainty.

Joseph Chingwa: Social Songs

First Love Song. Joe Chingwa sang this composition of his in the 1948 Harbor Springs Hiawatha pageant and was very proud of it. It is in traditional style.

|: ki:yadık' weiya meikweínimakʿ :| benosna nindagóšina
There is   someone I am thinking of   I were there I wish

wɑsa   ižiatʿ   meikweínimakʿ
Far away where the one is   I am thinking of

Jane adds that freely translated, the text reads: "I am thinking of someone. I wish I were there, where the one is I am thinking of." As all love songs of this area, this one is chanted in slow and sustained notes, in smooth descent. But the last phrases are a staccato monotone like the second part of the War Chant.

Second Love Song. This song is rendered not only with feeling but even with schmaltz, and with fond dwelling on each note—in two-thirds the tempo of the First Love Song, one-third the speed of the average Odawa song. Joe Chingwa reported that "this was a favorite love song of the Odawa and Ojibwe. It has been recorded a number of times and been published with English words. Love songs typically were sung by women or played on the flute by men. Indian flutes were used only for love songs." Female rendering can be questioned, notably in view of the text.

|: čigobeidíbikʻ onéndia :| agamiszíbi   onéndia
All night   I am gone   Across the river I am gone

The same text and melody were recorded in Garden River Reserve half a century ago as part of the Hiawatha pageant (Burton 1909, 203). It is a traditional chant, disseminated by means of the pageant. Perhaps it originated in the neighborhood of Garden River.

The usual descending sequence is handled dexterously. Of the two halves of the melody (A and B) the first always rises and falls, the second descends, once to the second of the scale, twice to the main tone. Each part A commences a third lower, but continues with variable intervals. Part B uses a cadence we will often encounter on the tones of 54 21.

Courtship Dance. This song, which was used in the Hiawatha pageant for a Courtship Dance, may originally have had a different function. It is a strange tune, with its high semitone and with the treatment of the lower fifth as the initial and penultimate note. It is based on the triad known to European harmony. The words are also strange—

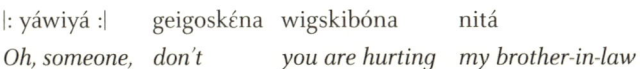

|: yáwiyá :| geigoskéna   wigskibóna   nitá
Oh, someone,   don't   you are hurting   my brother-in-law

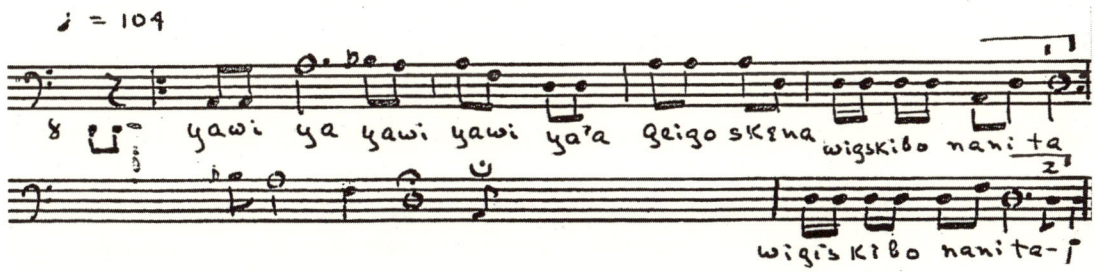

Wedding Dance. The Drinking Song, which served for this purpose in the Hiawatha play, has already been discussed and the dance description was quoted in the previous chapter. Evidently for the play it was necessary to select miscellaneous suitable tunes and social dances for the scenes of courtship and wedding, because of the aboriginal lack of such dances. None of the writers mentions any, and Baraga even specifically denies any custom of dancing at weddings (Baraga 1837, 160).

Social Dance. This accompaniment to a social dance in the play has an enigmatic text—

|: gegeitʻ sà :| nananéiwa
It surely is   intermittent breezes

Its structure resembles that of the Second Love Song, except that its two parts are coupled into two long sections, making four equally long phrases. But its rendering is fast, with the usual duple drum beat and a rhythm of the Hoot Owl Song type. As against the symmetrical structure, the tonality shifts from a 54 21 scale in the first half of the song to a triad scale in the lower second half.

Gambling Song. This song was also sung in the *Song of Hiawatha* plays given in Petoskey and Round Lake some years. During the singing, a gambling game was in progress—an old Indian game played with a bowl and counters. Either a man or a woman could sing the song. The counters used were two men, two fish, two snakes, and two brass discs, inscribed. Each side or contestant had a bowl in which the counters were placed. Bowls were then emptied on a skin on the ground. Points were counted according to how many counters fell right side up, with so many points for fish, and so on. There was also a good deal of additional betting, for high stakes such as clothes, canoes, and so on. The humorous laconic text is as follows:

|: gegɛtígo   manádseo   mákʼki :|
you betcha! homely   the toad

The musical motif is equally compact, consisting of a combination of two eighth notes and a "Scotch snap" or a snap and a quarter note. In the first rendering, this motif descends in four installments; then it wavers on the second and main tone for four measures. The second and the third rendering take six measures to descend and hover on the low main tone—the only song with this terminal monotone. The figure of the snap is also unusual and the compass of thirteen tones exceeds any of Joe Chingwa's frequently bold descents of twelve tones.

♩ = 104

16

gegetigo   manadseo   manadseo   maʼaKʼKi

gegetigo   manadseo   manadseo   maʼaKKi

You betcha   ugly is   the toad   – Chingwa

Joseph Chingwa: Ritual Songs

Of the ritualistic life cycle songs, the Naming Song is included in the discussion of Odawa feasts, as is the Ghost Dance. The former has an unusually clear-cut form for an improvisation, within the pattern of steep sequential descent. It combines the bold features of several of Joe Chingwa's songs—the large intervals of the Pipe Song, the snap and rapid figure of the Gambling and Drinking Songs. It has two musical motifs.

The Ghost Dance, on the other hand, is conservative in rhythm and compass and rises as well as falls in its cascading. The terminal phrase, an octave below the first one, typifies Chingwa, but in this case it is puzzling and creates an enigmatic scale. But for this coda the song would belong in the triad category. The coda produces a kind of upside-down scale. The particular rhythmic motif will be discussed later on in connection with intertribal characteristics.

Medicine Chant. This is also a puzzling tune, because of one single note, the F#. If that F# were a G, we would have an archaic two-part song within the 54 21 scale. It occurred to me that Joe Chingwa might inadvertently have raised the F# to a G or lowered the G to an F#, but he sings the cadence 53 21 in each of the four renderings. Such a cadence does not exist in any of the aboriginal songs studied either in Michigan or elsewhere. If it is an old chant, there was a slip-up somewhere.

Joe Chingwa claims it is traditional: "This chant belongs to my granddad and was taught him by his mother. His granddad was said to have heard the chant and gotten the receipt for the herbal medicine in a vision. A prescription for something. Chant he sings as making it. Sings to spirit of plants when gathers and when makes. Would get up and dance in one place as drummed. [Has special beat, but Joe doesn't know this.] In a way was bragging of medicine. All Indians have their special songs about different medicines. The chant is supposed to be sung four times, as were all Indian chants to make them valid. Fast seven to eight days, got vision."

|: šáškobinéši wεbágamaganiyá :|
green bird   (a kind of herb)

Eagle Dance. This song is categorized under the rubric of ritual songs, instead of under an earlier animal category, because this only bird song of Joe Chingwa's resembles the Medicine Chant, and also because it provides an interesting comparison with David Kenosha's Eagle Song, which follows. Like the Medicine Chant, it contains two very short themes, the first one a preliminary high soar, the second one a descent. It is repeated exactly four times. But it poses no tonal problem, contains no puzzling semitone. It is clearly pentatonic within its narrow six tone compass. At first glance its rhythm and contour seem to resemble the first part of Kenosha's Eagle Song, but Chingwa's is in a triad scale (5 3 1) and Kenosha's is in a quartal scale (54 21). Chingwa's is concise and definite, Kenosha's rambling. The texts are entirely distinct. Chingwa's goes as follows:

|: nimigónimágʻ   nibabámiwinigó :|
my feathers   are carrying me around

Jane Ettawageshik adds the following gloss to the performance: "solo eagle dance, such as Fred does. Traditional Odawa song, accompanied by tom-tom."

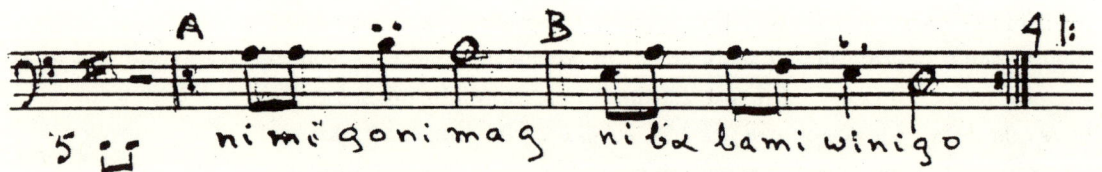

Joseph Chingwa: Summary

Joe Chingwa seems to have two main sources for his repertoire: his ancestors and the Hiawatha play. The former type, which includes songs like the first War Song, the Medicine Chant, and the Eagle Chant, uses short themes with narrow compass and follows the precept of four repeats. The latter type, which includes the Wedding and Gambling Songs, shows a steep descent of twelve to thirteen tones and rapid, syncopated rhythmic motifs.

Throughout Chingwa's repertoire, his vocal quality shows the influence of his acting career and resembles a white man's baritone. The large natural range might explain the compass of the Pipe Song or at least might have influenced his preference for large-scaled songs like the Wedding Song.

David Kenosha: Bird Songs

Eagle Dance. This song serves as accompaniment to the Eagle Dance, already described, even though by David Kenosha's claim the tune is Odawa but the dance comes from the West. At any rate, the text eloquently carries out the dance's sense of approach from a distance:

Odawa (phonetic):	binæšiwə́k	|: togo :| šənók	wasa	bionǰípawok
(Kenosha's spelling):	binesiwuk	togo tokoshenuk	wasa	beonjibawauk
English (exact):	birds	are coming	from far	they arrive

(Free): The birds are coming. They're coming from a long ways.

Woodpecker Song. David sings this song among friends such as the Kenoshmegs. Louise Kenoshmeg in particular is very appreciative and always laughs. David too thinks the words are very funny. The humor is much more subtle than in the Drinking Song and testifies to keen bird habit observation.

poposǽ	kipotó kóžešin	mæmǽgwaiget kagáwis atíkonír̨
woodpecker	got his bill stuck	He was pecking on a hemlock knot

hi i i i hi

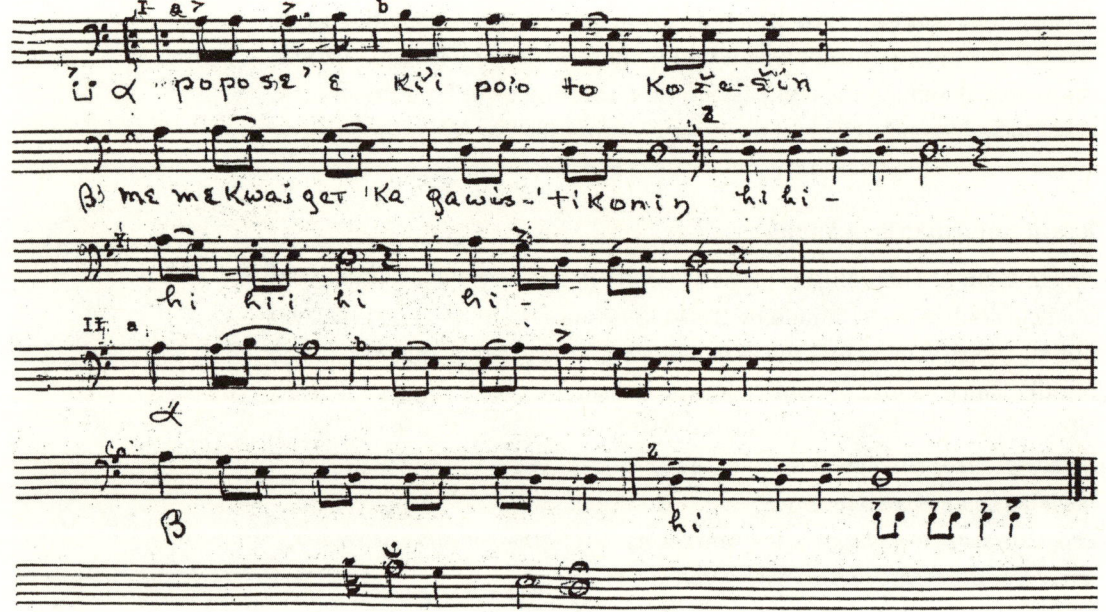

David Kenosha: Animal Songs

Bear Song. The song and text about the little lost cub have been quoted along with the dance with which they are associated. These three songs can be discussed together because of their similar form and scale. The first line of the Woodpecker Song illustrates the formula:

- *Phrase a.* High introduction on fifth and sixth of scale (like Joe Chingwa's Eagle Dance). Rapid start on eighth notes, then a hold.
- *Phrase b.* Stepwise descent from sixth or fifth to second; even eighth notes. Stepwise means: 65 54 42.
- *Phrase c.* Concluding phrase from fifth to main tone, eighth notes, hold.

The melodic outline and rhythms are simple; the scale of 54 21 is consistent. Yet a structural analysis is frustrating because of vagueness in repetitions. The second and third verses of the Eagle Dance are alike, but they differ from the first verse. At times it varies the rhythm with a dotted figure ( ). The Woodpecker Song is more variable and further loosens up the form by a [vocable] interlude on the main tone and another one with a melody. The Bear Dance is completely irregular from verse to verse and furthermore interpolates melodic nonsense syllable verse.

Harking back to the Hoot Owl Song, the same formula determines the four descending phrases but with an extension on account of the octave's range.

David Kenosha: Social Songs

Walking on the Green Grass. "Walking on the Green Grass," which was used with the women's dance in the Sun Ceremony, again varies the formula with each repeat. The second and third lines are similar, especially in the first halting phrase, but the others expand or contract, requiring vowel duplication in the text. This text alternates with a line of nonsense syllables [vocables], four lines of nonsense, and three of text. This gay "heya heya" plus the rapid tempo cheer up the tune in accordance with its hopeful and also wistful utterance from a lover to his sweetheart.

    he heya heya heya heya he . . .

Odawa (phonetic):	nǽngodiŋ	gabémosemin mægwe šásko komegág
(Kenosha):	nengoding	kapamocemin megwe shakomegag
English (2 trans.):	Some day	we'll be walking on the green grass
	Some day	we'll have a walk around the green grass sod

Maple Sugar Song. Here is another love song, addressed to the sweetheart at sugar making time and also singable at any maple sugar bee. Like in the previous love song, a rapid tempo lifts the tune to a gaiety befitting a happy season. The skipping rhythm enhances this. Its variant on the formula (a a b c) within an octave's compass is more accurately repeated than in the other David Kenosha songs. Verses three and four differ somewhat from verses one and two because of the text rhythm. All four verses conclude with a legato slower coda naming the sweetheart, in contrast with the staccato body of the song. The first two words rhyme so perfectly as to suggest a conscious word play. Note that the glottal stops are caused by rhythmic reiteration.

|: ngimákawan   nindémǝkwan   gágogwe wé'eya :| ninimušǽnso
I found it   *my spoon*   *with the crooked neck*   *My sweetheart*

|: ngaĵipákwe'esan   ngáša' ama'an   gayigé'eya :| ninimušǽnso
I'll cook   *I'll feed her*   *she'll be satisfied*   *my sweetheart*

David Kenosha says of this song, "This guy he's making maple sugar (*anishinabek zisbakwat*). After the sugar done harden up, he took the bowl here, he took the stick and goin' like this (stirring) making a fine sugar and grind it. And he says, 'I found my spoon with the crooked neck.' And he said, 'I'm going to cook, I'll feed my sweetheart this sugar.'" Another time Kenosha translated *ninimušǽ* as sister, but sweetheart is the usual meaning.

Drinking Song. David Kenosha's dignity extends to the tune and text of a drinking song. Compare it with the Chingwa-Albert-Garden River version. Its tempo is rapid but does not speed up to sixteenth note figures. The phrasing is completely irregular as against the other men's exact sequential repetition. Its sequential descent, confined within a sixth, is governed by the Kenosha formula in a rather free pattern—a c b c b c; at the end, b b c.

It is also meant for a beer party. "Well," says Kenosha, "I'll call on my brothers and sisters to join with me, and to drink with me."

Native Songs by Modern Singers

|: nijikiwædók opíšayok :| |: owabámišik :| ndawémadok opíšayok owabámišik
my dear brothers come over see me my sisters come over see me

kaminikwé:mæ wabížayók ndawémadok píšayok kaminikwé:mæ
lets have a drink come to see My sisters come over let's have a drink

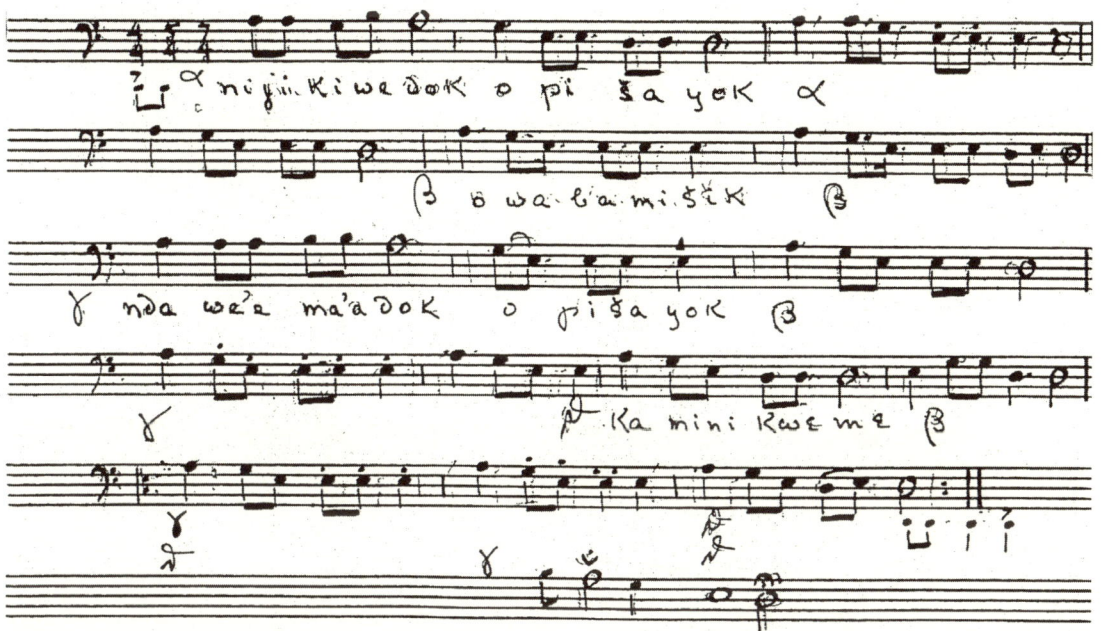

David Kenosha: Summary

There is every reason for faith in David Kenosha's assertion that his songs are Odawa. They are limited largely to a small group of animal and social songs with a specific 54 21 scale sequentially descending within a sixth or octave by a recurrent formula, and with a recurrent simple rhythmic motif. Semi-improvised songs, like the Scalp Song, follow the same formula. Within this pattern his structure is variable and vague, much in contrast with Joe Chingwa's. He contrasts with Chingwa also in vocal quality, with an Indian throat, and a light, often staccato attack. Like his dancing, his singing is traditional, graceful, and uniform.

Whitney Albert (Blue Cloud): Animal Songs

White Pigeon Song. Though listed with animal songs, this melody has necromantic associations, by virtue of its textual implications.

|: mi:mí:gwanag deyohági :|
feathers (of) white pigeon

110 The Art of Tradition

The feathers are witched into the body of a victim for bad medicine. This could still happen, for there are still Indian sorcerers and "bear walks" in Michigan, unknown to white people.

Raccoon Song. This is a comedy song for teaching youngsters how to dance. That's what "šaša" is for. Raccoon says,

[: |: essibə́n   nindigó   :| babámodéseani :] |: šą̌šą̌ šą̌šą̌ :|
Raccoon I am called walking around sideways (sound of dancing bells)

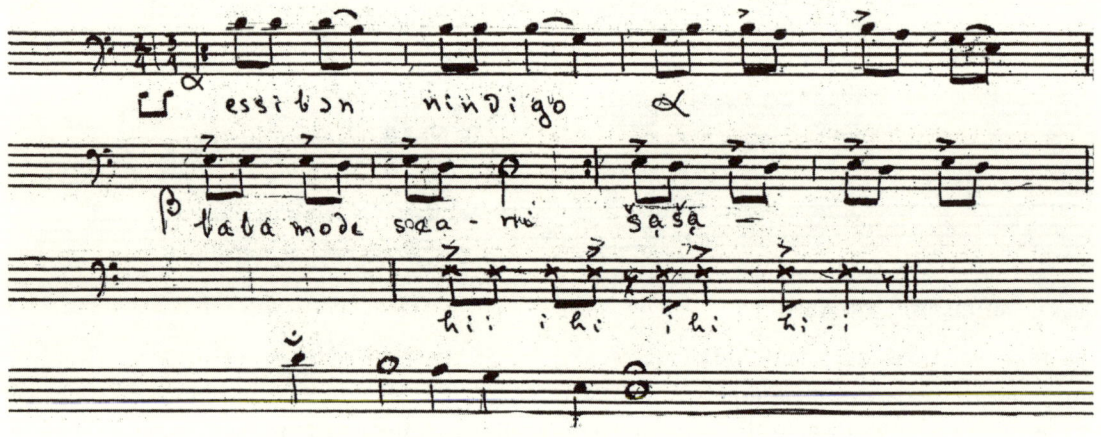

Rabbit Song. Youngsters are also taught dancing to this tune. Blue Cloud could not quite explain the strange and supposedly comical text, though he devised it.

[: A. maničiwigǽdowani   wábos wigiwámiŋ B. |: píndigeiá :| :]
I don't know what would happen to me   in rabbit house   when (if) I enter

　　　" "   gígabo wigiwámiŋ   " "
　　　" "   (some animal) house   " "

All three songs concentrate compact and symmetrical melodies in four short phrases, rising and falling but generally descending within an octave's range. The first two are most alike with their five tone scale of the 54 21 type (Hoot Owl Song scale). The Rabbit Song centers its three tones on the main tone, the lowest tone dipping to the fifth below, in the 5 3 1 5 scheme of a bugle call. It is not precisely sequential, for the second half brings new material and this part B repeats. The complex rhythm is caused by the rapid text syllables. The first and third songs conclude with a cell of two short yelps, the second with the syncopated coda of the Hoot Owl Song type—both of the coda types peculiar to Whitney Albert.

Whitney Albert (Blue Cloud): Occupational Songs

Fox Hunter's Song. Before a hunter goes out to track a fox he sings this song to help him find the track and to follow it and catch the fox. It is a very old chant and is connected with hunter's medicine.

A. |: ǫni wákəšæ :|
Where (is) fox?
(Hunter sees tracks going away)

|: hi' i' i' i' :|

hi hi

B1 |: ænomí: káwiya wákəšæ :| 4×
I see the track (of) fox
B2. |: ænomí bǽtobæ wákəšæ :| 2×
I see him running fox

B3. |: wawiágabato wákəšæ :| 4×
I see him running fox
B4. |: dædæmíneowa wákəšæ :| 4×
I catch up with him fox

Perhaps this compulsive song should be grouped with animal tunes, for it is identical in character with the Rabbit Song and suggests similar antiquity and purpose. It is more archaic and repetitious, is limited to a fifth compass, and after the first note, to a play on 3 and 1.

112 The Art of Tradition

Tracker's Song. This time the hunter is anticipating the pursuit of a deer. Albert translates the text as follows: "In the morning when I start in hunting, looking down on the track, I see a four-pointer deer."

|: ǰibmižáži   nikɪwegá káwiya məškodɛŋ :|
this morning   I'll be seeing his track on the plain

kičenæsowa   kónæ   ningawábama   kógižeb
big crotch   horn   I will see   early in the morning

Despite the similar compass, the style of this hunting song contrasts with that of the previous hunting or animal songs. The fundamental theme descends gradually but with variation in each of the six descents, not only in level but also in contour and length in accordance with the number of text syllables. The first and last lines play in the same small range of 1 2 1 7 1. The first and second lines include two notes (5 and 3) that do not reappear in the rest of the song, which has a 4 2 1 scale.

The Absent Trapper. Another hunting song is in this same style of theme and variation, on a basic 4 21 scale expanded to an octave's compass. It uses the same peculiar weaving on adjacent notes and cadence on the leading tone and main tone, ending on a sustained note. But its variations are more extensive. Of the twelve phrases, the first and eleventh are the same; the sixth and tenth (same as line 6 of the Tracker's Song), 2, 5, and 9 are similar (see line 3 of the Tracker's Song). The complex pattern of thematic alternation (aa'bcde b'cde ac") does not entirely coincide with the alternation of lines of text. In every musical respect these songs are unique, except in the "stepwise descent," which recalls David Kenosha's mannerism—75 54 42 21.

The text says nothing about a hunting charm. It cheers up the wife of an absent trapper.

|: ǰižážigo   ginigıwǽbini   gúšnabe :|
It's long ago   left home   your man
(since your husband went away)

kéget   šíguža   mígana   mówikeŋ   banige   giniginábəmæ
don't   fear   don't   cry   went away   your husband

báma báma   dadagwišín   ginábəmæ   gágo sáki pipičí gamowa
by and by   will arrive your husband   when the porcupine is fat

gégo gégo mówikeŋ báma báma ... ǰižážigo ... bani ...
don't cry

Says Albert, "The husband went out hunting, was gone too long. Another man came and sang this encouraging song, told her not to cry, he'd return, in the fall when the porcupine is nice and fat."

Canoe Song. Blue Cloud's third hunter's tale has a much more clear-cut form of three descending variants of the same theme, reminiscent of the David Kenosha formula and the Hoot Owl Songs, but with several differences. A call (y) is occasionally interpolated and the entire scheme is aba'byc abcyc abc, the final phrase combining b and c. This is one of the few songs with a skipping rhythm and one of the very few starting with an upbeat. The pattern of text alternation corresponds pretty well to musical phrases.

|: nindadagámagišín :| |: bina:kinábinada o:šin :| yúwa
I can't get across the river *Come and get me* *(express distress)*

Whitney Albert says of the song, "A man comes to water, calls to one on the other side to take him across in his canoe."

Whitney Albert (Blue Cloud): War Songs

Brave Song. This is a warrior's boasting song, a sort of contest song.

|: gawiyo nása nindaginǫ́na'a :| wægwæ æwisæmǽn éndogwe ǽndia nina
anyone *I can talk to* *(if) anyone smarter is than* *I (am)* *I*
(If anyone sings better than I, I can talk to him)

116 The Art of Tradition

Grass Dance. The first song belongs to a traditional style in a conservative scale of 654 21, though its structure is not archaic and the drum beat is in triple instead of the usual duple time. The form could be called ternary, as the first two phrases and the last two are alike and the central section is a bit different, playing on a middle level. Text and musical phrases correspond. The second song represents the erratic improvisatory style of improvisation for show dances. It descends steeply in fourths and fifths with "Scotch snaps," no two descents being alike. The vocal quality affects the strident Plains style, in contrast with Blue Cloud's usually subdued manner.

    heya ha heya ha (no meaning)

Whitney Albert (Blue Cloud): Social Songs

Cousin Song.

|: ǰižážigo :| ningiwábamaban   kitástina   (kinimušénsina)
long ago   *I saw him/her*   *our male cousin*   *(our female cousin)*
(It's a long time since I've seen my cousin)

Red Blanket Song.

|: waboyánes   májido :| megwa ekwabák   kıwanibámin
blanket   *I carry*   *in foliage*   *we'll go to sleep*

"   "   ninimušǽ   nin wíjiya
         my sweetheart   *I will take (carry)*

This tune and its text may have derived from the similar but not identical Garden River Red Blanket Song (Burton 1909, 210).

Whitney Albert (Blue Cloud): Ritual Songs

Medicine Song. A medicine man is looking for an herb and can work either good or bad magic with it.

|: aweminéndineha   gagwéjemi' iyan :|
what is that   you are asking me for?
ojípkægini'i   gagwéjemi' iyan
(name of root)   you are asking me for

|: awæminéndineha gagwejemi'iya
ojíbwe makadǽ məškimodǽ gagwéjemi' iya :|
Ojibwe black medicine you are asking me for

The theme and variations structure and recurrent 1 7 1 cadence are reminiscent of the Tracker's Song and the Absent Trapper Song. But the concluding phrase in each line recurs like a refrain, and the rhythm is more complex. The immediate reaction of all Indians to this song is "Catholic chant." Before conceding this, however, it is best to examine the peculiarities of this unusual tune. The dip to the seventh or the fifth below would be quite possible in Native song, but the four adjacent whole tones, adding up to a tri-tone in the second line, are unusual in any kind of folk music and unheard of in Indian music. In the fourth line the cadence is 6 1. These two lines provide a composite scale with all the notes of the octave. A further digression from the other Odawa songs is the opening on a lower note than the conclusion. Finally, the crowding of many syllables into a small space is fairly common in the Native songs—for instance, the Rabbit Song, but without a change of tempo. Here it has the effect of a retard ending on a long note, as in liturgies. All of this confirms the first impression of ecclesiastical influence, of a blend of styles. Blue Cloud could offer no explanation of blend in a magical song.

continued

Whitney Albert (Blue Cloud): Summary

Both in repertoire and style Whitney Albert surpasses even Joe Chingwa in variety. He knows ancient animal songs, comedy songs, recent social songs, and ecclesiastically oriented chants. He renders them with appropriately varied expression from staccato to sustained. His vocal quality more closely resembles the Indian throat of the Iroquois than does that of the other singers, at times even suggesting terminal pulsation. He often ends with typical Indian calls, usually of the eastern variety. His texts are interesting and complicated and preoccupied with various phases of Indian activity, not only related to animals but human occupations and incidents. Though some of his songs are derived from Chingwa and a few show songs are superficial improvisations, most of his repertoire is traditional, with a creative reflection of his own personality.

Eli Thomas

Though Eli Thomas is eminent as a singer of hymns and though his Native songs were taught by Blue Cloud, he has developed his own style. He has a preference for sustained notes preceded by a grace note in his codas (Hoot Owl Song) and his War Dance and Grass Dance improvisations. This preference and his generally sustained legato quality are doubtless due to hymn influences. Two of his recordings deserve special comparative mention, the former being a complete improvisation and the latter being a free rendering of a bona fide song. They are a War Song and a Drinking Song.

War Song. The free rhythm and general descent accord with Whitney Albert's War Song type. But the initial rise in all phrases except the first and the final retard are Thomas's own mannerisms. The scale is surprisingly conservative: a traditional 54 21 scale within an octave.

   heyo heyo (burden syllables [vocables])

Drinking Song. This unique song also has the features of initial rise from the lower fifth and final retard, also a 54 21 scale. Its rhythm has no counterpart—first the introductory drum beat, then the syncopation of jazz, rather than Indian type. Its text, too, differs from that of the other drinking songs—a curious text for a strict Methodist teetotaler:

   |: (o)žám   niminikwé   wénje nimigóyan(a) :|
   Too much   I drink   therefore I am disliked
   I drink too much, that's why they don't like me.

Eli Thomas confuses the issue with his associated story about his grandfather: "My grandfather sing this song when he was a young man. While he was singing, pretty soon he looked in this direction, there he sees a quail comin'. He look in that direction and see another. He look back, see another. There he was up against it. That's the song."

Thomas also has a monopoly on hybrid hymns, which are included in chapters 5 and 6.

Thomas Shalifoe

Thomas Shalifoe lives a day's drive north of the nearest Lower Peninsula Indians. He recorded only a few Native songs, because of mechanical troubles. Yet his few songs must be included, both for their patterns and their rendering. The pattern resembles the David Kenosha formula in two instances—the Deer Song and the Social Song. The former particularly descends very like the first Hoot Owl Song, with a similar rhythm and phrasing. But the scale is tertial with a quartal texture—that is, a 4 3 1 superimposed on a 5 3 1. The third song is reminiscent of Blue Cloud's Raccoon Song, plus a syncopated figure. Though successive renderings vary somewhat, the form is clear-cut. The tempo is crisp and the rhythm infallible. These are incidentally marked not by a drum but by foot tapping as for square dance fiddling (Shalifoe had no drum). The vocal resonance is superior to that of any of the other, younger singers. In some ways Shalifoe is the best of these Indian singers.

Deer Song.

|: máno máno dimá:ja :| wawəskǽšæ   n'dó:dæ:m haha wiha ho'ahe
Let him go   *the deer*   *my pal*

The term *n'dó:dæ:m* suggests relationship with a respected clan animal, but it was not familiar to Thomas Shalifoe in that association.

Social Song.

wáka nægodiŋ nínda íkwewæ |: wígiwe wígıwasiŋ :| waha'i'a haha
Some day I'll take my woman   *(into) birchbark lodge*

Shalifoe laughed after this song.

Partner Song.

|: wégonæ   nindángwæ   bádudaŋ :|
What (is)   my sister-in-law   packing?

Thomas Shalifoe also knows the Hoot Owl and Drinking Songs on the comparative plates, in variant versions. Recordings of these and other songs of his may yield interesting conclusions; they reflect a vigorous personality.

Comparative Analysis

Musical characteristics could be analyzed in technical detail. However, for the present purposes the most essential features are tabulated according to methods used in my previous publications and manuscripts. Scales, melodic rhythms, and tempi are concentrated together on sheets representing the individual singers. Structures and contours are represented by typical songs. With some exceptions, there is a surprising degree of correspondence between these features and the subject matter of the song; also there are definite distinctions between the singers.

The scales show the entire melodic material of each song according to tone frequency (whole tone most frequent) and labeled as to initial

(︶) , final (⌢), and sometimes semi-final (𝄈) notes. Obviously, they show the range. In composite songs the extraneous scale is written upside down. The four predominant scale types are (1) a tertial 5 3 1 scale; (2) a quartal 54 21 type; (3) a widely spread 8 4 1 or 8 5 1 scale; and (4) composite and indeterminate scales. Usually they contain additional notes. They are written with the tonal gaps shown in the spacing and, as much as possible, around D as the focal note (necessitating some transposition).

The rhythmic symbol is written to the right above each song scale and the tempo to the left. The rhythm represents only the most typical unit: (1) a half note stands for a slow sustained melody; (2) two quarter notes for a melody composed mostly of even notes; (3) fast units; and (4) syncopations for a predominance of that figure, always in connection with other rhythmic patterns.

Scales - 1. 5 3 1   2. 5 4 2 1   3. 8 5 1   4. Composite
Tempi   - 62-96   100-112   over 112
Rhythms -

Key to Structural Labels

A, B	separate themes
a, b, c	related themes with usually identical rhythms, differentiated by varying levels are sometimes contours
a, a′, etc.	considerably varied yet essentially same themes
8 5, 4 1, etc.	beginning and ending note of a phrase (octave and fifth, fourth and main tone); 5 indicates the fifth below the main tone
x	introductory call
y	interpolation; Y melodically important interpolation
z	final call; Z melodically important coda
α, β etc.	lines of text

In some songs the labeling is obvious; in others it is arbitrary—namely in certain kinds of variations (as David Kenosha's).

A study of the entire song collection showed that the majority of songs fall into certain types: (1) a repetitious type consisting of one or (usually) two themes repeated; (2) a sequential type descending as a rule from an initial to a terminal note, sometimes with some rising as well as falling, other times always downward; (3) a theme and variations, falling and rising type; and (4) some erratic songs fitting into none of these patterns.

The contours visualize the melodic trends and so closely express the structures as to fall into the same types. However, every single song, it was found, has a different contour, a different design of rise and fall. The most typical ones are drawn in their broad outlines, not note for note.

Many fine points cannot be shown in any of these tabulations—notably dynamic coloring, subtle rhythmic figures, upbeats, and so on. They could but do not include drum beats, for these are with few exceptions double quarter notes.

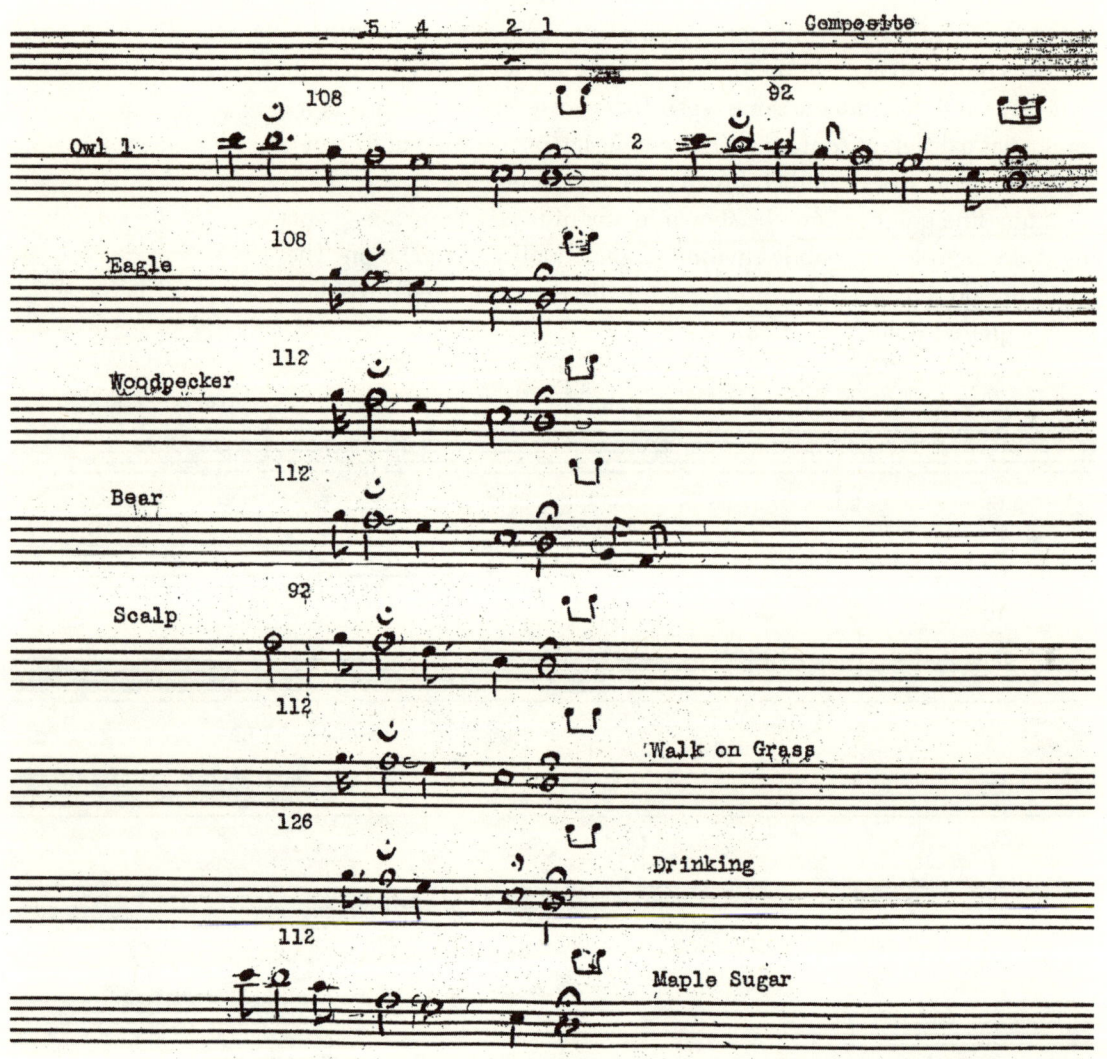

STRUCTURE   CONTOUR

Joe Chingwa

1. Repetitious Type

    Medicine 4 |: A -5 6 1   B 2 4 1 :|

    Eagle   4 |: A 5 6 1 B 2 4 1 :|

2. Sequential Type

    War 2   A 8 5. 4   B 1
         4 |:   A 8 5   4 1   B 1
            |:   A 8 4   4 1   B 1 :|

    Love 2   a 8 9 2   b 4 8 1   c 2 5 1
         2 |:

    Wedding   a 12 10   b 11 2 8   c 10 10 2 8   d 8 10 3   b 3 5 1   z
         2 |:

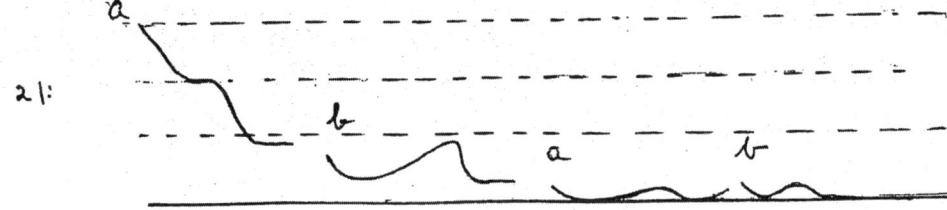

4. Irregular Type

    Gambling   a 13 6   b 5 3 6 3   a 2 1   b 2 1
                a' 13 8 10   a" 9 6   b 5 3 6 3   a 2 1   b 2 1

         2 |:

David Kenosha

1. Repetition
   none
2. Sequence
   Eagle   I a 5 6 5 c 4 1 |: b 2 5 c 5 1 :|

   3 |:   II a 5 6 5 b 4 2 c 5 1 b 5 2 c 5 1

   Woodpecker I |: a 5 6 b 6 2 :| c 5 1 z 1
                           Y 5 2 5 1
   2 |:   II   a 5 6 5 b 4 5 2 c 5 1 z 1 2 1

   Hoot Owl 1 a 8 9 5 8 b 5 6 4 c 6 2 d 5 6 1
   3 |:

3. Variations
   none
4. Unusual
   Hoot Owl 2 A a 8 9 5 b 7 8 1 B 8 1
   3 |:

Fred Ettawageshik

4. Unusual   A 8 2 5   B 11 1
              A 8 5 C 5 1 B 5 1 a

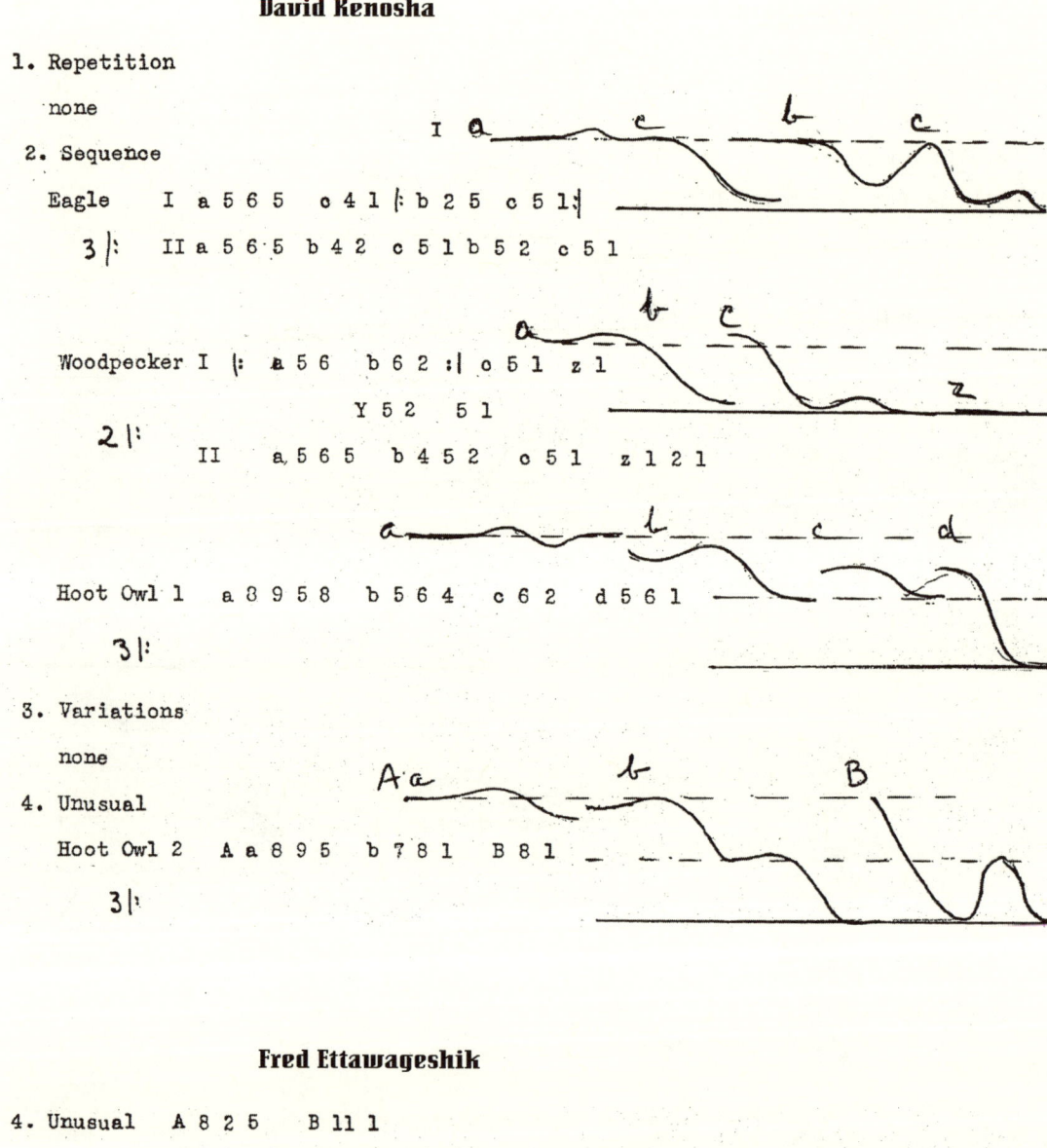

Whitney Albert

1 Repetition

   Fox Hunt 4 [: A 5 1 ∦ B 3 1 ∦ :]
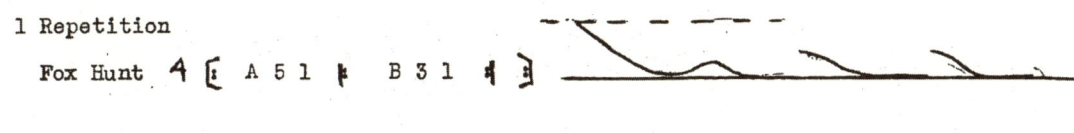

   Rabbit 8 [: A 8 1 B 5 1 B' 1 5 1 :|
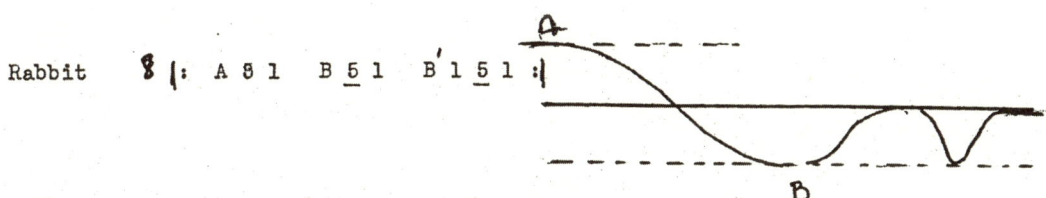

2. Sequence

   Hoot Owl 4 [: a 8 ′5 8 b 5 6 1 c 4 1 :| z 1
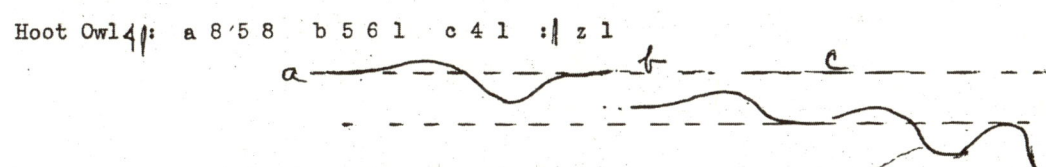

   Drinking I A a 8 5   b 6 1   c 1 3 1   B 1 2 1
       2 [: II A 8 5   b 6 1   B 2 6 1
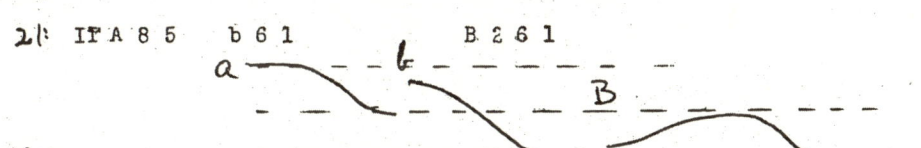

3. Variations

   Tracker   a 4 5 4   b 4 5 1   b' 2 4 1   c 1 5 1
                                  b" 1 4 1   c 1 2 1
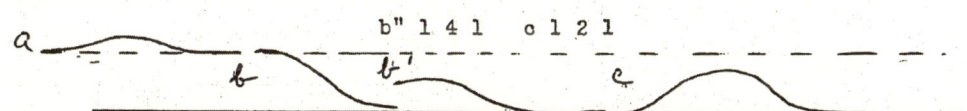

   Medicine A a 5 1   b 2 3 6 1   a' 1 4 5 6   b' 6 1
         A' 5 1   B 2 7 1   A" 5 1   B 1 3 7 1 z
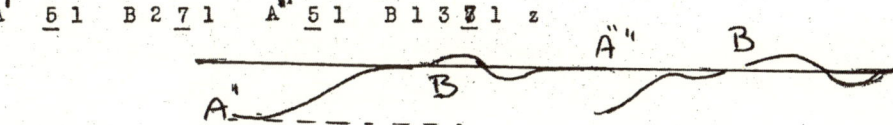

4. Erratic

   War x A 11 8 A' 8 5   A" 8 9 8   B 8 5   C 5   C' 1
      x A 11 8   B' 8 1   B" C' 1   C" 5 1
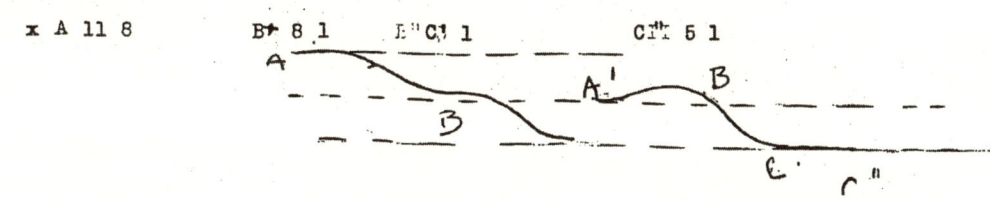

Formal Aspects and Subject Matter

The scales and other formal aspects are unevenly divided among the songs. Their distribution is as follows from among the forty-nine songs:

		N = 49 songs
Scale	1—rituals and animal hunt	8
	2—animals, social	26
	3—war, peace, social	10
	4—supernatural and miscellaneous	35
Rhythm	1—(long notes) mourning, love, rhapsody	4
	2—(even quarter) animals, social	28
	3—(fast) animal hunt, social	7→
	4—(syncopated) war, peace, social	10
Tempo	1—(slow) mourning, love	5
	2—(medium) animals, social, war	24
	3—(fast) animals, social, war	20
Structure	1—supernatural, hunt, social	6
Contour	2—animal, love, war, social	21
	3—hunt, war, social	4
	4—ritual, war, social	8

Half of the songs (not always exactly the same half in each category) belong to the 54 21 scale, with even quarter note rhythm, medium to fast tempo, and sequence. These all include animal songs and some social songs. Second is a combination of acrobatic scale (8 4 1) with fast speed and syncopation, sequential or erratic. These are war, peace, and social songs. The former are usually traditional, the latter often recent or newly come from western style. Scale 1 connects with rhythm and tempi 1 and 3, respectively sad and in animal pursuit.

Starting from the point of view of subject matter (original song function), the associations are as follows, with exceptions:

Supernatural/rituals:	Scales 1, 4	Rhythm 1, 2, 4	Tempo 1, 2	Form 1, 3, 4
Animals and hunt:	Scales 1, 2	Rhythm 2, 3	Tempo 2, 3	Form 1, 2, 3
War and peace:	Scales 3, 4	Rhythm 4	Tempo 3	Form 2, 3, 4
Social:	Scales 2, 3	Rhythm 1–4	Tempo 1–3	Form 1, 2, 4

That is, rituals are either very limited and slow or erratic and complex in rhythm and form. Animal songs follow a more uniform pattern of clear-cut and fairly limited scales and rhythm, in lively tempo and variable, but mostly sequential form. War songs consistently use acrobatic scales, daring rhythms and tempi, but a variety of forms. Social dances and songs fit into every type except the limited and composite scales. Their ubiquity in all categories suggests either that they are old tunes that became secularized or that new tunes were based on old models, in addition to composition in daring styles. By this approach, we again stress the conspicuousness and consistency of the animal and war types.

Individual Styles

One glance at the scale tabulations will show the contrasts between the singers:

- *Chingwa:* All scales, but preference for acrobatic; all rhythms and tempi in extremes; usually moderate speed; preference for tremendous range. His structure all types except theme and variations.
- *Kenosha:* Limitation to 54 21 scale with one exception; even rhythm and moderate to fast tempo. Structure sequential.
- *Albert:* All types of forms, but preference for 54 21 scale; simple or to fast duple (♩) rhythms; average to fast speed. A great variety of structures. Huge range and rhapsody only in war type.

Thomas, like Blue Cloud and Shalifoe, entirely tertial (vs. Kenosha) but sequential structure.

Textual Adaptation to Melody

Rhythm and Accent. In David Kenosha's Native songs, the spoken version is more condensed and rhythmically more erratic than the sung phrase in each case. The accent, virtually imperceptible in the song, tends toward the end of the spoken phrase; the strongest, terminal accent is also the highest melodic point. Thus speech has none of the descending, sequential qualities of the song. The spoken tempo is slightly faster than the sung. It becomes more rapid in comparison, because the speech omits syllables ... [ms. illegible].

Eagle Dance

Phrasing. The texts fit to musical themes in many ways, shown by labels. Sometimes phrases correspond exactly, even in some of Blue Cloud's theme and variations type songs. For instance, in his Trapper's Song, they correspond:

    a a' b c d e   b' c' d e a' c'
    α α β γ δ ε   β' β' δ ε α γ

In the Canoe Song, however, they are shifted somewhat:

    a b a' b y c   a' b c a' b c y c a' bc
    α α β α y α   β α α β α α y α β' α β

The same words may repeat throughout the song (Hoot Owl Song); two phrases may take turns freely (Deer Song); or new words may fit each phrase and verse (Hunter's Song).

Expressiveness. The literary quality of these songs brings up the question, "Does the subject matter determine the musical characteristics, scale, and so on?" One might be inclined to favor such a theory in listening to the plaintive Joe Chingwa songs about Jibiabos' departure to the spirit land and the singer's yearning for his lady love; then, in contrast, the vigorous injunction to light one's pipes. They do indeed contrast in every musical respect. But then we look at the scales and see that the second Love Song and second War Song have identical scales and even identical weighting, and we have to conclude that the lyrical versus virile expressions must be due to other factors: rhythm, tempo, rendering.

In Blue Cloud's repertoire, we admire the incisiveness of the Rabbit Song, the lilting of the Canoe Song, and the frenzy of the War Songs, each with a different scale, rhythm, and structure. On the other hand, the bad medicine Pigeon Song and the jocular love song "Red Blanket" agree in every formal respect except the nature of the musical theme.

In David Kenosha's songs the scale and tempo certainly have no effect on the song content, for they are distinguished only by their weighting between an eagle coming from afar, a little lost cub, and a dangling scalp. Even the rendering is similar and would give no clue about the contents to a listener unfamiliar with the language. Kenosha's Drinking Song, while similar to Blue Cloud's and Thomas's in scale and structure, differs from them in rhythm and vocal quality.

Examples could be multiplied, but they would confirm the observation that expressiveness is first of all a personal matter, the result of artistic rendering. Secondly, it can be affected by the tempo and the rhythmic quality and to a lesser extent by the weighting of the tones. It has absolutely no connection with the scale and apparently none with the structure. As is shown in the listings of forms and subject matter, many categories are included within one scale or structural type. But we have noted a certain homogeneity in animal songs and in war songs, and find confirmation for the contrast between these two types in the realm of sheer expressiveness.

A clue to their distinction may be sought in their cultural import, the animal songs belonging to a hunting complex and the war songs to a largely imported war complex. The next step is to review all the cultural and historical factors connected with song and dance and to relate these to the formal aspects, notably scale and structure.

Comparison with Songs of Other Tribes

On the basis of stylistic comparisons the Michigan songs can be placed in the jigsaw puzzle of Woodland music. They can be placed in historical perspective less securely because of the recent nature or reliable transcriptions. Exact duplicates cannot be found anywhere except at Garden River Reserve. In general, we must deal with similar types. As a starting point we use the categories of repetitious, sequential, and acrobatic songs, with a fourth very small category of composite songs.

Repetitious songs are of the type sung chiefly by Blue Cloud—the Rabbit and Hunter's Song, for instance. They use a narrow tertial scale, with lively rhythm, in two parts, the second being repeated usually four times. They are mostly animal songs. This type of song was recorded as Fish Dance at Lac du Flambeau in 1952. Among the Menominee, Densmore found a number of animal songs so old "that only the oldest singers remembered them," such as the Rabbit, Fish, Raccoon, Hunting Medicine, and Partridge Dances (Densmore 1932, 59, 189–90). These have perservered, though with changes, as shown in my 1956 tape recordings of Menominee secular songs. Once magical, these are now social dances. The Iroquois have a few similar songs, for instance in the Chicken Dance, but no analogies as striking as those of the Menominee. Possibly others are hidden away among other tribes.

Sequential songs of David Kenosha's type use a 54 21 scale within a sixth to a ninth, with even rhythms in clear phrases descending to the main tone. Blue Cloud and Eli Thomas use this type, and Joe Chingwa only occasionally, for animal and occupational song (Hunt Song and Corn Song) and several convivial and love songs. Burton recorded some of this type at Garden River Reserve: Wabano, Buffalo, Owl, Caribou, Morning Star Songs (Burton 1909, 240–57) and also the Love Song. Some of my 1952 field recordings are sequential: at Lac du Flambeau, for instance, a Swan Dance; at Tama, Iowa, a Buffalo and Shawnee Dance. Densmore has published a Lac du Flambeau Maple Sugar Song (Densmore 1913, 231), and Nettl a Shawnee Pumpkin Dance approaching this type (Nettl 1953, 280). Some Iroquois Eagle Dance songs use this scale but a different structure; likewise some Fox Pipe Dances (Kurath and Fenton 1953, 250, 292); and likewise some unpublished 1952 recordings. Tutelo Spirit Release and Harvest Songs at times show more sophisticated development of the same tendencies (Kurath 1954a, 92, 104–5; Kurath 1953b, 154, 158), as do some of the Iroquois Death Feast Songs (Kurath and Fenton 1953, 155–61). The closest analogies can be found among the Iroquois, with almost identical patterns to the "stepwise" melody, in some women's medicine rites with animal tutelaries, the Dark Dance and Changing Ribs, some Bear, Buffalo and Raccoon Songs, and above all, a number of Thanksgiving Songs (*ganeo'ǫ*) in the body of the rite during the dancing (see examples in Kurath 1951b, 1952a, and 1952b). This last is of particular interest in view of the similarity of the step with Kenosha's two-step.

Acrobatic songs, favored by Joe Chingwa and by powwow improvisations, descend steeply in numerous installments, down twelve to fourteen tones, with a preponderance of fourths and fifths, often with syncopated rhythms, "Scotch snaps," or their equivalent in grace notes. Among the Iroquois such songs are rare, appearing only occasionally in Wasase and Scalp Songs and as introductions to some cycles as Eagle and Thanksgiving Dances. The most common phenomenon of this type is the upside down scale (8 6 4 1), such as Chingwa's second War Song. This characterizes a Seneca Wasase Song (by Cowry, no. 1); a Meskwaki Soldier Song; and Northern Arapaho songs transcribed by Nettl, including an unpublished Soldier Song and a published Skybird Song (Nettl 1954, 195). Some use Chingwa's trick of reiterating the theme on a lower octave—for instance, a War Song from Lac du Flambeau by Fred Lacasse. Densmore transcribed such acrobatic songs from Lac du Flambeau (Densmore 1913, 185–95), all of them War Songs, and has published extreme cases of seventeen-tone compass from the Teton Sioux Grass Dances (Densmore 1918, 195–99). Chingwa's Pipe Dance Song descends with intervals as bold as any; but none of his songs show the rhapsodic structure of these Siouan songs. In that respect the improvised Grass Dance Songs by Blue Cloud and Eli Thomas emulate the Plains style.

Composite songs, which have scattered representation in several repertoires, shift from one tonal nucleus to another. A shift such as the one in Blue Cloud's Tracker's Song is rare indeed, encountered only in two Seneca songs, the second Shake-the-Bush and Cowry's second Strike-the-Stick (Kurath 1951b). Atonal songs like Joe Chingwa's Jibiabos and Coward's Song have not come to my attention elsewhere.

The 4 3 1 cadence of these two songs deserves special mention despite its rarity in Michigan. Thomas Shalifoe tends toward this scale in the Deer Song. Garden River Reserve singers recorded some for Burton (Burton 1909, 226, 236). A Lac du Flambeau singer recorded a Hoot Owl Song for Densmore (Densmore 1913, 135). Barbeau found some among the Huron at Lorette, Quebec (Barbeau 1915, 248). In the seventeenth century Sagard wrote down several Huron songs by the do-re-mi method, deciphered as 4 3 1 melodies (Sagard-Théodat 1866, 291). Elsewhere the 4 3 1 cadence has been located only in Tutelo Harvest Rite Songs (Kurath 1953b, 156–58).

The gumming is of the type prevalent among the Iroquois and Central Algonkians—in fact, generally in the eastern Woodlands. The few digressions from the simple duple beat are David Kenosha's prelude to the Bear Dance and the Swan Dance and Eli Thomas's Drinking Song; they appear original rather than traditional. There are no iambic or rhapsodic beats such as prevail in the Plains and have penetrated to the Wisconsin Ojibwe.

Among various negative properties may be mentioned the rarity of female singers of Native songs in Michigan, the absence of antiphony even in the Snake Dance as against the prevalence of this form in Iroquoian and southeastern songs, and the absence of pulsation and of other typically Indian mannerisms.

A review of these intertribal analogies suggests several layers—an archaic animal-hunting type shared with the Menominee and other Ojibwe, a residue probably from very ancient contacts; a less archaic sequential type with wider diffusion among the Iroquois and Central Algonkians; and an acrobatic type that points to the west, specifically the Great Plains. The 4 3 1 type raises the tantalizing hypothesis of Huron origin and limited diffusion to the Upper Peninsula and Upper Ohio. Of these the sequential type appears most typical—perhaps a Central Algonkian pattern accepted by the Iroquois and Tutelo.

Some Notes on the Association of Dance and Song

- *Prehistory through nineteenth century:* Dances always accompanied by song, accurate timing; singing without dance at individual and domestic rituals
- *Twentieth century until 1953:* Decreasing connection; until 1953 dance accompanied by drums alone; singing in Odawa Eagle Dance and Ojibwe War Dances
- *1954:* Increasing connection; five dances song accompanied among Odawa, as yet no increase in southern Michigan
- *Two reasons for decreasing association:* Paucity of singers, lack of rehearsals

1. *Ancient Odawa-Menominee (possibly wide substratum):* Animal and hunt songs, repetitive 5 3 1 scale; Blue Cloud
2. *Central Algonkian:* Animal and social songs, sequential 54 21 scale; Kenosha, Blue Cloud, others less (Legacy to Iroquois?)
3. *Huron:* Spirit songs in 43 1 scale; Chingwa, Shalifoe less
4. *East and Southeast:* none
5. *Northern Mississippi:* Chingwa, Pipe Song
6. *Great Plains:* More recent war type, acrobatic songs; Chingwa, improvisations; Blue Cloud and Eli Thomas
7. *White men:* liturgical Medicine Song of Blue Cloud

New compositions constantly coming into being in dance, to a lesser extent in song—Quignon, Ettawageshik, Blue Cloud, Chingwa.

The Christian Legacy

CHAPTER 5

Odawa Feasts

↦ *In this first of three chapters exploring the relationship between Christianity and Anishinaabe cultures, Jane Ettawageshik narrates how by the 1950s important Odawa ritual traditions had become consonant with key moments in the Christian liturgical year: All Souls', Epiphany, and Lent. An indigenous practice of honoring the dead by feasting them became associated with All Souls' "Ghost Suppers." The conferring of an Odawa name—a crucial rite of passage from aboriginal times—had become a tradition belonging to Lenten suppers. But this chapter does not content itself with a simplistic explanation that the feasts were only nominally Catholic—that they were really just Odawa ceremonies, thinly veiled. Instead, the author explains that these practices are complex, at once fully Christian and fully Odawa. They are also wonderful exhibits of the creativity, grace, and improvisation at the heart of tradition, as is seen in the practice of Epiphany "Bojoing" (Bozho!, a greeting)—neither aboriginal nor the fruit of missionary endeavors—in which members of the community call at each other's homes for sweets, stories, and laughter. Both authors spend energy trying to gauge whether such practices are aboriginal or derived from missionary influence, but the chapter is at its truest when it simply observes the inherently improvisational nature of tradition, where a person with the cultural competence of Fred Ettawageshik makes the annual Epiphany call at the Coopers' home to "play a traditional game of cribbage with Vincent."*

Any discussion of Odawa ceremonialism naturally centers around feasting, for the feast has always been an important part of Odawa ceremonial life and is almost all that remains of the old patterns today. One could assume that the Odawa so loved to gorge themselves that the frequent feasts, which Champlain wrote that the Odawa gave "more than other tribes" (Champlain 1929, 98), were indulged in simply to satisfy the palate. A more realistic approach, however, reveals that Odawa feasts, like those of other Anishinaabe tribes, were affairs of religious import. Thus each bite of the first sturgeon of the season was dedicated by the host and his guests to the host's personal *manido*; every bear feast placated the mysterious bear; and the white dogs, so carefully reared and ceremonially eaten, were "fed" to the sun and moon.

Perhaps the nature of Odawa feasting is best expressed by my husband, Fred Ettawageshik, who at one time wrote to me concerning the modern Feast of the Dead or Ghost Supper:

> I did notice, though, this important point. . . . It is, that when one takes an extra portion of food to eat, it is in memory of someone (some ghost) just remembered. This, however, does not hold true in every case, because there are those who just eat and eat for no reason at all other than just to eat.

How true perhaps of all ceremonial feasting, including our own Western survivals!

The modern Odawa in the Harbor Springs–Cross Village area of Michigan have retained certain aboriginal feast patterns, but have transposed and added others. The present ceremonial calendar must begin with the New Year–Epiphany celebrations, for they are considered the most important functions by the Odawa themselves. Following the Epiphany supper, called the King's Supper, or *kwáŋjigeŋ* (at the finding things in food), and complementary to it is a feast called the *Tabándaŋ* (at the paying off) given just before or just after Lent. The naming ceremony in which children are given Indian names usually takes place at one or the other of these feasts.

Then in the fall, starting on November 1 and continuing sometimes for a week, come the Ghost Suppers, the only survivals of the great Feast of the Dead. Indian wakes are also given, and until recently a Huckleberry Feast was held in July. Other ceremonial occasions observed today are either intimately associated with the above-mentioned feasts or are typically Western, such as marriage festivities, birthdays, Christmas, etc.

Nowadays, too, there are the summer powwows and pageants performed for tourists. Here the feasting pattern has been lost, of course, and singing and dancing are featured. The modern dance performances are discussed in some detail by Gertrude Kurath in chapter 4. She is the only one capable of describing the dance intelligently, so I will say no more concerning this feature of modern Odawa life.

New Year – Epiphany Celebration

An outline of the sequence of events at the New Year–Epiphany ceremony is as follows:

I. Beggar's procession
   New Year's Eve: Young men sometimes accompanied by girls go from house to house shooting guns ("shooting the Matchi Manido" [bad spirit]). The leader carries a bag for gifts of food. Some of the food is eaten later at rendezvous.
   New Year's Day: Children make their visits, begging for food.
   January 2–5: Adults beg food, January 5 being the old persons' special day. Games such as cribbage may be played.
II. King's Supper, January 6, a potluck affair given at the home of someone descended from chiefs or sub-chiefs
   Corn soup always served; also cakes containing coins and beans
   Catholic prayer in Odawa said by host
   Formerly, New Year hymn sung
III. Naming of Indian children may occur at the King's Supper
   Indian song and dance accompanies
IV. *Tabándaŋ* feast, given in February or just after Lent. The host is the person who finds a dime in the fried cakes passed at the King's Supper.

My first participation in the New Year ceremonies took place in 1947, in extremely cold, stormy weather. The thermometer went down to twenty degrees below zero and the harbor at Harbor Springs was frozen over. (The harbor does not usually freeze over until a month later.) There was what seemed to me (coming from Philadelphia) a phenomenal amount of snow—beautiful, dry, dazzling snow—whiter than I had ever seen snow before.

Unfortunately, I missed the beginning of the New Year–Epiphany celebration in 1947, so I will describe the typical New Year's Eve festivities in which I participated when I married and moved to Harbor Springs.

This past New Year's Eve (1953), for instance, my husband and I had just gotten the children to bed when a little after 8:00 P.M. we heard three shots fired on our lawn. Immediately a band of young men and women, led by the young man who had fired the shots, knocked loudly on our front door. When my husband opened the door, the leader, who carried a large burlap bag, shook hands with him, saying, "Happy New Year! *Bojo!*" The others, some fourteen of them, followed suit, shaking hands first with my husband and then with me.

They all found seats. Some were in the living room, and we served each of them a small glass of wine and some cookies. After chatting for a while with us, the leader arose, so I presented him with some food for his bag. Almost any kind of food may be given, for the perishable items are eaten a little later that night by the group of *bojoers,* while the canned goods are kept for use at the King's Supper. Some of the old people still make and give the *bi·mátaganagan,* New Year bread or twisted fried cakes about six or eight inches long. These may be sprinkled with maple sugar, if it is available.

Then the leader shook hands with me and again said, "Happy New Year! *Bojo!*" One by one, each of the others shook hands with me and my husband, saying "*Bojo!* Happy New Year!" and out they went again to make another call. They did not walk to the next house as *bojoers* used to do, however, for there were several hot rods parked outside!

Every household visited by the young beggars is expected to attend the great feast on Epiphany, the King's Supper, and if possible to contribute additional food for the occasion. Not every family is visited—only those whose ancestors were chiefs of the Odawa or who have achieved some measure of importance to the Indian community.

New Year begging or *bojoing* is also referred to as *nimkodátiŋ* (at the dancing), as is the entire week of visiting and begging that follows New Year's Eve. The use of the term by the Michigan Odawa and the Ojibwe of Michigan's Upper Peninsula is interesting, implying as it does that the beggars formerly danced during their visits.

After all the houses have been visited, the *bojoers* in Harbor Springs go to the Joseph Kishigo's home where the King's Supper is always held nowadays. Joe, who drives the snow plow and performs other labors for the city, is descended from a long line of Odawa chiefs. His mother before him was hostess at the King's Supper, but at eighty-seven she has been unable in recent years to perform this monumental labor.

Joe's wife, Elizabeth, has prepared coffee for the *bojoers,* who arrive about twelve midnight. The contents of the burlap bag, which the leader has carried during the visits is examined and sorted out. Such foods as doughnuts and other breads are eaten by the *bojoers* and the Kishigo family around their large dining table. As in every devout Catholic home, the grace before meals is said in Odawa by Joe before the group begins to eat. Later, canned goods and other similar foods are stored away by the Kishigos to be brought out for the King's Supper.

Shurtleff describes the New Year's Eve customs as she observed them in Cross Village:

> One of the most interesting of these practices takes place on New Year's Eve. Early in the evening a group of men, equipped with horns and guns, assemble and pass through the streets of the village. Before certain houses, particularly those which belong to descendants of the chief, they stop. After blowing on the horns, they shoot many times into the air. This is called "Shooting the Chemanido," which name is a shortened form of Matche-manido, the Evil Spirit, or Devil. The Indians believe that if the Chemanido is shot in this manner on New Year's Eve, he will give them less trouble during the ensuing year. (Shurtleff 1940, 36)

Indians questioned in Harbor Springs substantiated Shurtleff's statement that the guns are shot off in a mock killing of *Matchi Manido*.

After the rendezvous at Kishigo's, the young Harbor Springs *bojoers* disperse to their homes or join some private party celebrating the New Year in typical American style. A word, though, about the formation of the group in Harbor Springs: the leader in recent years has been John Gasco by mutual consent. When John's wife had a baby in 1952 on New Year's Eve, the young men, who take the lead in the activities and are often unaccompanied by the girls, got together, talked over the situation, and chose another young man to lead them. Without Johnny, however, their spirits flagged. The new leader could round up only two other young men. The little group arrived at our house with long faces and bellies too full of liquor to make the New Year's Eve visiting very entertaining. We were wondering about them as they set out by car over slippery roads for the next stop, but they made it and, in fact, finally accomplished the whole round of visits without incident. Ordinarily the young *bojoers* are not drunk, so this sad spectacle was quite unusual.

When the group arrived in 1950 led by John Gasco, he reported that he had had to get a permit to shoot off the gun, although the shells used are blanks. We had a new police chief in Harbor Springs at the time, who had heard rumors that the "Indians have wild celebrations on New Year's Eve and shoot off guns." When the police chief questioned some of the Indians, he was referred, of course, to Johnny, who explained the custom to him and told him that blank shells were used. The police chief insisted, however, on giving Johnny a written permit and told him to notify the police every New Year's Eve before setting out and to get a permit. Actually, as the police chief believed, it is a good idea, for should the group be questioned by anyone, John has only to flash the official permit now.

On New Year's Day the children begin their rounds of *bojoing*. This is their special day, although they may make visits on other days throughout the week also. Early in the morning—often too early for the comfort of those who may have been celebrating the night before—Indian children are seen in little groups, going from house to house, each child carrying a paper bag. When a door is opened to them, each child shakes hands with everyone in the household and says, "Happy New Year! *Bojo!*" They are given fruit, candy, nuts, cakes, and cookies for their bags, and in some homes they are also served food to eat before they leave for the next stop. As they depart, each child, no matter how small, shakes hands once more with everyone and says, "Happy New Year! *Bojo!*"

Some of the Indian families make elaborate preparations for the calls of the children. The *biʼmátaganagan*, New Year bread, is baked; little cakes beautifully frosted or cookies cut in interesting shapes are served; apples or oranges, which some can scarcely afford for their own families, are proudly given to the children. If the day is extremely cold, children may even be served cocoa or weak green tea and one of the three kinds of corn soup still made by the Odawa. It behooves one to have plenty of food on hand for the children, for one never knows whether to expect ten or even fifty children on New Year's Day.

When the children have completed their calls, each little group usually gathers in the home of one of the children, the bags are opened and the contents greedily devoured. During the remainder of the week, the adults make their calls, with January 5 being reserved for the old people, though others may call on this day also. Preferences and traditions have grown up in certain families regarding which household to call on. My husband, for instance, always calls on the Vincent Coopers, where he plays a traditional game of cribbage with Vincent.

I accompanied Fred on his *bojo* call to Cooper's house during a field trip to Harbor Springs in January 1947. We started out on foot from Fred's house, where I stayed during that visit, with Fred's sister, Julia Black, acting as chaperone. Julia stayed behind to keep the home fires burning, necessary because the temperature stood at sixteen degrees below zero on a sharp, clear night. Fred's old home was below the bluff that divides downtown Harbor Springs from the section on the hill. The Coopers live on the bluff, about a mile away. I was not so cold as I expected to be when we finally arrived at our destination, but cold enough to find the warmth and coziness of Coopers' small home very welcome indeed. The steaming *wiškobíminakʼ* (parched corn soup) and delectable lemon meringue pie we were served were completely unforgettable.

After we had eaten, Fred and Vincent played their games of cribbage, while Vincent's wife Betty, her ten-year-old daughter, Ruth Ann, Vincent's mother, and I looked on. As I recall it, Vincent was champion that year, beating Fred three games out of five. Of course, this made our stay at

Coopers' so long that we did not have time to visit another household that evening. We left at about 10:00 P.M. with the customary handshakes and *bojos* and carrying our paper sacks into which Betty had put apples and cookies.

Of the New Year-Epiphany celebrations and the culmination in the King's Supper, Fred Ettawageshik gave the following account in 1946:

> At New Year's there is a week's festival. Everyone goes "bojuing." They go from house to house, say "Boju!," and shake hands with everyone. They sit around minutes or hours depending upon who they are and the circumstances. The hosts may bring out a bottle if they especially like the callers. Everyone sits around and talks over the drinks. Gifts of candy, cookies, nuts, and apples are made. When the callers are ready to go they say, "Bojo! Bojo!" and shake hands. They take what they are given in a bag or a bag is provided. As a child, I always carried a bag.
>
> At some homes I always play cribbage, the winner being the first to win three out of five games. This often means that I stay longer when cribbage starts. Some families used to serve a glass of beer—home brew.
>
> The climax of the festivities is the King's Supper held on Epiphany, the week after New Year's. At one time a headman (a chief or sub-chief) used to give this supper, but now the supper is a potluck affair. The neighbors pitch in and bring something to make it a success. They may bring beans, spaghetti, corn soup, a loaf of bread, a canned vegetable, etc.
>
> The King's Supper is given by just one family now—Joe Kishigo's. Formerly, Joe's mother, Victoria Cooper, used to give the supper. It is traditional in their family because their ancestors were sub-chiefs.
>
> For the supper, Joe's wife, Elizabeth, makes small fried cakes or bread cubes about one inch square. Into one fried cake she puts a dime, in another a nickel, and in another a penny. In some of the others she puts a bean, although most of the fried cakes do not have anything in them. These are passed to the guests following the supper. The person who finds a dime is given the honor of sponsoring a complementary supper within the next few weeks or some time after Lent. The person who gets the nickel is assistant host at the complementary supper, while the one who finds the penny is expected to contribute his aid also. Those who get the beans may invite guests and may contribute some dish for the occasion.
>
> The term for New Year's greeting other than *bojoing,* which is derived from the French word bonjour, is *nimkodátiŋ.* Any day of the New Year-Epiphany week may also be called this. The very start of the festivities is on New Year's Eve. People go around shooting a gun. They shoot three times in the air and shout, "Happy New Year!" Then they go into the different houses

and shake hands. One or two of them carry bags into which they put the presents they are given—fruit, pastry, etc. They used to start at midnight or just previous to this. The callers on New Year's Eve don't stay too long at any one house. They pick out different places and slight those that are not too well liked. They shake hands and say, "Happy New Year," as they leave too. After they make the rounds, they meet at an appointed rendezvous and spread out the contents of the bags. The host provides the beverage.

The next morning, bright and early, the kids start going out. This is their day. They don't miss a house, except where an old grouch is living. They are afraid to go in there. This will go on all day. There will be two to three or possibly as many as eight to ten in a group, the children very seldom going alone. One day I remember seventy-five to one hundred children called, but my dad was well prepared for them with penny candles, cookies, and other things tasty but not too expensive. The children do not wear masks or costumes, nor do any of the other callers who come later. People probably painted their faces at one time.

Then next day, the grown people start going out. The last day before the King's Supper is for the older people to visit

The King's Day is called °*ki·magíčikak*,̧ while the supper given on that day is called *mkwánjigεŋ* (at the finding of things in food), which refers, of course, to the coins and beans cooked in the fried cakes.

During the week before the King's Supper, Elizabeth Kishigo is a busy woman—getting together enough dishes and silverware, making corn soup, baking, and preparing other foods. Her four daughters assist her, as do her sisters, some of whom live in Harbor Springs. Her sister-in-law, Amelia Kishigo, who lives across the street, is always helpful. Of course, many of the guests will bring some kind of food for the supper, but when one considers that there may be as many as one hundred or more persons present and that the responsibility for the success of the affair is Elizabeth's, it is still a large undertaking. Yet, during all the time that I have observed Elizabeth, a small, plump, jolly woman, I have never seen her the least bit flustered or even overly fatigued. Very few other women in the community, white or Indian, would be capable of managing such an affair with so much natural grace and common sense.

When the King's Day arrives, the guests begin to congregate at the Kishigos' about 6:00 P.M. for the first "setting" at the table. Joe Kishigo, the host, always sits at the head of the table for this serving and says a Catholic prayer in Odawa—the Lord's Prayer, the Hail Mary, or the Glory Be to the Father. At subsequent settings, someone who occupies Joe's place says the standard Grace Before Meals in Odawa.

The table has been filled with bowls of food, and other bowls may be passed to the guests by Elizabeth and her daughters or by other women who have volunteered their assistance. At the first King's Supper I attended, in 1947, we had, among other dishes, *wiškobíminakᶜ* (parched corn soup made with whole kernels of Indian corn, kidney beans, and beef), *pinagsíginakᶜ* (corn soup made with hominy, diced potatoes, and beef), mashed potatoes and hubbard squash cooked together, boiled Navy beans, white bread, pieces of pork cooked with a thick broth, spaghetti, carrots, chicken stew with dumplings, coffee or green tea, cole slaw, canned fruit, pies, and cakes.

At this feast, I remember that Joe Kishigo, who is a great comic, would take up a bowl of food and say, "Will anyone have any more of this loblolly goulash?" He made us all laugh throughout the meal with his stream of comments, half in English and half in Odawa.

As soon as the first table is through eating, some of those assisting Elizabeth clear the table and commence to wash dishes, while others reset the table for the next setting. This, of course, continues until all the guests have eaten, the cooks and assistants finding time to eat something themselves at one setting. There is no prescribed order in which the guests are served or in which they sit at the table, although Elizabeth always places the guests at the table.

After each setting is through eating, Elizabeth brings out her best dish, a silver bowl, containing the fried cakes, and passes it to each of those at the table. Anticipation is on each face, and everyone immediately breaks open his fried cake to see if he has gotten anything in it. There are "ohs" and "ahs" and some disappointed expressions of *kágego*! ("nothing!"). Finally, however, one hears the voices rise, and many of the guests who are waiting to eat or still tarrying come rushing over to the table as they hear, "So-and-so got the dime!"—or perhaps, the nickel or the penny. There are congratulations to the lucky person, who will be host at the payoff feast, or *Tabandáŋ*. The opened fried cakes are left on the table, and the next group comes forward to be served.

Any food remaining when the King's Supper is concluded is kept by the host or distributed to friends or relatives. As the guests leave, they shake hands with everyone nearby and say, "*Bojo*!," just as they did on their arrival.

When questioned about the custom of passing the fried cakes, Elizabeth Kishigo said:

> The three coins in the cakes represent the Three Kings—the dime, the First King; the nickel, the Second King; and the penny, the Third or Black

King (*me-ka-te-wi-jed Ogima,* according to Fred Ettawageshik). The second king will be the host at the *Tabandáŋ* in case the first king can't do it. All those that get beans must bring a dish to the payoff supper.

The beans are called *mem-skwa-ki-sid* (the bean with the little spots on it). They are not necessarily Indian beans—any small bean may be used. You estimate the number of guests. This number is then cut in two. That's how many beans you use. You have to leave the necessary "blanks." One of my daughters always makes a list of all those that get coins and beans. This is so the host at the *Tabandáŋ* will know who to call on for help with the *Tabandáŋ*.

Elizabeth Kishigo also said that when her family was still all together they used to sing a special song about the three kings at their King's Supper. She comes from a large family who still own their government-granted farm at Five Mile Creek, north of Harbor Springs. The song is found on page 120 in the old hymnal translated into Odawa by Father Baraga in 1858 and titled, *Katolik Anamie-Misinaigan.* Many of these old hymnals and others published around this time are cherished in Indian families. They were formerly used in church services, which up until about 1910 were conducted in the Odawa language. Nowadays they are used mainly at Indian wakes. Gertrude Kurath, in her section on hymns in our joint publication, "Memorial Feasts and Hymns of Catholic Odawa Indians" (*Library Bulletin,* American Philosophical Society, 1955) analyzes this hymn and a number of others.[1]

Fred Ettawageshik translated the words of the Three Kings hymn[2]:

> Api Jesus ga-bi-nigid,
> *When Jesus was born,*
>
> Wi-bi-nodjimoinang,
> *To come and heal us,*
>
> Mi api ga-bi-nagosid
> *It (was) then it came into sight*
>
> Apitchi gwanatch anang;
> *A very beautiful star;*
>
> Nisswi kitchi ogimag
> *(The) Three Kings*

O gi-wabamawan dash;
They saw it then;

Kitchi wassa gi-aiawag,
Very far distant they were,

Gisiss wendji-mokissed.
The sun where it rises.

The hymn is a long one with six verses in all. Fred's English translation of the remainder of the verses is as follows:

> *They went to learn about,*
>   *Those Three Kings,*
> *The Holy Father's Son*
>   *Who was born on earth.*
> *Now then, let us all go*
>   *To the city of Jerusalem;*
> *They said immediately*
>   *Those Three Kings.*
> *So then they really went,*
>   *Thus there Jesus*
> *They looked for him,*
>   *So they could worship him.*
> *But Jesus was not there*
>   *In the city of Jerusalem:*
> *For he was born in Bethelehem*
>   *In poverty.*
> *Therefore, let us go there,*
>   *We will see him there*
> *The Holy Father's Son;*
>   *So that is what they said.*
> *They went there and found him*
>   *In the stable;*
> *They prayed to him,*
>   *They adored him.*
> *And they gave to Jesus*
>   *Incense,*
> *And gold*
>   *To make him very beautiful.*
> *Then after they worshipped him*

> *Jesus, the Great King,*
> *Once more they returned*
> *Far away where they came from.*
> *Then they went and told the story*
> *The Three Kings*
> *Back to where their homes were,*
> *That He was born*
> *The Holy Father's Son,*
> *To come and heal us.*
> *Let us adore him forever,*
> *Because we love him very much.*

Most of the Indians themselves have no explanation to offer for the New Year-Epiphany ceremonies except to say that they are dedicated to God and to the Three Kings. They know that the custom is certainly not "all Indian," yet they remember always having observed it. My husband, Fred, however, has concluded that the festivities were inspired years ago by the French Jesuits.

But are the New Year–Epiphany celebrations entirely Christian with only a slight Indian twist? Or is the custom of ancient Indian origin influenced later by Christianity?

Diligent searching by both Gertrude Kurath and me has failed to uncover any reference from the seventeenth century that describes any such important ceremony among the Odawa at that time of year. As previously mentioned, the village and inter-village celebrations were held in the spring and fall and occasionally in the summer. Feasts and ceremonies in the winter were usually of necessity small affairs to which ten or twelve or possibly twenty persons came, for in the winter the families were scattered about on their various hunting grounds.

Occasions for feasting arose in the winter—before and after a hunting expedition, because of significant dreams, to prevent or cure sickness, and at times of crisis such as the birth and naming of a child or the death of a relative. Thus, Father Allouez wrote that the Odawa invoked their principal divinities or manidos "whenever they went out hunting, fishing . . . or on a journey, with ceremonies which he termed appropriate only for sacrificial priests" (Kinietz 1940, 291). Allouez wrote that, having completed a successful hunt:

> One of the leading old men of the Village discharges the function of Priest, beginning with a carefully-prepared harangue addressed to the Sun—if the eat-all feast, which bears a certain resemblance to a holocaust, is held

in its honor. He declares in a loud voice that he pays his thanks to the Luminary for having lighted him so that he could successfully kill some animal or other—praying and exhorting it by this feast to continue its kind care of his family. During this invocation, all the Guests eat, even to the last morsel; after which a man appointed for the purpose takes a cake of tobacco, breaks it in two, and throws it into the fire. Every one cries aloud while the tobacco burns and the smoke rises aloft; and with these outcries the whole sacrifice ends. (Kinietz 1940, 291)

The priest mentioned above might very well have been a chief or venerable old hunter who in his youth dreamed of the sun, which became his personal manido or guardian spirit. After successfully killing his first bear, or deer or other animal of the season, he gathered together a group of men—perhaps ten or twelve—to celebrate the event and give thanks to his manido. The "eat-all" was a common feature of such occasions and was supposed to demonstrate the manliness of the hunters. In another section of his journal, Allouez writes:

They deem the most common cause of illness to come from failure to give a feast after some successful fishing or hunting excursion; for then the Sun, who takes pleasure in feasts, is angry with the one who has been delinquent in his duty, and makes him ill. (Kinietz 1940, 304)

In case of sickness, a "juggler" was usually summoned, who went through a certain rigmarole, pretending to draw out a stone or worm that had been causing the sickness. He would display this and tell the patient he was cured and that he must give a feast (Kinietz 1940).

Perrot's description of the bear feast and hunt says that a war chief makes up a party of young men and gives a feast during which he announces that the wants to go on a bear hunt and invites his guests to accompany him. The host at such a feast does not eat but only drums and sings his own songs. He may have fasted for eight days before the occasion in order to make the bear favorably disposed to being killed.

On the day of the hunt, all the hunters blacken their faces with charcoal and fast until evening when they eat lightly. As soon as a bear is killed, the one who has killed it lights a pipe and thrusts it in the bear's throat and blows smoke through its nostrils. Then he cuts out the bear's tongue string, which he puts in his pouch and keeps until later. The bear is then cut apart in a certain prescribed manner.

When an extra large bear is killed, it is set aside for a solemn feast. Some of the remaining bear meat may be eaten at the hunting camp. After such a meal is finished, each hunter takes from his pouch all the tongue strings he has and places them "over a brazier with great respect and many invocations." As the tongue strings cook, the hunters say that if they make a squeaking noise (which Perrot reported they almost invariably did), it is a sign that the hunters will kill more bears.

After the bear hunt is finally concluded, the bears are taken home to be divided up among the families (who presumably are on the same or adjoining hunting grounds). If any strangers are present, they are also given a share, in typical generous Indian fashion.

For the bear feast, the entire animal is cooked. The chief invites twenty men to attend. The chief cooks borrow the great kettles that are reserved for such feasts and are kept outside the wigwams except on such occasions. Every part of the bear except the blood is cooked, the blood being seasoned with grease.

When the bear meat is cooked, the chief cooks get the names of the guests from the chief. They take a wooden stick to each guest and say, "You are invited to a feast at the house of so-and-so." The guests go, carrying their own dishes and spoons. Strangers sit next to the host, or if there are no strangers, the chiefs sit next to him. The host dedicates the feast to his personal manido, and the assistants serve the guests. Three or four of them must eat the head, the blood and the haslet; others must eat the fat. This ensures that the god of the earth will grant to the village his favor and abundance.

All of the oil or broth must be drunk and every piece of meat eaten, for this is an "eat-all" feast. Some hunters died from excesses in eating at such feasts. Those who successfully completed the ordeal were congratulated by the spectators and their families, who said that truly they were men (Blair 1911–12, 1:127).

The earliest reference to New Year celebrations, per se, is made by Schoolcraft (1848) in the body of a myth narrated by "Nabinoi, an aged Odjibwa Chief." The story is a mythological history of the Ojibwa and is called "Mash-kwa-shakwong, or the Traditionary Story of the Red Head and his Two Sons." Toward the end of the myth, Nabinoi says:

> There was in those ancient times an annual meeting among the Indians, resembling the French New Year's Day, which was generally observed on the new moon's first appearance, Gitchy Monodo gesus. The Indians of our village would visit these of another, and sometimes meet one another dancing; and on those occasions they would exchange bows and arrows, their rude axes, awls, and kettles, and their clothing. This was an annual festival, which was duly observed by them. (Schoolcraft 1848, 115)

According to Verwyst, the Ojibwe name for January is *Kitchi-Manito-gisis* (Verwyst 1901, 409). This then would definitely place the celebration mentioned by Nabinoi as occurring sometime in January. Nabinoi also related that the festivities were observed "four generations ago." If one figures a generation to be thirty years, this would place the time as early in the eighteenth century. At that period many of the Odawa and the Ojibwe were resident at Mackinac Island and under the influence of the French. Later, around 1742, the Odawa at Mackinac Island moved to L'Arbre Croche because of overcrowding and exhaustion of the soil (Kinietz 1940, 230–31). Here, in the "land of the crooked tree," which their descendants still occupy, the Odawa were guided for over twenty years by Father du Jaunay, a remarkable man whose influence was so pronounced that the Odawa became almost completely converted to Catholicism.

It is interesting to note that the New Year–Epiphany custom in its modified form seems to have survived only among the Odawa of L'Arbre Croche (Harbor Springs–Cross Village area of Michigan). Gertrude Kurath, in her work with the Ojibwe of Mount Pleasant, Michigan, did not discover any memory of such a celebration. Near Baraga, in Michigan's Upper Peninsula, Gertrude questioned Thomas Shalifoe, eighty seven years old, who reported that the Ojibwe there have a children's beggar procession on New Year's Day and refer to the New Year as *nimkwadading* (a form of the word "to dance" and used by the Odawa for the entire week of festivities). Shalifoe also remembered a squaw dance that was formerly performed at the New Year. He said, however, that there were no other ceremonies observed at this time of year by the Ojibwe.

Since the custom has not been recorded recently among any of the other tribes in the area that came under French influence, we will have to infer, perhaps erroneously, that it is still in existence only among the Odawa, though the Upper Peninsula Ojibwe still retain some remnants of it.

The situation regarding the New Year–Epiphany celebrations would appear to be this: In the early eighteenth century the Odawa and Ojibwe who lived near French missions and forts adopted and modified the French custom of New Year greeting and gift giving. They were receptive to the idea partly because generosity and hospitality were esteemed as great virtues among them, so much so that a family might impoverish themselves so that a guest's every want might be supplied. (Kinietz 1940, 249) They were also receptive because of their great inclination toward feasting and celebrating on almost any occasion that seemed at all out of the ordinary. No doubt the constant insistence by French Catholic priests and such Frenchmen as Perrot that French ways were better than Indian also strongly influenced them.

That the influence was French seems assured because of the period in which the custom first appeared and because the New Year was celebrated similarly in France in the eighteenth century and, indeed, is still so observed in France today. The influence could also have been Austrian, for several of the Jesuit missionaries were Austrians.

Among the L'Arbre Croche Odawa, the custom probably grew in importance after the 1850s, when the Odawa began to give up their semi-sedentary life and to remain all year in their villages. This is probably why Blackbird does not describe as elaborate a celebration as that observed today. He writes of the custom for the period of the 1830s:

> At the New Year's eve, every one of the Indians used to go around visiting the principal men of the tribe, shooting their guns close to their doors after screaming three times, "Happy New Year," then bang, bang, bang, altogether, blowing their tin horns and beating their drums, etc. Early on the New Year's morning, they would go around among their neighbors expressly to shake hands one with another with the words of salutation, "Bozhoo," children and all. This practice was kept up for a long time, or until the white people came and intermingled with the tribes. (Blackbird 1897, 50)

During the 1850 period, the Odawa also began to give up completely their most sacred institutions, such as the Midéwiwin and the Wabeno, both of which are little more than vague memories today. Such ceremonies were once held in the early spring, often at the sugar camps in conjunction with Feasts of the Dead, Sun Ceremonies, Dream Dances, and many other festivities in which a beggars' procession played a part, at least in the early nineteenth century (Blackbird 1897, 45). It is quite possible that some features of the great spring festivities may have been transferred to the New Year–Epiphany celebrations at this time.

In what follows, Gertrude Kurath has prepared a list of the various features of the New Year–Epiphany celebrations, showing their provenance among certain neighboring tribes and in Europe, as well as among the Iroquois, [and found the celebrations] are mobile [with respect to the calendar], due to [variations in] the weather. Gertrude concludes from this that the Odawa New Year–Epiphany celebrations represent a survival of the Sun Ceremonies formerly held in the early spring.

It is my contention that in the eighteenth century, at least, the Odawa and the Ojibwe observed the New Year–Epiphany celebrations *in addition to* the early spring festivities, so that the former cannot be considered a substitute for the latter. I do believe, however, that as the spring festivities were discontinued in the nineteenth century, the Odawa clung to the New Year–Epiphany celebrations and may have even elaborated upon them in a last desperate effort to preserve something "Indian" among them.

Notes on the New Year Feasts[3]

Beggars' Procession

I have found no reference to beggars' processions or to masked doings for the early Odawa and Ojibwe. The nearest is Blackbird's nineteenth-century comment on the children who go about during early spring during the Feast of the Dead (Blackbird 1897, 45). This omission is strange, for I have found the following references from tribes to the east and the west.

Huron. Champlain observed, "They parade (frenzied medicine men) while the feast is being prepared for the maskers." In another place he describes "the beggar maskers, men and women, visiting each other's villages much as they (the Iroquois) now go from house to house at Midwinter." Sagard added an observation about their bearskin garb (Fenton 1951, 413).

Iroquois. Masks derived from Huron between 1648 and 1656 (Fenton 1951, 416).
 Beggar masks of modern ritual (Fenton 1941, 409–10).
 Spring and autumn housecleaning, receive tobacco—False Face Procession (Fenton 1941, 425–26).
 At Midwinter, "a band of outlandishly dressed little boys wearing beggar masks may visit . . . soliciting or pilfering food and tobacco for a feast" (Fenton 1951, 424).
 At Onondaga Valley, Nedrow, N.Y. False Face Procession is ten days after end of Midwinter festival, hence early February—maskers receive gifts of white and brown mush, bread, Indian tobacco. Children also make beggars' rounds on New Year's Eve.
 At Six Nations Reserve also children's rounds. False face procession at beginning of Midwinter festival, which may be early January (Onondaga) and early or middle February (Cayuga and Seneca).

Menominee. Dog or Beggars' Dance in spring at sugar camps, termed *anamow'iwin*, grotesque birchbark masks; beg sugar, tobacco, corn, syrup, gifts; dance property of Wolves' Society (Skinner 1915, 210–11).
 anamowin (Densmore 1932, 187–88)

Minnesota Ojibwe. Maple Sugar Begging Song (Densmore 1913, 231).

Garden River [Ojibwe] Reserve. Maple Sugar Begging Song (Burton 1909, 224).

Parry Island Ojibwe. Begging Dance, men and women. (Jenness 1935, 100).
Women's Dance at Sugar Festival, beg gifts.

Europe. Dance processions from house to house common in western Europe; feature noise, masks, begging. Most similar to Indian are in Austrian Alps. These are called *Perchten* (after pagan goddess Berchta, custodian of the dead) or *Schemen* (meaning "masked figure" or "apparition"). "Von Martini bis Aschermittwoch ziehen mannigfache Umzugsgruppen durch das Land . . . Sie wünschen Segen . . . und umhalten dafür Gaben" (Wolfram 1951, 45–54). The *Perchten* of Salzburg are identified with the "wild horde," leaps, staves. Perchtennacht is January 5–6. The dance is clockwise. Grotesque wooden masks, animals, white-painted faces, demons, called *Schlachten Perchten,* fight beautiful spirits, *Schönperchten.* At Carnival often *Schemen* with masks and *Faschingsläufer.* This is winter solstice magic to drive out evil spirits and ensure fertility and good crops.

Similar customs prevail in England and are associated with Sword Dances and in the spring with Morris Dances. Face blackening is featured.

In Czechoslovakia boys seek alms and sing songs (Duggan, et. al 1948, 98).[4]

Cake

Indigenous. No reference was found to cake associated with Midwinter rounds. False faces receive mush and bread. Iroquois have special cakes at their Feast for Dead, however (Fenton 1951, 147).

Europe. In France and Germany, Twelfth Night cake contains a bean or kernel of corn. He who got it was king, and the first slice was dedicated to God or Virgin Mary. In Estonia, cake is offered to the dead. In France, at Epiphany, there are parties with a large cake containing a small doll or effigy. Whoever finds it is king or queen, and a slice is saved for first beggar. At New Year, there are family reunions, feasting, and exchanges of gifts (Duggan et. al 1948, 134).

At Midsummer in Brittany, they bake cakes with images that bring good luck. There are processions, pilgrimages, and so-called "pardons" (the latter rather at Corpus Christi). At New Year, there is much feasting, but no dances.

Feasting

Feasting is widespread in America and Europe. Iroquois have communal feasts. Europeans hold family feasts at New Year.

Hand-shaking

This seems to be a European custom, not observed in ancient Indian references (Blackbird 1897, 50).

Association with the Dead

This is a feature of the Odawa Feast of the Dead and the Iroquois-Huron dance for the dead. In Europe, Twelfth Night maskers commonly represent ghosts.

Combat

Schoolcraft mentions this at indigenous Sugar Maple gatherings. Jane Ettawageshik relates that Odawa shooting on New Year's Eve is to "combat" the evil spirit. Combat was also a common feature of European Midwinter dances.

As for the dates of these events, early sources make no reference to Midwinter festivals among Michigan Indians. Maple Sugar gatherings are commonly mentioned. These combined many features—meetings of Wabeno, Midéwiwin, war dances, hilarity, feasting—and people came from near and far. Blackbird mentions a feast for the dead at maple sugar time (Blackbird 1897, 45). The dates of such Iroquois celebrations were variable.

In Europe, especially Austria, Midwinter doings lasted (and still do) from December 6 to Carnival, centered around Twelfth Night. In France, Carnival opens January 1. In warmer countries, such as Italy, such doings are always in January. In colder countries, like England, they are held in spring. Thus festivals of regeneration are movable, depending on climate.

Probably there has been no general Odawa Midwinter feast, though there may have been family gatherings for feasting. Maple Sugar camp meetings combined feastings, beggars' processions, war dances, and apparently also dead feasts. This would have coincided approximately with European Carnival. The date being movable among both the adjacent Iroquois and the distant Europeans, a shift from late February to Twelfth Night would have been simple.

Certainly, the present Odawa feast contains in attenuated form the essentials of the Austrian Midwinter processions, minus masks, the begging being the most evident feature. The cake is certainly derived from European prototypes.

Naming Ceremony[5]

Many of the Odawa still have their children christened with Indian names, though some have abandoned this custom. Names are given to children by a chief or other prominent person usually at the King's Supper or at the *Tabandáŋ*. Occasionally a child is named at one of the summer powwows. The naming ceremony is referred to as *Wiąwįsǫ* (He or She Will Get a Name).

The parents or grandparents choose the name, which is usually that of an ancestor but may also be selected because of some peculiar circumstance attending the birth of the child, his place of residence, etc. Children may be christened when they are babies or when they are in their teens. Even adults may be christened, and white persons are occasionally adopted and given Indian names. It is one of the latter adoptions that I will describe first, for I was fortunate enough to record a naming chant in connection with the ceremony.

The adoption was, in fact, my own, which occurred at the King's Supper in 1947, previous to my marriage to Fred Ettawageshik. Fred and I had eaten at the first "setting" of the table, and following the passing of the cakes, Fred arose, saying in Odawa that he had something to say. He took his horn rattle from his pocket and stood by Joe Kishigo, the host, drawing me over beside him. Fred made a speech in which he said that it had been decided to give me an Indian name because I had spent considerable time among their group the previous summer trying to record the fast-dying Indian customs and language. The name chosen he said was *Wabanókwe* (Dawn Lady or Lady from the East) because I came from the east. After a few concluding remarks, Fred turned to me, shaking his rattle, and said in a loud voice, "*wabanókwe dajánkaso!*" ("Shall be called *Wabanókwe!*")

Then he said quickly to me, in English, "Follow me!" and he started to dance forward in a step-hop step, shaking his rattle.

Fred's naming chant was recorded later in 1948, when I was in Harbor Springs on a field trip sponsored by the American Philosophical Society and had a wire recorder with me. Along with other songs and legends recorded then, the naming chant and Fred's speech announcing what the name would be are now a part of the record library of the American Philosophical Society. Gertrude Kurath supplied the musical transcription.

The dance that Fred and I did was of necessity short because at that time Kishigo's home was very small and there were many persons crowded together in one room. We simply danced across the room and back to our starting point, thus concluding the ceremony. Afterwards many of the guests congratulated me and came forward to shake my hand, called me *Wabanókwe*, and said words in Odawa that I could not understand. Fred and I left shortly afterwards and I felt that I really had become an Odawa. It was quite an occasion!

In 1950, at the *Tabandáŋ*, our little boy Frankie, eight and a half months, was named *Nakwegíšik* (Noon Day) after his grandfather, Joe Ettawageshik. The namer was Mitchell Mastaw, who also named a little girl at this time. There were certain differences noted in this ceremony as compared with my own. Mitchell, too, shook a rattle and said *"Dajánkaso"* ("Shall be called so-and-so") as he held Frankie, but before starting to dance forward, Mitchell waved his rattle to one side then another and the witnessing guests gave a shout of approval. Then he pointed his rattle toward the doorway opposite him and said, "Let the name go through!" Mitchell told me that he said this because it signified that the name would "go on and on," carried by Frankie throughout his lifetime, then by one of his sons and so on in future generations. Mitchell pointed his rattle toward the south in this part of the ceremony, but the direction was apparently meaningless.

At this ceremony, too, most of the guests joined in the dancing. The Kishigos, who helped give the feast, had enlarged their house, and the ceremony was conducted in the living room, where there was space enough for a number of persons to dance. Mitchell led the dance, of course, carrying Frankie, chanting, and shaking his rattle. Others, both men and women, followed him in step-hop-step in a clockwise circuit of the room. The same procedure was repeated when the little girl was named.

A person giving a name is called *énos"winkɛt,* while the one receiving the name is referred to as *wewąwisát.* A namer is usually a chief or prominent person in the Indian community, almost always an older man. When parents want to have a child christened, they usually visit the person they have chosen to name the child. They tell him that they would like to have him give their child such-and-such a name at the King's Supper, the *Tabandáŋ,* or occasionally at a summer powwow. If the namer is unable to perform the christening at the desired time, the event is either postponed or the parents choose someone else to do the naming.

At the christening the parents, of course, are always present as are a number of other relatives. If dancing follows the christening, the relatives always take part, and others present may join in also. No present or payment is made to the person giving the name or to the child, though formerly gifts were made both to the namer and to the child being christened.

In the old days a person was sometimes named as a result of the vision of the namer or of the parents, or because of the first things seen or heard following the birth of the child. There are few instances of this type of naming today. No one is referred to in ordinary conversation by his Indian name but is called by the Christian name given at his Catholic baptism or by an English or Odawa nickname. Nor are persons referred to by the relationship term, which may be implied in the names of ancestors that they take, such as "grandfather" or "aunt." The latter would seem to have been true at one time.

The table on the following page gives names of Indians in Harbor Springs and the vicinity, the namer, and the occasion on which the name was given.

In the list of names, where the occasion and the namer are in question, the bearer of the name was usually an older Indian who was probably named as a baby at a family gathering or at one of the village celebrations. One of the reasons that I was able to obtain relatively few Indian names is because so many of the Indians in the area are related so the same names recur in different families. As I have said, names are usually ancestral in origin.

I know of only one recent instance of a child among the Harbor Springs Odawa having been named apparently as the result of a vision. This occurred at the *Tabandáŋ* in April 1947, when Fred Ettawageshik named

Odawa Feasts 163

WOMEN'S NAMES	OCCASION	NAMER
Sǫdési·kwe	?	?
Adowákwe (Odawa Woman)	King's Supper	Father
Bi·mačınókwe (Lady Saves Lives)	King's Supper	Fred Ettawageshik
Šaŋgwéčıkwe (Mink Lady)	?	?
Pabjınókwe (Running Water Lady)	King's Supper	Fred Ettawageshik
Baktigókwe (Lady of the Rapids)	?	?
Wánkwe (Lady of the Mist)	*Tabandáŋ*	Mitchell Mastaw
Šıbósɛkwe (Lion Lady)	?	?
Masékwe (Walking Lady)	?	?
Bısékwɛ (Rise Up from Sitting Position)	?	?
Nigánbikwe (Leading Lady)	?	?
Šawanókwe (South Wind Lady)	?	?
Kò·'tagíjıgòkwe (Around the Sky Lady)	?	?
Ižıgátɛ (Moonlight)	Odawa Summer Powwow	Joe Chingwa (grandfather)
Naŋgókwe (Star Lady)	Family feast	grandfather

MEN'S NAMES	OCCASION	NAMER
Nódın (Wind)	?	?
Kɛtkómık (On Top of the Ground)	?	?
Nakwegíšık (Noonday)	*Tabandáŋ*	Mitchell Mastaw
Pipigwé (Little Hawk)	King's Supper	Alec Kishigo
Wasagíšık (Bright Sky)	?	?
Anamíkwam (Trouble)	?	?
Epangíšımo (West)	Odawa Summer Powwow	Joe Chingwa (grandfather)
Mabıs (Vine Growing on the Ground)	?	?
Pítčɛns (Little Robin)	*Tabandáŋ*	Fred Ettawageshik
Manísano (Warrior from Tribe)	?	Paternal grandfather
Čıŋ:wə (The Roar of the Storm)	?	?
Bódᵐse (Chicken Hawk)	?	?
Kagéčıwan (Everlasting River)	?	?
Mtígojiman (Wooden Boat)	?	?
Sawábık (Copper)	?	?

fourteen-year-old Don Davenport *Pítčɛns* (Little Robin). Donnie's maternal grandfather, who died previous to the event, had told Donnie's mother that *Pítčɛns* was to be Donnie's guardian spirit and that if Donnie should ever find a coin in his fried cake at the King's Supper he should be christened with this name. Donnie got the nickel, I believe it was, in his cake that year, and so some time before the *Tabandáŋ* his mother asked Fred to perform the naming ceremony. It seemed a very appropriate name, too, for Donnie at the time was a round, fat little boy with very light tan skin and bright red cheeks.

Another case of a modern christening performed under unusual circumstances was that of Dorothy Sagataw, now about twenty years of age. When Dorothy was a baby, her parents took her to visit her paternal grandfather, an Ojibwe medicine man from Stonington, in the Upper Peninsula of Michigan. Dorothy cried so much during the visit that the old man suggested that if she had an Indian name it might quiet her.

The grandfather set about making hominy soup, *pinagsíginak*, chanting as he cooked it. Then with the help of the women present, he prepared a feast for the entire family. Before anyone started to eat, the old man took Dorothy in his arms and danced around the table, singing his own personal song, which he always sang on ceremonial occasions. He bestowed on Dorothy the name *Naŋgókwe* (Star Lady).

There have, of course, been a number of changes made in the naming ceremony performed by the Odawa today as compared with the early accounts of such occasions. One of the most notable changes is the lack of gift giving in the modern ceremony. Here is Perrot's account of the naming feast among the Odawa and related tribes:

> When a child, either boy or girl, has reached the age of five or six months, the father and mother make a feast with the best provisions that they have, to which they invite a juggler with five or six of his disciples . . . The father of the family addresses him, and tells him that he is invited in order to pierce the nose and ears of his child; and that he is offering this feast to the sun, or to some other pretended divinity whose name he mentions, entreating that divinity to take pity on his child and preserve its life. The juggler then replies, according to custom, and makes his invocation to the spirit whom the father has chosen. Food is presented to this man and his disciples, and if any is left they are permitted to carry it away with them. When they have finished their meal, the mother of the child places before the guests some peltries, kettles, or other wares, and places her child in the arms of the juggler, who gives it to one of his disciples to hold. After he has ended his song in honor of the spirit invoked, he takes from his pouch a flat bodkin made of bone, and a stout awl, and with the former pierces both ears of the child, and with the awl its nose. He fills the wounds in the ears with little rolls of bark, and in the nose he places the end of a small quill, and leaves it there until the wound is healed by a certain ointment with which he dresses it. When it has healed, he places in the aperture some down of the swan or the wild goose. (Kinietz 1940, 276)

This account does not, of course, specifically say that a name was given the child at this time, though one would suppose this to have been the case. Charlevoix described a somewhat different ceremony:

> The act which terminates their state of infancy is the imposition of the name, which amongst the Indians is a matter of great importance. This ceremony is performed at a feast, at which are present none but persons of the same sex with the child that is to be named; during the repast the child remains on the knees of its father or mother, who are incessantly recommending it to the genii, and above all to him who is to be guardian, for each person has one, but not from the time of birth; they never invent new names, each family preserves a certain number of them, which they make use of by turns; they even sometimes change them as they grow older, and there are some which cannot be used after a certain age, but I do not believe this practice to be universal; and as it is the custom amongst some nations on assuming a name, to put themselves in the place of the person who last bore it, it sometimes happens that a child is called grandfather by a person, who might well enough be his own.
>
> They never call a man by his own name when they speak to him in a familiar manner; this would be a piece of great impoliteness, they always name him by the relation he bears to the person that speaks to him; but when there is neither affinity nor consanguinity between them, they call one another brother, uncle, nephew, or cousin, according to the age of either, or in proportion to the esteem in which they hold the person to whom they address themselves.
>
> Farther, it is not so much with a view to perpetuating names that they renew them, as with a view to incite the person on whom they are bestowed, either to imitate the great actions of the persons that bore them, or to revenge them in case they have been killed or burned; or lastly to comfort their families: thus a woman who has lost her husband or her son, and finds herself thus void of all support makes all the haste in her power, to give the name of the person she mourns for to some one who may stand her in his stead; lastly, they likewise change their names on several other occasions, which it would take up too much time to mention minutely. In order to do this there wants only a dream, or the prescription of some physician, or some other reason equally frivolous. (Kinietz 1940, 277–78)

The ceremony described by Charlevoix, which was attended only by members of the same sex, seems to have followed a puberty fast, as the child's guardian spirit is mentioned. Nowadays, the puberty fast is a thing of the past, and an Odawa is lucky if he receives one Indian name, let alone several of them.

According to Joe Chingwa, it was customary in the nineteenth century for a father to choose the name for his child. He was influenced in his choice by the first thing seen or heard following the birth of the baby. The name Chingwa, for instance, which is a family name now, was originally picked for Joe Chingwa's paternal grandfather by his father because it was storming when the baby was born. Chingwa (*čingw*) means "the roar of the storm—the rumble of thunder and the vibration of the earth." Such a name would have been bestowed on the baby when he was several months old at a naming feast conducted by a chanter.

The Payoff Feast

As previously mentioned, the *Tabandáŋ*, or "Payoff Feast," is given by the person who receives the dime in his fried cake at the King's Supper on Epiphany. As there is only one King's Supper given in Harbor Springs today, there is, of course, only one payoff feast. It is given just before or just after Lent.

Soon after the King's Supper, the prospective host and those who have found the nickel and the penny in their fried cakes get together to discuss the date for the Tabandáŋ. When the time for the supper is established, the host obtains the list of those who have received beans from Elizabeth Kishigo. As the date approaches, the three "kings" (i.e., those who received the coins) or their female relatives busy themselves with preparations for the feast. The host may call on those who have received beans to aid him, and he has a right to expect them to bring some food for the occasion. The only requirement as to food is that corn soup must be served, especially *wiškobíminak,* the parched corn soup.

Word soon gets around the community that there is to be a *Tabandáŋ* on such and such a date. Attendance at such a supper is usually larger than at the King's Supper, for all those who received beans may invite guests, and in practice guests may be brought by anyone.

The *Tabandáŋ* is a very informal affair and is never spoken of with reverence as is the King's Supper. In recent years the *Tabandáŋ* has often been given in the basement of a nearby Town Hall, followed by square and round dancing upstairs. When I mentioned the informality of one of these affairs at the Town Hall to Dave Kenosha, he said, "Oh, yes, after all, it's just the *Tabandáŋ*."

When the feast is given in a private home, the procedure followed is similar to that at the King's Supper, except, of course, that the *bojoing* and handshaking are omitted. When it is given in the Town Hall, it resembles a church social. There is occasionally square dancing in the homes also, if there happen to be enough musicians present, although most homes are too small for much dancing.

The first *Tabandáŋ* I attended was given in May 1948. It had been considerably delayed because the hostess was living in Detroit and had difficulty getting up to Harbor Springs for the event. The supper was given at her uncle's house (Joe Kishigo) and was really managed by Elizabeth Kishigo and her sister-in-law, Amelia, the hostess's mother. Like all modern Odawa feasts, the supper began promptly at 6:00 P.M. and there were a number of settings at the table.

With the consent of Elizabeth Kishigo, I took the American Philosophical Society wire recorder with me to the supper and made a recording of a part of the conversation during the event. This is now a part of the record library of the American Philosophical Society. The quips and comments of Joe Kishigo stand out in this recording and are just as comic now as they were then. The conversation is in the strange admixture of Odawa and English that one hears at such affairs.

Following the supper, I asked if the group would sing some Odawa hymns, though of course this is not regularly a feature of the *Tabandáŋ*. The suggestion, however, was met with enthusiasm. Elizabeth Kishigo got out her old hymnal; her sister, Hattie Sagataw, rushed home to get hers. Soon Hattie was playing the piano (by ear, for the tunes of these old hymns are not recorded in the old hymnals), and as the Indians warmed up to the task, more and more of them joined in the singing. We all had a very good time and the occasion has been mentioned to me several times since by Indians who were there. Certainly it does seem that singing should always be a part of such Indian gatherings.[6]

The term used for this supper, *Tabandáŋ*, appears to be an old Anishinaabe term for feast. Champlain in 1612 mentions attending *une solemnelle tabagie* among Anishinaabe Indians (Champlain 1929, 3:253). In fact, Champlain uses this term several times in his *Voyages* to refer to a feast, whether it be Anishinaabe or Huron. Although the term is somewhat different from the present one, Fred Ettawageshik says that it is derived from the same stem, meaning "to reciprocate or pay off."

Such a term for a feast is very appropriate among the Odawa, for a feast was very often given as a means of "paying" for something. Thus, the bear feast paid the bear for his kindness in letting himself be killed, a man paid his manido for his cure in sickness by giving a feast, etc. It is also a part of Odawa custom to return favor for favor; thus those who brought gifts for the deceased at the time of his death were paid back later by the family with gifts and a feast (Kinietz 1940, 281).

It seems that at the present day the numerous *tabagies* mentioned by Champlain are preserved only in the *Tabandáŋ* and the few other suppers still given by the Odawa.

It is possible that the entire cycle—New Year, Epiphany, *Tabandáŋ*—may represent survivals of the ancient Sun Ceremonies among the Odawa, as Gertrude Kurath believes. The *Tabandáŋ* itself, especially when given after Lent, corresponds in time to the spring festivities described by Blackbird (Blackbird 1897, 45). There is no reference other than Shurtleff's to the *Tabandáŋ* in its present form, so we have no way of knowing for how many years the Odawa have observed it (Shurtleff 1940, 36). It seems probable to me that with the passing of sun worship, along with the Midéwiwin and the Wabeno, the Odawa may have added the *Tabandáŋ* feast to the New Year–Epiphany celebration in its present form.

Huckleberry Feast

Until very recently the Odawa at Cross Village celebrated a huckleberry feast, according to Shurtleff. Such a feast was apparently not remembered by any of the Odawa who were my informants. Of this feast, Shurtleff writes:

> Another feast which was formerly observed but is gradually being forgotten is the huckleberry feast. This was held early in July when the blueberries, or huckleberries, were beginning to ripen. Usually on Sunday the Indians would walk out to the sand plains to the northeast of the village, and gather small pails of the first berries. On the following day a group of men assembled at the cemeteries and cut the grass and weeds. Then the women brought the pails of berries. All seated themselves in the cemetery, and ate some of the berries, and left some on the graves for the dead to eat. (Shurtleff 1940, 37)

Such first fruits ceremonies are obviously very ancient with the Odawa, as they are with other Anishinaabe tribes. Densmore (1929, 124) writes that they are still held by the Minnesota Ojibwe, and Kinietz (1947) mentions them at Lac Vieux Desert in Michigan's Upper Peninsula.

Ceremonies connected with first fruits varied from such simple celebrations as that mentioned by Shurtleff to the elaborate Odawa bear feast described by Perrot in the seventeenth century. They were all designed to give thanks to the manidos for their blessings made evident by the harvest or by success in hunting or fishing. In the case of animals the feasts were given also to placate the beasts for the loss of some of their "relatives" and to insure future success in hunting. The ghosts, who were ever in the minds of the Odawa, were frequently included in the feast by means of food offerings in the fire or, as in the huckleberry feast, through food placed on the graves.

Corpus Christi

After the defeat of the French in the French and Indian Wars, the Odawa of L'Arbre Croche were without missionaries until the Catholics reestablished a mission at Seven Mile Point in 1827. This was soon followed by a mission at Cross Village. Many of the Indians who were said to have "reverted to paganism" in the absence of priests soon became converted to model Christians, celebrating the Catholic Holy Days with fervor. Corpus Christi was an important event and is described by Shurtleff in Cross Village:

> In the early history of the town the celebration of Corpus Christi was the most colorful event of the year. This celebration greatly resembled the pageantry of this day, and other religious festivals, in South America at the present time. In preparation for this day tall fir poles were set up at intervals in the streets. The branches had been removed from these trees, except for a few inches at the top where the tip of the tree still remained. These poles were connected by ropes on which were attached all the gay and gaudy fabrics at the command of the natives. Arrayed side by side between the poles might be found bright plaid shawls, lengths of gaudy calico, and quilts with a predominance of turkey red. Several booths of shrines were set up along the streets where the procession was to pass. The line was formed after preliminary service in the church, and as it passed through the streets stops were made at the various shrines, and then the procession returned to the church. In later years these processions took place only on the church grounds. (Shurtleff 1940, 38–39)

Gertrude Kurath compares this observance of Corpus Christi with the Argentine Sumamao celebration on the day of San Estaban, December

26, "which in South American would equate with the summer solstice in Michigan, that is approximately Corpus Christi." Kurath writes in an entry on the same in the *Standard Dictionary of Folklore:*

> On the day of San Estaban, December 26, el santo, the image of the saint, is placed on an altar . . . An avenue of arcos leads up to the altar, i.e. trees stripped of their branches except for a tuft on top, and coupled into arcos or arches by cords hung with ichas (cakes in puppet form) . . . During the third part, la Quila (generous gift), the populace demolishes the arcos, seizes the ichas, and feasts on them.

Gertrude tells me further that "the Sumamao is a vestige of a pagan harvest rite. The seizing of the cakes reminds one of the Iroquois elevation of the cakes at the end of the Dead Feast."

At the present day Corpus Christi is celebrated only by church members.

Ghost Suppers or Feast of the Dead

Beginning on November 1, the Odawa in Harbor Springs and vicinity have a series of Ghost Suppers, or *Jibiyasé' kwewak'* (They are Cooking for the Spirits), lasting until November 7. They are given in memory of the deceased and the guests are thought to represent ghosts and to be eating for them. Some also believe that the ghosts themselves attend the suppers. Stories are told of persons who have seen ghosts going to a supper or heard them rattling the dishes on the table. Fred Ettawageshik writes:

> The Indians go from one supper to the other, until they have made the rounds. Etiquette requires that they eat at least a little of each kind of food offered. After the last guest has been served, the remaining food is left on the table until midnight, or in some cases until morning so that the spirits may come and feast. . . . Some of the older Indians who are imbued with a profound belief in the significance of this custom have claimed to have heard the dishes rattling after everyone had retired for the night, saying that the spirits had come and feasted. Others have seen apparitions of people preceding them on their way to these suppers. There is the story, and a true one, of a man while passing an old burial ground, having seen a group of people going ahead of him on his way to a "Ghost Supper." Thinking that here was a chance for some company, he tried to overtake them,

but no matter how fast he walked, they remained always the same distance ahead of him. Then his attention was attracted from the rear, and when he looked again, the people in front had disappeared from view. He said that they were near enough so that, had they been real people, they could not possibly have gotten out of sight so soon (Fred Ettawageshik 492–93).

Elizabeth Kishigo adds:

The souls are free from Hallowe'en to November 2. Spirits come as a wind passing about one and a half feet from the ground. They must be fed or they pass on to the next house. The food eaten is in memory of the dead.

The order of events at a Ghost Supper and preceding it are the following:

I. Decoration of Graves (on All Saints' Day)
   - Wooden crosses at head of graves repainted white or replaced by new ones
   - Wreaths of wire and crepe paper made and placed on the cross
   - Food left on the graves (rarely now)
II. Ghost Suppers (from November 1 to 7)
   - First setting of table in individual homes at 6:00 P.M. for about ten persons. They are usually invited by card or orally by host and should be the same age and sex as departed relatives—"take their places."
   - Other guests at subsequent settings are unidentified "ghosts." They are expected to eat a little of everything. Corn soup made with Indian corn always served.
   - If any food remains after the supper, it is left on the table until morning for any "ghosts" who may not be satisfied.

Some time before All Saint's Day the family graves and crosses are inspected. The grass on the graves may be cut, old paper wreaths are removed from the crosses, and the crosses may be repainted. If the crosses are rotting away, new crosses are made to be placed on the graves with paper wreaths on All Saint's Day. On this day, too, a very few families in Burt Lake and in Harbor Springs still follow the old custom of leaving food on the graves of relatives. One family in Harbor Springs places a little candy on the grave of a beloved child.

The job of making and painting the crosses falls to the men. The white crosses (*jibiatigók*') placed on Indian graves are usually about six feet long with a crosspiece of approximately two feet. My husband, Fred, has made many of these crosses for friends and relatives because he has machinery designed for woodcutting and shaping. The crosses replace the wooden markers showing the inverted totem of the deceased, which are still used by many Ojibwe and other Anishinaabe tribes.

I recall one cross Fred made for a funeral in the Gasco family, our neighbors at that time. Fred was not requested to make the cross until the day before the funeral and as he was busy, he did not complete it until evening. None of the Gasco family offered to paint the cross, so Fred applied one coating of white paint. Unfortunately, the paint was not quite dry in time for the funeral, but one of the men in the Gasco family carried the cross in the funeral procession anyway.[7]

The work of making wreaths is undertaken by women. Wreaths are called simply *wawaskonéyan* (flowers). Of the wreath-making in Cross Village, Shurtleff writes:

> For weeks before this day (November 1) the women and girls spend much of their time making the wreaths which are to be used for decorating. The wreaths are made on a foundation of wire about eight or ten inches in diameter, wound with colored paper, and closely circled with paper flowers. Before the manufacture of crepe paper, these flowers were made of tissue paper, which kept its color for many weeks. Now they are made chiefly of crepe paper, which tends to fade more quickly. Attached to the wreaths are streamers of paper about three or four inches in width and about two feet in length.
>
> On the morning of November 1, the Indian women may be seen hurrying through the streets with bundles under their shawls. Upon arriving at the cemeteries, they remove the bleached remains of the wreaths of the previous year, and place on the crosses the gay new wreaths. By afternoon the cemetery is a riot of color, and the slightest breeze adds much to the spectacle. It is traditional in the village that it is certain either to rain or snow on November 1, thus hastening the process of bleaching the wreaths. The Indians believe that the dead wear the wreaths which they have placed on the crosses; and the living often dream of seeing them thus adorned. (Shurtleff 1940, 37–38)

On the evening of All Saints' Day there will be at least one Ghost Supper given in Harbor Springs and possibly several. A few of the guests are special and receive invitations; word simply gets around to others, who come or not as they desire. The specially invited guests represent certain departed relatives of whom the hosts are thinking especially. They should be about the same age and the same sex as the departed. If the deceased was a child, the child who represents him will be urged to eat candy and other foods he may have especially liked. Or perhaps a man might be served a certain kind of wine because the departed relative he represents was fond of it. Besides these special foods or beverages, the invited guests, like all other guests, are expected to eat a little of everything else that is served.

The specially invited guests are not told which ancestors they represent. Sometimes the guest himself decides this. Thus, old Victoria Cooper told me when we invited her to a Ghost Supper in 1949 that she would be my husband's mother. We have been invited several times to Ghost Suppers by card or orally by some member of the host's family. Even if the time of day is not specified, we always know that we should be there at 6:00 P.M. for the first setting of the table, for the invited guests are always served first.

The host always sits at the head of the table, while the guests are seated in no particular order. After the host says the Catholic Grace Before Meals in Odawa, bowls of food are placed on the table by the host's wife and her female assistants, usually relatives. Frequently a large kettle or bowl of *wiškobíminak*, parched corn soup, occupies the center of the table.

As at all modern Odawa feasts, the only food required is corn soup. Of the myriad other foods a host must supply, even a partial listing makes it obvious that such suppers are usually costly affairs. At the Ghost Supper that Fred and I gave in 1949, assisted by my sister-in-law Julia Black, we served, among other dishes, *wiškobíminak*, chicken, meat loaf, hubbard squash, carrots, lettuce and tomatoes, cole slaw, pickled beets, cucumbers, celery, mashed potatoes, potato salad, spaghetti, relishes and jellies, bread, pies, cakes, jello, beverages, and candies. We fed almost sixty persons and had very little left over to leave on the table for any dissatisfied ghost who might call during the night!

This is quite the customary type of menu for a ghost supper. Sometimes it is augmented by venison, rabbit, porcupine, duck, or other meat that may have been recently shot by the host or canned by his wife the year before. One must have a variety of foods so that the palates of all the ghosts will be pleased. Every guest is expected to take a little of each kind of food served.

Of course, there is a certain amount of "keeping up with the Joneses" involved in the giving of a Ghost Supper. No one wants to appear less able than his neighbor to give a fine supper honoring his departed ones. Some families impoverish themselves for weeks in order to have the very best supper possible.

Many of the "ghosts" at a Ghost Supper are experts on the subject, for they will go from house to house where the suppers are being given and may also attend other suppers throughout the week. Any guest is always welcome. Dogs and cats, however, are not. Victoria Cooper rebuked me sharply for giving some scraps to a starving cat that ran into our kitchen during our Ghost Supper. To the old people, at least, the food is reserved only for the human ghosts whom they represent. Shortly after eating, the guests prepare to leave and are expected to compliment the host on the fine supper and thank the hostess.

Although there is laughter and often a great deal of conversation and visiting at a Ghost Supper, I have never witnessed dancing and singing as reported by Louise J. Walker. Nor is there a procession to the cemetery on All Saints' Day in Harbor Springs or Cross Village today. Walker writes of the Cross Village ceremony:

> Except for the women who cannot leave the kettles, a few old men and women, and those who are sick, practically every Indian in the vicinity walks in the procession. When the services at the cemetery are over, the Indians give themselves up with utter abandon to visiting, dancing, and feasting. For many of them, these days are a homecoming and their only opportunity to see friends who are distantly located. (L. Walker 1949, 428)

Both the procession and the dancing mentioned have not been in practice in the memory of my husband, who is fifty-eight and was born in Harbor Springs. Old Victoria Cooper, however, remembers that there used to be dancing at Ghost Suppers but cannot describe any of the dances.

Wright, describing the ceremony for the early twentieth century, says that the dancing and singing accompanied the feasting. He calls the feast *Tu-san-wung*, derived from the French "Tout Saints." He writes:

> When the repast was about half over, all present would repair to some high eminence and build a fire, around which they would dance and shout at the top of their voices; occasionally the men would go to the edge of the hill and shoot volleys up into the air, with the words, "amo awda," "Let us drive him away!" referring to the evil spirit. After the atmosphere was thought to be cleared, the natives would go back and finish their feast.
>
> Those who gave it invited, besides others, one person for each dead relative they had. These especially favored ones were supposed to personify the departed relatives, and the more they ate the better were the host and hostess pleased. Food was also placed on the graves, and if in

a few days it had disappeared, it was a token that the dead were pleased and had eaten it; if it still remained at the end of a certain period, it was said that the spirits were angry and another feast would have to be given to satisfy them. The one who found a bean or a small coin that was previously placed in cookies that were passed at the table, would be the one to give the next feast. (Wright 1917, 87–88)

Wright's is the only reference I have seen to the passing of special cakes or cookies at an Odawa Ghost Supper. The baking of beans and coins in small fried cakes is reminiscent of the practice at the King's Supper on Epiphany, the one who finds the dime being the host at a return feast. One might be tempted to believe that Wright had confused the two ceremonies (he does not mention the New Year-Epiphany celebration) were it not for the fact that he was part Odawa and must have participated in Ghost Suppers himself.

The association of cakes with the dead is, however, not at all unusual as Gertrude Kurath points out. Gertrude writes me that specially baked cakes or breads are made by the Iroquois at the Feast of the Dead held in the autumn and that in some European countries cake is offered to the dead at this time of year also. None of the modern Odawa, however, have any memory of such cakes or cookies at a Ghost Supper.

Wright also refers to the shooting of the evil spirit at the Ghost Supper or Feast of the Dead. This custom, too, is now associated with the celebration of the New Year in Harbor Springs, but it seems to have considerable antiquity at the Feast of the Dead, for seventeenth century accounts refer to shooting and wild yelling at this time.

The lighting of a fire and the dancing and singing mentioned by Wright are also survivals of older practices. One wonders if on such an occasion the Odawa might not have sung and danced to the Ghost Song Joe Chingwa sang for me in 1948. Joe thought that this was possible himself. The song was recorded and the words translated by Joe at that time for the American Philosophical Society collection. Gertrude Kurath has made the following transcription:

ndasánəwɛs
I am playing

yaia   wiya   ya´iya ya wiya
is here somebody is here somebody

ndasánəwɛs ndasánəwɛs
I am playing I am playing

In all probability this song and others now forgotten were sung and danced when the Odawa celebrated their Feast of the Dead in Blackbird's youth in the early nineteenth century. At that time, the ceremonies were held in the early spring in conjunction with the Midéwiwin, the Wabeno, Sun Ceremonies, and other festivities. At some time in the nineteenth century, then, the Odawa must have transferred their Feast of the Dead to November in order to conform with Christian practice. Blackbird writes:

> Early in the spring we used to come down this beautiful stream of water (Muskegon River). In our long bark canoes, loaded with sugar, furs, deer skins, prepared venison for summer use, bear's oil, and bear meat prepared in oil, deer tallow, and sometimes a lot of honey, etc. On reaching the mouth of this river we halted for five or six days, when all the other Indians gathered, as was customary, expressly to feast for the dead. All the Indians and children used to go around among the camps and salute one another with the words, "Ne-baw-baw-tche-baw-yew," that is to say, "I am or we are going around as spirits," feasting and throwing food into the fire—as they believe the spirits of the dead take the victuals and eat as they are consumed in the fire.
>
> After the feast of the dead, we would all start for L'Arbre Croche, our summer resort, to plant our corn and other vegetables. At the crossing of Little Traverse Bay at the point called "Kitche-ossening," that is to say, "on the big rock," all the Indians waited until all the canoes arrived, after which they would all start together in crossing the bay. When about half way across they would begin to salute Arbor Croche by shooting with guns, holding them close to the water in order that the sound might reach to each side of the bay, to be heard by those few who always made their winter quarters around Little Traverse Bay . . . After all the Indians arrived and settled down, they would again have a prolonged merriment and another feasting of the dead and peace offerings. Grand medicine dances, fire dances, and many other jubilant performances my people would have before they would go to work again to plant their corn. I distinctly remember

the time, and I have seen my brothers and myself dancing around the fires in our great wigwam, which had two fireplaces inside of it. (Blackbird 1897, 45–46)

John Tanner, writing earlier in the nineteenth century, has a brief note about the Feast of the Dead, but does not mention at what time of year it was held:

Je-bi-naw-ka-win. Feast of the Dead. This feast is eaten at the graves of their deceased friends. They kindle a fire, and each person, before he begins to eat, cuts off a small piece of meat, which he casts into the fire. The smoke and smell of this, they say, attracts the Je-bi to come and eat with them. (Tanner 1830, 2:286)

Gertrude Kurath has found several references to a Feast of the Dead in a work of Father Baraga's, in which he speaks of food being eaten on the graves of departed friends and relatives. Baraga also mentions that the Indians sang and danced at such a time and that the spirits of the dead saw them and rejoiced (Baraga 1837, 294).

The best description of the ancient Odawa Feast of the Dead, of which the modern Ghost Supper is the only survival, is that of Cadillac. He writes about the custom as he found it among the Huron and the Odawa who were living at Mackinac Island in the early eighteenth century:

This is the way in which they hold their feasts for the dead. They erect a hut about one hundred and twenty feet long, with new bark which never has been used before. They set up a maypole at each end and another in the middle, taller than the others. These poles are oiled, greased, and painted; at the top of each is a prize, which belongs to the person who can first reach it and touch it with his hand. They then enter this new hut, in which there are several tiers, and bring the bones of their relatives, in small bags or wrapped very neatly in strips of bark. They set them out then, from one end to the other, and heap gifts upon them of all their finest and best possessions, and generally whatever they have got together in the previous three years. Meanwhile, the cooking pots are constantly on the fire, full of meat, for anyone to eat who likes. They make a continual noise, night and day, with drums or by striking the pots or the strips of bark with sticks. They go out from time to time and surround the hut, firing muskets and howling until the whole air quivers; then they re-enter, bedaubed with black. Finally, the same tumult goes on for three days and three nights; but, before the time has quite expired, they make presents to those who have been invited to the feast of all that belongs to the dead, that is, of all the booty with which the bones were covered. When this has been distributed they go out for the last time and surround the hut, uttering great howls; they fall upon it with heavy blows with sticks and poles, making a desperate clatter, and break all the bark in pieces. When that is done, the women are ready with faggots of fir-branches, and they put a layer of them on the ground from one end to the other of the place where the hut was. At the same time they kill a large number of dogs, which are to them what sheep are to us, and are valued by them more than any other animal, and make a feast of them. But, before eating, they set up two great poles and fasten a dog to the top of them, which they sacrifice to the sun and the moon, praying to them to have pity and to take care of the souls of their relations, to light them on their journeys, and to guide them to the dwelling place of their ancestors. This idea proves that they believe in the immortality of the soul. The feast being thus concluded, each takes the bones of his relations; they carry them all in their hands and take them to stony places, hollow, rugged, and unfrequented; they leave them there, and that is the end of the ceremony. After that, the dead whose feast they have held are never spoken of again in any way, and they remain in perpetual oblivion. (Kinietz 1940, 283–84)

Seventeenth-century authorities differ somewhat in their descriptions of the Great Feast of the Dead, some saying, for instance, that it was held every year, others that the interval was three years. Secondary burial in a cave or large pit is usually a feature of the ceremony, yet strangely enough Perrot's excellent description omits it. Unlike many of the other observers, Perrot tells us that the Feast of the Dead was held in the spring, as it was in Blackbird's youth.

It seems quite probable that in the late seventeenth century, some of the Anishinaabe bands were already changing the pattern of the Feast of the Dead. Indeed there is evidence even in early seventeenth-century reports that the custom had reached its height throughout the entire area where it was observed and was already on the way out. Brebeuf for the Huron speaks of dissension, which caused some villages to hold their ceremony separately, although it was considered preferable for all villages to participate in the feast and to invite neighboring tribes. Thus it was believed that the Huron villages were united with each other and with other tribes even as the bones of their ancestors were united in secondary burial (Kinietz 1940, 110).

By the end of the century we find that the Huron who were with the Odawa at Mackinac were giving their feast every three years instead of the customary Huron period of ten to twelve years. Among the Odawa whom Perrot knew, the feast had shrunk in magnitude from an inter-tribal affair to a village ceremony held annually. Perrot reported that the French were urging the Odawa to give up the custom because it was too costly. Many of them had already apparently ceased to include secondary burial as a feature of the feast.

Certainly by the time of the French and Indian Wars, the Ojibwe appear to have forgotten many of the features of the ceremony, which were probably included in their Feasts of the Dead at an earlier time. Thus Wawatam and his Ojibwe friends, who adopted Alexander Henry, were unable to offer any satisfactory explanation for the multitude of human bones found in the cave on Mackinac Island in which Henry hid (McCoy 1945, 148–49). If the Feast of the Dead with secondary burial had been practiced within the memory of any of the Ojibwe associated with Henry, they could surely have described the custom to him.

One must look to archaeology for a picture of the antiquity and possible early distribution of the Feast of the Dead. Unfortunately, there are few known sites at which such a specific practice can clearly be demonstrated. Greenman considered the Younge site in southeastern Michigan an ancient Huron or Huron-like burial ground because of the arrangement of the skeletons and disarticulated bones, and also because of the odd placement of the post holes surrounding the bones. Most of the burials were secondary and many of the leg and arm bones were perforated, probably showing that they had been hung up for display before reburial. The post holes immediately suggested to Greenman the long scaffolds that Brebeuf describes at the Huron Feast of the Dead, which were erected along the edge of the large burial pit. Gifts were placed on the scaffolds and the bones tied in fur robes were hung from poles attached to the scaffolds. Fully articulated skeletons were placed beneath the scaffolds and covered with gifts of robes, beads, axes, etc. At the appointed time, the bones were dropped into the pit, the skeletons were carefully lowered, and the gifts were placed over all (Kinietz 1940, 115–16).

Greenman estimates the age of the Younge site to be not more than two to three hundred years before the discovery of America. He equates it in time, roughly, with the Owasco focus in New York. Human remains and burial types are also similar to those at a site on the shore of Lake St. Clair, near Mt. Clemens, Michigan (Greenman 1937, 91–96).

Schoolcraft describes several burial grounds he inspected which may have been connected with the Feats of the Dead. One of these, on Isle Ronde at the western extremity of Lake Huron, contained many human bones that "appeared to have been gathered from their first or ordinary place of sepulture and placed in this rude mausoleum" (Schoolcraft 1848, 319). The skeletons were all buried longitudinally, arranged in order in a wide grave or trench. They were laid north to south instead of west to east, the latter being the custom of the Ojibwe in Schoolcraft's day. Ojibwe Indians whom Schoolcraft questioned concerning the site had no explanation to offer. One, however, said he believed the burial ground to be contemporaneous with the bones in the caves of Mackinac Island.

Another mass burial was examined by Schoolcraft north of the head of Lake Ontario, forty-two miles from Dundas in Ontario, Canada. Here he found long, wide trenches and rude vaults containing many secondary burials, as well as implements and large brass kettles (Schoolcraft 1848, 325). The brass kettles, of course, would date this as a post-contact site.

Other sites that quite probably could be explained by the Feast of the Dead are the ossuaries at Moyaone and at Piscataway Creek, where there were known villages and forts of the Powhatan Confederacy in the early seventeenth century. Of these and other similar sites in coastal Maryland and Delaware and in Virginia, Karl Schmitt writes: "A last holdover of mound burial, but now developed into a definite ossuary type of burial, may occur in the Piedmont region of Virginia, as evidenced by the excavation of Thomas Jefferson" (Schmitt, 67–70).

Most ossuaries, Schmitt writes, predate contact, while the later sites include European artifacts. Also found in some ossuaries are shell masks, some of the "weeping" or "lightning eye" type attributed to the southern death cult. The practice of secondary burial of disarticulated bones is found in the mountain and Piedmont areas in the Middle Woodland Period and was apparently diffusing to the coast. Schmitt feels that the ossuary type burial may represent a continuation of an initially Hopewellian practice (Schmitt, 68).

If Schmitt is correct and the archaeological sites he mentions do represent evidence of the Feast of the Dead complex, we may assume, perhaps fancifully, a history of the ceremony to be:

1. Out of the Hopewellian mound complex toward the end of its glory was born a great preoccupation with the dead and the belief that the dead must be buried with great ceremony in one communal spot.
2. Tribes who were moving north and east were either descendants of the Hopewell people or influenced by them. For some reason these tribes ceased to erect mounds for burial and instead developed the Feast of the Dead type of ceremony. Such tribes became semi-sedentary, living in areas where the soil or the game might become exhausted, necessitating the removal of villages to new locations.

Before removal, the old village site was cleansed and purified by removing all of the dead from scaffolds or graves and re-burying them ceremonially in a common pit, trench, or cave. Gradually the practice became compulsory after the lapse of a certain number of years—ten to twelve among the Huron, three among the Odawa, etc.

3. By the time the Huron reached their northern Ontario home, where they were found by Champlain, they had developed the Feast of the Dead into an elaborate complex, the most important of all their ceremonies, and a means of rekindling and proclaiming the spirit of unity among the various Huron villages as well as with neighboring tribes (Kinietz 1940, 100). Such tribes as the Neutral and Tobacco Nations and the Potawatomi probably also considered the ceremony of prime importance. Toward the east, the tribes of the Piedmont spread the ceremony as far as the Atlantic coast.

4. The Odawa and Ojibwe, pushing west and south to the northern Great Lakes and carrying a simple culture typical of the northeast where the Feast of the Dead was unknown (Cooper 1934, 279), adopted the ceremony, possibly from the Huron, before contact times. In the seventeenth century the Feast of the Dead had achieved a wide distribution among tribes around the upper Great Lakes (Kinietz 1940, 283).

5. Yet even the earliest records of the Feast of the Dead show signs of its ultimate breakdown. By the early eighteenth century, secondary burial had apparently been discontinued among many of the tribes. By 1763 this feature of the ceremony had been completely forgotten by the Ojibwe and probably by other tribes. The large inter-tribal ceremony became successively an inter-village affair, a village celebration, and at last in modern times a series of family suppers with friends and relatives in the role of "ghosts." Sometime after the middle of the nineteenth century the surviving rites were shifted from the spring to the fall to conform to Christian mores, at least among the Odawa.

In its present form, the Feast of the Dead or some similar ceremony has a wide distribution on the American continent and in many other parts of the world. It would be much too large a task to discuss these ceremonies here. Such a wide distribution certainly argues for the antiquity of the idea and for man's basic fear of and respect for the dead.

Of course, among the different peoples who hold a Feast of the Dead the emphasis is often on different features. Thus the Maskódens families, according to Skinner, hold a Feast of the Dead every spring and fall when the type of residence is changed. The husband lights a fire in the new residence, and dogs are sacrificed and ceremonially eaten by the guests. Food for the ghosts is cast into the fire (Skinner 1926, 269). Among the Fox, several different types of dead feasts are given, some of them more in the nature of gens festivals. There were also a number of other dead feasts, which are known now only by archaic names (Michelson 1918–19, 357). In Italy, as in Harbor Springs, food is left on the table for the ghosts; and in many parts of Europe food is placed on graves.

So in the modern Odawa Ghost Supper we find the remains of the great Feast of the Dead, but perhaps more important than this we see an almost universal picture of the mind of man when confronted with the unknown country of death. For everywhere the great ceremonies at death and following it, when stripped to their essentials, have to do with man's belief in and compulsion to placate the soul or ghost. Whether the ghost is more satisfied with corn soup or Mulligan stew is a matter of local interpretation.

Wake

All of the Odawa in Harbor Springs and vicinity are buried today as Catholics with the usual Christian burial. The only feature of the actual interment that may be considered Indian is the use of the wooden cross at the head of the grave. This particular use of the cross was, however, taken over from the Jesuits and replaces the wooden markers with inverted totem formerly used.

Many of the modern Odawa are accustomed to holding a wake, or *Nibabim* (People Are Holding a Wake), in the deceased's home or the home of a relative. In 1948, I attended a wake given by Clara Lasky in Good Hart for her brother, Clarence Gibson, a bachelor about forty-five years old. Of this ceremony, I wrote the following in my field notes:

> I went in a taxi from Harbor Springs (fifteen miles) with Elizabeth Kishigo (a first cousin of the deceased) and Katherine Kiogima (half-sister). Katherine took her four-month-old baby, Johnny. We carried food with us to help out the family giving the wake, as this is customary. We arrived about 9:45 P.M. and found a large crowd of men, women, and children already gathered together in the small home.
>
> Friends and relatives, Clara Lasky's daughter among them, had prepared pies, potato salad, meat loaf, coffee, etc. (no corn soup!). Most of

those there were relatives—a brother, Mose Gibson, had come from Detroit with his wife.

The corpse was laid out in one room in a grey coffin on a raised carpeted base. There were metal crosses at each end of the coffin on quite massive bases and a large sheath of flowers on the corpse. A large metal crucifix with a blue cellophane covering was framed on the wall directly over the coffin. Large candles also stood at each end of the coffin and one in front of it. Directly in front of the coffin was a lectern where the chanter knelt to lead us in the rosary.

There were chairs in rows in the room and we sat here after standing and viewing the corpse. Other persons were in the kitchen or in the living room—there were only three rooms in the house. Sarah Frances, a woman of about seventy, led us in the rosary. She wore a bandana around her head and a long loose print dress; also a short tan coat, which she did not remove. She used a prayer book and hymnal written in Odawa; others there also had prayer book-hymnals, all of them old and printed at various times by the Catholics during the nineteenth and twentieth centuries. Elizabeth's was printed in 1904 at the Holy Childhood School in Harbor Springs, and was borrowed from a cousin for the occasion.

After the rosary, we sang hymns, singing all verses if the tune could be remembered well enough. (Hymnals include no music.) Sarah Frances led the singing in a high, clear voice, others following as best they could. Singing was a cappella. Hymns are called *Anamie-nagamonan,* according to Baraga.

About midnight, food was passed on trays to us by the deceased's sister and her daughter. A short grace in Odawa was said, Sarah leading. Then we ate and were quite merry. Sarah caused laughter by punning in Odawa. Combination English-Odawa conversation, mostly the latter.

After eating, we sang more hymns. Left about 1:00 A.M. by taxi. Others would remain all night, though there were few there except Clara and her daughter when we left. Funeral the next morning.

Some of the hymns sung at this wake appear in chapter 7. The tunes are remembered by many of the old people, who consequently become changers or leaders in the singing.

CHAPTER 6

Ojibwe Methodist Camp Meeting and Hymn Singing

⁃ *Gertrude Kurath's scholarship in this chapter is important—perhaps unique in its own day—for the way she construes Native language hymnody to be an Anishinaabe musical tradition in its own right, not simply a performance of cultural and religious assimilation. From the late 1820s, Protestant missionaries among the Anishinaabeg vigorously promoted translations of evangelical hymns into Native languages as effective tools in what they considered the civilizing process, for missionaries believed that Native people would imbibe the messages of the hymn texts in the practice of singing them. In addition, hymnody was to distinguish itself from all other Anishinaabe music making in that it would involve neither drumming nor dancing. Indeed, certain Native clergy in the nineteenth century, such as the Methodist preacher Peter Kahkewaquonaby Jones, were instrumental in this work of translating, although they were more optimistic than most Anglo-American missionaries that the Ojibwe and Odawa languages could give voice to the nuances of Christian theology.*

Those Anishinaabe who identified with Christianity heartily embraced this practice of hymn singing in their own tongue, much to the delight of missionaries eager for indications that their labors were bearing fruit. But Ojibwe and Odawa hymn singing, as Kurath depicts, was hardly a straightforward outcome of the missionaries' designs of a cultural revolution. Native language hymn singing, along with the encampments in which it happened, had become central activities of Michigan's Anami'aajig (those who pray), as Christian Anishinaabe people referred to themselves. But it was through these practices that Anishinaabe people made the Christian tradition their own, and this was largely beyond the range of missionary discipline and control. As is suggested by Kurath's documenting of four distinct versions of a translation of "Jesus, My All, to Heaven Is Gone," Native hymnody had a complex life in the oral tradition. Native hymnals, like those generally found among evangelical Protestants in the nineteenth century, included texts alone, indicating only the meter that would help adept singers set the text to any number of tunes. Anishinaabe singers clearly held fast to this practice well into the twentieth century, setting Native language texts to a variety of tunes they retained in memory. Kurath even documents one hymn atypically performed by Eli Thomas with drum accompaniment. For Anishinaabe people like Eli Thomas and the Pamps, hymn singing and camp meetings had become curiously traditional, woven seamlessly into the larger fabric of an Anishinaabe way of life in the twentieth century.

When Jesuit Catholicism was at its height about a century ago, Methodism picked up momentum among the Indians. It owed a spectacular spread not only to the spiritual preparations of Catholicism, but in particular to the type of ritual, the type of song, and the conditions and date of acceptance.

The camp meeting pattern of Free Methodism started the wave of conversions, and it continues to grow in intensity as a more significant form of worship than the formal church service. It is run by the Indians themselves in both languages. Its life blood is the series of hymns sung in Ojibwe or English by the entire congregation. Such meetings move from place to place all summer long, lasting from five to ten days in each place. Indians assemble from all over Michigan and western Ontario, Muncie, Ohsweken, and sometimes from Iroquois reservations in western Now York. Many, like the Pamps and Glenna Rickard, wander from meeting to meeting. One such meeting I attended at Mount Pleasant on September 6, 1953, is forthwith described and illustrated in full, hymns and all. Judging by the Indians' statements and by Louise Walker's description of a Greensky Hill meeting, this event was typical but also particularly gala, well-attended, and spirited (L. Walker 1950).

The hymns recorded on this occasion have been supplemented by solos or small group recordings at odd times by Eli Thomas and friends, always sung a cappella. All of the texts, from books by Peter Jones and William Soney, have been identified and mostly translated by Eli Thomas and Betty Pamp. The tunes of the camp meeting have almost all been traced; those of Thomas's repertoire remain largely anonymous. These songs, integrated in their setting, play a clear-cut and contemporary role.

During the entire week before Labor Day, a wooded knoll on Isabella Reservation is the site of the largest Indian evangelist meeting in the state. Anishinaabeg and some Iroquois assemble from both peninsulas and from adjacent Ontario. On the occasion attended, three hundred came from local farms; seven hundred arrived for a day by chartered bus or pitched their tents in a circle for the duration of the meeting. A large group arrived from Walpole Island, Ontario, with preacher and choir, for the day before Labor Day.

Preachers, self-appointed evangelists, and laymen worshipped in an open wooden tabernacle with plank benches facing a crude raised platform. Most of the time the congregation or featured musicians sang hymns in Ojibwe or English, either unaccompanied or accompanied by Lucy Pelcher's or Ford Soney's piano, sometimes with steel guitars and an accordion, and on Sunday evening also with a saxophone. On Sunday afternoon, children and adults stepped on the platform for a performance of their special hymns. All three or four daily services featured witty bilingual sermons by local or visiting ministers. All of these events were recorded, thanks to Eli Thomas's interest.

A communion service and series of baptisms on Sunday afternoon honored two white ministers as officiates and preachers. Both came from Mount Pleasant and had been adopted into the tribe.

Meals were prepared in the adjacent community building by the Ladies' Aid Society, which managed to efficiently serve the long line of visitors. Neither Indian dancing nor square dancing is permissible at any of these meetings. But the conversions entail highly emotional, rhythmic activity, walking, clapping, and swaying in a complex group counterpoint. The last Labor Day service concludes with the singing of the Doxology in a huge circle with joined hands. Except for the language, the Doxology, like other hymns, is harmonized according to the hymn books.

Free Methodist Camp Meeting—Isabella Reserve

Sunday, September 6, 1953

Adult Sunday School, 10:00 A.M.
1. Responses for September 6; "On Possessions" read by: *Preacher and congregation, Jim Peters of Isabella Reserve leading*
2. Hymn (Ojibwe)
3. Sermon on Responses (alternately in Ojibwe and English)

Revival Service, 11:00 A.M.
1. Bells
2. "O For a Thousand Tongues," version 1 (Ojibwe): *Congregation*

Group of men and women near platform clustered around kneeling convert, shouting "Merciful Jesus," "May God bless you," "Shawendagoze," "Save this poor sinner," "Thanks," "Amen." Three kneel, others walk back and forth. Continuation of shouting without hymn.

3. "More, More about Jesus" (English): *Piano and congregation*
4. "O For a Thousand Tongues" (Ojibwe): *Piano and congregation* (Tune: "I Would Not Be Denied")
5. Announcements (English): *Quignon*
6. "Constantly Abiding" (English): *Piano and congregation*
7. "All Hail the Power" (English): *Piano and two girls*
   "There's a Crown for You" (English)
8. Sermon (bilingual): *Jim Peters, Walpole Island*
9. Collection, to "Jesus, My All" (Ojibwe): *Congregation*
10. Prayer (Ojibwe): *Selkirk Sprague, Bradley*
11. Doxology (Ojibwe): *Piano and congregation*
12. Benediction (Ojibwe): *William Soney, Walpole Island*

Lunch, 12:30 P.M.
Served in community house or al fresco. Mr. and Mrs. Enos Willis of Charlevoix joined us.

Children's Sunday School, 1:30 P.M.
1. "Sweet Bye and Bye" (English): *Steel guitars, Roy Chevis and John Colgrove*
2. Questions on Bible (English): *Preacher and children*
3. "Nothing but the Blood of Jesus" (English): *Children*
   "I Would Not Be Denied" (English)
   "What a Friend I Have in Jesus" (English)
4. Admonition (English): *Preacher Jim Peters, Mount Pleasant*

Communion Service, 3:00–5:00 P.M.
1. "'Neath the Old Olive Tree" (English): *Guitars, accordion, voices (Chevis et al.)*
2. "When I Can Read My Title Clear" (Ojibwe): *Walpole Island Choir and Ford Soney, piano*
   Unidentified hymn (English)
3. Address: *Guignon*
4. "O For a Thousand Tongues" (Ojibwe): *Mrs. Chamberlain* (Tune: "At the Cross")
   "Meet Me There" (Ojibwe): *Margaret and Mrs. Chamberlain*
5. "O Wonderful Jesus" (English): *Child, guitars*

Ojibwe Methodist Camp Meeting and Hymn Singing

6. "Jesus, My All, to Heaven" (Ojibwe): *Congregation, piano*
7. "There Is Something Within" (English): *Mrs. Shomin*
8. Two hymns (English): *Congregation*
9. "O For a Thousand Tongues," v. 3, 4 (Ojibwe): *Congregation*
10. Communion—Baptisms (English): *Rev. McKinney, Mount Pleasant and deacon*
11. Sermon, *Walpole Island Choir*
12. "I Want to Walk in the Path" (English): *Congregation*
13. Benediction (Ojibwe): *William Soney, Walpole Island*

Jesus, My All, to Heaven Is Gone
Text: John Cennick (1718–55); tune: Lowell Mason (1835); translation:

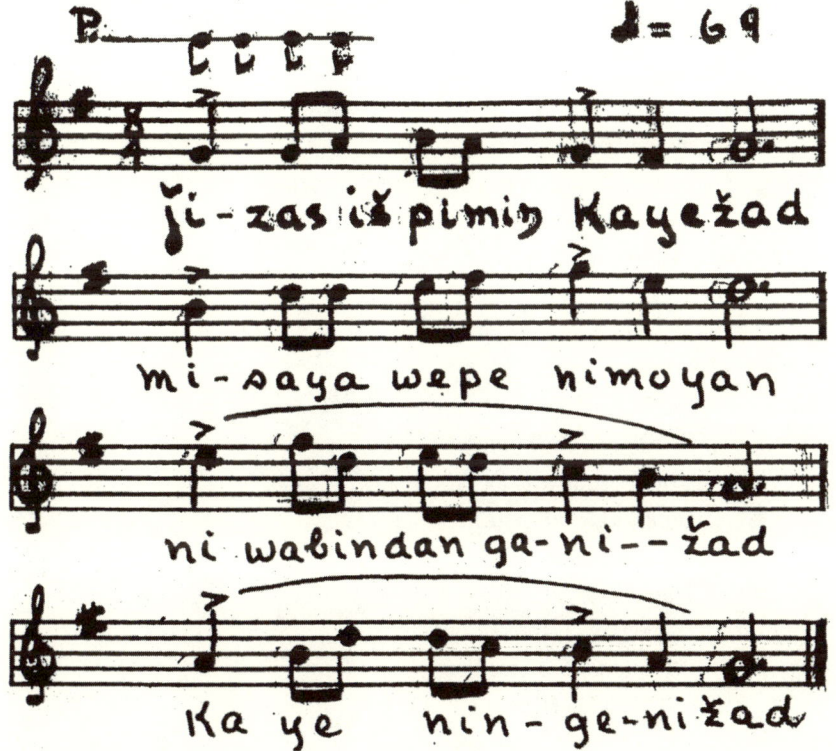

Peter Kahkewaquonaby Jones (P. Jones 1854, 110–13).

1.
Jesus, my all, to heaven is gone;
    He whom I fix my hopes upon;
His track I see, and I'll pursue
    The narrow way, till him I view.

Jízas íšpimiŋ káyežad

Jesus   heaven   he went
    mísə   *yawœpénimoyan*
    I'm the one   depending on Him
niwabindán   *gá:niyežad*
I've seen it (where)   He went
    káye   *ningéniyežayad*
    That's   me going the same way

2.
The way the holy prophets went,
    The road that leads from banishment,
The King's highway of holiness,
    I'll go, for all His paths are peace.

gá:nežawá:d   *ka:nibwɔ́kadik*
Wherever went   the prophets (saints, wise)
    mi:kǫ́s kuyɔ́k œnimənik
    The road is made straight (goes way straight up)
káye ninkemá:didóyan
I'm going to follow (that road)
    mi:kǫ́s kǽče šawéndawik
    The road (is) happy (blessed)

3.
    míso' o   *ká:miné:žiyan*
That's the one   that was lacking me
    káyunje   *kidimá:giša:n*
    Poor   weak
ki:kénimasiwók   *ma:bə́*
Before I knew Him   (that one)
    ki:žé mənedó   *owisá:n*
    Great Spirit   His Son

O For a Thousand Tongues to Sing
Text: Charles Wesley, 1740; tune: "Ortonville," by Thomas Hastings (1784–1872); rendered: verses 1–6, v. 5, 6, 6, text of Doxology. Slows down from 88 to 72 in course of singing.

1. O for a thousand tongues to sing
    My great Redeemer's praise!
The glories of my God and King,
    The trumphs of His grace.

o bǽgiš kíči íngo:dwók
I wish there was a hundred
nijiníšinábæg
(of) my Indians
činenágáma-təwəwád
So they could sing
    niŋgižé mənedúm
    To my manido.

2. My gracious Master, and my God,
    Assist me to proclaim

To spread through all the earth abroad
    The honors of thy name.

ningí:či nosǽ   wí:jisǽn
O my father,   be with me
    čiwé:ndəmágeyon
    [Assist me to proclaim]
o ma'ǽni:gúk ká:migək
    O whole universe (earth)
    ǽžiŋ wǽbižiyən
    How great you are.

3. Jesus, the name that charms our fears,
    That bids our sorrows cease
'Tis music in the sinner's ears.
    'Tis life, and health and peace.

jízəs—ka:bi:nándawi:nəŋ
Jesus—was the one that
    ka:gá:sisbí:ŋwayenəŋ
    Cures us and wipes our tears
kegǽtče minǫika:yo
O that great name
    kanó:ji:moyinəŋ
    That saved us from sin.

4. He breaks the power of cancelled sin,
    He sets the pris'ner free,
His blood can make the foulest clean
    His blood availed for me

wí:nsə ogí:mə mą:žiyán
He's the one that licked (overlorded)
    máji məni:dóšən
    The evil spirit (devil)
ki:bezíwǽbinámonəŋ
The one that spilled
    wi:n   jí:zəs omiskwí:m
    His,   Jesus's, own blood

5. Look unto Him, ye nations; own
    Your God, ye fallen race;

Look, and be saved through faith alone,
    Be justified by grace.

o ǰí:zəs   kanawábəmik
On Jesus look
    o nišiná:beduk
    O ye Indians
iná:biyuk tǽbwatəwik
Believe in him, look upon him
    čibimá:diziyæg
    Then you'll live

6. See all your sins on Jesus laid,
    The Lamb of God was slain;
His soul was once an off'ring made
    For every soul of man.

ne ǰí:zəs obimundá:nən
Jesus is the one that's carrying our sins
    we:nišígoyegun
    That's going to destroy us
kákinə činújimayæg
All that you may be saved
    ǰí:zəs   kiyúnǰine
    Jesus he died.

O For a Thousand Tongues, version 2

*Piano by Lucy Pelcher; tune: "I Would Not Be Denied," by C. P. Jones (*Songs of Spiritual Power*, 107).*

Bilingual Sermon by Jim Peters

You've got to love your brothers, that's the main things. (... Ojibwe ...) This camp ground (... Ojibwe ...) that great promised land. You're wasting time. Why don't you go cast that mountain down, that mountain that you made between you and your brothers and sister. (... Ojibwe ...) You've got to have a straight way. (... Ojibwe ...) You can't climb that mountain. (... Ojibwe ...) That is the main thing. (... Ojibwe ...) Because you've got that mountain between him and you, and that's got to be cast down. If you want to have light in your soul. You can't go in that kingdom of God because you can't climb that mountain. (... Ojibwe ...) There's no place for you in heaven ...

My brothers, I don't have much time. (... Ojibwe ...) I would like to say a few words, but I don't have time. (... Ojibwe ...) (An inextricably mixed passage). I'm always the same. (... Ojibwe ...) But I do (... Ojibwe ...) when God comes in my heart. Amen. This isn't the way to serve God. (... Ojibwe ...) By my own experience, when God comes in a person's heart. (... Ojibwe ...) (Yea) Because the light that comes in his heart. (... Ojibwe ...) He's in darkness.

But when that sin is taken out, the light of God is in him. (Amen) I wasn't asked to preach. (... Ojibwe ...) What I like to do, I like to speak to my own people. (... Ojibwe ...) The more people the better, I have a chance to speak to them. (... Ojibwe ...) (Anecdote greeted by laughter)

We're in God's temple. (... Ojibwe ...) This is God's temple. (... Ojibwe ...) This is the house of prayer (... Ojibwe ...) *kiče manitu*. Maybe I don't have to tell you (something about food in Ojibwe).

Now that costs a lot of money. (... Ojibwe ...) When I was in Canada, when I came back, I gained a lot of weight. (... Ojibwe ...) (Laughter) So it costs a lot of money to feed that many people. I remember one time (... Ojibwe ...) we had seven or eight hundred strangers. There was 900 in Ohsweken (Six Nations Reserve). (... Ojibwe ...) One bag of potatoes for one meal. Next meal another bag. Three bags of potatoes every day. Now that costs a lot of money. (... Ojibwe ...) We get good meals. (... Ojibwe ...)

God is asking you (... Ojibwe ...) because you know every dollar you make, God owns that ten cents out o' that dollar. (... Ojibwe ...) (Laughter) Preachers and all, I'd like to see 'em give ten percent ... that's good. (... Ojibwe ...) We're gonna take an offering. Give all you can. God is asking you to give. (... Ojibwe ...) Give what you can now, some other time you give him some more, then you won't owe God anything. Give all you can, to help the chairman pay that grocery bill. Some of you is eatin' four dollars a day (Laughter), that's right. Now, there's quite a bunch of us here. (... Ojibwe ...)

And at this time I want every preacher to stand on his feet and remain standing. You is willing to do what God wants. (... Ojibwe ...) Man or woman, I want him to stand till I get through counting ... One, two. ... etc. fifteen. I know the preachers. Sixteen, seventeen. ... twenty-two. Now, that's 22 dollars. We want those preachers to come here and put their dollar bills in this hat, all the preachers. (Laughter) Now when you get through I'm going to count this money. (Laughter)

(Collection, piano starts tune, then singing.) Now while the choir's singing, we're going to ask this side to come. Ready with your money? Amen. (Procession to front, to deposit coins in hat.)

Jesus, My All, to Heaven Is Gone (second tune)
Piano, choir, then congregation; text: John Cennick, 1718–1755; tune: not identified, similar to "Olive's Brow," by William R. Bradbury; translation: Peter Kahkewaquonaby Jones (P. Jones 1854, 110–13).

Doxology[1]
Piano and congregation. (Only second half recorded.) Text: Bishop Thomas Ken (1695); tune: "Old One Hundred," by Louis Bourgeois; Geneva Psalter 1551; translation: Peter Kahkewaquonaby Jones (P. Jones 1854; attached to many hymns as coda).

Praise God, from whom all blessings flow,
> Praise God, all creatures here below;

Praise Him above, ye heavenly host
> Praise Father, Son, and Holy Ghost.

má:mayu: wamá:dama:bə
Give Him the high honor (thank Him)
> *wǽnǰi šawéndagəziyǫ*
> That's the one that blesses (blessing flows, you can't run out of it)

> *wé:yosimint wékwisimint*
> The Father   the Son
> > *káye panižíd ojičág*
> > Also the Holy Ghost (the awful clean spirit)

Benediction
By William Soney (trans. Betty Pamp).

> *kineŋkiyáŋ mandó ežædawéndamin*
> We have done what you commanded
> *či dápine má:ŋdemáŋ kidimá:ŋdemá:ŋ miskwí:m*
> to take   this   sacrament   (blood)
> *kwimændegæ megwéč   žawendá:min*
> we are   so thankful for mercy
> *wi:sá čiškæniwæŋ demǽ:ndina:n*
> let our minds   be new (clear)
> *wæn či miskówežiya:n činǽŋkiyá:ŋ ežædawendámin.*
> to be stronger   to do thy will and your command.

English: May the grace of our Lord Jesus Christ, and the love of God, and the fellowship of the Holy Spirit be with you now and forever. Amen.

At this point, hymns were practiced on steel guitars, accordion, and later on saxophone and piano till suppertime.

Communion Service

'Neath the Stars of the Night Walked the Savior of Light
Tune and text by B. B. McKinney.

> In the garden of dew-laden breeze . . .
> > (Choir: |: 'neath the old olive trees :|)
> > Went the Savior on his knees:
> "Not my will, Thine be done," cried the Father's own son,
> > And he knelt 'neath the old olive trees.

When I Can Read My Title Clear (Walpole Island Choir)
Text: Isaac Watts (four verses sung); tune: "Lingham" (in second half, the soprano and bass overlap in canon form); [phonetic transcript translation:

Peter Kahkewaquonaby Jones (P. Jones 1854, 86–87); translation by Betty Pamp, December 11, 1954.

1. When I can read my title clear [when I am certain]
    To mansions in the skies,
 I'll bid farewell to every fear
    And wipe my weeping eyes.

api kwaiak wendamonin [uh pee qua yuh quan duh mon in]
When I am certain
    ispimiŋ ežaya:n [ish pe ming e zhah yon]
    to heaven   I am going
kə kina   awaskiwinən [kuh ke nuh uh gwuh skee win un]
all   of my trials
    ninbakewiduna:n [nin bah ka we doo nun.]
    I will lay aside.

2. Should earth against my soul engage,
      And fiery darts be hurl'd;
Then I can smile at Satan's rage,
      And face a frowning world.

mi:sawa akiŋ ayəgin [me suh wah uh keeng a yuh gin]
even though these earthly things
      mamiganigoyan [mah mee gah ne go yon;]
      might fight me
kabapišnindagosasi [kah bah pish nin dah go sah see]
still I will not be afraid
      maci mənizaiwin. [mu je mon e ze win.]
      the evil spirit.

3. Let cares like a wild deluge come,
      Let storms of sorrow fall;
So I but safely reach my home,
      My God, my heaven, my all.

pučgopigo təmigwinək [pooch go pe go tah me gwee nuk,]
even though there may be many
      migoskadiziwin [me go skah de ze win;]
      trials and troubles
ningawidadəwešinsa [ning uh wee da duh gwe shin suh]
still I will make it
      išpimiŋ kadayon. [ish pe ming ka dah yon.]
      heaven where I will live.

O For a Thousand Tongues, version 3

Mrs. Chamberlain (a white woman who married an Indian). Ford Soney of Walpole Island, who accompanied, asked, "Shall I play the piano in English or in Indian?" and this to much laughter. Text: solo part same as O bægis in morning service, three verses used. Chorus, in English, by congregation, same as for Watts's hymn, "At the Cross." Thomas says this chorus can be added to other hymns. It is at times sung in Indian, Ažedewatigong. *It was rendered with great enthusiasm, and the chorus was repeated. Tune: by R. E. Hudson, 1885, usually used for "Alas and Did My Savior Bleed."*

Meet Me There (Child of Sorrow, Child of Care)

(Mrs. Chamberlain and eldest daughter Margaret). Tune: Unidentified, of late nineteenth century, revival style; text: In none of the available hymn books. Same pattern of solo and chorus, but chorus sung in Indian. Translation: (Soney n.d., 4).

1.
kinəwakiškéndəmeg
ye that are sorrowing
    sažibéndamoyuk sá
    take courage   indeed
apénimoyak, kižé mənidú;
depend on the great spirit;

2.
meník nanəmíziyeg
those of you
    məskəkwéndəmayuk sa
    that are determined
kagawidukágowa o ǰízas
will receive help from Jesus

Chorus:
pama:pí: iwidí:
after a while   over there
    kəməndómigonan ǰízas   iwidí
    we will be called by Jesus   over there
čiwidápəməŋ   osa gi'iwáwin o ǰížas
to feast with him   in the love of Jesus
    kawəwéžetəmunaŋ   íšpimiŋ
    that he has prepared   in heaven.

O For a Thousand Tongues, version 4 (congregation)

Text: Charles Wesley, verses 3 and 4. Tune: "Elizabeth," by George Kingsley (1811–1884).

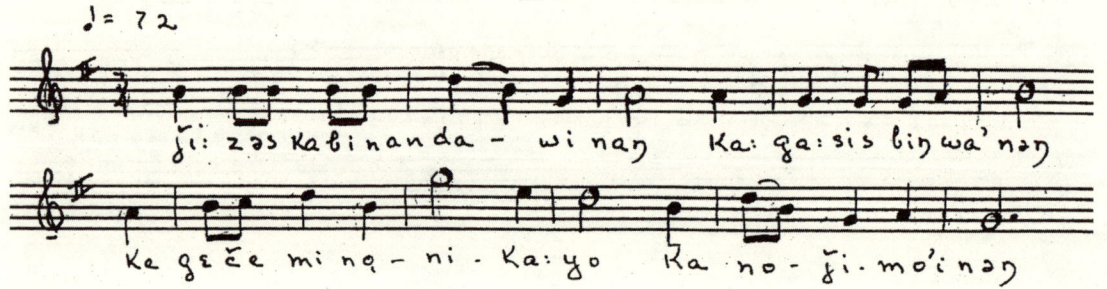

Communion, Baptism, Sermon

This ceremony followed white customs and was in fact conducted by a white minister assisted by his white deacon. The Walpole Island Choir sang softly during silent actions. This was not recorded. For the communion the congregation came forth and knelt by the rail at the platform in groups of twenty, adults then children. Two young Indian girls held trays with cubes of bread and wine in tiny glasses. The minister handed these out with the customary prayer, "Do this in remembrance of me." Then he gave each group a blessing.

The rite of baptism started with three small children, then one of the girls who had carried a tray, then a group of half a dozen small children. All of this was conducted with great solemnity. The long sermon in English referred to Rev. McKinney's adoption into the tribe but otherwise had no ethnological interest. Rev. and Mrs. McKinney departed immediately after their share in the ceremony and left the concluding hymn and benediction to the Indians. the service concluded with "I Want to Walk in the Path of the Savior," a revival hymn.

Separate Hymns

Jesus, My All, to Heaven Is Gone
(Jesus Ishpemiŋ) (Eli Thomas). Drum accompaniment: "Grandfather Song." Recorded: Hastings (August 16, 1953).

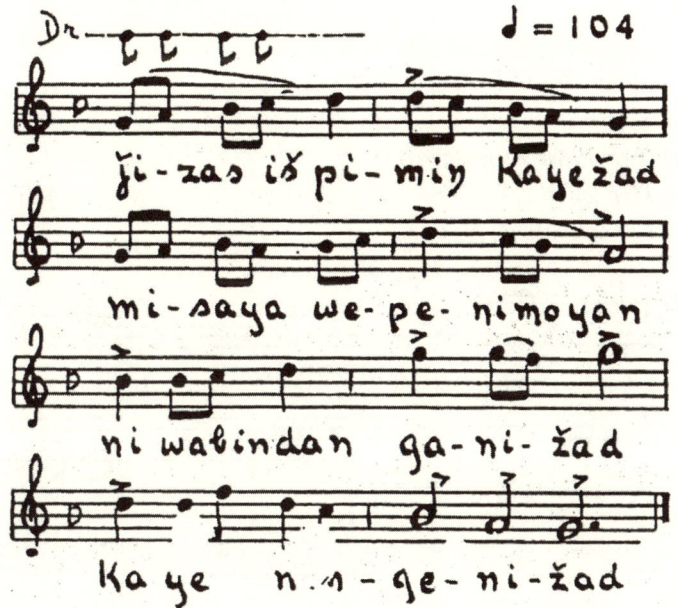

Jesus, My All, to Heaven Is Gone
(Eli Thomas and Whitney Blue Cloud). Recorded: Mount Pleasant (July 2, 1954).

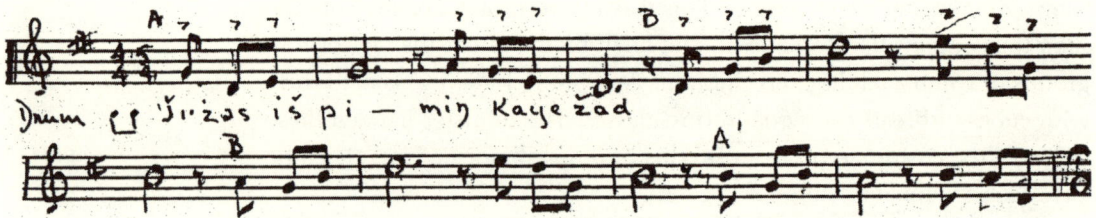

Jesus, My All, to Heaven Is Gone
(Mr. and Mrs. Thomas) a capella. Recorded: Ann Arbor (November 4, 1953).

Hymns Sung at Informal Gatherings

O for a Thousand Tongues to Sing
"O begiš kiče iŋgodwok" (Betty and Joan Pamp, Glenna Rickard). Recorded: Ann Arbor (September 14, 1954).

This fifth version of "*o begiš,*" by Betty and Joan Pamp and Glenna Rickard, resembles with variations a tune by S. Hubbard published in *Favorite Methodist Hymns* with the text "How precious is the book divine." This recording is of particular interest because it is coupled with another rendering in the Seneca language. Mrs. Lyons, a recently converted Cattaraugus Seneca, accompanied the Pamps in the September visit to my home and sang two hymns common among the Ojibwe, this one and a second version of "*Jesus Ishpemiŋ.*" Her vocal quality betrayed her recent adherence to the longhouse, in its meekness, the frequent slurs, and the difficulties with the interval of a semitone. In comparison, the Ojibwe voices sounded thoroughly acculturated.

The five versions of this text do not include a transitional, half-Indian setting, but they exhibit historical variety, ranging from the fine chorale by Hastings of over a hundred years ago to the revival tunes taken from "At the Cross" and "I Would Not Be Denied."

Come Ye Sinners
(Eli Thomas). Recorded: Ann Arbor (November 4, 1953)

Thomas said of the translation, "That's a preaching in itself, the way we've got it expressed." But he remarked, "We say it more plainer. We don't beat around the bush like the white poets." The tune is anonymous.

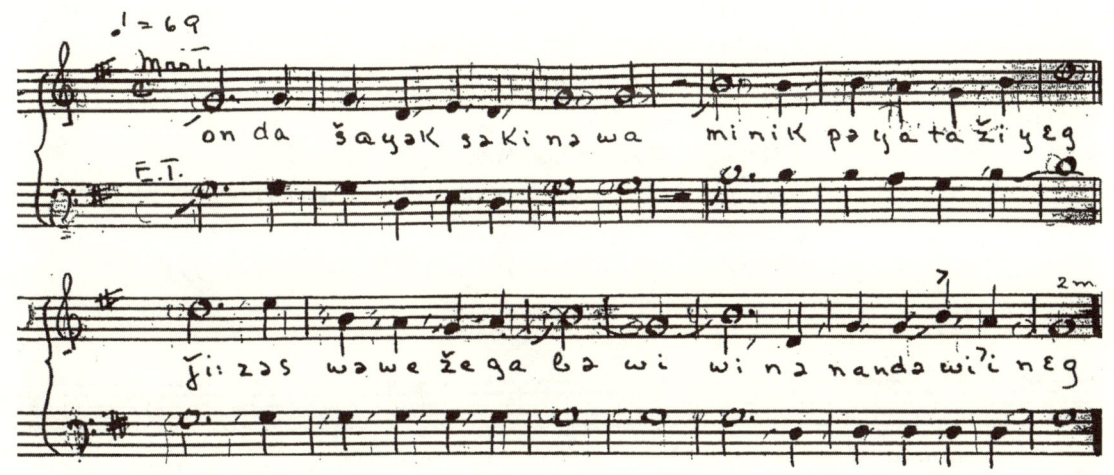

1.
ondášayək sakínəwa   minίk pəyátaziyeg
come all   everyone ye sinners
   jίzəs   wawežegábəwi   winəná:ndə wί'incæg
   Jesus   is ready to   make you whole (so you can go on)

2.

/: /: *ma:škawési* :/   *kœbizawéni:menœg* :/
  he is able, he is strong   the one that's going to bless you

3.

kedimágiziwegwœnsa   *má:no'odápinamuk*
all you that are poor   may take heart
(he's poor when he is a sinner)
     gižé mənidó ogíči   *ošawénjigewinən*
     the great god is a gift,   is going to give you a blessing

4.

/: /: *wenipáš sə* :/ *kišpinadá:ma:dišuk* :/
  that's free (you need pay nothing for it) if you take the blessing

5.

kégo žawanimokœgun' pamá:či'encendamœg
don't hesitate don't wait much longer
     nóngom činədówenimœ   *kidincenimegowa*
     now to-day is the time   that he expects you

6.

/: /: *kimí:nigum* :/   *má:bə*   *kíči ojičág* :/
  it is given to you   that   holy spirit

God Moves in Mysterious Ways
(Eli Thomas). Tune: "Evan," by William H. Havergal (1793–1870). Text: William Cowper (1731–1800). Translation: Peter Kahkewaquonaby Jones (P. Jones 1854, 112–15). Recorded: Ann Arbor (November 3, 1953).

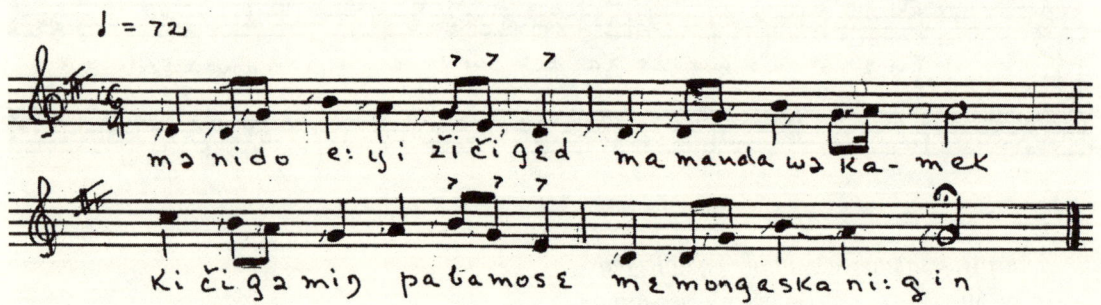

1. God moves in mysterious ways
       His wonders to perform;
He plants his footsteps in the sea,
       And rides upon the storm.
Deep, in unfathomable mines
       Of never-failing skill,
He reassures up his bright designs,
       And works his sovereign will.

mənidó   e:yižíčigœœd   məmá:nda:wəkamík
God   whatever he does   it's a wonderful thing
kəčígəmiŋ pəbámasœ   məmóŋ áškanigin
the ocean he walks upon   when there's a storm
gečídəmiməgádinœ œwoni wáčiwœn
his love is great and deep
a:pejé'owə yákwœndon   kižé widǫkagœd
he knows how he's going   keep up with it

2. Ye fearful saints, fresh courage take
       The clouds ye so much dread
Are big with mercy, and shall break
       In blessings on your head.
Judge not the Lord by feeble sense,
       But trust him for his grace;
Behind a frowning providence
       He hides a smiling face.

kínəwa səkwe ta:jiyœg   məškəwœndəmiyuk
you are the one I fear   have faith
təwába:sin gewánakod   na:škajœ'goyœg
the black clouds   will blow away (the one that's troubled)
ká:win enœndágoziče   œwœži'oya:šən
he doesn't expect them to be his children
kewi mənidó dogowa   šanagizí:yaŋgun
he's a great God   he's helping his children

3. His purposes will ripen fast,
       Unfolding every hour;
The bud may have a bitter taste,
       But sweet will be the flower.
Blind unbelief is sure to err,

    And scan his work in vain:
God is his own Interpreter,
    And he will make it plain.

wəyé:bə təyežíčigœ   manda éyinœnduŋ
he'll do whatever   that is good
kákinə čiwéškobitod   ma:min wa:ságəngin
he's going to make it sweet   that's bitter
nətá:ba:ta:yé:waməgad   agǫwatəmowin
that always gets you into trouble   the doubt
kéget dəš wí:ngo tədebwa   mənidó œkidód
surely I'm glad he'll do   God whatever he say.

A Charge to Keep I Have

(*Chi anokitonan*) *(Betty Pamp and others). Tune: unidentified. Text: Charles Wesley. Translation: Peter Kahkewaquonaby Jones (P. Jones 1854, 102–5). Recorded: Mount Pleasant (July 2, 1954).*

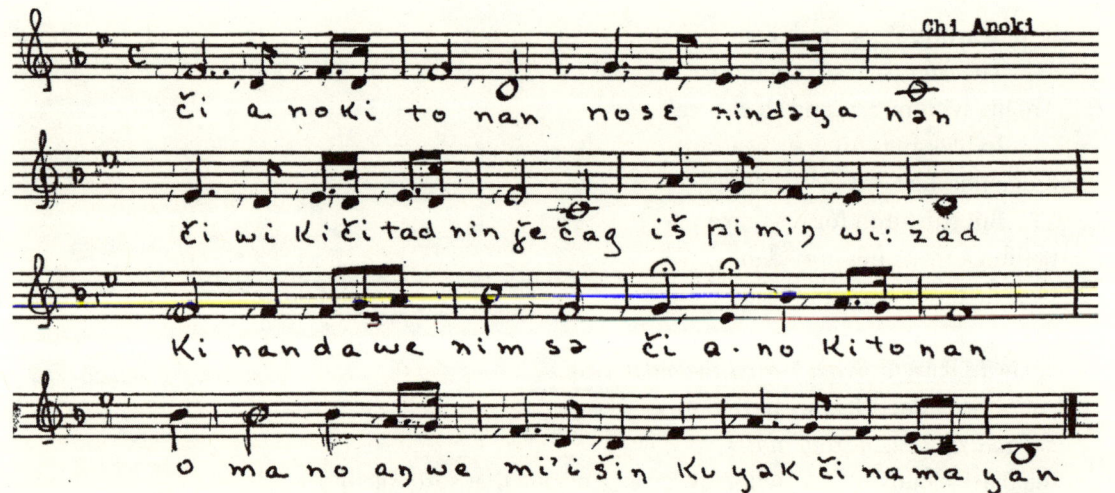

1. A charge to keep I have,
    A God to glorify;
A never-dying soul to save,
    And fit it for the sky.

či anókitonan,   nosœ nindəyanən
to work for thee,   o father I have
    či wíkičitad ninječág išpimiŋ wí:zad.
    that it might prepare my soul heaven to go.

2. To serve the present age,
   My calling to fulfill;—
O may it all my powers engage
   To do my Master's will.

kinandáwenimsə   či anókitonan
you want me   to work for thee
   o máno angwe mišin   kuyák či'námayan.
   Oh, be careful with me, perfect I may pray.

3. Arm me with jealous care,
   As in thy sight to live;
And O thy servant, Lord, prepare
   A strict account to give.

wáweže išínsa či agasánimoyan
Prepare me to think humbly
   či dakižétayon,   noscé,   apinakwáskunan.
   that I might finish, father, when I meet thee.

4. Help me to watch and pray,
   And on thyself rely;
Assured, if I my trust betray,
   I shall forever die.

widukáwišinsa   či akawébiyon,
Help me   to watch for thee
   kaye či anámeyan   wibimá:diziyan.
   and to pray   so that I might live.

Come Thou Fount of Every Blessing
(*Ondá šansá*) *(three versions). Tune: Set to three anonymous tunes. Text: Robert Robinson (1814–1887). Translation: Peter Kahkewaquonaby Jones (P. Jones 1854, 64–67).*

Version one uses a curious technique, with Eli Thomas carrying the tune in a lower voice and Mrs. Thomas providing the harmony in a higher pitch. The four-phrase melody was adapted to the stanzas as written below. Version two, sung in unison an octave apart, is twice as long, with eight phrases of the same rhythm but different melody from version one. It could accommodate twice as many lines. Version three, harmonized in three parts by four singers, has another rhythm repeated in eight phrases. The singers were Mr. and Mrs. Thomas, recorded at Hastings, Betty Pamp, and Glenna Rickard. The tempo, slow to begin with, retarded in the course of the singing. Neither of these verses resembles the printed tune to this text in *Favorite Methodist Hymns* attributed to Asabel Nettleton.

1. Come, thou Fount of every blessing,
    Tune my heart to sing thy grace;
Streams of mercy never ceasing,
    Call for songs of loudest praise.

Ondá šansá tebénda:mán *kíči šawénǰigewin*
come along bring all you have, great blessing
  wawéšitun nindœnéniš *činanágəmatonan*
  prepare my heart that I may sing.

2. Teach me some melodious sonnet,
    Sung by flaming tongues above;
Praise the mount—I'm fix'd upon it:
    Mount of thy redeeming love.

kikí:nu 'imowišinsá *íšpimiŋ* *nágəmawad*
show me (teach me) in heaven the song they sing
  kíči mægwéč mæǰœnéyan *kežawǽnǰigiwœniŋ*
  I thank you for keeping me in great blessing.

3. Here I'll raise mine Ebenezer,
    Hither by thy help I'm come;
And I hope, by thy good pleasure,
    Safely to arrive at home.

kikídəwašínsəyoma *češí bœnǽkɛtona:m*
you have come that I may stretch my arms
  œnœníniwœnadášgo wi:yuw: niwgi:wœ
  if you want me I will go back home.

Partial Camp Meeting Calendar

Comparable to the Native ceremonial schedule, an evangelist calendar, differing from year to year, can be drawn up. This partial list holds good for 1954.

March 14–April 1	Athens Indian Mission Church	Jack Pamp
June 20–27	Zeba Holiness Camp Ground	
August 15–22	Zeba Methodist Camp Ground	
August 8–15	Oscoda Camp Ground	
August 8–15	Greensky Hill Mission	
August 15–29	Athens Mission Camp Ground	Jack Pamp
August 29–September 6	Isabella Reserve Camp Ground	Jim Peters
September 15–19	Walpole Island Camp Ground	William Soney
October 22–30	Athens Mission Church Revival	Jack Pamp
October 23–31	Greensky Hill Mission Church	Warren Pamp

White Holiness

July 15–25   Ball Road Tabernacle, Ecorse Rd.; D. C. Pegler Indian preacher, Rev. A. Bass from Isabella Reservation. Betty Pamp and other Indians in attendance.

Transition to Evangelism

The apparent gulf between aboriginal song, dance, and ceremony, and modern evangelism was bridged in several ways. First, after the way was prepared by the Roman Catholic missionaries, Christian ideas continued fermenting even during their temporary withdrawal. Second, the ancient summer conclaves served religion and sociability much as the camp meeting does today. Third, economic conditions around 1823 cried for a revival. The fur trade had left poverty and drunkenness; treaties had pillaged Indian domains. In this time of need there arose a leader, half Mississauga and half Welsh, raised in pagan practices, yet baptized in a Mohawk Episcopal Church. After many failures to obtain a puberty vision, Peter Jones, Kahkewaquonaby, was converted to Methodism during a camp meeting at Ancaster, Ontario (P. Jones 1861, 7–9). After an English preparation for the ministry, he devoted his life to evangelism among his own tribesmen on River Credit Reserve and in seventeen Ontario missions. He translated hymns, prayers, and the New Testament. Soon his influence reached Michigan.

    Although his followers agreed that Christianity had lifted them out of the miry clay, the old shamans noticed that the white man would, after coming out of his praying house, continue to drink, fight, and cheat. Many Indians clung to their old ways until well into the twentieth century. However, the Indians who followed Peter Jones did find some security, and became relatively clean, sober, and industrious.

The Midéwiwin and Wabeno rites discontinued in eastern Michigan about 1910. Eli Thomas remembers them from his boyhood near Bay City. A few harmless beliefs remain among the old-timers, such as tobacco offerings during a thunderstorm. Native dances and songs were completely condemned, along with sorcery. Evangelism came to form the reality of the Methodist Anishinaabeg's religious life. It has swept many of them into greater fervor—even fanaticism—than currently is the case among their white neighbors.

Educated Indians took charge of the preaching. Even women were soon admitted into the ministry—for example, Betty Malone, former preacher at Hannahville. Although, as in former days, the sexes have duties specific to them, the women are on an equal footing with the men in the organization and in the music. They are active as missionaries and delegates. They are content to follow the imported forms and idioms.

The Catholic service, led by white preachers, has shed Indian elements. The Protestant services, though led by Indians and conducted in their tongue, yet are modeled on white patterns. Betty Pamp tells of the camp meeting organization in an interview of December 11, 1954:

> **Betty Pamp:** Usually the local church body appoints a chairman, a camp president, and they appoint all the officers. Usually the Ladies' Aid takes care of the cooking and feeding of the people that come from other places. And this camp president is then responsible for finding places for people to stay that come in to visit.
>
> **Gertrude Kurath:** Who was the camp president last year?
>
> **B.P.** For our meeting here it was Harold Jackson.
>
> **G.K.** He's not a minister?
>
> **B.P.** No, it's just someone from the congregation, usually.
>
> **G.K.** What's the program chairman?
>
> **B.P.** That's the camp president.
>
> **G.K.** That was Benedict the year before?
>
> **B.P.** Yes.
>
> **G.K.** What do you mean, the different officers? How do you appoint the work?
>
> **B.P.** Well, the camp president appoints a committee to clean up the grounds. That committee is responsible for keeping up the grounds. They usually all get together and have a bee and get the grounds ready.
>
> **G.K.** Sort of a work cooperative?
>
> **B.P.** Yes.

G.K. How important are the women? Can they have offices, can they preach?

B.P. Yes, now it's just the same as with the men. The can do just about anything.

G.K. You organize them just like the white church?

B.P. Yes, the church too, is just the same as the Methodist.

G.K. It has nothing to do with the clans?

B.P. No, not now. It used to.

CHAPTER 7

Hymn Tunes and Texts

→ *In this chapter, Gertrude Kurath complements the previous one with a deeper inquiry into the textual and melodic content of the hymns and a broader survey of Native Christian hymnody. Here, too, Kurath documents how those affiliated with the Christian tradition brought their Native heritage together with the Christian narratives and practices that missionaries introduced. Whether Catholic or Protestant, hymns made considerable room within the colonizing confines of missions, reservations, and assimilation policies, for their distinctive tunes are uniformly of Euro-American origin. The texts are by and large prayerful attempts by Native clergy to render the Christian concepts and narratives in Ojibwe and Odawa. The drum and dance so elemental to traditional Anishinaabe music are conspicuously absent. Kurath's notation documents how Ojibwe and Odawa Christians performed the Christian songs in distinctive Anishinaabe idioms in distinctively Native settings. We learn, for example, that since 1910, hymnody was almost exclusively tied to the ritual setting of the funeral wake. The slow a cappella chanting of hymns in these all-night gatherings could be entrancing, setting the tone and rhythm for the Anishinaabe idiom of mourning and spiritual reflection. Hymn performances also were drenched with meaning, simply because they were sung in Odawa and Ojibwe languages and the politicized context of assimilation policies and boarding schools militated against the very survival of those languages. Native language hymnody incorporated Christianity solidly into the discursive universe of Anishinaabe religious thought, and this affirmed for those Anishinaabeg who identified with the Christian tradition what the missionaries typically denied: that one could be both fully Anishinaabe and fully Christian. Similarly, near the end of the chapter, Kurath documents how ritualized speech in such liturgical settings took on a cadence and pacing that flooded the specific Christian discursive content with uniquely Anishinaabe associations.*

Hymnody inevitably accompanied Christian practices. The Catholic and Protestant hymns have independent origins, histories, melodies, and texts, although they share linguistic terms for concepts. In the chapters on Catholic feasts and Methodist camp meetings, numerous examples give color to the proceedings. The examples in this chapter illustrate the problems of the two separate hymn sets.

Catholic Hymns

The Catholic music played an important part in the conversion of the Indians. The surviving feasts, the reports of obsolete festivals, and the arrangement of the hymn books show that the *Anamie-nagamonan* [Prayer Songs] were adapted to every event in the Catholic calendar and to every act of worship. They were devised for *Kitchi-ogimagijigak* (New Year), *Anwenindisowini* (Lent), *Tchibaigijigad* (All Souls' Day), *Niba-anamiegijigad* (Christmas), and *Eukarisitiwin* (Eucharist), and for eulogies to Jesus and Kitchitwa Marie, the Blessed Virgin. At these and other festivals and at weekly church services, the hymns were sung in the Native language. Since 1910 they have bean limited more and more, and now they serve chiefly at wakes.

The occasions and the texts were similar in all of the Catholic communities, although several expressions differ in the Odawa and Ojibwe words. Latin liturgies were common to all. The song types agree, and often the melodies coincide. But many local tune variants have developed even in adjacent settlements such as L'Arbre Croche and Burt Lake. The Cross Village and Harbor Springs singers often sing different tunes to identical words from versions by Whitney Albert, Margaret Lambert of St. Ignace, Mary Weeden of Nahma, and Thomas Shalifoe of Baraga. Also, they differ in large and small details from the melodies collected and published by Fr. Paul Prud'homme and Fr. Desautels (Prud'homme 1931). Susan Shagonaby has remarked on this local diversity. In good folk song tradition, the variability also extends to individual renderings.

Some of the versions are accessible for exact study. Others have been limited to listening sessions. A comparative study must be left to the future. For the present, the selections and a few comparisons will be used in unraveling the provenance.

In the wilderness around the Great Lakes, Jesuit "black robes," who followed on the heels of the first explorers, noticed that the Native religion consisted "mainly in singing to the beating of drums," for worship and recreation, and in joy and suffering (Kenton 1925, 58–59). They considered the religion a rank superstition and the music lacking in sweet harmony. They called the nature spirits demons, but they showed good sense in replacing the sun symbol by Jesus, Nokomis by Mary, and Native music by attractive Gregorian chants. They turned to the children and through them appealed to the adults. By 1644, Huron converts enthusiastically sang Christmas hymns (*Jesuit Relations,* 25:113, 211). Soon afterward they harmonized in four voices (*Jesuit Relations,* 28:249). The Native drum and flageolet found counterparts in the drum and fife played by French soldiers for the blessing of the bread (*Jesuit Relations,* 45:131).

By 1672 the French Jesuits had learned the Native languages and were translating Latin and French texts into these tongues. Fr. Druillettes, pastor of the mission at Sault Ste. Marie, wrote: "They are assiduous in saying their prayers in the Church . . . and take pleasure in chanting beautiful hymns in their language" (*Jesuit Relations,* 57:207). The *Jesuit Relations* refer frequently to plainsong, to Pange Lingua for the Sunday before Lent, the Magnificat, Te Deum, Miserere, and Gloria Patri for Palm Sunday (*Jesuit Relations,* 48:231), and to the Vexilla and Exaudiat at a large intertribal meeting near the Sault (*Jesuit Relations,* 55:107ff.). Fr. Pierre Cholenec mentions the eighth mode used in chanting a hymn to the Virgin (*Jesuit Relations,* 60:283). He thereby justifies an assumption that these early Indian hymns were the modal chants handed down in the Catholic Church and published in the *Liber Usualis* (Society of St. John the Evangelist 1934). In 1671, Fr. André mentioned responsorial rendering of the chants at Manitoulin Island:

> No sooner had I begun to have these sung in the Chapel, accompanied by a sweet-tuned flute, than they all came in crowds so that I let only the girls enter the Chapel . . . thus we sang in two choruses, those without responding to those within. (*Jesuit Relations,* 55:147)

Fr. André was the first great hymn popularizer all the way from Manitoulin across the Upper Peninsula to the Menominee Indians near Green Bay of present Wisconsin. He spent 1682 in St. Ignace and then returned to Canada. One of his reports not only shows his attitude but reveals several secrets of his success. He had the children learn French airs, and he himself composed melodies for their use:

> The reason why he was so eagerly sought was found in certain spiritual songs that he was wont to have the children sing to French airs, which

pleased these Savages extremely . . . This success . . . made him resolve to assail the men through the children, and to combat idolatry with souls of extreme innocence. In short, he composed songs against the superstitions that we have mentioned, and against the vices most opposed to Christianity; and after teaching the children to sing them to the accompaniment of a sweet toned flute, he went everywhere with these little Savage musicians, to declare War on Jugglers, Dreamers. (*Jesuit Relations,* 56:129ff.)

The transition from plainchant to French folk melody began in the seventeenth century. Though the *Jesuit Relations* grew less specific on music and although they discontinued by 1790, the process probably continued in the missions that persevered. In some areas the priests withdrew, only to reappear in full force in the early nineteenth century. The Odawa were converted rapidly after 1823; the Upper Peninsula Ojibwe more slowly and later.

In most missions French influence continued. But L'Arbre Croche was assigned a series of Austrian and German prelates, both Jesuit and Franciscan, from 1831 to 1889: Fr. Friedrich Baraga, the sympathetic Fr. Francis Pierz, Fr. Ignatius Mrak, Fr. Seraphim Zorn, Fr. Louis Sifferath, and the energetic and eccentric Prussian, Fr. Bernard Weikamp (Shurtleff 1940, 24–30). The most important figure in hymn propagation was Baraga, a Slovene native of Carniola, who spent 1831–1833 in L'Arbre Croche, then moved to the Upper Peninsula, became Bishop of Marquette, and often returned to L'Arbre Croche. Fr. Dejean had published a hymn book in 1830, but Baraga studied the language intensively, wrote a grammar, translated hymns and scriptures, and widely encouraged reading and singing in the Native languages. His name is on many a battered title page of *Anamienagamonan.*

In his large area of activity he appears to have introduced folk tunes from his native Austria, side by side with or in place of the earlier French and still earlier Gregorian melodies. This theory will appear in musical form in a moment. The consolidation of Austrian influences under his successors would account for some of the differences between L'Arbre Croche and Upper Peninsula tunes.

Very few of the hymn tunes can be positively identified. But they bear stylistic earmarks that place them as European folk tunes and in some cases suggest the national origin. The three traditions can be illustrated by comparing two examples.

"Jesus Wegwissiian" was recorded in Baraga by Thomas Shalifoe, with a melody unlike either version in Prud'homme's collection (Prud'homme 1931, 179) and also unlike the Ave Maria Stella, which is quoted as the air for its singing. But one of the Prud'homme tunes shows its derivation from Ave Maria with a change to the major key. Ave Maria (Prud'homme 1931, 329) is in the Aeolian mode or the eighth ecclesiastical mode (Bas 1906, 25 ff.). Its derived melody has the Indian words that enlist Jesus and Mary against the powers of darkness. The third part of the example, Shalifoe's tune, uses these Indian words, read from one of Baraga's hymnals. But it is in the Dorian mode, with the regular meter and regular division into phrases of four measures each. It is the only recorded melody that is not in the modern major scale, and its quality is more fluent than that of the L'Arbre Croche melodies. The Dorian mode is a more archaic scale than our major scale, or Ionian mode. It persists in some older European folk songs and in French songs of Canada, such as the voyageur song "V'la l' bon vent" (Barbeau 1946, 38). It may be derived from one of the French tunes introduced by André, or from one of André's compositions in the folk vein.

Shalifoe sang all ten verses, with his particular dialectic pronunciation. Eight verses were translated freely by Thomas Shalifoe, Jr., and more exactly by Fred Ettawageshik.

Jesus Wegwissiian

Text and Ettawageshik's Translation [*Shalifoe's Free Translation in italics*]

1.
Jesus wegwissiian
Jesus who art the son
    Mojag gaie bekish
    Forever may you
Gagigangowisan
Take good care of me
    Kiminowinigo.
    So I will be happy
        [Jesus the son
        Take care of me
        So I may go to heaven]

2.
Gwanatch Marie, gijig
Lovely Mary, this day
    Gepakakonaman,
    Shield me,
Inenimishinam,

Remember us,
> *Gij'gong tchi igaiang.*
> To heaven so we may go.
>> *[Beautiful Marie*
>> *Take pity on me,*
>> *So I can be with you in heaven.]*

3.
Eve sa nitam ikwe,
Eve behold the first woman,
> *Ningi-nissigonan,*
> I descended from,
Kin kiginigia
You were born,
> *Gabimadjiiangid.*
> So I could go on living.
>> *[He put me here on earth*
>> *To worship you,*
>> *You made me*
>> *So I could go on living]*

4.
Marie, abiskon
Marie, deliver
> *Neta-batadidjig,*
> The sinners,
Wassenemaw gaie
Remove indeed
> *Tebikadisidjig.*
> The powers of darkness.
>> *[God, put your collar on,*
>> *So the sinners can follow you.]*
>> [Shalifoe apparently mishearing]

5.
Miwitawishinam
Help us
> *Anotch maianadak,*
> Against evil,
Bidawishinam dash
Bring us verily

Mojag wenijishing.
Always the good things.
> *[Tie us up*
> *So we can stay put where we are,*
> *And bring us the good things often.]*

6.
Wabanaishinam
Look upon us
> *Eji-ogimik Jesus,*
> Thou that art the master Jesus,

Kinki ginigia,
You were born,
> *Tchi widagwishinged.*
> So I might arrive (in heaven).
>> *[Look upon me*
>> *Blessed Jesus*
>> *You made me*
>> *So I can make my way to heaven.]*

7.
Ki sagiig Jesus,
Thou beloved Jesus,
> *Kiga-babamitag.*
> May I obey you.

Kejewadisiian,
Be kind,
> *Jawenimishinam.*
> Have mercy on us.
>> *[Beloved Jesus,*
>> *Have pity on me.*
>> *So I can serve you on earth.]*

8.
Kin gagangowiian
Take care of me
> *Tchi bimadisiiang*
> So I may go on living

Kaginig gijigong
Always in heaven

Tchi wabamag Jesus.
So I may see Jesus.
[Preserve me
After you make me good
So I can see Jesus.]

A hymn for the Eucharist, "Sagitoda Jesus wiiaw," shows a similar plainsong origin and change to folk melody, but it has a different kind of pattern. The printed text bears a caption, "Sur l'air Pange Lingua," and thereby suggests that formerly the Odawa words were sung to this ecclesiastical chant in the Phrygian or third mode. One of the versions in Prud'homme's collection is fitted to the chant, which appears later in the book with the Latin text (Prud'homme 1931, 146, 319). The melody recorded by David Kenosha evidently was introduced after publication of the 1858 texts, hence by Baraga on a return trip or by one of his successors. It is in the major diatonic scale, with a rigid form of four phrases with four measures each, the four phrases grouped as A A' and B B'. The recurrent rhythmic theme descends sequentially in B. The structure, phrasing, and very theme recall the Austrian national anthem, "Gott erhalte Franz den Kaiser," composed by Joseph Haydn in 1797 and taken over later as the German "Deutschland, Deutschland über alles." It fits into the style of Austro-German folk songs that are the likely origin of both the hymn tune and the anthem.

Another hymn tune of L'Arbre Croche has an even stronger Austrian flavor. "Mamoya wamada" is a hymn of thanksgiving, recorded by Jane Ettawageshik at a New Year Feast of the Kishigos, with Hattie Sagataw at the piano. It appears to be a variant of a folk dance known in Austria and Bavaria as "Siebenschritt" and in Czechoslovakia as "Ctyri Kroky" (Four Steps). One need only compare the B part of the Odawa tune with the second half of three folk dance tunes, which are twice as fast as the hymn: "Siebenschritt," "Ctyri Kroky," and Humperdinck's folk-derived "Bruederlein, komm' tanz' mit mir," from *Hans and Gretel* (Duggan, Schlottman, and Rutledge 1948, 57, 103).

The newer, folk-like melody of "Jesus wegwissiian" is more anonymous than the medieval chant, which was composed by St. Thomas of Aquinas in 1263 for Holy Communion, Corpus Christi processionals, Matins and Vespers, and the forty Hours (Julian 1892, 878). Excerpts from the first and fourth verses give its content, relating to the Communion rite:

1.
Pange, lingua gloriosi
Sing the glorious body broken,

> *Corporis mysterium*
Sanguinisque pretiosi
Sing the precious blood . . .

4.
Verbum caro, panem verum
Word made flesh, the Bread of nature
> *Verbo carnem efficit . . .*
> By a word to flesh he turns . . .

The Odawa text paraphrases the Latin freely. David Kenosha understood the contents but was unable to translate exactly. So Fred Ettawageshik provided an interlinear translation.

"Sagitoda Jesus wiiaw" [Pange lingua gloriosi]

Odawa with Fred Ettawageshik's Translation [*Kenosha's Commentary in italics*]

Sagitoda Jesus wiiaw
Let us cherish Jesus' body
> [*That's about the precious heart, his body. We thought of it, his body—his body is holy.*]

Ketchitwawandawadinig;
It is holy;
> [*And his blood . . . it's like we think a lot about his blood.*]

O miskwim manadjitoda,
His blood, let us glorify it, (make it beautiful)
> [*When he was killed he poured that blood out. He done that for us*]

Gasiginan apinassind
He poured it when he was killed,
> [*When he was hanging on the cross, they had him in court and put the crown of thorns on his head, his blood dripping all over him. He done that for us, when he died on the cross.*]

Kigisiginamagonan,
He poured it for us,
Tchibaiatigong ginibod.
On the cross he died
Win Jesus bwa mashi nibod
Before Jesus died
O Wikeman wikanissan

He invited his apostles (to a feast)
Odinan dash: Nongom niiaw.
He told them thus: This day my body.
> *[And then he told them about his body.]*
> *[Before he died, he invited his apostles to have supper with him.]*

Gigishpinadaganiwan;
Let us come together;
> *[Like you'd buy something.]*

Tchibwa mashi nissigoian,
Before I am killed,
Ganapine wikondida.
Let us sup together.

Odawan pakwejiganan
Thus he took bread
Obigonan, ominan dash:
He broke it and gave them saying thus:
> *[(Reads Mark 36:26) And as they were eating, Jesus took bread and blessed it, and brake it and gave it to the disciples, and said: Take, eat; this is my body.]*

Mi anawi pagwejigan
Although like bread
Eji-nagosid, odinan:
It appears, he said;
Geget niiaw atemagad.
Indeed my body is there.
Anaming mananigog
Breath of life it gives you.

For the second Austrian-type hymn of praise, "Mamoya," there is no known Latin prototype. In fact, the origin of the words remains obscure. The text for I changes from verse to verse. The text for II recurs as a chorus—a common feature of these hymns.

Two typical hymns, recorded by David Kenosha and Susan Shagonaby, were at one time meant for Christmas ("Kakina minawasida") and for the Blessed Virgin Mary ("Kagenig Kije-manito"). Their central ideas, as translated by Fred Ettawageshik, are much akin.

I.
Kakina minawasida

All let us make merry
> *Ki mino nondagemin:*
> He was pleased to hear us:

Kinawind gi-ondji-nigi
For us he was reborn.
>> CHORUS:
>> *Kije-manito Ogwissan.*
>> The Holy Spirit's Son.

II.
Kagenig Kije-manito
Always, Holy Spirit,
> *Kigi-bi-sagiig, Marie;*
> She loved you, Mary;

Bwa mashie ondadissiyan
Before you were born
> *Ki gi-makwenimig*
> He thought of you who are a virgin.
>> CHORUS:
>> *Gagangowiian*
>> You who are Virgin
>>> *Marie eninijiminang,*
>>> Mary who is like us,
>>
>> *Gwanachiwiian,*
>> Who is beautiful,
>>> *Nadamawishinam.*
>>> Help us.

"Mojag Anamiewin"

A hymn rendered by Blue Cloud fits the chorus or refrain into another pattern equally characteristic of European folk songs. The changing verse is A A and the chorus is B A, making a ternary form.

1.
Mojag anamiewin
Always faith
> *Babamenindanda,*
> Let us be mindful of it,

Kiji-manito   eta

God   only
    Kitchi sagiada.
    Let us greatly love.
        CHORUS:
        Machi bimadisiwin
        Evil ways
            Anotch maianadak,
            Anything evil,
        Enigokodeiiang
        With our whole heart
            Kakina webinanda.
            All throw it away.

2.
Memanitowisidjig
False gods
    Agonetawadag;
    Let us not believe them;
Ka-bamenimassidag
Do not pay attention to them,
    Matchi magoshejig.
    Bad they who gave feast.
        CHORUS

Not all of the hymns float in a three-century-old haze. "Adeste Fideles" resounds in all churches and schools at Noël. A hymn to the Virgin is set to the tune known in this country as "America," in England as "God Save the King," in Austria as "Heil, Kaiser Josef," and in Germany as "Hail Dir im Seigerkranz" (Schmalstich n.d., 88). It is not very old, being composed in 1743 by Henry Carey and taken over by Austria and Germany in 1781 and 1793, but it antedates Odawa hymnody. This same text, "Wenijanissimiang," appears in Prud'homme's text with essentially this same tune (Prud'homme 1931, 230), but at the printing of the hymnals it was set to "L'air Nous Vous Invoquons Tous," and it was heard in another setting from Whitney Albert, Margaret Lambert, and Mrs. Weeden. The first verse proceeds, with David Kenosha's translation, as follows:

Wenijánissimiiang
Treat us like your children
    Genawenimiiang

Take care of us
Gwanatch Marie;
Gracious Mary;
   Ganodamawishinam
   Speak for us
Kinwegimigoian
We love you like our mother
   Jawenimishinam
   Have mercy on us
Gwanatch Marie.
Gracious Mary.

In his rendering, as in "Kitchitwa Marie" and others, Kenosha takes metric liberties—a significant point that implies changes away from prototypes through centuries of individual variation.

Concordance of Odawa Hymns in Paper

Recorded Hymn Texts and Tunes

NAME	SUNG BY	RECORDED BY	LOCATION	TUNE
Emamiaieg	Kenosha and Shagonaby	G. Kurath	Harbor Springs	*Adeste Fideles*
Kakina	Kenosha and Shagonaby	G. Kurath	Harbor Springs	
Api Jesus	Kishigo and Kenosha	Edwin Burroughs	Harbor Springs	
Epitoweng	Kishigo and group	J. Ettawageshik	Harbor Springs	*O l'Auguste sacrement*
Mamoya	Kishigo and group	J. Ettawageshik	Harbor Springs	*Benissons à jamais*
Sagitoda	Kenosha	G. Kurath	Cross Village	*Pange lingua gloriosi*
Gagengowiian	Kenosha and Shagonaby	G. Kurath	Harbor Springs	
Kitchitwa Marie	Kenosha and Shabonaby	G. Kurath	Harbor Springs	
Gwanatch Marie	Kenosha		Cross Village	*Nous vous invoquons tous*

Methodist Hymns

While the Catholic hymns remain in part enigmatic—despite the tantalizing clues of the captions "Sur l'air," perusal of numerous folk song volumes, and consultations with musicologists and Fr. Prud'homme—the Methodist hymns have for the most part been traced to Wesleyan composers. A few remain anonymous. The documentation, which starts with the eighteenth century, and the known facts of hymn-singing practices, white and Indian, explain the eccentricities of the Protestant repertoires and suggest a similar explanation for the Catholic hymns.

The Wesleyan tunes and texts were disseminated in the South in the eighteenth century and moved north in the course of several waves of revivalism during the nineteenth century. Many of the melodies were compositions by followers of Wesley, but some are older. Bourgeois's setting to the Doxology in 1551 was derived from a secular chanson, a "jocund and lively air," just as Catholic vernacular hymns derived from dances (Foote 1940, 14–15). Many of the older Wesleyan tunes were inspired by the splendid Moravian hymnody (Foote 1940, 144). Some of the best ones (for instance, "Uxbridge"), though they appear in the hymn books, are now rarely sung by white congregations and were not identified by the choir masters I consulted. The older Indians prefer these older tunes.

These older tunes were the ones propagated by Peter Jones after 1823, together with his translations. Apparently, anonymous creations also came into being with modal scales such as the Grandfather Song, which Eli

Thomas sings to drum accompaniment. This is a minor tune in the Dorian scale, known only to Eli.

As revival followed on revival, cheaper melodies were fitted to the old texts of Watts and Wesley, and sentimental verses came into being before and after 1900, such as Hudson's 1885 setting for "Alas and Would My Savior Bleed" and the English hymns rendered by the children in English.

The many musical versions of the self-same texts, such as "Jesus My All" and "O For a Thousand Tongues," are explained by the custom of fitting together various texts and melodies as long as the meters corresponded. Such interchangeability was most prevalent until 1855 (Foote 1940, 191). It is still common among the Indians, while white congregations adhere to the printed combinations. In view of such flexibility in the face of the early printed music of Methodism, an even greater flexibility would appear likely in the case of the unprinted Catholic hymns. Another kind of development was observed by Burton at the turn of the century—namely, the Indians' gradual transition from Native quality to conventional rendering. Burton heard several old men singing hymns with slurs, pulsation, and an Indian throat (Burton 1909, 136–37). He even recorded and transcribed a sample by William J. Shingwauk. At the same time, the younger people sang like white congregations (Burton 1909, 279–80). A little of this old style still adheres to David Kenosha's a cappella singing, while the Methodists of all ages have adopted the standard renderings and ordinary harmonization.

In addition to all these variant developments there are some quaint contemporary oddities. Eli Thomas may change a revival tune. Or he may combine a Wesleyan text with a modern popular song and an Indian drum beat. Younger men, such as Jack Neomi and Roy Chevis, sing with a hillbilly twang copied from radios, along with their guitar accompaniments. Then there are the secular instruments: the accordion and saxophone.

Several of these tendencies can be illustrated by versions of "Jesus My All," the Grandfather Song, and Thomas's variations on an anonymous revival tune and his setting to "Travellin' Down to Mexico" with drum. These can be compared with the standard Wesleyan settings by Lowell Mason, featured at the Mount Pleasant revival.

From Native Song to Hymn

The chasm between Native dance song and hymn is just as deep in the Methodist communities as in the Catholic. In scale, structure, and contour the two hymn categories present a similar picture. But to widen the gap, the Methodists commonly harmonize their songs. As in the Catholic hymnody, the resemblances are limited to the preference for sequential treatment and the strophic division into clear-cut phrases ending on a sustained note. But the contours are consistently divergent, bow in the case of the hymns, cascading in the Native songs. A study of the scales, however, suggests a point of contact and a process of transition by means of the Grandfather Song. The following chart typifies two kinds of Native scales, a transitional scale, and three kinds of hymn scales.

1. The tertial Native scales, as in Chingwa's Medicine and Eagle Songs, contain only five tones, begin on a high note, and end on the lowest main tone: 6 5   3 2 1.
2. The quartal scales, as in the Hoot Owl Songs, Kenosha's Eagle Song, and Blue Cloud's Brave and Pigeon Feather Songs, have these same characteristics but lack the third and are thus even further removed from the diatonic scale: 8   6 5 4   2 1.
3. The scale of the Grandfather Song includes both the third and fourth in its six tones; it is distinguished most radically by the beginning and ending on the same lowest main tone: 8 7   5 4 3 2 1.
4. The complete diatonic scale begins and ends on the same lowest note of some hymns, such as the first two versions of "Jesus My All": 8 7 6 5 4 3 2 1 7.
5. In a diatonic scale, much of the melodic material dangles below the tonic, as in "Mojag Anamiewin" and version five of "Jesus My All": 6 5 4 3 2 1 7 6 5 (4 3).
6. The scale is "gapped" so as to include only fine tones, as the first version of "O For a Thousand Tongues," or six tones as "God Moves": 6 5   3 2 1   6 5.

One could reverse the process and compare these scales with those of Native songs in a hypothetical European scale, namely:

David Kenosha, Second Hoot Owl Song	987654	21	6 tones
Whitney Albert, Medicine Song		3 217654	7 tones

The former plays above the tonic, like most Native songs and some hymns; the latter dangles mostly below, even more than most hymns. They differ from the true Native songs in lining up more than three tones in succession, due to the filling in of the scale. However, this is not the only feature distinguishing the Native from the transitional and European melodies, as there are five-tone hymns.

The melodic contour of the two styles contrasts. All of the Native songs except Blue Cloud's Medicine Chant have a descending trend, but the hymns rise as much as they fall, sometimes even more. The device of sequential development is common to both, but in the Native repertoire it is always descending, as in "Sagitoda" and "Mamoya" A, and in hymns it is just as often ascending, as in "Mamoya" B.

Structurally the two types share the preference for the number four, in Native songs limited to the number of song repeats and in hymns extended to the number of phrases, the number of measures in a phrase, and often the number of beats in the measure. The hymns are much more rigid in pattern and generally boil down to a form of A A B B, or A A B A, with regular metric divisions of duple or triple time. However, both types prefer simple rhythmic motifs of even or dotted notes, with complex rhythms only in special Native song types. The accompaniment of drum or piano perseveres in an even beat. The Native songs never slow down at the end as do the hymns, and they rarely drag along at a slow tempo.

The Gregorian chants, with their free meter and modal scales, may have provided a transition, as did the Grandfather Song. Even so, the jump was a wide one. As the Anishinaabeg apparently used no antiphony, this device was likewise new. And the adoption of harmony required a radical musical adjustment. Probably the Christian music sounded as strange to the Indians as the Native songs did to the missionaries. But the Indians were more receptive to novelty. An equal flexibility is manifest in the literary aspects, in devising suitable texts in the Native language, and in combining Algonkian terms with European melodies.

The Texts of the Hymns

Concepts within Terminology

A sympathetic student of Indian ways, Henry Rowe Schoolcraft once said, "They appear, by their words, to live in a world of spirits. Aside from the direct words for Father, as the universal Parent, and of Maker, and Great Spirit, they have an exact term for the Holy Ghost; and he who has ever heard a converted Indian pray, and can understand his petition, will never afterwards wish to read any philological disquisitions about the adaptation of their languages to the purposes of Christianity" (Schoolcraft 1851, 453–54).

The majority of Native songs show quite different preoccupations from those expressed in the hymns, but some songs of medicine societies uttered exalted invocations—for instance Wabeno songs (Burton 1909, 247–48) and Midé songs (Densmore 1910, 113–18). For some Christian concepts the translators found equivalent Native terms; for some they had to modify the application; and for some they had to coin words. On a number of terms the Catholics and Methodists have agreed; on others they are at variance.

The concept and the name of the supreme deity find two equivalents: *Keche manedo* (Great Spirit) and *Kesha manedo* (benevolent spirit) (Copway 1851, 154).[1] Other names have been adapted to hymnody—*Nosæ* or *Kosena:n* (Our Father), *Tebenege* (ruler, or Lord), and *Ogima* (chief); and in the Doxology, *Weyosimint* (he who is the father). The conceptual enigma will be further discussed in the final chapter.

In the Doxology, the Son is called *Wékwisimint* (he who is the Son). In Catholic hymns he is called *Kižé mənedó ówissan* (Great Spirit's Son). Usually he is called Jesus in both sects, but with a different pronunciation—*jésus* in Catholicism, *jízəs* in Methodism, respectively French and English pronunciations. His role as intercessor is significant, perhaps due to Native preferences for a middle man, and his prominence in hymnody vies with that of the Father.

Jesus' mother, the Virgin Mary, is ignored in Methodist hymnody but is prominent in Catholic verse as a powerful and merciful mother and intercessor. In the aboriginal pantheon she may have been foreshadowed by Nokomis, Grandmother Earth (Jenness 1935, 108), or by the beautiful woman, the sun's sister, who might appear to a vision-seeking youth (Schoolcraft 1845, 8–10). Her invocations are taken from everyday human experience—*wenijanissimiiaŋ* (we your children), *genawenimiiaŋ* (take care of us), etc.

The Holy Ghost, third member of the Trinity, is not termed a manido. Rather, it is the *pánižid ojičág* (superlatively clean ghost). In fact, none of the minor spirits are called manidos. Saints, who occur only in Catholic prayers, are *kíčitwawendagósid* (the blessed). Angels serve as intercessors and protectors in both pantheons. To the Catholics they are *anžéniyok,* an Odawaization of the English term. To the Methodists, they are *íšpimiŋ žéwis aníšinábek* (heaven its Indians), perhaps in recognition of their anthropomorphic qualities.

Evil spirits have several linguistic equivalents. In "Jésus wegwíssiian," they are *tebíkadisijig* (powers of darkness); in "Mojág anamiéwin," they are *memanitówisijig* (false gods), meaning the Native deities. Satan is a manido, an evil *mači manido,* bobbing up as humorous *Chemanido* in Odawa New Year celebrations. It is perhaps significant that only the supreme deity and those who became Christian demons are addressed as manidos in prayers and hymns, although according to Schooloraft, manido is "a generic term for spiritual agency" (Schoolcraft 1851, 55–56). The Jesuit missionaries came to recognize the function of these agencies in nature by 1700 (Kinietz 1940, 287–88). The converts and translators evidently recognized the distinction between angels and "other minor or guardian spirits whom they court in their first dream of fasting . . . in the shape of quadrupeds, birds, or some inanimate object in nature, as the moon, stars, or the imaginary thunderers" and to whom they paid special homage (Warren 1885, 65). Both are clearly distinguished from *jibám* (soul) and *jičág* (ghost); *jibám* was particularly handy for discussions of salvation.

All of these spirits, which in Native lore inhabited the surrounding world, had to be moved to heaven. For this new place of bliss, the Odawa Catholics use *Wákwing* or *Gíjig* (*ciel*) and the Protestants use *Ishpeming*. Good spirits have been moved upward, and the evil spirit had to move his habitation under the earth (Blackbird 1897, 79). This is *anámakamig*. Eli Thomas explained that *'nəməkəmik* means "under the ground" or "cellar." That's where the underground monsters live. But as a place of eternal torment for the souls of misdoers it formed no part of Native beliefs (P. Jones 1861, 102).

For actions that predestined the soul for either place, the hymns show various attempts at linguistic substitutes. Sin could be *gagibádisiwin* (folly), *batádowin, mačí dodámowin* (evil action), or *mačí bimádisiwin* (evil ways). To Catholics and Protestants alike, *jawéndagosi* recurs both for "happiness" and "mercy." They have synonyms, such as *wišéndam* (glad), *ineniwíshinam* (remember us), and *gagigangówinan kiminowínigo* (take care of me so I will be happy). It is to this end that the Catholics sing *manajiáda* (let us honor him or her) and *mamóya wamáda*, (let us give praise). Prayers might seek to avert physical miseries, as in aboriginal times, but the emphasis has shifted to moral issues. The Indians had moral codes and twenty-one precepts that Blackbird likens to the Ten Commandments, and they could suffer from the infringements (Blackbird 1897, 103–5). But these issues were not the aim of all religious rites, as they were among the Christian descendants.

A few more adapted terms are listed below:

žawéndagósiwin	communion
enámiewin	prayer, Christianity
enámiad	Christian (pronounced by Thomas *'nimə'ed*)
enámiajig	believers
enámia kížig	Sunday (prayer day)
enámia wigómig	church (prayer wigwam)
enámiassig	pagan (negative of Christian)
sa:sá:giwičigœ	pagan sacrifice (Methodists also Christian sacrifice)
debweiendamowin	belief
kotagiídisowin	penance
pinízewin	redemption
aźedeátig, čibaiátig	cross
enámiewatig	cross (prayer stick)
pakgížigad	Easter (*pâques*)
wabigónigížigad	Corpus Christi (flower day)
jízəs kinígid	Christmas (Christ was born)
məkátewikwanaie	priest (black robe)

wenidjanissimíyang	we your children
sagiáda	let us love
manadjiáda	let us glorify
nagamóda	let us sing
jawéndagosi	charitable
enígokodeiiang	with our whole hearts

These are fitted into the regular song meter and structure. If the number of syllables does not come out even with the number of notes, a vowel may extend over several notes, as in the refrain of "Mojag anamiawin," or it may be contracted, as in the last word of this refrain. The natural accent may have to be shifted, as from *mačí bimádiziwin* to *máči bimádizíwin* or from *kágenig kižé manitó* to *kagénig kíže mánitó*.

Text and Melody

Obviously both Odawa and Ojibwe have no set rules for either intonation or rhythm. They thereby could be much more easily adapted to imported songs than could a tone language. They raise no problem such as that related by Eunice Pike about the Mexican Mixtecs. This tonal language demanded hymn tunes that followed the tonal pattern of the words. Adaptation to tonal languages in hymnody has been described by Cowan and Davis (1955). In Odawa and Ojibwe, the words as spoken may fit in rhythm, accent, and contour to a tune, or they may have to undergo violation.

In Thomas's hymn that follows, the relative contraction of speech is also apparent. The rhythm is irregular and different for each line, in contrast with the recurrent pattern of the song. The accents, two for each line, are near the beginning of the word, the stronger one being in the second half of the phrase. Thus the melody, which here also reaches its high point at the accent, falls to a main tone at the end of each line. Only one song version adheres to this pattern of accent—namely, the Grandfather Song, which formed an early transition. None of the tunes have any connection with the spoken melody, except, by chance, the first line of version four. Nor does their octave's range correspond to the compass of a fifth in the speech. The tempo is very much slower than that of speech, the Grandfather Song being closest with its moderate tempo. In general the hymns use each syllable, except for version three in the last line. This tune contracts *géniyežayad* to *génižad*, just like the spoken line. But the shifts of phrasing and accent produce peculiar distortions, as in version four of *jizás išpí—miŋ* and the breaking up of *o ——wépenimoyan*.

236 The Art of Tradition

Invocations do less violence to the Native patterns, as they are not restricted by a tune. They may adhere to a monotone or chromatically descend. They may rattle off faster than natural speech. But they make no adjustments in the accents.

Liturgical Speech

From this and other studied samples, it would appear that liturgical speech undergoes major changes: breakneck speed, a monotone descending in a chromatic scale to the end, and rhythmically spaced accents frequently at variance with natural accent. It is impossible to say whether this derives from Native liturgical practices or from Christian influences.[2]

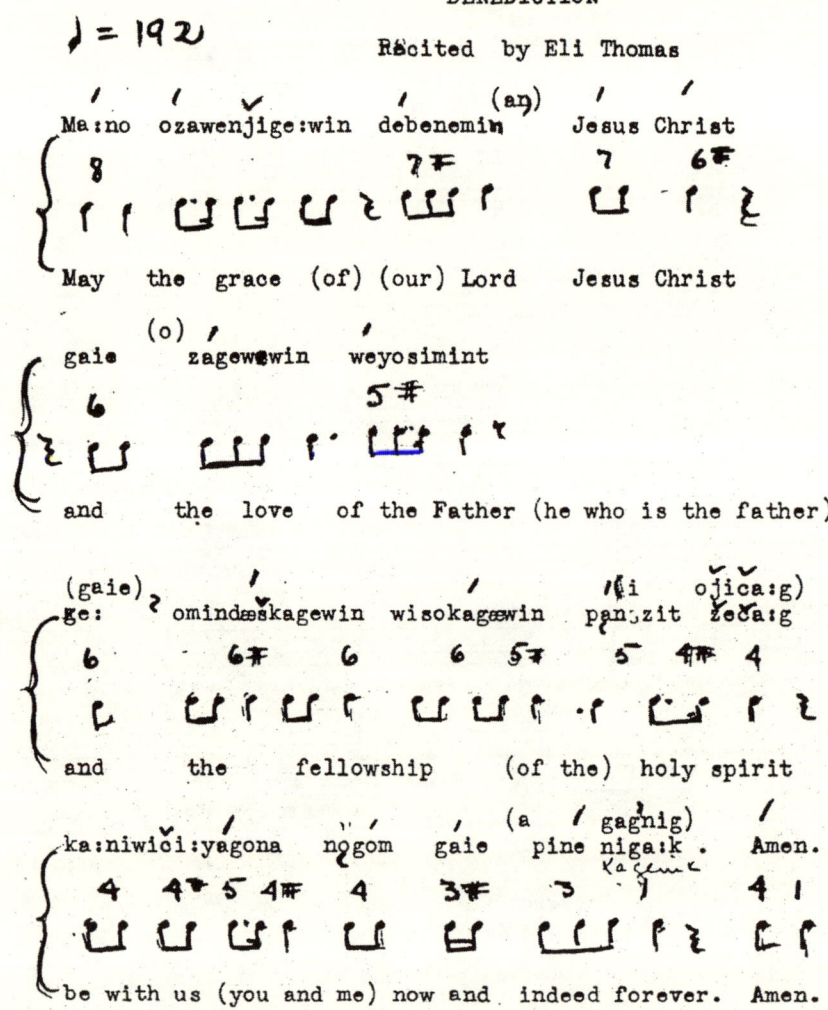

Omitted syllables are found in parentheses above word.

Beliefs

CHAPTER 8

Indigenous Lore

➣ *For this chapter Jane Ettawageshik assembled a body of local knowledge to which she referred in the original manuscript as Odawa "superstitions." This unfortunate word choice, of course, bears an implicit value judgment, which Ettawageshik clearly rejects. Under the category "superstition," the author contents herself with gathering a miscellany of recorded lore without eliciting—or even suggesting the possibility of—the fuller Odawa worldview that places that body of lore within the framework of an indigenous logic. By contrast, the anthropologist A. I. Hallowell, in a germinal essay, "Ojibwa Ontology, Behavior, and World View," took pains to identify a worldview in which his Northern Manitoba Ojibwe consultants' lore about bear walking and other putatively supernatural phenomena made sense (Hallowell 1955). Appealing to the structure of the Ojibwe language and sociolinguistic remarks made by his subjects about the workings of the language, Hallowell argued that no clean and clear distinction obtains in Ojibwe thought between the natural and the supernatural.*

Be this as it may, Ettawageshik documents here the continued vitality of aspects of that traditional Odawa worldview in the mid-twentieth century, even while she identifies the hybrid nature of the worldview of her consultants. As with dance and song, local knowledge in the oral tradition such as we encounter here proceeds according to what Pierre Bourdieu calls "the logic of practice" (Bourdieu 1987). Rather than concern itself with theoretical orthodoxy, such local Odawa knowledge was deeply practical, woven into the complicated lives of twentieth-century Odawa people who drew on it resourcefully to make do as well as to make meaning.

Traditional knowledge in the service of healing classically proceeds according to this practical logic, and the section entitled "Plant Lore" addresses the distinctively Anishinaabe knowledge of Michigan's flora in the service of healing. Joe Chingwa is the author's source for this herbal knowledge, and he in turn credited his grandfather, Mkkwániwi, for most of it. Ettawageshik proceeded with the assistance of a number of botanists in identifying the Linnaean classifications of the plants. Readers should be advised that Jane Ettawageshik voiced some concerns to her son Frank about the proper identifications of some of the medicines in this chapter.

The Odawa superstitions in this chapter have been divided into three categories: (1) those of obvious European origin; (2) those that may be European but are shared by the Odawa (Indian-European); and (3) those which are definitely Indian.

European

Salt will drive snakes away because "snakes hate salt." If one puts a baby down on the ground while attending to some duty, a circle of salt should be scattered around the child, so the snakes will not come near. Likewise, salt is sometimes put at a doorway to keep snakes from crawling into a dwelling, and anyone planning to walk through a field where there are likely to be snakes should put salt in his shoes before starting out.

It is a bad sign to spill a glass of beer on the table.

A bird beating its wings against a window pane bears a message for someone.

The seventh son of a seventh son will be gifted with the ability to prophesy.

If two persons walk around opposite sides of a post or a similar object, they must say, "pins and needles" to avoid a quarrel.

A rooster crowing in the yard has a message, either good or bad.

If chickens run for cover when it first starts to rain, it will clear up soon. If they stay outdoors, it may rain for hours.

If you tell your dream before breakfast, it will come true.

When you see a shooting star, put your hand in your pocket and say "Money, money, money," and you will find some money in there that was not there before.

Indian-European

Thunder casts thunderbolts from the skies that can be found occasionally and are a sign of good luck.

A woodpecker pecking on the chimney or roof is bad luck.

Tobacco will keep moths away from woolens. So it is a good idea to put cigar butts in woolen bags and similar objects.

A bat in the house is a bad omen.

If a man lights a fire in a stove and it goes out, this is a sign that he will have a lazy wife.

A ring of light around the sun or moon is a sign of an approaching storm.

Blinking stars mean that there will soon be a wind storm. ("*nɪngakéné:o nango*—blinking star," said Joe Chingwa.)

To cure a goiter hold a live garter snake out straight with one hand at the head and the other at the tail and rub it across the goiter seven times. The goiter will then shortly disappear.

Indian

Do not insult old persons because they might be sorcerers or "bear walks" (*mkkwábamosɛd*, "they walk like the bear") and would revenge themselves against you.

If at night a person sees a queer light that seems to bounce along, or any other odd-acting thing, he should quickly put some sand or dirt in his mouth to avoid being bewitched.

Old women may drive away ghosts from deserted houses merely by going to the house alone and saying quietly, "Here, go away from here. No one lives here now. Go away!" This feat is said to have been accomplished only recently by an old Odawa woman in Harbor Springs at a house where strange noises and voices were sometimes heard.

Robins and blackbirds, especially when seen at night, are bad omens. They might be "bear walks."

All animals have their own plant medicines. This is the plant near which they may usually be found.

If a person hears the sound of Indian tom-toms in his dreams, it is a sign that someone will soon die.

Whenever lives are lost on Lake Michigan the sound of an Indian drum is heard beating, one beat for every life lost.

Speckled trout can turn into lizards or salamanders. Some persons never eat speckled trout because of this and consider them bad luck.

No one should tell stories in the summer time, lest the toads sleep with him.

Children should not blow poplar whistles in the spring because they might call up the snakes. (Joe Chingwa said that his story "The Magic Arrow" explained the origin of this saying.)

If a person bites into a live green (grass) snake, it will protect and strengthen the teeth. In case any poison gets into the teeth, it will not harm the person but will harm anyone bitten.

A crescent moon with a star between the points is a sign of war.

If a storm blows up from Cheboygan, it will not stay. (Generally true, perhaps because Cheboygan is south of Harbor Springs where the informant lived.)

If a snapping turtle gets hold of you, it won't let go until it thunders.

If you turn a toad over on its back, it will thunder.

A captive who lives with his captors and then returns to his own people will not live long.

A person with tuberculosis can be cured if carried during the early stages of the disease to the top of one of the Seven Sisters' sand dunes at the head of Little Traverse Bay, Michigan.

Anyone who climbs to the top of Sleeping Bear Point near Frankfort, Michigan, will have a long life. The climb must be made from the lake side of the dune, Fred Ettawageshik says.

In obtaining a strange white growth sometimes seen on tall pines and used in making a medicinal salve, the branch on which it is found must be shot down because the growth is alive and might be damaged otherwise.

If a door seems to open of itself, it is Nanabojo opening it. He wants to take a good look inside the house.

On days just after a fall of fine snow one sometimes sees a little swirl of snow carried down a street or across a field by the wind. This is Nanabojo running swiftly by.

If a person is looking for something but cannot find the right size or shape and first picks up one thing and then another, he is told to make up his mind and not to be like Nanabojo. Joe Chingwa said this saying was based on an episode in his myth about Nanabojo and Jibiabos, for Nanabojo tried first one stick and then another before finding the right one for an ice hockey game with the bears. In the meantime, the bears had slain his brother.

On very cold nights when old Indians see brilliant northern lights they say, "Nanabojo is poking the fire." Some believe that in a few days there will be milder weather, while others say that it will become even colder. In the summer, when bright northern lights are seen, the old Indians say, "A sign of rain and also chilly days after."

During a shower, when thunder rolls up and the sound seems to stop at the zenith, it will continue raining for a while. If the sound of thunder passes on across the sky, it will stop raining shortly. (*Mišumsinánikꞌ žagwiwak*, or "Grandfathers, they pass through," according to Fred Ettawageshik.)

Bear Walking or Sorcery

The term *mkkwábamosɛd* (he walks like the bear) is used to describe a type of sorcery similar to that attributed to the seventeenth century New England witches or the "loup garou" of the French Canadians. Bear walking is also known by this name among the Ojibwe of the Upper Peninsula of Michigan, where similar stories of their powers are told (Dorson 1952).

A bear walk is an evil person who has the power to change into animal form, often a bear, hence the name. In this guise, the bear walk, who is jealous of all handsome, healthy, and successful persons, visits a victim in order to destroy him. He (or she) goes like a ball of fire, or like a will o' the wisp, casting a greenish light wherever he moves. Some informants say that bear walks make this light by using the phosphorescent punk wood. Hence almost any Odawa, though he may stoutly deny believing in bear walks, feels a superstitious fear if an unexplained light is seen moving about in the fields or woods.

As he goes on his errand of destruction or sometimes theft, the bear walk emits cries that resemble that of the bird or animal form he has assumed, yet are just different enough that one may be forewarned if one listens closely.

A victim has only to see the bear walk to fall mysteriously ill; if the bear walk visits him four times, he will probably die. Meantime, if the bear walk has been discovered and wounded by the victim's family, some person who was practicing this witchcraft will be found at his home, wounded in the same spot.

Betty Cooper says of bear walks:

> Bear walks make evil medicine and make a wish that a sick person gets worse. If you are traveling at night and see a light—greenish yellow—and you get near it, you might see a dog or a bear or a bird. If you try to shoot the animal, it has to get back home. The person might have a mark on

them. When near to a bear walk, people become paralyzed, perhaps with fright. The bear walk might be a turkey or owl, if seen flying. Whatever it is, it leaves a track. They used to use bird form because they could get away quicker. They have a funny sound—sort of a high-pitched, crying sound.

Some old people nearby said they saw a bear walk at night. It usually appeared after twelve midnight. They heard strange sounds near the woods. The man shot at something.

The bear walk is always an elderly person—a man or woman.

Last summer a man in Petoskey was sick. The people sitting with him heard strange sounds, quite far off. They seemed like the sounds of a turkey to some of them; to others like something else. The man finally died in the hospital of a mysterious sickness that could not be diagnosed.

The bear often works against a successful person of whom he is jealous.

Fred reports that those who believe in bear walking say that bear walks almost always work at night:

They take off their clothes and seem to assume animal form. Dogs and cats thought to be *mkkwábamosɛd* are still sometimes shot. They spit fire and seem to bounce along. There is a bitter medicine to counteract the effects of a bear walk that may be obtained from a *midewátsit* (wise doctor).

The *mkkwábamosɛd* say a sort of chant, go through a certain hocus-pocus, cause misfortune and disease to the victim. I had a poplar tree near my home at one, time which was cut down by a woman, a neighbor, who thought she saw weird green lights in it. She rushed up with an axe and cut it down before she could be stopped.

My mother once saw a green light on the house wall at night. She ran at it and it gave her a chase. It proved to be a luminous bug, bigger than a firefly.

A dog with enlarged teats is often said to be a bear walk. The children of a bear walk are said to die off before the bear walk does, but this is not borne out by fact. I do not believe in bear walking myself—if anything, it is a form of hypnotism.

If a dog or other animal, a bear walk, is shot at night, the next morning some guilty human will be found wounded. The bear walk must always be home by morning. They can go into houses without opening doors. Ghosts, on the other hand, must always open doors.

Some time ago it is said that a person was sick and a priest was called. He, of course, did not believe the family's story that the sick person had been bewitched and that the house was "infected" with the evil presence.

However, he walked three times around the house, blessing the ground by sprinkling holy water. The next morning a nude woman was found lying within the circle he had made.

There was another case of a woman found nude near a white man's woodshed. When approached, she said she was "caught in a trap." She rushed away, forgetting to take her medicine bag with her. (They sometimes carry bags of powdered herbs.) She came back the next day for her bag.

A bewitched person can tell when the bear walk is approaching, though it may be invisible to everyone else. The victim says, "Here she comes!" This is usually at a certain time of night.

Bear walks sometimes operate in groups of two or three. To become a bear walk, you must take herb medicine, which can be bought.

A transformation was witnessed by my maternal aunt. She saw the bear walk—a woman—who was stripped to the nude put a large bear skin across her chest and over one shoulder. She sang a chant as she did so and eventually seemed to become a bear. In this way my aunt got the bear walk power herself, though she did not use it. The power is usually gotten for a fee and is almost never revealed to anyone unless it is bought.

The bear walk may also be a man. A white man coming through the woods alone once heard a strange chanting. He went to the spot from which the noise came and found a nude Indian man singing and dancing.

The bear walk is usually over fifty-four or so. A child is never a *mkkwábamosɛd* and young people are seldom accused of bear walking.

In a talk that Fred Ettawageshik gave during one of Dr. Frank Speck's classes at the University of Pennsylvania in 1926, he included this additional information about bear walking:

Bear walks can travel long distances in a short time. They make four visits to a victim, the fourth one being fatal. The victim becomes hypnotized, losing all power of life so to say. They do not come to until the bear walk's visit is complete . . . There was one case where a person threatened another with witchery and was struck down. The threat was to take effect before sunrise and it did. The victim was visited two times, but did not stay at home thereafter to foil the attempt . . . There was another case where a dog was trailing a man, spitting fire at intervals. The man, bravely, turned and kicked the dog in the jaw. Next day a woman in the village suffered a painful jaw.

Indians are suspicious of an animal or bird that comes during the night. Robins and blackbirds are ill omens. Some can detect the presence of the *mkkwábamosɛd* by the charring of the earth. The turkey is another type. The penalty for failure to take one victim each year is the loss of one immediate member of the family. Cases are known where only one survived. To spit fire, the *mkkwábamosɛd* blow on fire wood, *pakkwanatik*. They carry small sacks around their necks containing medicines—corn, sea shells, sometimes worms will be drawn from the victim in affected parts. Snakes may be called by the bear walk to produce poisons. For this, the bear walk must have snake weeds. The Indians are very cautious when in the vicinity of a patch of such weeds. They are fern-shaped, but low and clustered, and called snake medicine. They possess no good medicinal qualities. Before starting on a journey bear walks perform certain rites in the darkness outdoors or indoors and in the nude. They make appeals to their spirit helper and to the animal into which they wish to change. They usually dance in a circle.

There was one case—at a wake a dog-like creature prowled around the house. It was shot and jumped straight up in the air about six feet. When it landed, it disappeared instantly. A few days later an old gent died about fourteen miles away with a wound in the mid-body. He said that a board with a nail on it sprang up and struck him in the body. He was seriously ill for several days and refused to go to the hospital. The family covered up the case. (Notes given to me by Speck, 1947)

Further information about bear walking was given to me by Christine Otto, who said:

There was a man drowned at Manistee River who had medicine buried at Capemish. There were four stones around the place and a queer light, only seen at a certain time of year—I forget when. One night I went with my father and brothers to investigate, but when we got near the light it went out. We were frightened and ran back. If that medicine had been dug up without the owner's permission, it would have caused disease or death. Later, before his death, the owner asked someone to dig up the medicine. We found the stones pushed aside and a hole dug, but no medicine or bag. After that there was no light there. This Indian witchcraft is the work of the devil. Old women with eyes bloodshot are under suspicion. They get bloodshot eyes from dancing around the fire at night. They become animals, invisible.

Three children in a family died in one year. It was quick consumption. An owl was seen near the house acting strangely. People fall asleep, except the person being bewitched, when the animal comes. It is hypnotism. I don't know what the animal does to its victim. A medicine bucket made of wood was dug up when a man was putting in a cellar. It contained long string of insects, human ears, and so on. It was under the house flooring and was dug up. The man destroyed it because he was afraid to have it around. Bear walks pound up herbs in a medicine bag of skin.

When a person's death was attributed to bear walking, it used to be customary for a group of male relatives and friends to watch over his grave to prevent the bear walk from stealing a finger, toe or other part of the corpse. If the bear walk did not do this, it was thought that he would die himself. Graves were watched for eight days and a fire was lit; after this period it was too late for the bear walk to make his visit.

Susy Shagonaby told about hearing a strange-sounding owl (*kukuku*) on the roof of her home several years ago. She knew it was a bear walk and was very frightened. She had been told of a place in Canada to buy medicine to counteract bear walk sorcery, so she sent for some of it. She was horrified to learn, however, that the medicine was so powerful that it would eventually kill the bear walk and his family, but she decided to use it anyway to protect her own family. Suzy says:

> I heard the owl coming one night so I got the medicine and burned it—it was a powder. There must be four pinches of it. I threw it in the stove and heard the owl choke and cough. Then it left, flew off. The medicine works round and goes back to the bear walk. First he loses his job, then everything—his children, his stock. He must pay a sacrifice for his sins. Then eventually it takes his own life.

Several informants told me that both *wíkɛ* (*Acorus calamus* or Sweet Flag) and *mánwɛgʻ* (*Osmorhiza lons*) are used as charms to ward off the *mkkwábamosɛd*. The roots are dried and kept on a shelf or even hung over the doorway.

According to Susy, the original bear walks got their evil power from the great sea serpent, *miši ginébik*, the embodiment of all evil in Odawa mythology. She described the serpent as an enormous snake with a head like a horse or cow and horns:

> This serpent started all bear walking way back. Then it was handed down. Those that wanted the serpent fasted 40 days. The serpent came out of the water and they shaved his horns to get medicine from them.

Erminie Voegelin writes that many other tribes believe that power, usually for evil, is to be found in the horns of the great serpent. The heart of the serpent is also considered especially powerful.

> In the east and southeast the great horned underwater serpent with one red and one green horn is a powerful, mysterious creature who could be lured to land and to his death by shamans, only when they used the most powerful of all medicines, the ashes from the fireplace of a hut occupied by a menstruating woman, or a few drops of menstrual blood. When the body of the serpent was burned, his heart refused to burn, and was cut up and used thereafter, always alive and quivering, as a witch medicine. (*Standard Dictionary of Folklore*, 2:1029)

Several persons whom I know personally have been accused of bear walking. Not long ago Susy Shagonaby told me that a man from Good Hart, now dead, was a bear walk. In telling about him she revealed that bear walk power resides in their equipment and that bear walks have feasts:

> John ——— was said to have died of a heart attack. He was found sitting nude with a "bear walk strap" on. It was three fingers wide, made of buckskin, and had feathers in it, also human teeth, etc. He got this strap from his grandma. His power is in this belt. If it's not in use, the power in it will destroy you. You can counteract this by giving a feast for the belt once a year. Bear walks of the same sex get together and have a feast at night, every fall.

Susy could not give any further details about the bear walk belt or the feast, but she said that a woman in Good Hart had the belt. I questioned this woman, but she denied all knowledge of such a strap or belt and spoke highly of the accused man.

All over the world one finds, of course, a superstitious fear of witches and the belief that they can assume animal form at will. So widespread is the belief that there seems no need to quote references here. The term *bear walking*, however, seems to be confined to Michigan. At least the only other source in which it is mentioned is Dorson for the Ojibwe of the Upper Peninsula of Michigan (Dorson 1952). Most similar is the Pomo term *bear doctor*, used to describe evil persons of a similar character (Barrett 1917).

One important point that became evident to me in looking through the literature since I first learned of bear walking in 1946 is the number of cases in which the bear is connected with the cause or cure of sickness. Probably, as Hallowell said when I mentioned this to him, it is a natural outgrowth of the great respect and veneration shown the bear wherever the animal is found. The Odawa certainly shared in this belief, and the bear feast was an important occasion among them.

It is interesting to consider only a partial list of the peoples who connect the bear with sickness, either as a curative agent or as a bearer of disease or sometimes both:

1. Keresan, Tewa, and Zuni curing societies have the bear as patron. Shamans can become real bears and go after death to live with the bears in the spirit world. Bear gave man the aster root, a powerful medicine (*Standard Dictionary of Folklore*, 1:125).
2. "The Sioux also value especially the medicines given to mankind by the bear. They regard him as the chief of all healing animals, partly because his claws are so well adapted to digging roots and partly because benevolence from an animal usually considered ill-tempered takes on particular significance" (*Standard Dictionary of Folklore*, 1:127).
3. "In India bears are believed to be powerful against diseases; children are given a ride on a bear's back to ward off disease, or sometimes one hair from a bear is hung as an amulet around their necks" (*Standard Dictionary of Folklore*, 1:124).
4. Ojibwe, Odawa, and other tribes who had the Midéwiwin featured the bear as a prominent patron, and the candidates for membership spoke of following "the bear path" (*Standard Dictionary of Folklore*, 1:126; Hoffman 1891; Densmore 1929).
5. The bear clan among the Winnebago is the second most powerful clan. They act as sergeants-at-arms and are also called on when there is sickness in the village. They have a feast, chant and dance, and visit the home of the sick person. Their power comes from the bear guardian who only appears to members of the bear clan (Radin 1915–16, 228).
6. The Menominee believe that the Great Underground Bear can join his power to that of the common bear for the benefit of the sick (Densmore 1932, 86).
7. Among the New York Iroquois, the curing aspect of the bear is found in all tribes. The bear society is female.
8. The Pomo bear doctor is similar to the Odawa bear walk. Barrett got a confession from an actual bear doctor, who also presented him with the bear skin she had used. A similar type of sorcery and evil-doing is said to be widespread in California at the present time (Barrett 1917, 443–65).

Such a widespread belief that the bear is somehow connected with sickness is probably in part due to diffusion, but must also be caused by the very nature of the bear itself and man's reaction to the animal. The way in which such a phenomenon as bear walking could presumably have developed is very well demonstrated in one of Hoffman's Midéwiwin charts in which a second degree Midé is shown capable of performing evil as well as good (Hoffman 1891, plate IIIB). A rough figure of a bear is drawn with bear tracks on either side of it, "impressions of which are sometimes found in the vicinity of lodges occupied by his intended victims." Trees are shown on either side of the figure to "signify a forest, the location usually sought by bad Midé and witches" (Hoffman 1891, 169).

Of such an evil Midé, Hoffman writes, "He has the power of assuming the form of any animal in which guise he may destroy the life of his victim, immediately after which he resumes his human form and appears innocent of any crime. His services are sought by people who wish to encompass the destruction of enemies or rivals, at however remote a locality the intended victim may be at the time" (Hoffman 1891, 168).

Hoffman goes on to explain that a Midé of the second degree was especially powerful because the *migis* or magic shell was placed on all his joints and his "heart . . . filled with magic power." He could see and hear for great distances and could also transport himself quickly to any spot. "Therefore he is sought after by hunters for aid in the discovery of and capture of game, success in war, and for the destruction of enemies, however remote may be their residence" (Hoffman 1891, 237).

Evil Midés used charts similar to hunting charts when preparing to act. Hoffman reproduces such a chart, which was drawn by a Midé on birchbark in 1884 and was used in a ceremony at White Earth, Minnesota (Hoffman 1891, 238). The chart shows the Midé, the person who asked for his help, the Midé drum, the victim lying prone, with vermillion daubed in a spot representing the heart, and off to one side of the lake more than one hundred miles away, where the victim lived. It also shows the degrees of the Midé, although Hoffman states that this is not necessary. "By a strange coincidence," Hoffman writes, "the person against whom vengeance was aimed died of pneumonia the following spring . . . and his death was attributed to the Midé's power, a reputation naturally procuring for him many new adherents and disciples" (Hoffman 1891, 238).

It seems quite probable that, among the Michigan Odawa and Ojibwa, as the Midéwiwin came into disfavor the power of the Midés for evil became emphasized over their power for good. Jenness writes that on Parry Island the Midéwiwin is generally considered evil now and that if one finds a piece of equipment suspected of connection with the Midéwiwin, it is best destroyed or not touched at all (Jenness 1935, 88). The "bear walk belt" and the "medicine" mentioned by Odawas to me may very well be in this class. Certain it is that the Catholic priests did all in their power to destroy and discredit medicine bags and other "superstitious articles," holding them up as works of the devil (Willets 1948, 105–7).

In many acculturated societies it has been found that there is a period shortly after the adoption of the new culture in which sorcery in some form is rampant. Honigmann, writing about witch fear among the modern Kaska, says, "As a product of stress, the belief in interpersonal malevolence is comparable to other social excrescences which have been exhibited whenever traditional ways of living have been threatened or blocked by unavoidable circumstances" (Honigmann 1947, 239).

At times, Honigmann points out, the disturbed society turns to "revivalistic, messianic, or renaissant movements"—thus the Ghost Dance Religion, the Peyote Cult, and so on. Other societies in which the personality background differs become fraught with sorcery and witchcraft (Honigmann 1947, 239).

Whether or not there are those who actually make a practice of bear walking is not known to me. Various informants insist that there are, but I have not obtained an admission of sorcery, as Barrett did from his Pomo informants, an elderly man and his wife who wished to help wipe out their sins by their confession. Barrett was told that the bear suit he got from them was worn to commit robbery and various evil doings, even including murder (Barrett 1917, 443–65).

One hopes that bear walking in the Harbor Springs-Cross Village area is in a class with the "bogey man"; it seems to me that this is the case among most Odawas. I feel sure, at least, that the belief in bear walking is less strong now than it was fifty years ago, for most of the actual cases mentioned to me happened in the past. There is every reason to think that the belief may disappear entirely in a few years, for the Odawa are becoming more and more an integral part of the white community.

Other Types of Sorcery

Nindəwágę (I am out looking for something or someone). According to Susy Shagonaby, the sorcerer sends his evil spirit out, causing his victim to lose his will to succeed. *Nindəwágę* is just a force, not a real person like a bear walk.

Sympathetic Magic. Fred says that some evil persons will draw an image of a victim in the sand and will thrust a stick or a pin in its stomach. This is supposed, of course, to make the real victim ill. Likewise, a witch or sorcerer may thrust a pin in a person's footprints at the same time uttering a curse. The victim is then said to develop a lame foot. Christine Otto gave an example:

> My grandmother once had an old lady visitor, whose feelings she hurt. The old lady left in a huff, so my grandmother told my Aunt Julia to head her off. Aunt Julia hurried ahead and saw the old woman drawing figures of people in the sand. She threw medicine on the drawings, sang and danced around. My aunt and her daughter broke up them drawings with sticks. To be on the safe side, they built a fire over the spot.

This type of sympathetic magic is, of course, worldwide and takes many different forms. It crops up in one way or another in all societies. I recall hearing of an anthropology student at the University of Pennsylvania who took a photo of a southern mountain girl on a field trip. Several weeks later the girl's brother appeared at his dormitory demanding in no uncertain terms that the picture be returned immediately and in good condition. Fortunately, there were no pin pricks in the photo!

Love Charm. Sympathetic magic is also used sometimes in preparing a love charm as well as powdered "love medicine." In the summer of 1946 Christine Otto showed me a crudely carved figure of a man about two inches tall, which she said she had found wrapped in a newspaper with some powdered herbs under the mattress of an old woman, recently deceased. Christine said the figure was a charm. The old woman had slept on it and the medicine with it was supposed to draw back a lover who had gone away somewhere. Neither Christine nor her husband could identify the herbs used with the charm.

Christine added that the woman was a neighbor who gathered herbs and sold them. When Christine was young she had accompanied the woman on herb-gathering trips and had heard her sing chants over them. She would never reveal her secrets to Christine, however. The old woman and her husband, with no spare cash for liquor apparently, had died from drinking a mixture of antifreeze and wine! Christine had found them both dead on the floor of their house.

Joe Chingwa told me that the flower of the "little thimble" plant (*kandi' gwaswás*) may be dried and pulverized for use as a love charm. "It can bind a man to you or a wife to a husband," Joe said. Christine swore that packets of love medicine were formerly sold in drugstores for five dollars each.

No other herbs used as love charms were mentioned to me, but Dorson identifies an Upper Peninsula Ojibwe love powder as made from the root of the Bluebell, the male plant being used on the women, the female plant on the men. Another informant told Dorson that canary root was used as a love powder and also as a hunting charm to draw deer and bear (Dorson 1952, 35–36).

Hunting and Fishing Charms. A number of informants told me that "medicine" is sometimes rubbed on fish hooks to make the fish bite. Jennie Chingwa said she had gone to the woods once with Joe for a certain kind of leaf, which he crushed against his fishing hooks. She said that Joe got a good catch that day and she supposed that the medicine helped. Jennie said that she would be unable to identify the herb used.

Hunting charms were once elaborately prepared; they included charts, medicines, songs, and dances. No Indians today make use of any of the older charms that I know of, but Joe Chingwa told me that his father once participated in a hunt in which medicine was used to ruin the luck of some members of the party.

> A man furnished all of them on the hunt with tobacco. He had a bowl eight to ten inches across with tobacco in it. My dad was only eighteen or nineteen years old and it seemed like he couldn't get enough of the tobacco. He could hardly wake up the next morning. All that smoked it were the same—Sogat, John Devurnay, MacMillen. I forgot to say this was in the Black Lake region. Well, they finally got up, but they couldn't even see a deer. Those that hadn't smoked the tobacco, though, by gol, they got lots of deer—fifteen or twenty deer. The man with the tobacco, who was the boss along with *Pakí sigan*, said to save the deer hearts.
>
> That night it was John's turn to cook. He made *pinábo,* potato soup with deer hearts. Each one had his own wooden bowl and spoon. *Pakí sigan* ate and said nothing, but Jim (the man with the tobacco) called him down. MacMillen then knew what was what and told. There's an herb deer despise. When you smoke it the deer get your scent and leave before you see them. You need to have some deer hearts for the herb to take full effect.
>
> After this their luck changed a bit, perhaps because the hunters ate so little of the deer hearts. My father shot a deer, but it only had three horns, one prong on one side, two on the other. It was a freak. The next day he shot another one through the stomach, but didn't get it as he knew it would bleed to death. Jim said that night that he'd shot a deer through the hips. My dad had to help him, as Jim was the boss. So my dad didn't have time to get his.

Herbs and Other Medicinal Remedies

The modern Odawa still retain a remarkable knowledge of herbal medicine, considering that Western medicinal remedies and practices have been universally embraced. The Odawa seem to hold that Western medicine is simply an addition to the old proven remedies, an enrichment perhaps but certainly no reason for discarding the latter. Many of our Western doctors might be the first to agree with this view, for is there not a constant search for new remedies, new wonder drugs, some of which have been discovered through the old medicines themselves?

Not long ago Joe Chingwa's wife, Jennie, was suffering from a particularly stubborn diarrhea, which her Petoskey doctor was unable to cure. Various remedies were tried, but the diarrhea persisted. One day Jennie decided to try an Indian medicine—black cherry bark tea. She brewed the tea and drank about two cups of it. Almost immediately she found relief and was able to tell her doctor the following morning that she was cured. Jennie's doctor at any rate agreed that perhaps modern medical science could still learn something occasionally from Indian medicine.

Indeed, the white man in the Central Woodland area owes much to Indian medicine already. Many a trapper and many a trader have been saved from death by the kind attentions of his Indian friends and their herbal knowledge. True, such really beneficent remedies were often administered by medicine men who capered about in grotesque fashion, but their medicines were more often than not efficacious nonetheless.

Cadillac, after condemning the "jugglers or charlatans" who seemed to believe that all sickness was caused by witchcraft, wrote:

> Nevertheless, one thing is quite certain, namely that the Indians are most skillful and very experienced in healing all kinds of sores and wounds, of whatever kind they may be, by means of simples, of which they have an excellent knowledge. They also have remedies or burns, frostbite, and the stings and bites of snakes and other venomous animals; but the best of it is that they stop and drive off the mischief as quickly as it came. They are very good anatomists; and so, when they have an arm or any bone broken, they treat it very cleverly and with great skill and dexterity, and experience shows that they can cure a wounded man in a week better than our surgeons can in a month, perhaps because the former have better remedies and are more straightforward, while the others are actuated by the desire to turn their talent to their own profit. As to venereal diseases, they laugh at them, for those who are attacked recover in ten or twelve days at the furthest, by taking certain tasteless powders, which they swallow in

hot water, and for this reason one never sees a woman among them who has syphilis; but they are malicious enough to refuse to teach the French their secrets, though they do not refuse them their remedies in case of need. (Kinietz 1940, 307)

Perhaps no other Indian groups had such extensive knowledge of medicinal herbs as the Indians of the Central Woodlands. There were the common herbal remedies known to everyone; then there were the medicines known only to the medicine men and women, most of them members of the Midéwiwin or the Wabeno societies. Besides the great store of herbal remedies handed down by the practitioners of the Midéwiwin, new remedies were constantly being discovered and were said to be given by manidos in visions along with the necessary songs and dances. Hoffman wrote concerning the medicinal knowledge of the Ojibwe Midés:

> It is interesting to note in this list of herbal remedies the number of infusions and decoctions which are, from a medical and scientific standpoint, specific remedies for the complaints for which they are recommended. It is probable that the long continued intercourse between the Ojibwa and the Catholic Fathers, who were tolerably well versed in the ruder forms of medication, had much to do with improving an older and purely aboriginal form of practicing medical magic. (Hoffman 1891, 197)

It should be added that Indian remedies also augmented Western medicinal knowledge as a perusal of our early U.S. Pharmacopoeia shows.

There were various degrees of skill and knowledge obtainable by medicine men, even as there are in modern medicine. It is assumed that the Odawa Midéwiwin had four degrees [of membership], as did the Ojibwe, but there is little description of the Odawa society. Modern Odawas have almost completely forgotten the Midéwiwin and can give no adequate description of it. Christine Otto of Petoskey, now in her late fifties, said that she saw a performance of the Midéwiwin at Mackinaw City when she was six years old.

> I was with my father and mother at Mackinaw and saw this meeting. It was held under a sort of canopy of boughs. There were three drums and the members danced around. Some "pointed" their medicine bags at the others with a peculiar yell. I thought this was funny and laughed. There was dancing and singing. My father couldn't go inside to watch because he wasn't a member of the society.

Some of the herbal remedies still known to the Odawa probably stem from the Midéwiwin and Wabeno societies, although most of them have undoubtedly been fairly common knowledge for generations. Much that was good passed away with the Midéwiwin; what has been retained is found in some remedies and probably in the strengthened belief in and practice of sorcery.

There are still medicine men among the Odawa, although today these men or women do not employ singing and dancing or other ritual along with their medicines. One simply visits such a person, if able to do so, describes the ailment, pays for the medications, and may be given a small portion of pulverized herbs, wrapped up in newspaper and tied firmly with cord. The doctor then tells the patient how to prepare the medicine and how much of it to take. One always pays for the medicine before receiving it and using it in order to show one's faith in the doctor.

There are no fixed rates for a medicine and the payment is often a token one, for even one's best friends must always pay for medicine or its effectiveness will be impaired. One old man named Sákko, who had a chest of medicines, once took a pair of rubbers as payment for a medicine, Joe Chingwa told me. More common payment is some form of tobacco, whisky, blankets, or money.

Almost every Indian family also keeps herbal medicines on hand in the home, the pulverized medicine done up in packets, the whole plants from which a tea is usually made suspended in paper bags from hooks in the shed. Some families grow the more common herbs, such as *wíkȩ* (Sweet Flag, *Acorus calamus*), a remedy for colds, in their gardens. Drugstores in the area carry *wíkȩ* and other common herbs chiefly for their Indian customers.

Herbs are gathered at any time of year, but mainly in the summer and spring, often in the course of family expeditions to pick mushrooms or berries. "Some of the old people," Joe Chingwa said, "would go out and be gone all day long. An old woman at Cross Village, when my wife and I visited her, had shelves of wrapped up medicine. Herbs are like male and female. They work together for man. Male grows on high ground; female is smaller and grows on low ground. Strawberries are medicine—if they are all male, they don't bear."

Unless needed immediately, the herbs are hung in bags to dry. Later on those that are to be pulverized are mixed in the proper proportions and ground into a powder. It used to be customary, some informants say, to pulverize medicine in the *potágan* (mortar) with the opposite end of the pestle, *baškwanátik,* from that used for pounding corn. Fred Ettawageshik says that a buckskin sieve is used when making powdered medicine.

When an herb is pulled up or any part of it taken for medicinal purposes, one must always put a little tobacco in the ground and say, "*Nókamıs, bi·nda'konín*" ("Grandmother, I am offering you a smoke"). This is an offering for the Great Spirit, some say; others believe that the tobacco is intended for Grandmother Earth, who controls all growing plants. Nowadays, a cigarette or a little chewing tobacco is often used, for the Odawa have not smoked Native tobacco for many years.

Up until the turn of the century, individual medicine men still sought the aid of the manidos more directly than through the tobacco sacrifice. Joe Chingwa said that his grandfather, Mkkwániwi, would go off in the woods by himself with his drum. He would fast for several days until he had a vision in which a manido would appear to him and reveal the prescription for a medicinal remedy along with a song and dance. After this, every time Mkkwániwi prepared the medicine or administered it, he had to sing the song and do the dance he had learned from the manido. Such songs are discussed by Gertrude Kurath in chapter 4. Mkkwániwi also told Joe a way to test the strength of a medicine:

> You test poison with poison. A medicine man got reptiles, poisonous, and other poisonous things. He, himself, and other braves danced on them, after they had put medicine on themselves. The idea was to show that his medicine was better. If it failed, the medicine man died.

A similar idea must have been in the minds of the members of the Wabeno cult when they put a special preparation on their hands and arms, enabling them to reach into boiling syrup or toss fire brands around without being burned. Tanner wrote that the medicine used for this purpose was made from yarrow (*waw-be-no-wusk*) and an unidentified herb growing in the West. He also said that yarrow "in the form of a poultice, is an excellent remedy for burns" (Tanner 1830, 94).

The old-time medicine men also used considerable psychology to aid in curing their patients, as this account by Christine Otto shows:

> Once I called on a *sagima* or medicine man, John Miksabi, to look at my daughter, Mary, who was about ten then. She felt sick and was having convulsions. After a few days, John came. He seemed to be in a daze or trance. He talked in a whisper, looking at Mary. After a while he said to call him back in two weeks. Then he said Mary would grow up well and get over convulsions. He said to make her a certain kind of dress, a blue dress with a white collar and another collar on top cut in scallops. He said he had had a dream, a vision, and he had seen Mary this way in his dream. He said

Mary was to wear that dress to pieces. John asked for a blanket, whisky, and tobacco in payment and so we gave him a blanket and some money to buy the whisky and tobacco. John gave us some powdered *obšiškan* and said for Mary to take a bath in this every other night. Mary got over her convulsions in a short time.

Several remarkable cures have been mentioned to me, the most amazing perhaps being that of one of my in-laws whose right leg was severely crippled almost from birth. When she was a young child, her mother took her to the leading doctors in Petoskey who x-rayed her, gave her medication and crutches, but ended by concluding that she had tuberculosis of the bone and that her leg must be amputated. The child's mother, horrified, of course, by this verdict, called on an Indian medicine man in a last desperate attempt to save her daughter's leg. My in-law, who prefers not to be mentioned by name, remembers only vaguely the visit of the medicine man. She says that he sang and danced while shaking a rattle. Then he gave her mother a powdered medicine to be dissolved in water. Her crippled leg was bathed in this mixture for several weeks and began slowly to become stronger. After a month or two the crutches were discarded and at the end of a year the child was able to walk and run about like other children. Today this woman, now in her fifties, has no limp and appears to have normal use of the once crippled limb. Neither she nor anyone else I have questioned can suggest just what was contained in the Indian medicine used to cure her.

Another story of a cure through the use of an unidentified herb was related by Joe Chingwa:

At Honor, Michigan, a white man in a logging camp had creeping paralysis and shook. An old Indian man and his wife were getting herbs every day near by. They called, "Hey, old man!" He answered in a deep voice, "What do you want?" He was told they had a sick man so he went to the man's shanty. They talked in Odawa when they saw the shaking man in bed—"Very sick man." He turned to his wife, said something. "Tomorrow we come back," he told the men. Next day they came carrying a gallon pail. Each wanted a cup and drank out of the pail to show it wasn't poison. Then the Indian filled a cup and told the sick man to drink it and often—"Two pails you drink. Four days I come back. See you." The sick man did what he was told to do. On the fourth day he could feel the disease going out the end of his toes. In two months' time he hadn't shook. In three months his hand was steady. In four or five months he could go to work.

On the first pay day he went to see the old Indian man. "What do you want?" the man asked. The old Indian man said, "Don't want nothin'." So the man bought groceries for them—did this often. As for the kind of herb, this old man would only say, "Lots of it in the woods." It was quite bitter, whatever it was.

The following is a list of medicinal herbs and trees that were mentioned to me by various informants. I am indebted to Mr. Carl Wright of Harbor Springs for the botanical identification of many of these trees and plants. Others were identified by the Botany Department of the University of Pennsylvania, and one was identified by the Botany Department of Haverford College.

List of Plants Arranged according to Botanical Name

BOTANICAL NAME	COMMON NAME	USE
Abies balsames, Mill	Balsam Fir	Colds; cuts; sores
Acer saccharium, Marsh	Sugar Maple	Poultice for sores
Acorus calamus	Sweetflag	Colds; lameness; magic; heart medicine
Aralia racemosa	Ginseng	Heart medicine
Arctium lappa (minus?)	Burdock	Heart or blood medicine
Carpinus carolinianum	Ironwood	Colds; sores
Chamaecyparis thyoides	White Cedar	Colds; indigestion
Chimaphila umbellata	Prince's Pine	Blood medicine; diuretic
Epigea repens	Arbutus	Blood medicine, diuretic; arthritis, rheumatism
Fagus americanus, Sweet	Beech	Cuts; sores
Fragaria americana	Strawberry	Jaundice
Gaultheria procumbens	Wintergreen	Jaundice; arthritis; blood tonic
Larix americana	Tamarack	Colds; sores
Nymphaea odorata	Waterlily	Lameness
Osmorrhiza lons	Sweet Cicily	Cuts; magic
Pinus strobus	White Pine	Sores
Polygala senega	Seneca Snake Root	Blood medicine headache; colds
Prunus pennsylvanica, Linn.	Red Cherry	Blood medicine; female medicine (?)
Prunus serotina	Black Cherry	Colds; diarrhea
Rhus coriaria	Sumac	Rupture
Rumex crispus	Yellow Dock	Diarrhea; constipation
Sambucus ?	Elder	Colds; sores
Sanguinaria canadensis	Bloodroot	?
Sassafras, Karst	Sassafras	Blood medicine; sedative
Sorbus americana, Marsh	Mountain Ash	Blood medicine

Trillium grandiflora	Trillium	Stomach tonic
Tsuga canadensis	Hemlock	Colds
(Plant of *Umbellifer* family)	?	Headache; sedative
Valeriana uliginosa	Valerian	Heart medicine; headache; tonic
Viburnum oculus	?	Colds; stomach ache

[*Editor's note:* Question marks were placed in text by original author to indicate uncertainty about the proper Linnaean identifications or medicinal applications. The reader is also advised that the author voiced at several points subsequent to drafting the manuscript that she lacked confidence about the accuracy of this list of medicinal knowledge.]

List of Plants Arranged according to Native Name

NATIVE NAME	MEANING	COMMON NAME
Bakwan		Sumac
Ɛnsınabésiwan		Ginseng
Gagágowiš		Hemlock
Gɛgin'dɛ́bɛ	Pointed head	Balsam fir
Gížikˈ	Hot (?)	White Cedar
Kəndəmǫ́		Waterlily
Kobənággaǫš		Mountain Ash
Mananǫs		Ironwood
Ma'nwɛgˈ		Sweet Cicely
Maškigojípəkę́s		Seneca Snake Root
Mıktógɛ	He has a scab on the ear	Arbutus
Mı́škwajíbik	Red root	Bloodroot
Mıškozíwaškˈ	Red, bitter-tasting plant	Plant of Umbellifer family
Mkadewıgwásɛs	Black bark	Red Cherry
Monbánmiš	Tree growing in water or well	Tamarack
Nɛnégwəkamıš	Not two leaves alike	Sassafras
Odémın	Heart berry	Strawberry
Okawémıš		Black Cherry
Páštəmo		Trillium
Sanámıš		Sugar Maple
Sawémıš		Beech
Sagadébowe		Burdock
Šəškwándiš	? (*Viburnum oculus*)	
Síbowɛ	River plant (?)	Valerian
Šíŋgwəkˈ		White Pine
Wábado	White	Fungus
Waˈiáskobakˈ	Shining leaf	Prince's Pine
Wíkɛ		Sweet Flag

Winsíbugǫ	Wintergreen
?	Yellow Dock
?	Elder

[*Editor's note:* Question marks in text indicate the author's uncertainty about identifications.]

A number of plants and medicines were mentioned to me that could not be identified. These include:

- All of the ingredients of *obšíškan,* a medicine for colds, headaches, and convulsions. Valerian and Seneca Snake Root and an herb called *sawánkadǫs* are included in it.
- The Star Flower, which may be *Trientalis americana,* is used to make a poultice for sores. This may also be "a high-stem plant with a white flower" that is employed in making an eye wash.
- An unidentified herb that was used in treating tuberculosis.
- A species of tobacco used on cuts.
- A plant like a wild grape, called *pičígagogas,* from which a tea is made to treat high blood pressure.
- *Bebísəgibagak*ʻ or *memákadewəkogádeak,* two names for the same herb, sometimes called "Black Leg," a plant with a black stem, fine leaves, and roots like a crow's foot. It is used to make a female medicine.
- *Kinebigáminagaǫš* with "leaves as big as fingernails, almost bluish, very deep green. It has a red berry and grows low against the ground." It is used in treating female disorders.
- *Šə́škoniš,* a "female medicine. When you break the stick it is green on the bark. Grows high."
- *Káoš,* "sort of a vine in the woods, an evergreen, three and one-half feet high. It has regular needles like balsam and is a female medicine."
- The "little thimble" plant, *kandìgwaswą́s,* a plant used to prevent conception. A tea is made from the roots and a love charm from the flower.
- Wild Poppy, *nεpέmškiki,* seeds are crushed and put in water as an anesthetic or sedative.
- *Mεskwasan* grows two to three feet high in the sand and is used with sheep tallow as a salve or for rouge.
- *Bastáʻigan,* a plant with a big leaf, used to draw out inflammation.
- *Sabankak,* "like red osier," mentioned as medicinal herb.
- *Tigkwəkikaǫš,* an evergreen shrub, used as a tonic.
- A species of thistle is used for headaches.

- An herb was known to counteract rattlesnake bite.
- A species of Goldenrod was supposed to have protective powers against smallpox.

Classification of Diseases and Injuries Treated by the Odawa

Nervous System (Convulsion, Headache, "Creeping Paralysis")

- A Plant of the Umbellifer Family *(Miškozíwašk)*. The stems are cut and dried and boiled in water to make a tea for headaches or for use as a sedative. Sage or sassafras may be mixed with it. Christine Otto says that "a little fish with a dog face that lives near the shore, tapers toward the tail, about two inches long—looks a bit like mosquito larva—has this herb as its medicine. It is a sedative, panacea."
- *Obšíškan.* This is an "all-around tonic" for colds, headaches, convulsions. It consists of a number of powdered herbs, including valerian, Seneca Snake Root, and an herb called *sawánkados*. In one case, it was dissolved in water and used to bathe a girl who had convulsions.
- Thistle. The roots or the whole plant of an unidentified species of thistle are pounded up, put in the hand, and used like snuff. "It makes you sneeze" and is especially good for headaches.

Circulatory System (Heart, Blood; also for Rheumatism, Arthritis)

- *Epigea repens*, Arbutus. The leaves, roots, and stems are boiled in water for about one to three minutes and used as a blood tonic for kidney and bladder trouble, arthritis, and rheumatism. It is sometimes mixed with Prince's Pine and Wintergreen. The strong tea is diluted with a large quantity of water and drunk off and on during the day or for two days so that the system is cleansed.
- *Chimaphila umbellata*, Prince's Pine. The whole plant is used to make a tea for a blood tonic. It is also good for low blood pressure or high blood pressure. Fred was once asked by a man to cure his wife of low blood pressure. Fred told the man about Prince's Pine and showed him the plant in the woods. He told the man that he must put a little tobacco in the ground when removing the plant. The man used a cigarette, took some of the plants, and steeped them as directed. His wife drank the tea mixed with water and in three days' time her blood pressure was up.
- *Gaultheria procumbens*, Wintergreen. This is used with Prince's Pine and Arbutus to make a tea for a blood tonic.

- *Aralia racemosa, Polygala senega, Valeriana uliginosa, Acorus calamus.* The roots of these plants are boiled together in water to make a tea, which is then strained through a cloth and is drunk instead of water for a day or two. A heart medicine.
- *Pičigagogas.* An unidentified plant like a wild grape from which a tea was made to treat high blood pressure.
- *Arctium lappa, Prunus pennsylvanica,* Linnaean (Linn.), *Sorbus americana,* Marsh., Sassafras, Karst. The root of the burdock is boiled with bark from the red cherry, mountain ash, and sassafras trees to make a tea for use as a blood tonic. Joe Chingwa said that it was "the same as vitamins."

Respiratory System (Colds, Lung Trouble, Tuberculosis)

- *Prunus serotina.* The outer bark is cut in strips and boiled as a tea for sore throat. It is sometimes mixed with balsam bark.
- *Tsuga canadensis.* A tea sometimes called "Michigan tea" is made from the smaller boughs, which are steeped in boiling snow water for one minute. Fred says that the boughs must not be steeped too long or the tea will be oily. This is drunk for pleasure or as a protection against catching cold. Strips of hemlock bark are boiled in water as a cold remedy.
- *Larix americana, Chamaecyparis thyoides, Carpinus carolinianum, Prunusserotina, and Sambucus* (Elder?). Strips of bark from these trees are boiled together in water as a remedy for colds.
- *Viburnum oculus.* Stems are boiled in water to make a tea for colds. Has a laxative effect also.
- *Acorus calamus,* Sweet Flag. The root is shaved into water and boiled into a tea, or the root may be chewed. A remedy for colds.
- *Abies balsamea,* Mill. Bark may be boiled with black cherry for colds.
- *Obšíškan.* A mixture of powdered herbs that may be used to treat colds.
- Unidentified herb. Known to "old Indians as a cure for tuberculosis, but they won't reveal it," Christine Otto says. Joe Chingwa said that patients with tuberculosis used to be carried to one of the Seven Sisters hills at the head of Little Traverse Bay, where the Indians were able to nurse them back to health if they were not too far gone.
- Prevention of colds. Joe Chingwa's grandfather, Mkkwániwi, as a boy was made to cut a hole in the ice on the harbor and dive in three times to make him hardy and safe from colds. His grandmother used to stand near the fire with a poker to keep him from seeking its warmth.

Digestive System (Indigestion, Acute Gas Pains, Diarrhea, Constipation)

- *Prunus serotina.* Strips of bark are boiled into a tea to cure diarrhea.
- *Viburnum oculus.* The stems are boiled into a tea for use as an antispasmodic and mild laxative.
- *Rumex crispus.* The root is made into a strong tea to cure diarrhea; if weakened with water and drunk for several days it also cures constipation.
- *Chamaecyparis thyoides.* Use cedar cones or needles to make a tea for the relief of sharp gas pains.
- *Trillium grandiflora.* Use the bulbs to make a tea for a stomach tonic.

Urinary (Diuretics, Kidneys, Jaundice)

- *Epigea repens, Chimaphila umbellata,* and *Gaultheria procumbens.* Besides their use as a blood tonic, these are also used to cure bladder and kidney trouble.
- *Fragaria americana.* The roots are sometimes used with wintergreen roots to make a tea used in the treatment of jaundice.

Skin (Inflammation, Sores, Cuts)

- *Osmorrhiza lons.* The root is used to make a salve for cuts. When pulverized it "gives off a sweet-smelling odor." It is also considered a charm against bear walks (sorcerers).
- *Abies balsamea,* Mill. Balsam pitch, *bagi·ó,* especially that in bubbles on the trunk, is used for healing cuts, sores, and so on. Fred Ettawageshik uses this remedy, and it is very effective.
- *Trientalis americana* (?). The root is dried and pounded up in a mortar. It is mixed with water to make a poultice for sores and cuts.
- *Fagus americanus,* Sweet. The dry beech leaves that remain on the trees in the winter are used to make a poultice for sores. Species of tobacco, moistened in the mouth, were used to make a poultice for cuts and sores.
- *Wabado.* This fungus is crushed and made into a poultice for sores. It was also highly prized as a magic article and was carried in medicine bags. Fred says that it grows high up on pine trees and that the Indians used to consider it "alive" so they shot it down with their bows and arrows.
- *Bastá'igan.* An unidentified plant used in making a poultice to take out inflammation.

- *Pinus srobus, Larix americana, Abies balsamea,* and *Sambucus* (?). A poultice made from the barks of these trees is used to draw out inflammation. Twigs are cooked in water until the bark peels off. Then the sticks are removed and the bark is cooked until it is soft. The water is then drained off and the remaining mixture is applied as a poultice. Joe Chingwa's mother once made such a poultice to treat an old medicine man, Sákko, who had an infected, gangrenous foot. "My father got the boughs for it," Joe said. "It killed Sákko's fever and helped to keep him alive for two or three weeks, but the fever came back. It was too late and he died. My father said that if he had known about it several months back, the treatment might have saved him."

    Pine rosin may also be used as a poultice, and pine needles, powdered and mixed with Vaseline, may be used for the same purpose. Christine Otto said that her sister was covered with sores at one time. "My dad went for pine needles. He dried them in the oven and sent for some Vaseline, which he mixed with the powdered needles. He put this on the sores and in a few days' time the sores started disappearing. Her skin peeled but it cured her."
- *Acer saccharum*, Marsh. Some part of the maple is used in making a poultice for sores. It is pulverized in the mortar and sifted.

Diseases of Women

- *Bebísəgibagak‛* or *Memákadewekəgádeak, Kinebigáminagaǫš, šóškoniš, Káǫš, Prunus pennsylvanica*, Linn. These may be used alone or combined to make a tea for female disorders. The whole plant is used, and in the case of the cherry, also the bark.
- *Kandıgwaswą́s*, Little Thimble. Roots are steeped to make a tea to prevent conception.

Diseases of Bone (Lameness)

- *Nymphaea odorata*, Plant of Umbellifer Family, *Acorus calamus*. These three were used in the following way to cure lameness, according to Joe Chingwa, who was cured of a lame hip when he was twelve or thirteen years old by Sákko. "The needles on the waterlily are poison. If the skin is jabbed with one you can feel the sting of the poison. Sákko made a spear from them. The needles are not bigger than three-eighths inch long. Sákko put one on the end of a three- or four-inch-long cedar stick. Then he jabbed at the sore spot four times. Then he made a pulverized medicine of *wíkę* (*Acorus calamus*) and *miškozíwašk* (Umbellifer) roots, put this on wet gauze, and put the gauze over the place that had just started to swell. He comes regularly once a day for four days. The medicine counteracts the poison. It feels like ice. After four days, then he quits for four days. Then he comes another four days and then he is through. Old Sákko cured me of the lame hip this way. I was cured for life, even played baseball afterwards."

Tonics

Generally includes many of the plants listed in the first five categories.

Contagious Diseases (Smallpox)
- Goldenrod—*škodekánmiš,* Fire Plant. Joe Chingwa's grandfather told him that those who drank a tea made of goldenrod instead of water during a smallpox epidemic escaped the disease.

Rupture
- *Rhus coriaria.* Leaves are crushed to make a poultice for ruptured navel in babies. Joe Chingwa's son had a ruptured navel, and when he told an old Indian woman about it, she said, "That's easy to cure. Go and get sumac leaves and pick them in crimson. Crush the leaves until they're fine and put them on wet gauze, and put it over the rupture and it will heal. It did, too."

Soreness of Eye
- *Bastá'igan*—unidentified plant with a big leaf. The leaf may be placed over the eye with a gauze covering to remove inflammations, or the leaf may be crushed and made into a salve.
- *Trientalis americana* (?). The root may be pulverized and mixed with water to make a poultice for sore eyes or it may be made into an eye wash. Christine Otto says that it is a good medicine but that it is a black snake medicine also and so it is difficult to get.

Relief of Pain

- Plant of Umbellifer Family. A tea is made of the dried stems for use as a sedative.
- Wild Poppy, *nεpέmškiki*—Unidentified. The seeds are crushed and put in water to steep. The tea is used strong as an anesthetic; when weakened it is given to children "who can't sleep."

Rattlesnake Bite

Remedy is supposed to have been known to old Indians.

CHAPTER 9

Odawa Myths

→ *For this chapter, Jane Ettawageshik compiled a rich collection of Odawa language stories from the oral tradition, invaluably transcribed and translated in interlinear fashion by her husband, Fred Ettawageshik. Gertrude Kurath augmented this with the "tales of the water, soil, and beasts" she collected; they are included at the end of the chapter. Like the chapters on song and dance, this chapter shows how Odawa narrative knowledge and practice defy easy classification regarding what is traditional and what has changed in light of modern circumstance. In the stories that follow, the deep mythic past, the historic past, and familial lore mingle together, distinguishable but not separable from one another.*

This collection includes some versions of the more sacred stories of Anishinaabe people, those associated with the trickster and culture hero Nanabozho (Nanabojo in text), and other stories that make reference to a time beyond ordinary time, the "long ago," and that consequently strike modern Western imaginations as myths. But the story time of our Odawa storytellers also includes events and people of the not-so-long ago, more conventionally viewed as "history" rather than "myth." We learn, for example, about Mkkwánıwi, Joe Chingwa's grandfather, who lived in the Upper Peninsula but who continues to live a larger than life existence in the stories told about him. Similarly, we hear extensively about the Maskutens, a people from whom some Odawa claim direct ancestry but who claim a kind of mythic presence in the stories told about them. The Odawa storytelling documented by the authors makes reference to timely events and timeless truths alike.

There is an important indigenous distinction to be noted in this repertory, however. It corresponds to the author's distinction between "myth" and "legend," though the latter would more accurately also include history and lore. Ojibwe and Odawa speakers hasten to tell of the significance of the distinction between aadizookanag (myths) and dibaadjimowin (tales or news), a semantic distinction that is also a grammatical one. Aadizookanag are animate in gender, which means they are categorically alive, and grammatically are referred to by the pronoun he/she, not it. They are considered by Native speakers (along with their characters) to be living and powerful, if nonhuman, persons who are part of the moral universe of persons, having the capacity to exert power and involving their own code of respect. Another common English reference for these animate stories about Nanabozho and other manidoog (manidos in text), or spirits, is "Winter Stories," stories that are only to be told when snow lay on the ground. Dibaadjimowin, which the authors identify as "tales," are no less vivid as narratives and can involve mythic or "supernatural" occurrences—not just relations of experienced events. However, they are inanimate in gender and do not incur the same ethical code that aadizookanag entail for their telling.

As the stories of both classifications make clear, humor plays a crucial role in Anishinaabe narratives. This is especially true of the stories about Nanabozho, the trickster whose name still brings a chuckle when uttered among Anishinaabe people. Nanabozho is the bringer of culture, a compassionate champion of human beings and life in general against its monstrous foes. But curiously, he is not uniformly good. Instead he is amoral: an innocent, a buffoon, a drifter, and an opportunist who follows his insatiable appetites for food, sex, and a good nap into all the wrong places and situations. Sometimes he wins and sometimes he loses; but somehow he always seems to survive and reappear in another story. Take, for example, the account of "The Origin of Red Osier," in which Nanabozho instructs his rear end to keep an eye on the ducks he is cooking on an open fire while he naps. Of course, the ducks are stolen, and in his anger, Nanabozho places his rear on the open fire until, burning, it bleeds, compelling him to seek relief by rubbing it on a bush, which ever after takes on the color red.

What is one to make of such a curious story, knowing that Nanabozho is considered among the more sacred of beings? Students of trickster narratives in Anishinaabe and other cultures point out that the deep significance of these story cycles is not obviously available to those of us thinking in modern Western terms (Vizenor 1984; Vecsey 1988; Gross n.d.; Hyde 1998; Radin 1976). Anthropologists point out that tricksters often emerge as the key models of myth for human behavior and endurance among hunters and gatherers, people who must learn to live in and with nonhuman nature, outwitting it at its own game to survive rather than striving to transform it into something else, like a forest into a field of grain. Ojibwe authors Gerald Vizenor and Lawrence Gross carry the insight forward to the recognizable, claiming the trickster and his stories as the lifeblood of Anishinaabe culture and spirit, the key resource in surviving dispossession and colonization

(Gross n.d.; Vizenor 1984, 1988). Like other personifications of the sacred powers that give, sustain, and take life, Nanabozho is a fickle figure, holding both good and bad, both sacred and profane, and both mischief and honor, in delicate balance. Unlike "an isolated and sentimental tragic hero in conflict with nature," Gerald Vizenor writes, the trickster "survives as a part of the natural world; he represents a spiritual balance in a comic drama rather than the romantic elimination of human contradictions and evil" (Vizenor, 1984, 4). The ability to outsmart the established systems—economic, bureaucratic, educational, and military—that constrain Native lives, to deftly seize opportunities when they arise, and ultimately to laugh at tragic experience is for Vizenor the key to what he calls Anishinaabe "survivance."

To appreciate the wider associations attached by Native people to the stories that follow, one must approach them as a vigilant and resourceful reader. Aadizookanag and dibaadjimowin alike are stories accessible to all, carrying various layers of meaning and fulfilling various functions in concrete moments of social storytelling, and the reader must keep in play a wide range of meanings. "The Origin of Red Osier," for example, surely tells us about more than the origin of red osier. It does explain a phenomenon of nature by giving an account of its origin, and this is, of course, an important function of many of these stories. But at the same time, it confers significance on the experience of that phenomenon, relating our idiosyncratic experiences of the world to a broader framework of meaning. This need not mean that Odawa stories, like the myths of any tradition for that matter, wholly resolve or explain away the riddles of human existence. For example, in "Nanabozho and His Younger Brother Fight the Bears," we encounter one account of the origin of human death, as the bears avenge their grandfather's murder at the hands of Nanabozho by killing his younger brother during an ice hockey match. But the story offers no tidy rational reason for death: Nanabozho decrees his brother must move on to live in a place other than earth, when the brother he has thought dead and mourned for four days reappears. Finally, these stories model appropriate behavior, often by laughingly depicting inappropriate behavior. In the case of "The Origin of Red Osier," children are reminded to stay away from fire; those of any age are reminded of the ill consequences of sloth and of blaming someone else for one's own mistakes. Because in an oral tradition all tellings are situation specific, a story could carry poignant meanings to a given audience in a given moment that are inaccessible to the reader of this chapter sitting quietly in a chair.

The variety of meanings potentially at play in a telling is matched by the variety of functions a telling fulfills. Stories that are told in various times and spaces can soothe hungry stomachs, redirect attention, reassure unsettled nerves, confront unrepentant offenders, and subvert social tensions with laughter, even as they explain the world, teach moral lessons, or confer meaning and orientation to experience. They can facilitate social exchanges between people and thereby constitute community. Not least of all, stories can make life beautiful.

If the stories that follow appear somewhat flat on paper, we can use our imaginations to make their possibilities come alive. If we discover conflicting information among the stories, as with the two accounts of the primordial murder of Nanabozho's brother—one by bears avenging a prior offense by Nanabozho and the other a more malicious murder by the "Spirit Lions" in the water—we should accommodate the way in which the oral tradition allows for variant stories without suggesting their mutual exclusion. To bring these stories off their two-dimensional confinement on paper, we can also hearken to Jane Ettawageshik's observations about the storytellers and the texture of their storytelling. Here, for instance, is an account of Joe Chingwa's gifts:

> Thus, he had a special gift for describing the out-of-doors, probably because he loved it so. His choice of words and his delivery were such that one actually shivered if he told about an incident that happened on a cold wintry day! . . . None of the English translations of Joe's stories are adequate. Even when I was able to take the story down, word for word, as in the case of the "Defeat of the Maskutens," I could not record the depth of voice, the well-placed pauses, and the other characteristics that made Joe a really superb storyteller.

And here, Jane's account of old Victoria Cooper:

> It was fascinating to watch Victoria as she talked, for she often illustrated a point with her hands. Thus when she described characters going up a hill, she would demonstrate their course with her hands. Or if she told of a bird flying, she might flap her arms to show how it flew, then slowly bring her hands down to her lap to indicate that the bird had alighted.

These and other observations appear in Jane Ettawageshik's rather lengthy introduction to the body of narratives. Readers interested primarily in the narrative content of the stories are directed beyond the interlinear translations to each story's end, where, with the generous assistance of Matt Hooley, I have attempted freer English renditions of the authors' translations at hand.

Introduction

The myths and legends in the following collection were recorded between 1946 and 1954 from Odawa informants living in Emmet County, Michigan, the site of the old Indian settlement of L'Arbre Croche. They form the first collection of this type ever made for the Odawa, per se, although certain Odawa myths were included in seventeenth-century accounts of the tribe and also are to be found in the works of such authors as Schoolcraft, Blackbird, Assikinak, and Wright.[1]

That many of the old myths and tales have been forgotten by the very acculturated Odawa today goes without saying. In fact, there are very few persons now who remember any stories at all. Some know that there are stories about Nanabojo or that the "Odawas once had a big battle with the Maskutens," but they are unable to give more than the bare outline of the plots of such tales.

Thus, I was fortunate indeed to find three excellent storytellers who remembered many myths and legends, as well as a woman, Susy Shagonaby, who knew a fragment of a song that was once included in the Odawas' most popular semi-historical legend, "The Defeat of the Maskutens." Several other persons knew a story or two, and I was able to record them.

From Victoria Cooper, now eighty-seven, I obtained a number of stories, told in Odawa and recorded on wire for the American Philosophical Society in 1948. Unfortunately, only one of these tales has been translated. In the same year, Joe Chingwa told myths and legends in Odawa, one of which was transcribed with interlinear translation, while for most of the remaining stories I obtained fairly good English translations. Fred Ettawageshik, my husband, read from a prepared Odawa script when he recorded myths and legends for the American Philosophical Society in Philadelphia in 1947. These stories have been translated by Fred and are included in this collection along with one that Fred recorded and then translated in 1948.[2] I made phonetic transcriptions with interlinear translations of three other stories told by Fred. Odawa stories may be divided into the myths proper, most of which have to do with Nanabojo, and the legends and tales, the latter being animal stories, tales of the supernatural, and historical and semi-historical ends. The dividing line between myths and tales is, of course, somewhat arbitrary, but in general the myths are of a cosmological character, while the legends describe events presumed by the Indians to have occurred after the world was given its present form by the manidos or spirits.[3]

In the old days the people used to gather around a good storyteller and listen to his tales by the hour. They would pay him with a bag of tobacco or some other similar gift. This was usually in the winter, for the days were often dreary and food was scarce, and the nights were bitter with cold. Furthermore, it was considered bad luck to tell stories in the summertime. Fred Ettawageshik says that if a person was telling stories in the summer, an old woman might interrupt him and say, "*i:ya! asoké maba. m'kakín nongo gawipémagon!*" ("Ha! This person is telling a story. Now a toad will sleep with him!") Joe Chingwa told me that the saying applied to all of the "creatures": to snakes, toads, lizards, and so forth who are active during the summer and able to hear anything that is said, while in the winter they are sluggish and torpid. All of these "creatures" are thought to be evil, Joe reported, and it is feared one of them might be insulted by a story and "take revenge" on the one who told it.[4]

So in the winter, the storytellers, who were often the chiefs and medicine men as well, told the ancient stories and the new ones they had learned from other tribes. Some of the myths came to be connected with certain rites, such as the origin and prescribed order of events in the Midéwiwin. Others described the adventures of the great manidos—how they subdued monsters and created the world as the Indians knew it. Often a myth or tale contained lessons in natural history or in the moral code of the Odawas. Some of them described historical or semi-historical events.

Nowadays, the stories are told summer or winter, and almost purely for enjoyment. The good storyteller is a popular person, as he is everywhere, who has many visitors and is often treated to supper or given a gift, usually of food. In the questions his listeners ask him about his stories, one may sometimes detect a sort of nostalgia, even a trace of belief in the old religious ideas expressed in the stories.

Myths

The Nanabojo myths include many stories or incidents in the culture hero's life that are told in common with other Central Algonkian Indians. There are, however, several of the myths for which no exactly similar versions exist elsewhere. Fred's story of "How the Bear Lost Its Tail," for instance, contains elements of the Hoodwinked Dancers motif, the attempt to fly and the fall into the stump, which are known to many Central Algonkians (Fisher 1947, 240–47), but the attempts of the bear to reach Nanabojo in the stump and the loss of the bear's tail when he scrambles out after being jabbed by Nanabojo are new incidents in this section of the Nanabojo cycle. In the Indian recreations of the ancient European story, of course, the bear usually loses his tail while fishing with it through the ice (*Standard Dictionary of Folklore*, 1:126).

Joe Chingwa's version of the death of Nanabojo's younger brother is unique in its inclusion of his visit to the bear family, the killing of the bear grandfather, and the feeding of sausages made from the bear's intestines to his two grandchildren. The bears' revenge for this crime is to entice Nanabojo's younger brother, Jibiabos, into an ice hockey game played with war clubs during which Jibiabos is killed. The discussion that follows, about death and Jibiabos's journey down the Path of Souls to the west, is well known and is told by the Ojibwe, Potawatomi, Fox, and Menominee (Fisher 1947, 241).

The only versions of the first section of this long myth that are at all similar to Joe's story are told by the Menominee. It is the bears in Menominee myths who are Nanabojo's enemies, and it is the death of the bear chief that causes the flood. In one of the Menominee versions, Menabush [a variation on Nanabozho], "a little white rabbit," assumes the disguise of a tall pine tree from which he observes a ball game played on the ice between the white and grey bears. Menabush wounds the enemy bear chief and later kills an old woman, the *mita* or guardian of the bear's sick lodge, dons her skin, and visits the sick bear chief and kills him (Chamberlain 1891, 199–200). Then, the ice having unaccountably disappeared, the narrative follows the flood and earth diver motifs in the usual sequence found in the Central Algonkian Nanabojo cycle.

The incident of the killing of the guardian of the sick lodge, usually Toad Woman, is strangely omitted from both Odawa versions of this part of the Nanabojo cycle. It may, however, be included in Victoria Cooper's story of Nanabojo, for which I have no adequate translation as yet.

The Menominee description of the flood itself is also the most similar in its wording to the Odawa version told by Fred. In both, the hero climbs the highest mountain, then the highest tree, but is only saved by the intervention of the Great Spirit, who causes the waters to cease rising higher. In this connection, it is interesting that many of the Menominee religious concepts are almost identical to those of the Odawa but differ somewhat from those of the Ojibwe. Likewise, Gertrude Kurath finds that Odawa music is in many respects more similar to that of the Menominee than that of the Ojibwe. Because, according to Menominee tradition, several of their clans originated in Michigan (Skinner 1913, 9–10), it is interesting to speculate that the two tribes may have at one time shared a common culture. One must remember, however, that the modern information on the Ojibwe is mostly from the Minnesota bands and that little has been obtained from the Ojibwe of the Upper Peninsula of Michigan or the region of Sault Ste. Marie, whose culture one would expect to find almost identical with the Odawa.

The Death Chant that Joe Chingwa includes in his version of the Nanabojo cycle is actually an Ojibwe song, Joe said, pointing out as proof of this the fact that the Ojibwe word for west, *gabi:náŋ*, is used instead of the Odawa word, *ɛpangíšimok*, which is given in the story itself. Gertrude Kurath, in chapter 4, analyzes this death chant, which she finds somewhat unusual.

To return to Fred's version of the flood, it is followed by the usual earth diver motif but concludes with Nanabojo creating men from clay that he bakes in an oven, instead of with the description of the animals forming the earth in its present form under Nanabojo's direction, the more usual ending. Actually, Fred has told the incident of the Creator making men of clay as a separate story, but he says he included it in the Nanabojo myth because at the time it seemed to fit into the story. Eli Thomas, an Ojibwe, told Gertrude Kurath this story, and, according to Welpley (1932), it is also known to the Eastern Cree.

Of the remaining Nanabojo stories included here, the "Creation of Mackinac Island," "Why the Birches Have Knobs," "Why the Great Lakes Are Receding," "The Story of the Leeks," and "The Origin of the Choke Cherries" are found in John Wright's collection and of course are also told by many other Central Algonkian tribes (Wright 1917; Fisher 1946, 240–47). Fred's story, "Why the Birch Has Streaks," is similar to Ojibwe, Algonquin, Cree, and Blackfoot versions of the tale (Fisher 1946, 246). "The Bear's Skull" story is widely distributed in the Central and Eastern Woodlands. Michelson recorded the story from an Odawa informant (Michelson n.d.), while Speck's version from the Timiskaming Algonquin is almost identical (Speck 1915, 4). The incident of Nanabojo bumping into the trees while in the bear's skull is not only ridiculous; it is also a lesson in natural history.

Nanabojo's attempt to fly with the geese is known to the Cree, Ojibwe, Menominee, and Blackfoot (Fisher 1946, 245). The incidents in the "Origin of Red Osier" in slightly varying forms are found in stories of the Ojibwe, Algonquin, Cree, Potawatomi, and Fox (Fisher 1946, 241), while the suggestive version of Nanabojo and his wives has parallels in other culturally related tribes. The latter tale was related by Joe Samuels of Cross Village, who was considerably inebriated at the time.

Fred Ettawageshik also tells the story of the diluted maple syrup, although I do not include a version of this incident here. It seems that at one time the maple trees produced pure syrup, but Nanabojo, thinking that this made life too easy for the Indian, urinated in the syrup, thus diluting it. This incident is also known to the Ojibwe.

Joe Chingwa's tale of the "Creator and the Ten Talents" was told to him by his wife's grandfather, a Potawatomi from southern Michigan. Joe said that he once heard an Oneida or some other Iroquois Indian tell this story. I have not found it included in any folktale collections. "The Snowball," another of Joe Chingwa's tales outlined here, seems to be a version of the defeat of winter by spring, a widespread story known to the Ojibwe and the Menominee among other tribes (Schoolcraft 1848, 85–86; Hoffman 1896, 216).

Tales and Legends

Supernatural Tales

Included here are tales of the underwater snake, of the origin of corn, of the giant bear who became Sleeping Bear Point near Frankfort, Michigan, and of Bagog, the skeleton. Many of these stories have been recorded for other tribes, though the ones that describe the formation of local landmarks are known only to the Odawa.

The story "Bagog, the Skeleton" is recorded by Speck for the Timiskaming Algonquin and is also known to the Timigami Ojibwe, both of whom believe that when Bagog is heard rattling, it is an omen of death (Speck 1915, 22, 81).

The legend of Sleeping Bear Point has been recorded by Wright for the Odawa, and is still a favorite story (Wright 1917, 15). Less well known among the Odawas is the legend of the corn, though Weer recorded a somewhat similar version from Fred's father (Weer 1940, 25). The story that Fred tells was related to him by Joe Chingwa, from whom I recorded a lengthy version of the tale, which included a prophecy that the ground on which the Odawa lived would one day be lost to them. Schoolcraft's Odawa myth of the origin of corn is quite different and is apparently the myth on which Longfellow based his description of the gift of corn to Hiawatha (Schoolcraft 1848, 175–78). Gertrude Kurath obtained still a different tale from one of her Michigan informants. Some other tribes in the area tell similar stories, but probably because of the comparatively recent introduction of corn, such stories are usually of a fragmentary nature.

"The Man Carried Off by an Eagle" was related by Jim Cooper, son of the old woman, Victoria Cooper, who told me so many stories. Jim said that Chief Thunder Cloud, an Odawa of Cross Village, told him this story when he was a child. It is an abbreviated version of the widely distributed Roc tales found all over the world. In their discussion of the Iroquois Eagle

Dance, Fenton and Kurath give several versions of the myth, some of which describe the origin of the Eagle Dance (Fenton and Kurath 1953, 80–90).

Joe Chingwa's story of "The Magic Arrow" was also probably at one time connected with the Thunder-Eagle-Sun concept among the Odawa. In this story, the magic arrow probably causes misfortune because it was made from a snake, an animal still considered an evil being by the Odawa. I have not found the story recorded elsewhere.

Animal Stories

Some of the short stories included in this section show European influence, but at least one of them, "The Story of the Robin," has been a favorite tale of the Odawa and Ojibwe for many years and is purely Indian. Tanner gives this tale in his account of his life with the Odawas (Tanner 1830, 2:306). It is also included in four of Schoolcraft's works (Hallowell 1946, 139). The lesson in the story—that one should not wish for too much importance for oneself or for one's children—is an expression of Odawa philosophy that is found in other stories also.

Like the Ojibwe, the Odawa did not consider the robin the gay harbinger of spring, as do Europeans, but instead the red-breasted bird was considered a false prophet. According to Joe Chingwa, the robin comes early in the spring, promising warm weather, but the truth of it is that it usually snows after his arrival. His song is not "Cherries! Cherries!" but rather "I have ten sons-in-law and only one daughter!" ("*mdáswakʿ ningwanakʿ béšigo daš ndánisę!*")

The story "A Girl Married to a Dog," which is summarized here, is known in some form by other tribes and is listed by Fisher for the Passamoquody, Fox, Menominee, Blackfoot, and Cheyenne (Fisher 1946, 252). The "Little Bear" stories, or incidents, were told to me by Clara Cooper, an old Odawa of Harbor Springs, who said they were true stories. She said that in the old days, the Odawas frequently kept bears—especially cubs—as pets, and that they were as fond of them as they were of their dogs.

"The Cricket and the Ant" is, of course, the Aesop fable of the "Ant and the Grasshopper," but in this case the ant gives the cricket some food. It would be inconceivable to an Indian that anyone who was hungry should not be given food by those who were well fed. Fred's story "The Legend of the Serpent" is also a European tale in the "Bear Food, Ungrateful Serpent Returned to Captivity" tradition (Thompson 1946, 226). It is probable that such stories came to the Odawa through French missionaries and traders, whose influence on other aspects of Odawa culture is pronounced. Fred learned this story from Joe Chingwa.

"The Fastest Bird," also given only in summary, seems to be a European story, but I have been unable to find any references to it.

Semi-Historical Legends

These stories include tales of murder and kidnapping by the Saginaw Indians, several versions of the war with the Maskutens, the origin of the Underground Indians, and biographical material about Mkkwánıwi, grandfather of Fred and Joe Chingwa.

"The Defeat of the Maskutens" tales are by far the most popular stories among the Odawa today. The most usual version describes briefly the location of the main Maskutens village at Indian Gardens near Cross Village, the Odawa war party against the Sioux, the defeat of the Odawa by the Sioux, the mockery of the mourning Odawas by Maskutens braves, and the subsequent battle between the Maskutens and the Odawa in which the Maskutens were virtually annihilated. This is the story told by Fred, which I transcribed phonetically and he translated.

Susy Shagonaby tells a variant of this story in which the chief of the Odawas is said to have been Pak'sígan, an ancestor of Susy's. She describes the Odawa council ring and says that Pak'sígan called for volunteers to fight the Sioux (Winnebago?) in a song, part of which Susy knows and which is included in the story. The remainder of Susy's story is similar to the one Fred told. The tale was recorded in June 1954 by Edwin Burrows of WUOM at the University of Michigan. Gertrude Kurath transcribed the song and discusses it in chapter 4.

Joe Chingwa's story of the defeat of the Maskutens concerns the vision of a Maskutens boy during his puberty fast in which the eagle warns him that his people will lose their lands. The first battle between the Odawa and the Maskutens is merely mentioned, and the story continues with a description of the final siege between the remnant of the Maskutens tribe and the Odawas at Benton Harbor.

These stories about the Maskutens are, of course, said by the Odawas to be true. They all agree on the location of the principal Maskutens village at Indian Gardens, and most of them say that a remnant of the tribe fled to the vicinity of St. Joseph or Benton Harbor, where a second battle occurred. Oddly enough, though, there is no historical reference to the existence of a large Maskutens settlement in the northwestern section of the Lower Peninsula of Michigan. However, Champlain refers to warfare between the Odawas and the "Asistaguerouon" or "Fire People," a "distant ten days' journey" or two hundred leagues westward from the Odawa villages, located at that time probably on Manitoulin Island and around the shores of Georgian Bay (Champlain 1929, 3:96–100). The Asistaguerouons have been tentatively identified as the Maskutens or Potawatomi, according to Kinietz. Sagard also mentions the warfare between the two tribes, saying, as did Champlain, that the Neutrals were allied with the Odawa. "Several of the *Jesuit Relations*," Kinietz writes, "mention the continuance of this warfare in later years" (Kinietz 1940, 308).

When the Potawatomi were first contacted in 1634 by Nicollet, they were living near the Winnebago at Green Bay. In 1642, Lalemant reported that some of the Potawatomi "who had abandoned their own country had taken refuge with the inhabitants of the Sault." By 1653 some of the Odawa with the remnants of the Huron "were reported taking refuge with the Potawatomi and allied tribes at Aotonatendie, which was three days' journey south of the Sault of the St. Mary's River" (Kinietz 1940, 309). During the remainder of the seventeenth century the Potawatomi are located in various villages along the western shore of Lake Michigan. By the eighteenth century, with the founding of Detroit, Potawatomi villages were found also in southern Michigan.

In the Maskutens story given by Blackbird, he writes that the great battle occurred when the Odawas were living on Manitoulin Island and the Maskutens in what later became the Odawas' L'Arbre Croche. The two tribes, Blackbird writes, were confederates and "called each other 'brothers.'" The Maskutens were peaceable Indians who never went on the warpath. They were great cultivators of the soil, "making the woodland into prairie as they abandoned their old worn out gardens which formed grassy plains" (Blackbird 1897, 90). Their name means "the prairie people."

Blackbird's account makes it plain that the Maskutens were the original inhabitants of the Cross Village and Harbor Springs area, but Joe Chingwa denied this, saying that the Odawas lived there first. He said that the Maskutens came from somewhere else and asked the Odawas for territory in the region. Joe described the Maskutens as having high foreheads and being very shy. He said they always hid when visitors came to their villages. Informants usually say the Maskutens lived in underground houses, which are variously described as resembling the hogans of the Navaho or the sod lodges of the Pawnee. Some informants insist that one may still see holes in the ground at Indian Gardens where these houses were situated, but this I have never seen myself.

It is a fact, though, that arrowheads, axes, and potsherds may still be collected from the surface of the ground at Indian Gardens. Archaeologists have not discovered evidence of any extensive village site there, but of course no intensive work has been undertaken in the area. Weer and Greenman have both visited the Indian Gardens region, and Greenman reports several sites nearby that have never been thoroughly investigated (Weer 1940; Greenman, personal communication).[5]

None of this, of course, solves the problem of whether or not there were Potawatomi villages in the northwestern section of Michigan's Lower Peninsula at any time. It is conceivable from the historical evidence that there were, particularly as the legends told by the Odawa concerning the Maskutens persistently locate the tribe in this area. It may be that the great battle referred to in the legends occurred about the time the Odawas returned from the west in 1670 to live again on Manitoulin Island (Kinietz 1940, 309), or it could have occurred very early in the century.

Quimby is of the opinion that the Potawatomi were probably the protohistoric inhabitants of Michigan:

> At the beginning of the historic period the Odawa, Huron, and Ojibwe were recent arrivals in the area. They were products of a westward drifting of peoples, although it is possible that they had moved eastward out of the area at a much earlier date. The Potawatomi had recently moved westward and later they reentered the state along with the Miami. But thinking primarily in terms of the westward drifting of tribes that can be inferred from all of the sources cited by Kinietz (1940), it looks as if the Potawatomi moved westward just prior to the beginning of the historic period. And they would be the best suspects as a native population. (1952, 99–107)

I have discussed the tale of the defeat of the Maskutens at length because it is the one bit of cultural heritage that every Odawa knows today, whether or not he is informed about any other aspect of his ancient mode of life. And it is told so vividly, as though the battle had happened the day before yesterday. Under the circumstances, it is strange that this warfare, which occurred upwards of three hundred years ago, should be so fresh in the memories of the Odawas, while more recent events have been completely forgotten.

By the early nineteenth century the Odawa, Ojibwe, and Potawatomi formed the "Three Fires" confederacy, while the Maskutens, or Prairie Potawatomi, were removed, eventually to the far west. Were the latter the people with whom the Odawas fought? Legends of all three tribes agree in describing their close relationship, which is probably why the modern Odawa deny that the Maskutens of Indian Gardens were the Potawatomi.

There is one Odawa legend, however, in which war with the Potawatomi is specifically mentioned. This occurs in a long myth recorded by Gatschet in Baxter Springs, Kansas, in 1887, which has never been published (Gatschet n.d.). Gatschet's Odawa informant described the relationship between the three tribes, saying that the Ojibwe were called "older brother" because they were more numerous. The Odawas would not fight with the Ojibwe but they did fight with the Potawatomi in a battle that lasted until noon, when the chiefs said that it was enough fighting. There were more Potawatomi killed than Odawa, so the Odawas were considered older, and they called the Potawatomis their "younger brother." The Odawas then told the Potawatomis never to fight alone again because they would become even younger, or smaller in numbers. They said that if the Potawatomis undertook a battle by themselves, it would do them no good to come to the Odawas crying for help. So after this, the three tribes thought of themselves as three bodies in one, and together they warred against the Delaware, Sac, and several other tribes.

The Underground Indians described in Fred's story, which follows the Maskutens myths, are sometimes identified with the Maskutens (Wright 1917, 25), though Fred says that the Undergrounds were located somewhere in the west. It is possible that they were the Pawnee, who were often taken by the Odawa as slaves and sometimes married into the tribe. In fact, the word "Pani" for Pawnee in the seventeenth century was synonymous with "slave" because so many of the Pawnee were enslaved by the Odawa and other tribes (McCoy, 121–22). At any rate, Fred traces his ancestry from the Undergrounds, as did Blackbird, who is called Black Hawk in Fred's story, this being the correct translation of his Indian name. The *pipigwé* (little hawk), Fred's totem, is said to have been a totem of the Undergrounds, and it eventually belonged to many famous Odawa chiefs, all of whom traced their descent from the Underground boy captured by the Odawas.

Joe Chingwa's tale of the Odawa cousins captured by the Sioux presumably happened some time during one of the many wars between the Odawa and the Sioux, as did his story of the Sioux captive. At various times during the seventeenth and eighteenth centuries the Odawa were at war, both with the Winnebago and with the Dakota Sioux. None of the tales specify just which Siouxan-speaking peoples are involved.

The stories of enmity between the Odawas and a "Saginaw band" of Indians in fairly recent times are difficult to explain. The Ojibwe are the most recent inhabitants of the Saginaw Valley, but there are no records of warfare between them and the Odawas. It is probable that the tales are oral records of events that happened many years ago when the Sac are said to have lived in the Saginaw Valley. Indeed, the word "Saginaw" is derived from their name. It is also possible that the tales may describe expeditions of retaliation and revenge undertaken by one family group against another for some insult, imaginary or real. Tanner's account is replete with such episodes, though, as in Joe Chingwa's story of Dané'zi, the problem was usually settled by an exchange of gifts between the families involved.

"The Chief with Seven Sons," though it is said to be a true story by Joe Chingwa who told it, seems to be influenced by European tales, if for no other reason than the prominence of the number seven. I do not know of any similar European story, however.

The material about Mkkwánıwi has been recorded in Odawa in a series of long stories. The English versions of these accounts are very unsatisfactory and fail to import the romance that Joe Chingwa and Fred Ettawageshik connect with the life of their grandfather. Mkkwánıwi was apparently a somewhat fabulous person, whose exploits in hunting often take on an almost supernatural character. As Joe Chingwa talked vividly about him in the very house where the old man died, one could almost feel his presence. For the moment, one forgot that it was the twentieth century and that a modern wire recorder was taking down all that Joe said. For the storm was howling over Lake Michigan as Mkkwánıwi and his grandparents fought to keep their canoe from overturning, or again one was with the lonely hunter and shared his uneasy feeling that "all was not well" in his isolated camp at Indian River. Some day a biography should be written of this remarkable man, who seems to have made such a great impression on the hearts and memories of Fred Ettawageshik and his cousin Joe Chingwa.

Narrators

Joseph Chingwa

As already mentioned, Joe Chingwa was a vivid storyteller who could keep his listeners spellbound for minutes or even hours. This well-known chief, dead now, was in his sixties when I knew him. He was rapidly losing his eyesight but was still passionately fond of fishing and even of hunting. He had a special gift for describing the out-of-doors, probably because he loved it so. His choice of words and his delivery were such that one actually shivered if he told about an incident that happened on a cold wintry day!

None of the English translations of Joe's stories are adequate. Even when I was able to take the story down, word for word, as in the case of the "Defeat of the Maskutens," I could not record the depth of voice, the well-placed pauses, and the other characteristics that made of Joe a really superb storyteller. Joe had little education, but he had read a good deal and was a natural orator. He seldom used his hands when he talked, achieving the desired effect in his stories by his wording and the intonations in his voice. His stories are rich in detail and are consequently very long in the Odawa versions. He was not above including almost anything that he thought would enhance his effect or make the tale more clear or exciting. He dwelt at length on certain episodes in which danger or enchantment was being described in order to keep his audience in suspense.[6]

Victoria Cooper

This old woman, now eighty-seven, speaks little English, though she attended schools where English was taught in her youth. Her tales were all told in Odawa while her son, Jim, was present to answer in English any questions that I might have to ask. My knowledge of Odawa is still too limited for me to be able to judge Victoria's storytelling ability. From the one translation that Fred Ettawageshik made, I should say that she tells a story very well, indeed.

It was fascinating to watch Victoria as she talked, for she often illustrated a point with her hands. Thus when she described characters going up a hill, she would demonstrate their course with her hands. Or if she told of a bird flying, she might flap her arms to show how it flew, then slowly bring her hands down to her lap to indicate that the bird had alighted. It's quite probable that Victoria does not ordinarily make so much use of her hands in telling a story and that she did so with me because she knew that I understood very little Odawa. If so, she was successful, for her motions did often make the tale more understandable to me.[7]

Fred Ettawageshik

Like Joe Chingwa, Fred Ettawageshik is an excellent storyteller, but he depends on a few well-chosen words to produce his effect, rather than on repetition and detail as Joe does. He is at his best when describing a ridiculous situation, a peculiar twist of character, or the conflict between two different personalities. He has a dry humor, subtlety, and wit about him, which he often imparts more by what he omits than by what is actually said. His stories are swift-paced, vigorously told, sometimes brief, but always enjoyable. I have heard Fred tell the story "How the Bear Lost His Tail" many times, for instance, yet I always find myself listening as though I had never heard it before.

When Fred is given an audience to speak to (the larger, the better), whether he is going to tell a series of stories or give a speech, he knows just what to say and how to get his listeners in the palm of his hand. I once introduced him to a large group of young children to whom he told stories. Ordinarily, such an audience might have been filled with wriggles and chair scrapings, but there was not a sound while Fred spoke. It was as though he had commanded them to be silent. Afterwards, though, when Fred invited the children to come forward for a lesson in Indian dancing, their shrieks of delight were ear-splitting.

In his stories, Fred is quite outspoken, calling a spade a spade and a rump a rump. He does not gloss over physical actions or characteristics that might offend the sensibilities of his listeners, as Joe Chingwa sometimes does. In this sense, his stories seem more primitive, more like the ancient legends that they purport to be than Joe's do. There is also less European influence manifest in Fred's tales, either in their trappings or in their plots.[8]

Myths

Note: Readers interested in freer English renditions of the translations are directed to the end of each story. The editor rendered these from Ettawageshik's English interlinear translations, and thus they are not direct translations from the original Odawa.

Nanabojo and His Younger Brother Fight the Bears[9]

Iya'a sa	*nıwí*	*dıbádjma*		*Nanabojo*	*anıš gana*
About himself	that (him)	I am going to tell		Nanabojo	so

Nanabojo dıbádjmigosıtˤ		*miwa*	*žanda*	*gaškımadəsıtˤ*
history of Nanabojo I'm going to tell		him	here	the first to live.

nıwi	*dašgo*	*widəbadjma*	*nıwi gana*	*gawijıdanokímajın*
those	thus	I am going to tell you	those	those he lived with

gana gewi	*iya'a*	*ndaš*	*nıwi*	*wɛsi'ín*	*makkwán*	*mínawa*
those	about	thus	those	animals	bears	and (again)

wawaškɛšwan	*mínawa*	*gana*	*anınd gana wɛsiín gána*	*bebıžıájıkˤgána*
deer	again	also	other animals	he lived with

nandaš mkkwán oginsís'tagon gána *manda anbóı'jat‛*
Thus bears they could understand him this he goes to visit them

gana čıkítəngıba akononat‛ *bɛ́ško gana*
to say (what he said) when he spoke in conversation the same as

gi:nıwɛɛžıkanóndi:ŋ migažígənonát‛ nıwɛ Midášgɛ ɛngodıŋ
him when we speak he spoke to them them. So once

anıboi'ját manda
when he went to visit them these

angatəgamkwán gɛgo minawa b'mígowan aniš
household of bears very again friendly (nice to his face) maybe

gıgsígodigénàn ške: gana gimjá' aošıwɛ
they were afraid of him. Really he was very active (supple)

ske:gána Nanabojo mıdaš gıwɛ ıwɛ dıbadjmótgak
really was Nanabojo. So then there she starts to tell a story

nıwɛ kwéwın ɛndənjıŋ ıžıwɛ́ ni:šıwan maba kwe
those mother of family she lives there. Two that woman

nijánseyan anidáš manda wıdıgémaganan kawıyásiwan
children. At that time this husband he is not home (there)

maba kwe maba Nanabojo nıwɛ nia'dısad‛ nıwɛ mıš
this woman this Nanabojo her when he arrived him. So
  gi:wɛ
  seemingly

nıwɛ kwewan atıbádjmonit‛ "*maba ge nos*
this woman she commences to tell a story. "This my father

kiwési wıgona maba ápıtči opıžíšıgo
old man he is this very very much
  adombıžénıman
  they make too much noise for him

nanda gwiwissan" angunanganga'kıtˤ "makwǫ́sag daš gıwȩ
these boys," she says. "Little Bears thus them

anbaškamgısınıtˤ gana gwiwisȩ́s beíka makwǫ́sag
they play boisterously together. Boys wait, look bears

gana gei:gana wisasámsɛ nıwi nínıwe bodwin" dıbádjıge
  overbearing that man (make fire?)," she told

gana niwɛ maba kiwési ejıboasɛendıŋ Mdaš kažıkˤ kıteyaŋ
  Him that old man So? cat?

dawajno mıngo nawa sa gana čısıtómbıtˤgewi ske:gana wédatˤ
  surely he made a home

miwe nabe kıšəwɛnajınágadowén mangi mıšıgo maba kiwési gažım nıwɛ
  this old man

naŋga midaš kašítšgeyaŋga kíkˤ pian giwɛ žıton gıtəwewatˤ odɛ
  So make? there

maba kiwési anıš mıšıgo gagıštəwángıtˤ migo
this old man so when we have completed it for him then

gikˤ pit gìbindodágosıtˤše kınáge íwadatˤ
he left for the country he yelled all he went to live.

gínagodowènmana daš gana kıtawídagènan. Sa nanda
We took care of him thus they must have said. So this person

kwéwın maba Nanabojo tıbášmat táogatˤ anıš Nanabojo géwi
woman this Nababojo he is being told to. So Nanabojo

mjíawıš géwi miwa gana gewi gi'kɛnəmatˤ
he is crafty, resourceful him. So then he he knew

odɛ gadagóšnınıtˤ mkkwokiwésian ɛndánıtˤ "í:dıkˤ"
there when he arrived bear old man made his home. "Seems to be,"

ganéndaŋ "gegɛtˤ sána maba gwonájıwȩ
he thought, "Surely is (oh, for goodness sakes!) this one handsome

mkkwokíwɛsi   apıčıgego   winanno   ta:ʿadam'nápogosę̨"
bear old man   very much   fat   he would taste very good,"

nɛndamsa   "anišgǫ   mkkwokíwɛsi   maba"   midaš   i:dıkʿ
so he thinks,   "Well then   bear old man   this."   So then   it seems

gažınéndam   "ıwɛ   gegétıgo   nga'ogim'nana   mabagǫ
he thought.   "There   surely   I will slay him secretly   this

mkkwokíwɛsi"   nɛndam giwę̨   míšıgo   gegétı   ga'ošítšıgɛtʿ
bear old man,"   he thinks seemingly.   Well, so   surely   he did do it

ángodıŋ gowídıkʿ gǫ   migižátʿ   odɛ   ɛndánıtʿ
Once   he went   there   his home (he who lives there)

nıwę̨   nıtagósıŋaᵃ   kwéškagatʿniwɛ
that one.   As he arrives (indicates question)   he meets me

škwandémwenıŋ   nıwɛ   ɛndánıtʿ   "ani   mina   Nanabojo   (a)bínsian"
in the doorway   his   his home.   "Well   so   Nanabojo   you come to

          dıgodigénan   sa   nıwɛ   mkkwokíwɛsian
kill me,"   he probably said to him   himself   that   bear old man.

"a: nıš   gona   babámosę̨"   dınan   askona
"Oh, only   just   I am out for a walk,"   he says to him   so

maba Nanabojo   Migo   žážıgo gǫ   gikénmıgan   ıžıwę̨
that Nanabojo.   So   already (before)   he knew him (it)   there

bınjižatʿ   nıwɛ   mkkwokíwɛsian   míšıgo   gegéte   maba Nanabojo
when he came   him   bear old man.   So   certainly   this Nanabojo

gažıčgɛtʿ   gigimnana   nanda   mkkwokiésian   mínawa
he did it   he killed him secretly   this   bear old man.   Moreover

i:dıkʿ   gipkwánatʿ   giansatʿ   mínawa
it seems   he starts to skin him   after he killed him.   Then

gıgıkíškuodaŋ   wías   mínawa   gege   nanda
he starts to cut in quarters   meat.   Then   also   these

naggızian   gıbínškwadanan   ge
intestines   he starts to fill the intestines up with meat   (and)

nanda   gábintotˤ   εsčígewatˤgana   nongo gana
these   after he cleaned them   as they do   now

banškwé:jikˤgana   wábəmag   nángad'naŋ gana
they fill the intestines   as I see them   sometimes.

midaš   i:dıkˤ   énεndam gó:'wε   manogóšandaŋ   ngá'iya
So then   it seems   he thinks   he wants to stay there   there

bama gana   maba   gi:gitamákˤ   mabagǫ
a while   this one   he ate all the meat   this one

mkwakíwεsi   mijimdábiwá   gi'néndam   anganınbóıčakˤ
bear old man.   He would come to the shore,   he thought,   he intends

         giwε nanda   gebínmajikˤ   kiwésian   nεndam   í:dıkˤ
to visit   this   those who own him   old man,   he thinks   it seems

maba Nanabojo   anıš   miš   bama   gágadaŋ   kına
this Nanabojo.   Well,   so   a while (after)   he had eaten it   everything

wías   nıwi   gimdabıtˤ   ganebìndagáwakˤ
meat   him   he came to the shore.   He will visit them (stop in),

gınεndám   daš í:dıkˤ   míšıgo   gegétε   maba   ıžíwε
he thought,   thus it seems.   So   surely is   this   there

kwe   nanda   weositˤ   nanda mkwokiwésian   Migo   ıžíwε
woman   this   he was the father   this bear old man.   So   there

gapanəjídigošıŋ   anıš
he arrived at the place where he intended to stop.   Well,

gıčımənıwabəmígoan   ságiwǫ   nanda   éndanjın
they are very glad to see him   it seems   this   at their home

makkwág'əganda   gawi ganda   anıšnábεsi:wakˤ   Mıš   maba
bears these   (they are)   they are not Indians.   So   this

The Art of Tradition

Nanabojo énat͡ʃ nanda kwéwan "gɪtánawikawebítonɪm
Nanabojo he asks her this woman, "I would like to stay with you

gana ma gegána swogwan mage:gana ni:'gwan nánogwan ge:gana
maybe three days, maybe four days, five days maybe.

gìkonanbabáwàbandan kínago nágego
I am looking over the land (cruising around) everything

babawábadan góna žánda ki:ɛndo'kiŋ Midaš žanda
I am looking over here that is on this earth. So here

čimɛndamamba jɪnjajíyamba"
I would like very much to stop here, place to go and come."

dɪnadagénan sa maba Nanabojo nandá kwéwan "anɪš
he told her himself this Nanabojo this woman. "Well,

kɪta:dɪníssa" otegó:n skɛ nanda
he is obliged (free) to stay," she says to him surely this

kwéwan maba Nanabojo "kášwi gana nɪmíŋgɪgésim
woman this Nanabojo "Not we do not have a large room

gana miš gana widanísian žánda gana gwiwissak͡ʃ
for him so if you want to stay here boys

nɪš eyáwogɪk͡ʃgeni gɪtawípemak͡ʃ" odɪgodigénan
two that I have you could sleep with them," she told him

sa nanda kwéwan anɪš nižíwan maba nɪjánsan kwe
herself this woman Well two this children woman

makuo:sák͡ʃ "ahao! migo ɪwɛ" dɪnádɪgenan daš maba
little bears. "All right! So there," he told her thus this one

Nanabojo, "migo ɪwɛ nga'kšɪmnowɛndam go jɪwipɛmogw
"So there I will be very glad to sleep with them

ganda makkuo:sak͡ʃ" kədo i:dik͡ʃ sa anɪš míšigo ɪžɪwɛ agínɛgadaŋ
bear cubs," so he says. So there he leaves it

ıwɛ maškımat'ami gego   *bíndenık'*   *ızıwɛ*   *nággži*
the bag (pack)   the sausages are in it there   bologna

gabinškwádıngıŋ   *anıš mísagana*   *wísnınıt'gana*
those that he filled.   Well, so   whenever they ate

widóbəmat'   *ɛžiwísniwat'gana*
he ate with them whatever they ate

gewi gondámkwot'   *mıdaš giwɛ ıwɛ ko*   *ganıbáwajı*
he sits down with them. So it seems then after   every-

gana ma   *ɛšpitadibıka*   *mi mába Nanabojo*
body went to sleep sometime night   so this Nanabojo

iyabıžéyaŋ   *mandá máškəmat'* *Mi* *amijıt'*   *ıwɛ ko*
starts unraveling this pack.   So   he starts to eat the

wías *mínawa* *nanda naggəži* *kabimškwádıngıŋ* *mišgɛ*
meat and also that sausage   that he had filled.   So

nanda mkkósan   *mamɛsskwəmígoan*   *"geginawa*   *na*
those little bears they wanted some too. "Something (question)

manda *gwımíjənawa"*   *dinandıgénan* *daš* *ángodıŋ ko*
this   do you want eat?" he said to them. Thus once

asagiwɛ   *mkkǫsák* *ganda* *wimíjınawa* *wɛ'i:yai* *mkkwa*
it seems like bear cubs these   they want to eat that   bear

naggiš   *bánskwadɛk'*   *anıš misa*   *maba Nanabojo*
intestines they are stuffed, filled. Well, so   this Nanabojo

gigikíškodɛmawat' *bɛbángı gana mánda* *nággiš* *"ahao*
he cut some off   small portion   sausage. "All right,

manda gégi" *odinádıgenan*   *"nıwɛ bejík'mkkǫsan"* *mínawa*
this here,"   he said to them. "Him first bear cub."   And then

anínd *gigiškodaŋ* *manda* *gegi*   *gi:mo:šıgǫ́*
so   he cut (more) this one something he did this secretly

aniš	nbáwakʿgana	wenijánsıjıkʿ	"gegɛtʿ sa géna ganda
since	they are sleeping	for the children.	"Surely those

kwiwisɛsakʿ	omɛ̀npıdánawa	mkwa nággiš	Mišgɛ
boys	it tastes good to them	bear intestines.	So

ga'ıškwəgıdámınıtʿ	kína	wıngègıdámákʿ	manda" dınantəgí
after they ate it,	All	eat it all, every bit	this," he said to

	maba Nanabojo gewɛ	manda	mkkǫsakʿ	Miš ge	ganda gwisiwɛsakʿ
them	this Nanabojo	those	bear cubs.	So	those boys

í:dıkʿ	gaškwa	gagadamawatʿ	ganda makkǫsakʿ	nıwɛ
it seems like	after	after they ate it up	those cubs	them,

"gikwe:jĭmatʿ"	nıwɛ	Nanabojo	"ani kíno	nakkigıdánawa
"Did you eat it?"	(to) those	Nanabojo,	"Well, all of	what (sausage)

	ıwɛ̨ ga' šamınagokʿ"	dınadıgénan sagóna	gi:močı
I gave you	the did you eat?"	he says to them	secretly

wiboinóndagatʿgɛnıwɛ		nik'əgówan	ganda mkkǫsakʿ
lest they hear him (they told?)		their parents	those cubs.

"ɛya kínago	gígıdana"	kıdowan	ıšıwɛ	nanda makkǫsakʿ miš giwɛ
"Yes, all	we ate,"	they say	there	those cubs. So

maba Nanabojo	enátʿm	nıwɛ	makkǫsan "kìnıstopwə́wa'na
this Nanabojo	he says to them	them	cubs, "Do you recognize

	gímišamısawa"	dınan giwɛ	aniš gašıwi
the taste	of your grandfather"	he says to them.	Well,

ganda mkkǫsákʿ ge	wínowa	ginsıs'táwasiwan
those cubs	they themselves	they did not understand him.

andodıŋ škona	maba Nanabojo	majatʿ gana	pınɛ ɛnsogižıgakʿ
Once	this Nanabojo	he leaves	regularly every day

mosé	bama gana	nákšınıkʿ	adogásıŋ	miš	gíwɛ ángodıŋ
he walks.	Later		evening	he returns. So	seemingly once

gamajánıtˤ   ganda   mkkǫ́sakˤ   mi giwę nıwę̨ˤ gašíwan énawatˤ
after he left those cubs   so it seems her   their mother they say to,

"*gego šagıwɛ dašmigona ıwę̨ Nanabojo*" *dınánwan   niwę̨ gašwan*
"Something   he feeds us   Nanabojo," they said to her   their mother.

"*apıčıgo   nappogatˤ   wías   šowádjıgego   nággažı   žınaggatˤ*"
"very good   it tastes   meat.   It looks like intestines   it looks like"

ıwę̨" ıkıdo sagigiwę maba   bejíkˤ mkkǫ́s "aníš beka"   kídow n
he says   I guess   this   first   cub.   "So, wait," she says

sagíwę nıwę̨ gášwan   manda   mkkǫ́san "Kiš ma nóngo nidadıbıkˤ
I guess her the mother   these   cubs,   "If   now   tonight

samənigˤiwę̨ gego kína kıdángego   ngáwabandan
he gives you that all   do not eat it. I want to see it.

gego   ní:go   maba Nanabojo" ndınénıma kído idıkˤsa
Something   I suspect   this Nanabojo," she said, she said, I guess

maba kwe   maba wɛnijánsıtˤ nanda mkkǫ́san "aniš mkkwo go" gewi
this woman   these children   these cubs.   "Well, bear"   her

maba kwe   aniš gana iwę̨ dıkídowe   kwe   áškıdo:yá "Gego
this woman   so   the I just said woman she said. "Something

nongo kína gıdángégo   gí:moš   nongo kakıdónawa   ıwę̨ wías
now   all   do not eat all secretly   now   you save some that meat

ge šamnıgˤ   o'tígowadıgenan sa" ganda   mkkǫ́sakˤ
   he gives you to eat.   Be sure to save some." these   cubs

nıwę̨ gášwan   "ahao   aniš mısa gego"   ma'pí
      mother. "All right!   well, so   something."   After a while

maba Nanabojo ıwę̨   nondádıbıkˤıwę̨   kınagánbawatˤ
this Nanabojo   some time in the night after all went to sleep

mige mínawa abıžean   ıwę̨ maškˤ mat   migo mínawa
so   again   he starts unraveling   the pack.   So   again

mijıtˤ wías mkkwo wías mínawa iwɛ nággıš gabínskwadan
he starts to eat meat bear meat again the sausage he filled with.

mínawa gipakwékadɛmawatˤ ıwɛ gwiwissan ıwɛ nággıš məmámənıkˤ
Again he cuts the meat up the boys the sausage a certain

gana gáškɛ ganda gwigisɛsak kína
amount (he cuts off) I guess. So these boys all

gogıgıdazínawa (kína ıwɛ) aniš gigó:wana
they did not eat it all so she warned them not to eat

nıwɛ gášwan kawi kína jimítsıgowa wiwábadan
her their mother. Not all you should not eat. She wants to see it

maba ıwɛ kwe ıwɛ godowɛndıg í:dıkˤ ıwɛ wías gégo
this the woman that thing whatever this meat something
   dınɛnmanıgo
   she said

nanda Nanabojúan maba kwɛ miš gıwɛ gamajánıtˤ
this Nanabojo this woman. So seemingly after he had gone

Nanabojúan gıšép mimaba "gogwéjımatˤ" nıwɛ mkkǫ́san "ani
Nanabojo morning this, "Did you eat?" her cubs "Well

kıšámagowa na mínawa wías dıbık Nanabojo?"
did he give you to eat some more meat in the night Nanabojo?"

dınádıgenan "ɛya" "kínanago kigıdánawa" "ka ngíškuo:nan
she said to them. "Yes!" "All did you eat it?" "No, I saved

géni" kído sage maba bejıkˤ mkkǫ́s "migo geni
some," he says this first cub. "So some

gimoč go:geni ngi'kídowan pangi ıwɛ," kído í:dıkˤsa
secretly some I hide little bit," he says it seems

géwi bejıkˤ midaš gıwɛ gi'nat maba kwɛ nıwɛ
that one. So, seemingly she told them this woman those

nijánsan nıwę̧ "tagašguó:nadıkʿ ıwę̧ gaškwándamık"
children   "Let's go and get it   what you did not eat,"

dınàdıgénan sa   "kanabádjəgo   maba nıwę̧   kiwésian
she said to them. "Maybe, I guess so this   old man

Nanabojo   giwansádıgenan"   kído sa   í:dıkʿ   maba kwe
              I believe he killed him," she says it seems this woman

anıš mi mába   kwe   nıwę̧ ó:san   Misıgo   daš me   ganda
well so this   woman   her father. So   thus   those

gwiwisę̧sakʿ agıbítuowatʿ ıwę̧ mkwa nággiš   giwábandan   maba kwe ıwę̧
boys   they brought that bear sausage. She saw it   this woman

"gegétɛ̧   mkkwo wías sa manda" kído   giwę̧   migɛgo žažıgo
"Certainly bear   meat this,"   she says seemingly. So   after

maba kwe   gá'kčimowıtʿ   "mıgo gegétʿa   maba Nanabojo
this woman   she started to cry; "So certainly   this Nanabojo

ná'   nıwę̧ kiwésian   í:d kʿ   agíwansatʿ"   kıdo
him   old man   it seems he has already killed him," she says

giwę̧   anıš ganda   daš   mkkwag   agosáwan   nıwę̧
it seems. So there   thus   bears   they are afraid of him him

Nanabojo. "anıš gana   genapínanago"
            "So   what can we do to him (to get even)?"

kıdowak   ši:d kʿ gana   amaʿojíʿtəwatʿ gana
they said   it seems.   They are huddled together hold a council

gewi   ę̧čıwatʿ   deʿčıwak gǫ   i:dıkʿge   wínawa
those they are assembled   they were quite a few it seems   them

ganda mkkwakʿ "gasıwígo maba Nanabojo   kıda'kškíasına
these bears   "Impossible this Nanabojo,   we cannot hurt him

gegǫ   jıdódowan   Nanabojo" kıdo   ške
something   they want to do something   Nanabojo," he says one of these

maba bejık‛ "*kaógogego géjık‛ škę ngoba apıčígo majaíyawıs*
this first one. "Nothing we can do. Very much clever, crafty

maba" kído i:dík‛sa maba gantámigıgodat‛mkkwə
this person," he says it seems this one the first speaker bear.

bejık‛ "*škɛgo" mínawa gígigod*
First, "What can we do?" Again (another?) he got up to speak

mkkwə "*gikɛ́ndanwini gešítčıkandıba*
bear. "I know how we could fix him (get even with him)

jiáštəwàyan" kído i:dık‛sa "*anıš gıdádıbàjım sa"*
to take revenge on him," he says it seems. "Well, let's hear what

         nadıkša maba bekıdód ıwę "*aᵃ*
you have to say," so they tell him this they say. "Oh,

komíŋ sa škékabadiŋ sa pakkwákwat‛ kawepadána žánda
on the ice first ice ball game (like hockey) here

gana nongo šəškwadejık‛ kwakat‛sa kawɛ́podangık‛ iya'ín kanokasnánın
now skaters ball they hit it. Some we will use

paggamáginan" kído i:dík‛sa maba škígıbadıŋgo "*ɛpıčı gonačəwaŋ*
war clubs," he says it seems this first one. "While it is good

mkkwam mıwę pijítogogıwę jí'tuowaŋwa
ice (bears?) so it is clear the time to play the game with

Nanabojo gewi gona ędočıt‛ gegwínawę ɛnčiaŋ aniš gıt‛čımę gǫ"
Nanabojo them his group his own group. Well, quite a few of us,"

kído i:dık‛sa maba gágodat‛ "*mıdašgo manda pí:gǫ*
he says it seems this speaker. "So this time
   bębɛšogoní'yaya
   close huddled

gana míwę anjída nıwę čímeyan
so intentionally, purposefully him younger brother

ji:wépədoŋ	aniš	widámɪno ɪgǫ		géwi	ábɪdɪkˤgǫ géwi
we will strike.	Well,	he is going to play		him	surely

mabá	Jibiábos	ɛnínd	miwa Nanabojo	čɪméyan"
this one	Jibiabos	what he is called	his Nanabojo's	younger brother."

gíntanəgamó	giwɛ̨	maba škínɪwɛ̨	apɪčɪgéno	kwanážɪwɛ
he was a good singer	seemingly	this young man	very much	handsome

kínage	gíbosɪndàgo:nˤ	bematsɪnjɪn	ánagamatˤ
everyone	listened to him	the living ones	when he sang.

Midaš ɪwɛ̨	í:dɪkˤ	giwɛ̨	ganda mkkwák	ganéndəmowatˤ
So	it seems	seemingly	these bears	what they thought (it was

	"missa mába	gɛnəsánˤ	aniš	kawimamɪda
their intention)	"So this one	we will kill him	well	we cannot hurt

Nanabojo	mjaíawɪs"	míšɪgo	gigičákanawatˤ
Nanabojo	he is very supple."	So	they had already made up their

	mɪwɛ̨	apikwə́kwatˤ	wépadamon
minds (plans were made)	so	when the ball	when they strike it

kómɪŋ	mɪwɛ̨ apíjɪnsan		maba Nanabojo	čímeyan
on the ice	so when we kill him		this Nanabojo	younger brother

gikɪdo i:dɪkˤ		"ahao!"	aniš nomákɪžɪgo	manda gǫ
they said seemingly		"All right!"	Well time went by	this

mápi go	i:díkˤ	níksenagˤ	mígɪabadɪŋ manda
after a while	it seems	cold weather	ice freeze over this

čígome	ɪžɪwɛ̨ éndawɪtˤ	gegɛtígo	gigwanádjɪwan
lake (Michigan)	there where they live.	Surely	it was very smooth

	go iwɛ̨ kwam	í:dɪkˤ	miš gíwɛ̨	wɪdámɪnowatˤ
(pretty)	that ice	I suppose.	So seems like	they are ready to play

manda kwə́kwat	giwépodàmawat	kómɪŋ	žážɪgo	gigiža'konígewakˤ
this ball	they are going to hit	on the ice	already	they have made

298 The Art of Tradition

wasíšıgewatˤ   *gegɛtı*   *giwę*   *maba*
up their minds   what they are going to do.   Surely   it seems   this

gewi   *Jibiábos*   *wıdámınąˌ*   *aháo!*   *amígo ıwę*
person   Jibiabos   he is going to play.   All right!   so now

nɛndamok sa   *i:d kˤ*   *gánda mkkwak*   *migǫ*   *jiáštowaŋ*   *Nanabojo*
(after) they know   it seems   these bears   so   revenge   Nanabojo

"*migo nongo wagewépıdan*   *pággamagan*   *Jíbiabos*"
"So   now   we are going to hit   with war clubs   Jibiabos,"
    kıdowìdıgénakˤsa
    so they said so.

migęgę   *maba Nanabojo*   *kawıgego*   *pággamagan*   *manž i:dikˤgewi*
So   this Nanabojo   not any   war club   whatever

kadódəmokwè   *íta ıwę*   *abaggámagan*   *migi*
he does not know what he did with it   whatever   his war club.   So

wɛpıjinakˤ   *gımájiptotˤ*   *mtígwakıŋ*   *pandápəkweyáŋ ıwę*
before he can play   he started to run   to the woods.   He ran
    abàggámagan
    his war club

wan'ókəsıt   *géwi*   *wiwidó'kəsıtˤ*   *aniš*   *enádjəmın*
he realizes he must have   so that   he can play.   Well   this story

daš gó'ko   *Nanabojo*   *bejıkˤgo*   *manda*   *pággamagan*   *agínıp kwèyaŋ*
thus   Nanabojo   first   this   war club   he chiseled out

migegago   *degíštotˤ*   *miginondɛ*   *anıwábadoŋ*   *mi*   *ngojɛ*
almost   he has completed   so   he was dissatisfied.   So   away

mínawa   *gipaggadaŋ ıwę*   *mi mínawa bejıkˤ*
    he threw away the war club.   So   another first

(agi)nındáwabadan   *angojɛ gana*   *paggamágan*   *jibkwéangıba*
I (he) looked for it   away   war club.   He chisels out another

wikášgɛ gǫ gana *agímkan gana* *wa'nokasıtˤ* *i:dikˤ*
Later, after a while he found it the one he could use it seems

kamınwábandan *i:dikˤ* *wa'nokasıtˤsa gana*
he saw something satisfactory it seems he could use.

giwèwipətátˤ *i:dikˤ* *giıšıtotˤ* *ıwɛ paggamágan* *mıš*
he hurried it seems he had to finish the war club. So
   aginímdabitˤ
   he went to the shore

žažıgo ge:gana *škàkamigədínəgoba* *odɛ* *dɛːˈkošıŋ*
after the game was all over there at the place

kómıŋ *kagogego* *wíya* *wabamatsı* *angoji* *aniš daš*
on the ice. No one someone he did not see anywhere. So

gana *panánıbowıtˤ* *odɛ kómıŋ* *taiá*
probably as he stood around there on the ice surprisingly
   gimámənonabandànan
   he discovered

wínsısan *mıtátenıkˤ* *midaš i:d kˤ* *agíːdapınaŋ*
strands of hair they strewn around. So it seems he picked them up

niwɛ *taiá* *ıwɛ* *wégwagɛ* *mınıwɛ* *wínsısan*
those. Surprisingly the he knows (understands) those hairs

Jibiábos ka'ɛnínd *mi* *žážıgo* *ganda mkkwakˤ*
Jibiabos belong to. So (time past: earlier) those bears
   aginsawatˤ
   they killed him

taiá *gegɛtˤ sa gena* *škɛːndam* *awa* *Nanabojo* *wıkanéyan*
surprisingly. Surely sorrow him Nanabojo his brother

ogínsımın *miš gɛgi* *gibámadematˤ*
had been killed. So he started out walking and crying

sadáwendaŋ gana *ɛnınıˤ* *gwánəga'nıkˤgego* *nangodıŋ* *gana*
in sorrow. So on the fourth day momentarily as he was

abmademat‛	*gana ábamosɛt‛*	*migɛ*	*gibɩgənónagat‛*
walking and crying	as he is walking	so	he came and spoke to him

nɩwɛ Jibiabosan	"*aniš*	*wɛnjímowɩyan*	*nsaí yɛ*"
him Jibiabos.	"What	are you crying for	my older brother"

dìgodɩgénan	*daš*	"*ge abɩsa wininibɩmádɩs*"	*kídowan*	*gɩwɛ*
he said to him	thus.	"I myself, I am still alive,"	he says	to him

"*Ka wigìgibɩmátsisi*"	*dɩnan*	*škɛ*	*maba Nanabojo*
"No, you are not alive,"	he says to him	so	this Nanabojo.

"*ki:nsɩgósanìnɩwɛ*	*odɛ api*	*kwɔ́kwat*	*gadənákkamigak‛*
"you know they killed you	there where	the ball	where they held the

gaťpɩnɩnígoyan"	"*ayam*	*bɩmádɩs sago*"	*odígowan*
game where they killed you."	"Oh,	I'm alive still,"	he tells him

kɩwɛ nɩwɛ šímeyan		"*kawi:wi*	*kawi:gínowɩt‛*	*mátsiwɩn*
so him younger brother.		"Oh, no,	not in this life	life

eyamaŋ	*gɩdaiyási*	*géyabi*"	*dinan*	"*ši:dɩk‛*
(that we have)	you haven't got	some (more),"	he says to him.	"So

pɩkansab	*matsɩwɩn*	*gídaiyán sa*	*ani gana*	*gegi'žɩwɛkak‛ iwɛ*"	*ganda*
different	life	you have	so	it cannot be so"	these

énɩnd bojɩk‛	*neyab mínowa*	*jɩbɩpškabɩwat‛*	*žanda*
those that die	return again	they will never come back again	here

aki	*jɩbɩbɩmádɩsɩwat‛*	*kasago*	*wɩka*	*taižɩwébsɩno*
earth	they rise up and live over again.	No	never	it cannot be so.

"*Kigàmmajása*"	*dɩnadigénan sa*	*maba Nanabojo*	*šímeyan*
"You leave!"	he said to him	this Nanabojo	to his younger brother.

"*kawigɩwábasi*	*aniš kawi*	*manda madsíwɩn*	*odaiyási*	*ge:yabɛ*
"I do not see you	so not	this life	you do not have	anymore

bɩkanbimádsɩwɩn	*manda sa šímɛ*	*ka'ižá*	*épangìšmak*
different life.	This younger brother	you go	West.

geni žawatˢ   *pama*   *anıšnábɛkˢ*   *genınbojıkˢ*
Those (that die) they will follow   after a while.   Indians   the dead

míkan   *kanižıtón*   *geni*   *žaíyan*   *kanıwàbzagákowakˢ*
road   you build   them.   You follow   you must make a mark on the trees

mtıgokˢ   *mi*   *ódę*   *gɛˈtanamásıyan*   *gegi*   *mi wodę*   *kína*
trees.   So   there   you will sit and sing   him alone.   So there   all

anıšnábɛkˢ   *bama*   *gewi*   *žáwatˢ*   *ahao!*   *majan*
Indians   after a while   they   they will follow.   All right!   you go now

daš   *gigánınıgam*   *békıš*   *kıgábasınduo:nˢ"*   *aniš mısa*
thus.   You sing   at the same time.   I will listen."   So

Jibiábos   *gamájatˢ*   *épangišmokˢ*   *ıžatˢ*   *mandaš miga*
Jibiabos   he starts to go   West.   He is going.   So this

niˈnaˈaŋ   *enımážatˢ* *("ngagojınnagamm"):*
what he sang   he starts. ("I will sing": narrator):

       Manó: *nína*   *nıngámaja*
       All right,   I, myself,   I am going away.

       Manó: *nína*   *nıngámaja*
       All right,   I, myself,   I am going away.

       Gabínaŋ   *nıngaˈíža*
       To the West   I am going.

    Here Joe Chingwa gave a short ending to the myth, which he later asked to have deleted in favor of the following:

misa Jibiábos   *agímajatˢ*   *Nanabojo*   *gegi*   *božɛndawatˢ*   *nıwi*
So Jibiabos   he is gone.   Nanabojo   so   he listened   him

šímeyan   *nidɛptáogosınitˢ*   *gıškana ge*
younger brother   he could hear his voice at a distance.

agigčıbogámanmadınıkˢ   *dıbíško*   *škę gana*
A great gust of wind came through the forest.   Same   thus

wíya   škɛdaŋ gana migíwɛ gágənɪwɛg   manda tígwə:kɪŋ
someone to say   after the sound ceased this   in the woods

bɪnéšiakˤ wesíakˤ   mɪš gɪwɛ   gabonánmàd:nɪkˤ
birds   animals. So   it seems   after the wind ceased (calmed down)

maba Nanabojo   kawigɛgéyabɛ   ginóndawasi   nɪwɛ
this Nanabojo   he did not hear him any more he did not hear him

šímeyan   midaš ɪwɛ   gibónɛndan
younger brother. So   there he calmed down (got normal)
   gagɛgéyabɛ
   not any more he heard him.

gɪškɛndasi   ɛžiyápa gana gížiatˤ
He is not sorrowful   once again   he became normal.

mínawa   wodɛ   ɪwɛ jíbiakˤ   enɪnágadowatˤ
Then again there   the souls, ghosts they followed

manda mí:kan iya'i gɪwɛ   témagatˤ ɪžɪwɛ 'démɪn   mi ganda
this trail   it seems it lies there. Strawberry so those

gíwɛ   anɪšnábɛkˤ enínɪbojɪg enɪmíjəwatˤ jɪbwa
seemingly   Indians   the dead   they feed on just before

nitɪgšnɪwatˤ   ɪžíwɛ
they get to where they are going (their destination)   there.

anɪš mɪsa Nanabojo gibonéndaŋ   kawigéyabɛ   gɪškéndəsi
So   to be calmed down   not any more   he is not sorrowful.

anɪš mɪsa ekwəg manda   dɪbádjmowɪn čɪmigwétč   gabasíndowiɛgˤ
Well, so end   this   story.   Thanks very much for listening.

Nanabozho and His Younger Brother Fight the Bears:
Free English Rendition

I am going to tell a story about Nanabozho, about the first one to live. Thus I am going to tell you about those he lived with: the bears and deer and all of the animals. Of these, the bears could understand Nanabozho, and he was able to speak with the bears in conversation, in the same way we speak to each other. So once, when Nanabozho went to visit a household of bears, they were friendly and nice to his face, though perhaps quite frightened of him. Indeed Nanabozho was nimble and tricky. So the mother bear, whose husband was away, leaving her alone with her two children, commenced by telling Nanabozho a story:

> "My father is very, very old. And these, my boys are way too loud and boisterous for him when they play, even though he was at work making them a home. I told them, 'Boys, wait! You're overwhelming that old man bear!' So we went away, and when he finished the home for us, he yelled and he left for the country and we took care of him that way."

Nanabozho, ever crafty and resourceful, listened to the tale and pondered the possibilities. Nanabozho thought, "Surely, this old bear is very handsome and fat and he would taste really good. Perhaps I will go there and slay this old bear secretly, and eat him." And so he set about the task.

Nanabozho went to the house where this old bear was living, and arriving at his door, discovered him standing there waiting for him. The old bear looked at Nanabozho and, knowing of his cunning, suspected he had come to eat him. But Nanabozho reassured him, "Oh, I'm just out for a walk." But before long, Nanabozho accomplished his task. In secret, he killed the old bear and skinned him. Then he cut the meat into quarters and filled the bear's intestines with some of the meat, to make sausages, as one sees people doing nowadays.

Having thus prepared the meat, Nanabozho decided he would stay there and enjoy his meal for a while, and he ate until the old man bear was all gone. Then he thought that he might return and visit old man bear's family. So, when he had finished the meat, he came to shore and stopped at the home of the old bear's daughter. The family was delighted to see him—they are clearly not Indians—and so Nanabozho, seizing the present mood, asked:

"I would like to stay with you, three, four, maybe five days. I am wandering about the land, surveying all there is, and I would like to have this place to come and go for a while."

"Well," she said, "feel free to stay here, but we do not have a large room for you to sleep in. You could sleep with the boys, in their room."

"All right! I will be very glad to sleep in the room with your two bear cubs!" he said, setting down his backpack, full of his fresh sausages. Whenever they ate, he sat down with them. And at night, after everybody went to sleep, Nanabozho reached in his pack and ate the meat and the sausages he made. The little bears wanted some too.

"Do you want something to eat?" he asked the little bears, and they said they wanted to eat those sausages. So Nanabozho cut off small pieces and gave some to one bear and then to the other, all very quietly because everyone was sleeping. And they thought it tasted good.

"Well, did you eat every bit of what I gave you?" Nanabozho whispered, so their parents wouldn't hear.

"Yes, we ate everything," they replied.

"Do you recognize the taste of your grandfather?" he asked. But his wit was lost on the befuddled cubs.

Every day, Nanabozho would leave in the morning, only to return very late. Once, while he was gone, the cubs told their mother, "Nanabozho feeds us some kind of meat, which tastes very good." "It looks like intestines," the first cub added.

"Wait," said the mother. "If he gives you the meat tonight, do not eat it. I want to see it first. I suspect this Nanabozho is up to some trickery. So be sure to save some for me to see." So the cubs, excited in their new scheme, waited for Nanabozho to return. Some time that night, he did, and once everyone had gone to sleep, he unraveled the pack, and ate the bear meat and sausage. Again, he cut up some meat and some sausage for the boys. But they remembered what their mother told them and did not eat it all.

The next morning, after Nanabozho left again, the mother asked the boys if he gave them some meat and if they had saved some. The first cub said, "Yes, I secretly hid some." And she looked at the saved morsels. "This is bear meat!" she said, and began to cry. "I think that this Nanabozho has killed the old bear, your grandfather."

So those bears were very afraid of Nanabozho. "So what can we do to get even with him?" they asked themselves. So they called together a large council of bears and huddled together. The first bear to speak said, "We can't hurt this Nanabozho, he is too crafty and clever." But the next bear seemed more hopeful. "I know how we could take revenge on him." "Well, let's hear what you have to say," the rest said.

"As soon as there is the first ice on the lake, we can play *kawepadána* (a game like ice hockey). Some of us can play with war clubs. When the ice is good and clear, a good-sized group of us can challenge Nanabozho and his group to a game, and surely Jibiabos, Nanabozho's brother, will come. We can huddle close together on purpose and strike his brother." Jibiabos was not as tricky as his brother but was a handsome and renowned singer, whom every living thing loved to hear.

So they made up their minds. "Since we cannot kill the cunning

Nanabozho, we will kill this one during the game." Soon enough the ice froze over the lake (Lake Michigan), and it was smooth, beautiful ice, and they were ready to play. The game had been proposed, and it seemed likely that Jibiabos was going to play, so they planned to beat him with their war clubs during the game: the bears' revenge was set.

When the game was to begin, Nanabozho could not remember what he did with his own war club. So he ran into the woods to make a new one, chiseling it out of wood. However, when he finished, he was dissatisfied with it and carved out a second. By the time he had finished and returned to the shore of the lake, the game was over. Everyone was gone. All that was left, in fact, was some hair strewn around on the ice. Taking the clumps of hair in his hands, he realized that they belonged to his brother, Jibiabos.

So, long ago, those bears had killed Nanabozho's brother, and this filled him with sorrow, and he walked around weeping for several days. On the fourth day, suddenly Jibiabos spoke to him.

"Why are you crying, older brother? I am still alive."

"No, you are not alive," Nanabozho replied. "Surely you know they killed you there where they played the game on the ice."

"Oh, I am alive still," insisted Jibiabos.

"No, you are done with this life that we have." Nanabozho said. "Now you have a different life. It cannot be that those who die return again. They will never rise up, come back, and live over again on earth. It cannot be so. You must leave. I will not see you any more in this life. You have a different life. Go to the west. All those who die will follow you after a while. Make a path for the dead people who follow you by marking the trees as you go. This way you will not sit and sing alone; because the people can follow."

"All right. Go now!" Nanabozho commanded, "and sing as you go, for I will listen!"

And so Jibiabos started to go west. And this is what he sang as he left:

> *Manó: nína nıngamája*
> *Manó: nína nıngamája*
> *gabináng nınga'íža*
> (All right, I am going away.
> All right, I am going away.
> To the west; that's where I'm going.)

So when Jibiabos had taken leave, Nanabozho could hear his voice in the distance. Then a great gust of wind came through the forest, and as it did, there was no sound of birds or animals in the woods. After the wind calmed down, Nanabozho could not hear his younger brother anymore, and he too became calm. His sorrow ceased and he took to normal.

Ever since, souls of the dead follow this trail, and strawberries lie along the path for the dead to eat on the journey to their destination.

So, Nanabozho, he calmed down and ceased being sorrowful. Well, so this is the end of the story. Thanks very much for listening.

Nanabojo Anishinaben Ogiijiad [Nanabojo Creates the Indian][10]

Nanabojo   oshemeian   iian   manido   shibjin
            his younger brother those   Spirit   Lions

ga-ansigon,   miiwi   Nanabojo gi-andowa bamad.
he was killed by   so then   he looked for them.

Tibeiw   dash   abmosed Nanabojo, mi-wi giawabamad
On the beach   then   he walking   so he saw them

shibjin   anawindj   adam-inonid.   Epitchi
lions   far out on the water   playing they.   While

anana go-dawendag   dash   mindj-edig   ge ijitchke gwe
he thinking about them   then   how   what he could do

tchishki apa   besho   jiwi be jamid   niwi   "Mongwan"
he to make them   near   for them to come.   That one,   "Loon"

dash   nanita   abmissewan,   midash   iniwi
then   just happens   him flying by   so then   him

ge-kwedji madjin   ga ishkwa   winda mowad   ga ijiweb isinid
he asks him,   after   he told him   what happened to him

oshimeian.   "gawindamon ge ijitchkeian,"   digon
his younger brother.   "I'll tell you how to do it,"   says to him

niwi   Mongwan.   "Wode   ga onanibo,   gidji keing
that   Loon.   "Over there   you stand (yourself),   like a stump,

dash   ga-ojina gos.   Ga-miiab migog   dash
but   you will look.   You will look strange to them   thus

giwi   manidog,   ka ge bapish   gab-madjisi,
those   monsters,   but you must not   move in the least.

ga-winda mon   dash   besho   biiawad.   Midash
I'll tell you   but   near   as they come.   So then

dji ba-mod   nagan sid."   Miiwi   Nanabojo   gi-ojina gosid
shoot him   the leader." So then   Nanabozho   he went and looked like

adjike-ing.   Midashgo   gegeti,   besho   gi-webi-bijawad
a stump.   So then   really   near   began coming they

shib jik   awi binda kend mowad   awi-dji-ken.   Kawika
lions   they coming to find out that stump.   Never

awam da sinawa   ijiwi   awi-dji-ken   djigi bigad sing.
they did not see it   there   that stump   ever to stand there.

Apitchi   dashgo   besho   abiia-nid   miwi
Very   so then   near   as they get,   so he (that one)

"Mong"   ajinad   Nanabojoian,   "Ahow!   abamo
"Loon"   he says to him   Nanabojo,   "Okeh!   shoot him

awi   nagansid."   Gabamod   dash   Nanabojo
the (that) the leader." After he shot him then

niwi   shibjin,   kitchi-tang shki gewan   miwi
that   lion   he kicks very much   so the (that one)

bish   gitchi swe iia gamisemigog,   migego   webimosh kang.
water   splashes very much,   so also   it begins to flood.

Amadjip tod Nanabojo,   apitchigo   ano kiji kad
He begins to run   very, very   although speedy he

migo   gaiewi   eshkwe iang   ebidana-simgag   awi   bish.
so   also   behind   coming along   that   water.

Ajibik-kong   ano gida kiwep tod,   migo   gaiewi   ijiwe
Mountain   although he ran up,   likewise   also   there

awi   bish   enidana-simgag.   Mtigon
the (that) water   coming right along.   A tree

nigodagwi siweptod—   migo   gaiabe   gaiewi   awi bish
he climbs up—   likewise   still   also   that water

enipiskam gadnig.   "We wit   madji gin"   ejinad
coming just as fast. "Hurry   you grow,"   (he) says to him

niwi mtigon   kago mamda   ano gini-bi-god
that tree   although   it grew very fast

awi mtigon,   migo-bodj   gaiewi   ijiwi
that tree   just the same   also   it there

enidana simgag   awi   bish.   Midash   Nanabojo
coming right along   that   water.   So then

gi gwedji mad   Gitchi-manidon   djiwin-gashka-to-nid   awi
he asks him   Great Spririt   for him to stop it   that

bish.   Migo   pabige   gi-naga-sem-gadnig.
water.   Right then   immediately   it stopped.

Aji nabin   tabashish Nanabojo   miwi   giwabamad
He looking   down   so then   he saw them

wesinsan   pama-daga-dinid.   Apitchi   dashgo
little animals swimming about.   Very   so then

gi aja wemiman.   Miwi   gi an-do-mad   besho
he felt sorry for them.   So then   he called to them near

dji-wi-bi-ja-nid.   Midash   gi-kano nad,   awinda mowad
for them to come.   And then   he talked to them,   telling them

epitchi   jawenimad,   "Aki   gaiji-ton
how very   sorry he felt for them.   "Land   I'll make

ganada-mo   dash."   Anish   gitchi   min-nwe-da-mog
you will help me   but."   Well,   very   they are happy

we-sin-sag   awi iia-mawod   miniwa   awi-dawad.
the little animals   they to have   again   place for them to live.

Gitchi- anwa dji wag   dash   awi-nadama-gewad.   "Gago gim
Very   they are willing   thus   for them to help.   "You will dive

dash,   dji-dawam-da-meg   negawika.   Gin-nitam"   dinan
then,   you will look for   ground.   You first,"   he says to him

amik-wan.   Miwi   Amik   ge-go-gid.   Tchiga-nwesh
the beaver. So he   beaver   he dived.   A long time

anendi.   mawipi   bima-kobise   jajigo
he is gone.   After a while   comes floating up   after

ganibo dji.   Nanabojo   ano-dowam-dang   anindj-ing
he had died.   When he tried to look   in his hands

negawike,   kagego.   Midash   giones-sendwad   niwi
ground   not any.   So then   breathed life into them   that

Amik-wan.   Iia   dash   miniwa   Shang gwe shi
Beaver.   A(that)   thus   then again   Mink

ano-kodji-ton.   Giono-wito   dashgo   gaiewi.   Anibina
tried to do it.   He failed to   but then   he also.   Several

anowikodjito-nawa,   midashgo   nasab   ga-ijiweb-isiwad.
tried to do it,   but then   the same   it happened to them.

Apitchi shkwadj   dash,   miwi   Nanabojo   enad
Then at the very last   then   so he   he says to him

Shushko ian,   "Taga,   gin-tam."   Miwi   Shush kon
Muskrat,   "Well, then   you next."   So   he Muskrat

gi-gogid.   Mamo go gonwesh   dash   ginendi   awi
he dove.   Longer time than   but   he was gone   that

Shushkon.   Benishgo   gi-webi-nanisa-nendang   Nanabojo
Muskrat.   Until then   he began to (be) sorry

Wika   dashgo   miiwi Shushkon gibimok sed
Later   but much   so he   Muskrat   he came to the surface

apitchigo   iiekose. Anindji sing   anabid Nanabojo,
so very   tired.   In his little hand he looked

apitchigo bangishe   nega wike gim kan. Miso Nanabojo
so very   very little ground   he found. So

gi oji tod aki.   Gaishkwa ojitod   aki,   miwi
he made   land. After   he made   land, so then

ginendang   anishinaben tchiji ad.   Ganid nang
he thought   Indians   to make them.   After he molded

negawike   miwi negwapkin ganing gi tod.   Osam dash
ground   so he in the oven   he put it. Too   but

wiba,   gigidi nan.   Apitchi dash   gi-waban siwan.
soon   he took him out.   So very   but   he was very pale.

"Miwi gonda ge-wabshki-wedjik."   Kadashgo
"These will be palefaces."   But he is not

deben dasi.   "Miniwa gakodjitod" ishkidod. Tchi weweni
not satisfied. "Again   I'll try it," he says.   So carefully

ganadnang   negawike, gi negwap kinang.   Nongo
he molded   ground.   (He put it in the oven?). This time (Now)

dash gego   anashkwe god, miwi   gajinenda mod
but   something   distracted him, so he   he forgot him

niwi.   Migo bama   waban dang sagaptenig, wewib
(that one). Only   when   seeing it   smoking   hurry

gisagadi nad.   Jajigo   dash ganwad so nid,
he took him out. Only after but   he caught fire

tchim-kade-wak-gosi-wan dash. Anindj   ajinokasod, Nanabojo
burned very black   but.   His hand   using he

miwag di-be binad	*niwi,*	*minongo*	*awendji*	*bisagan di bed*	
rubbing his head	him,	so now	wherefore	his hair is curly	

iwi mkade wiias sens.   Kadashgo gaiabe debendisi
him little black meat (Black Person). Is not still not satisfied

Nanabojo.   "Gaiabe goding ga-godjiton,   nongo dash
Nanabojo   "Again   once   I'll try to do it, this time but

apitchigo   gawing ges" ajinendag   Nanabojo. Miiwi
be very   careful"   he thinks   Nanabojo. So then

miniwa ginadinang negawiki. ginegwapkinang
again   he molded   ground.   He put into the oven.

papitchin   dash nongo   negwe-wam-dan
Every little while but   this time peeks at it

ako wam dang   weweni   wim-sawa-kade nig.
watching over it very well baking into a nice tan.

Eni-mino pitan demig   dash miiwi
Just as it attains the right shade then so then

gigidanag   ijiwi negwapkin ganig "Be!" eshkidod,
he takes it out there (of) the oven.   "Ah!" he says

gitchi bapinendang Nanabojo "migonda   ge anishinade-widjig.
very happily   Nanabojo "and these   shall be the Indians.

ge-ishimeiianig!"
They shall be my brothers!"

Nanabojo Anishinaben Ogiijiad (Nanabozho Creates the Indian): Free English Rendition

Because Spirit Lions had killed his younger brother, Nanabozho went to look for them. He was walking on the beach and saw them playing far out on the lake. So he started to think about how to get them to come in from the deep, nearer to him. Just then Loon happened to be flying by, and so Nanabozho told him the story and asked for his advice.

"I'll tell you how to do it," that Loon said to him. "Stand over there and be very still, like you are a stump. You will look curious and thus they will come over to check you out, but you must not move in the least. I'll tell you when they get very near, and you can shoot the leader."

So, Nanabozho went to the spot and stood very still, like a stump. Soon the Spirit Lions came very near to look at the stump that they had never seen there before. When they got very close, Loon said to Nanabozho,

"Okay! Now shoot the leader!" So Nanabozho did this, and the wounded Spirit Lion leader kicked so hard, his splashing began a flood. Nanabozho began to run away, just ahead of the advancing waters.

Although he ran up a mountain, the waters still followed closely behind, and so he climbed a tree on its peak. Still the waters came at his heels, so Nanabozho told the tree to start growing, which it did. But still the waters rose. Finally, Nanabozho asked the Great Spirit to stop the water, and in a moment the flood stopped. Looking down from his tree, Nanabozho could see animals swimming in the water and he felt very sorry for them. So he called them close to him and told them how sorry he felt: "I will make you some land, but I need your help." The animals were very happy to hear they would have somewhere to live again.

"Dive down and bring back some land. You first," he said to Beaver. Beaver dove and was under water for a very long time. After a while he floated to the surface, dead. Nanabozho looked in his hand, but did not find any earth. So, he breathed life back into Beaver and told Mink to go down next, but he failed too. Several others tried next, but the same thing happened again and again.

So Nanabozho said to Muskrat, "Well, you go now." And so Muskrat dove and he was gone longer than any other animal had been. Soon Nanabozho felt very sorry, thinking the animal dead. But much later, Muskrat came to the surface, very tired. Nanabozho looked in his little hand and found a very, very small pinch of soil. So, from that, Nanabozho made land.

Then Nanabozho thought to make people. After he molded earth he put it in the oven, but he took it out too soon, so that man was very pale. "These will be palefaces," Nanabozho said, but he was not satisfied. "I'll try again," he said. So he carefully molded ground and put it in the oven. This time, something distracted him, so he forgot that one in the oven. He took him out, but only after that one had caught fire and burned very black. With his hand, Nanabozho rubbed his head, so now the "little black meat" has curly hair. But Nanabozho was still not satisfied. "I'll try it once again," thought Nanabozho, "but this time I will be very careful." So then he molded ground, put it into the oven, and this time he watched over it very well, baking it into a nice tan. Just as it attained the right shade,

Nanabozho took it out of the oven. "Ah," he said, well pleased, "these shall be the Indians. They shall be my brothers."

Nanabojo and the Bear's Skull[11]

Nanabozó	apágiwɛsɛtˁ		mkkwán	ginansán	gaíškwəpkwànatˁ
Nanabojo	is out hunting.		Bear	he killed.	After he skinned him

míwɛ	gímınozıwatˁ	wiwèbıwísnıtˁ		daš	mtígoan	sibwoiɛškánıtˁ
so	he cooked him.	As he starts to eat		thus	tree	it squeaking

ginaškwégoan	wip'kwémat gǫ		mkkwán	wiwèbowísnıtˁ
it disturbs him.	As he is about to bite		bear	as he starts to eat

mínawa	siboiɛškánıt	mtígoan	Midáš	gıgidagwíšit	wió:gadısgàkwanatˁ
again	it squeaking	tree.	So then	he climbed	so that he could

	wodɛ́	ašwákˁsínowat		giwɛ	mtígokˁ
release	there	they learning (caught in trap)		those	trees.

mišgažìnso:njíškosıt		odɛ	ɛpítči:atˁ		daš	odɛ
So he caught his hand		there	while he is staying.		Thus	there

iya'an	mí:nᵃganakˁ	ginóndawanˁ	mıptuó:n tˁ	ginanondaósıtˁ
some	wolves	he heard them	running (they).	He yelled and yelled

Nanabojo,	"Geigó	žánda	bižápkegak"		ížınatˁ
	"Don't (not)	here	they come" ("don't come here"),		he says

"Odɛ	níkeya	nípatuo:kˁ"	midaš	mi:nᵃganak
"There	in that direction	you run."	So	wolves

ginéndəmawatˁ	"Tága!	Odɛ	ožada	Nanabojo	ıžiát		ganama
they thought,	"Aha!	There	let us go	Nanabojo	where he is.		Perhaps

geígo	tayánadıkˁ	odɛ	wamijıŋ"	kıožáwatˁ	odɛ
something	he may have	there	to eat."	They went	over there.

giwábamawatˁ	ıžıwɛ	mkkwán	žažıgo	gamınòsəjín		gıgıdámwawatˁ
They saw him	there	bear	already	after it was cooked.		They ate

niwę mıdaš gamájawatᶜ   mıwę Nanabojo gíškıtotᶜ
it all him. So   after they left so   Nanabojo he succeeded

(stutter) wıgòdísnaŋ nıŋj odę sódɛnıkᶜ   mtígoan
       in releasing hand there where it was caught tree.

gibınísbozatᶜ   kwa'tánıgıdàzo   mtígoan   anonádamowatᶜ
He came sliding down. He was very angry at the tree. Although

           gıssonjıskágonıtᶜ   mtígǫsan   gibkwɜ̀kobınatᶜ
he helped them, they trapped his hand. Little trees he pulled up

         giačıpášızewat   niwɛ   wıgwaskémajıg Mi nongo
by the roots. He switched them those birch trees.   So now

wénji passážıwatᶜ   wıgwaskémajıg gaıškwɜ passažéwatᶜ
why they are bruised birch trees.   After   he switched them

daš nıwę mtígoan mıwę gimdáwamadan na Nanabojo na geíwi wías
thus them trees   so   he sought   Nanabojo he also meat

wímijıtᶜ   kašıgo geígo   mígowetta kanan ıžıwɛ
he to eat. Not something (nothing) only   bones there

ɛ'tén:gın   Midaš giwábadaŋ í:ya'i   mkkwá
they lying (found) there. So then he saw   something bear

ndıp "A! Migámıjın ıžıwę gabíndodɛtᶜ ızíwę" išinéndaŋ
head. "Oh! So I'll eat it there. I'll crawl in there," he thought

giwę   kwenanágodowɛndaŋ daš mınj í:dıkᶜ wəsítšgegwę̀
(I guess) seemingly he contemplating   thus how I guess how he will

      widébınaŋ ıžıwę bínžnaŋ dıbáŋ   wímijıtᶜ Mıdaš
do it to reach there inside of in the head he to eat. So then

dawač nɛbagǫsıŋ gižıdızatᶜ   gıbíndodɛtᶜ   ıžíwɛ
     little snake he made himself into. He crawled in there

gígčıwàwisnıtᶜ   ıžambidaš níbına gíwisnętᶜ gáıškwawìsnıtᶜ
He ate and ate a lot. Too much all   he ate.   After he ate

giánawıto	*wiságanodɛt‛*	*Midaš*	*ıžıwɛ̨*	*dıban*	*gibatásnınıt‛*
he failed	he to crawl out.	So then	there	his head	it became stuck

géwi	*mkkwandıp*	*iyá!*	*gípəmosɛt*	*mtígoan*	*məpitáok'šıŋ*
also	bear's head.	Oh!	he walked	trees	he bumps and bumps from

	atáokškuo:wat	*mtígoan*	*migwéjımat*	*nıwɛ̨*	*"wɛnéšgin‛"*
tree to tree.	He bumps	trees.	He asks	them,	"which kind

		"I:y'a sa	*nin*	*ndawó*	
you (which kind of tree are you?)."	"Some kind	myself I	I am	

wígabìmıš"	*migikéndaŋ*
basswood tree." ("The kind of tree I am is basswood.")	He then knew.

ɛsámwasa	*nopəmıŋ*	*ıžiat‛*	*Nanabojo*
Too far	in the deep forest	so thereabouts	Nanabojo

nımaját‛	*maópi*	*mínawa*	*mtígoan*	*nıptáoksiŋ*	*"wɛnéšgin‛"*
he is going.	Later on	another	tree	he bumps.	"Which kind are you?"

ıžínat‛		*"Sıngówək sa*	*daš*	*nikánıgo"*	*kıdoaw*
he says to him.	"Pine tree	myself	thus	I am called,"	he said (says?)

géwi	*nıwɛ̨*	*mtígoan*	*Miwɛ̨ daš*	*nikéndaŋ*	*Nanabojo*	*čígomıŋ*
also	him	tree.	So thus	he knows	Nanabojo.	To the big

níkeya	*nižat‛*	*maópi*
sea (Lake Michigan) in the direction of	he goes by.	Later on

gǫ nisákìwɛ̨	*mínawa*	*mtígoan*	*nıptáokšıŋ*	*kwéžımat‛*
he walks downhill	another	tree	he bumps.	He asks

niwɛ̨	*"wɛnéšgin?"*	*"gıžık‛*	*sa*	*daš*	*nıkás"*
him,	"which are you?"	"Cedar tree	myself	thus	I am named."

"O"	*kído sa*	*Nanabojo*	*miwɛ̨*	*mìnowéndaŋ*	*míšıgo béšo bišıŋ*
"Oh!"	he says	Nanabojo.	So	he is glad	finally near to the water

nítıgošna	*maǫ́pıgo*	*móštuo:n*	*zıdáŋ*	*iya'í*
I am approaching.	Later	he feels	at his feet	a kind of

mišašk   mi maópi   bɪš   nìpagamádɪgatˤ   ɛškamgo
hay.   So later   in the water   he begins to wade.   Gradually

nawɪŋj   nìtɪgósɪŋ   maópi   zamgoníndəmánɛ
out farther in the water   he is arriving.   Later on   too much deeper

bɪš   wibəmádɪgatˤ   Midaš   giwɛbimádɪgatˤ   anɪšnábɛn
water   for him to wade.   So then   he began to swim.   By the Indians

daš   gidebábəmìguo:n   "nákša   odę   makkwá"   kɪdowak
thus   he was seen at a distance.   "Notice   there   bear,"   they said

gɪwę   "təgá o:nsadá"   kídowatˤ   Miginaskáwawatˤ
them.   "Let's go and kill him,"   they said.   So they went

            gànidɪmnéwawatˤ   mi   gi:čɪbaŋdɪbéwawatˤ
after him.   When they overtook him   so   they gave him a hard blow

                niwę   Nanabojóan   gidašk'dibègənámawatˤ   ɪžɪwę
on the head   him   Nanabojo.   They cracked open his head   there

mkkwándɪp   Nanabojo   gigwəgádɪgàptot   pínɛ
bear's head.   Nanabojo   he waded ashore a-running.   And so

tɪgwəkɪŋ   ginímbatotˤ   míwę
in the woods   he went a running.   That's all.

Nanabozho and the Bear's Skull: Free English Rendition

Once, Nanabozho was out hunting. He killed Bear, skinned him, and cooked the meat to eat. But just as he began eating, nearby trees started to squeak. Nanabozho tried again to eat, but the trees continued to squeak, disturbing him. Nanabozho climbed the trees so he could untangle the branches, but as he was in the tree his hand was caught in the branches. While he was up in the tree, he heard some wolves running through the forest. Not wanting them to take his meat while he was in the tree, he yelled at them, "Get out of here! Go away!" But the wolves, hearing him, thought perhaps he was hiding something to eat, and ran to the camp. When they got there, they saw the freshly cooked bear meat sitting on the ground, and so they ate it. After they had gone, Nanabozho finally released his hand out of the tangle and got down from the tree. He was very angry at the tree, who had trapped him after he had been trying to help them. So he uprooted the little birch trees and began to switch them, giving the trees welts, and this is why they are now called bruised birch.

When he had finished he looked down and saw that there was not any meat left of his bear, only bones. However, he did see the bear head laying there on the ground. So he turned himself into a snake and slithered into its mouth and began to eat. Nanabozho ate and ate until he was too large to get his head out of the bear's head. He started to slither along, and as he did, he kept bumping into trees. After each bump, he asked, "What kind of tree are you?"

"I am Basswood Tree," said the first. And so Nanabozho knew that he was still deep in the forest. Sometime later he ran into another tree.

"What kind of tree are you?" he asked.

"I am called Pine Tree," it responded. Thus Nanabozho could tell that he was on his way toward the big lake. After a while longer of walking, he bumped into another tree.

"Which tree are you," he asked again.

"I am named Cedar Tree." So Nanabozho was sure that he was finally near the lake's edge. And sure enough, a few steps later he felt the water at his feet. He waded further into the lake, until he began to swim. Some people on the shore could see the great bear's head swimming through the water.

"Let's go kill that bear," they said. They came after Nanabozho, and when they had overtaken him, they hit him hard on his head. The bear's skull cracked open and Nanabozho ran ashore and into the woods. That is all.

Origin of the Red Osier[12]

Angoding	*Nanabojo*	*tchinibina*	*shishibeian*	*giansan*	*gaiskwabianwod*
Once	Nanabojo	great many	ducks		he killed. After he

	miwi	*giangowod.*	*Ashkode*	*giajitod*	*"taga*
cleaned them	so then	he buried them.	A fire	he made.	"Meanwhile

gonkawenba	*gepitchi*	*minosiwod"*	*ajinendong*	*miwi*	*tchigashkodeng*
I'll nap	while	they cook,"	he thinks.	So	near the fire

gigowishmod	*ashkodeng*	*nikeija*	*ajidieshing*		*"kawabim*
he lay down,	the fire	toward	facing his rump.		"Look after

            giwe"   aginod   ogiang   epitchi   tchinbad
(watch)   them,"   he says to   to his rump.   While   big sleep (he sleeps

          miwi   Anishnabeg   gibidigoshnowod   wabamowod
hard   so then   Indian people   they arrived.   Seeing them
   sagagodeshninid
   legs sticking out

shishibeian   gekidiwod   "taga   miwada   giwe"   gagidamwawod
ducks   they said,   "Let's   eat them them." After they ate all

miwi neiab   gepotkisidowod   kadensan   gweshkosid
so   same way   they stuck around   little legs.   When he awakes
   Nanabojo
   Nanabojo

makwenimod   shishibeian   asigidgodenod   kawiia!   kwatangidaso
he remembers   ducks.   Taking hold of legs,   not any!   Being very

          Nanabojo   "tawatao"   asginododiang   "gitchiweweni
angry   Nanabojo,   "Shame on you,"   he says to his rump,   "Most thoroughly

gakinomon   nongo. Iwe   giagonetwien"   Midosh   Nanabojo
I'll teach you   now.   You   you did not mind me."   And so   Nanabojo

gemadibid   ijiwe   ashkodeng   tchidijagiso!   dash
he sat   there   on the fire.   He gets an awful burn!   Thus

ano-gisidisod   gitchi   miskwiew nindji   Nanabojo
he tries to wipe himself.   Very   bloody   his hand.   Nanabojo

gisindisod   mitigonsing   sagitchi-ing   miwi nongo
he wiped himself   on little shrub   on the outside.   So now

miskwabiminagons   awendji   miskosid.
red osier   why   it is red.

Origin of the Red Osier: Free English Rendition

Once, Nanabozho killed many, many ducks. He cleaned them, buried them, and then made a fire.

"While they cook," he thought, "I'll take a nap."

So he lay down with his butt facing near the fire.

"Look after them," he said to his butt.

He went to sleep and slept so hard that he did not see some Indian people when they came up and saw the ducks' legs sticking out of the ground.

"Let's eat them," they said.

So they ate the ducks and put the legs back into the ground. When Nanabozho awoke, he remembered the ducks and pulled them out of the ground. When he realized they were gone, Nanabozho was very angry.

"Shame on you, butt!" he said. "I'm going to teach you now! You did not mind me!"

So Nanabozho sat on the fire. He got a terrible burn, and when he tried to wipe himself, his hand got very bloody. So, he tried to wipe himself on the outside of a little shrub. And that is why the red osier is red.

Wendji Takwaniwed Makwa Asokewin (How the Bear Lost His Tail)[13]

Megwa Nanabojo tchigabig abmosed apa giwi sed.
While   on the beach he was walking he was out hunting.

Apitchi gaie mibkade bekij-ge-mina-na-gada-wendam
Soon and he got hungry and also he was thinking about

mindj-edig-pitch ge wis nigwe. Nagatch dash-go miwi
at what time he will eat. Later on then so then

giwa bamod jishibeian nawindj babam shka nid. "Ta-ia
he saw them the ducks out at sea floating around. "Oh! no!

misa jiwiseniia," aji nendang giwe. "Ani-dash
so now I will eat," he thought so (seemingly). "But how

edig ge-ijitch-geiia jiwi-debini-gwa." Mi dash giwebi
then shall I do to catch them." So then he began

dewewad dakon. Miniwa giwebi nagamtawad niwi
drumming his pail. Again he began singing to them those

jishibeian. "Besho bijag! Besho bijag! ishka-iiain
ducks. "Near come! Near come! New

nagamo- winan-bida mo nim." Kadash-go ieshkat- gi-babamitaksin.
songs   I bring you."   But not   at first   did they listen to him.

"Kego   jakego wode,"   kido   bejig jishiben. "Gego
"Do not go   over there," he said one   duck.   "Something

gadodagona wi   Nanabojo. Anish   apitchigo gaiewi
he will do him.   But then very much he also

mino tagosi angamod   Nanabojo. Mi dash eshkam besho
sounds good when he sings.   So then   nearer (and) nearer

gibijawad jishibeiag. Mi dash Nanabojo enad,
they came the ducks. So then   he says to them,

"kida-tchi pa-ki-no-nim go-go-gieg." Anish   nita go giwag
"I could beat you all at diving."   But then   they are good divers

gaiewi   jishibeiag. "Ahow,   ida nitchi ma sa."
they also the ducks. "All right, we will have a contest."

dinawan   Nanabojoian. "Giinwa nitam," dinan
they say to him Nanabojo.   "You all first," he says to them

Nanabojo, "Mi dash gaieni."   Apitchi   tchi-ga-gogiwag
          "So then I will be next." Very much do much diving

jishibeiag, tchi wasa anin   pamko   jiwewag.
the ducks, very far   some of them swim and dive around.

gaish kwa tawad   dash, "Ahow gintam"   dinawan
After they finished then, "All right, you next," they say to him

Nanabojoian. Mi so   Nanabojo gi go gid. Epitchi
Nanabojo.   So now   he dived. Then while

pamkojiwed   Nanabojo, mi gig dinang-pindag ning saba bisan
he was diving   so   he took out his pocket strings.

Gi webi   ta-ko-bin-wad kadenswan. Mawipi   mi-giwebi
He began   tying their   little legs. After a while they began to get

Odawa Myths 321

sega-siwad   jishibeiag. "Taga   kogada   ajonda" ishkid awad.
alarmed   the ducks. "Let us go away   here,"   they said.

Ga gisik kewad   mi ijiwi   migodj jing   gaiewi Nanabojo.
As they flew away so there   he is hanging he also

ishpiming eshkam, mtigwaking nikeia.   Apitchi   ni segissi
high (and) higher, the forest towards.   Very much he is scared

Nanabojo. Ja gwenimo wi bigidna ma kwid, osam   ishpiming
Nanabojo. He is afraid to let go,   too far high

miia. Barna dashgo apitchi   ni wisigindjish   saba bisan
he is. Later but   very much   hurting his hand   strings

mi gibigidna ma kwid. Tchi jik-keing   wim-binak-dining   ga-jibin-sed.
so he let go.   A large stump   in the hollow   he fell into.

Migo   batashing. Epitchi   nanaga dawendang   mindj edig
So now he is stuck. And while he was thinking about how   then

ge-ijitch-ge-gwe dji sagan noded mi gi mondang gego
he would do   to crawl out   so he heard   something

migas bidj gem gadnig godjing. Ma-ma-dwen-gadni gaiego.
scratching   outside. It was grunting   also

Mawipi-go   moj-ton   webi-godwi-sim-gadnig. Ishpiming
So after a while he feels   it beginning to climb. Up high

anabid Nanabojo, kitchi makwan bigno wabmigon.
he looks   a large bear   looking at him.

Miwiksha   binis bosnid   niwi makwan. Gegetsa na
Really (actually!) he slides down that bear.   (Ah!)

anendam Nanabojo, anish na-edig nongo gejitch geia.
he thinks   now what   now   will I do?

eshkam   gaiewi   besho bidnisi   makwa.
And more he (also) near   he is getting bear.

ga-nan-kib-dod   mtigons,   Nanabojo mi giba biiad.
After he pulled out stick (sliver)   so he waited for him

makwan. Wibiianid   eko deb niked, mi gik-tchi-pi-dak-di iewad!
the bear. To be where he could reach, so he pricked him in the rump!

Whoosh! an new wan   eni madji odeptonid, mi
        he grunts (he sounds) as he starts crawling, so

gi sagan we nod. Eni-bashto-ded   makwa miso
he grabs his tail. As he crawls over the edge the bear so

gajigishka bo denig sawanagon. Miwi   nongo makwa
it gets cut off   his tail.   That's why (so) now   the bear

wendj   gish kan wed.
therefore has a short tail.

Wendji Takwaniwed Makwa Asokewin
(How the Bear Lost His Tail): Free English Rendition

Nanabozho was out walking on the beach and hunting, and soon he became hungry and started to think about when he would be able to eat. A little later, he saw some ducks floating around just off the shore. "Ah ha! Now I will eat," he thought. "But how should I catch them?" So he started drumming on a pail he was carrying and singing to the ducks, "Come near! Come near! I'll bring you new songs."

    At first the ducks tried not to listen to him. "Do not go over there," they said. "He will do something to us." But the song sounded so nice, and they soon came closer to him. Nanabozho said to them, "I bet I could beat you at diving." The ducks were very good divers, and so they said, "All right, we will have a contest." Nanabozho told the ducks to go first, and so they dove very deep and swam a long ways. When they were done, they came back and said, "All right, you next!" So Nanabozho dove, and while he was under water, he took out his pocket strings and began to tie them to the legs of the ducks. Eventually the ducks were very alarmed. "Let's get out of here," they exclaimed, and took off. When they flew away, Nanabozho was carried into the sky by the string. The ducks went very high, flying toward the forest, and Nanabozho began to get very scared. But soon the string started to hurt his hand and he had to let go. He fell into the hollow of a large stump in the forest.

He was stuck. So he began to think of ways to crawl out. Then he heard scratching on the side of the stump. At the same time, he heard grunting, and soon he could feel an animal climbing on the outside. Nanabozho looked up and saw a large bear starting to slide down into the stump. Nanabozho was very worried, so he decided to pull a sharp stick. He waited for the bear, and when he was close enough to reach, he stuck him in the rump. The bear hurried out of the stump, and as he left, Nanabozho held on to his tail. When the bear crawled out, his tail was cut off, and that's why the bear now has a short tail.

Awendji Pepe Ja Biiasing Nongo Wigwas
(Why the Birchbark Has Streaks)[14]

Agoding	*Nanabojo apa-giwe-sed*	*makwan*	*gib-min-san*
Once upon a time	Nanabojo he was out hunting,	a bear	he killed him (it).

ga-ishkwa pakwanad   dash, miwi   gi-mino-so-wad megwa dash
then after he skinned him   then, so then he cooked him while then

wi-mad   miwi   wi-gwas-ke-mijin gi-anash-kwe-god
he is going to eat him. So then a birch tree   it annoyed him

se-bwe-eshka-nid ajinoda-ni-nig.   Anabid   ish-pe-ming miwi
it squeaking   when the wind blew. He looked upward   so then

gi-wabamad asindawk-shi-nid   bejig mitick sawak-sinid
he saw him him being squeezed one   tree   in the crotch
  wi-gwas-ke-mi-jing
  in the birch tree

mi dash gi-go-dagwisid wi-ogwi-tak-onad   epitchtad dash misa
so then   he climbed it he went and released it while   then and then

ga-ji-so-te-nig anindj   ijiwi. Apitchi ga-gwa-sa-gen-dam Nanabojo.
it was wedged   his hand there. Very   he was angry.

migo bama anod-ininig   miniwa gi-ish-kitod awi-mod   anindj
Then after the wind blew   again   he was able to he take away his hand.

ga-bimisi-bisod   gagwa-tan-gida-so   Nanabojo. "Tawataw"
after he slid down (it) he was very, very angry   "I'll fix you!"

ajinad. Gapakwa nindji-nid   mitigosen   mi-iwi
he said. He doubled up his fist (at) the little tree. So

ge-gitchi-paj-ije-wad   niwi wi-gwas-ke-mijin kitchi pasans-iwan
he switched them hard   that   birch tree.   It was very bruised up

epita gan-a-mad.   "Be!" dinan   "dash miiwi
(because) he hit them so hard. "So!" he said to him "then   so then

nongo pine   ge-iji-na-go-siieg"
now   always   you will look like this."

Awendji Pepe Ja Biiassing Nongo Wigwas [Why the Birchbark Has Streaks]: Free English Rendition

Once Nanabozho was out hunting. He killed a bear, skinned him, and cooked the meat to eat. When the wind came up, though, the birch tree next to him started squeaking. He looked up and saw that another tree was caught in the crotch of the birch tree, and so he climbed up to release it. While he was up in the tree he got his hand caught and became very angry. After a while, the wind blew, and he was able to release his hand from the tree, and so he slid down. Nanabozho was still very angry and yelled at the tree, "I'll fix you!" and doubled up his fist. So he switched the little birch tree very hard, and it was badly bruised. "So!" said Nanabozho, "that is how you will always look!"

Sas-swe-minan Asokewin [The Story of the Choke Cherries][15]

Agoding Nanabojo tchgii-sibing   abmosed.   Abing
Once   along the river   he walking. In the water

anina-bid   mi-giwam dang
now and then he looking   so he saw

gitchi-wenadj-wang-gin wigwas-minessan. Niwa-gadji-tad
very nice looking   little cherries.   As he stooped over

dash awidebinang niwi   miso! gajibko-bised.
but   to reach   them (those) So!   he fell into the water.

ga-gawa-dagad	*dash*	*ishpiming*	*anabid*	*miwi*
After he waded ashore	thus	up	he looked	so

giwam dang mtigo-sing ajigo-denig. Indj-kigod
he saw   on little tree hanging.   They made him angry

iwi gi-iej-migod,   kowa-tesninig abishing   eta.
those they deceived him, reflecting   on the water only.

"Tawatow!" eshkidod, mi gibkwak-binad mtigosan.
"Pshaw!" he says   so he pulled up   that little tree,

Sas-swe-webinang wigwas-minessan. "Nongo endji,"   kido
Scattering about   little cherries,   "Now   therefore," he says,

"Da-mama-kide-winon nonda, miniwa   dab-kwendjka-gem-gadon."
"They will be black   these   and also   they will cause to choke."

mi nongo sas-swe-minan nonda wedji-jin-kadem-gog.
so now   choke cherries these   why they are called.

Sas-swe-minan Asokewin (The Story of the Choke Cherries): Free English Rendition

Once Nanabozho was walking along the shore of the river. Now and then, he looked into the water, and eventually he noticed some very nice looking little cherries. He bent over to pick them out of the water, but fell in. When he waded ashore, he looked up and saw the cherries hanging in a tree above the water. They made him very angry because they had deceived him. "Pshaw!" he said, and pulled up the tree, scattering the cherries. "Now they will be black and they will make people choke when they eat them." This is why they are now called choke cherries.

Tchigamin Awendji Eni-gagatchibi Iamigag (Why the Great Lakes Are Receding)[16]

Agoding   Nanabojo gaishkwa wis nid   miwi
Once upon a time   after he finished eating so then

tibeiw   gi-gawish mod, aminwa te nig   awinbod.
along the shore he lay down   where it was sunny he to sleep.

Miwiko   Nanabojo ga-nita-do-dang   gaishkwa wisnidji
That is what   he usually did that after he had eaten.

Ano-nita-wis-sinid   Nanabojo migo-bodj   pine
Although he was a big eater   just the same all the time

miabidji-bkaded.   Nongo   dash gi-sami-tchinba
he is always hungry. This time but   he slept too hard.

migo-bama   mosh-tod adkibig-shing   gi-basigwin-sed.
It was only after he felt   he lying in cold water he quickly got up.

Awamdang   gik-tchi-boji ned   awi-ondji   bish
He seeing that he very nearly lost his life because that water

amosh kan nig. Miiwi   Nanabojo gi-des si nike nid,
flooding.   So then   he spread out his arms,

miwi edang   iwi bish,   "Nongo-ondji   ga-webi
so   he says to that water, "From now on   you will begin

eskate   binishgo   eta   dji sibi wens wiian."
drying up until then only   you will be but a tiny stream."

Midash   nongo   awi bisan awendji
Therefore now   the lakes   the reason (why)

eni-gagatchi-bi iamigag.
lakes are becoming smaller and smaller.

Tchigamin Awendji Eni-gagatchibi Iamigag (Why the Great Lakes Are Receding): Free English Rendition

Once, after Nanabozho had just finished eating, he lay down along the shore of the lake in a sunny spot to take a nap. That was what he normally did when he had just eaten. Although Nanabozho was a big eater, nonetheless he was always hungry. But this time he slept too hard. It was only after he felt cold water around him that he awoke, and he realized that he very nearly lost his life because of the flood. So Nanabozho stood up, spread out his arms, and said to the water, "From now on you will begin to dry up until you are just a tiny stream." That is why the Great Lakes are becoming smaller and smaller today.

Nanabojo gaie Jigog-wiji-sag Asokawin (Nanabojo and the Leeks)[17]

Agoding   megwa   apa-giwi-sed Nanabojo.   Minon-debkaded
Once   while   he was a-hunting   he gotten hungry

dash   miiwi   ga-ijik tchimad   jigog-wijisan.
thus so then he ate a lot   little onions (leeks).

Iwipi   dash gi-wishkbis wag   agiwi jigog wijisag.
At that time   but   they were sweet they   little onions.

Ga-ishkwa-debsinid   dash Nanabojo miiwi
After his hunger was satisfied then   so then

gigno-wabamad   niwi, "Anish eji-nikasieg   shemek?"
he looked at them those, "What are you named my little brothers?"

dinan   dash. "Mi-meen gabwi sa digo mi"
he says to them thus.   "so we are called,"

kidawan   aniwi jigog-wiji-sag. "Ho!" kido Nanabojo
they said them   little onions.   "Ho!" he says.

Ga-isiji-nad   anin niwi, miiwi   bako-nang
He took a handful some them, so then behind his back

gaininad.   Gik tchi bog-djinad!   "Be!"   kido
he put them. He broke wind on them! "So (There)!" he said.

Nanabojo. "Mi-nongo pine   ge-endji   tchiwi-sigis-ieg."
            "So now   always wherefore you will have a strong taste."

Nanabojo gaie Jigog-wiji-sag Asokawin
(Nanabojo and the Leeks): Free English Rendition

Once, while Nanabozho was out hunting, he got very hungry and ate a lot of little leeks. They were very sweet, and so he asked them, "What are you named, little brothers?"

  "We are called *mi-meen gabwi*," the little onions said.

  "Ho!" he said, and took a handful and put them behind him. He broke wind on them and said, "So! Now you will always have a strong taste!"

Wendji Bkogwad Anin Mtigog gaie Wigwaske-mijig Wendji Missokwiwad (Why Some Trees Have Knobs on Them and the Birches Grow in Clumps)[18]

Megwa Nanabojo ab-mundang   odji-man
While   he was carrying on his shoulders boat

mtigong   pitaksin-nik   miiwi   ga-pag-nigod. Apitchigo
on tree   it bumped against so that it threw him. Very much

gindj-kadesi.   Ga-basigwid   dash, miiwi   ga-pakwak-nindji-nid
he became angry. After getting up then, so then he made his fist,

gik-tchi-wep-towad   niwi mtigon. Migo   pabige
he struck a great blow   that tree.   So that   immediately

gibibko-ginid   gaiewi   dash segisi-wad
it became swelled   and also thus   they were frightened

wigwaske-mijig gi-maniwi-pawewag. Midash   nongo anin
birch trees   fled together they. Therefore now   some

mtigog   wendji bkogig-wad   minawa   gaie
trees   why they have bumps (or knobs)   more (also) and

mi-wendji   miso-kisowad   wigwaske-mijig.
therefore   they grow together   birch trees.

Wendji Bkogwad Anin Mtigog gaie Wigwaske-mijig Wendji Missokwiwad (Why Some Trees Have Knobs on Them and the Birches Grow in Clumps): Free English Rendition

While Nanabozho was carrying a boat on his shoulders, it bumped against a tree and threw him back. Nanabozho was very angry, so when he got up, he made a fist and struck a very hard blow on the tree. The tree swelled up, and the birch trees around it became frightened and fled together. That is why now some trees have knobs on them and why birch trees all grow in clumps.

Dibadjmowin—Wi Nanabojo Ogiijitod Odenang [Legend: Creation of Mackinac Island by Nanabojo][19]

Anida-goshing   Nanabojo tchigamin miwi ogiijitod ajigan,
When arriving at   large lake, so   he made bridge,

gitchi sinin   gainokas djin. Gadka mid   dash, miiwi
huge boulders   he used.   After he crossed but   so then

gik tchi noding,   gibi gwa sing   ajigon.
the wind blew very hard. It blew to pieces bridge.

Gabo nan mak   gi-nide-deb bagwin de nen   minis sensan.
When the wind stopped, they were lying in the water little islands.

Miijiwi   awenda dag   awi Odenang   bejig
So it is there it comes from that Mackinac Island one

minis sens   nongo   ejiini kadem gog.
little island now   it is called (named).

Dibadjmowin—Wi Nanabojo Ogiijitod Odenang [Legend—Creation of Mackinac Island by Nanabojo]: Free English Rendition

When Nanabozho arrived at this large lake, he decided to make a bridge, to cross it, out of huge boulders. When he crossed his bridge, the wind started to blow very hard, and it blew the bridge into little pieces. When the wind stopped, they lay in the water as little islands. So this is how that little island now called Mackinac Island came to be.

Nanabojo Flies with the Geese[20]

Nanabojo was up with the wild geese in Canada in the wild rice marsh. It was time to fly south and the geese told Nanabojo they were leaving. Nanabojo wants to fly south with the geese so he kills one of the geese and the others tell him they will make him a coat. They had a trial flight in a circle, the gander taking the lead.

The gander tells Nanabojo to fly with his eyes shut when they take the V formation. Nanabojo asks how he will know then which way to fly. The gander told him to fly in the inside of the V so he will know how to go.

As they fly along, the gander tells a story to the young ones. Nanabojo is interested. He opens his eyes just a little. The gander knew it, so Nanabojo shuts he eyes. Later he does it again and immediately fell to earth.

This explains the geese's method of flying, as they change from the V formation to another. It is because Nanabojo opened his eyes that they only fly in the V formation for a short time. It also explains why geese fly in a V formation with one bird in the center.

Nanabojo lived at the time of the great prehistoric animals. Nanabojo slew the animals that were harmful and told them they must live underground. Nanabojo patrolled the beaches of Lake Michigan, Huron, and Superior—all the way to Niagara Falls. Some distance west of St. Ignace at Nɛdóbemá, High Roll Away, Nanabojo saw a serpent and killed it with his bow and arrow.

Nanaboju[21]

Nanaboju? He was the guy who built these islands here. He got that island, $wak^a šás$ (Fox). Nanaboju built a passage from Tempest Point to $wak^a šás$ light and Skillagalee. Come high water, rough—wind too, high winds—$zamči˙ni˙wi˙da\ nudın$ (high wind) at White Shoals. Nanaboju's aim was to build a passage across—a sort of bridge. But he couldn't make it—too rough.

Nanaboju was quite a man with women. He did his work over there on these islands—maybe a week at a time. (He was) disgusted. Well, disgusted, (he) come back. He'd go back and oversee—way round where (he) started from and back. He knowed where he was going. Sure, he knows where he left off. He has a sweetheart some place.

Maybe he made good—maybe not. He would tell his wives—he has so many wives, not only one. He would tell his wives what a wonderful man he was. He was going to build a natural bridge! Perhaps he had seven wives.

Nanaboju got home in the evening. They'd have (a) meeting (with) a campfire, nice supper, lots of eats, lots of ladies. He was the only one (man). I think he was a Mormon. First thing they'd make up the mattresses (arrangement side by side demonstrated with hands). All he'd move is his pillow—from wife to wife for seven nights. What was going on, I don't know.

He was very important. He almost succeeded in connecting the islands. You can see how shallow the water is (between them). What happened to Nanaboju? He went away. No one ever knew where—so much business on his mind.

The Ten Talents[22]

After the creation of the world, Creator made the four races of men: the Black people, (*kadeíwias*, "black meat"); the yellow race (*weisáweis*); the Indian (*anišnábɛ*); and the Whiteman (*čimókiman*).

There were just the four men of different races and they lived together in one household.

The Creator says to the Whiteman, "I am going to give you ten talents. Go out into the world and see what you can do."

He said the same thing to the black man and to the yellow man and the red man. They all went out into the world.

Later the Creator calls them back to give an account of themselves. The Whiteman still had ten talents, as did the yellow and black men. But the Indian only had nine talents. He told the Creator that he had made fun of one talent and had destroyed it. The Creator became angry.

"You go out into the world," he says. "Make utensils from stone. From the skins of animals, make your clothing."

What was the talent the Indian destroyed?

The Snowball[23]

Once there was a man who became tired of seeing so much snow. He kicked at the snow and cursed it. Shortly after, the snowflakes started falling— *pabiwéppa*. The man ran into his house, but soon something hit the house. It is a huge snowball. The man builds a fire, as frosty air fills his home. Day after day, night after night, it kept snowing and the snowball got larger. The thaw came when he was completely exhausted. The snowball kept wetting and putting out his fire. He won by the skin of his teeth.

The Indians always said not to make fun of the snow. It is okay to play in it though.

Legends: Supernatural

Man Carried Off by Eagle[24]

A man was one day standing out in the woods. Suddenly an eagle swooped down, clutched him with its claws, and carried him off to its nest in the mountains on a cliff. Here the man was dropped. He found himself in the nest with the little eaglets. Every day the eagle would carry deer and other animals to the nest and drop them there. It would then fly away. Several times the eagle tried to kill the man, but he learned to protect himself by crawling into a crevasse in the cliff when the eagle approached.

While the eagle was gone, the man made deerskin clothing for himself and the eaglets out of the deer the eagle had brought. One day the eagle flew down and noticed the clothing. The bird was very pleased. As a reward, the eagle took the man back to earth in its claws and left him in the same spot where he had been captured.

The Magic Arrow[25]

Once there were two white people, a young man and woman, who were taking a walk on a hill near Petoskey. The young man found a small, crystal clear arrowhead of remarkable beauty, which he kept and prized highly.

The young man did not know it, but he had found a magic arrowhead that had brought both good fortune and tragedy to its owner many years before.

It seems that once there was an Indian boy, a poor orphan, who was adopted by an old woman. The boy had few toys—just a small bow and arrows, a dugout canoe (*nɛpogamagan*), and a few other possessions. He learned to swim and to stay under water longer than any of the other boys.

When the orphan boy was eighteen years old, one summer the Indians in his village had a field day. There were contests in swimming, climbing trees, paddling a canoe without making any noise, archery in which the contestants shot at a moving target, and making imitations of animals and birds. The young orphan got a high score in all the contests and won an eagle feather for it.

The Indians had to win their eagle feathers, you see. Perhaps they saved a life or won many contests. The chief of the tribe had a beautiful daughter and he wanted her to get married. The chief declared that his daughter's suitors must be between eighteen and thirty years old and that the one chosen to be her husband must bring him a white eagle. So the word passed around.

The old woman, the guardian of the orphan, heard of this and brought up the question one night to her adopted son.

The boy said, "She won't look at me because I'm poor."

"Yes," said his adopted mother, "but if you get the white eagle—if you do, our people here will help you build a home and prepare for your bride."

"But," cried the boy, "I haven't any really good arrows, though my bow is all right."

"Well," the old woman told him, "I have a friend—"

"What is a friend?" the young man interrupted.

"A friend will be there when he sees you in need," the old woman told him. "He'll do anything to save your life. This man is a magician. He has a large place filled with many curios—gold and silver, perhaps from other tribes."

So the old woman goes to see her friend, the magician. She tells him about her adopted son and his desire to marry the chief's daughter. The magician pities the young man and says he is going to help him and will make him a good bow and arrows. A good bow, he says, will shoot one hundred yards, four hundred feet with a good shot.

Now the magician had a pet in the house, a rattlesnake. The magician would play a flute, a *podájigànsan,* a real flute of cedar, holding it out to the side. The rattler was kept in a jar, and as the magician played the flute the rattler slowly came up out of the jar. The magician takes the snake in his hands and holds the snake horizontally. He kneels with the snake before a magic fire and sings his magic song. Slowly he raises the snake toward heaven and when he completes his magic song there is no more snake, for it has turned into an arrow with a shaft as straight as a dye, fully feathered and with an arrowhead almost transparent. The magician gave the arrow to the old lady for her son. She takes it and tells the young man that with this it would be impossible to miss anything he shot at.

So with his new bow and magic arrow the young man set off to hunt for the *wàbskibınéssi,* the white eagle. He was very proud of his new bow and arrow. First he saw a hawk, which he killed easily. Then he tried a more difficult shot on another hawk and was successful again.

The young man went home and told his mother, "I am ready."

By now there were other Indian suitors out hunting too.

The young man's mother got everything ready for his trip. He was gone four or five days. At first he did not see an eagle of any sort, so he returned discouraged.

"There is no such thing as a white eagle," he says to his mother.

But she is wise. She says, "If you wish to bring home a white eagle, you must go up to the mountains."

She meant that he must go to the Rockies.

Her son decides to go and she prepares for him. After he got to the Rockies he saw all kinds of eagles, but no white eagle. He is getting discouraged by things that he'll try one more day, for his mother had told him that he would see a white eagle.

On the tenth day, he climbed a high mountain. Hours passed. He is far above the timberline. Towards the end of the tenth day, he saw the white eagle coming, circling, but far out of range, although coming in his direction. In order to get the eagle in range, the young man had to climb even higher. He climbed fast and watched the white eagle at the same time. He climbed until he thought he was in range of the eagle as it slowly made its circle.

"Here is where this arrow is to prove its merit," the boy thinks. "I'll try it."

As the white eagle came around to make its circle, the young man drew his bow and lets the arrow go. The arrow went up toward the sky like a streak of lightening. It pierced the eagle. Slowly the eagle starts to fall earthward, but it fell far below the boy and disappeared though the trees.

The young man was so happy. He climbed down swiftly, perhaps even fell part of the way, but got down as quickly as he could. He got his bearings and found the eagle at last. He was a happy man. He comes home. He is on his way home and at last arrived and brought the white eagle to his mother. She says to take it to the chief.

The young man takes the eagle to the chief, who accepted it although he knows that the young man was poor. The people of the village built the young man a home and gave him everything he needed.

But as happens in many a lifetime, there is something this young man didn't know: the princess had a secret lover. The young man didn't know it, but the neighbors told him. His wife was good to him, however, and they got along well, so he couldn't believe it.

One day, the young man told his wife that he'd be gone on a longer hunting trip. He is going to see for himself whether she has a secret lover. So instead of going hunting he made a circle and came back to the lake. No one saw him.

That evening, close to sundown, he saw a canoe coming toward shore and heard voices. Someone was paddling the canoe and there were two passengers—his wife and a young man.

All the joy he had went out of him. First thing he thought of was his magic arrow. The canoe came opposite him. He took his arrow and thought, "I am known never to miss."

His wife was singing, probably "My Bark Canoe." He let the arrow go. Wherever it hit her, it killed her instantly. He commanded the young man to come to shore and he did so, begging for his life.

The youth did not hurt his wife's lover. He picked up his dead wife from the bottom of the canoe and took her back to her father. He told the chief why he had killed her.

The chief said, "My son, did you consider the price of the crime that you have committed?"

The young man answered, "Yes."

Then the chief gathered all the warriors and told them they must torture the young man to death. So that's what the warriors did, treating the young man with the utmost cruelty. Afterwards they took his body to a high hill and buried him there among the pines. At night his spirit would come out of his grave and would sort of patrol that hill overlooking the village.

One hundred years passes. This time there is no more Indian village and also there is no more great pine forest. But still when night came the unfortunate young man's spirit would patrol that hill. It was here that the two white people found the fine arrowhead. It was the one that killed the young man's wife.

Bagag Dibadj'mowin [The Story of Bagag, the Skeleton][26]

Agoding	anishinabens	enidid-semgadnig	awi-pitch
Once upon a time	a young Indian	when the time came	at the time

anendag-osiwad   anishinabensag awi-mkadeke-wad
it was thought proper for them young Indians   for fast they

wijita dis wad   jiwiapwad-mowad
to prepare themselves so then they dream about that

nigani bimadisiwin. Miiwi   maba   anishinabens
future life.   So then this person young Indian

giajad   mtigwa-king giojistod   wigwamens wa itchi
he went in the forest he made ready little lodge where at

mkadeked. Giktchi   ishpendiso   dash
fasts he. Very much highly thought of himself so

maba   anishinabens gi-bagosendam aptichi-woshime
this one young Indian. He was wishing very much more

awi pitenda-gosid. Eshkwa medwas-gongag dash miiwi
to be thought of he. After   tenth day   thus so then

gi apowed. Getchi sigingwe wan gitchi kiwesian gawabadjin
dreamed he. Very wrinkled faced very old man   he saw

bidasmosenid, bi bapawan gaie. Miiwi
walking towards him, came a-smiling and. So then

ginsidwi nadsod edig waniji-nagosid. Kadash
recognized himself, probably what he will look like. Not

monda gimin-nwe-dasin. Miiwi ginendang woshime
this he did not like it. So then, he thought, furthermore

jiwi-mkadeked, kadashgo naj miniwa gi-apowesi. Nagatch
he would fast, but not again more he dreamed. Later on

dash eni-messinin, miiwi gi-anda-ken-min
then when he was missed, so then to learn about him

onabawad anishinabeg wigwamesing Mi giwabamawad
looked they Indians in the little lodge. So they saw him

jing-gish-ninid ijiwi, jajigo gwa-nand-moba kadashgo
lying there. Already he had starved, but not

pabige gi-masiwan. Apitchigo dash gig-nibim-gadni
immediately removed him. Very but was very rapid

wiiassim niba-tem gadnig. Kadashgo anishinabeg
flesh his drying up it. Not but Indians

gi-pamendasinawa awi bagog. Nagatch dash megwa
they did not bother that skeleton. Later on but while

dabikag mi giwebe-ktchi noding mi monda kanan
it was night so began big wind blowing so these bones

awebi-ba-sing, nidawesem gag dikonan, migego
beginning to blow up, they spread out branches, so also

webi-tching-gwe-wemgog. Mi-nongo wendji kidong mtigog
began roaring they. So now why it is said trees

tching-gwe-we-wad aj noding, "Bagog! pambiso!"
they do roar wind blowing, "Skeleton, flying about!"

Bagag Dibadj'mowin (The Story of Bagag, the Skeleton): Free English Rendition

Once there was a young person who had reached the customary time to prepare himself for a fast, so that he could dream about his future life. So this young man went into the forest and made a little lodge where he could fast. He thought very highly of himself, this young person, and he wanted to be well thought of when he returned. Thus it was that on the tenth day of fasting, he had a dream. He saw a very old man walking toward him, smiling, and the young man recognized that this was himself in his old age. But he did not like this vision, and so he thought he would continue fasting in order to have yet another dream. But he did not have another dream. Later on, he was missed in the village, and some others came to look in the lodge to learn what had happened to him. They found him lying there, having already starved to death, but they did not immediately remove him. His flesh was drying up very rapidly on the bones, but they did not bother that skeleton. Later on, during the night, a big wind came up and blew the bones into the branches of the trees where they began to howl. So now that is why the trees are said to howl in the wind: "Bagag! Pambiso!" ("Skeleton! Flying about!")

Legend of Harbor Point[27]

Jajigo   iiaing   bitok migag   singa biing   giiia
Long ago where   underground on the point of land was there

tchi-manido.   Nano god nong   dash anishinabeg
big monster (spirit). Now and then   thus   Indians

gi wabama wan. Agoding dash megwa anishinabeg
they saw him. Once   then while   Indians

amishka wad   miwi gi mokitag wad   niwi manidon.
a-riding in their canoe so he sneaked up on them that spirit.

Sasswe sinid   dash gi-gagawita wishka magwan dotchi-manwa.
Being playful then he went round and round   their boat.

Awewe-bas sidod do sawana gon mi! agoding gaji-bindja-godenig
Swinging about   his tail   so   once   it fell into their boat

do-tchiman ingwa. Ganawad nag   bejig   anishnabe
in their boat.   As he took hold one   Indian

awagakwatonsim mi   gikitchi-wepotamowad   sawangon, mi
his little axe   so   he struck very hard   his tail,   so

ga jigishka-mowad   sawangon. Nongo   dashgo   gaiabe
he cut off   his tail.   Now   and so   still

be bang gishe   mitatem igad   awi manidon   biwabik.
small amounts is here and there that spirit   iron.

Miskwi-biwab kong gi anan deni osawanagon, apitchi   gaiego
Like copper   was colored   his tail   very   and also

gikitchi wasko deni. Jajigo   dash   nondj-giganwa kon gadba
very much shiney.   Long ago but   it was much longer

awi aki. Nongo dash awendj   da kon gag. Awi   manido
that land. Now   but   wherefore   is short.   That   spirit

osam   edig   ga-maga-iian-ked wode   endad
too much seemingly he dug too much   there   where he lives

anama kamik. Mi-gaongji   kiswa bigsemgag   anin   awi aki.
underground. That is why   it sank into the water   part of   that land.

Legend of Harbor Point: Free English Rendition

Long ago, under a point of land [in Lake Michigan] there lived a big spirit. Every once in a while, the people who lived nearby saw him. Once, while some people were riding in their canoe, the big spirit sneaked up on them. Being playful, he swam around and around their boat, swinging his tail so that one time it even fell into the boat. One person took hold of the tail and struck it very hard with his ax, cutting it from the spirit's body. The tail was copper colored and very shiny, and so even now small pieces of that spirit metal can be found here and there. Long ago, that point of land was much longer, but now it is short, because the spirit dug so much underneath the point of land where he lives. That is why the land there sinks into the water.

The Legend of the Manitou Islands and Sleeping Bear Point[28]

Agoding kitchi jajigo   iiaing   agaming   Wisconsin
Once   long time ago out where across the sea

aki   nongo ejnika-demigog, baka dewin gidago, apitchigo
land   now   it is called,   hunger   existed very much

gisnagad gibati-nad   gaie nibowin. Makwa miniwa
difficult plentiful (much) and   death.   Bear   also (and more)

nij   makonsag,   tibeiw,   nibina so-gwan gib-mosewag.
two   little bears (cubs) on the beach   many   days   they walked.

Manpi   agaming   bagosend-mowad   wibi-jawad.
Over here across the sea they were wishing to come here they.

Mawipi   nises-sesnand-monid   makonsan. Miiwi
After a while whimpering with hunger they little cubs. So then

gi-gijen-dang   makwa ji-manen-dong jidka-mada-gawad.
made up her(his) mind bear   to attempt   they to swim across.

Mi-gibko-biwad,   eedowi-ing   bi-ianid   makonsman.
They waded into water,   on either side they came   her little cubs.

Madja-wad! kitchi-wasa wi-ija-wag.   Mawipi   mi
Going away! very far   they are going. After a while so

biiek-sinid   makonsag. "Keta-nam-sig" ajinad
they become tired   cubs.   "Try hard they," she says to them

makwa,   "Kago   aniwi wasa geiabe."   Mijigo
the bear, "Not   very far   yet (still)." Soon

bidebam-damwad   aki. apitchi-dash-go gaiewi
they come within sight   land. Much but so   they also

eshkam   ninin-wiswag   makonsag. Gonama-dash-go
gradually become weaker they   cubs.   Perhaps but just

midasswe ta-bagano-wang gaiabe wida-goshnowad,
ten   miles away   still (yet) for them to arrive,

mi gi-ano-witod   bejig makons gig-osa-bid!
so became exhausted they one   cub   so he sank!

Wiba   dashgo miiwi gaiewe wi bejig
Very soon but   so then he also that one

giano-witod,   gig-osa-bid gaiewi. Apitchigo
he became exhausted, so he sank   also.   Very much

ish-ken-dam   makwa. Kadash-go gego   gaiewi
heart broken (saddened) bear. But nothing something he also

wajitch-ked.   Ga-gawa-dagad   dash makwa. Miiw
could do he (she). She (he) waded ashore thus the bear. So

tibeiw   gija-gish-ing. Ajinabid wode   abing
on the shore she lay down. Looking out there on water

gadpine-nid nidjan-se-san.   Bisaga-bim-gadni,   nij
where they died her children. They come to surface two

minis sesan. Mi-dash-go   gaiabe wendjish-gishing
little islands. So thus (then) still   wherefore he lies

ijwe nongo awi makwa, akowabimad
there now   that bear   guarding (looking after them)

niwi   nidjan sesan.
those (them) her children.

The Legend of the Manitou Islands and
Sleeping Bear Point: Free English Rendition

Once, long ago, in the land called Wisconsin across the great lake, there was terrible hunger and many people died. A bear and two little cubs were trying to leave that place and come around the lake where there would be more food. They walked for many days on the beach together, but after a while the two little cubs began to whimper with hunger and so the bear decided to try and swim across the rest of the lake. They waded into the water, one cub on each side of the bear, and they swam off into the lake a long way. After a while the cubs began to get very tired, and so the bear said, "Try hard, the land it not very far." And very soon they did come in sight of land. But gradually the cubs got weaker, and only ten miles away, one cub sank into the water. Soon afterward the other also drowned. The bear's heart was broken, but she could do nothing. She waded ashore and lay down, looking out on the water where her cubs had died. Eventually, both of them came to the surface as two little islands, and so the bear still lies there now, looking after her children.

Minadóbígǫ Asokewan (Devil's Pond Story)[29]

Šásgo	čimókimanık	číbawǝ bi·gamkí·wakʿ	káwe	ajanda
In the past	White people	before they arrived here	not	here

apitčí	anišňábɛkʿ	kidna'ki·si·okʿ	Apitáyaiŋ	niké·ya
very	Indians	they did not live here.	Middle Village	hereabouts

ošmé·	ki·nendánawa	wi·dnakkí·wat	í·ya	mínadobígǫ
more	they thought (of)	(to) live there.	At	spirit pond

gi·katánawa	ajánda	í·ya	mínadobígǫ	ganjí·k
they were afraid of it	here	at	spirit pond	because

tamawátko	kinondánawako	ode·	ge·gǫ	minawa	godiŋ
they were afraid	they heard	there	something.	Again	once

'ko	gí·či·bí·mskojiwan	ojiwé·	biš	kage·gi·kendá·ksino
too	big water in whirlpool.	There	water	it was not known

gakwi·ndámamıgakʿí·wɛ	oŋaʷwodíŋ	anišinábe	kinóndawa	maŋgwan
how deep it was there.	Once	Indian	he heard	loon

áwodè	amsitáwgsinit	"tǝgá	gowábama"
over there	making call (yell).	"Guess	I will (go and) see,"

gí·wɛ	ajinéndaŋ	ᵐneságe·wɛt
so	he thought.	(as) He came within sight (of something)

daš mí·we   gì·wabe·mát   gogi·nɛt   anᵃwí·babi·yát
thus therefore he saw him (her) diving (he dives). He tried to

              wi·bi·mòksé·nit   *kàgonáš Midéš*
wait (for him) (to) come to (the) surface never.   Then

ki·nóndawat   áwodè   čígamɪŋ   mí·we   beki·š
he heard him over there on (the) big lake. Therefore along with

kanjik   tame·wát   mánpi· ni·ké·ya   abamosé·ẁat
because   they were afraid (of it) here   hereabouts (while) they

            ajánda anišhabɛkʿ ki·ġhamowawak   abɪnóji·yakʿ
were walking here   Indians   they were forbidden children

awí· ba baškomgisiwat.
so   as they make a noise.

Minadóbigǫ Asokewan (Devil's Pond Story):
Free English Rendition

In the past, before white people arrived, not many Indians lived here. Most preferred to live in the area of Middle Village, as they were afraid of a spirit pond here. They heard sounds come from this spirit pond and were afraid of some great whirlpool. It was not known how deep the pond was. Once, a man heard a loon calling from the pond and thought, "I guess I'll go over there and see." When he came near the lake he saw the bird dive and decided to wait for it to return to the surface. The loon did not come back up, but the man heard it over on the big lake nearby. And so people were afraid to come near the pond, and their children were forbidden to make any noise while they were walking here.

Legends: Animal Tales

Ginebik Dibadj-mowin (The Legend of the Serpent)[30]

Megwa anishinabe apa giwi sed   mi gianon dawad awiia
While   Indian   was hunting he   so heard he   someone

ananonda gosinid. Ajibikong   dash adnita gosiwin.
yelling.   From the mountain thus yelling (calling),

"Bi nada moshin! bi nada-moshin!" madwekidwan   giwe.
"Come, help me! Come, help me!" hear saying him (her) seem to.

Mi giwebi   gida ki wed.   Apitchigo, sanag adini
So he started climbing the hill. Very   difficult

iwi   sini kam gadnig. Gada goshing ednitagosinid niwi
there rocky.   He arrived   he heard him   that one

gitchi ginebagon ijiwe bimabik jinon. "Anidash,"
large snake   there lying coiled up. "Now what?" ("How about this?")

ejinad wi   anishinabe. "Nada-moshin," digon   niwi
says he that Indian.   "Help me,"   says he that one

ginebagon. "Manda asin gidakwan, da sos
snake.   "This stone pry it up, under something fallen.

Gitchi weweni   dash gada bamon." "Ahow,"   kido
Very good (well) thus I will pay you." "All right," he said

anishinabe. "Matig ga nadin." Mi gi ni saki wed
Indian.   "Pole I will get." So he went down hill

anishinabe. Matig gam kang,   miniwa   ge-gidaki-wed.
Indian.   Pole   after he found once again he climbed the hill.

Nongo dash mi gegeti nian misid.   Anish, kitchi
Now   thus   so very   having hard time he. Well, large

matik sawi   bem da badang   kitchi asin gaiewei
pole indeed he is dragging along large stone that which

wagida kwang.   Gada gojing   miniwa,   mi
he is going to pry. After he arrived there once again, so

giwebi   gida kwang wi   asin egatch   dash-go
he began prying up   that stone carefully then

tchibwa apitchi sonad niwi ginebagon. Ga sagano den nid
before further trapped that one snake. After crawled out he

dash miwi monda egod, "Anish gan-sin
thus so then this said to him, "Therefore I will kill you

sa, miwi gaiewi niniwi ejida-bama-diiang
surely, so then and (also) we the manner we pay each other

gishpin awiia anada-mon-gid, miwi niniwi
if someone for having helped, so then we

ginebago-iiang enak-oni-gewin ej-sing." "Beka." dinan
among us snakes the law written." "Wait!" says to him

anishinabe, "kasa-gona mamda monda djitsh-kemba. Kawin
Indian, "you hardly can't this do this. Not

aniniwi anishinabewiang dodj-tchige-semi monda."
ourselves being Indians ever do this."

"Mi-sago-eta wi gaieni ge-jida-ba-mon-namba," kido
"So certainly only that and me only way I'll pay you," said

wi ginebik. Migo win-si-god niwi ginebagon
that snake. Really going to kill him that snake

wi anishinabe. "Beka" miniwa ishkidod wi anishinabe,
the Indian. "Wait!" again he said the Indian

"awi bejigog iji okwedji-mada nitam." "Ahow,"
"that horse we go ask first." "All right (yes),"

kido ginebik. Mi niwi bejigogijin akwedjimawad,
he said snake. So that horse asked him,

"Anish gaie-gi gejitch ke-amba," ajinad wi anishinabe.
"What and you would you do?" said to him the Indian.

"Maba ginebik gi anada-mowa, mi-dash nonga awa
"This one snake I helped him, so then now he

awanji-dji-insid." "Kago-gwetch gi-kenda-sin ge-ijin-kweta-mon-namba,"
would kill me." "Do not hardly know how to answer you,"

kido wi bejigog iji. "Monda gaieni dijiwe-bis,
said the horse. "This and me

eko-bimadisiia dogiman anada-mowa, nonga dash ni-kaiia
all my life my boss helped him, now then getting old

eni-an-witoiia wi-noki-tawag, miwi winsid.
becoming unable I work for him, so he would kill me

Wiba go da-bida-simose dji-wi-bin-sid." "Beka," kido
Very soon he come walking to kill me." "Wait!" said

ginebik. Aptichige anishinabe gwin-wi-nendam.
snake. Very much Indian does not know what to think.

"Beka, miniwa," ishkitod Adebab-amad wagosheien
"Wait some more," he said. He sees yonder fox

besho mipto-nid. "Awi- nitam wagoshen agwedjimada
near by running. "Him first fox we ask him.

mindj-dashgo-edig gekidod miwi ge-ijitch-geia."
Thus whatever he will say so that I will do."

"Ahow," kido ginebik, "mi dash nongo shkwatch."
"All right," he said snake, "so but now last time."

Anishinabe webi nanonda-gosid, "Madjan! Madjan!
Indian began yelling, "Come here! Come here!

shime," ajinad niwi wagosheian. Mi gibi-ajad
my brother!" said to him that fox. So came forward

wagoshen. "Ani dash," ishkadod wagoshen. "Maba ginebik
fox. "Now what?" he said fox. "This snake

ginada-mowa wode aji-bikong, kitchi sin
helped over there on the mountain large stone

ason-god," kido anishinabe. *"Da-gin-sigon-go*
falling on him," he said Indian. "Would have killed

abwa-nada-mo-giba. Gikitchi-noki, kitchi-matig ga-gidaki-weda-badma
before helping. Did work hard large pole dragged up hill

wa-nokas-iia wi sin wi-gwi-da-kwa-ma. Tchi-we-weni
for me to use that stone, for me to pry that. Very well

gada-bamon gaie giji-wa-winda-mak. Midash nongo
pay you and he promised me. So then now

winsid." Wagoshen agona-wabamad ginebagon. "Gegeti na,"
he would kill." Fox looked at him snake. "Is that so?"

dinan. "E" kido ginebik, "miwi gaie
he said to him. "Yes," he said snake, "Therefore and

niniwi eji-tabamadiang gishpin awiia anada-mongid."
ourselves how we pay if someone have helped."

"Kago-gwetch monda nis stota sin" kido wagoshen. "Taga
"Not hardly this understand," he said fox. "Please

miniwa winda-moshin." Anish, mi-sa miniwa tchi-weweni
more tell me." Then so more very well

ano-dibadj-imod anishinabe. Ga-gijitod, gijib-diben-diso
tried to tell Indian. Having finished, scratches head

wagoshen, miniwa mik-agwe-se. "Taga ajada wode," kido
fox, more shakes head. "Please, we go there," he said

wagoshen, "ga-owam-dan manda ga-ondji-jiwe-bak." Gada-gosh-nowad
fox, "I go see this where it happened." When they arrived

"mi ajonda" kido anishinabe. Geiabe-go sa-gak-sinni matig
"So here," he said Indian. And still sticking out pole

gano-kasod anishinabe. "Taga dashgo kino-mo-shin ga-ijishnan
he used Indian. "Ah, then show me how you lay

| ajonda" | dinan | | niwi | ginebogon | wi wagoshen. | Miso |
| here," | says to him | that | snake | | the fox. | So then |

| ginebik | egatch | gi-nego ded | wi-bwa | jib-shkang | awi |
| snake | carefully | crawled under | lest | he jar | that |

| asin. | Weweni | ga-iji-shing | | ginebik. | Mi awi |
| stone. | Very well | after he arranged himself | snake. | So the |

| wagoshen | ajib-binad | anishinaben | einad, | "Ahow, |
| fox | nudges | the Indian. | He said to him, | "All right, |

| gondj-djwe-binan | awi asin." | Gi-gandj-djwe-binang | awi | sin |
| push forward | that stone." | So he pushed | that | stone |

| anishinabe. | Gi-apsi-konad | niwi | ginebogon. | Bi-nisaki-wewad |
| Indian. | Completely crushed | that | snake. | As they walked down hill |

| apitchigo | bi-gitchi-megwetch-wian | wagoshein | anishinabe. |
| very much | very great thanking him | fox | Indian. |

| "Kitchi-weweni | gada-ba mon" | dinan. | "Batinad |
| "Very very well | I will pay you," | he says to him. | "There is plenty |

| midjim | enaiiang, | batinawag | gaie | baka-kwaiiang." |
| food | at our home. | There are plenty | and | chickens." |

| "Kago mamda | nongo | dja-iamba," | kido | wagoshen. | "Bama goding |
| "I cannot | now | go there," | he said | fox. | "After a while |

| ga-bija." | Ni-gitchi | bopi-nendam | anishinabe | ni-giwed |
| I will come." | So very | happy | Indian | he goes home. |

| Wika | dashgo | goding | megwa | wisniwad, | anonda wawan |
| Later | but then | once | while | they eat, | they hear |

| baka-kwa-iian | kitchi anwatonid. | Kwi wi sen | gan-wad-inang |
| chickens | making great commotion. | Boy | he took hold of |

| bashk-sigan | ni-sagi-djipto. | Wagoshen | gitchi | babam-inaj-kawan |
| gun | he ran out. | Fox | much | chasing around |

baka-kwaiian,   baka kwa gamagong.   Eni-gidji-biwed   wagoshen
chickens,   in chicken house.   As he flees   fox,

"Bang!" anwe-we-sige   kwi wi sen.   Mi-gaiewi   gi daba-ged
"Bang!" sounded like   boy.   So he also   he paid

wagoshen   ano-anada-mowad   wi-djib-madsi-man.
fox   he tried to help   his fellow man.

Ginebik Dibadj-mowin (The Legend of the Serpent):
Free English Rendition

While a man was out hunting one day, he heard someone yelling from the slope of a mountain. "Come, help me! Come, help me!" he heard the voice say. So the man started climbing the hill, and it was very rocky and difficult to climb. When he got near the voice, he saw a snake lying coiled up under a rock. "How about this?" the man said. The snake said, "Help me! Pry this fallen stone up off of me, and I will pay you very well." And so the man said, "All right, I'll get a pole," and he went down the hill again. When he found a pole he climbed the hill once again. It was very hard climbing because the pole was very large and hard to drag, but when he got there he began to pry at the stone very carefully, so that the snake was not hurt any more. The snake crawled out from under the rock and said, "Now, I will kill you, because that is the customary way that we snakes repay each other when we have been helped."

"Wait!" cried the man, "you can't do that! That is not the way that Indians repay each other!" But the snake insisted, "This is the only way that I can repay you," and he was about to kill him when the man stopped him again.

"Wait, first we should go ask that horse."

"All right," said the snake.

"I helped this snake and now he wants to kill me. What should I do?" the man asked the horse.

"I don't know how to help you. I have worked for my boss my whole life, and now that I am getting old, he wants to kill me, and soon he is going to come and do it," the horse replied.

"I still don't know what to do," said the man, "but wait a little longer. Let's ask that fox first."

"All right," the snake said, "but this is the last time."

So the man yelled, "Come here, come here, my brother!" and the fox came over to him.

"Now what?" asked the fox.

"I helped this snake on the mountain over there. A large stone had fallen on him and he would have died if I hadn't dragged a pole up the mountain and pried the stone off of him. He promised to pay me very well, but now he wants to kill me."

"Is that so?" asked the fox.

"Yes," the snake said. "That is how we pay those who have helped us."

"I don't understand this," said the fox. "Please tell me more."

So the snake told it again. When he finished, the fox scratched his head and said, "Please go over there, so I can see where this happened." When they arrived, the man said, "Here!" and pointed to the stick still stuck under the stone.

"Ah," the fox said. "Now show me how you were laying." And so the snake carefully crawled under the rock again. Then the fox nudged the man and said, "All right, push the stone forward again!" And they pushed the stone and it completely crushed the snake. As they walked down the hill, the man thanked the fox many times.

"I will pay you very well for this. Go to my house and there are plenty of chickens there to eat."

"I cannot go there now," said the fox, "but later I will come." The man went home very happy. But later, while he was eating with his family, they heard the chickens making a great commotion. His son took his gun and ran outside and saw the fox chasing the chickens around. As the fox ran away the boy shot him, and so he repaid the fox for helping his fellow men.

Pitchi Asokewin [The Story of the Robin][31]

Agoding	anishinabe	ogwis san	nidit sem gading
Once upon a time	Indian	his son	when the time came

wimkade-ke-nid	gaie	awi apwadang	nigani bimadisswin,	miiwi
for him to fast	and	dream about	further life,	so then

gi-mi-tchi jita ad.	Miiwi	anishinabens	gi-obin-da-ged
made great preparations.	So then	young Indian	he entered

wigwamensing	monda	ondjita	wenenda gwag.	Midasswe-sogwan
in little lodge	this	purposefully	intended for.	Ten days

dashgo	manda	mkadekewin	adjitam-igad.	Maba dash
therefore	this	fasting	usually lasts.	This but

anishinabe pago send man ogwissan woshime   iwi
Indian   wishes for him his son   moreover him

gitchi-piten da gosinid. Midash   ga-ishkwa midasswe-sogonigadnig,
be very important.   So then after   ten days were over,

maba   anishinabe epitchi mashko wen dang ogwisson
this one Indian   very   determined   his son

wi-kitchi-ijia-nid   gi-kan simod gaiabe   jiwi-mkade ke nid.
to be very important   urged   further for him to fast.

Jajigo   gaiewi   dash gi-midasswe-sogon gadni gako
Already   it has been but   ten days past   since

webi-mkade-ked wi anishinabens. Niwebi   tchi-bkade
began fasting   it little Indians. He begins very hungry

dash gaiewi.   Mano   dashgo   gaiabe   wi-wik-odjiton
thus he is (also). Any how   but then further will try to

owi mkaded. Kano   eko bimadisid gi kino mo wasi
he to fast. Did not   all his life   he was thought

awi bisind awad   nikagon.   Wiba   dashgo   eni-apitchi
he listen to them his parents. Very soon but then getting very

kitchi-bkaded miiwi   nian wendji ged.   "Sham shin! bakade!
very hungry, so then he giving up hope. "Feed me!   I'm hungry!

Sham shin! bakade!"   "Bama wab-and," kido   anishinabe
Feed me!   I'm hungry!"   "After tomorrow," he said   Indian,

"Gitchi weweni dash ga-sha-min." Apitchigo   dash gaiewi
"Very well   then I'll feed you." Very much   then and he

maba   anishinabens bkade.   Miminwa ish kodod, "Sham shin!
this one young Indian hungry! So again he says, "Feed me!

bakade!   Sham shin! bakade!"   Epitchi kidod   dash
I'm hungry! Feed me!   I'm hungry!" While he's saying then

Manda, iiai   miskwi wabagan jajo nan ka ka nang. Epitchi
this,   that thing red   clay   he rubs on his chest. While

gagik-kamad   dash mi-wik-sha   ninwe ijiwe Pitchiwan
while advising   but   and right then then   then   Robin

ga-nindji-pisa gwinid. "Cheep! Cheep! Cheep!" ni-kidowin.
he arose from there.   He goes saying.

Midash   edig   nongo awi   "Pitchi" anishinabewid
so then   seemingly   now   him   "Robin"   being Indian

awendji   nita-anoji tchi kong wigwaman.
wherefore likes to be around   houses.

Pitchi Asokewin (The Story of the Robin): Free English Rendition

Once there was a man whose son approached the age when it was time for him to make preparations to fast and dream about the rest of his life. So the young man went into the lodge built for this purpose. Usually people fasted for ten days, but this boy's father wanted him to be very important, and so after ten days he insisted that his son fast longer. His son had begun to be very hungry but agreed to fast more because he had never thought to disobey his parents. However, as he became more hungry he began to lose hope. "Feed me! I'm hungry!" he cried. Finally his father said, "After tomorrow, then I'll feed you." But the boy was already starving and begged, "Feed me! I'm hungry! Feed me! I'm hungry!" And as he said this, he rubbed some red clay on his chest. Just then a robin appeared from where he was sitting and the boy's words changed to, "Cheep! Cheep! Cheep!" So that is why Robin always likes to be around houses now.

The Cricket and the Ant[32]

The cricket, *ojigáwεsa*, doesn't sow or reap. He sings all summer, starves all winter. The ant, *έnnagǫs*, is small but works hard. The cricket is hungry so he visits the ant.
　"What did you do all summer?"
　"I sang."
　"Why don't you sing now?"
　"I'm hungry."
　The ant gave the cricket some food.

The Girl Married to a Dog[33]

The girls at puberty used to fast in little lodges. One girl had a dog she wanted to take with her. Her parents let her have the dog with her.

Afterwards the girl married the dog. She moved to Fox Island and took this dog with her. Later some Ottawas found her lodge (*waganogan*) on Fox Island, where no one had ever lived. She had two offspring from this dog. The offspring had human faces and bodies of animals. They could only say, "*anısnabe.*"

The Ottawas came back and told the girl's parents. Her brothers, maybe two, went to find out about it. One brother murdered his own sister, the dog, and the children.

After this the Ottawas passed a ruling that there could never be a human being who would live with animals. They gave the island the name *nımǫnıŋ* (dog place).

Makkwons (Little Bear)[34]

An Indian family long ago had a little bear as a pet. They used to feed him corn soup with maple sugar in it in his own little dish. They sugar was kept in a little box about ten inches square. The bear knew the box of sugar was his. Whenever the box was empty, they would open it and show the little bear that there was no sugar left. When they did this the little bear would eat his corn soup without the sugar, although he preferred it sweetened. But if there was no more sugar left in his box and they did not show the little bear that it was all gone, he would refuse to eat his corn soup and would turn over his dish in disgust.

Another Indian man—and my grandfather knew the man, so this is true—had a little bear as a pet, as had many other Indians in those days. One day the man said in a joking manner to the little bear, "When you get big, I'm going to kill you." But the little bear believed him and he was sad. Later in the day the man went hunting and on his return he saw a terrible sight—the little bear had jumped into the fire and had been burned to death! He had committed suicide. This proves that bears could understand Indian.

The Fastest Bird[35]

Once all the birds were racing to a Pacific island where there were many nuts. The first one to get a nut won the race and also won the chief's daughter in marriage.

The kingbird was very fast and the eagle also was fast. There were many other birds, many of them very swift. Then there was the crane, *šagi*, who flapped along very slowly.

When night came all birds stopped to sleep, but *šagi*, who doesn't sleep much, kept right on going. He passed all the others and was the first to get a nut. He won and also won the chief's daughter.

Legends: Semi-Historical

The Maškóde Indians[36]

Iye'ák'	*Šɪmnibámkuŋ*	*bešo*	*kid'nakkɪwak'*
A kind of	at Seven Mile Point (apple place)	near	they lived

anıšnábɛk maškuo:deyák kižínkàzıwak' aŋgodíŋ daš
Indians   Maskuten   they were called.   Once   thus

ɛpaŋgišmók' gipamigasıwak' Odáwak' Nadowéssan gımigánawan
out West   they were fighting   Ottawas   Sioux   they fought them.

gimažáwak'   daš   bɛškabiwát'   daš
They were defeated   thus   while they were returning   thus

egátč gona bıbəmíškawat'   šɪmnibámkuŋ
slowly   as they were gliding by in their boats   at Seven Mile Point

bešú mi. . . .   gisadédnmowat' angam'tuo:áwan
near (stutter)   they feeling sad   they were singing for

wi:jɪnɪšnábɛwan   gansɪnjík'   wodɛ   Nadowɛssi:kíŋ
their fellow Indians   who were killed   over there   Sioux land.

Iyaak'   daš   gipab' áwan   Maškuó:déyak' ɛškanígajık'
A kind of   thus   they laughed at them   Maskuten   youths.

guo:na Mi   bekíš   giwɛ   geyi   gipamsɪníwawan
So   along with   seemingly   also   they throw stones at them

nıwɛ Odawan mi gɪnškáčiwat'   Odáwak' gapıgíwewat'
those Ottawa.   So they became angry   Ottawas   after they returned home.

daš míwɛ gigižéndamowatˤ   čɪmokítˤwawatˤ
Thus so   they made up their minds. They decided to sneak up on them

                 Maškuó:deyan gaɪškwá   natuó:watˤ   makkasɪnwan
and surprise them Maskutens.   Afterwards they repaired moccasins.

mínawa gɛ   gižíˤtawatˤ   mi gɪmokítuowatˤ
Again   also after they got ready so they sneaked up on them

Maškuo:déan gigčiabínčawan   daš   gegágo gajagənanáwatˤ
Maskutens.   They bitterly attacked them. Thus almost they killed

            iya'ɪŋ daš Sú:nyan   gipaʷwewakˤ iye'akˤ
them all. At (to) thus St. Joseph they fled   some (those)
  Maškuo:déan   midáš
  Maskutens.   So

maʷpítč   gominawá angodɪŋ   wikágo:na giánjɛ   mokítuowatˤ
about the time again   once again later on and again they sneaked

              Odáwak nɪwɛ mínawa gi:čɪmigánawatˤ
up on them. Ottawas those   again   they gave them a big fight.

midaš ɛpangíšmak   níkeya   gipówewatˤiya'akˤ
So then they went West in the direction of they fled to

Maškuo:déyakˤ Míwɛ.
Maskutens.   That's all.

The Maškóde Indians: Free English Rendition

Near Seven Mile Point (called "Apple Place" in Odawa) lived some people called the Maskutens. Once, many Odawa people were returning from the west where they had been fighting the Sioux. They were defeated and so they returned slowly, and as they glided by Seven Mile Point in their boats, they were singing for their friends who had been killed fighting in Sioux lands. As they passed through, some Maskuten youth laughed at them and threw stones, making the Odawa men very angry. When they returned home, they resolved to sneak up on the Maskutens and surprise them. They repaired their moccasins and sneaked up on the Maskuten village. The Odawa warriors bitterly attacked the Maskutens, nearly killing them all. Some of them fled west to St. Joseph. Later on, the Odawa men again snuck up on them, and again they attacked the Maskutens. Those Odawas gave them a good fight, so again the Maskutens fled west. That is all.

Legend of Škodęs, a Maškódęš Boy[37]

A young boy called Skodęs was once fasting in a little lodge away from the main Maškodęš village. He had a vision that caused him to get out of his bed and go to Round Lake. (This was near Eight Mile Harbor.)

He looked out over Round Lake and saw an eagle that had a serpent in his beak. The eagle had almost raised the serpent from the water.

The boy stood on the beach and watched. The eagle saw him and said, "I'd like your help, and I will help you in return."

The serpent said, "Do not help the eagle. He has no power. I have more."

The boy didn't know which one to shoot.

The eagle said, "If you help me now, you'll be great here."

The serpent said, "The eagle is lying. He can't help you. If you help him, you will never travel on water because the other serpents will be 'laying' for you."

This scared the boy, so he shot the eagle.

Before the eagle went down, he said, "I want to remind you—where you live now, there will be nothing—not even as much as you dogs."

The serpent left.

Later the Ottawas drove the Maškodęš out—clear down to Benton Harbor, where there was a small band. Here the Maškodęš dug a hole in the ground for safe-keeping like a funnel. A big tree (150 feet long) hung over the funnel-shaped place.

The Ottawas said, "They'll fight to the last man. We'll cut the tree down at night."

One man could hit the tree trunk once or twice with an axe (without being shot by a Maškodęš' arrow). Since the tree hung over the funnel-shaped place, it wouldn't take much to cut it down. Finally after several nights, while the arrows were flying thick, the tree began to croak. The Maškodęš in the hole knew it was the end and started to cry.

The leader told the Ottawas like this, "When a person sits at the table and eats and keeps on eating, after a while he gets enough and if he overdoes his eating, he vomits. So we'd like to have you do the same thing."

So the Ottawas left them alone and told them to come out. The Ottawas told them to leave the area and not to come back. I don't know where they went—north, south—but they left.

Kiwe wigi wa meiag (Underground People)[38]

Jajaie   agiwandoba-niwa go bane   Otawag
Long ago while they were out scouting Ottawas

gibinawa goba   bejig anishinabesan agita kana wad
brought   along they   one   little Indian   set him free they

ajonda Odawa nang tchibi dana kinid. Kiwewiga wama dash
here   Ottawa land he came to live.   Undergrounder thus

giawe   awi   gwiwisens. Gini tawi gid "Odawan"
he was that boy.   He grew up   "an Ottawa"

ogioji niman.   Giondadi siwag abino-dji iag.
he became an in-law. Were born they babies.

Giodawa wiwag   dash ondji   megwe Odawa
Became Ottawas they   thus   therefore among Ottawa

gidaji nitawi giwad.   Kiwe-wigiwa meian osiwan,
while they were growing up. Undergrounder   their father,

Odawa kwen dash ogashi wan. Gegeti   gioni jishe
Ottawa lady but   their mother. Certainly he was good

anini giwi sewi nini. Ginita   nan do ba ne
man   hunter.   He was good at scouting

awidji wad   nenda bani djin "Odawan." Gionendan
he was going with them   scouters   .   "Ottawa." He forgot

kiwe wiga wa mewid.   Ga ondji   inin dwa
he was Undergrounder. Wherefore they were called

kiwe wiga wa me, giwani kadeni aki(aking)   ga da wad.
Undergrounders, it was dug out in the ground where they lived

Odawaka niwan gaie wanika ning   gidawan.
              and hollowed out place he lived.

Mi iji we   nibina wenda disi djig   minik
that is where many   where they originate as many

"Edawigijik"   egoing   daweman, wikaneian.
"Ettawageshik" we are called, his sister, his brother,

oji she ian, omisho misan   gaie "Edawigijik"   kakina
his uncle,   his grandfather, and "Ettawageshik" all of them.

gaie "Makadebi nessi" enin djig   ijiwe
And "Black Hawk"   who are called there

ondji gewog   kiwe wiga wa me ga inin djig
they changed homes Undergrounders   were called they

anishinabeg kawi bagona wisi djig, gegi-badisi-djig
Indians   they were not wild,   those who are bad

gaie ogi-awisi wag. Ogi-nitawigito nawa wamidji-wad.
and they were not. They raised   what they would eat.

Gi nan da-wenji gewag gaie winawa gaie onakoni-gewin
They sought to learn and they   and law

ogi-ojito-nawa. I-nwe-win gaie winawa eta gi-inwe-wag.
they made.   Language and they   only they spoke.

Ogi-odemina-wan   "Pipi gwe (ian)" mi dash naning-go dinong
They had for totem "Little Hawk"   so then once in a while

kiwe-wiga wame ian ga-ogitisi-midjig ga-ondji jini kanin dwa
Undergrounders   your ancestors   why they were called

"Pipi gwe iag." Eshkam   gibati newag.   Kishpin
                Gradually they became many. If

gego   bejig iji-madji-do-dang, Odawag   dash
something one   does wrong,   the Ottawas then

widiba konawad, gaie winawa "Pipi gweiag"
they bring to trial and they

mawandji diwag   adiba-kona-mowad odad-awinwa.
they gather together to judge   their actions

mam awe "Odawag" nagan-sidjig. Nibina kiwe-wiga-wama-ian
together "Ottawas" leaders.   Many   Undergrounders

ga-ogitisi midjig aniniwag gi-ogima wi wag tchi bwa
your ancestors   men   they were chiefs before

migading Odenang 1812— ga-ishkwa-migading gaie
the war   Mackinac Island after the war   and

binish nongo anemia. Nin-gidekenimag go anin.
until   now   recently. I can remember some of them.

Paul Edawigijig ogi-iji-she-inan,   ogima "Oning-gwi-gaian"
              he had for uncle   Chief   "(Wing)"

"Makade benessi"   dash de-de-bi-na-we wikaneian.
"Black Hawk (Blackbird)" but   half-   his brother.

Minawa bejig "Wau-ke-so" "Maka debenessi" owika neian
Also   one   his brother

ogima. Gida-pine Manitoba (Canada) 1820. Win dash
chief.   He died at   Him but

"Makade benessi" ogi-niganisi-kandawan   Odawan
              he assumed leadership over them the Ottawas

anawe   "Pipigweian" agi-ogiti simid   misode
although   they were his ancestors all over

Wagina kising.   Ginibo   June 1861. Nijing
Crooked Tree land. He died June 1861. Twice

gana-ning gishkak aki   Wagi-naki-sing   ogi-nagada-nawa
after it quaked   land Crooked Tree land they left it

Odawag edna kiwad.   Epang gish mok gi-ija wad,
Ottawas where they live. Out west   they went,

mi dash awadibe nibina gawad pine wad,
so then over there many they died there

agi-maie-kish-nok. "Saw kaw kee" *ogima wigo ba.*
the land was too strange for them. "Growing out" was then Chief.

gaiewi awode giwad pine.
He also over there he died there.

Mi nijing Odawag gi-kitchi ajish-kawd
So twice Ottawas very greatly set back

Enda tchi wagobane. Nitam mamakisiwin
from their past number. First time disease (smallpox)

gega gadja-gina-nigo-wad Wagina kising.
almost they killed them off Crooked Tree land.

Kiwe wigi wa meiag (Underground People): Free English Rendition

Long ago some Odawa men were scouting and they brought back a little boy and set him free to live with them in Odawa country. The boy was called "Undergrounder." He grew up as an Odawa, became an in-law, and had children. His children became Odawas since they grew up among the Odawa, and because their father was Undergrounder and their mother was an Odawa woman. Undergrounder was a very good hunter and scout among the Odawas. He eventually forgot he was an Undergrounder, a name that referred to the hollowed-out place he made to live. That is where many of us named Ettawageshik come from: his sister, his brother, his uncle, and his grandfather. All people called Ettawageshik and Makade binessi (Black Hawk) come from Undergrounders. These people were not wild or bad. They raised everything that they ate. Many of them learned about and helped make laws and a language that only they spoke. Their totem was *Pipigweian* (Little Hawk) and so they were called Pipigweiag. Soon there were many of them. When someone did something wrong, the Odawas brought them to trial and the Pipigweiag came together to judge them with the Odawa leaders. Many Undergrounders, your ancestors, were these chiefs from before the war on Mackinac Island in 1812 even until very recently. I can remember some of them.

Paul Edawigijig had an uncle—and half-brother—who was Chief

Oning-gwi-gaian Makade benessi (Blackbird Wing). Also, his brother Wau-ke-so Makade benessi was a chief. He died in Manitoba in 1820. But he, Makade benessi, assumed leadership over the Odawas even though his ancestors were Pipigweiag and they lived in Crooked Tree land. He died in June 1861. After the land quaked twice in Crooked Tree land, the Odawas left where they lived and went west.[39] Many people died then, because the land was unfamiliar, and the chief, Saw kaw kee, died there too.

So, twice was the Odawa population set back in numbers. The first time, smallpox had almost killed them off in Crooked Tree land.

Two Cousins Captured by the Sioux[40]

Once there were two young men who were cousins. One of them, the weaker one, had refused to fast (at puberty). Well, they got captured by the Sioux.

The Sioux had a big celebration. They put up stakes in the middle of the village, as they planned to burn the boys. They put piles of pine wood around the stakes—a sort of pyre.

The boy who fasted said, "We'll live!"

The other boy said, "No!"

The first boy, the one who fasted, said, "In a vision I saw wind and water. (He meant rain.) The wind and the rain will come and put out the fire."

The next day the Sioux were making fun of the boys in the chief's tipi. The Chief comes out after doing this and lights the fire. But it starts to rain. It rained and rained. A heavy wind came and blows the flaming sticks away.

The Sioux were out of luck. They didn't try again that day. The next morning, before the old women came with the wood (for the pyre), a nice young girl came out of her buckskin tipi. She came out and looked at first one of the boys and then the other. She had a knife in her hand. She looked at the weaker one and then at the other. She cut the cords of the stronger one who had fasted and released him and took him to her tipi.

Then another girl came with a knife to the weaker one. She cut the cords and took him by the arm to her tipi.

The two boys had to marry these girls and then they were just as much adopted into the tribe. One girl had a brother and he told his brother-in-law that he would like to go hunting. They went together everywhere. (This was the weaker one of the two boys.)

One day the weaker young man saw his cousin and said that he would like to go home. The other said that he would not leave his wife.

"She saved my life," he said.

The next day the weaker cousin started to hunt with his brother-in-law, but they went toward the east. He told his brother-in-law that he was going to leave and thanked him.

But it is usual if a person left after being captured and living with another tribe and came home that he would not live long.

The Sioux Captive[61]

This is a story of the primitive life. It was all right—sunshine and rain. There was a man named Mıškóagə (Red) at Manistique near Escanaba. He went to hunt the Sioux. His group killed a family of Sioux isolated somewhere.

Mıškóagə went and got drunk and he would mock the Sioux boy, the only one left. He would imitate the voices and ask the Sioux boy who made the noise. It was his mother who had been killed.

The boy would say, "That was my mother."

The other Ottawas would say, "Don't tease him like that," and he'd say, "He's only a slave. He doesn't know anything." But the neighbors said, "Yes, he did."

Well, the boy grew up and talked Ottawa. Mıškóagə had a daughter, Babanák'kwe (Walnut Tree), sort of a princess, seventeen or eighteen years old. He also had a younger daughter about twelve.

In social gatherings Mıškóagə always got drunk. One night he was on his way home with a companion, singing maybe war songs. As he got to the door of his log house, a young man came running out. Mıškóagə ran and overtook him but let him go. Then Mıškóagə called his oldest daughter, but there was no answer. As he neared the house, he heard a dripping sound. The Sioux boy had cut off her head and the blood was dripping. He had tied the head on the old man's musket and planned to take it, but he didn't have time. The younger girl had run outside and crawled into the wood pile. She was too scared to come out at first.

Word was passed around about it. The Sioux boy had taken revenge. The Indians had a root cellar always, where they kept potatoes, syrup, canned stuff, etc. They were usually some way back of the house. This Sioux went to a root cellar back in the hills. He lived there on the stuff in the cellar. Later he sneaked off to another village and made his way westward. Perhaps he got there.

Sogat [Three Legged][62]

Once an Ottawa Indian at Seven Mile Point stopped along the trail to tie his moccasin and was ambushed and killed by Indians from Sagina. An only son of Sogat went to Sagina and retaliated—killed someone maybe. An Indian (from Sagina) came for Sogat next spring. Sogat had fled to an island. The Indians usually attacked at four o'clock in the morning because it was cool then. They wanted to get Sogat alive. The swallows overhead swooped down and warned Sogat. Three birds seemed to say, "Get away from here, Indian. You're going to be killed." Sogat told his wife to throw stuff into a canoe and they fled again. There were a dozen attackers or more, but the wind changed from an east wind and Sogat escaped. This was in 1855 or 1856. They are still after Sogat.

Kidnappers from Saginaw[63]

Aníš mi ságiwę misa jıdabájmo:yą́ šánda
What (so then) so seemingly so I shall tell here

gašowébdággobanei čišažigo Kawiwiya žanda iyábžkiwɛtˤ
what happened then long time ago. No one here one who is white

giási migwéˑtta anısnábɛkˤ gaèiyá:jıkˤ žanda gá:odɛ́tˤtojıkˤ
was here only Indians were present here here those who came

Midaš ıwę bınódjiakˤ gibaˑtı́nnawakˤ goˑna
to town. So then young children there were many (and)

čaiyąsakˤ góˑna miˑwɛ gınni:žwáswəpangízwaddìkˤ
big children (and) (about) was seven years old, I guess

kwíwisęs padámınowakˤ daš gıwę́ oští ódę
boy. They are playing thus seemingly there over there

nıkéya manda miˑkán ɛnınımákˤ žanda ganna
in the direction of this road the way it goes here

odɛnaŋ Padamnowatˤ iya daš mánda šigobí:msakˤ
into town. They are playing thus this little evergreens

daš kakína kibɪdákšowakʿ   íya'akʿ   giškandogó:sakʿ
but nothing they were growing (alive) of a kind little cedar trees.

Padamnawatʿ   bɪnó˙ jiakʿ gwiwisę̄sak Mí˙sa   išɪwę̄
They out playing children boys.   So that at that place (there)

anıšnábɛn gibɪdagóšnɪnɪtʿ   migowɛ˙'tə́ no˙nž   iwę̄   sɛsíkzitʿ
an Indian he arrived (came) that only   slightly there older

miwá   gabɪnnawadɪnɪn gibɪnwódjabɪnɪn gimajíptwanawatʿ
that one he was taken up. He was snatched. They ran off with him.

Manda gɪdáki wódɛ gimɪpáttowatʿ gigajɪbówewat Miš wodę̄ mon
That hill there they ran by they fled.   So there (?)

ɛškwe˙í   kimjɪgannáwan nɪkánɪŋ   niwɛ niš Miš
behind on either side they held him by the arms him two. So

gibmɪtwánawatʿ   giba...   gigamodawakʿ   niwɛ bɪnódjian
they ran with him (stutter) they were stealing him. Children

kwiwisę̄san mɪdaš ganda ižwę̄ eyabínɪkʿ   wadokwabínikʿ
boys   so then those there those who were here who were

        migo wewipʿ   gibɪdabájowatʿ   žanda
playing with them very   very soon they came and told here

daš gánna odɛnwę̄ ́sɪŋ   gibɪnwádjɪbɪnnɪn   wodę̄
thus   in the little town (that) he was taken (snatched) there

ɪwę̄   škɪnígɪš Midaš   giwę̄   ogánda   anɪšnábɛkʿ kína(kakina)
that one youth. So then seemingly those who Indians all

gima... wewibago gimandópɪdawatʿ   gi...   Baš'kəsɪganan
(stutter) right now they rushed together (stutter) Guns

ginwàdanámowatʿ   kɪnagógègo wa'účgèwatʿ
they grabbed them anything   they used as weapons to strike with

ɪgo   baš'sɪganan ginwajə́bɪdowatʿ Mɪdaš
(superlative for emphasis) guns   they snatched.   So then

gımajíptowatˤ	*Gináganàwan*	*daš*	*niwę*	*niwę*
they ran off.	They trailed (tracked)	thus	him (or they)	that one

sa	*kabıgamódəni:jín*	*bınódjian I!*	*mandašigo*	*gwiák'go*
very one	who stole	child. Oh!	(certainly)	straight

mandę	*bęjık*	*nıwę*	*bıs:san*	*wɛndagó:gın oštɛgó:odę*	*wəgwəsęskákˤ*
this	one	him	lakes	located at beyond there	where there is a

	mi ódę	*i:díkˤ gigabawatˤ*	*giwe*	*anıšnábɛkˤ*
birch grove.	It was	there maybe	so they camped	those Indians

pìgamodawátˤ	*bınódjian*	*Miš wodę*	*manpi*	*ɛškweˤi*
they coming to steal	children.	Over there	here	either side

mıjıgnáwatˤ	*miš gunda gewi*	*gimajíptowat*	*gagamodámınıjıkˤ*
they holding him (them)	so	they ran off	they who stole from

bınódjan	*Nınıwák*	*nibınagǫ*	*kàwigopangíšę go*	*Mınikˤ sago*
children.	Men	many	not just a few.	As many as

ga:iyawágobàne	*ižıwę*	*gigajıptwónowatˤ*	*nıwę*
that were staying there	there	they ran off with him (them)	that

bınódjian	*Mıdaš*	*ginınanondáoziwat*	*giwę*
child.	So then	they were calling	those

sa nɛndonnewadjıkˤ	*kwiwisęsan*	*gabıgamot'njın*
themselves those who are searching	boys (boy?)	that which they stole.

nanondaósiwatˤ	*mínıwa*	*ginimadwézigewakˤ*	*Baš'ksíganan*
they were yelling	again.	They were shooting at intervals.	Guns

gibaš'ksigéwakˤ	*Naganáwan*	*daš niwę*	*boɛšáganigadɛ*
they shoot off.	They were trailing	thus them.	He was bare-legged

gɛ maba bınódji	*migowétta*	*bababígiwi:anɛs*	*égowat*	*manda*
also this baby.	Only	little shirt	he wore	this

gikwégıdòne
this long (length of shirt—to waist—was illustrated by narrator).

Odawa Myths

opíčigo   ginagá:awan   migo gis ...   gibapasgoʷdeá'kožıŋ
Very much they were cruel to him. So   (stutter) his legs were all

mégowε̨   tatakágomiškε̨ iwε̨   bınódji   kwíwisε̨s
scratched up among   blackberry briars that baby. Boy

mıptwónın   miš wodε̨ manpi ganna minòndamáwatʿ
they were running with him so   over   there   they are hearing

giwε̨ gεžabá:adjıkʿ   bınódjian abınanondaósınıtʿ
those whom they are fleeing   child.   They coming yelling

mínawa bımmadowézigenıtʿ   opıčıgó bınwá'tıwan
again.   They coming making noise with guns, very much they coming

        mí: nıwε̨ bεmənaškàgowádjın   Miš wodε̨   bεšo
noisily. So then they running after them. So   over there near

ıžígo bıdənewèzıgéwan   nıwε biabapassí:gεnjın
near reports of guns coming them they who are making the shooting.

wínsawak   go   manžıgó   i:díkʿ
They are going to be killed undoubtedly. Whatever maybe so

wanapnanandwane   midaš gi:iyáwatʿ
they wonder what's going to happen to them. So then

midaš ıžígo sagızíwakʿ   gíwε   gagəmòjıjíkʿ   bınódjian
so then now they are afraid them   those who stole child.

Migo iya'ıŋ gajıptágganawatʿ megowetʿ tatakágomiškε gigadwεbınawatʿ
It was there they threw him   only   briar patch   they pushed him.

gigajıpiwewat odε   daš   gibıggábawatʿ   wəgwəsε̨skakʿ
They fled   there then where they camped   where there are birches.

čimanəwa gipáttawatʿ mi wodε̨ gapowewatʿ   Miš gunda
their canoe they ran to so   there   where they fled to. So

bεmınaškágejıkʿ   giwabamawat ıžıwε níwε bınódjian iži:ánıtʿ
those who are pursuing   they saw   there that   child.   He is there

mɛgowę tatakágomıškɛ anıš mıško gınopškawat' kwežımawat'
among briar patch. Well so they stopped. They asked him

ani... anıpídaš gíwɛ gigajıpıwéwak' "mišgo žanda gajippágsiwat'
(stutter) where them they fled. "So here they threw me

megowɛ tatakágomıškɛ" opčıgego mıskwiwákogade skınígıš
among briar patch." Very much his legs are bloody youth

gıbabasgó deyákojın baggwašágınısdɛ:gɛ Midaš
where his legs were scratched up. He was also bare-footed. So then

mıškogɛ giyewat' ıžíwɛ nınıwák agıgčíməmadwesıgéwat
they stayed there there men. They made a lot of noise shooting.

ežıskítowat'igo mínawa nanondáosiwak' mišgo ganda
As much as they could again they yelled. So them
  gigajıbáwewat'
  they fled

mi wodɛ gapawewat' čimanawa gingagámowat'
so over there they fled to their canoe where they left it
  gibıgmó:dawat'
  they came to steal

niwɛ bınódjan Anıš mišgo gi:bonábomındwa
that child. So therefore they stopped looking for them.

Kıšpin gɛgo dodwawapá gonama:gé sàwapá migo
If something they did to them supposing they killed him so

'kına odɛ winabıgamówapá giwɛ anıšnábɛk'
all there they would all have gone there them Indians

wiwansìndáwa gıwɛ gagamójıjık bınódjian kadaš gišıtšgesiwàk'
go and kill them them they stole child. Not they did not

ıwɛ migo beka gajıpskabwó:nawat' gibıtú:nawat' nıwɛ
there so quietly they returned him. They carried him that

bɪnódjian gibɪgiwénawat⁽	Mɪdaš ganda	gigčɪségsiwat⁽
child. They brought him home.	So then	they were very

	ganda sa	Ságina nɪnɪwak⁽ giwɛ	gadódɛngɪk⁽
frightened	so these themselves	Saginaw band. Them	they did it

ɪwɛ	Ságɪna	gabɪnjɪbádjɪk⁽	miš gɪgčɪsésiwat⁽
there	Saginaw	those who come from	so they were very scared.

Kašwika	mínawa	gidótsiwak	ɪwɛ pané:go	gi:ndáosiwak'
Never	again	they did it not	there. All the time	they were trying to

čɪgamódawat bɪnódjian	Odáwan	čɪgamòdamáwat⁽
they to steal child	Ottawa.	They want to steal from them

bɪnódjian ginskénmawan	nɪwɛ Odáwan	gipággojɪk⁽ wàwan
child. They hated them	those Ottawas.	They provoked them

Ságina nɪnɪnwak⁽	wagwɛndɪgé:nak⁽ganna	ganda Ságina
Saginaw band.	Whoever they are	them Saginaw

nɪnɪwak kawigikɛnmasik⁽	missa gibskabwówɪnɪn	maba
band not I did not know them.	So they returned him	this

bɪndójian gibagiwéwɪnɪn	ka:ŋikénmasi
child. They brought him home.	I did not know (him)

gažɪnkasat⁽ wɛnijansé:ɪt⁽	Misa gažɪwɛ̀bədágəbane	ɪwɛ.
what they called him whose child.	So that is what happened	there.

Kidnappers from Saginaw: Free English Rendition

What I will tell you here happened a long time ago. No whites were here, only Anishinaabeg. There were many younger and older children then and some of them, including one boy about seven years old, were playing over there near this road that goes into town where there are now those little cedar trees. While they were out playing, an Indian arrived, only slightly older than that seven year-old boy, and snatched that boy up and ran away with him over that hill, holding him by his two arms. Soon the boys that had been playing went and told the rest of the town that the boy had been taken. So, many people from the town rushed together, grabbing whatever they could use for weapons, including guns! So they ran off, and tracked him, that one who stole the child. Surely he had gone straight toward a lake that stood beyond a birch grove, and the pursuers thought the people who had come to steal the child had been encamped there. They were holding him on either side, but they ran off, all those many men, ran off with that child.

So then the pursuers were yelling again and shooting guns at intervals, trailing the marauders. The boy was bare-legged, too, and was only wearing a little shirt, only to the waist. His kidnappers were very cruel to him, and so his legs were all scratched up by the blackberry briars as they took him away from their pursuers whom they could hear getting closer. Soon the kidnappers could tell the men from the village were getting very close and could hear the guns and thought that they would surely be killed. They were afraid, so they threw the child into a blackberry briar and ran away to their camp. The men from the village soon saw the child in the briar and so they stopped and asked him where the kidnappers went. The boy told him that they had thrown him into the briar patch. His legs were very bloody and scratched, and he was bare-footed. The pursuers stayed with the boy, though they still made a lot of noise shooting and yelling. The kidnappers fled in their canoes, where they had left them. The men from the town would have gone after them, but the kidnappers had left the boy and not killed him, and so the boy was just carried back to the village. So the people from the town were frightened that the Saginaw would try again to steal another child from the Odawas. They hated the Odawas. Whoever those people from Saginaw are, I do not know them. But they left the child so he could be brought home. I never knew the child who was stolen. That is what happened there.

Dané·zi[44]

Dané·zi was a young Ottawa who fell in love with a girl who refused to marry him. He threatened the girl and said he would take her life if she continued to refuse him. Once out on the trail, the girl forgot something. She went back for it and happened to meet Danézi. He got the better of her with a knife.

Dané·zi fled to Washtenaw County and was never found. He returned an old man. He must have been one hundred years old when I saw him. My grandpa (we were related to Dané·zi) didn't dare go to Seven Mile Point where the murder happened as he was afraid of revenge. There may have been an exchange of gifts between Dané·zi's family and the girl's family.

The Chief with Seven Sons[65]

Long ago the Indians went to the St. Joseph area to hunt, before Chicago was there. It was a swampy land. Sagowang village was at St. Joseph. A man, his wife, and their fourteen- or fifteen-year-old daughter had their winter quarters there. The man went to where Chicago is now to trap muskrat. The girl goes down with a birchbark bucket for water and she doesn't return. The Indians found the bucket at the water's edge.

Later, Ottawas coming home from the Plains ran into some Indians who had kidnapped the girl. They saw her and were told that she was taken to become the wife of the oldest son of the chief with seven sons. They said to tell her father not to worry. These Indians lived somewhere in the southwest.

The father gets up a band to go and get his daughter back. They rode on ponies. The girl gets to the southwest, but the chief had moved farther west for some reason. The Ottawas follow and finally met (the other Indians).

The two groups are friendly, so the chief gives a big feast. They had a special place for them (the Ottawas) to eat. They had buffalo meat, fish, prairie chickens.

Shortly after the father of the girl ate, he died, though he was probably not poisoned. The Ottawas buried him there. The chief with seven sons claimed the pony. The Ottawas had no claim on the girl so they went back to Sagowag.

The chief in the southwest decided to have a wedding of his son and the Ottawa girl. He gave a big feast and there was much dancing and singing. But just an hour or two before the wedding was to take place, the oldest son died.

The second oldest son thought he'd marry the girl then, and the date was set for the wedding. But he died too in the same way.

Then the third son said he'd marry the Ottawa girl, but he too died as the others had done.

The fourth son said he'd marry the girl and the time was set, but he died too. So did the fifth and sixth sons. The seventh son said he'd try it. He was the last son left, but he died too. So nobody got the girl.

The Ottawas found out about this much later at Haskell Institute. Some Ottawas saw an old woman in a blanket who looked like someone they knew. They said, "*kegagonɛstagona*" (I almost know you). She answered them in Ottawa and told them the story.

This is a true story, not a made-up story.

Mkkwániwi (Louis Bear or Louis of the Bear Clan)[66]

Mkkwániwi was my grandfather and also Fred's. He was a great hunter, a chief, and knew a lot about medicines. He was called Mkkwániwi because of his power over the bears. He could go to a bear's den and call to a bear to come out. The bear would come out! He belonged to the bear totem.

Mkkwániwi's father died when he was a boy, and his mother remarried. His step-pa didn't like him, so he went to live with his grandparents. To prevent his having colds in the winter, his grandma used to cut a hole in the ice and make him run to it and dive into the cold water. She made him do this three times. His grandma stood with a poker to keep him from getting too near the fire.

Mkkwániwi also used to say that you should get a snake, a green snake, as green as grass. He would pick up the snake and bite it. He said the slime on the snake protected your teeth. If you do this, your teeth will always remain sound. If snake poison got in your teeth, it didn't harm you, but would anyone else you bit. Girls used to do this too and they had a wonderful set of teeth. Skeletons show this. If a boy refused to marry a certain girl, she'd bite his face. The mark on him would show that he had lied to some girl. It spoiled his looks.

Mkkwániwi told me that Indians had stuff they put on arrows that caused hemorrhage.

When he was a boy of twelve, he went to a little lodge to fast. He dreamed of his future life and saw an old man with a long beard. The man looked at him a long time and smiled at him. He had white hair and a wrinkled face. The man looked familiar. It was himself. Because of this, Mkkwániwi always said that he would have a long life. (He died at about 86 year in 1910 at the home of Fred Ettawageshik's parents in Harbor Springs.)

Mkkwániwi was great hunter and was very strong. He once grappled with a deer, got it by the horns, and succeeded in throwing it to the ground and killing it with his knife. He could also call the bears from their dens. He shot lots of bears—that's why he was called Mkkwániwi, Louis Bear. He used to talk about a bear called *giẑéko*, a running bear that stood up when it ran. It was the same color as a brown bear, only bigger. Mkkwániwi said it broke off branches and sat on them. It would follow a person.

Mkkwániwi was once hunting at Roscommon. There were two dogs with his hunting party. They camped at a spot where there was hemlock flat above them. They had just untied their horses at a spring when the dogs started to chase something. The dogs chased the animal or whatever it was for a way and then it turned and came toward them. The dogs stopped a couple of hundred feet from the hunters. Someone suggested taking a light to see what the dogs had cornered. So a couple of fellows went. They found a porcupine up in a tree. Whatever the dogs had been chasing had run across the path of the porcupine and then the dogs came and the porcupine went up into the tree. So the dogs stopped and barked at the porcupine. Mkkwánıwi always said that porcupine had outrun the dogs!

Mkkwánıwi's brother died in the spring of his life by sudden death. He was buried somewhere here (at Harbor Springs) or at Seven Mile Point. Everyone said that he was a victim of the *mkkwábomosę* (bear walk or sorcerer). The *mkkwábomosę* will go to the grave of his victim, take the heart or tongue, and preserve it. If they didn't do this, they died themselves. ("I don't believe in bear walking," Joe said.)

So Mkkwánıwi selected some men friends and relatives to watch the grave for eight days to prevent this. During the fourth day and night they almost fell asleep. It seemed like the person who killed him wanted to get to the body and was making them sleepy. The eighth day and ninth night was the worst. It was very, very hard to keep awake. They would get up and keep moving all night long. The *mkkwábomosę* was making sounds in a peculiar way.

Some people on Seven Mile Point did the killing. A suitor of a girl in the family heard the conversation of these people by accident.

One night later at Burt Lake (where Mkkwánıwi lived), Mkkwánıwi told his wife and daughter, "We don't sleep tonight. There's someone coming." The same people were coming for him because he guarded his brother's grave. There was a fire in the log house—you could see the door in the light of it. My father, who was about five or six, slept between his parents. He said he could see the door open a little—then a little more. A figure stuck its head through the door. It looked like a dog.

Mkkwánıwi was not asleep, but he felt paralyzed. Finally he managed to move his big toe. The dog was staring at him. When he moved his toe that person who looked like a dog saw him moving his toe. When Mkkwánıwi moved both feet, the dog back out. When it was out of sight, Mkkwánıwi got up quick. He got his gun that he always kept over the door and had loaded. He looked out the door and saw the dog. It might have been a man in a dog's skin.

Mkkwánıwi had a pig pen and there was a road leading up hill from it. The dog was on this road. Mkkwánıwi shot at the dog, but his aim was too low. Then he took out after him. Some ways up the trail a tree had blown down. The dog paused there and made a noise like man—I remember that tree. He got by the tree before Mkkwánıwi could get his hands on him, but Mkkwánıwi told him, "By gol, I'll get you if you ever come back again!"

After that they were afraid of Mkkwánıwi, that bunch. A short time later that whole family died off, one right after another.

Mkkwánıwi at Sleeping Bear Point[67]

Once when Mkkwánıwi was a young man he was going south for the winter hunting with his grandparents and some others in canoe. They were caught in a dreadful storm on Lake Michigan. Their canoe had a sail on it and the wind which came up was turning the canoe about like a top. Huge waves were dumping water into the canoe. Mkkwánıwi dipped water from the canoe, the front man paddled, the back man steered.

Suddenly his grandma, who acted as captain, cried out, "*Niwi, waganédiš*" ("Louis, What is it?"). She was looking toward the shore, where she seemed to see some Indians. Then his grandma said to him, "Take heart! You will soon be there safely!"

She had a vision and it came true. For the canoe finally was washed up safely on the beach near the Sleeping Bear sand dune. There were no Indians, but they found several *waganóganan,* the temporary framework for houses that could be used by any Indians.

So they stayed there a while and Mkkwánıwi decided to try to climb Sleeping Bear. It is very high and very hard to climb. The Ottawas believed that anyone who could climb to the top of Sleeping Bear, from the side of the dune facing the lake, would have a long life. There are odd-shaped stones at the top that the Indians think are magic. Mkkwánıwi climbed Sleeping Bear, but he didn't take any of the stones at the top. He had his bow and about a dozen arrows. He had a difficult time, clinging to the hanging bushes, but he finally made it. It was so high that Mkkwánıwi couldn't shoot an arrow to the bottom of it. The arrow only went half-way down. He tried all his arrows and he was strong.

Mkkwánıwi and the Murder Trial at St. Joseph[68]

Now I am going to tell another story about the Ottawas when they were going to their winter quarters in the south in the fall. The reason that I want to tell about this Mkkwánıwi is that he was raised the old Indian way.

Well, once Mkkwánıwi was going with the Ottawas in the fall to the St. Joseph region to hunt. When they arrived there, they heard about an Indian trial that was to take place. Some Indian there had killed another Indian of his own blood. He did not mean to kill him. The two Indians got to fighting and one struck the other too hard with his knife and he died. Well, so this Indian he was arrested. He killed a man of his own blood.

So about the time the Ottawas arrive, it seems those who are already there are going to try this Indian. Well, they all came together in one spot, when they arrived there at their winter quarters, at the place where the trial was to be. It was too small a place for all the Indians, so they said to clear away more ground so they would have enough room to sit down and listen to the trial of the murderer.[49]

Mkkwániwi at Burt Lake[50]

At the green corn husking one year, each man had to tell a story. My grandad told this story. First you should know that Michigan was almost uninhabited then. Detroit was just mushrooming out.

One old man who had hunted many places told a story. He said that there used to be elk and wild turkey and plenty of other species of game. This old man said he was never scared in his life, though he was often alone because he was a hunter and trapper.

Then it was up to my granddad. He said he made his living by hunting and trapping in his younger days. He once had a trap-line from Indian River to Mullet Lake. He trapped otter, fisher, and marten because they were the prettiest animals. There was no sale for beaver and muskrat then.

The Indians at the mouth of Indian River had built a log cabin in case of a storm, so they could stay in it for shelter. Anyone was welcome to use it. It was just a log house.

One time late in the fall, my granddad had picked up his traps and had loaded them and his furs in his canoe. He came down the river and there was a north wind blowing. He could have crossed over to the Indian village at the end of Indian River, but he decided to stay at the point (where the log shelter was) because it was too rough.

He went into the pine forest and gathered dry limbs for a fire. It was becoming dark and the heavy sea seemed never to cease. He built a wind break. He always carried a bear robe, so he got it from his canoe and made a bed of it. He made his evening meal and afterwards sat down to smoke.

It was getting dark, awful dark. Every now and then, Mkkwániwi threw wood in the fire. The night wore on. He was becoming uneasy (*mansosagana*). He got up and walked around the shelter, but he couldn't see anyone. He went back and lit his pipe, but he couldn't sit still. Something was "crowding" him. He had never felt this way in his life.

He said, "I will take the windbreak down," because the fire was an attraction that could be seen a long way.

There used to be a marsh there with cattails and high grass. Mkkwániwi went in the marsh across the river in his canoe. He had an old muzzle-loading rifle with him. He waited but nothing showed up. It seemed like hours. Finally he felt better and slept as he sat in his canoe.

"When I woke up," Mkkwániwi said, "it was daylight. First thing I thought, I'm going back to the log house."

He went back across the river to the log house. Where the beach was smooth, he found all kinds of moccasin tracks, cut different on the soles (from Odawa moccasins). These men had come after he went to sleep. Everywhere he had gone in the woods, they followed his tracks, but the tracks always went back to the log house. They couldn't figure out where he was. They had finally given up.

Tales of the Waters, Soil, and Beasts[51]

The proximity of water was an important feature in determining Indian home sites, not because of the scenery but because of the food supply in the form of fish, the attraction of game, aquatic fowl, and other birds, and transportation facilities. The waters could be dangerous as well as beneficial. The Great Lakes particularly could be awesome by their expanse and depth and could be menacing during a storm. It is no wonder that much belief and ritualism centered on the waters and evoked monsters of the air and the deep.

Many Anishinaabe legends have been told and retold since the days of the first white immigrants. Their distribution and variations have been studied by Jane Ettawageshik. However, a few tales outside of her realm of the Odawa are told here in the words of the narrators, some of which have been often repeated and some of which are less well known. The first one is a creation legend reminiscent of the seventeenth-century story of spontaneous human origin from the foam and sun at Mackinac (Kinietz 1940, 299). It was recorded by Anthony Chingman (Chinginushcum, Fast Runner), an Odawa related to the Kishigos of Harbor Springs, but resident in DeWitt, just north of Lansing.

People Arise from the Waters and Discover Fire[52]

Indians recently discovered themselves here in America. They didn't know what land it was or where they were. They were standing on the shore of an ocean. It was kind of sandy, the shore. They were standing in the sand and the sand covered their feet and came clear up to their ankles. They finally worked themselves loose and walked around. That's where their mind started. They remember that far back. These people were full-grown; there were no children. They began to move around and walk around the shore where they were.

Finally they were just about gettin' sick, didn't feel good. They began to wonder what they were goin' to do. Then a voice came to them and said they should get a certain bird. They look around and see all kinds of animals and all kinds of wild game there. So they hunted this bird and they found it. Well, they didn't know how to kill a bird. They finally smothered it to death in order to eat that bird. They try to eat the bird, but it didn't taste good. So they gave up on the hopes of eatin' for a while.

They just got around to wondering what they were going to do. Then the voice came to them and told them to go to a certain tree. There'd be dry limbs there. When they got the limbs they must place two limbs on the ground cross-ways. Then they followed the instructions closely and brought them limbs back. They set them on the ground and set them cross-ways. Then they sit there and watch, to see what was goin' to happen. Finally they got impatient.

Finally they took these two limbs they had and rubbed them together. They felt at them, they was gettin' hot. So they kept on doin' that. Finally they got smoke out of them. Then they rubbed a little faster and then they got a blaze. That's how they built their first fire. Then they cooked this bird that they couldn't eat before.

Many are the beliefs about monsters living under water or in bogs, particularly the Great Serpent. They were conquered by thunders who in many ways benefited man, despite the terrors of wind and lightning (Hinsdale 1925, 24–25). Here is an unknown legend.

The Serpent at Manidu Island[53]

Manidu Island or Devil's Island is beyond the point of Keweenaw Peninsula. Long time ago when Indians used to fish and hunt there, when they passed between the mainland and the island, someone would disappear. For years people were afraid to go across. Going from village to village, some never reached there.

A serpent lived on this island, called Manidu or Devil.[54] There was a passage between the island and the mainland, a tunnel. There is a swamp on the island; if you walk on it, it shakes as far as you can see. They claim that's where the serpent lived.

After the Indians knew what was harming them, they had a big feast, they called the doctors together. They decided the only thing that could kill this was thunder. They had a big feast to the thunder. The storm chased the serpent into the island, it went into a cave. Lightning chased and killed him. I don't know how far down it goes; the water is black, though it's Lake Superior water.

We still believe that thunder kills snakes; also fast animals like a weasel, it has to hide when it's lightning. We don't offer tobacco to the thunder, but we've seen people do it. Old people on Lake Superior, when there was a thunderstorm, threw tobacco on the water.

All writers on the Anishinaabeg have similar tales. Fred Ettawageshik and Eli Thomas have special versions. Thomas also can tell about beliefs and incidents of the present day. Here are several stories of his and also one in which Eddie Jackson, a seventeen-year-old youth, joined during their Ann Arbor stay in November 1953.

Thunders Destroying Serpents[55]

Eli Thomas: Now, long time ago you know about the thunders. When a thunderstorm comes from the west, we always put tobacco on the fire, always, we do that yet. And we talk to that thunders, we talk to 'em, "We-e-ll, we're glad you've come, grandfathers (we call 'em grandfathers). Protect us, give us good luck!"

So then, we believe if it wasn't for them, the underground serpents, the underwater serpents would come up. They could go all over, they'd come out. We still believe that they kin come out. If we don't have no thunderstorm, they'd come out. According to our legends what the great ancestors been tellin', some day they're going to come out and they're going to be on the ground.

There, west of Mount Pleasant, they captured a thunder. The thunder and that big snake, they fight. The big snake got the best of that thunder, so he took him under there, on that little lake west of Mount Pleasant called Cold Water Lake. When it's going to storm, we could hear that roar, some roar like a thunder underground. He's in there yet.

Gertrude Kurath: How do you say "underwater monster"?
E.T. *Mishiginebik*, big snake. The snake has horns on it, just like a deer.
G.K. How do you say "underwater snake"?
E.T. *Namiking*, under water, under the earth. Could be a big snake, as big as a wash tub maybe. They're long, maybe forty feet long. They have horns on their head. They seen them in the lakes, dangerous lakes, some places they seen them, but not to be seen every day.

There are some lions underground too. They don't come out till later on, before the end of the world. That's what our grandparents say. It's a story that the thunders won't have no more power to chase them back, so that will be real close to the end.

G.K. Do the Indians still believe it?

E.T. They were quite a prophet people. That was a prophecy, not religion, that's what's going to happen.

The thunderstorm, we call it an electric storm. We don't know nothing about it. They say that hot air and cold air come together and make it lightning. No, we don't believe it thataway yet. That's how far they go in college education. We don't believe it.

We still put tobacco on the fire when a storm goes by. We still believe that will protect us from those animals, they won't come out of the ground, they're just like lambs, they won't hurt nobody.

G.K. You're not afraid of the thunderstorm?

E.T. Oh, no.

G.K. What does it look like?

E.T. They're big birds, *nimikí or binéš*. *Binéš* means "big bird."

G.K. Tell me about the time you were picking blueberries.

E.T. I strongly believe that the thunders are taking care of us yet. I seen a lot of rattlesnakes that time. The clusters of them berries were about an inch and a half thick. All I had to do was scoop them in a pail, and the pail filled in no time. Nice day, nice sunshine, no clouds no place. I was pickin' berries. Pretty soon I heard a noise in the front of me in the brush. I paid no attention. I seen them gettin' ready to snap. I said, "Now, snake, don't do that. I just want to pick berries." Pretty soon I heard one on the other side of me and on the other side too. Pretty soon I heard them all around me. Then all at once I heard that thunder roar and it poured right down—what they call a cloudburst. We didn't see no clouds no place to warn us that it's going to storm. So that's protection.

G.K. What do you call a rattlesnake?

E.T. *Mœdəwœwœ.*

G.K. And a rattle?

E.T. *Mœdəwœwœ.* That's a rattle or a rattlesnake.

Eddie Jackson: There's an underwater monster up there in that there school section near Grayling. Kids were swimmin' out there one time. Folks seen somethin' comin' close to shore. There was no breeze to blow it into shore. The kids saw it was a monster.

G.K. Did it eat the kids?

E.J. No. My brothers and sisters all went out there. They took them home to my grandmother. They don't like kids to go swimmin' there.

G.K. Where is that?

E.J. School section. They've got a tourist camp out there.
G.K. Do the tourists go swimming there?
E.J. O yea, I guess they told them, but they wouldn't believe it anyway.

Eddie, quite a modern youth, is fond of animals, as are many of his friends. He proposed an interview on Ojibwe animal names. He told about his hunting expeditions near Houghton Lake, for rabbits, deer, and black bears. He is also fond of fishing, as are the other boys. But for him and the modern Indians it is more of a sport than a necessity.

To the aboriginal Indians, fish, birds, and game of the waters and deciduous forests were a necessity of life (Hinsdale 1925, 16). Much of their ritualism and their mythology centered on these creatures. Here are two tales by Thomas, one his version of a well-known Nenebush creation legend and one an animal origin story.

Deluge Legend of Nenebush [Nanabozho] and the Animals[56]

That's a story of a hero, a story like Noah. Nenebush he made a boat, just like Noah many years ago. He sent beaver first, he went down and down. Beaver (that's *amík*), he couldn't stand it, he came back. Then he sent that bird called andiver (*jižibe*), that's a duck, he couldn't stand it. He give up. Then he sent the loon, another bird that can dive. The loon (*amáŋ*), pretty near like a goose, a great big bird. When it's going to storm, surely enough he'll make a noise—*hooo*—because he's the one, the animal that's taking care of the underground monsters, he's a-watchin' them, that loon. Then when it's going to storm, he'll make a noise. He sent that one out but he couldn't make it. Then he sent *žeskǫ*, the muskrat. He said, "Muskrat, you go down, see what you can make of it." *Žeskǫ* went down, down, down. He reached the sand alright, and then he fainted. When he fainted he put his claws tight into that sand. Pretty soon that *žeskǫ* come up, pretty near dead. Nenebush says, "He's got some earth on his finger. We'll increase the earth so it'll be earth."

So that's why we have earth now. That's the story. That's religion, an old story.

Among the many variations of this tale, Perrot credits the Great Hare with the recreation after the deluge and mentions three animals—beaver, otter, and muskrat (Kinietz 1940, 299–301). Jones told of the loon, otter, beaver, and muskrat and centers the tale on Nanabush (P. Jones 1861, 33–35). Blackbird and Wright abbreviate to beaver and muskrat, and Ettawageshik also has his version (Blackbird 1897, 76–77; Wright 1917, 149).

Story of Porcupine[57]

Now, a long time ago there was an Indian. He lived in the woods all by himself. He had an evil spirit, spirit ain't no good, that's the kind of spirit he had. He wanted to go to war all the time. So one day he got to thinking about making arrows. He made arrows all the time. Pretty soon he filled his wigwam. So then he said, "I must try my arrows." So then he took 'em outside, took a big pile, and began to shoot them up in the air one by one.

First the arrows went up in the air. And then he began to look up at the one he shot up first. Pretty soon he seen that first one he shot coming down straight at him. He made a dodge like that—"EE." Another come—"EE." Another one—"EE." I guess that's all of them. He picked up his arrows. He stooped down and one fell on his back. He began to walk on all fours. And then that poor Indian turned to porcupine.

There are relatively few tales about the plant kingdom. Though corn was raised within limitations (Hinsdale 1925, 22–24), there are several origin myths. Thomas's differs from the following story by Ettawageshik.

The Origin of Corn[58]

We have an old story that I heard from way back, how the corn originated. Now a long time ago these two people, not too old, they had a boy, about that size. They felt sorry for him and loved that boy. So this boy, he died. That was the only boy they had, these people. When they die, you can't do nothing. "We must bury him outside of our wigwam."

So they buried him. He stayed under on the west side. The lady she went up there. They fixed up that grave. One day they got up. A tiny thing come up, about this size. They looked, something come up on that grave. They fixed that. Four done come up this high. They fixed that. Some corn come up.

The legend says the man had a dream. He fasted and said, "My seed will never die." He dreamed about many people. They took the corn; it had long ears. They said, "We will not eat this corn; we will keep it and increase it." The dream came to the old man, and he said, "My son, as long as Indians live in the United States, we shall be there." That's the dream he had.

So today there's Indian corn, no matter if it's a small group of people, they have Indian corn. The farmers plant it now. I don't know how true the story is. I kind of believe it.

It is interesting that the Ojibwe tale speaks of male instead of female origin, in contrast to the Iroquoian tale. The uses and recipes of corn products are virtually the same as the Iroquoian.

Corn Soup[59]

Eli Thomas: We call this here (a white ear of corn) *saságwœmin,* Indian corn. It's all white, don't mix it up with the other; plant it alone. We braid it and hang it up. (So do the Iroquois.) We make corn soup out of it, *məndáminawok.* We pound it to a powder. We mix it with maple sugar.

Gertrude Kurath: Do you use it for special occasions?

E.T. We make hominy out of it. We take some wood ashes (nowadays they burn coal). You get some wood ashes, white ashes, you put that in there, maybe one quart, real ashes. The black will come up, scum. Stir it again till it's all mixed up. Put the corn in, maybe two quarts, cook a half hour, then you watch it. When it peels, the heart comes off of it, it's time to quit. Wash it, maybe four or five times. You cook that. Make it the goodest hominy. You can put venison in there, or maybe short ribs, pork ribs—you call it *kinipízenewok;* then you get corn soup.

This tale followed a question about a Green Corn ceremony. Said Thomas, "The Green Corn Dance, we have what we call the Green Corn Dance at the end of July, when we plant corn," and dropped the subject. He explained neither the ceremony nor the later calendar date for planting.

He and Mrs. Thomas were explicit on ordinary secular uses of corn soup but remembered little about ceremonial uses, which have become more legendary than the myths. However, Thomas has some recollections of the procedure of the Wabeno wizard society, entirely from hearsay.

"But a long time ago they (the wizards) reach into the bottom of the kettle, into the corn soup while it's boiling, put it in a dish. Now they have to have a long spoon." That was the "early dawn" dance.

Medicinal Herbs

It is difficult to decide whether the medicinal use of herbs belongs in the realm of legend, superstition, science, or religion. Perhaps it is best to say that it used to reach into all of these realms and that it was a significant stimulus to the development of songs and dances. Jane has made such a careful study of this phenomenon that her materials need hardly be supplemented. Nonetheless, the importance of the subject may warrant a few quotations from informants outside of her territory. Every Indian volunteers a few traditional remedies.

Dave Kenosha casually mentioned the use of a ground pine brew for colds—a remedy known also to the Iroquois—and a concoction from wild dogwood bark for diarrhea and women's complaints. Thomas Shalifoe, Jr., quoted wintergreen against summer complaint, birchbark extract for the cure of cancer, and squirrel tail to stop blood. The doctor chews the squirrel tail, *jidemowanuk*, and places it on the wound. This remedy saved the life of many a lumber jack within Shalifoe's memory. Thomas says, "We people modern, we don't use that medicine any more," but he well remembers a magical use of herbs.

"You've heard about witchcraft, bear walk. They have what you call the 'Kokoko' owlskin. They say you put medicine in, howl like an owl, dance around the fire four times, all at once you'll be flying. It's nothing to travel from here to Chicago."

But "the young people, they honor their old people on account of that medicine." This statement probably harks back to ancestral times when older people's authority was maintained by means of medicine power.

Tobacco

On the uses of tobacco, Eli Thomas is more explicit, though he knows of no legendary or historical accounts. To Kenneth Pike's question about tobacco, he answered, "We had Indian tobacco. I don't know whether we crossed a weed. We use regular what they plant now." And again, "He sacrifice, like putting a whole carton of cigarettes into the fire, so that he could learn. I don't know how many people could do that." He and his contemporaries know that they were important and widespread among Indians, but that tobacco and peace pipe came from another tribe. Western origins are claimed by a number of scholars, including Kurath and Fenton (1951) and West (1934).

Several vital plant products, such as maple sugar and wild rice, do not seem to be represented in legend or lore, except for a Nanabojo legend about the watering down of maple sugar (told by Fred Ettawageshik). However, the strawberry features in stories of the trip to the spirit land. Also a body of water, a river, forms an obstacle. Here is Eli Thomas's version with a somewhat perplexing prologue about a cradle.

The Strawberry on the Road to the Spirit Land[60]

Eli Thomas: Then a dream came to one person many years ago. He was carrying the little baby, maybe about walking. He had that cradle (board) with him, pulling it. He was having a time, it got stuck on the limb, he had to work it along to get it loose. He had an awful time going to the happy hunting grounds.

From then on, these people thought, "Maybe that's a bad way of getting ready." They knew that cradle was sin. Doing that to the small children, which they belonged to the happy hunting grounds anyway, but they put them in the cradle to make them straight and be big warriors. Then they stopped using that cradle

From then on, when a person dies, they always have eight days before they could send him away to the happy hunting grounds, like you and me we're going west, you're going to meet difficulties. They tell them, "You're going to cross one river. That river on the edge of it you'll see a boat. You get on there. That'll take you across."

About halfways, you'll see a great big *odę́min*. That's a heart, it's always alive. Other word we could have is a "big strawberry." *Odę́* is a heart. You stop there and there'll be a wooden spoon that you'll use to take just a little bit of that big strawberry and get filled up. From then on you'll make it across. That's how they get to the happy hunting grounds. They have to eat so they won't starve before they get there.

Gertrude Kurath: Do they get to the happy hunting ground after they eat the *odę́min*?

E.T. Yes.

G.K. The good people and the bad people, they get there just the same?

E.T. They never talked about the bad people. Only they talk about the good people.

G.K. What do they find there?

E.T. They're in there for the time being, and then from there there'll be a big judgment . . . It would be a purgatory or first heaven, a paradise.

G.K. What goes on there? What do the people do?

E.T. They go out hunting. Everybody's happy.

G.K. What do you call the happy hunting ground?

E.T. *Abungíšmok.* That means, out West.

Thomas's remarks about sin and purgatory, Christian touches, have not been located elsewhere. But the *odę́min* and the river have often been mentioned (Baraga 1837, 179–83; Warren 1885, 73, 102–3; Kurath 1954a, 97–99). Generally the passage over the river is described over a rolling log (Jenness 1935, 108–9). The general attitude seems to have been one of pleasant anticipation of a land that abounds in reward (Schoolcraft 1852, 68), a land of eternal summer. In a northerly latitude it is a natural result of hard winters to conceive of heaven as a warm and sunny spot and hell as cold and icy, in contrast to the teachings of a religion derived from the Near Eastern deserts. This was noted by Baraga (1837, 181).

But the realm of Indian fantasy must be left to Jane, and these tales must remain as mere supplements to her collection and her analysis. They will conclude with an amusing variant by Eli Thomas on a familiar recent origin legend. This was never recorded but was tossed in during lunch, and it is retold in my own words. It leads into the major objective of this book, for it shows the Indian's observation of a phenomenon evident to any music investigator.

The Creator Sings for the Three Races

The Creator made men out of earth, out of clay. Now he shaped a small image of a man and put it in an oven to bake. He let it bake and meanwhile he sang a song. Then he pulled out the man, but he saw that he was still white; he wasn't done. "This will be the white man," said the Great Spirit.

Then he made another man and put him in the oven. "This time I will surely bake him long enough," he said. So he sang three songs. When he pulled out the figure, he was all black, all scorched. He had roasted too long. "This will be the black man," said the Creator.

He decided to try again and made another figure. This time he sang two songs and when he pulled out the man, he was just right, nice and brown, not too light and not too dark. So the Creator was pleased. "This will be the red man, the Indian," he said. "These will be my people."

So that is why the different races have different colors. That is also why the white man cannot remember and invent songs as well as the Indian or the black man. And that is why the black man is the best singer in the world, because the Creator sang three songs while he was baking. But the Indian too learns a song right away and remembers many, many songs from way back, while the white man has to practice and use a sheet of paper with notes on it to remember his songs.

Story of a Deer[61]

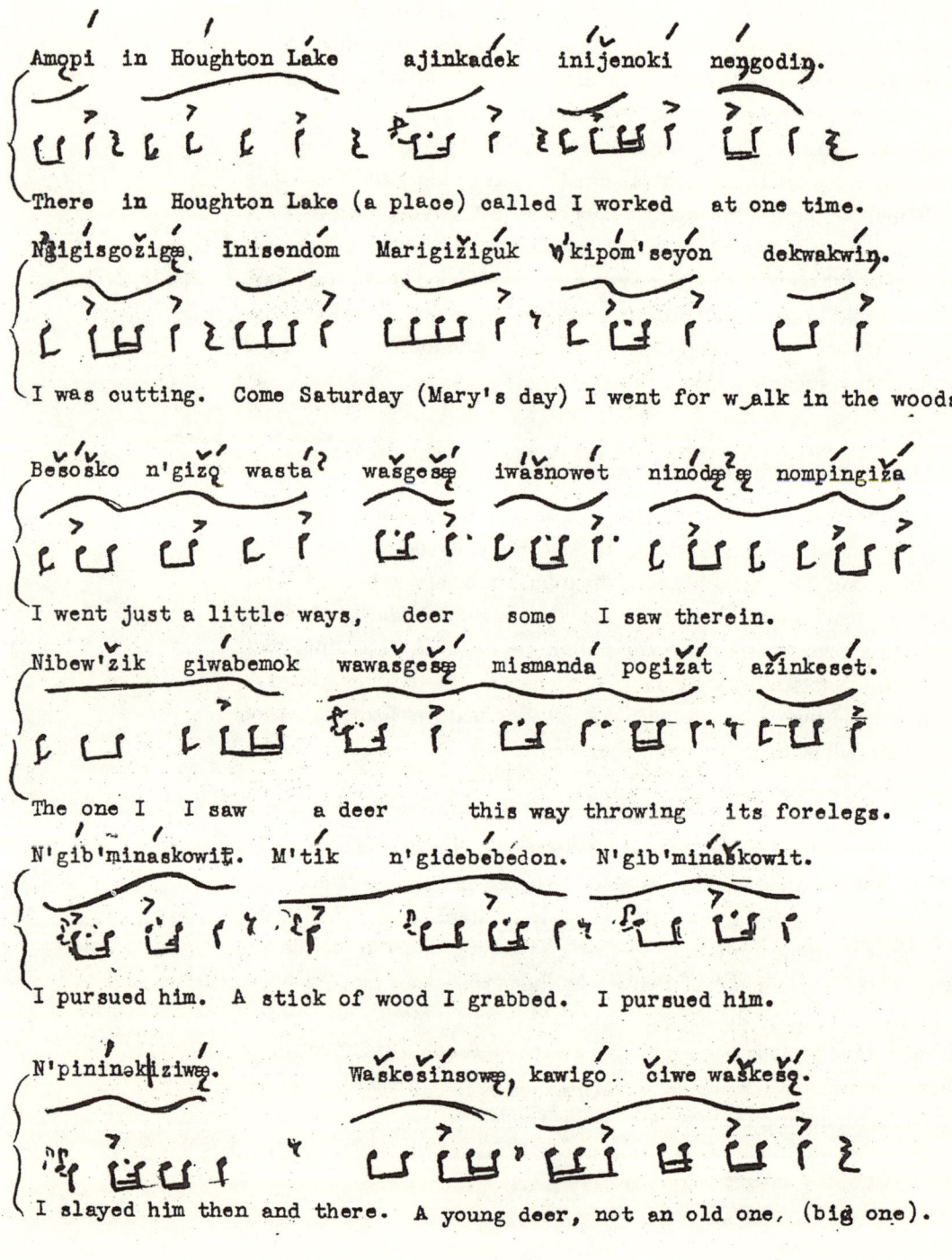

Amopi in Houghton Lake ajinkadek inijenoki nengodin.
There in Houghton Lake (a place) called I worked at one time.

Nāigisgozigæ. Inisendom Marigiziguk n'kipom'seyon dekwakwin.
I was cutting. Come Saturday (Mary's day) I went for walk in the woods.

Besosko n'gizo wasta? wasgesæ iwasnowet ninodæ nompingiza
I went just a little ways, deer some I saw therein.

Nibew'zik giwabemok wawasgesæ mismanda pogizat azinkeset.
The one I I saw a deer this way throwing its forelegs.

N'gib'minaskowit. M'tik n'gidebebedon. N'gib'minaskowit.
I pursued him. A stick of wood I grabbed. I pursued him.

N'pininekiziwæ. Waskesinsowæ, kawigo ciwe waskesæ.
I slayed him then and there. A young deer, not an old one, (big one).

Miwæ iziwæ n'gib'g'konok. Gwan mino'odæ.

So there I skinned it.   Liver, also heart.

Miwæ nki'izayo in housetrailer. N'gijibekwæ:, geigate n'giminiwisid'n.

So I went to a housetrailer. I cooked it, ineed I ate well.

Anomiyo gomanda gi'izuwewet monda Mt. Pleasant enikayo.

Very recently   this happened over there Mt. Pl. way.

Keget izayo miwæ gib'mensək waškešæ. N'gibimoče mena:skewa,

Indeed thus   I killed a deer.   I ran   after him.

N'giga:zedeb'gena:mok m'tik. Manenet pogizat azinkezet.

I managed to strike him with a club. That way throwing his forelegs.

N'gidebkino migatpenenək iziwe waškešæ. Geiget n'giminiwisid'n.

I managed to strike   slayed him there, the deer. Indeed I ate well.
him,

♩ = 120.

Translation by Fred Ettawageshik

Interpretation

CHAPTER 10

Interpretation

❧ As an editor working from the perspective of the twenty-first century, I find this is a curious and difficult chapter. The authors constructed the chapter as a kind of yardstick of Anishinaabe tradition against which to measure the extent and nature of culture change documented in the preceding chapters. The chapter was drafted by both authors, with the exception of the "Conclusions" section, for which Kurath alone was responsible. In effect, much of the chapter complements chapter 8 on indigenous lore, as it presents a miscellany of more overtly religious beliefs and ceremonial practices from the Anishinaabe past. The authors glean their "data" for this effort from references in ethnographic and missionary sources on Odawa and Ojibwe ceremonial traditions, a move that frankly is problematic, since missionaries and ethnographers documented traditions that were already registering change in light of contact with Europeans, their trade goods, their religion, their music, and their microbes. The reader also can discern in this chapter another difficulty of trying to isolate such a yardstick outside of history, for the authors make numerous references to contemporary Anishinaabe circumstances that work against the authors' comparative aims.

In light of these problems, it is perhaps unsurprising that the central claims made by the authors in the concluding remarks of the chapter and book are generally unsupported by the body of the book. Their central claim is that "aboriginal religion" was by then "only a memory" but that in the realms of "sorcery" and "herbal medicine" the "old religion is maintained." Surely in the 1940s and 1950s many of the old ceremonial complexes had been successfully suppressed by overt policies and subtler processes of assimilation and missionization over the previous hundred years. But from the perspective of the twenty-first century, after thirty years of dramatic spiritual and cultural resurgence of Anishinaabe traditions, the authors' claims are misleading. And this is ironic, because the authors clearly would have been delighted to have been proved wrong about the end of Anishinaabe religion. One could envision Gertrude Kurath and Jane Ettawageshik as two smiling ancient women in lawn chairs at a contemporary Midéwiwin ceremony. What's more, the conclusions seem to obscure the ways in which the body of their research on practices of dance, song, and storytelling continue to carry on Anishinaabe tradition, albeit in modified form. How are we to read this chapter then?

I would suggest we can square the authors' mid-twentieth-century observations and conclusions and bleak prognostications about the future of Anishinaabe culture by critically examining the way the authors use the concept of religion. It is clear from what follows that religion for the authors is fundamentally about beliefs and that the system of aboriginal Anishinaabe beliefs had given way to a Christian theology. Given this posture, the authors must interpret the persistence of the many practices—singing, dancing, healing, etc.—as hollow, formal, habitual practices that no longer give reliable expression to an intact system of aboriginal belief.

What if we were to rethink the priority of religious practices, though? Contemporary religious studies scholarship has emphasized that outward practices need not be seen simply as following from or expressing inner beliefs or emotional states. Often they are prior to those inner beliefs and emotional states, and this is particularly true of indigenous or primarily oral religious traditions. Making room for this possibility, we are better situated to appreciate the significance of the persistence of Anishinaabe practices associated with the sacred, and perhaps to see how they can provide the infrastructure for the resurgence of the belief systems two decades later. This is hardly mere theoretical speculation about the nature of religion. It helps retool the way we imagine the Anishinaabe tradition, which Anishinaabe people hasten to point out is no religion but rather a "way of life," a set of practices that are informed by beliefs but that include the material concerns of economic, political, medical, and ecological life as well as the spiritual. One could observe, for example, that the Midéwiwin ceremonial complex or other facets of the Anishinaabe way that outsiders have understood as religious phenomena were fundamentally concerned with "healing" and not solely matters of a "Great Tradition" concerned with universal, otherworldly, spiritual matters.

Thus readers are advised not to accept the authors' conclusions that religion was only a memory by 1950 and that only traditions of healing remained intact, for practices of healing, and other practices recognizing sacred power and bringing it to bear in life (what the authors unfortunately label "sorcery" and "superstition"), had always been the warp and woof of Anishinaabe religion.

Interpretation

The aboriginal religion is to a great extent only a memory among the Odawa today. The important manidos or spirits are still known by name. Their nature and characteristics can be described. But they have been almost completely supplanted by the Catholic God, the devil, the saints, and the angels. The dualism inherent in seventeenth-century Odawa religion has been emphasized and focused on God and the Devil; animism has been virtually lost in favor of a belief in omnipresent God.[1] In the chapter 5, we have shown how most of the old ceremonies have been discarded or made to conform as much as possible to Christian holy days.

In two realms of thought and practice, however, much of the old religion is still maintained: sorcery and herbal medicine. A third category might be superstition, though what has survived often carries no more weight than that in the action of a white person who knocks on wood to avert bad luck.

In the seventeenth century the Odawas, like other Anishinaabe people, believed in a great, universal power, or manido, which manifested itself in lesser manidos. Like a coin, the power in the universe had two sides, good and evil, and by his actions man called forth one side or the other. Through fasting and ritual acts, the intentions of a particular manido or of the universal manido might be revealed to man, who must then take the course prescribed for him. The spirit seen in visions induced by fasting usually became the personal manido of the supplicant. This was particularly true of the manido seen during the puberty fast, which lasted anywhere from four to ten days and was required of both boys and girls.

Each person acted individually in his relations with the manidos, but there were some men and women who might be especially chosen by a manido or manidos to carry out their wishes. These men became the priests of the Midéwiwin, the "jugglers" of the shaking tent, the seers and the medicine men and women. They also became great war chiefs or hunters or fishermen. In fact, anyone who distinguished himself for some reason in his tribe was thought to have received his power from his manido.

But the manidos did more than endow the Indian with power for its own sake, for the good and great manidos also gave him his moral code, his spiritual and emotional release, and offered him as it were his key to the natural order of the universe. Living as he did a rough and primitive life in the forests and swamps, the manidos spoke to him in terms of the out-of-doors. Ancient myths tell how Nanabojo, the great hunter and fisherman, commanded the Odawa to be generous and hospitable, not to be greedy, and to honor one's family. Blackbird adds a number of additional moral precepts of the Odawa, listing altogether twenty-one of them. They include all of the Christian Ten Commandments and a number of others having to do mostly with kindness, generosity, and cleanliness (Blackbird 1897, 103–5).

Since there was no Bible and no well-organized religion, each Indian was more or less free to interpret for himself what he learned from his elders through talks, speeches, and mythology. In fact, he was encouraged to "get religion" himself through visitations of the manidos in dreams and visions. It must have been somewhat comforting to believe, in lieu of our concept of God, that for each and every Indian—no matter how impoverished, ill, or poor in spirit—there was a manido or guardian spirit who would throughout his life offer practical advice in hunting and warfare as well as in more spiritual matters! It is no wonder that in several of the legends recorded the importance of proper fasting to obtain a good vision is emphasized.

Because their lives were ruled by dreams and visions, there were few fixed holy days among the Odawa, Ojibwe, and Potawatomi. The sun manido was customarily honored in a long ceremony sometime in the spring or fall, when Grandmother Earth and Nanabojo were also feted in performances of the Midéwiwin and Wabeno societies. But at any time of the year, if one's manido demanded it in a vision, one had to prepare a roast in its honor and perform the dances and songs revealed by the manido. If one did not do so, failure, sickness, and even death might result.

Ritual and ceremony are described in the chapter on feasts (chapter 5), Indeed, they are thus described throughout this book, for religion cannot be separated from dancing, singing, and feasting in Michigan Indian culture.

Aboriginal Ceremonies

Great Tribal Ceremonies

- *Maple Sugar Gatherings in March.* Beggar, social dances, death feast, war preparations; Mide, Wabeno, Jesikon meetings with song and dance.
- *Sun Ceremony (Painted Pole, Sasagiwǽčigœn).* June or repeatedly during summer for each harvest? Offerings, dances, and songs by everyone; prayers of thanksgiving, feasts.
- *Special Feast for Dead (fall, after frost).* Contests, songs, dances, offerings, burials, feasts.
- *Clan Feasts.* Winter and early spring without dance? Early fall with dance?

Seasonal Ceremonies of First Fruits

- *Strawberry:* June or July
- *Raspberry:* July or August
- *Huckleberry:* August
- *Corn Husking:* September
- *Wild Rice:* August and September (Upper Peninsula only)
- *First Animal Kill:* November
- *Bear Feast:* any time in winter, especially in January
- *Animal Propitiation:* any time during winter

War Dances

Aboriginally only in warm season; after eighteenth century, any time

Pipe Ceremony

Any time

Intertribal Adoption

Any time

Family and Private Rites and Rites for Crises of Life

- *Naming:* song, dance, feast
- *Puberty dream:* song, feast
- *Boy's first kill:* offerings, song, feast
- *Courting:* song
- *Cure:* song, dance, feast, invocations, jugglery
- *Wakes:* song, feast
- *Memorial feasts:* song, dance, feast, and other features

Sacred Societies

- *Jesikon:* any time for war, drought, cure, etc.
- *Midé, Wabano:* spring and probably also fall

Ceremonial Procedure

- *Preliminaries:* invitation by messenger; food collection
- *Offering at dance place:* food, clothes, etc.
- *Song and dance:* women, men, general assembly
- *Feast:* dog meat or venison, corn soup and mush, maple sugar, wild rice

Dance and Music

Early writers do not give systematic lists, but they occasionally mention the Calumet Dance and various types of War Dances, women's dances, and the Midéwiwin. They tell of invocations to the thunder, lightning, serpents, panthers, bears, and other animals (Kinietz 1940, 287–88), and to the sun and air, which remained prominent well into the nineteenth century (P. Jones 1861, 97).

A century ago many writers reported on the prevalence of Native songs and dances. "The worship of the Great Spirit consisted mainly in singing and dancing," observed Andrew Blackbird (Blackbird 1897, 29). According to Frederic Baraga (1837, 192), "The religious customs of the Ojibwe and other northern tribes consist now in certain chants and dances." Still earlier, in 1703, Baron Lahontan said, "The Ottawa invoked divinities whenever they went out hunting, fishing, to war, or on a journey; offering them sacrifices, with ceremonies by Sacrificial priests" (Kinietz 1940, 291). Lahontan described the huge summer ceremonies. In 1626 Biard made the following, more general statement: "Among the savages who had any religion, it was only a coarse fetishism, the practices of which were most commonly reduced to dances, fastings, and feasts; and these were in almost every case regulated by the dream, interpreted by the sorcerers of the tribe" (Blair 1911–12, 1: 47).

Thus dance and song were connected with every phase of life. Their precise functions are evident in a few listings of traditional repertoires. Closest to home, George Boyd, an Indian agent at Mackinaw, listed the current dances in 1822: War Dance or Strike the Post, Pipe, Buffalo, Dog, Begging Dances, Fire Dance (Wabeno), and Medicine Dance (Mide). (Kinietz 1947, 92). In less detail, Blackbird mentioned at the spring gatherings, "Medicine Dances, Fire Dances, and many other jubilant performances" as well as Ghost Dances at L'Arbre Croche (Blackbird 1897, 29). Songs and often dances featured in feasts listed by M. Edwin James and Peter Jones. Both mention the *Weendahsohwin Weekondewin* (Naming Feast), *Jeebanakawin* (Feast to the Dead), and *Ooshkenetahgawin* (the first fruits offering of the season or of a young hunter). James adds the *Metaiwekoondewin* (Medicine Feast), *Wainjetahwekoondewin* (for obtaining a dream), *Menissekoondewin* (for war), *Gitchewekoondewin* (Great Feast[2]), and *Chebahkoochegawin* (hunter's medicine bundle) (Tanner 1835, 2:344–51). Jones mentions the Midéwiwin and Wabeno and Jesikon separately, as do all writers of the period. He lists the *Sahsahgewejegun* (Painted Pole Feast), *Kahgageshee* (Crow Eat-all Feast), and *Unemoosh* (Dog Feast) (P. Jones 1861, 97).

Although the list of manidos is legion—for almost every natural phenomenon was thought to have its manido—the principal manidos and those still known by name today are described below.

Manidos and Their Worship

The Great Spirit, Gitchi Manido

There is, of course, considerable question as to whether the aboriginal Odawa had formulated their beliefs to such an extent that they arrived at the conception of the Great Spirit. Cooper has concluded that the concept of the Great Spirit was aboriginal among the Anishinaabeg (Cooper 1934); Allouez and other Jesuits generally agreed that it was not, Allouez in particular implying that the sun was the principal divinity (Kinietz 1940, 285).

In the myths and ceremonies recorded in the seventeenth century, the Great Spirit is seldom mentioned, although this power is referred to in prayers such as that given by Lahontan in connection with the Sun Ceremony (Kinietz 1940, 290–91). Later myths, obviously influenced by Christianity, depict the Great Spirit in the role of Father and Creator, like the Christian God, as in the latter part of the story of the flood, and in the legend of the "Ten Talents."

The Great Spirit, as described by Fred Ettawageshik, was "invisible, omnipresent, omnipotent." He was the creator of the universe and of the world before the flood. Other manidos, such as the sun and moon, have been given their form and function by the Great Spirit. Fred says:

> In case of a threatening storm, old Indians put tobacco or hemlock boughs in the fire. This is an offering to the manido of the wind or the snow or whatever it may be—or to the Great Spirit. The spirits or manidos are part of Gitchi Manido. They are in a subordinate position to Gitchi Manido,

who rules them. It is somewhat similar to Christianity, when one says, "God is three in one."

This controversial concept is variously interpreted. Fr. Cooper regards the Anishinaabe Supreme Being as a personal being, a supernatural force, a being who remained invisible yet has a wife and children, who is distinct from guardian spirits (Cooper 1934, 37–39). Originally God was simply "Manitu," and "Kitci Manitu" came with the missionaries. "My Father," "Our Father," "Master of Life," and "Thou Who Standest" (not used in hymns) are probably aboriginal. There is no hint of relationship to the sun or any other heavenly body. But Skinner considers the Chief of the Powers above as formerly the same as Sun and mentions that Fr. André for the Menominee replaced the image of Sun with the image of Christ (Skinner 1915, 79–80, 88–89). William Jones (1894, 190) speaks of an unsystematic belief in a cosmic, mysterious property . . . everywhere in nature. Chief Blackbird states, "Odawa and Ojibwe Indians were not what we would call entirely infidels or idolaters; for they believed that there is a Supreme Ruler of the Universe, the Creator of all things, the Great Spirit, to which they offer worship and sacrifices in a certain form" (Blackbird 1897, 14).

These differences, no doubt in part due to subjective attitudes of the writers, also certainly reflect the change that had been continuous since the seventeenth century, when Allouez stated that "the people believe that it is this God who is the master of our lives" (*Jesuit Relations,* 54:203) and when Perrot dubbed the principal divinities the Great Hare, Sun, and Devils and Ragueneau claimed that they recognized no sovereign (Kinietz 1940, 286–88). The aboriginal beliefs evidently approached Christianity closely enough for some sort of understanding and for the appropriateness of the term selected by the nineteenth-century writers; and by the time of Baraga's and Jones's translations, the concept had been sufficiently adapted for fitting inclusion in hymns under the term *Kiže Mənido.* It is likely that change is still taking place and that the faith of the older, Indian-speaking people differs somewhat from that of the youths.

The same could be said of other terms that reflect increasing analogies and that will come under more rapid scrutiny. One sometimes says "Nanabojo or Gitchi Manido." Whether Nanabojo is conceived of as the son of Gitchi Manido, like Christ is the Son of God, is difficult to say.

Fred also described how an old medicine man in fairly recent times called on the Great Spirit for rain—and got more of it than he wanted:

An old man was asked to make rain. He said he would and asked that someone go out and find him a cedar stick about two foot long that grew on the tree pointed toward the east. One was obtained from a nearby swamp, and the man took it and pointed it toward the east. He had built a fire and he stood there and said a chant of some sort and danced. Then he threw the stick as far as he could toward the east. A short time later, a great dark cloud was seen coming across the sky from the east. As the cloud got over head it began to rain, harder and harder, until there was a cloud burst and really too much rain!

Fred cannot explain the importance of the east in this story. Perhaps it helps to substantiate Allouez's contention that the Great Spirit was the sun, for the latter is commonly associated with the east in Indian belief. On the other hand, had the old medicine man heard, perhaps on his radio, that a storm was due from the east?

Mose Gibson, an Odawa from Harbor Springs, also tells about an Odawa who prayed successfully to the Great Spirit—this time for snow so the skiing would be good. Mostly, however, when Odawas speak of the Great Spirit it is in the past tense, while the Christian God is ever with them for they are devout Christians.[3]

Matchi Manido, the Spirit of Evil

Like its opposite, the Great Spirit, this all-pervading power may not be an aboriginal concept among the Odawa. It is mentioned less often even than the Great Spirit in seventeenth-century accounts. According to Fred, Matchi Manido is the invisible power of evil, whose agents are the serpents and other reptilian creatures.

The Sun, Kišis

Little memory of the sun as a powerful manido is retained today, although in ancient times the sun may have been the most important manido. Recognition of the sun manido is made in the powwows and pageants performed for tourists when Sun Dances are given and the pipe ceremony is conducted (see Gertrude Kurath's descriptions in chapter 3). It is also possible that underlying the New Year-Epiphany ceremonies and the *Tabandáŋ* feast is an indirect worship of the sun but whether this is true of the Native ceremonies any more than it is of corresponding Christian ceremonies is difficult to estimate.

The Odawa conceived of Sun as a man and of the moon as his wife or sister, although this anthropomorphic character been lost today. They were both thought to be good manidos. Schoolcraft (1848, 82–84) gives an

Odawa myth that describes the adventures of a young man who was taken to the sky during a fast by the sun's sister, the moon. He marries the moon and every day accompanies the sun on his path across the sky. Their food consists of the offerings of white dogs made by the Indians on the earth below. It was probably through this myth that the Odawa explained the custom of using white dogs as sacrifices at Sun Ceremonies. Until recently the Ojibwe of Parry Island still observed the white dog feast to the sun and moon every fall (Jenness 1935, 32).

Although in later works on the Ojibwe a similar conception of the sun and moon is given (Jenness 1935, 32), earlier references often speak of the sun and moon as material objects. Peter Grant wrote that the sun and moon are metal and are carried by a manido upon their courses (Kinietz 1947, 154). There is also a similar reference in Schoolcraft's *Indian in His Wigwam* (Schoolcraft 1848). One is tempted to speculate from such descriptions that the Ojibwe and the Odawa may have at one time differed in their conception of the sun and the moon. The Menominee, on the other hand, believe like the Odawa that the sun is the moon's brother and that both are shaped like human beings (Hoffman 1896, 209–10). As previously mentioned, the Menominee and the Odawa share many of the same concepts.

The manner of propitiating the sun as described in historical references is quoted in chapter 5 and in Gertrude's description in chapter 3 of the modern Odawa recreation of the Sun Ceremony. The sun was also one of the more important Odawa totems (Michelson 1911, 338; from Gatschet's notes).

Sun Ceremony[6]

The principal ceremony was probably held in the spring in conjunction with medicine rites, the Feast of the Dead, and occupational rites such as the Maple Sugar Dance. Jenness (1935, 32) describes a Sun Ceremony for the Ojibwe on Parry Island, which is held in the autumn and includes the sacrifice of white dogs to the sun and moon, a practice of the Odawa also.

The sun in its course around the cardinal points has motivated the Great Lakes choreographic patterns. He was the great patron of war, commander of the thunderbirds for the Ojibwe (Copway 1851, 30), Potawatomi (Blair 1911–12, 2:291), and Odawa (Blair 1911–12, 1:48). "Their most intelligent priests tell us, that their forefathers worshiped the sun; this luminary was regarded by them . . . as the symbol of divine intelligence, and the figure of it was drawn in their system of picture writing, to denote the Great Spirit . . . in the Medicine Dance, and the Wabeno Dance," Schoolcraft wrote (Schoolcraft 1848, 204). He was worshipped by the Huron (Barbeau 1915,

273) and the Menominee, who identified the sun with the Great Spirit, *Matč Hawatuk* (Skinner 1915, 79; Curtis 1952, 178), or with the East God in the Wapuno rite (Densmore 1932, 41ff.).

The Odawa reflect worship in their surviving Sun Dance as well as in the direction of dance movement. Writing about the Anishinaabeg of Manitoulin Island, Jenness says that the Great Sprit arranged the course of the sun, and he made it "travel from east to south, and south to west and he intended that everything should go in the same direction. Medicine and laymen alike must follow the course of the sun in dancing" (Jenness 1932, 30). They must gather plants and pass the pipe sun-wise. But sorcerers and evil spirits go the other way. Kenosha confirms this theory.

Moon (Night Sun)

What I have said above concerning the sun also applies to the moon, for the two were linked in Odawa conception. Aside from the idea that certain crops should be planted during certain phases of the moon, nothing at all remains of ancient beliefs concerning the moon. There are also several superstitions about the moon and stars that could conceivably hark back to old religious practices.

Earth, Aki

The earth is referred to as "my grandmother" (*nókəmis*) and is thought to have given birth to all plants and trees, except the poisonous ones. She is honored in the pipe ceremony and was also important in the ritual of the Midéwiwin at one time (Hoffman 1891, 85–86). Nanabojo's grandmother or mother in some Anishinaabe myths is said to be the earth, and this may also be true of the Odawa, though the only myth I recorded describing the birth of Nanabojo has not as yet been translated. *Aki* is still honored by Michigan Indians. When an Odawa is gathering herbs for his medicines, he always leaves a tobacco offering for the earth, saying "*Nókəmis, bindàkonín!*" ("Grandmother, have a smoke!"). According to Fred, this is still done today. Fred says it does not matter what kind of tobacco is used—it could even be a cigarette.

Cardinal Directions

Little description of the four cardinal directions is given by the Odawa. They figure in the pipe ceremony and probably formerly played a part in other ceremonies. Winds and directions also are honored in the offerings of tobacco and hemlock boughs made by modern Odawas when a bad storm is brewing. Gertrude Kurath reports that Odawa dances are always performed in a clockwise direction, indicating that some directions were more important than others.

Nanabojo is often identified with the east and in the myths describing the origin of the Ojibwe Midéwiwin. He is said to have procured the magic *megis* shell in the east. As the god of the east, Nanabojo is also sometimes identified with the sun in Anishinaabe thought. The Wabeno cult, too, must have been connected with the east because of its name, but the modern Odawa remember nothing of this.

Joe Chingwa said that the south wind was a brother of Nanabojo but could not describe him. However, Jenness reports that an aged Odawa living on Parry Island told him that Shauwanigizik (Southern Sky) was the originator of all totems. This "appears to have been an Odawa tale not current among the Ojibwe and Potawatomi of Georgian Bay," Jenness writes (Jenness 1932).

> Shauwanigizik, who created the birds, the animals, and the trees, sent them to bless the Indians, and those who were blessed by the bear, the caribous, etc., took these animals as their totems. Indians who were blessed by the hemlock adopted the eagle because that bird constantly nests in the hemlock tree; and for a similar reason those who were blessed by the cedar became the squirrel clan. The children of these early Indians inherited their fathers' totems. It was the sun who bestowed on each clan its special style of face painting. Hence in life the Indians painted their faces to please the sun; but they decorated the faces of the dead with their clan paintings to please the sun's sister, the moon. (Jenness 1932, 9)

"The Happy Hunting Ground" is thought to be situated in the west, and it is here that Jibiabos, Nanabojo's younger brother, rules as chief of the dead. Nanabojo is also said to have gone west when he departed, promising to return.

Joe Chingwa said that the north manido wore a fur robe and snowshoes and that the snowshoes could be heard making a squeaking noise when he walked. North was generally considered a bad manido because he brought cold and storms, while east, west, and south were thought to be good manidos.

Of the cardinal points, west, Schoolcraft wrote, "called Kabeun, has priority of age. The East, North, and South are deemed to be his sons, by a maid who incautiously exposed herself to the west wind" (Schoolcraft 1848, 215). The Midé revered four manidos, representing the four points among the Ojibwe and the Menominee (Densmore 1913, 143; Hoffman 1896, 92). This tribe associated many animals with the four directions: the bear, great owl, fox, and others with the east; the otter with the south; the eagle and thunderbird with the west (Hoffman 1896, 90–92).

The Michigan Calumet Dance, like all pipe invocations, addresses the four winds and heaven and earth. According to Eli Thomas, "When he points north, it's the north wind, it brings nice tracking. The east wind brings nice rain; the south wind brings nice warm weather. We have a lot to do with the wind. *Abungismowanodin* comes from the spirit land, it brings nice weather." This symbolism combines with the former belief in the sacred character of fire. "One of the most curious opinions of this people is their belief in the mysterious and sacred character of fire . . . Their national pipes are lighted with this fire. It is symbolical of purity" (Schoolcraft 1848, 205–6).

Tobacco offerings and smoking were featured in all ceremonies from Allouez (Kinietz 1940, 292) to Peter Jones (1861, 114), in invocations, dance, councils, witchcraft, and adoptions (Hinsdale 1925, 104) and in Woodland and Plain to the distant Crow (Lowie 1935, 269–73). "Every tribe of Indian far and near deposited their pipe of peace with the head chief of the Odawa nation as a pledge of continual peace and friendship. Every pipe of peace contained a short friendly address if there was an outbreak among these tribes . . . a general council would be called and the pipe of peace would be lighted up, and a short address . . . would be repeated in the council by one of the speakers and then reconciliation must be had" (Blackbird 1897, 95). In individual feuds the Michigan tribes also preferred a calumet to make peace for a wrong, a killing, etc. Gifts of guns, blankets, and horses were presented, and a "long pipe" was handed around by the medicine man, each man saying, "mesagwayuk" ("that's right") (Wright 1917, 73–74). In 1680 the Three Brothers used calumets for father-son relationships. In 1690 the Odawa sent the Iroquois redstone calumets for negotiations. In 1710 Odawa sang a song of joy at a peace pipe delegation. But no dance is reported till 1765 on the occasion of Pontiac's attempted entrance into Detroit (Kurath and Fenton 1951, 158, 166–67, 186). Whether the song and dance resembled today's, nobody knows.

Raudot's celebrated description of a Calumet Dance in 1709 probably refers to the Miami (Kinietz 1940, 346). The Michigan type of Calumet Dance is a direct development from the invocation pattern. It differs and probably always differed from the exhibitionistic type of the Central Plains—and of the Anishinaabeg across Lake Michigan, the Ojibwe, and the Menominee (Densmore 1932, 184–87, 293–96)—a type which was shared by the Winnebago (West 1934, 1:249). It also differs from the type with two or four contestants in a peculiar alternate pattern of song and movement—that of the Fox and the Lac du Flambeau Ojibwe (observed)—a type traceable to the Pawnee and Omaha and now functioning among the Iroquois as Eagle Dance (Kurath and Fenton 1951). This distinction holds for both the dance and the song.

The presentations to the sun and earth are mentioned in Marquette's famous description of the Illinois "Calumet of the Sun Dance", but the combat features are absent in Michigan (Kurath and Fenton 1951, 273). The closest analogy is to the northern Plains versions of the early twentieth century—the Blackfoot All-Smoking Ceremony with quadruple presentation to the sun (to four songs repeated four times) and the Plains-Cree invocation of the pipe keeper (Kurath and Fenton 1951, 274). The analogy extends to the steeply descending song type, although that of the Odawa is less rhapsodic than that of the northern Plains.

Nanabojo

There has been so much written about this culture hero that it seems unnecessary to describe him fully here. Suffice it to say that Nanabojo is credited with originating the earth as the Indians know it and with the transformation of various monsters into animals. He is also said to have taught the Indians all that they know and to have given them many of the material objects that figure into their culture. He is at once a god, a creative genius, a solemn judge, and the basest sort of trickster. There are still many stories told about him by modern-day Odawas.

Nanabojo seems to have been identified with the east, perhaps even with the sun. Perrot, however, spoke of the "Great Hare," who seems to have been the same character and who created the world from a grain of sand obtained by the muskrat during the flood. Perrot writes:

> After the creation of the earth, all the other animals withdrew into the places which each kind found most suitable for obtaining therein their pasture or their prey. When the first ones died, the Great Hare caused the birth of men from their corpses, as also from those of the fishes which were found along the shores of the rivers which he had formed in creating the land. Accordingly, some of the savages derive their origin from a bear, others from a moose, and others similarly from various kinds of animals (Kinietz 1940, 301).

Rasles wrote that the Great Hare left man to return to the sky, "his usual dwelling place, leaving directions that his descendants' bodies should be burned and their ashes scattered that they might more easily rise to the sky. He warned them that failure to observe this would result in the snow covering the earth and the lakes and rivers remaining frozen, whereby, not being able to catch fish, they would all die" (Kinietz 1940, 298). The hare totem was apparently the only one that burned the dead; others placed the dead on scaffolds or buried them in the ground until the time of the great Feast of the Dead when all the bones were cleaned and re-buried in a common pit. In many of the myths about him, Nanabojo is also confused with the Great Spirit. Thus in the conclusion of Fred's story about the flood, when men are created, Fred says that one could just as well substitute "Great Spirit" for "Nanabojo."

This controversial manido is mentioned in a number of present-day Odawa superstitions. He is also credited with originating the Midéwiwin, but as I have said, very little memory of this medicine society is retained today.

Thunder or Thunderers, Nimki or Mišumsinánik'

Many confusing concepts of these manidos prevail today. The thunder is at once a single manido, an invisible and powerful spirit beneficial to men and animals. But thunder also is a whole group or band of "thunderers," who are sometimes thought of as men or souls and are called *mišumsinánik'* (the grandfathers). Fred says that the thunderers are ancestors of the Odawas, who have been taken up into the sky by the other thunderers. Thus when a thunderstorm immediately follows the death of an Odawa, it is said that the thunderers have come to carry his soul to the sky. Susy Shagonaby reports that boys who used to fast at puberty were considered very fortunate if they received the thunder as a spiritual helper. Thunder sometimes appeared as a man to such persons. She says, "Only those having thunder power can see the thunder man."

But the thunderers are also conceived of as eagles or thunderbirds. No description of their appearance was given to me, except that they are large and in this guise wage an incessant war on the evil serpents.

The Menominee, too, stress the anthropomorphic character of the thunderers and think of them as ancestors whom they call "grandfathers" as well as eagles or thunderbirds. According to Densmore (1932, 6), the Ojibwe conceive of the thunderers as birds, but not as men. In this respect, the Odawa concept of the thunderers is identical with the Menominee but not with the Ojibwe. An old Odawa, Mitchell Mastaw, said regarding the thunderers:

A man was hunting by himself. He fell asleep at the bottom of a hill. Heard strange voices and shouting, so he goes up the mountain and the noise gets louder. Pretty soon he come to a big man. The man says, "Who are you?" So the hunter tells him his name and he says, "Hey, what's going on here?" "Come with me," says the big man. He leads the hunter on up the mountain and soon he saw a lot of big men. They are eating great big snakes. He is about to ask something more, but the big man says, "Now you better get out of here or you'll lose your head!" The man had seen the thunderers.

If one were to ask an Odawa today, "Do you worship the thunder?," he would, of course, say that he did not. Yet there is a feeling of kinship and even sometimes of reverence expressed in his attitude toward the thunder that is certainly not found among neighboring white people. Thunder and lightning are never feared by an Odawa. They will always point out the benefits such storms bring. Another Odawa, Betty Cooper, expressed it this way:

Thunder is the spirits of the dead—especially the first sound of thunder. The first sharp thunder in the fall is the younger spirits going back to the Happy Hunting Ground in the west. Thunder is honored by Indians.

Fred Ettawageshik elaborates on this:

Thunderers are spirits of ancestors, our grandfathers or *mišumsinánik.* Also when a man dies it is said that he joins his elders in the skies. The spirits of the dead become thunder, fish, birds. The thunderers may do harmful acts because they are displeased about something; also they may strike at times to protect the Indian.

An Indian hunter was returning home with a *máskmut* (woven basswood bag) on his back filled with game. He felt something stirring in the bag and saw a snake's head above the top of the bag. He tossed the bag on the ground some distance from him. Thunderers struck the bag and killed the snake—*nimkik giwɛbtawáwat* (thunderers struck him).

The Odawa also believed, like many Europeans, that the thunderers cast thunderbolts, which appeared in the form of stones. Regarding these *nımki wɛbčıgéwınan* (thunder things), Fred Ettawageshik says that they are "small, round stones thrown by the thunderers. During a storm when you see a flash of lightning and hear thunder crackling and something is struck, if you go out, you will find the stones twelve to fourteen inches down in the soil. If you do not hurry, the stones will disappear. The stones are jet black and some are tan."

Fred has several of these stones, which have been handed down in his family and were once carried as magic objects in ancestral medicine bags. They were identified by the Geology Department at the University of Pennsylvania as water-smoothed quartzite. In the old days there must, of course, have been ceremonies that were connected with the thunder, although I know of no descriptions that had to do with the thunder alone. In a legend told to me in Odawa by old Victoria Cooper, the thunder is credited with the origin of the naming ceremony, but unfortunately I do not have a good translation of this story. The Eagle Dances and songs performed now for tourists may have at one time been connected with the thunder, as were many of the war ceremonies. The legend of the Maskutens boy in chapter 9 describes the enmity between the eagle (thunder) and the serpent, and it is probable that the eagle referred to in the story "The Magic Arrow" is the thunder. Thunder was also a powerful Odawa totem and is still known as such by the modern Odawa.

Great Serpent, Mišiginébikʽ

About the giant, mythological serpent, Susy Shagonaby says, "there is a giant serpent called *Mišıgınébıkʽ* (big, bad snake) with a head like a horse or cow, horns, and body like a snake. Its scales are copper."

The giant serpent and all reptilian creatures who are its agents are thought to be the embodiment of evil. Susy says that the first bear walks or sorcerers obtained their power from the giant serpent, whose horns they scraped to get their medicines. The medicine was handed down, or rather sold, from bear walk to bear walk through the ages. It is the basis of all their evil doings—the "underwater panther" of the Ojibwe, Menominee, Dakota, Omaha, and Ponca.

The giant serpent is said to have been seen at various spots in the Great Lakes in stories that remind one of these of the Loch Ness sea monster. Fred connects the origin of Harbor Point, a mile-long peninsula that forms the southwest side of the harbor at Harbor Springs, with the antics of the sea serpent in a story in chapter 9. He also tells about a party of Odawas who were out on Lake Michigan in their canoe and saw the huge coppery body diving over and under the waves. The Odawas were almost overturned, for the giant serpent cast the tip of his huge tail over their canoe, scraping off several copper scales as the tail slid back into the water.

Pieces of copper, said to have come from the giant serpent, have always been prized possessions of the Odawas. Allouez mentioned pieces of copper from Lake Superior, which the Odawas kept as "household gods." They were carefully wrapped up and were handed down in families for generations (*Jesuit Relations,* 12:65–66). Fred calls these bits of copper *manido biwábık̆* (spirit copper) and says that the Indians kept them "because they were so unusual." He has a small specimen of copper, which appears to have been daubed with red ochre and is wrapped in red cloth of the period around 1800. It was carried in the medicine bag of an ancestor.

Dablon reported that the Odawas and related tribes looked on Isle Royale with awe and would not go near it. They called it *Michipotin* and said that it was a floating island, always surrounded by fog, and filled with copper. Long ago, the Indians told him, four Indians landed here. They stone-boiled some meat, and as they left, they took slabs and pieces of copper, which they found in abundance. They heard a voice say, "Who are those robbers carrying off from me my children's cradles and play things?" Some said the thunder spoke; others that it was Missibizi, the god of the waters, or Memogouissiouis, "the marine people somewhat like the fabulous Tritons or the Sirens, who always live in the water and have long hair reaching to the waist." The Indians were afraid. One of them died immediately of fright and two others died later on the return voyage. Only one reached home. He told the story and died immediately. "The savages never visited the Island afterwards" (*Jesuit Relations,* 54:155–57).

Dablon's later death among the Indians was attributed by them to the fact that he boiled "copper in a crater" (*Jesuit Relations,* 54:157). The Missibizi referred to in Dablon's story is another name for the giant serpent, who was apparently conceived of as a sort of sea tiger. The Memogouissiouis, or marine people, are unknown to the modern Odawas.

In most of the Anishinaabe myths about the flood, it is caused by the giant serpents or sea lions, who kill Nanabojo's brother. In revenge, Nanabojo kills the serpent chief and the serpents then thrash their tails around, causing the flood (Fisher 1940, 240–41). This is the version of the flood given by Fred Ettawageshik. As previously pointed out, it is only in some Odawa and Menominee myths that it is the bears instead of the serpents who kill Nanabojo's brother.

When the Odawas set out on a canoe voyage, they always threw a white dog with his legs firmly bound or some tobacco in the water as an offering to the giant serpent. This was done in the hope that the serpent would be pacified and would not cause a storm on the lake. Fred says that tobacco was still used for this purpose until fairly recent times. There were, however, no important ceremonies dedicated to the serpent, except those reputed to have been held annually by bear walks. The Snake Dance described by Gertrude Kurath may have been used at one time to appease the giant serpent, however.

It was considered bad luck for a youth to dream of a serpent during his puberty fast, and he was usually asked to continue his fast in order to obtain a better vision. Susy Shagonaby said that a youth during his fast could erase the effect of a bad vision by "scraping his tongue with a cedar stick and trying again . . . Anyone having a vision of a snake during fasting tries to get another vision, as the snake is evil. One who accepts the snake will never have any living children." The misfortune that might result from such a vision is shown in the story of Skodęs, the Maskutens boy. The enmity between the serpent and the eagle or thunder is also demonstrated in the tale.

The conception of the giant serpent is quite universal among the Anishinaabeg, all of whom tell similar stories about it. These tribes also believe that thunder is the natural enemy of the serpent. Gertrude Kurath gives some additional serpent-thunderer lore.

Snakes, lizards, toads, and other reptilian creatures are considered the agents of the giant serpent and are looked on with superstitious awe. Fred said that his father would never eat speckled trout because he imagined that they could change themselves into lizards. It seems that a resorter at Wequetonsing, near Harbor Springs, once had a pool in which he kept speckled trout. Fred's father had often observed the trout here, but one day when he looked at them he saw that the trout had started to grow legs. After this, he never ate speckled trout again. Of the magical properties of lizards, Elizabeth Kishigo says:

> My aunt once saw a lizard in her cellar, where she had gone to get potatoes. She picked it up and threw it outside, quite far off. But she was no sooner back in the cellar again than she saw the lizard. Once more she picked up the lizard by the tail and threw it outside, but when she returned to the cellar, there was the lizard again. This time she picked up the lizard and threw it into the stove. "There!" she said, "Burn up, you ugly thing. This is the end of you!" After that, she did not see the lizard again.

The magical properties of fire to defeat evil and witchcraft are mentioned in a number of similar stories. Some of these beliefs about reptiles are influenced by European ideas; others purely Indian.

Bear, Mkkwá

The bear has always been considered a mysterious animal by the Odawa. They share this belief with many other peoples, as Hallowell (1926) has shown. It was customary to apologize to the bear before killing it and to hold a great eat-all feast in its honor. Bears are associated with causes or cures of sickness to some extent and the enmity of the bear people and Nanabojo is shown in the myth "Nanabojo and His Younger Brother Fight the Bear."

The bear was one of the principal Odawa totems. Kinietz quotes Rasles as saying that the Odawa were composed of three families: "Michabou or the Great Hare, that of Namepich or the Carp, and that of Machoua or the Bear" (Kinietz 1940, 246). The Kishkakons, or Cut Tails, a division of the Odawa tribe, was said to have the bear as its totem (Kinietz 1940, 247). There are Odawas today who claim the bear as their totem. The importance of the bear in Odawa belief is demonstrated by the number of myths featuring the bear that are still told today.

Turtle, Mišiki

This odd character, which is often mocked in the legends of the Anishinaabeg, is depicted as a slow-moving bungler, often obscene, who nonetheless possesses considerable power. A few modern Odawas remember that turtle played an important part in the performances of the "shaking tent," when his squeak-voice could be heard giving messages to the bear.

Owl, Kokoko (Horned Owl)

The owl at one time was important in the Midéwiwin, medicine bags often made of its skin. Nowadays it is connected with sorcery, and children are frightened by threats of owl "getting them," just as white American and European children are threatened with the bogeyman.

Windigo

The Windigo is featured as a cannibal spirit by more northerly tribes but also is known by the Odawa. He is conceived of as a wild man who carries off children. Fred Ettawageshik says that children used to be told not to wander away at night or the Windigo would get them.

There are a number of minor manidos who were honored by the Odawa on occasion. In fact, almost everything, animate or inanimate, that was at all unusual was conceived of as a manido or as having manido. Certain lakes, hills, and other natural phenomena ware also considered manido, such as the Sleeping Bear Point. Schoolcraft mentions odd rock formations that the Ojibwe honored as manidos (Schoolcraft 1848, 292), and "Allouez saw a group of Odawas blowing smoke into an . . . image a foot high" (Weer 1940, 23).

Any thing or any animal that was odd-shaped, deformed, or thought to be manido, or was otherwise misshapen, was regarded as a bad omen if seen, for example, while on a trip. Likewise, any bad dream was an omen of misfortune and often explained the seemingly unaccountable behavior of the Odawas. Perrot, Allouez, and other seventeenth-century observers frequently mention the great influence that dreams had upon the Odawa (Blair 1911–12, 1:238; *Jesuit Relations,* 57:275). Dorson (1952), writing of the Ojibwe of the Upper Peninsula of Michigan in 1952, still found them "dream-ridden," but I have not found this to be true among the modern Odawa.

Occupational Festivals

These include maple sugar dances and animal, bird, and fish dances and songs, etc. There is so little description of such ceremonies that one can only assume that they were dedicated to one of the leading manidos. Some of them were connected with first fruit ceremonies. The dances and songs that are still remembered are purely social now.

Dances and Songs for Birds and Beasts

The preponderance of surviving animal dances and songs and the persistence of associated myths and beliefs has deep roots in the past. Animals and the hunt remain significant to many of the men but nothing compared to their aboriginal significance in dreams, social organization, shamanism, and the problem of sustenance. All observers have remarked on the concept of animals as sentient beings with souls and as supernaturals or as actors in legends (Schoolcraft 1848, 212; Kinietz 1940, 286–88; 297ff.). All writers emphasized the totemic social structure, originating perhaps in the legend of people arising from the corpses of beasts (Kinietz 1940, 301). Jenness (1935, 8) reports animal clan feasts at Manitoulin until about 1920. Many times we read of magic songs for animals; rarely can we find mention of specific dance enactments.

This lack is most conspicuous in the case of the eagle and the snake, persistently referred to since the seventeenth century and still identified in folk belief with the beneficent thunder and the malignant underwater spirits. These beliefs extended to the Huron (Barbeau 1915, 53, 115–22, 154–60), Iroquois (Kurath and Fenton 1951, 50 ff.), Menominee, Delaware, and Shawnee, and, in fact, all the way from the Mississauga to Plains tribes

(Skinner 1913, 74–77, 79–80, 89; 1915, 201). Wapinamakin, leader of the thunderers, gave the thunder songs to the Menominee (Skinner 1913, 201); the Wyandot had many Snake Clan Songs; to the east the Iroquois and to the west many tribes from the Pawnee to the Pueblos have had Eagle Dances of varying antiquity. The popular Michigan Indian Eagle and Snake Dances are allegedly imported from the western sources, and only Kenosha's Eagle Song is Odawa. The Eagle Dances are either new compositions or imitations of southwestern prototypes via Wisconsin. The snake effigy idea derives from the Hopi; the snake-like meandering arrived from the southeast by way of Oklahoma and diffusion from there to Wisconsin Anishinaabeg (Kurath 1951a, 130–31).

The swan, which served the golden eagle in the higher Menominee pantheon (Curtis 1952, 178) and which is mimed by the Odawa in imitation of the Winnebago women (Densmore 1947, 75), appears nowhere in Michigan Indian tradition, despite the location on the migration route for wild swans (Kortright 1942, 78–79). An Owl Dance evidently did not come closer than the Menominee (Densmore 1947, 75); but Owl songs were transcribed with a different melody early in the century by Burton at Garden River Reserve and likewise by Densmore at Lac du Flambeau (Burton 1909, 135; Densmore 1910, 135). Eli Thomas remembers the connection of the Hoot Owl Song with medicine bundles—the *kokoko* or owl skin—part of a widespread custom. Blue Cloud specifically connects his White Pigeon Song with medicine.

Various birds have appeared as dream guardians. Birds of prey and falcons were imitated in the *Weendahsowin* or naming rite (Tanner 1835, 2:348). Similarly, the swan, woodpecker, crow, and bluebird (Schoolcraft 1848, 201; Davidson 1946, 303). This function is still operative, according to Kenosha, for the Hoot Owl Song, Woodpecker Song, and other bird and animal songs.

Animals have been associated well into history with the hunt (Kinietz 1940, 238, 322), which provided much of the food in prehistoric times and still features in the economy of Parry Island (Hinsdale 1925, 71–72; Jenness 1935, 13–15). "Boss" animals or supernatural prototypes were placated by shamanistic procedure, with medicine bag (*maškemod*), an image of man and animal, dreaming, and prayer.

Singing was always a necessary constituent. In the nineteenth century, as Jones remembered, "the hunter's medicine is made of different sorts of roots . . . a little of which he puts into his gun, that it may make the first shot take effect. He will also place a small portion of it in the first deer or bear's track he meets with, supposing that if the animal be two or three days journey off, they will come in sight of it in a short time . . . To render the medicine more effectual he will frequently sing the hunter's song, and I have known many a hunter to sit up all night beating his *tawagun,* and then at daylight take his gun and go in quest of game. This is generally done when an Indian imagines he has displeased the god of game, by not paying him that reverence that secures success in the chase. The first animal he takes he then devotes to the god of the game, making a feast, and offering part in sacrifice, by which he thinks to appease his wrath" (P. Jones 1861, 154). This is suggestive of Blue Cloud's Hunter's and Medicine Songs.

Very few authors describe animal dances. James inserts a group dance in his quotation of a hunting song text (Tanner 1835, 2:410–13). Copway remarks that "in their war songs animals are likewise represented in various attitudes. A rattle of deer hoofs is made, which is shook during the singing" (Copway 1851, 128). Among adjacent tribes, however, dance references abound—for instance, in all of Densmore's works. Some of these dances are simple pleasure imitations, as the Rabbit Dance (Densmore 1947, 75). The majority are magical—the Menominee imitation of a buck for hunting, buffalo mime in a circle for cure following a dream, and bear placation blended with a Sun Ceremony featuring a painted stake (Skinner 1913, 87, 138, 201; Skinner 1915, 213).

The bear is the most potent of the magic animals. In the Winnebago dream society of "Those Who Have Been Blessed by the Grizzly Bear," the men imitate the motions and cries of the beast, whirling around and stretching out their hands (Radin 1923, 347–48). The Meskwaki imitate the grizzly in clan feasts. The Iroquois maintain a curative bear rite with a dance resembling Kenosha's description of an ancient counterclockwise stomp for men and women (Kurath 1951a, 120–23). These, now unmasked, dances were hoary with antiquity when described by Champlain for Huron curing rites and have a tremendous diffusion in the haunts of the woodland bear and western grizzly bear (Kinietz 1940, 140–41; Hallowell 1926).

Other less formidable animal dances are more recent and more limited in their extent. The Odawa Buffalo Dance, despite buffalo absence in the state, was a pleasure dance in 1822 at Mackinaw (Kinietz 1947, 92). Its present enactment is more reminiscent of the Plains free mime (J. R. Walker 1917, 116; Catlin 1841, 1:186–87) than the counterclockwise linear side shuffle of the Meskwaki and Iroquois (Kurath 1951b, 16). Kenosha's Raccoon Dance also has no connection with the Iroquois foot twister (Kurath 1951b, 33).

Whitney Albert's Dog Dance apparently has no connection with traditional dog dances and rites. But these deserve brief mention because of their importance in ancient ceremonies and feasts. The Dog Dance was identified with the begging procession by men and women before a feast. At Parry Island, "Dogs are dancing, begging for something to eat," went the song. (Jenness 1935, 100) As part of the Maple Sugar springtime gatherings, songs were noted by Burton (1909, 224) and Densmore (1913, 231). The wider diffusion cannot be quoted in detail. The dog, especially a white dog, was a sacrificial animal throughout the Great Lakes area in the nineteenth century (P. Jones 1861, 97; Baraga 1837, 195). In the seventeenth and eighteenth centuries it was thrown to the god of the waters, in the Feast for the Dead (Kinietz 1940, 283–87). Such a sacrifice is accompanied by song at the Iroquois Midwinter festival, now in effigy, and continues as food offering in Meskwaki gens festivals. Such association has completely vanished in modern Michigan, for obvious humane reasons.

Less obvious is the complete absence of a Fish Dance, which remains as one of the most attractive items of the Lac du Flambeau Ojibwe and Menominee repertoire and also is a social dance of the Winnebagos and which perseveres at least as a song among the Menominee (Densmore 1932; Densmore 1947, 76, 191). None of the Michigan Indians remembers either or song or dance, even though they depended to a large extent on fishing for their living and still favor it, although even clan totems have been fish (Warren 1885, 42, 84–89) and family names retain that connotation—for instance, Kenosha meaning "pike."

Rites for Ceremonial Plant Foods

Whereas the male occupation of hunting dealt with animals, the largely female occupation of agriculture or food gathering concerned plants—maple sugar, wild berries, roots, corn, beans, and squash in Wisconsin and also wild rice in the western Upper Peninsula. All of the tribes centered one of their largest, if not the very largest, camp gatherings on the tapping of the maple trees, and these gatherings included social and war dances as well as meetings of medicine societies (Schoolcraft 1852, 55–56). There is no mention of special worship connected with maple sugar or even of its use as ceremonial food, as still occurs in Meskwaki gens festivals. But there are references to songs. Many of these songs deal with the Beggar's or Dog Dance and refer to sugar. One song—a jolly love song—is preserved in Kenosha's repertoire. There is no specific calendar of food spirit festivals, such as is still customary among the Iroquois, or even of dances. However, such festivals are suggested by the Oshkenetagawin, or first fruits ceremony, for wild rice, blueberries, raspberries, and strawberries, corresponding to the first fruit of the chase (Kinietz 1947, 56). Certain months were "moon of sugar, strawberries, whortleberries, rice harvest" among the Odawas and Menominees (Tanner 1835, 2:383–84). Shurtleff witnessed a blueberry feast, consisting lately only of ceremonial eating of the first berries. Any feasts and attendant dances or songs must have to have corresponded to the seasonal ripening. In the vicinity of Baraga, the September wild rice harvest was, according to Thomas Shalifoe, Jr., attended by songs like it was in northern Wisconsin (Keesing 1939, 22–23).

Maize ceremonialism also escaped the attention of writers. It is true, maize culture did not feature among the Ojibwe and was secondary among the Odawa. However, both Odawa and Potawatomi raised corn, beans, and squash, according to Charlevoix and Champlain, around 1700 (Waugh 1916, 5–6). The former claimed its reception from the Huron, the "granary of the Algonquians." But Hinsdale reports from excavations in territory that was presumably Potawatomi territory prehistorically at Charlotte near Hastings, that corn hills, hoes, spades, and other tools indicated early agriculture, and that mortars and pestles indicated similar preparation to that still customary for feasts (Hinsdale 1930, 73–75, 105).

The *Mondamin* or Spirit Grain gave rise to various origin myths still circulating. It occupied and still occupies many of the women. Corn planting, gathering, and husking gave occasions for merriment and thanksgiving, with the women as focal performers and the old chiefs as spectators. (Schoolcraft 1848, 179–80) Joking songs were improvised around crooked ears, *Wagemin*. But the only ceremonial and dance allusion concerns the Prairie Potawatomi in Kansas. Of the three great dances, "the first one, called the 'green bean dance,' is celebrated early in the summer, when the bean . . . is ready for the table. The second, the most elaborate of all, the 'green corn dance,' is celebrated when the corn is in its milk" (Blair 1911–12, 2:291). The third one, Thanksgiving, centers on the turkey. Perhaps these festivities are related to those of the Iroquois, via the Huron; perhaps they were received from the Shawnee during their Kansas residence (Schoolcraft 1852, 591).

The custom of offering and giving thanks for fruits of the soil and the chase was quickly transferred by the Jesuits. At Sault Ste. Marie in 1672, the converts were bringing the first corn to the church *(Jesuit Relations,* 67:207). Again, at the Native feast of the squashes at St. Ignace, Fr. Marquette asked the Indians to thank God in Christian prayer *(Jesuit Relations,* 67:251).

War Ceremonies

Making up for the deficiency of agricultural dance references, war celebrations fascinated all observers. In the spring and summer these celebrations were dedicated to the sun or the thunder. The ceremonies could be held before or after battle and often featured the calumet dedication and dance. Bishop Baraga devoted many pages to four kinds of War Dances (Baraga 1837, 223–35).

He spoke of the Recruiting Dance, which took place around a red-painted pole, to a drum. Old warriors start and invite young braves. Whoever joins the circle is considered a recruit. Baraga also cited the Boasting Dance, or recital of exploits by old warriors: "Le danseur s'avance en soutane tres lègérement et s'arręte au milieu de la place de danse. Il fait alors difference sauts y mouvements qui figurent la marche contre l'ennemi. Il se glisse alors tout doucement ça et la, s'arręte de temps en temps, puis se lance tout a coup vers un certain endroit, fait tous les gestes d'un homme qui se bat et qui tue son ennemi, saisit un des assistants, comme s'il fait voulait le faire prisonnier . . . Après cette representation, il se tient debout au milieu de la place et fait le recit de ses exploits." This is a realistic portrayal of ambush attack, killing, and taking prisoner. Third, Baraga observed a dance known as Strike the Post, a circular dance around several poles in a circle, with a human image carved on one end, possibly that of the enemy. The men jump with a fearful mien. "Les dancers sont pres'que nus, tenant d'une main une citrouille remplie de petits pierres, et d'autre une branches d'arbre; Ils sautent en faisant les gestes les plus éntranges et le tapage le plus effroyable autour de ces poteaux." Finally, Baraga observed the Victory or Scalp Dance held after successful expeditions. Women join in the singing. Other ceremonial procedures noted by Baraga include a chant of farewell before setting out, various taboos, and face blackening.

Of Copway's and Jones's descriptions, the latter is the more vivid. As in Baraga's account, warriors dance around a drum, brandishing tomahawks and throwing the body into all sorts of postures. Occasionally they strike a pole and relate war experiences. They enact a sham fight, tomahawking, scalping, and drinking the blood of the foe (P. Jones 1861, 133).

Early accounts are scantier. Sabrevois remarked that young Odawa warriors "often dance in a circle, and strike at the posts; it is in this dance that they recount their exploits; on such occasion they also dance the scout dance. They are always well adorned when they do this" (Kinietz 1940, 346). Warriors crop their hair and put on war paint. The chief exhorts them. They answer with a shout. The chief rises with quiver in hand and sings as warrior. His song is generally only a repetition of what was said in the harangue. They chant thus, one after another, especially those who want to take part in the expedition. Then they eat what was prepared. The day of departure on their revenge expedition the canoes are lined up, the chief stands and sings his invocation to his guardian spirit for a prosperous journey. The warriors answer "Che!" (Kinietz 1940, 252–53). These seem to correspond, respectively, to Baraga's Strike the Post and rally and farewell chant.

This individual chant receives frequent mention. At a feast for the warrior's pouch, *pindikossan*, the sponsor blackens his face and sings with two companions in honor of his guardian spirit. Then all feast on dog meat (Blair 1911–12, 1:62). The same author tells of another more violent sacrifice. During the singing of his chant he makes frightful contortions and goes back and forth many times with a partner. All answer "Ouiy." They throw coals and fire brands, feigning attacks (Blair 1911–12, 1:54). La Potherie mentions the identical procedure, with War Songs, going back and forth, gestures and violent movement, and fire brands. Three or so successive musicians and the chief perform. Then there is a feast (Blair 1911–12, 1:337–38).

Of other references, the Warriors' Dances in Lahontan's Great Sun Sacrifice need not refer to War Dances but rather to dances by the young and able men (Kinietz 1940, 290–91). Raudot's Discovery and Strike the Post Dances refer to the Miami (Kinietz 1940, 348).

By the seventeenth century, this was a well-established complex. Yet several authorities claim that the nomadic hunters were not warlike, that the Odawa and Ojibwe were rarely scalpers before the advent of steel knives (Hinsdale 1925, 24–25, 76–77). In the northern Woodlands, Indians struggled along during the winter in small groups and had no thought for war except as small revenge expeditions. Spring social gatherings vaunted exploits for personal glory (Hadlock 1947, 213, 217, 219–20). With the coming of agriculture men had more time for war and organization and a desire for land.

It is likely that most of the early war ceremonies prepared for personal expeditions, hence featured personal chants. The chain reaction of westerly migration after 1700 occasioned more intertribal and interracial conflict, scalping for pay, and organized wars like Pontiac's. The high point of this development finds expression in Baraga's times. Yet it was less elaborate than the Great Plains warrior rituals and societies. Very likely the development received impetus from the Sioux. The Iroquois have definite traditions concerning the Plains origin of their War and Strike the Post Dances, and they were more aggressive than the Anishinaabeg (Kurath and Fenton 1951, 108ff.).

Even after the war rituals ceased functioning, they remained in shows for their spectacular value. Jenness saw a War Dance on Parry Island with realistic staging of a mimic battle (Jenness 1935, 100). He also mentions the individual Medicine Song. They appeal to tourists as real Indian manifestations and are a must in all shows.

In reviewing the various descriptions of warrior ceremonies and placing them next to Odawa and Iroquois survivals, the persistence of types is amazing. Baraga's rally would seem to persevere in the song by Susan Shagonaby regarding the Maskutens. The War Dance and Strike the Post are ubiquitous, but with a loss of realism. Tomahawk and Scalping Dances have their foundation in both the War and Scalp Victory Dances. The individual chant perseveres in the Iroquois Personal Chant, or *adonwe*, and perhaps in Chingwa's old War Song and Blue Cloud's Brave Song.

The Green Grass Dance is a curious phenomenon. The Plains Grass Dance is a fairly recent development from an old Plains war complex. Originally it included a dog feast. It retains the war idea and an attenuated movement pattern but is misunderstood by Eli Thomas as to function and origin. The songs, strange to say, fit the Grass Dance type. The most recent developments of this complex—the Powwow or War Dance, the war contest of the Midwest and West, diffused from Oklahoma—has missed Michigan (Kurath 1956b). Its present costume of feather bustles also fails to have reached the peninsulas, even though tribes on the other side of Lake Michigan have accepted this.

Aboriginally, war dance, song, and ritual played into other phases of religion. They were connected with the sun, thunders, birds and beasts, the dream and medicine bundle complex, and the pipe of peace, but not the cardinal points; also with adoptions and death.

Rites of Passage and Crises of Life

Songs and ceremonies, but not always dances, accompanied all rites of passage and crises of life: birth, puberty visions, the first hunt, courting, illness, and death. Marriage alone received no such sanction. Naming and death involved larger ceremonies with dancing. Adoptions were a common sequel to wakes and often concerned war captives who replaced a dead warrior of the tribe. Regularly after a year of mourning a person was adopted to assume the offices of a dead chief or to replace a young person; he had to be of the same age.

Dream Feasts

These are mentioned by Tanner as *Wain-je-tah We-koon-de-win*. (Tanner 1830, 1:286) They could be held at any time of year that a person had a significant dream which compelled him to give thanks to his manido.

First Fruits

Besides the first fruit ceremonies already considered there was also a feast held after a boy killed his first game. It was given by the boy in honor of his manido, which he had obtained in a vision during his puberty fast, and according to Tanner was called *O-skin-ne-ge-tah-ga-win* (Tanner 1830, 1:287).

Individual Medicine Rites

Rites, feasts, songs, and dances were performed as the result of a dream or vision during a fast. They were used when treating a patient, when picking herbs, or when preparing a medicine. Most of those who owned medicine songs and dances were members of one of the medicine societies, but any individual favored with the requisite visions could also become a medicine man. Tanner mentions a feast called *Che-bah-koo-che-go-win* (feast for his medicine) and writes that it occupied a whole day every spring and autumn. "Each good hunter spreads out the contents of his medicine bag in back of his lodge . . . feasts his neighbors in honor of his medicine . . . solemn and important" (Tanner 1830, 1:287).

Though the modern peninsular medicine rites are reduced, on the one hand, to herb lore, and on the other, to bits of clownery, the ancient medicine rites were so important as to warrant a summary. These rites could be special cures by individual medicine men with herbs, song, and sometimes frenzied dance, or by a group. These were prevalent in the early accounts. The shaman performed juggling feats, foamed at the mouth, and threw himself around as though possessed (Kinietz 1940, 376). Again, "the sick man is placed in the hands of doctors who suck with cries and frightful yells to the sound of a drum." A great noise was made "by several boys and girls who sing and dance around" a sufferer (Kinietz 1940, 347). Iroquois men and women of today effect cures by such a round dance but without a great noise.

The Midéwiwin

More frequently, Medicine Dances are meant to refer to shamanistic societies, which embrace many other features besides curing—namely, the Midéwiwin and Wabeno fraternities. The Midé, which still has adherents in Wisconsin, includes in its elaborate procedures almost all aspects of Anishinaabe religious concepts: the cardinal points in the four patron manidos of the east, south, west, and north; animals in the songs and in the bear mime recurring four times; and the sun-wise course of the dances themselves (Hoffman 1896, 92, 99–103; Densmore 1910, 40, 76–77, 143). Its preliminaries can feature an initiation to fill a vacancy by death and a ceremony at the grave (Hoffman 1896, 71ff.). War has no place. But the pipe fosters comradeship.

The Midéwiwin rites were held in the early spring or in the summer in conjunction with other ceremonies. There is little description of the Odawa Midéwiwin, but it is assumed to have resembled the Ojibwe. The latter has been discussed in detail by Hoffman (1896) and by many others, so it seems unnecessary to describe it here. Certain aspects of the Midéwiwin may survive in the Odawa belief in bear walking (sorcery), which is discussed in chapter 8.

The Wabeno

Members of this society were frequently referred to as "fire walkers" because of their ability to walk on hot coals or embers, toss burning brands in the air with their bare hands, and even appear to swallow fire. Their ceremonies were held at night, usually in the spring in conjunction with the Midéwiwin. Wisconsin Potawatomi and Menominee, until recently at any rate, celebrated with sorcerers' exhibitions and dances by a large assembly. The Menominee Wabenos invite friends to a feast for the tutelary daimon and spend all night in boisterous song and dance and in fire handling and other tricks (Hoffman 1896, 151–57). Jenness noted that on Parry Island, the feasts were open to all and were held for prestige. "With a tambourine, a wabeno advanced to the center of the wigwam, all fell in line, danced and sang around a central fire. The wabenos took turns leading" (Jenness 1935, 63). They plunged their hands in boiling water.

The boisterousness is confirmed by various writers. Other reports relative to the Midé and Wabeno differ. One old Ojibwe Christian regarded the Wabeno society as wicked, consisting of mere braggadocio, and not ancient (instead an invention by a Potawatomi) (Schoolcraft 1848, 116, 211). On the other hand, a Meskwaki ritualist, Wilson Roberts, considered the Wabeno society as the older and claimed that the Meskwaki abandoned the Midé but retained the Wabeno because of the degeneration of the former.

The songs of the Midé are plentifully preserved; those of the Wabeno only meagerly (Burton 1909, 247). The dancing seems to have consisted in circular stomping. It has not been observed.

These societies have been important not only because of their all-inclusiveness. The Midé in particular will also throw light on the acceptance of Christian ideology by its precepts and mythology. By its origin legends, it also will give a basis for ritual chronology. Namely, the shell or *megis* was brought from the great eastern salt water by three migrations (to Montreal, the Sault, and La Pointe) and reposed at the last place three generations before the white man (Warren 1885, 78 ff.).

The Jisako, or Seer

The famous "shaking tent" of the Anishinaabeg has been adequately described by many authors.

Ceremonies Connected with Death

Regarding belief in an after life, most modern Odawas merely say that Indians go to the Happy Hunting Ground, but they cannot describe it further. Joe Chingwa, in his myth of Nanabojo and Jibiabos, describes the origin of death and the Path of Souls and tells how Nanabojo commanded Jibiabos, "the sweet singer," to rule over the dead in the west. Joe also mentions the giant strawberry, which the souls feasted on during their long journey to the Happy Hunting Ground. The strawberry and the Path of Souls were also mentioned to Gertrude Kurath by Ojibwe informants.

Seventeenth-century accounts all agree that the Odawa, like other Anishinaabeg, believed in immortality. There are quite elaborate descriptions of the Path of Souls and the Happy Hunting Ground. Thus Perrot wrote:

> All the savages who are not converted believe that the soul is immortal; but they maintain that when it is separated from the body it goes to a beautiful and fertile land, where the climate is neither cold nor hot, but agreeably temperate. They say that that land abounds with animals and birds of every kind, and that the hunters while going through it are never in danger of hunger, having only to choose what animals they will attack, to obtain food. They tell us that this beautiful country is very far away, beyond this earth; and it is for this reason that they place on the scaffolds

or in the graves of the dead, at their funerals, provisions and weapons, believing that the souls will find again in the other world, for their use, and especially in the voyage which they must make thither, whatever shall be given to them in this world.

They believe, furthermore, that as soon as the soul has left the body it enters this charming country, and that, after having traveled many days, it encounters on its route a very rapid river, over which there is only a slender tree trunk by way of a bridge; and that in passing over this it bends so much that the soul is in danger of being swept away by the flood of waters. They assert that if unfortunately this mishap occurs, the soul will be drowned; but that all these perils are escaped when once the souls have reached the country of the dead. They believe also that the souls of young people, of either sex, have nothing to fear, because they are so vigorous; but it is not the same with those of the old people and the infants who have no assistance from other souls in this dangerous crossing, and it is this which very often causes them to perish.

They relate to us, moreover that this same river abounds with fish, more in number than can be imagined. There are sturgeons and other kinds of fish in great numbers, which the souls kill with blows of their hatchets and clubs, so that they can roast these fish while on their journey, for they no longer find therein any game. After they have traveled a long time, in front of them appears a very steep mountain, which closes their path and compels them to seek another; but they do not find any way open, and it is only after experiencing great suffering that they finally arrive at this fearful passage. There two pestles of prodigious size, which in turn rise and fall without ceasing, form an obstacle most difficult to overcome; for death is absolutely inevitable if while making the passage one is unfortunately caught under (them)—I mean while one of the two pestles is falling. But the souls are very careful in watching for that fortunate moment when they can clear a passage so dangerous; yet many fall in it, especially those of old persons and little children, who are less vigorous and move through it more slowly.

When the souls have once escaped from this peril, they enter a delightful country, in which excellent fruits are found in abundance; and the ground seems to be covered with all kinds of flowers, the odor of which is so admirable that it delights their hearts and charms their imaginations. The short remaining which they must traverse before arriving in the place where the sound of the drum and the gourds—marking time for (the steps of) the dead, to give them pleasure—falls agreeably on their ears, urges them on to hasten directly thither with great eagerness. The nearer they approach it, always the louder becomes this sound; and the joy which the dancers express by their continual exclamations serves to delight the souls still more. When they are very near the place where the ball is held, part of the dead men separate from the others in order to meet the newcomers, and assure them of the great pleasure which their arrival generally gives to the entire assembly. The souls are conducted into the place where the dance is held, and are cordially received by all who are there; and they find there innumerable viands, of all flavors, everything of the most delicious taste, and prepared in the best manner. It is for them to choose whatever pleases them, and to satisfy their appetites; and when they have finished eating they go to mingle with the others—to dance and make merry forever, without being any longer subject to sorrow, anxiety, or infirmities, or to any of the vicissitudes of mortal life. (Kinietz 1940, 292–93)

There are hints in modern information and in older accounts of the Odawa that they believed to a certain extent in the transmigration of souls. As already mentioned, the first Indians were sometimes said to have originated from the bodies of fishes, birds, and animals, from whom their totems were also derived and then passed on from father to children. Fred Ettawageshik, in his description of the thunderers, says that souls become thunder, fishes, and birds. Allouez wrote that the Odawa "believe, moreover, that the souls of the departed govern the fishes in the lake; and thus, from earliest times, they have held the immortality, and even the metempsychosis of the souls of the dead fishes, believing that they pass into other fish's bodies. Therefore they never throw their bones into the fire, for fear that they may offend these souls, so that they will cease to come into their nets" (*Jesuit Relations*, 12:89).

Occasionally one runs across a reference that implies that the soul might also be reincarnated in human form, although there is nothing as clear-cut as the Fox belief that humans have two souls, one of which, "the small soul," may be reborn four times. The Fox offer this as an explanation of "what makes people think they have existed previously" (Michelson 1918–19, 358–59).

It is an odd fact that although all the surrounding tribes believe that man has two souls, the Odawa credit him with only one. Most Anishinaabeg believe that, after death, one soul lingers near the grave and must be given gifts of appeasement. A second soul, the *jibi,* sets out on the Path of Souls for the Happy Hunting Ground in the west. It is only this latter soul, the *jibi,* in which modern Odawas believe. Probably they have lost the concept of the second soul due to the influence of Christianity.

Wakes and Memorials

These events could be family affairs or huge tribal feasts. This complex is discussed in full by Jane Ettawageshik, but its dance and song aspects deserve additional comments. The Ghost Dance described by Chingwa imitated ghosts. The corresponding dances among the Iroquois, and apparently other neighboring tribes, are completely abstract, with a slow halting step by a circle of women (Kurath and Fenton 1951, 165). Early writers are very vague as to the choreography. Baraga, in a sweeping statement about funeral feasts, says, "et il en est qui alors chantant et dansent au son du tambour" (Baraga 1837, 294).

Perrot gives us some idea as to the seventeenth-century form. Immediately after the arrival of the guests, "they begin to dance to the noise of a drum and of a gourd which contains some small pebbles, both keeping the same time. They dance from one end to the other of the cabin, returning after one another, in single file, around three spruce-trees or three cornstalks" (Blair 1911–12, 1:86–87). This continues for three days.

Similar concepts unite the Great Lakes tribes in the beliefs concerning the soul, in mortuary customs, even in the prevalence of the number four (Kurath 1954b, 97–99), at Six Nations Reserve, on the Menominee Reservation (Skinner 1915, 212; Densmore 1932, 51ff.), and at the Meskwaki settlement in Iowa. Both the songs and the dances share common procedures. Surviving rituals can perhaps tell us something about ancient practices. The men's chants with two striking sticks at Iroquois wakes may throw light on the seventeenth-century interment singing by young men with staves in their hands (Kinietz 1940, 294–96). The Iroquois women's songs at the Ohgiwe may be related to the mournful female songs of 260 years ago (Blair 1911–12, 1:79). Specifically, one of the Ohgiwe songs bears a striking resemblance to Chingwa's Ghost Dance song.

Restoration of Mourners

A widow or widower mourned for a year at the end of which he attended a feast and ceremony given by his in-laws in which he was clothed in new garments and given freedom to marry again (Blair 1911–12, 1:70–74). Though the period of mourning may vary, this is a widespread practice found among the northeastern Algonkians as well as in the Central Woodlands and among the Iroquois. No particular time of year is specified for the Odawa ceremony. Jenness (1935, 106–7) reports that the Ojibwe of Parry Island release mourners at the Feast of the Dead held in the fall.

Adoption

This ceremony, in which the name of the deceased was passed on to someone who "takes his place," was important in Odawa culture. Perrot writes that a solemn ceremony was held six months after the death of a chief, during which a new chief was given the name of the deceased. Frequently the new chief set off soon after on a war foray with a party of volunteers in order to demonstrate his prowess and prove that he was worthy of his new name. Perrot describes it as follows:

> As for the women, girls or boys, a similar usage prevails, (the adopted one being) of the same age and sex (as the dead). The one to be adopted dresses up, painting his face with vermillion. The parents of the dead man are in his cabin. At the outset three persons are requested to sing and beat the drum. The adoptee immediately enters the cabin of the departed, dancing. He offers presents composed of peltries or other goods "to the nearest relative of the deceased and continues dancing all day to the drum." During his dance, he is stopped occasionally by the parents of the departed who adorn him with necklaces, etc. At the end of the dance, he is given food and additional presents. The adopted person then assures his now family that he will always render service to them and will endeavor to take the place of the one whose name he has assumed.
>
> At the outset, three persons are requested to sing, and to beat the drum, keeping time with the measure of their song. The person, whether man or woman, who has been adopted immediately enters the cabin of the departed, dancing; and after he has offered presents, composed of peltries or other goods, to the nearest relative of the deceased person . . . , he continues dancing all day to the sound of that instrument. During this time the parents of the departed stop him occasionally in his dancing, to place some adornments on his body or neck . . . When the dance is ended, they give him food, with various presents, in memory of him whose place is taken and who thereby comes back to life (Blair 1911–12, 1:85).

This widespread custom was especially important among Great Lakes tribes and has shown corresponding tenacity. At Manitoulin it was the last Native dance ceremony to persist (Kinietz 1947, 108). At Harbor Springs this dance alone is still featured in true ceremonials. The original richness and the nature of the patterns can be inferred from the modern Iroquois condolence and adoption rites, one derived from the Tutelo; and from the Meskwaki adoptions, during which men dance in a circle and women bounce up and down in place (W. Jones 1939, 69–71).

Factors Aiding Christianization

The practice of puberty visions for the sight of a guardian spirit must have been an important factor in adaptation to the new religion. The voluntary endurance of deprivations and even suffering no doubt prepared the ground for the Catholic fasts and acts of penance (*Jesuit Relations*, 27:209). The dream cult corresponded with Christian aspirations toward communion (Baraga 1837, 199). Says a Native about the experience, "While in the presence of the object, the individual has a vague sense of something strange. The most common experience seems to be that of being overwhelmed by an all encompassing presence" (W. Jones 1894, 183–84). Does this already show Christian influence?

In their approach, the Indians were always the receivers, blessed and pitied by the spirit in the vision (Hallowell 1947, 564). The desire to see God facilitated conversion, said Allouez (*Jesuit Relations*, 51:489), and predisposed the converts for the rites of initiation—namely, baptism (Schoolcraft 1845, 456).

The naming rites of the two religions have much in common. In particular, Indian ceremonies of adoption paved the way for the concept of the individual's rebirth as well as of divine resurrection. A seventeenth-century Indian song went, "He who is to bring me back to life is he who consoles me" (*Jesuit Relations*, 32:311).

The Midéwiwin contained much that made Christian ritual acceptable—for instance, the *megis*, which resembled the host; the *midewatig*, or pole, which foreshadowed the crucifix, the priestly function of the leaders as intercessors and administrators; and the sacred character of the ceremonial lodge, analogous to the church as a place for offering and worship (W. Jones 1894, 189).

Sacrifices in Large Public Meetings

The public festivals prepared the way for the democratic Free Methodist meetings, which are guided by initiates but which allow each individual, women as well as men, an expression of faith and thanksgiving. Aboriginally, these meetings combined ritual features, songs, prayers, and particularly sacrifices known to Christians.

They were social as well as religious. They ushered in a time of rejoicing—the summer and the end of the winter's hardships, worries, and starvation; they gave thanks for harvests and beasts, and they prayed for future bounty. Indian bands came from near and far to camp on open grounds, to feast, and to celebrate the exclusive rituals of the Wabeno and Midéwiwin societies. Drum and rattle echoed (Schoolcraft 1851, 95–96).

Offerings of tobacco, dogs, and furs, and later on offerings of firewater, pervaded all activities private or tribal. These were offerings to the guardian spirit or to the sun and other members of the spirit pantheon.

These gatherings persisted into the nineteenth century, as did the painted Pole Feast called *Sahsahgewejegun*—the spreading out to view of the supplicant's desires by tying offerings to the top of the elevated pole. The Indians of today speak of sacrifice as *sasagiwejigæ*, in the sense of offering. Peter Jones used both senses in his comment, "In illustrating the nature of the great atonement to my pagan countrymen, I have often made reference to their own sacrifices" (P. Jones 1861, 96).

The Symbol of the Sacred Pole

The Anishinaabeg were not given to the worship of idols, but they understood the symbolism inherent in visible objects. The Catholic statues fit better with the ritualism of tribes such as the Aztecs, with their carved and sculptured images. But the symbol of the cross, common to all sects, had many Native antecedents.

The first antecedent was the *aẑedeatic*, or grave post, with the family totem upside down, usually representing an animal or bird (Schoolcraft 1852, 49, 66; Baraga 1837, 289). The Painted Pole for the *Sahsahgewejegun* feast was painted red or black and surmounted by sacred feathers and tobacco (P. Jones 1861, 97). No doubt this is the type referred to by Blackbird, in his telling of making the spring offering to the Great Spirit by presenting cast-off garments erected on a pole.

Another antecedent was the *midewatig*, which took two forms: one a horizontal pole with gifts from the candidate, the other a smaller medicine pole carried in procession (Densmore 1910, 40–43, 48; Warren 1885, 77). Copway (1851, 160) said that this latter pole had painted on it the representation of the Great Spirit.

Third, the *Manido* poles, or individual medicine poles, still in use among the Wisconsin Potawatomi, consists of a peeled cedar sapling with stripes, tobacco, and ribbons, as is used for the *Sahsahgewejegun* (Ritzenthaler 1953b, 156–57). These could be in across shape (Densmore 1910, 248). Baraga claimed that some of these were surmounted by a human head, so he termed them idols (Baraga 1837, 195). Similar small ones, he said, were kept in the huts as guardian spirits.

Two final antecedents to the cross could be found in the greased poles for the Feast of the Dead and in the war posts, either single ones for Strike the Post or an entire circle (Kinietz 1940, 270, 282; Copway 1851, 128; Baraga 1837, 214).

Of these, the *Ažedeatic* and *Manito* poles reminded the missionaries of the crucifix. In particular, Fr. Marquette saw at Green Bay "a handsome cross erected in the center of the village" (Kinietz 1940, 215). By 1642 the Jesuits had the Hurons framing a great cross in the early spring, adoring it and offering thanks for preservation through the winter (*Jesuit Relations*, 27:213). By 1673, Fr. André had them believing that the image of the Menominee cross brought the Menominee a good catch of sturgeon (Skinner 1913, 79–80). The cross could fulfill all the functions of the medicine poles in curing illness, bringing success in expeditions, and protecting from harm in the manner of amulets.

More recently, in mixed religious observances the cross has been used as symbol in the western Great Lakes Dream Dance (Skinner 1913, 176). On the other hand, the aboriginal painted pole survived in the Corpus Christi processions of twentieth-century Cross Village.

Thus, although many differences remained, many features abstract and concrete had conditioned the Anishinaabe mind for Christian teachings.

Dance and Music as Factors in Christianization

The dance must immediately be discounted as a negative factor. At first Marquette and other priests did not forbid dances, except for a few like the Huron Bear Dance (*Jesuit Relations*, 57:255), but they regarded them with disfavor. They substituted processions, shows, and dramatic performances about unbelievers hunted in hell by fiends (*Jesuit Relations*, 45:129, 155; Parkman 1902, 252–54). But unlike the Jesuits and Franciscans in Mexico, they made no provisions for their amalgamation with church festivities and encouraged their transference to social, political, and theatrical functions. The first two functions persevered until the turn of this century but are now all but defunct; the third role flourishes. This important element of Native religion would have formed a barrier against Christianization and was decried by the evangelists.

Music, on the other hand, served both religions and had to surmount only stylistic obstacles. Plainsong eased the transition to folksong and hymn styles, which have shed Native mannerisms.

Conclusion

Before restating and answering the problem, this chapter will survey the present state of affairs and the processes of change in Michigan Indian customs.

In modern life, religion, the arts, and economy are separated in accordance with dominant white pattern. Except for the Lac Vieux Desert Ojibwe, who fit into Wisconsin ceremonialism, the descendants of the Three Brothers—the Odawa, the Ojibwe, and the Potawatomi—are Christianized. Catholics hold lakeshore settlements in both peninsulas, from Cross Village to Petoskey, St. Ignace, Bay Mills, Nahma, and Baraga (formerly near Hart). At Zeba, Methodists and the Church of God divide adherents. In the Lower Peninsula the largest Methodist center is at Isabella Reserve, with other centers from Petoskey to the Leelanau Peninsula, near Athens, Alto, and Oscoda. In the Upper Peninsula, Hannahville is Methodist. The two sects have developed different types of adjustment due to different tenets, forms, and missionization.

The Indians of all sects express their Native and acculturated attitudes in various gatherings. Native or quasi-Native survivals are exhibited to white audiences at public shows, which also provide occasions for Indian visiting. The survivals include dances, songs, stories, and crafts. The dances and songs show much individual and local variation, particularly as between the Odawa and Ojibwe. The dances and songs have lost so much of their aboriginal import that they can be understood only by a wide search into their temporal and spatial relationships, by comparison with these arts through the last three centuries and within adjacent tribes. This search is often impeded by vagueness as to the nature of the dances and songs and at times as to their tribal identification. But it leads to some conclusions.

The Catholics retain family feasts and memorial customs that blend the old and new religions. Until recently at Baraga and Nahma, and still at L'Arbre Croche, the Odawa families celebrate New Year and the Feast of the Dead with partly Native customs, and they sing Odawa hymns at wakes. Until recently the Native elements and the hymns extended to other calendric festivals and to regular church services. These can be interpreted in the light of prehistoric ritual and of the Jesuit missionaries' methods of conversion. The Jesuits substituted plays for dances and hymns for Native songs.

In contrast, the Methodist missionaries clamped down on ancient customs and continue to discourage folkloric revivals. The present adherents, as the early converts, find emotional uplift in their summer-long camp meetings. Although they run these according to white patterns, they perpetuate early Anishinaabe fondness for camp circles, cooperative working and feasting, and democratic organization. The older people prefer hymns in the Native language. The women find satisfaction in their important roles as evangelists.

The Indians have bridged a wide gulf in three centuries, changing from aboriginal religion to Christianity, from Native dance and song to hymnody. Each generation has lost more of the old ways. Today only the elders adhere to any real belief in Native lore; only elders know of Native remedies and Native legends; only they command their languages.

The vastness of the change becomes all the more apparent in the study of the aboriginal ritual patterns. At the same time, this study and its resultant reconstruction reveal common elements in the two religions, and they help explain the transition.

To the first inhabitants, religion, art, and economy were interlocked. In the forests, prairies, and waterfronts they were dependent on the natural resources; they regarded them with respect and endowed them with supernatural power. They accompanied every occupation and life crisis with invocations, dances, and songs. In the winter small groups feasted together; in the summer large bands met for festivals and for rituals of secret societies. Some of the ,vision quests for deities and sacrificial customs blended nicely with Christian approaches. Others were incompatible and had to disappear. The Native animism became meaningless as forests and game shrank and as an industrial economy took over. The more westerly Messianic cults did not reach Michigan Indians; no Dream Dance or peyote cult prolonged adherence to pagan faith. Adjustment to Christianity inevitably accompanied adjustment to the white man's way of life.

Now to restate the problem—what is the adjustive value of the religious customs, residual, blended, or modern?

From the point of view of the dollar norm, only the powwow pattern is directly lucrative, and that only within a limited group. The other types of gatherings are self-supporting. Indirectly, however, religion has a beneficial effect—particularly Methodism, with its ban on liquor and consequent improvement of work capacity.

More important are the psychological effects of increased self-esteem for the performer, momentary glamour in the shows, and emotional release in revivals. Equally important are the social-nativistic effects of tribal cohesion and pride in being an Indian. Artistic and educational effects are secondary and result automatically from good and authentic presentation of Native lore.

These factors vary considerably with the individuals. Perhaps the economic and nativistic effects are in inverse ratio, the most conservative profiting least in dollars and cents. For all, however, the adjustive value of meeting with other Indians in some kind of festival is enormous. The religious significance today could be pronounced in inverse ratio to the degree of Native ingredients. That is, the more Native gatherings and practices evoke little faith or none at all, while the acquired religious patterns dominate the lives of the modern Indians.

Although statistics are still wanting, the various adjustive features could be lined up with the three major expressions of solidarity, the major types of gatherings.

ADJUSTIVE FEATURE	POWWOWS	ODAWA FEASTS	CAMP MEETINGS
Economic	Revenues	Potluck	Self-supporting
Artistic	Variable	None	None, except in song
Educational	Secondary	None	None
Personal	Considerable	Considerable	Considerable
Social	Significant	Significant	Most significant
Nativistic	Tribal pride	Tribal cohesion	None, except in language
Adjustive	Secondary	Historical	Primary
Religious	None	Partial	Primary

The conclusions would be that the conservative Indian finds satisfaction and adjustive value in all customs containing Native elements and involving contacts with other Indians. Likewise, one could predict that the next generation, which will complete the process to assimilation, will lose values peculiar to their ancestors.

From the ethnocentric point of view, the white student of culture can find much of value in these highly acculturated groups. He can learn about the processes of transition between alien and apparently incompatible ways of life. He can be impressed by human capacity for finding the way through a maze of alien patterns, for retaining at least the memory of ancestral lore, and for fitting into a changing world.

NOTES

Editor's Introduction

1. See, for example, Philip Deloria, *Playing Indian* (New Haven, Conn.: Yale University Press, 1998); and Frederick Hoxie, "Exploring a Cultural Borderland," *Journal of American History* 79 (December 1992): 969–95.
2. This song is also discussed in chapter 4.
3. For a fuller discussion of the Song of Hiawatha pageants, see Michael McNally, "The Indian Passion Play: Contesting the Real Indian in *Song of Hiawatha* Pageants, 1901–1965," *American Quarterly* 58 (March 2006): 105–36.
4. See Gregory Dowd, *A Spirited Resistance: The North American Struggle for Unity, 1745–1815* (Baltimore: Johns Hopkins University Press, 1992).
5. For a brief overview of missions to the Ojibwe, see Christopher Vecsey, *Traditional Ojibwa Religion and Its Historical Changes* (Philadelphia: American Philosophical Society, 1983).
6. See Keith Widder, *Battle for the Soul* (East Lansing: Michigan State University Press, 1999).
7. See Michael McNally, *Ojibwe Singers: Hymns, Grief, and a Native Culture in Motion* (New York: Oxford University Press, 2000), for a deeper exploration of this in northern Minnesota.
8. See Frederick Hoxie, *A Final Promise: The Campaign to Assimilate the Indians* (Lincoln: University of Nebraska Press, 1984); and Francis Paul Prucha, *American Indian Policy in Crisis: Christian Reformers and the Indians* (Norman: University of Oklahoma Press, 1976).
9. See Brenda Child, *Boarding School Seasons: American Indian Families, 1900–1940* (Lincoln: University of Nebraska Press, 1998).
10. See James McClurken, *Gah-Baeh-Jhabgwah-Buk The Way It Happened: A Visual Culture History of the Little Traverse Bay Bands of Odawa* (East Lansing: Michigan State University Press, 1991), 81–86.
11. The subtleties of this religious idiom are comparable to religions of East

Asia, especially the Confucian tradition.

12. See Walter Hoffman, "The Midéwiwin or Grand Medicine Society of the Ojibwa," in Bureau of American Ethnology, *Seventh Annual Report to the Secretary of the Smithsonian Institution (1885–86)*, 143–300. Washington, D.C.: U.S. Government Printing Office, 1891.

13. See Vecsey, *Traditional Ojibwa Religion and Its Historical Changes*; and John Grim, *The Shaman: Patterns of Religious Healing among the Ojibwa Indians* (Norman: University of Oklahoma Press, 1983).

14. See Thomas Vennum, Jr., *The Ojibwa Dance Drum* (Washington D.C.: Smithsonian Institution Press, 1982); and Beverly Diamond et. al., *Visions of Sound: Musical Instruments of First Nations Communities in Northeast America* (Chicago: University of Chicago Press, 1994).

15. From remarks made by Larry Plamondon at "A Gathering of Cultures" symposium, Eastern Michigan University, Ypsilanti (January 1999).

16. Vecsey, *Traditional Ojibwa Religion and Its Historical Changes*, 4.

17. See A. Irving Hallowell, "Ojibwa Ontology, Behavior, and World View," in *Culture in History: Essays in Honor of Paul Radin*, ed. Stanley Diamond (New York: Columbia University Press, 1960).

18. See end of chapter 1.

19. See end of chapter 1.

20. The field of American anthropology in the early part of the century was significantly shaped by Columbia University's Franz Boas and his many protégés.

21. For criticisms of the ethnographic present of classic anthropology, see Johannes Fabian, *Time and the Other: How Anthropology Makes Its Object* (New York: Columbia University Press, 1983); and George Marcus and Michael Fischer, eds., *Anthropology as Cultural Critique* (Chicago: University of Chicago Press, 1986).

22. A number of antiquarian articles had been published on the texts of Native language hymnody, but the fuller life of hymnody in terms of musical structure, aesthetics, and performance has only been the subject of fairly recent studies. See Luke Eric Lassiter, Clyde Ellis, and Ralph Kotay, *The Jesus Road: Kiowas, Christianity, and Indian Hymns* (Lincoln: University of Nebraska Press, 2002); McNally, *Ojibwe Singers: Hymns, Grief, and a Native Culture in Motion*; Beverley Diamond Cavanaugh, "Christian Hymns in Eastern Woodlands Communities: Performance Contexts," in *Musical Repercussions of 1492: Explorations, Encounters, and Identities*, ed. Carol E. Robertson (Washington D.C.: Smithsonian Institution), 381–94; and Beverley Diamond, "Music and Gender in the Sub-Arctic Algonkian Area," in *Women in North American Indian Music: Six Essays*, ed. R. Keeling, SEM Special Series No. 6 (Bloomington, Ind.: Society for Ethnomusicology, 1989).

23. For a fine review and excellent new contribution to this literature, see Tara Browner, *Heartbeat of the People: Music and Dance of the Northern Powwow* (Urbana: University of Illinois Press, 2002).
24. See end of chapter 1.
25. See end of chapter 1.
26. See end of chapter 1.
27. For an elaboration on the centrality of the trickster and of trickster logic, see the work of Anishinaabe novelist and critic Gerald Vizenor, especially *Fugitive Poses: Native American Indian Scenes of Absence and Presence* (Lincoln: University of Nebraska Press, 1998).
28. Michael D. McNally, *Honoring Elders* in *Practicing Protestants,* ed. Leigh Schmidt et al. (New York: Columbia University Press, 2009); and (Baltimore: Johns Hopkins University Press, 2006).
29. A biographical sketch accompanies her article, "Panorama of Dance Ethnology," *Current Anthropology* 1, 3 (May 1960). Other details are from correspondence with her daughter, Ellen Kurath, January 2000.
30. Gertrude Kurath, "Research Methods and Background of Gertrude Kurath," in Kurath, *Half a Century of Dance Research: Essays by Gertrude Prokosch Kurath* (Flagstaff, Ariz.: Cross Cultural Dance Resources, 1986), 407.
31. Gertrude Kurath, "Dance, Music, and the Daily Bread," *Ethnomusicology* 4, no. 1 (1960): 1–8.
32. Kurath, "Research Methods and Background," 413.
33. Kurath, "Research Methods and Background," 410.
34. Speck's own ethnographic work concerned Algonkian speaking peoples of Maine and the Maritime Provinces of Canada. See *Penobscot Man* (Philadelphia: University of Pennsylvania Press, 1940) and *Naskapi: The Savage Hunters of the Labrador Peninsula* (Norman: University of Oklahoma Press, 1935).
35. Frank Ettawageshik, in conversation, August 8, 2002.
36. Frank Ettawageshik, in conversation, August 8, 2002.
37. The American Philosophical Society has for centuries served as a prominent sponsor of scholarly research in Native American languages and cultures.
38. See Deloria, *Playing Indian,* for a discussion of how nonnative Indian hobbyists, boy scouts, and other enthusiasts in the 1950s sought to perform what they took to be authentic Indian-ness and in so doing displaced the contemporary Native people in their midst and devalued their extant culture as "degraded."
39. Gertrude Kurath to Gertrude Hess, (A.P.A. Asst. Librarian), November 18, 1959, American Philosophical Society.
40. Gertrude Kurath, "Catholic Hymns of Michigan Indians," *Anthropological Quarterly* 30 (1957): 31–44; Gertrude Kurath, "Summertime is Powwow

Time," *Dance Magazine* 40 (1966): 40–41, 85–86; and Gertrude Kurath's notes to "Songs and Dances of Great Lakes Indians," Ethnic Folkways Record, Monograph Series LP 4003 (New York: 1956).
41. Public Law 103-324, 108 Stat. 2156, 104 Cong. (1994).
42. James McClurken, "Ethnohistory of the Little Traverse Bay Bands of Odawa."
43. Vander, *Songprints: The Musical Experience of Five Shoshone Women* (Urbana: University of Illinois Press, 1988).

Editorial Principles and Orthography

1. I am grateful to John Nichols for this cautionary note, given the importance of getting the orthography right for Anishinaabe communities.
2. I direct future community members and scholars interested in this work to the impressive 267 typescript pages of transcription and translation of additional stories from the Kurath Ettawageshik audio recordings (Spools I–V) undertaken by Howard Webkamigad of Algoma University College for James McClurken of Michigan State University.

Chapter 1. Peninsular People

1. The numbers of Odawas living in urban centers is certainly no longer small. As a result of the incentives offered by formal relocation policies at the time of this book's original writing and the inducements of the economy in years since, by the late 1970s, half of the Native Americans in the United States lived in urban areas.
2. The Midéwiwin, or Grand Medicine Lodge, is a ceremonial complex involving healing, divination, and recitation of sacred migration stories. The migrations were said to be the fruit of a vision in which the Anishinaabe were to follow a sacred migis shell.
3. See the editor's introduction for further discussion of the authors' perspective on acculturation.

Chapter 2. Public Festivals

1. A fuller account and analysis of the Hiawatha pageants can be found in Michael McNally, "Contesting the 'Real Indian' in *Song of Hiawatha* Pageants."
2. Later powwow culture would speak in terms of "regalia" rather than costume. That the provenance of much of the regalia is from outside the Anishinaabe cultures need not suggest a lack of authenticity. The Plains

provenance of much of the regalia stems largely from late nineteenth and early twentieth century gatherings that brought the Lakota Sioux and Anishinaabe together on reservations in Minnesota and the Dakotas and featured cultural exchange. Exchange and hybridism were elemental to powwow culture in this region long before the specific performances documented here.

3. As with "costume," the term "accessory" may suggest more showmanship than Kurath might have intended. Pipes are and were considered instruments of prayer and fellowship. Certainly some pipes were regarded as more or less sacred; nonetheless, the activity of making and carrying pipes was not a completely casual, completely profane matter.

4. This is perhaps evidence that Eli Thomas distinguishes his show from more ceremonial invocations with a drum.

Chapter 3. Contemporary Dance Patterns

1. Kurath's word choice, "make-believe," is potentially misleading here. Ceremonious action concerning pipes does not always involve actually smoking them. Moreover, it may be out of respect to the pipe that no ceremony is staged in this context.
2. A reference to "Tape Reel 6" is noted in the margin of manuscript here.
3. Kurath adds, "Is this a variant of Baraga Squaw Dance?"
4. Kurath adds, "See recording." Particularly in Upper Peninsula communities, but to some degree throughout Anishinaabe and Métis country in the United States and Canada, fiddling took root from musical exchanges in the fur trade years and developed into a proud form of music making and social dancing.
5. Given the strong biases of missionary and other colonial sources against embodied dance, Kurath's comments are subject to considerable inaccuracy about the particulars of early dance traditions gleaned from such sources.

Chapter 5. Odawa Feasts

1. The editor could not locate this proposed article.
2. Sung by David Kenosha and Eliza Kishigo (1954). For text, see Baraga (1858, 120). For melody, see variant in (Prud'homme 1931, 33).
3. This section was authored by Gertrude Kurath.
4. For more summaries of these customs, see "Berchta" and "Epiphany" in the *Standard Dictionary of Folklore*. See also Gertrude Kurath, "Mexican Moriscas," *Journal of American Folklore* 62: 97–98.
5. The rest of the chapter was again authored by Jane Ettawageshik.

6. The authors indicate that these recorded hymns are analyzed and discussed by Gertrude Kurath in her section on hymns in their publication "Memorial Feasts and Hymns of Catholic Ottawa Indians," *Library Bulletin*, American Philosophical Society, 1955. The editor was unable to locate this proposed publication.
7. At this point there is a break from lost pages in the original manuscript.

Chapter 6. Ojibwe Methodist Camp Meeting and Hymn Singing

1. A page detailing the song before the Doxology was missing from original typescript.

Chapter 7. Hymn Tunes and Texts

1. The variance is an orthographic one, not a semantic one, as Kurath's observation implies.
2. These formal stylizations of speech are common in formal Anishinaabe oratory, Christian or not. See Lisa Valentine, *Making It Their Own: Severn Ojibwe Communicative Practices* (Toronto: University of Toronto Press, 1995).

Chapter 9. Odawa Myths

Except where noted, these endnotes were the original authors'.

1. The following include one or more Odawa myths: Kinietz 1940, Perrot in Blair 1911; Schoolcraft 1848 (also other works of Schoolcraft); Blackbird 1897; Jenness 1935; Michelson 1931; Chamberlain 1891, 197–200; Tanner 1830; Assikinack 1858; Weer 1940; Wright 1917; *Bureau of American Ethnology Bull.* 30; *Jesuit Relation* vols. 51, 54–57; Wood 1918. See also the unpublished notes of Truman Michelson and Gatschett in the files of the Bureau of American Ethnology, which include several Odawa myths.
2. The Odawa script that Fred Ettawageshik uses is based on our English alphabet and his own interpretation of the way it should be used to write Odawa. He does not know just when he began to write Odawa. I am of the opinion that he was influenced by his father, Joe, who also wrote Odawa. The Odawa written by Joe Ettawaweghik is very similar, if not identical, to Fred's rendition.

    A number of Odawas write their language and there is considerable variation among them. The original desire to write Odawa was probably inspired by the Catholic priests. Blackbird speaks of his father in the early days of the mission schools, helping Odawas to learn to write by devising an alphabet that he called "Paw-pape-po" (Blackbird 1897). Old Victoria Cooper still remembers a little about "paw-pa-pe-po" and at one time had a little book explaining it.

It is probable that modern writers of Odawa owe a debt to Fr. Baraga, who translated hymnals and prayerbooks into Odawa in the mid-nineteenth century, yet I have not seen any recently written Odawa that is exactly similar to his. I have tried to pin Fred down a number of times about the origin of his Odawa script, but he usually ends by saying, "I write the words the way they sound to me."

3. The distinction to which Ettawageshik refers here is also a grammatical one. *Aadizookanag,* or what the authors call "myths," are grammatically animate, whereas the "legends and tales," or *dibaadjimowinan,* are gendered inanimate.—Editor

4. Use of the English term "evil" here is misleading; a more accurate word might be "powerful," for sacred power—or, by extension, a being with sacred power—is in many respects morally ambiguous.—Editor

5. Susy Shagonaby reported to me recently that many persons believe that Indian Gardens is still haunted by ghosts of the Maskódens. "When white people first came to live there," Susy says, "they grew squash and pumpkins in their gardens. One day the kids came running in and said they had seen 'them' trampling the squash and pumpkins. Only the kids could see them. So the grown people went out and found the squash and pumpkins all trampled and messed up. Others told about this too."

Susy also told about an experience her father had while driving his buggy through Indian Gardens: "Ater a while my dad heard someone following him. Whatever it was, it could go right through the woods where the horse and buggy couldn't. The horse began to rear up and then to gallop. He was just more than going. After my dad passed Indian Gardens, the horse calmed down. Dad had two different exile experiences like that in Indian Gardens."

6. Another tale that Joe recorded in Odawa but for which I have no translation is "The Fleet-Footed Woman," which describes the efforts of a sorceress to seduce a man from his wife. The Magic Flight motif is included. European influence is suspected in this story. Second, "Two Sisters" is a semi-historical legend about two sisters of the Harbor Springs band of Odawa. Also, Joe recorded a version of "The Origin of Corn," which is almost identical to Fred's story.

7. It is too bad that most of Victoria's tales have not been translated and that I do not even have adequate outlines of the plots to include with this collection. When the stories were recorded, Jim Cooper wrote down the English versions of a number of them. Unfortunately, Jim has mislaid this material.

They are important stories, which would probably give us a clearer picture not only of Odawa mythology but of their customs and beliefs as well. At least, however, they have been recorded on wire, though the laborious task of translating them remains. At the time, it seemed more important to me to record everything in Odawa, since the language is rapidly being forgotten. The following myths and legends from Victoria are included:

- "The Rabbit and the Lynx." This story describes the animals' comical adventures in a trickster type of tale.
- "Man Carried Off by an Eagle (Thunder)." This story is somewhat similar to the tale Jim told me previously and which is given in this collection. However, it contains a description of the origin of the naming ceremony according to the dictates of the thunderers.
- "Nanabojo Cycle." This describes the birth of Nanabojo, several of his adventures, and presumably the flood and earth diver motifs. It is a long myth.
- "Bear Walking." Bear walking is the Odawa term for sorcery and is discussed in chapter 8. In this story a bear walk in the form of an owl tries to bring harm to a family, who use magical means to protect themselves.
- "Bear Walking." This is another tale about sorcery, this time by one brother against another.
- "Family of Bears." Two children are kidnapped by bears.
- "Kidnapping of Child from Burt Lake Band."
- "Autobiography." This describes Victoria's early life at Wasson Grade, where she was born, her attendance at school, and the coming of the Catholic priests in the early nineteenth century. It gives a number of historical facts about Harbor Springs and the Odawas.

8. There are two other tales that I have heard Fred tell. In "The Theft of Fire" a great manido had all the fire in the world. The animals stole a ball of fire from the manido and took turns carrying it because it was so hot. First Coyote carried it, then Raccoon, then Rabbit. When it was Squirrel's turn, he dropped the ball of fire and it started to roll towards him. To protect his tail, Squirrel turned it over his back in a curl. Ever since then, Squirrel's tail has curled over his back.

   The theft of fire is told in some form or other all over the world. In the Indian versions it is usually stolen by a trickster hero, usually an animal, often aided by his friends.

   In "Why the Chipmunk Has Stripes on his Back," A chipmunk was testing a giant who lived far off in the woods. The giant chased the chipmunk and as the chipmunk neared the door of his house, the giant grabbed him in his hand. The chipmunk succeeded in wriggling free, but the giant's fingers left streaks on the chipmunk's back, which have been there ever since.

9. Narrated and translated by Joe Chingwa.
10. Written in Odawa and translated by Fred Ettawageshik.
11. Narrated and translated by Fred Ettawageshik.
12. Written and translated by Fred Ettawageshik.
13. Written in Odawa and translated by Fred Ettawageshik.
14. Written in Odawa and translated by Fred Ettawageshik.
15. Written in Odawa and translated by Fred Ettawageshik.
16. Text and translation by Fred Ettawageshik, 1947.
17. Written in Odawa and translated by Fred Ettawageshik.
18. Written in Odawa and translated by Fred Ettawageshik.
19. Written in Odawa and translated by Fred Ettawageshik.
20. Told by Joe Chingwa.
21. Told by Joe Samuels (Anımıkwαm); told to him by his grandfather.
22. Joe Chingwa heard this story from his wife's grandfather, a Potawatomi. He also heard it told by the Oneidas or some other Iroquois Indians in the East.
23. Told by Joe Chingwa. A longer version, recorded in Odawa, is in the American Philosophical Society.
24. Told by Jim Cooper. The story was told to him when he was child by a brother of Chief Thunder Cloud of Cross Village, an old man at the time, who had lived in Harbor Springs for a few years.
25. Told by Joe Chingwa. Recorded in Odawa also.
26. Written in Odawa and translated by Fred Ettawageshik.
27. Written in Odawa and translated by Fred Ettawageshik.
28. Written in Odawa and translated by Fred Ettawageshik.
29. Narrated and translated by Fred Ettawageshik.
30. Written in Odawa and translated by Fred Ettawageshik.
31. Written in Odawa and translated by Fred Ettawageshik.
32. Told by Joe Chingwa. Recorded in Odawa.
33. Told by Joe Chingwa. Recorded in Odawa in a longer version.
34. Told by Clara Cooper.
35. Told by Joe Chingwa. Recorded in Odawa in a longer version.
36. Narrated and translated by Fred Ettawageshik.
37. Told Joe Chingwa. Longer version recorded in Odawa.
38. Written in Odawa and translated by Fred Ettawageshik.
39. This presumably refers to the great earthquake along the New Madrid fault that shook the entire Midwest in 1809.
40. Told by Joe Chingwa.
41. Told by Joe Chingwa.

42. Told by Joe Chingwa.
43. Narrated by Victoria Cooper. Translated by Fred Ettawageshik.
44. Told by Joe Chingwa. Recorded in Odawa in a longer version.
45. Told by Joe Chingwa. The story was told to him by Charley Green, an old man from the Horton's Bay vicinity. It has been recorded in Odawa.
46. Told by Joe Chingwa. The way in which Mkkwánıwi's given name, číŋwə, was chosen for him by his father is mentioned in chapter 2. Gertrude has a transcription of Mkkwánıwi's medicine chant in music along with a description given by Joe of how Mkkwánıwi received the chant and how he used it. Many of the herbal remedies described to me by Joe were Mkkwánıwi's. It is also probable that Joe learned some of the myths and legends he told from Mkkwánıwi.

    Fred Ettawageshik says that Mkkwánıwi told him that he went hunting at one time far in the south where he saw large snakes wound around the tree limbs. On the day the old man died he was upstairs in one of the bedrooms in Fred's old home. He asked Fred's mother to make him a bowl of corn soup. He smiled when she brought it to him, took one spoonful, and died with the spoon raised in his hand.
47. Told by Joe Chingwa. Long story recorded in Odawa.
48. Told by Joe Chingwa. Recorded in Odawa.
49. The remainder of this story has not been translated. It describes the trial in which Mkkwánıwi was one of the judging chiefs. The murderer's relatives were compelled to make substantial gifts of food and clothing to the family of the murdered man.
50. Told by Joe Chingwa. Long version recorded in Odawa.
51. This concluding section was assembled and drafted by Gertrude Kurath, and thus appeared in their manuscript as a separate chapter. —Editor
52. Told by Anthony Chingman and recorded by Edwin Burrows at Hastings, August 15, 1954.
53. Told by Thomas Shalifoe, Jr., of Baraga.
54. "Devil" is an insufficient translation of Manidu, or *manidoo*, because the term implies a powerful spirit that is, in effect, amoral, not immoral or simply evil. —Editor.
55. Told by Eli Thomas and Eddie Jackson.
56. Told by Eli Thomas.
57. Told by Eli Thomas.
58. Told by Eli Thomas.
59. Told by Eli Thomas.
60. Told by Eli Thomas.
61. Told by David Kenosha. Translation by Fred Ettawageshik.

Chapter 10. Interpretation

1. One could question how accurately the authors' reference to *animism,* a belief that all living things have a soul, applies to aboriginal Anishinaabe religion, given the tradition's unifying concept of *Gizhe Manidoo* (Great Spirit).
2. The authors query whether this is the former Sun Ceremony.
3. This, of course, has not remained true, even if it was accurate at the time.
4. The authors pose the question of whether this is what Tanner calls the "Great Feast." See Tanner 1830, 2: 886.

WORKS CITED AND SUGGESTED READING

Entries designated by an asterisk (*) are those supplemented by the editor as references for editorial remarks in the text. These are by no means exhaustive of the extensive literature on the Anishinaabe since 1955.

American Bible Society. 1875. *Otoshki-Kikindiuin au Tebeniminung gaie Bemajiinung Jesus Christ* (The New Testament). New York.
Assikinack, Francis. 1858. "Legends and Traditions of the Odahwah Indians." *Canadian Journal of Industry, Science, and Art* 13:115–25.
Bald, F. Clever. 1954. *Michigan in Four Centuries.* New York: Harpers.
Barbeau, C. Marius. 1915. *Huron and Wyandot Mythology.* Memoir 80, Anthropological Series, 11. Ottawa: Government Printing Bureau for the Canada Department of Mines, Geological Survey.
———. 1952. "The Old-World Dragon in America." In vol. 3 of *Proceedings of the Twenty-ninth Congress of Americanists,* ed. Sol Tax. Chicago: University of Chicago Press.
Baraga, Fr. Friedrich. 1837. *Abrege de l'historie des Indiens de l'Amerique septentrionale.* Paris; A La Société des Bons Livres.
———. 1858. *Katolik Anamie Misinaigan.* Cincinnati.
———. 1878. *Theoretical and Practical Grammar of the Otchipwe Language.* Montreal: Beauchemin and Valois.
———. n.d. *Gijigong Ababikaigan: Katolik Anamie Masinaigan* (Holy Songs). St. Louis, Mo.
Barrett, S.A. 1917. "Pomo Bear Doctor." *University of California Publications* 12:443–65. Berkeley, Calif.
Barrows, Cliff. 1950. *Singing Evangelism: Billy Graham Campaign Songs.* Winona Lake, Ind.
Bas, Giulio 1906. *Über die Ausfuhrung der Gregorianischen Gesange.* Dusseldorf.
*Bell, Catherine. 1992. *Ritual Theory, Ritual Practice.* New York: Oxford University Press.

Benson, John T. 1947. *Songs of Spiritual Power.* Nashville, Tenn.

Benson, Louis F. 1915. *The English Hymn.* New York: Doran and Co.

Blackbird, Chief Andrew J. 1897. *History of the Ottawa and Chippewa Indians of Michigan.* Harbor Springs, Mich.

Blair, Emma, ed. 1911–12. *The Indian Tribes of the Upper Mississippi Valley and Region of the Great Lakes.* 2 vols. Cleveland, Ohio.

*Bourdieu, Pierre. 1987. *Outline of a Theory of Practice.* Trans. Richard Nice. New York: Cambridge University Press.

Browner, Tara. 2002. *Heartbeat of the People: Music and Dance of the Northern Pow-Wow.* Urbana: University of Illinois Press.

Burchenal, Elizabeth. 1929. *Five Folk-dances from Austria, Germany, Holland.* Boston.

Burton, Frederick. R. 1909. *American Primitive Music: With Special Attention to the Ojibways.* New York: Moffat, Yard and Company.

Cartwright, W., and F. H. Douglas. 1950. *Basic Types of Indian Women's Costumes.* Denver Art Museum. Leaflet 108. Denver: Denver Art Museum.

Casagrande, Joseph B. 1951. "Ojibwa Bear Ceremonialism." In vol. 2 of *Proceedings of the Twenty-ninth International Congress of Americanists,* 113–17. Chicago: University of Chicago Press.

Catlin, George. 1841. *The North American Indians.* 2 vols. London.

Chamberlain, A.F. 1891. "Nanibozhu among the Otchipwe, Mississagas and Other Algonkian Tribes." *Journal of American Folklore* 4:193–213.

de Champlain, Samuel. 1929. *Voyages.* Vol. 3 of *Collected Works of Champlain.* Toronto: Champlain Society.

*Child, Brenda. 1998. *Boarding School Seasons: American Indian Families 1900–1940.* Lincoln: University of Nebraska Press.

Conklin, Harold C., and William C. Sturtevant. 1953. "Seneca Singing Tools at Coldspring Longhouse." *Proceedings of the American Philosophical Society* 97:262–90.

Cooper, Fr. John M. 1934. *The Northern Algonquian Supreme Being.* Catholic University Anthropological Series, vol. 2. Washington, D.C.: Catholic University.

Copway, George. 1851. *Traditional History and Characteristic Sketches of the Ojibway Nation.* Boston: Mussey Company.

Cowan, Marion M., and Marjorie E. Davis. 1955. *Hymn Writing in Aboriginal Languages.* Norman, Okla.: Summer Institute of Linguistics.

Curtis, Martha E. 1952. "The Black Bear and White-Tailed Deer as Potent Factors in the Folklore of the Menominee Indians." *Midwest Folklore* 2:177–90.

Davidson, John F. 1946. "Ojibwa Songs." *Journal of American Folklore* 58:303–6.

Deardorff, Merle H. 1951. "The Religion of Handsome Lake, Its Origin and Development." In *Symposium on Local Diversity in Iroquois Culture,* ed. William Fenton, 77–108. Bureau of American Ethnology Bulletin 149. Washington,

D.C.: U.S. Government Printing Office.

Densmore, Frances. 1910. *Chippewa Music*. Bureau of American Ethnology Bulletin 45. Washington, D.C.: U.S. Government Printing Office.

———. 1913. *Chippewa Music*. Bureau of American Ethnology Bulletin 53. Washington, D.C.: U.S. Government Printing Office.

———. 1918. *Teton Sioux Music*. Bureau of American Ethnology Bulletin 61. Washington, D.C.: U.S. Government Printing Office.

———. 1929. *Chippewa Customs*. Bureau of American Ethnology Bulletin 86. Washington, D.C.: U.S. Government Printing Office.

———. 1932. *Menominee Music*. Bureau of American Ethnology Bulletin 102. Washington, D.C.: U.S. Government Printing Office.

———. 1947. "Imitative Dances among the American Indians." *Journal of American Folklore* 60:73–78.

———. 1949. "A Study of Some Michigan Indians." *Anthropological Publications of the Museum of Anthropology (University of Michigan)* I:1–41. Ann Arbor: University of Michigan.

———. 1953. "Technique in the Music of the American Indian." Bureau of American Ethnology Bulletin 151. Anthropological Papers. 36:211–16. Washington, DC: U.S. Government Printing Office.

*Diamond, Beverly, M. Sam Cronk, and Francesca von Rosen. 1994. *Visions of Sound*. Chicago: University of Chicago Press.

Dorson, Richard M. 1952. *Bloodstoppers and Bearwalkers*. Cambridge, Mass: Harvard University Press.

*Dowd, Gregory. 1992. *A Spirited Resistance: The North American Struggle for Unity 1745–1815*. Baltimore: Johns Hopkins University Press.

Driver, Harold E. 1953. "Indian Tribes of North America." *Indiana University Publications in Anthropology and Linguistics*. Mem. 9. Bloomington: Indiana University.

Duggan, Anne S., Jeannette Schlottmann, and Abbie Rutledge, 1948. *The Folk Dance Library*. New York: A. S. Barnes.

Eggan, Fred. R. 1952. "The Ethnological Cultures and their Archaeological Background." In *Archaeology in Eastern United States*, ed. James B. Griffin, 35–45. Chicago: University of Chicago Press.

Ettawageshik, Fred. "Ghost Suppers." *American Anthropologist* 45 (1943): 491–93.

Evangelical Lutheran Synodical Conference of North America. 1941. *The Lutheran Hymnal*. St. Louis: Concordia Publishers.

Farver, Peru. 1938. *Corporate Charter of the Saginaw Chippewa Indian Tribe of the Isabella Reservation of Michigan*. Washington, D.C.: U.S. Government Printing Office.

Fenton, William N. 1940. "Problems Arising from the Historic Northeastern Position of the Iroquois." In *Essays in Historical Anthropology of North America*,

159–251. Smithsonian Misc. Coll. 100. Washington, D.C.: Smithsonian Institution.

———, ed. 1951. *Symposium on Local Diversity in Iroquois Culture.* Bureau of American Ethnology Bulletin 149. Washington, D.C.: U.S. Government Printing Office.

Fenton, William N., and Gertrude Kurath. 1953. *The Iroquois Eagle Dance.* Bureau of American Ethnology Bulletin 156. Washington, D.C.: U.S. Government Printing Office.

Fisher, Margaret M. 1946. "The Mythology of the Northern and Northeastern Algonkians in Reference to Algonkian Mythology as a Whole." In *Man in Northeastern North America.* Andover, Mass.: Phillips Academy, the Foundation.

Flannery, Regina. 1939. "An Analysis of Coastal Algonquian Culture." *Catholic University of America Anthropology Series 7*. Washington, D.C.: Catholic University.

Foote, H. W. 1940. *Three Centuries of American Hymnody.* Cambridge: Harvard University Press.

Free Methodist Church of North America. 1910. *Free Methodist Hymnal.* Winona Lake, Ind.

Gamble, John I. 1952. "Changing Patterns in Kiowa Indian Dances." In vol. 2 of *Proceedings of the Twenty-ninth International Congress of Americanists,* 94–104. Chicago: University of Chicago Press.

Gatschet, Albert S. n.d. Unpublished notes in Bureau of American Ethnography files. Washington, D.C.

Graham, Floy Irene. 1938. *Petoskey and Bay View in Ye Olden Days.* Petoskey, Mich.

Grand Rapids and Indiana Railway. 1912. *The Indian Play–Hiawatha.* Grand Rapids, Mich.

Greenman, Emerson F. 1937. *The Younge site; an archaeological record from Michigan.* Museum of Anthropology. Occasional Contributions, no. 6. Ann Arbor: University of Michigan Press.

Griffin, James B. 1952. "Culture Periods in Eastern United States Archaeology." In *Archaeology of Eastern United States,* 352–64. Chicago: University of Chicago Press.

*Grim, John. 1983. *The Shaman: Patterns of Religious Healing among the Ojibwa Indians.* Norman: University of Oklahoma Press.

*Gross, Lawrence. n.d. "The Liberating and Healing Power of the Trickster: A Case Study of Nanabush in the Anishinaabe Tradition." Unpublished manuscript.

Hadlock, Wendell. 1947. "War among Northeastern Woodland Indians." *American Anthropologist* 49:204–21.

Hallowell, A. Irving. 1926. "Bear Ceremonialism in the Northern Hemisphere." *American Anthropologist* 26:1–175.

———. 1946. "Concordance of Ojibwa Narratives in the Published Works of Henry R. Schoolcraft." *Journal of American Folklore* 59:136–53.

———. 1947. "Myth, Culture and Personality. *American Anthropologist* 49:544–56.

———. 1955. *Culture and Experience*. Philadelphia: University of Pennsylvania Press.

Hamilton, Charles. 1950. *Cry of the Thunderbird*. New York: Macmillan.

Hastings, Thomas and Lowell Mason. 1835. *Spiritual Songs for Social Worship*. Utica, N.Y.: Gardiner Tracy.

Hinsdale, Wilbert B. 1925. "Primitive Man in Michigan." *Michigan Handbook*. Ann Arbor: University of Michigan.

———. 1927. *Indians of Washtenaw County*. Ann Arbor: G. Wahr.

———. 1930. *First People of Michigan*. Ann Arbor: G. Wahr.

———. 1931. "Archaeological Atlas of Michigan." *University of Michigan Handbook Series 4*. Ann Arbor: University of Michigan.

———. 1932. "Distribution of the Aboriginal Population of Michigan." Ann Arbor: University of Michigan Press.

Hoffman, Walter J. 1891. "The Mide'wiwin or 'Grand Medicine Society' of the Ojibwa." In *Seventh Annual Report of the Bureau of American Ethnology, 1885–1886*, 149–300. Washington, D.C.: U.S. Government Printing Office.

———. 1896. "The Menominee Indians." In *Fourteenth Report of the Bureau of American Ethnology*, Pt. 1. Washington, D.C.: U.S. Government Printing Office.

Honigmann, John J. 1947. "Witch-Fear in Post Contact Kaska Society." *American Anthropologist* 49:222–43.

Hubbard, Bela. 1887. *Memorials of a Half-Century*. New York.

*Hyde, Lewis. 1998. *Trickster Makes the World*. New York: Farrar, Straus, Giroux.

Hymns Ancient and Modern. 1909. London: Clowes Sons.

Indian Gospel Crusaders. 1952. *Indian Gospel Light,* ed. Myrtle Pappas. Battle Creek, Mich.

Jenness, Diamond. 1935. "The Ojibwa Indians of Parry Island, Their Social and Religious Life." Canada Department of Mines, National Museum of Canada, Bulletin 78.

The Jesuit Relations and Allied Documents, 1610–1791. 1895–1901. ed. Reuben Thwaites. 73 vols. Cleveland: Burrows Bros.

Jones, Peter Kahkewaquonaby. 1854. *Ojebway Nuhguhmonun: A Collection of Chippeway and English Hymns*. New York: Carlton and Phillips.

———. 1861. *History of the Ojibway Indians*. London: Houlston and Wright.

Jones, William. 1939. *Ethnography of the Fox Indians*. Bureau of American Ethnology. Bull. 125. Washington D. C.: U.S. Government Printing Office.

———. 1894. "The Algonquian Manitu." *Journal of American Folklore* 17:183–90.

Julian, John. 1892. *A Dictionary of Hymnology*. London: John Murray.

Kellogg, Louise P. 1925. *The French Régime in Wisconsin and the Northwest*. Madison: State Historical Society of Wisconsin.

Keesing, Felix M. 1939. *The Menomini Indians of Wisconsin*. Philadelphia: American Philosophical Society.

Kenton, Edna, ed. 1925. *The Jesuit Relations*. New York: Albert and Boni.

Kinietz, W. Vernon. 1940. "The Indians of the Western Great Lakes, 1650–1760." *Occasional Contributions of the Museum of Anthropology of the University of Michigan*. Ann Arbor: University of Michigan.

———. 1947. "Chippewa Village." Cranbrook Institute of Science, Bulletin 25. Bloomfield Hills, Mich.: Cranbrook Institute of Science.

Kortright, Francis H. 1942. *The Ducks, Geese and Swans of North America*. Washington, D.C.: American Wildlife Institute.

Kurath, Gertrude P. 1951a. "Local Diversity in Music and Dance." In *Iroquois Symposium*. Bureau of American Ethnology Bulletin 149, 109–138. Washington, D.C.: U.S. Government Printing Office.

———. 1951b. "Seneca Song and Dance Style." Manuscript in the American Philosophical Society Library, Philadelphia.

———. 1952a. "Ceremonial Songs of Tonawanda Seneca Longhouse." Manuscript in the American Philosophical Society Library, Philadelphia.

———. 1952b. "Onondaga Ritualism." Manuscript in New York State Music Education Department.

———. 1953a. "Native Choreographic Areas of North America." *American Anthropologist* 55:60–73.

———. 1953b. "The Tutelo Harvest Rite." *Science Monthly* 76:153–62.

———. 1954a. "Chippewa Sacred Songs in Religious Metamorphosis." *Science Monthly* 79:311–17.

———. 1954b. "The Tutelo Fourth Night Spirit Release Singing." *Midwest Folklore* 4:87–105.

———. 1955a. "Modern Ottawa Dancers." *Midwest Folklore* 5:15–22.

———. 1955b. *Songs of the Wigwam*. Delaware, Ohio: Cooperative Recreation Service.

———. 1956a. "Pan-Indian Dances and Songs of the Midwest." *Journal of Health, Physical Education and Recreation* 27:44–45, 51–52.

———. 1956b. *Songs and Dances of Great Lakes Indians*. Ethnic Folkways Record and Monograph LP 1003. New York: Folkways.

*———. 1986. *Half a Century of Dance Research: Essays by Gertrude Prokosch Kurath*. Flagstaff, Ariz.: Cross Cultural Dance Resources.

*———. 1957. "Catholic Hymns of Michigan Indians," *Anthropological Quarterly* 30:31–44.

Kurath, Gertrude P., Jane Ettawageshik, and Fred Ettawageshik. 1955. "Memorial Feasts and Hymns of Catholic Ottawa Indians." Manuscript to be published in Library Bulletin. *American Philosophical Society*. [Editor could not locate].

Kurath, Gertrude P., and William N. Fenton. 1951. "The Feast of the Dead." *Iroquois Symposium*. Bureau of American Ethnology Bulletin 149, 1399–165. Washington, D.C.: U.S. Government Printing Office.

*Landes, Ruth. 1968. *Ojibwa Religion and the Midéwiwin*. Madison: University of Wisconsin Press.

Lanzelère, Claude S. 1936. *The Story of Michigan*. 2d ed. Lansing, Mich.: Michigan School Service.

Linton, Ralph. 1943. "Nativistic Movements." *American Anthropologist* 45:230–40.

Lowie, Robert H. 1935. *The Crow Indians*. New York: Farrar, Rinehart.

Lyford, Carrie. 1945. *Iroquois Crafts*. Washington, D.C.: U.S. Indian Service, Haskell Institute.

Mason, Bernard. 1938. *Drums, Tom-toms and Rattles*. New York: Barnes Co.

———. 1940. *Dances and Stories of the American Indian*. New York: Barnes Co.

*McClurken, James. 1988. "We Wish to Be Civilized: Ottawa/American Political Contests on the Michigan Frontier." PhD diss., Michigan State University.

*———. 1991. *Gah-Baeh-Jhabgwah-Buk--The Way It Happened: A Visual Culture History of the Little Traverse Bay Bands of Odawa*. East Lansing: Michigan State University Museum.

*McNally, Michael D. 2004. *Honoring Elders*. New York: Columbia University Press.

*———. 2000. *Ojibwe Singers: Hymns, Grief, and a Native Culture in Motion*. New York: Oxford University Press.

*———. 2006. "The Indian Passion Play: Contesting the 'Real' Indian in *Song of Hiawatha* Pageants, 1901–1960." *American Quarterly* 58 (March): 105–36.

Michelson, Truman. 1911. "Ottawa Gentes." *American Anthropologist* 13:338.

———. 1918–19. "Fox Mortuary Customs and Beliefs." In *Bureau of American Ethnology Fortieth Annual Report, 1917-18*. Washington, D.C.: U.S. Government Printing Office.

———. 1928. *The Buffalo-Head Dance of the Thunder Gens of the Fox Indians*. Bureau of American Ethnology Bulletin 87. Washington, D.C.: U.S. G.P.O.

———. 1931. "Three Ottawa Tales." *Journal of American Folklore* 14:191–95.

———. n.d. Unpublished notes in Bureau of American Ethnography files. Washington, D.C.

Morse, Jedidiah. 1822. *A Report to the Secretary of War of the United States on Indian Affairs*. New Haven.

Nettl, Bruno. 1953. "The Shawnee Musical Style." *Southwest Journal of Anthropology* 9:277–85.

———. 1954. "Text-Music Relationships in Arapaho Songs." *Southwest Journal of Anthropology* 10:192–99.

Nichols, John and Earl Nyholm. 1995. *A Concise Dictionary of Minnesota Ojibwe.* Minneapolis: University of Minnesota Press.

Parkman, Francis A. 1902. *The Jesuits in North America.* Boston.

Prud'homme, Père Paul. 1931. *Anamie Nagamonan* (Prayer Songs). Nipigong, Ontario.

Quimby, George I. 1952. "The Archaeology of the Upper Great Lakes Area." In *Archaeology of the Eastern United States,* ed. James B. Griffin. Chicago: University of Chicago Press.

Radin, Paul. 1923. "The Winnebago Tribe." *Thirty-Seventh Annual Report of the Bureau of American Ethnology, 1915–1916,* 33–560. Washington, D.C.: U.S. Government Printing Office.

*———. 1976. *The Trickster: A Study in Amerindian Indian Mythology.* 1956; New York: Schocken.

Ritzenthaler, Robert E. 1953a. "The Impact of Small Industry on an Indian Community." *American Anthropologist* 55:143–47.

———. 1953b. *The Potawatomi Indians of Wisconsin.* Bulletin of the Public Museum of the City of Milwaukee 10.

Roe, Frank Gilbert. 1951. *The North American Buffalo.* Toronto: University of Toronto Press.

Sachs, Curt. 1953. *Rhythm and Tempo.* New York: Columbia University Press.

Sagard-Théodat, Gabriel. 1866. *Histoire du Canada et Voyages.* 2 vols. 1636; Paris.

Schmalstich, Clemens. n.d. *Das Deutsche Volkslied.* Berlin: Bernbach.

Schoolcraft, Henry R. 1839. *Algic Researches.* 2 vols. New York: Harper Brothers.

———. 1845. *Oneota.* New York: Wiley and Putnam.

———. 1848. *The Indian in His Wigwam.* Buffalo: Derby and Hanson.

———. 1851. *Personal Memoirs of a Residence of Thirty Years with the Indian Tribes of the American Frontier* A.D. *1912–1842.* Philadelphia: Grigg, Elliot and Co.

———. 1852. *Information Respecting the Indian Tribes of the United States,* vol. 2. Philadelphia: Lippincott.

Shurtleff, Mary Belle. 1940. *Old Arbre Croche.* Cross Village, Mich.

Skinner, Alanson. 1913. "Social Life and Ceremonial Bundles of the Menomini Indians." *Anthropological Papers of the American Museum of Natural History* 15:1–165.

———. 1915. "Associations and Ceremonies of the Menomini Indians." *Anthropological Papers of the American Museum of Natural History* 13:167–215.

———. 1926. "The Mascoutens or Prairie Potawatomi Indians." *Bulletin of the Public Museum of the City of Milwaukee* 6:263–326.

Society of St. John the Evangelist. 1934. *Liber Usualis.* Tournal, Belgium.

Soney, William. n.d. *Ojibway Hymn Book*. Walpole Island, Ontario.

Speck, Frank G. 1915. *Myths and Folk-lore of the Timiskaming Algonquian and the Timagami Ojibwa*. Memoir 71, Anthropological Series, 9. Ottawa: Government Printing Bureau for the Canada Department of Mines, Geological Survey.

———. 1945. "The Celestial Bear Comes Down to Earth." *Sci. Publ.* 7, Reading, Penn.: Reading Public Museum and Art Gallery.

———. 1949. *Midwinter Rites of the Cayuga Longhouse*. Philadelphia: University of Pennsylvania Press.

Speck, Frank G., and G. Herzog. 1942. *The Tutelo Spirit Adoption Ceremony*. Harrisburg, Penn.: Pennsylvania Historical Commission.

Standard Dictionary of Folklore, Mythology and Legend. 1950. 2 vol. ed. Maria Leach. New York: Funk & Wagnalls.

Tanner, John. 1830. *A Narrative of the Captivity and Adventures of John Tanner*. 2 vols. New York: Edwin James.

———. 1835. *Mémoires de John Tanner*. 2 vols. Paris: Edwin James.

Tax, Sol. 1937. "The Social Organization of the Fox Indians." In *Social Anthropology of North American Tribes*, ed. F. Eggan. Chicago: University of Chicago Press.

Thomas, Cyrus. 1903. *Indians of North America in Historic Times*. Philadelphia: G. Battie and Sons.

Thompson, Stith. 1946. *The Folktale*. New York: Dryden Press.

Thwaites, Reuben G. ed. 1906. *Collections of the State Historical Society of Wisconsin*, vol. 17. Madison.

Tschopik, Harry, Jr. 1952. *Indians of North America*. New York: American Museum of Natural History.

U.S. Bureau of American Ethnology. 1907–1910. *Handbook of American Indians North of Mexico*. 2 vols. Bureau of American Ethnology Bulletin 30. Washington., D.C.: U.S. Government Printing Office.

*Valentine, J. Randolph. 2001. *Nishinaabemwin Reference Grammar*. Toronto: University of Toronto Press.

*Valentine, Lisa. 1995. *Making It Their Own: Severn Ojibwe Communicative Practices*. Toronto: University of Toronto Press.

*Vander, Judith. 1988. *Songprints: The Musical Experience of Five Shoshone Women*. Urbana: University of Illinois Press.

*Vecsey, Christopher, 1983. *Traditional Ojibwa Religion and its Historical Changes*. Philadelphia: American Philosophical Society.

*———. 1988. *Imagine Ourselves Richly: Mythic Narratives of North American Indians*. New York: Crossroad.

*Vennum, Thomas, Jr. 1982. *The Ojibwa Dance Drum*. Washington, D.C.: Smithsonian Institution Press.

Verwyst, Chrysostom. 1901. *Chippewa Exercises.* Harbor Springs, Mich.

*Vizenor, Gerald. 1984. *The People Named the Chippewa.* Minneapolis: University of Minnesota Press.

*———. 1988. *Fugitive Poses: Native American Scenes of Absence and Presence.* Lincoln: University of Nebraska Press.

Walker, J. R. 1917. "The Sun Dance and Other Ceremonies of the Oglala Division of the Teton Dakota." *American Museum of Natural History Anthropology Papers* 16:51–221.

Walker, Louise. 1949. "Indian Feast of the Dead." *Journal of American Folklore* 62:428.

———. 1950. "Indian Camp Meeting at Greensky Hill." *Journal of American Folklore* 63:96–97.

———. 1953. "The Legend of Indian Corn." *Trails for Juniors.*

Warren, William W. 1885. *History of the Ojibways.* St. Paul, Minn.: Minnesota Historical Society.

Waugh, F. W. 1916. *Iroquois Food and Food Preparation.* Memoir 86, Anthropological Series, 12. Ottawa: Government Printing Bureau for the Canada Department of Mines, Geological Survey.

Weer, Paul. 1940. "Ethnological Notes on the Ottawa." *Proceedings of the Indiana Academy of Science* 49:23–27.

Wolfram, Richard. 1951. *Die Volkstänze in Österreich und verwandte Tänze in Europa.* Salzburg: O. Müller.

Works Progress Administration (WPA). 1941 *Michigan: A Guide to the Wolverine State.* New York: Oxford University Press.

Welpley, Margaret N. 1932. *A Concordance to Cree Mythology.* PhD diss., George Washington University.

West, George A. 1934. *Tobacco, Pipes and Smoking Customs of the American Indians.* 2 vols. *Bulletin of the Public Museum of the City of Milwaukee* 17.

*Widder, Keith. 1999. *Battle for the Soul.* East Lansing: Michigan State University Press.

Wike, Joyce. 1952. "The Role of the Dead in Northwest Coast Culture." In *Proceedings of the Twenty-ninth International Congress of Americanists* 3:97–103. Chicago: University of Chicago Press.

Willets, Jane Esther. 1948. *Correlated Changes in Ottawa Kinship and Social Organization.* Master's thesis, University of Pennsylvania.

Wissler, Clark. 1915. "Costumes of the Plains Indians." *Anthropological Papers of the American Museum of Natural History* 17:39–91.

Wood, Edwin O. 1918. *Historic Mackinac.* 2 vols. New York.

Wright, John C. 1917. *The Crooked Tree.* Harbor Springs, Mich.

INDEX

A

Aadizookan, xxii, 270, 274–77, 437; distinguished from *dibaadjimowin*, 269–70; seasonal restrictions on, 242. *See also* Myths
Absent Trapper, The, 113
Accordion, 188
Acculturation, 27, 427–429; inadequacy of, as framework for culture change, xii, xxiii–xxv
Acrobatic Dance, 45
Adeste Fideles, 224
Adoption, 38, 41, 43, 423. *See also* Naming ceremony
Adoption Dance, 58
Aeolian mode, 217
Afterlife, 419–21. *See also* Death; Happy Hunting Ground; West
Ahgosa, Susan, 22–24
Alas and Did My Savior Bleed, 198, 227
Albert, Whitney (Blue Cloud), xxix, 17–18, 40, 42, 45, 46, 50, 71; and dance, 72, 73, 77, 83; and hymns, 202, 214, 223–24; song performances of, 93, 96–97, 133, 135, 229; song repertoire of, 109–20, 127, 130, 138, 416
Algonquin stories, 276, 277
All Hail the Power of Jesus' Name, 188
All Souls' Day, 214
Allotment, 18–19
Allouez, Fr. Claude, 11, 152, 396, 401, 405, 409, 424
American Philosophical Society, xxxvi, xxxviii, xlv, xlvi, xlvii, 92, 167, 273
Anamie-nagamonan, 216. *See also* Hymns, Roman Catholic
Ancestors, 404, 421
André, Fr., 11, 215, 396, 426
Anishinaabe: criminal justice of, 368, 373, 401; defined, xiv, 4; history of, 5; livelihood of, 4, 11, 18, 25; tradition, resurgence of, 389–40. *See also* Religion, Anishinaabe
Apteneben (Midsummer Festival), 45
Arapaho, 136, 137
Art. *See* Crafts
Asignok, Chief, 24, 273
Assimilation policy, xvii, xxv, 58
At the Cross, 188, 198
Athens, Mich., 22
Ave Maria Stella, 216

B

Bad River, Wisc., 26, 27
"Bagag, the Skeleton," 277, 335–36
Baptism, 201

Baraga, Mich., 24–26
Baraga, Fr. Frederic, xv, xlii, 25, 26, 150, 177, 216, 414, 415, 425, 437
Bartram, Fr., 15
Baseball, 42, 266
Basket weaving demonstration, 45
Basketry. *See* Crafts
Bass, Rev. A., 210
Baths, ice water, 370
Bats, 241
Beadwork. *See* Crafts
Bear Dance, 59, 68–69, 82, 88, 137, 411
Bear Feast, 142, 153–54, 169, 248, 393
Bear Song, 68, 88, 106
Bear walks, 110, 241, 243–51, 371, 381, 405
Bears, 275, 285–306, 321–22, 339–41, 373, 407–8; East, association with, 401
Beauty contests, 37
Beavers, 309, 378
Beggars' procession. *See* Bojoing
Begging Dance, 71, 158, 392, 394, 412. *See also* Dog Dance
Beliefs. *See* Religion, Anishinaabe
Bells, 66, 80, 187
Benediction, 196
Berries, 412. *See also* Strawberries
Big Village, 23
Bimaadiziwin (the good life), xxii
Birch (bark), 45, 323–24, 328
Birch, Mrs., 43, 72
Birds. *See* Bluebirds; Cranes; Ducks; Eagles; Geese; Kingbirds; Loons; Robins
Black, Julia, xxxvi, xlvii, 146, 173
Blackbird, Andrew (Mack-e-te-be-nessy), viii, xlii, 38, 176, 273, 280, 358, 391, 394, 425, 437
Blackfoot, 276, 278, 402
Blanket Act, 41, 43

Bluebirds, 410
Boarding schools, xvi–xvii, xxxiv, 213
Boasting Dance, 414
Bojoing, 143–48, 157
Bourasaw, Rose, 26
Bourdieu, Pierre, 239
Bow and Arrow Dance, 36, 72
Boy Scouts, 38
Boyd, George, 394
Brave Song, 115, 416
Bread making, 43
Bruneau, Antoine, 66
Buffalo Dance, 36, 52, 59, 70, 83, 84, 394, 411
Burrows, Edwin, 279
Burt Lake, Mich., 371–74. *See also* Mkkwánıwi, Louis
Burton, Frederick, 96, 136, 227, 410, 412

C

Cake, 158–59, 175. *See also* King's Supper
Calumet. *See* Pipe
Camp meetings, 6, 23, 25, 186, 427–28; as improvisation on traditional enclaves, 210, 424–25; Greensky Hill, 186, 210; Mount Pleasant, 186–212, 227; public role of women in, 211; schedule of, 209–10
Canoe Song, 115, 334
Carey, Raymond, 41, 44, 65, 80, 84
Caribou Song, 136
Carlisle Indian School, viii, 11, 21
Carp, 408
Ceremonials. *See* Festivals, Indian
Ceremonies, 392–94; first fruits, 393, 417; individual medicine rite, 417–18. See also *specific ceremonies*
Challenge Song, 75, 98

Chamberlain, Margaret, 188, 199
Chamberlain, Mrs., 40, 188, 198, 199
Charge to Keep I Have, A, 206–7
Cheboygan, Mich., 242
Cherokee, 22, 84
Cherry bark, 254, 259
Chevis, John, 42
Chevis, Roy, 188
Chicago, Ill., 369
Chickens, 343–49
"Chief with Seven Sons, The," 283, 369
Child of Sorrow, Child of Care, 199
Chingman, Anthony, 17, 42, 44, 45, 48–49, 374; story repertoire of, 375–76
Chingman, Malvina, 17, 42, 44
Chingwa, Jennie, 254
Chingwa, Joe, xiii, xvii, xxviii–xxix, 13–14, 38, 61, 63, 71, 79, 80, 239, 254, 267, 280; debt to Hiawatha play, 104; origin of name, 166, 439; on directions, 400; on healing, 257–58, 265; on hunting medicine, 253; song performances of, 93, 96–97, 133; song repertoire of, 98–105, 125, 129, 138, 416; story repertoire of, 286–306, 329–30, 331, 351–53, 360–62, 368–74; storytelling of, 272, 274, 277, 278, 283–84
Chingwa, Joe, Jr., 89
Chingwa, Louis, 89
Chingwa, Virginia, 37
Chipmunks, 438
Choirs, 188–89, 201
"Choke Cherries, Story of," 276, 324–35
Cholenec, Fr. Pierre, 215
Christmas, 214, 222, 224, 232
Church of God, 25
Clan. See *Doodem*
Clan Feasts, 392
Coldwater Lake, Mich., 376

Colgrove, John, 188
Come Thou Fount of Every Blessing, 207
Come Ye Sinners, 203
Communion (Eucharist), 187, 188, 201, 214, 232
Constantly Abiding, 188
Contest Dance, 43
Conversion, 187; music's role in, 214. See also Religion, Anishinaabe
Cooper, Betty, 145, 243–44, 404
Cooper, Clara, 278; story repertoire of, 352
Cooper, James, 277, 284, 437–38; story repertoire of, 331–34
Cooper, Ruth Ann, 146
Cooper, Victoria, 147, 173, 174; story repertoire of, 362–68, 404, 437–38; storytelling by, 272, 275, 284
Cooper, Vincent, 146
Copper, 338, 405–6
Corn, 41, 43, 277, 379–80, 412, 413, 437
Corn Dance, 39, 45, 72, 81, 83, 84, 85, 380; Potawatomi, 85
Corn Grinding Dance, 43
Corn grinding demonstration, 43, 45, 50
Corn Husking Feast, 393
Corn (Dance) Song, 136
Corn Soup (parched), 146, 171, 173, 380
Corpus Christi Feast, 169–70, 232
Costumes. See Regalia
Courtship Dance, 79, 101
Courtship (Dance) Song, 101
Cousin Song, 117
Coward's Song, 98, 137
Coyotes, 438
"Cradle in the Other World," 45
Crafts, 11, 33, 40, 41, 44
Cranes, 353, 410
"Creation of Mackinac Island," 276, 329

Creation story. *See* Flood myth
"Creator and the Ten Talents," 277
Cree, 276, 402
Cribbage, 146
"Cricket and the Ant, The," 278, 351–52
Cross, 424–26
Cross making, 171–2
Cross Village, 11, 14–16, 27, 65, 71
Crow (Indians), 401
Crow-Eat-All-Feast, 395
Crows, 410
Culture change. *See* Dance; Religion, Anishinaabe; Songs
Curtis, Dan, 25

D

Dakota, 5, 6, 25, 137, 249, 279, 282, 353, 361–62, 415
Dance: Anishinaabe compared with other Indians', 85–6; culture change and, xxvi, xxx, 46; diminished ritual significance of, xxvi, xxvii, 46, 80, 211, 426; functions of, 58; gestures in storytelling, 284; healing and, 257; humor and, 58, 71, 76, 78; postures of Woodland, 84; prohibition on, 187; provenance of, 52, 409–10, 413; song, association with, 92, 138. *See also specific dances by name*
Danézi, 368
Davenport, Donnie, 163–64
Death, 271, 274, 335–36, 381–82, 403, 425; origin of, 296–301, 419
Death Chant, 276, 301
Deer, 253, 370, 384–86. *See also* Hunting medicine
Deer, story of, 384–86
Deer Dance, 36, 71, 82
Deer Song, 122, 137

"Defeat of the Maskutens, The," 272, 273, 283
DeJean, Fr., 216
Densmore, Frances, xxv, 136, 137, 168
Detroit, Mich., 10, 373, 401
Devil's Island. *See* Manidu Island
"Devil's Pond Story," 341–42
Devurnay, John, 253
Directions, 399–400. See also *each cardinal direction*
Diseases, 262–67. *See also* Healing
Doctoring. *See* Healing
Dog Dance, 43, 71, 394, 411–12
Dog Feast, 395, 415, 416
Dogs, 245–46, 278, 352, 370, 371; offering of, 406, 412, 425
Doodem (*n'dó:dœ:m;* clan; totem), 122, 282, 398, 408, 409, 412, 425
Dorian mode, 217
Dougherty, Rev. Peter, 23
Doxology, 187, 195–96
Dream Dance, 51, 156
Dream Feasts, 417
Dream guardians, 410, 414, 424, 425. *See also* Eagles; Snakes; Thunders
Dreaming, xix, 241, 335, 409; centrality of, to religion, 394; Christianity and, 424; future and, 349–51, 370; healing and, 257; power of, xix; snakes and, 407; songs gifted through, 103–4; names gifted through, 162, 165; thunders and, 403. *See also* Puberty fast
Dress, 257–58, 332. *See also* Regalia
Drinking Song, 18, 96, 101, 108, 121, 123, 135, 137
Druillettes, Fr., 215
Drum, xx, xxi, 50–51; dream dance, 51; in dreams, 241; tom tom, 43; log, 43, 51; with hymn, 201–2
Ducks, 2, 317, 319–21, 378

E

Eagle Dance, 16, 37, 41, 43, 45, 52, 59, 65–67, 81, 84, 88, 410; of Iroquois, 136, 278; and thunders, 405

Eagle feathers, 332

Eagle (Dance) Song, 65, 104, 105, 134, 229

Eagles, 331–32, 332, 353, 355; thunders and, 403; West, association with, 401

Earth. *See* Grandmother Earth

Earthquake of 1809, 357

East, 399–401

Easter, 232

Economy. *See* Anishinaabe, livelihood of

Elders, 58, 83, 335; animal, 286, 288; naming by, 160, 162; oral tradition and, xxix, 392. *See also* Cooper, Victoria; Mkkwánıwi, Louis; Sákko

Elizabeth, 200

Elk, Billy, 40, 61, 80

Elk, Elijah, 19

Epiphany. *See* King's Supper

Epitoweng nagamoda, 39

Escanaba "Indian village," 26, 45

Ettawageshik, Frank, vii–viii

Ettawageshik, Fred, xvii, xxxiii, xxxiv–xxv, 12–3; on bear walks, 244–46; cribbage, traditional games of, 145; dances, 75, 83; naming ceremonies by, 164; performances by, 37, 39; songs, 95, 130, 138; story repertoire of, 306–29, 335–51, 356–59, 438–39; storytelling of, 284–85; translations of, 273

Ettawageshik, Jane Willets, xxxiii–xxxiv; involvement of, in planning festivals, 38; naming ceremony of, 160–61

Eucharist, 187, 188, 201, 214, 232

Evan, 204

Evil, 440. *See also* Matchi Manido

Exaudiat, 215

F

Face painting, 414–15

Falcons, 410

Farce, 71, 76, 78, 80

Farewell Dance, 79

Fast. *See* Puberty fast

Feast for the Dead, 142, 157, 159, 170, 175–82, 403, 392, 395, 398, 412, 422, 425, 427. *See also* Ghost Supper

Feasts, 141–83, 153, 168. *See also* Bear Feast; Corpus Christi Feast; Feast for the Dead; Ghost Supper; King's Supper; Tabándaŋ Feast

Festivals, Indian: hybridity of, xxvii, 31–32; motivations of, 53. *See also* Naming ceremonials; Pageants; Powwows

Fiddle, 16, 25, 82

Fire, 375, 407, 415

Fireball, 241

Fire Dance, 44, 45, 394, 418. *See also* Wabeno society

First fruits ceremonies, 393, 412–13, 417

Fish, 142, 242, 407, 408, 412, 421

Fish Dance, 136, 412

Fishing charms, 253–54

"Fleet Footed Woman, The," 437

Flood myth, 276, 303–11, 378, 395, 406

Flute, 333

Folk melodies, 215, 217, 220, 224, 226

Folk songs, 42

Folklore, Native, 240–43

Fox Hunter's Song, 111

Fox Indians. *See* Meskwaki
Fox Island, 330, 352
Foxes, 345–49, 401
Foxtrot, 81
Francis, Frank, 71
Francis, Sarah, 183
Francis, Victoria, 89
French folk melodies, 215, 217, 224, 226
Fungi, 264

G

Gambling Song, 102
Garden River, Ont., 38, 79, 98, 100, 117, 136, 137, 410
Gasco, Frankie, 37, 65
Gasco, John, 37, 145
Gasco, Richard, 37
Geese, 329–30
German folk melodies, 220, 224
Ghost Dance, 80, 82, 103
Ghost Song (for Ghost Supper), 175–76
Ghost Supper, 16, 80, 142, 156, 170–82; ancestors represented by guests at, 173; archeological accounts of, 179–81; cross making and, 171–72; dancing at, 174; historical accounts of, 175–79; menu for, 173
Gibson, Clarence, 182
Gibson, Mose, 183, 397
Gilbert, Margaret, 15
"Girl Married to a Dog, A," 278, 352
Gitchi Manido, 395–96
Gloria Patri, 148, 215
God, translation of, 230–31
God Moves in Mysterious Ways, 204–5
God Save the King, 224
Gott, Erhalte Franz den Kaiser, 220
Grand Rapids, Mich., 11
Grand River, Mich., 10
Grandfather Song, 226, 227–29, 230, 233–35
Grandmother Earth, 257, 392, 399
Grass Dance Song, 116–17
Grave Post, 425
Great Serpent (Mišiginébikʼ), 375, 405–6. *See also* Spirit Lions
Great Spirit. *See* Gitchi Manido
Green Grass Dance, 42, 43, 77, 85, 120, 416
Greensky, Peter, 23
Greensky Hill, 22–24, 186
Gregorian chants, 230
Gross, Lawrence, 270
Guardian spirits. *See* Dream guardians
Guitar, 42, 187, 188
Gwanatch Marie, 224–25, 226

H

Hail Mary, 148
Hallowell, A. I., xxiv, 239, 248, 407
Handicrafts. *See* Crafts
Hannahville, Mich., 26, 45, 211
Happy Hunting Ground, 400, 404, 419–20. *See also* West
Harbor Springs, Mich., 11
Hart, Mich., 17, 20
Haskell Institute, 25
Hastings, Mich., 18, 22
Hawk, Little, 282, 357
Haydn, Joseph, 220
Healing, 241; animal spirits and, 411; clothing and, 257; dance and, 257, 411; disease classification of, 262–67; doctoring and, xix, 256, 257–59, 417; fungi and, 264; herbal, 254–67; persistence of, 391; shaking tent ceremony and, 393, 417; song and, 257
Hemlock, 400

Herbs, 252–67, 380–81; gathering, 252, 262, 266, 399; gendered nature of, 256; hunting and, 253; identification of, 260–61; indigenous classification of, 256, 266; medicines proper to animals, 241; remedies with particular, 259–60, 261–66; unidentified, 261–62. See also *specific herbs by common name*

Hiawatha, story of, 45

Hiawatha pageants, vii, xii–xiii, xxviii–xxix, 13, 18, 36, 38, 49, 63, 79, 80, 96, 98, 102; shaping repertoire by, 104

Hockey, 271, 274, 296–99

Hoffman, William, 250, 255

Holy Child School (Harbor Springs), xxxiv, 12, 26, 38

Holy Cross Church (Harbor Springs), 38

Hominy soup, 164

Hoop Dance, 39, 41, 52, 80, 84

Hoot Owl Dance, 40

Hoot Owl Song, 42, 43, 44, 45, 60, 88, 94–96, 106, 120, 123, 229, 409

Hopi Snake Dance, 38

Homestead Act of 1975, 11

Horses, 344, 369, 373

Houghton Lake, 384

"How the Bear Lost His Tail," 274, 284, 319–23

Howard, James, 22

Huckleberry Feast, 142, 168–69, 393

Human origins, 276, 306–311

Humor: dance and, 59, 71, 76, 78; in performances about missionaries, 45; sacred and, 271, 417; song and, 122; stories and, 270–71; storytelling and, 284. See also Drinking Song; Nanabozho, cycle of stories of; Red Blanket Song; Wedding Dance

Hunt, 393, 395

Hunt Song, 136. See also Buffalo Dance; Deer Song; Rabbit Song

Hunter's Dance, 41, 43, 71–72

Hunting medicine, 253–54, 294, 395, 410, 417

Huron (Wendat), 6, 137, 157, 177, 280, 398

Huron, Lake, 329, 330

Hymn singing, xxv, 15–16, 20, 23, 183, 213–14, 427; as Anishinaabe music, 185; at funeral wakes, 25, 26, 183, 210, 214; at informal gatherings, 202–9; at King's Supper, 150–51; at Tabándaŋ Feast, 167; early descriptions of, 215; vocal quality of, 227; Odawa, 183

Hymns: books of, 216, 437; contrasted with Native songs, 227–30; and liturgical calendar, 214; Native language, 24, 26, 38, 140; and oral tradition, 185; Protestant, 185–211, 226–27; Roman Catholic, 213–26; translation of, 213, 215, 230–33; tunes of, 216. See also Jones, Peter Kahkewaquonaby

I

I Want to Walk in the Path of the Savior, 189, 201

I Would Not be Denied, 188, 193

Indian Reorganization Act of 1934, xvi

Indian River, Mich., 373

Invocations, 236–37

Iroquois, 5, 10, 48, 65, 84–85, 136–38, 186, 210, 249; dances, 411; funerary customs, 422; hymns, 203; narratives, 277

Isabella Indian Reservation, 7, 18–22, 40–41
Isle Royale, 406

J

Jackson, Eddie, 45, 63, 77, 376, 378
Jackson, Harold, 211
Jackson, Mrs., 72
Jackson family (Mt. Pleasant), 40
James, M. Edwin, 394
du Jaunay, Fr., 11
Jazz, 16
Jenness, Diamond, 400
Jesikon. *See* Shaking Tent Ceremony
Jesus, My All, to Heaven is Gone, 185, 188, 203, 227–29, 233; Native text and translation of, 189, 195, 201–2, 233–35
Jesus Wegwissiian, 216; Native text and translation of, 217–20
Jibiabos, xiii, 13, 135, 137, 242, 296–306, 419; dead, ruler of, 400
Jitterbug, 81
Jones, Peter Kahkewaquonaby, 186, 208–9, 394; hymn translations by, 189, 196, 197, 204, 206, 207; on traditional customs, 401, 414, 425

K

Kagenig Kije-Manito, 222–23
Kakina Minawasida, 222–23
Katolik Anamie-Misinaigan, 150
Kenosha, David, xlv, 15–16, 18, 27, 36, 39, 46, 53, 88, 166, 381, 399; and dance, 59, 61, 65, 68, 69, 74, 80, 81, 82–83, 86; and fiddle, 82; and hymns, 220–25, 227; song performances of, 95, 97, 133, 135, 229; song repertoire of, 105–9, 126, 129, 384–86; story repertoire of, 384–86
Kenoshmeg, Fred, 16, 36, 65, 105
Kenoshmeg, Louise, 16, 36, 65, 105
Kettle Dance, 36, 50, 52, 74, 88
Keweenaw, Mich., 79, 375–76
"Kidnappers from Saginaw," 362–68
King, Mrs., 42, 44, 65
King, Philip, 42, 44, 65
King, Victor, 84
Kingbirds, 353
King's Supper (Three Kings' Supper; Epiphany), 142, 143, 147–53; food typifying, 149; fried cakes with hidden beans or coins for, 149; hymn singing at, 150–51; naming and, 160
Kiogima, Gus, 37, 75, 88
Kiogima, Johnny, 182
Kiogima, Katherine, 182
Kiogima, Raymond, 37, 75
Kiowa, 76
Kishigo, Elizabeth, 48, 89, 144, 407; on Ghost Supper, 171; King's Supper with, 147–49, 220; Tabándaŋ Feast with, 167
Kishigo, Joe, Sr., 88, 89, 144, 374; King's Supper with, 147–48, 220; Tabándaŋ Feast with, 167
Kishigo, Veronica, 48, 89, 144
Kitchitwa Marie, 225
Knox, Cecilia Shagonaby, 17
Kurath, Ellen, xxxvi, xlvi
Kurath, Gertrude xxxi–xxxii, 38

L

L'air Nous Vous Invoquons Tous, 224
Lac Court Oreilles, 84
Lac du Flambeau, 136, 137, 401, 410, 412
Lac Vieux Desert, 168, 427

Lahontan, Baron, 38, 394, 396, 415
Lake Michigan, 283, 297, 325–26, 330–31, 337–38, 339–41, 371, 405
Lakota. *See* Dakota
Lambert, Margaret, 24, 214, 224
Langlade, Charles, 9
L'Anse, Mich., 25
L'Arbre Croche, Mich., 7–12, 20, 84, 96, 155, 169, 273
Lasky, Clara, 182
Leeks, 276
"Legend of Harbor Point," 337–38, 405
"Legend of the Manitou Islands and Sleeping Bear Point, The," 277, 339–41
"Legend of the Serpent, The," 278, 342–47
Lent, 214
Lightning, 241, 243, 376, 404
Lingham, 196–97
Linton, Ralph, 29
Little Bear stories, 278, 352
Little Thimble Plant, 252
Little Traverse Bands of Odawa Indians, vii, xviii, xxxvi, 5
Lizards, 407
Longfellow, Henry Wadsworth, xiii
Longhouse, 203
Loons, 341–42, 378
Lord's Prayer, 148
Love Medicine, 252–53
Love Song, 44, 98–101, 136
Lyons, Mrs., 203

M

Mackinac Island, xv, 3, 8, 9, 155, 177, 255, 329, 394
"Magic Arrow, The" 278, 332–35
Magnificat, 215
Malone, Betty, 26, 211

Mamoya Wamada, 220
"Man Carried Off by an Eagle, The," 277, 331–32
Manidos, 395–409. *See also* Gitchi Manido; Great Serpent; Matchi Manido; Nanabozho; Spirit Lions
Manidu Island (Lake Superior), 375–76
Manistique, Mich., 13
Manitoulin Island, 10, 11, 96, 215, 279, 399, 409, 423
Maple sugar, 276
Maple Sugar Begging Song, 158
Maple Sugar Dance, 398
Maple Sugar Festival/Gathering, 45, 108, 159, 392, 412
Maple Sugar Song, 108, 136
Marriage, 352, 369, 416
Marquette, Fr., 11, 39, 401, 413
Mary (Virgin Mary), 214; hymns to, 215, 216, 218, 222–23, 224–25, 231; indigenous understandings of, 231
"Maškóde Indians, The," 353–55
Maškódedens, 8–10, 269, 273, 279–81, 353–55, 415; and Feast for the Dead, 181; ghosts of, 437. *See also* "Defeat of the Maskutens, The"
Mason, Bernard, 72
Masto (Mastaw), Mitchell, 89, 403–4
Matchi Manido (Maji Manidoo), 145, 397, 437
May God Bless You, 188
McClurken, James, xxxvi
McKinney, Rev., 189, 201
Medicine, 380–81; love, 252–53; fishing, 253–54; hunting, 253–54; persistence of, 391. *See also* Healing; Herbs
Medicine Chant, 103
Medicine Dance, 80
"Medicine Man" performance, 40, 43, 45

Medicine Song, 45, 229; of Whitney Albert, 118–20, 229
Meet Me There, 188, 199
Megis shell, 400, 419, 424
Melodies, French, 214, 217
Memorial Feasts (Restoration of Mourners), 393, 416–17, 422–23
Menard, Fr., 11
Menominee, 6, 25, 51, 136, 138, 157, 215, 244, 275, 399, 401, 402, 410, 412, 418
Mermen, 406
Meskwaki (Fox), 51, 84, 85, 136, 275, 278, 401, 411
Methodists, 20–24; Anishinaabe inflections on, 210–11; and dancing, 81, 187, 427. *See also* Missionaries
Miami Indians, 6
Michelson, Truman, 276
Michigan Folklore Society, 45
Michigan Indian Defense Association (MIDA), xxxv, 13, 14, 36
Michigan Indian Foundation, xxxv, 38
Middle Village, 8, 11
Midewatig (Midé Pole), 425
Midéwiwin, xvi, xviii, 17, 21, 51, 159, 250–52, 391, 392, 393, 418; bears and, 249, 418; dances and, 58, 418; decline of, 156, 210; degrees of, 255; directions and, 400–401, 418; early references to, 391, 394, 395; herbal knowledge of, 255–56; lodge, 424; Nanabozho and, 400; Owls and, 408; persistence of, 390; rebirth in, 424; songs and, 63, 230, 419; storytelling and, 274
Midsummer Festival, 45
Mikado, Mich., 17
Miksabi, John, 257
Mink, 309

Miserere, 215
Missionaries, xiv–xvi; comic performances about, 39, 45; Methodist, xv, 23–24, 186, 210–11; problematic interpretations of Anishinaabe culture by, 380; replacing Native forms, 215; Roman Catholic, xv, 7, 8, 11, 25, 26, 214–16
Mıškóagǝ, 361
Mkkwánıwi, Louis, 13, 103, 239, 269, 279, 283, 438; narratives about, 370–74; on herbal medicine, 257
Mojag Anamiewin, 223–24, 229, 233
Monsters. *See* Spirit Lions
Moon, 241, 242, 397, 399
More, More About Jesus, 188
Moreland, Lawrence, 24
Morning Star Song, 136
Mount Pleasant, Mich., 11, 376. *See also* Camp meetings
Mourning. *See* Death; Memorial Feasts; Wakes
Mrak, Fr. Ignatius, 216
Music. *See* Songs
Muskrats, 310, 378
My Bark Canoe, 334
Myths, 274–77; death's origin in, 275, 296–306; decline in knowledge of, 273; difficulty of translating, 272, 283; distinguished from tales, 269–70; functions of, 271, 273; humor and, 270; Nanabozho cycle of, 285–331; provenance of, 274–75. *See also Aadizookan;* Storytelling; Tales

N

Nahma, Mich., 26
Names, Odawa, 163, 165
Naming ceremonials, 36–39, 76. *See*

also Festivals, Indian

Naming ceremony, 38, 142, 160–66, 393; birds and, 410; early observations of, 164, 395; occasions for 162; thunders as bringers of, 405

Naming Song, 103

Nanabozho (Nanabojo), xx, xxvii, xxix, 242, 270, 273, 285–337, 391, 402–3; association with Sun of, 400; communicates with animals, 286; cycle of stories of, 274–77, 285–337; dance and, xx; death and, 419; East, association with, 400; flatulence of, 327; Midéwiwin, as source of, 400; relation of, to Gitchi Manido, 396; sexual prowess of, 330; transformation and, 313–16; transforms world after flood, xx, 270, 306–313. See also *specific stories*

"Nanabozho and the Bear's Skull," 276, 313–17

"Nanabozho Creates the Indian," 306–11

"Nanabozho Flies with the Geese," 329–30

"Nanabozho and His Younger Brother Fight the Bears," 271, 285–306

"Nanabozho and the Leeks," 327–28

Nativism, 29

Nazarene Church, 19

'Neath the Old Olive Tree, 188, 196

'Neath the Stars of the Night, 196

Neganagijig, 27

Neomi, Jack, 42, 84

Nettl, Bruno, 136

New Year Bread, 146

New Year Feasts, 25, 142, 143–47, 427; history of, 154–57; hymns and, 214. See also King's Supper

Newaygo Centennial, 44

Niagara Falls, 330

Nısawákwatʻ, 9

North, 400–1

Nothing but the Blood of Jesus, 188

O

O For a Thousand Tongues to Sing, 187, 188, 202–3, 227, 229; Native texts and translations of, 190–92, 193–94, 198–99, 201–2

O Wonderful Jesus, 188

Obšiškan, 258, 261, 262

Odawa Catholic feasts, 427

Old age, 335–36

Olive's Brow, 195

Omena church, 25

Onions, wild, 327–28

Optatus, Fr., 15

Orality, 392

"Origin of Red Osier, The," 271, 276, 317–19

Orthography, 436–37

Ortonville, 190

Osier, Red, 261, 270, 318

Ottawa Indian Stadium. See Naming ceremonials

Otters, 401

Otto, Christine, 17, 36, 42, 246–47; on herbal healing, 252, 255, 257, 265

Otto, Donald, 42, 48, 65, 66, 84

Otto, Foster, 17, 37, 42, 61

Otto, Mary, 257

Owl Song, 136. See also Hoot Owl Song

Owls, 381, 401, 408, 409

P

Pageants, 21, 22, 40, 428; Odawa Indian, 11, 12, 142; Marquette's

Landing, 39. *See also* Hiawatha Pageants; Wisconsin Dells

Painted Pole Feast, 392, 395, 425

Pakiísigan, Chief, 253, 279

"Pale Moon," 45

Palm Sunday, 215

Pamp, Betty, 22, 40, 72, 84, 210; and hymns, 186, 196, 197, 203, 206–7, 208; on camp meetings, 211–12

Pamp, Jack, 22, 84, 186, 210

Pamp, Joan, 48, 84, 203

Pamp, Warren, 210

Pamptope, Charles, 22

Pange Lingua, 215, 220–22

Papoose Dance, 43

Papoose War Dance, 43

Parry Island, 158, 410

Partridge Dance, 45

Partner Dance, 78

Partner Song, 123

Passamoquody, 278

Payoff Feast. *See* Tabándaŋ Feast

Pegler, D. C., 210

Pelcher, Isaac, 21, 40, 45, 61, 78, 84

Pelcher, Lucy, 72, 78, 193

Peters, Jim, 187, 188, 194–95, 210

Petonquet, Eliot, 26

Petoskey, Mich., 11, 13, 332

Philemon, Alex, 26, 27, 45, 53

Phrygian mode, 220

Piano, 187, 188, 195, 196, 220

Pierz, Fr. Francis, 216

Pigeon Song (White), 109–10, 135

Pike, Evelyn, xlv

Pike, Kenneth, xlv

Pipe (peace or ceremonial), 6, 49–50

Pipe Ceremony, 43, 45, 58, 62–63, 393, 399, 400–2

Pipe Dance, 17, 36, 41, 43, 52, 61–62, 81, 82, 88, 401; of Meskwaki, 136

Pipe (Dance) Songs, 18, 93, 137

Plants. *See* Herbs

Point St. Esprit, 10

Poles, Manido, 425

Polkas, 81

Pomo, 242

Pontiac, 401, 415

Porcupines, 43, 371, 379

Potato soup, 253

Potawatomi, 6–7, 21, 22, 26, 41, 275, 279, 400, 413; Maskutens as, 281–82; Sun Ceremony of, 398; Wabeno and, 418

Powwows, 27, 36, 42–43, 82, 86, 137, 142, 416, 428, 435

Prayer: benediction, 196, 236; transformative power of, xxiii; Odawa Catholic table grace, 144, 148, 173, 183; rosary, 183; vocal quality of, 236

Prayerbook, Odawa, 183, 437

Prud'homme, Fr., 26, 216, 224

Puberty fast, 165, 279, 335, 349–50, 360, 370, 391, 403, 407; Christianization and, 424; feast following, 393, 417; for girls, 352. *See also* Dreaming

Pueblo, 66, 84, 85

Q

Quignon, Benedict, 21–22, 40–41, 42, 59, 65–67, 71, 188, 211; compositions by, 138

Quignon, Johnny, 41, 44, 53, 65

Quillwork. *See* Crafts

R

Rabbit Dance, 411

Rabbit Song, 110, 119, 136

Rabbits, 402, 438

Race, origin of, 276, 310–11, 331, 383
Raccoon Dance, 70–71, 88, 411
Raccoon (Dance) Song, 110
Raccoons, 438
Radin, Paul, xxxix
Radio, 279
Railroads, 13
Rain Medicine, 396
Ramage, Jack, 65
Rattle, 51, 65, 77
Rattlesnakes, 377
Recruiting Dance, 414
Red Blanket Song, 117–18, 135
Red Ochre, 406
Regalia, 40, 47–49, 65, 66, 434–35
Religion, Anishinaabe: beliefs summarized, 391–92, 395–409; culture change and, xxiii, xxvi–xxvii, 28, 389–90, 427–29; decline (purported) of, 391; differentiated today from arts and economy, 427; difficulty of defining, xix, xxi; dreams and, 394; inseparable from music, dance, feasts, 392; integrated traditionally with arts, economy, 428; orality of, 392; persistence of, 28, 390; practices, as, 390; relationship to music and dance, xix, 46; sacred power of xxi; supplanted by Christianity, 391, 424. *See also* Dreaming; Manidos; Midéwiwin; Wabeno Society
Religious Customs of Modern Michigan Algonquians, xviii, xxxv–xxxvii, xlv
Rickard, Glenna, 72, 186, 203, 208
Rites of passage, 31, 416–17. *See also* Naming ceremony; Puberty fast; Memorial Feasts; Wakes
Ritual. *See* Ceremonies; Religion, Anishinaabe
Roberts, Wilson, 418

Robins, 44, 241, 278, 349–50
Rocks, 408
Rosary, 183
Roscommon, Mich., 370
"Rosemarie," 38, 41
Round Dances, 81
Round Lake, 355. *See also* Hiawatha Pageants

S

Sabuco, Mark, 45
Sacrifice, 425. *See also* Dogs; First fruits ceremonies; Tobacco
Sagataw, Dorothy, 164
Sagataw, Hattie, 167, 220
Saginaw, 19, 282–83, 362–68. *See also* Isabella Indian Reservation; Mount Pleasant, Mich.
Sagitoda Jesus Wiiaw, 220, 221–22. *See also Pange Lingua*
St. Ignace, Mich., 5, 9, 24, 25, 330, 413
St. Joseph, Mich., 10, 372
Sákko, 256, 265–66
Salamanders, 242, 274
Samuels, Joe, 330
Sarnia, Ont., 21
Sauk, 85
Sault Ste. Marie, 26
Save this Poor Sinner, 188
Saxophone, 187
Scalp Dance, 36, 37, 76, 80, 84, 414, 416
Scalp (Dance) Song, 109
Schloop, Rev. Lloyd, 21
Schoolcraft, Henry Rowe, xiii, 154, 230, 273, 277, 397, 398
Seaman, Betty Lou, 89
Sermons, 187, 194–95
Serpent. *See* Great Serpent; "Legend of the Serpent, The"; Spirit Lions
Seven Mile Point, 11, 353, 368, 371

Shaffer, James, 22, 42, 50, 84
Shagonaby, Charlie, 51, 69, 83
Shagonaby, Evelyn, 68, 83
Shagonaby, Kathleen, 72, 83
Shagonaby, Robert, 83
Shagonaby, Susy, xlvi, xlvii, 14, 68, 78, 83, 89, 251, 403, 405, 415, 437; hymns and, 222–23; storytelling and, 273, 279; on bear walks, 247–48
Shaking Tent Ceremony (Jesikon; Jisako), xix, 391, 392, 408, 419
Shalifoe, Thomas, 24–26, 78, 155, 381, 412; hymns and, 214, 217–20; song repertoire of, 121–22, 128, 133, 137; story repertoire of, 375–76
Shape-shifting. *See* Bear walks
Shawanessi, Jonas, 8–9
Shawnee, 6, 84, 136, 413
Shell. *See Megis* shell
Shield Dance, 36, 52, 75, 88
Shingwauk, William J., 227
Shomin, Mrs., 189
Shows. *See* Pageants
Sifferath, Fr. Louis, 216
Simonds, Elmer, 19
Sinágo Odawa, 9
Sioux. *See* Dakota
"Sioux Captive, The," 361
Skillagalee, 330
Sleeping Bear Point (Dunes), Mich., 242, 277, 339, 341, 371, 408
Smart, Frank, 27
Snake Dance, 36, 37, 42, 43, 45, 52, 81, 83, 84, 88, 137, 406
Snakes, 241, 242, 273, 330, 342–47, 370, 376–78, 404. *See also* "Legend of the Serpent, The"
Snow, 242, 331, 397
"Snowball, The," 277, 331
Sogat, 253, 362

Soney, Ford, 187, 188, 198
Soney, William, 186, 188, 196, 199, 210
Song of Hiawatha, xiii, 38
Songs (Anishinaabe; non-hymnody): compared with other tribes, 135–38; change in function in, 92, 210; Christianization as factor in, 426; contrasted with hymns, 227–230; formal aspects of, 123–132; and dance, 138; dream (personal), 103–4, 410, 415–16; expressiveness of, 135; healing and, 257; humor and, 122; hunting and, 410; performance styles of, 92, 133; provenance and diffusion of, 138; in storytelling, 301, 319–20, 384–86; compared to texts, 92, 132–33; transformative power of, xx
Sorcery, xxi
Soul, 419–21. *See also* Dreaming
South, 400–1
Souvenirs. *See* Crafts
Speck, Frank, ix, xxxiii, xxxiv, xlvii, 276
Spirit Lions, 272, 306, 337–38, 406
Spirits. *See* Manidos
Sprague, Selkirk, 188
Square Dance, 16, 24, 42, 81; at Tabándaŋ Feasts, 167; prohibited at camp meetings, 187
Squash, 413
"Squaw" [Ikwe] Dance, 25, 78, 155
Squirrels, 438
Stars, 241
Steel Guitar, 188
Stories. *See* Myths; Nanabozho; Storytelling; Tales
Storms, 243, 244, 283, 372, 376, 400
"Story of the Choke Cherries, The," 276, 324–25
"Story of the Leeks," 276, 327–28

"Story of the Robin, The," 349–50
Storytelling, 272, 273–74, 283–85, 286; song in, 301, 319–20, 384–86
Strawberries, 256, 259, 260, 382–83, 412, 419
Strawberry Ceremony, 393
Strike-the-Post Dance, 75, 83, 87, 98, 394, 414, 415, 416
Sturgeon, 142
Sun, 397–99; Gitchi Manido and, 395–96
Sun Ceremony (and "Odawa Sun Ceremony"), 51, 59, 68, 69, 75, 76, 78, 80, 107; ancient, 156, 392, 395, 398–99; contemporary, 86–89; reason for, 398; relation to New Year/Kings Supper/Tabándaŋ Cycle, 168, 397–98
Sun Dance, 52, 60, 86, 399, 402
Sunday school, 188
Sundog, 241
Superior, Lake, 330, 375–76, 406
Swan Dance, 36, 38, 52, 68, 83, 88, 136, 137
Swans, 410
Sweet Bye and Bye, 188
Sweet Flag, 247, 256, 259, 260

T

Tabándaŋ Feast (return feast; paying off feast), vii, 142, 166–68; history of, 167–67; naming and, 160; square dancing at, 167
Tales (*dibaadjimowin*): difficulty of translation of, 272; distinguished from *aadizookan*, 270; European influence on, 278; supernatural, 331–42
Tama, Iowa, 136. *See also* Meskwaki
Te Deum, 215

Tempest Point, Mich., 330
"Ten Talents" (legend), 331, 395
Terhaus, Fr., 26
"Theft of Fire, The," 438
Theology, 391–92, 395–409
There is Something Within, 189
Thomas, Eli, 18, 20–21, 26, 27, 40, 211, 232, 401; and dance, 63, 72, 77, 80, 83; and hymns, 120, 121, 186, 201–2, 204–5, 207–8, 226, 233–35; and song, 95; prayer of, 236–37; song repertoire of, 118–19, 128; story repertoire of, 376–83; storytelling by, 276
Thomas, Mrs., 41, 201, 207–8
Thomas Aquinas, 220
"Three Kings Hymn," 150–53
Three Kings Feast. *See* King's Supper
Thunder, 241, 243, 376, 404
Thunder Cloud, Chief, 277
Thunder things (thunderbolts), 405
Thunders (thunderbirds), 45, 375, 376–78, 398, 403–5; ancestors of Odawas as, 403; West, association with, 401
"Thunders Destroying Serpents," 376–78, 404
Timiskaming, 276, 277
Toad Woman, 275
Toads, 242, 273, 407
Tobacco, 257, 381, 425; as hunting charm, 253; offerings, 211, 241, 257, 262, 376, 395, 399, 401; storytelling and, 273
Tomahawk Dance, 416
Tracker's Song, 112, 137
Translation, 230–33. *See also* Hymns; Myths
Transmigration, 421
Traverse City, Mich., 12
Treaty of Washington, xv

Trickster. *See* Nanabozho
Trout, 242, 407
Turkey Dance, 42, 413
Turtles, 242, 408
Tutelary spirits. *See* Dream guardians
Tutelo, 136, 137, 138
"Two Cousins Captured by the Sioux," 360–61
"Two Sisters," 437

U

"Underground People," 279, 282, 356–60
Undergrounders (Underground Indians), 282–83, 356–60
Uxbridge, 226

V

Vecsey, Christopher, xxi
Verwyst, Chrysostom, 155
Vexilla, 215
Vision. *See* Dreaming
Vision Quest. *See* Puberty fast
Vizenor, Gerald, 270–71
Vocables, 98, 106, 121
Voyageurs, 217

W

Wabado (white fungus), 264
Wabeno society, xvii, 50, 159, 380, 392, 393, 398, 418; dances and, 58, 394; decline of, 156, 210; East, association with, 400; herbal knowledge of, 255–57; songs and, 136, 230
Wakes (funeral), 25, 142, 182–83, 422; adoptions often associated with, 416; hymn singing at, 183, 427
Walker, Louise, 24, 186

Walker, Rev., 24
Walking on the Green Grass, 60, 88, 107, 120
Walpole Island Choir, 188–89, 201
War Dance, 41, 44, 77, 79, 83, 84, 86, 120, 393, 394, 416
War Dance Song, 98, 120
Warrior ceremonies, 414–16
Warrior's Pouch Feast, 415
Watts, Isaac, 227
Weasels, 376
Wedding Dance, 79, 96, 101
Weeden, Mary, 26, 214, 224
Weikamp, Fr. Bernard, 15, 216
Welcome Dance, 37, 42, 44, 79
Wemigwase, Louis, 37, 76, 83, 88
Wemigwase, Mary, 39, 80, 89
Wemigwase, Richard, 36, 39, 48, 50, 53, 61, 69, 72, 75, 76, 83, 88, 89
Wemigwase, Richard, Jr. (Dick), 39, 48, 75, 80
Wenijánissimiiang, 224–25
Wesley, Charles, 190, 199, 200, 206, 227
West (direction of Path of Souls), 300–302, 382, 400–401, 420
What a Friend I Have in Jesus, 188
When I Can Read My Title Clear, 188, 196–97
Whirlpools, 341–42
White Dog Feast, 398
White Earth Reservation, Minn., 250
White Shoals, 330
"Why the Birch Has Streaks," 276
"Why the Chipmunk Has Stripes on His Back," 438
"Why the Great Lakes Are Receding," 276, 325–26
"Why Some Trees Have Knobs on Them and the Birches Grow in Clumps," 276, 328
Wild Rice, 412

Wild Rice Feast, 393
Willis, Enos, 23
Windigo, 408–9
Winds, 399–400. See also *specific directions*
Winnebago, 6, 15, 244, 282, 401, 410, 412
Winter, 277. *See also* Storytelling
Wintergreen, 262, 264
Wisconsin Dells, 7, 15, 27, 69, 74, 76
Wollenberg, R. A. C., 38
Wolves, 313
Women's Dance, 45, 52, 82, 83, 88, 107

Woodpecker Song, 105, 410
Woodpeckers, 241, 410
Wright, Carl, 259
Wright, John, 276

Y

Yarrow, 257

Z

Zeba Church, 25
Zorn, Fr. Seraphim, 216